The Devil on Screen

To six individuals who created very
different interpretations of the Devil:
Danny Elfman, Robert Helpmann,
Burgess Meredith, Ray Milland,
Vincent Price, and Jean Shepherd

The Devil on Screen

*Feature Films Worldwide,
1913 through 2000*

CHARLES P. MITCHELL

McFarland & Company, Inc., Publishers
Jefferson, North Carolina, and London

ALSO BY CHARLES P. MITCHELL
AND FROM McFARLAND

The Great Composers Portrayed on Film, 1913 through 2002 (2004; paperback 2010)

The Hitler Filmography: Worldwide Feature Film and Television Miniseries Portrayals, 1940 through 2000 (2002; paperback 2009)

BY PAUL PARLA AND CHARLES P. MITCHELL
AND FROM McFARLAND

Screen Sirens Scream! Interviews with 20 Actresses from Science Fiction, Horror, Film Noir and Mystery Movies, 1930s to 1960s (2000; paperback 2009)

The present work is a reprint of the illustrated case bound edition of The Devil on Screen: Feature Films Worldwide, 1913 through 2000, *first published in 2002 by McFarland.*

LIBRARY OF CONGRESS CATALOGUING-IN-PUBLICATION DATA

Mitchell, Charles P., 1949–
The devil on screen : feature films worldwide, 1913 through 2000 / Charles P. Mitchell.
p.   cm.
Includes bibliographical references and index.

ISBN 978-0-7864-4699-5
softcover : 50# alkaline paper ∞

1. Devil in motion pictures—Catalogs. I. Title.
PN1995.9.D46 M58   2010   791.43'651—dc21   2002282598

British Library cataloguing data are available

©2002 Charles P. Mitchell. All rights reserved

No part of this book may be reproduced or transmitted in any form or by any means, electronic or mechanical, including photocopying or recording, or by any information storage and retrieval system, without permission in writing from the publisher.

Cover photograph ©2010 Photos to Go

Manufactured in the United States of America

*McFarland & Company, Inc., Publishers
Box 611, Jefferson, North Carolina 28640
www.mcfarlandpub.com*

Contents

Acknowledgments
vi

Introduction
1

The Films
7

Appendix One: Lost, Obscure, and Arcane Devil Films
305

Appendix Two: Television Devils
309

Index
313

Acknowledgments

I would like to thank the following individuals and organizations for their assistance and encouragement in the preparation of this volume: Bangor Public Library, John Berrien, Eddie Brandt's Saturday Matinee, Robert Brosch, William Chadwick, L. M. Garnett, Richard Gordon, Hollywood Book and Poster, Joe "Phantom of the Movies" Kane, Dewayn Marzigalli, Jean and Dick Norris, Paul and Donna Parla, Freddy Peralta, Michael Pitts, Bill and Cheryl Pitz, Ben Reeves, Robert Rotter, Vincent Schiavelli, Robert W. Schmidt, Dr. Ronald and Amelia Schwartz, Audrey Totter, the University of Maine's Fogler Library, and Video Screams.

I especially want to thank my wife, Roberta, for her help and assistance at every step of the process, from watching every single film reviewed, to reading my sometimes ragged first draft, to researching esoteric facts and reading obscure novels by Marie Corelli. Her patience has been beyond measure.

Introduction

> I know my course. The spirit that I have seen
> May be the Devil, and the Devil hath power
> To assume a pleasing shape. Yea, and perhaps
> Out of my weakness and my melancholy,
> As he is very potent with such spirits,
> Abuses me to damn me.
>
> *Hamlet*, act II, scene 2

The Devil has assumed many shapes, pleasant and unpleasant, on the page, on the stage, and on the screen. Ever since magician and cinema pioneer Georges Méliès first portrayed the Devil onscreen in 1896, his Satanic majesty has been represented in every genre including horror, comedy, musical, fantasy, satire, drama, and religious epic. He is depicted in an astonishing range of guises from the all-powerful and unconquerable agent of evil, the supervillain of all supervillains, to a reluctant component of God's divine plan forced to perform His dirty work. He can be terrifying or beguiling, charming or revolting, a comic stereotype or a symbol of repugnance, a despicable sadist or an honorable tragic hero. Like the nature of God, the nature of the Devil has stimulated an enormous number of volumes of philosophical and religious thought. It is not the purpose of this book to plumb the depths of these beliefs but merely to entertain by providing a thorough study of the Devil in cinema.

Whether you believe in the Devil or not, his image has probably been with you from your earliest days as the personification of evil. Dr. Paul Caras in his volume *The History of the Devil and the Idea of Evil* (1900) noted, "The dark figure of the Devil, that is to say a powerful evil deity, looms up as the most important personage in the remotest past of almost every faith." Most representations of the Devil on the screen are based on four specific literary sources, which we will briefly consider. The first is The Holy Bible, along with early sacred Jewish texts. Please note all quotations from biblical scripture are from the revised standard version. The Old Testament Book of Job and the New Testament Book of Revelation are especially pertinent to many screen presentations.

The second source is *The Divine Comedy* by Dante Alighieri (1265–1321), of which the first book, *The Inferno*, is a detailed description of all of the levels of hell. The Devil as presented by Dante is remote, but his personality is revealed by the punishment that he devises for every type of sin.

The third source is *Paradise Lost*, the epic poem by John Milton (1608–1674) which tells the story of the revolt of Lucifer and his transformation into the Devil. This extraordinary work can be interpreted as being sympathetic to the Devil, endowing him with tragic grandeur and dignity despite his overbearing pride. His honor and sense of independence are traits that have also been well mined in cinematic depictions of the Devil, especially the oft-quoted phrase "Better to reign in hell than serve in heaven."

The fourth and final source is the collection of works developed around the figure of Johannes Faust which date back to the sixteenth century. There are earlier medieval tales about characters selling their souls to Satan, but the concept coalesced in the Faust legend. The original tale portrays a scholar who makes a deal with the Devil, who uses the name Mephistopheles (literally, "not light loving"); after twenty-four years of pleasure and fame as a wonder-worker, Faust is torn apart by the Devil, who drags his soul to hell for eternal punishment. A number of variations appear in the various Faust stories. The English playwright Christopher Marlowe (1564–1593) used the story as the basis for his masterpiece, *Doctor Faustus*. The poignant last pages of the play, where Johannes Faustus is claimed by the Devil, rank among the finest in English literature. Other writers were also intrigued by the Faust legend, including Friedrich Klinger, Adalbert Von Chamisso, Christian Dietrich Grabbe, Nikolas Lenau, and Heinrich Heine. The most acclaimed version, however, is by Johann Wolfgang von Goethe (1749–1832), who labored over his version of *Faust* for more than thirty years. His play is regarded as the cornerstone of German Romantic literature, and in his concept, Faust instead of damnation finds redemption due to the purifying love of Gretchen (Marguerite).

The central element from *Faust*, the deal with the Devil, is also the essential ingredient in the plots of most Devil pictures. Other motifs, such as the crossroads, the legal pact signed in blood, and the possibility or struggle for redemption, occur again and again on the screen. A number of films brilliantly camouflage and recycle ideas from *Faust* in which the Devil does not appear except in a symbolic way. These fascinating films are loaded with many Faustian elements, some obvious and some rather subtle. In the science fiction film *The Black Hole* (1979), for example, when the Faustlike main character, played by Maximillian Schell, dies, he exclaims, "More light," duplicating the dying words of Goethe. The musical version of *Little Shop of Horrors* (1986) also reflects the Germanic legend, and the clever *film noir* starring Cuba Gooding, Jr., *A Murder of Crows* (1998), is based on Faust, tipping its hand when a serial killer uses the name Chris Marlowe as his pseudonym.

Another important offshoot of *Faust* and other literary works about the Devil is the story's impact on the great Romantic composers, including Carl Maria von Weber (opera *Der Freischütz*), Hector Berlioz (oratorio *La Damnation de Faust*), Franz Liszt (*Faust Symphony, Dante Symphony, Two Episodes from Lenau's Faust: Nocturnal Procession* and *Mephisto Waltz*, and countless piano works), Robert Schumann (oratorio *Faust*), Richard Wagner (*Faust Overture*), Charles Gounod (opera *Faust*), Arrigo Boito (opera *Mefistofele*), Ferruccio Busoni (opera *Doktor Faust*), and Gustav Mahler (*Eighth Symphony* with text from Goethe's *Faust*). A number of films used and adapted these musical works, particularly Liszt's *Mephisto Waltz* and Gounod's *Faust*. The original *Phantom of the Opera* (1925) utilized *Faust* as its operatic backdrop. The blockbuster *San Francisco* (1936) with Clark Gable, Spencer Tracy, and Jeannette MacDonald features a

Introduction • 3

Gounod's opera Faust *was showcased in the film* San Francisco *with Jeanette MacDonald as Marguerite. Tudor Williams (far right) is Mephistopheles.*

lengthy segment of *Faust* with MacDonald as Marguerite and Tudor Williams as Mephistopheles. In addition, Williams provided the singing voice for Boris Karloff when he performed Mephisto in Oscar Levant's opera *Carnival* used in *Charlie Chan at the Opera* (1936). While the operatic segments do not qualify these pictures as outright Devil films, they do illustrate the influence of the original literary sources.

They say the Devil is in the details, so the remainder of this introduction will concentrate on the structure of this book and the criteria employed in its writing. This filmography brings together and reviews motion pictures featuring the Devil. In tackling this subject, certain ground rules were applied to select the productions included.

First, the Devil must make a bona fide appearance and be played by a recognizable person. This standard eliminates a number of excellent Devil films, such as *The Mephisto Waltz* (1971), in which only the Devil's shadow appears; *Rosemary's Baby* (1968), where we catch only a fleeting glimpse of Satan's hands and eyes; *The Devil's Partner* (1957), in which only his hand is seen; *Incubus* (1965), where he appears vaguely in the distance; and *Asylum of Satan* (1972), where an unidentified actor in a cheap rubber Halloween mask makes a mini-appearance. Cartoons and animated features do not qualify, but telefilms are included. Films where the Devil shows up only in the form of a dog, such as *Devil Dog: The Hound of Hell* (1978), a snake, as in *Jaws of Satan* (1984), or a car, as in *The Car* (1977), are likewise omitted.

Second, it must be a feature-length film. All short subjects are omitted, including *The Devil's Cabaret* (1931) with Charles Middleton and *Simon of the Desert* (1965), Luis Buñel's forty-five-minute featurette that included a female Satan played by Silvia Pinal.

Third, the character depicted must reasonably be considered to be the actual Devil. Satan goes by many names, such as Lucifer, Beelzebub, Mephistopheles, etc. In some productions, these names refer to separate beings. This book includes films where major Devil figures appear. There are also some pictures in which the Devil is not actually identified but in which a character can be reasonably assumed to be the Devil, such as David Warner in *Time Bandits* (1981). Pseudodevils, however, are not eligible, such as those appearing in *Seven Footprints to Satan* (1929) or *Hellzapoppin'* (1941). The Antichrist is also not the Devil, unless the film depicts the Antichrist as being literally possessed by Satan himself as in *The Omega Code* (1999). *Holocaust 2000* and the *Omen* films are omitted, being outside these parameters. Also excluded are demonic possession films, unless Satan himself is doing the possessing. In *The Exorcist* (1971), for example, the young girl is actually possessed by Pazuzu, a relatively minor Sumerian demon.

Fourth, skin flicks, both soft and hard, are not included, so don't look for such efforts as *My Tail Is Hot* (1964), *Sinthia the Devil Doll* (1968), or *Satanico Pandemonium* (1978).

Finally, the film must still exist and be available to be seen by viewers. Every film in the main section of this book has been reviewed by the author on video, including rarities such as *Autopsia de un Fantasma* (1967) and *The Devil's Hand* (1942). (Some unseen, unavailable films are listed in Appendix 1.)

With these factors in mind, ninety-five films are covered in comprehensive detail in this book.

Each entry begins with the title as rendered in the print reviewed by the author, followed by the year of production and any commonly known alternate titles. Next comes a rating of the picture as a Devil movie. A film such as *Crossroads*, for example, may be regarded as a blues film or a Devil film. These ratings apply to the picture exclusively as a Devil film and should be interpreted in the following manner:

*Poor to Fair
**Fair to Good
***Good to Very Good
****Very Good to Excellent
*****Top of the Line

Note that in these evaluations, the rating used is a range, so half stars are not employed.

The performer who plays the Devil in each film is then highlighted. Production credits include the screenwriter, the cinematographer, the editor, the special effects chief, the composer, the producer, and the director. In some cases, several members of the special effects crew are listed. However, since in some recent films several dozen people are often recognized for their special effects contributions, only the supervisor or effects company is cited. Likewise, the list of executive producers can sometimes be lengthy, so only those of particular interest are included. The credit section ends with color indication and film length rounded off to the nearest minute.

The annotated cast list features the names of the performers followed in parentheses by the names of the characters they play in italics with a concise annotation. In *Alias Nick Beal*, for example, you will find "Thomas Mitchell (*Joseph Foster*, ambitious district attorney)." If the character is identified by a generic term, such as sheriff or minister, then it is not italicized.

The next section is the combined appraisal and synopsis, which includes the action of the picture as well as a critical analysis. The spotlight next turns upon the performances, concentrating naturally on the individual playing the Devil. Other performers also receive mention when their contributions are noteworthy. The final section consists of representative quotes or bits of dialogue, which help convey the flavor and character of each picture.

Lost, genuinely obscure, and arcane efforts are noted in the first appendix. The second appendix contains a brief look at some of the actors who have played Satan on television.

The index includes both individuals, themes and titles mentioned in the book. All actors who play the Devil are noted by an asterisk in the index.

Now that all the minutiae of the layout have been imparted, it only remains for the reader to plunge ahead. The landscape of Devil films has many strange byways and labyrinthian crossroads. Feel free to explore them all or selectively sample a few. Either way, I trust you'll enjoy the adventure — whether or not you come armed with bell, book, and candle.

The Films

Alias Nick Beal

1949   Rating: *****   Ray Milland as the Devil

Paramount. Written by Jonathan Latimer; Story by Mindret Lord; Photographed by Lionel Lindon; Edited by Eda Warren; Music by Franz Waxman; Produced by Endre Bohem; Directed by John Farrow. B&W, 93 minutes.

Cast

Ray Milland (*Nick Beal*, the Devil); Audrey Totter (*Donna Allen*, woman recruited by Beal); Thomas Mitchell (*Joseph Foster*, ambitious district attorney); George Macready (*Rev. Thomas Garfield*, minister and Foster's best friend); Geraldine Wall (*Martha Foster*, Joseph's wife); Fred Clark (*Frankie Faulkner*, corrupt political boss); King Donovan (*Peter Wolfe*, Foster's legal assistant); Henry O'Neill (*Ben Hobson*, judge, Reform party leader); Darryl Hickman (*Larry Price*, streetwise kid at boys' club); Nestor Paiva (*Karl*, bartender at China Coast Cafe); Charles Evans (*Paul Norton*, candidate for lt. governor); Maxine Gates (*Opal*, Donna's maid); Arlene Jenkins (*Aileen*, Foster household maid); Douglas Spencer (*Henry T. Finch*, murdered mob bookkeeper); Steve Pendleton (*Lt. Dodds*, investigator in Finch murder case); Erno Verebes (Foster's tailor); Pepito Perez (designer of Foster's campaign poster); Joey Ray (*Tommy Ray*, messenger boy for Beal); Percy Helton (lost soul working for Beal).

Appraisal and Synopsis

Alias Nick Beal is an unusually rich and rewarding picture that works on many levels. It blends elements of fantasy with *film noir* in updating Goethe's *Faust* to a mid-twentieth century American setting. It pulls this off quite successfully, largely due to a heavy reliance on atmosphere and superb acting from the principal stars. The director, John Farrow, had just completed *Night Has a Thousand Eyes* (1948), a masterful and rare amalgamation of the supernatural with the gritty realism of the *noir* style. In many ways, *Alias Nick Beal* is an extension of the mood and atmosphere of *Night Has a Thousand Eyes*. It also goes beyond *Night Has a Thousand Eyes*, abandoning any comic relief except for occasional black humor, usually supplied by Milland. There is also some cynical humor in the script, where many names are derived through subtle word play. The weak governor is named Lambert ("lamb"). Foster's assistant is Peter Wolfe ("*Peter and the Wolf*"). The leader of the independent party with a penchant for bad choices is

The original poster art for Alias Nick Beal *hid the real nature of the film.*

Ben Hobson ("Hobson's choice"). The political hack from the southern part of the state is Faulkner. All of these references are certainly deliberate as demonstrated by Nick Beal himself, combining the Devil's popular nickname of "Ol' Nick" with his alternate name of Beelzebub. The entire film is filled with entertaining surprises for the viewer, since much of the dialogue and action works on two or three levels at once, one of the film's best features. Other outstanding aspects include an exceptional musical score, moody and atmospheric cinematography with many fog-enshrouded scenes, and a unique and masterful set design. Most impressive is Donna Allen's apartment, which is apparently designed by the Devil. The surreal art over the fireplace and in the bedroom shows what meticulous care was lavished on the production. All of these elements combine to make this film a genuine classic.

Alias Nick Beal captures its audience from the opening credits, which depict a dark sky during a raging thunderstorm. Franz Waxman's music alternates between a brass choir intoning the hymn "A Mighty Fortress Is Our God" and a sardonic saxophone riff representing the Devil. This music sets the overall mood in a most compelling fashion. Milland's voice-over narrates that every man has a fatal weakness and as an example offers the story of Joseph Foster, who sacrifices integrity for power. Governor-elect Foster is on his way to his inauguration, but the Devil chooses to backtrack his story eight months, when Foster was a struggling district attorney. He is observed conferring with Frankie Faulkner, a corrupt downstate political hack. Faulkner suggests that if the DA drops his case against a local crime boss named Hanson, his political machine would support him in a race for governor. Foster throws him out after Faulkner says that Hanson's financial books won't be turned over as ordered since they have been accidentally destroyed in a fire.

The Reverend Tom Garfield drops by to visit Foster, and the DA confides that Faulkner and Hanson may have outwitted him. Foster escorts Larry Price, a youngster in trouble with the law, to the Garfield Boys' Club. At the club office, Foster has a heart-to-heart talk with Larry and persuades him to join the club. The young man agrees just as Martha Foster shows up. The DA tells his wife that he will probably lose the Hanson case. In frustration, Foster exclaims, "I would give my soul to nail him!" At that instant, a small lad enters the office and hands Foster a message that reads, "If you want to nail Hanson, drop around the China Coast at eight tonight." Foster says he doesn't even know the location of the China Coast, but Larry tells him how to get there.

The cafe is located on a wharf, and as eight o'clock approaches, it becomes enshrouded in a heavy fog. A sinister-looking man, whistling a mournful tune, appears from the end of the wharf and enters the cafe. He is dressed in an elegant business suit. He asks the China Coast bartender to bring two drinks, ginger ale and Barbados rum, to his table. The bartender says he doesn't have Barbados, but the man replies with confidence, "It's in a square bottle. You'll find it." Much to his amazement, the barman locates the unusual bottle. Foster enters the cafe and approaches the table, asking, "Are you the man who sent me the note?" The man motions for Foster to sit and offers him a drink. Foster replies, "Ginger ale," just as the bartender arrives with the drinks. "Here it is," the man says and pays the barman with a silver dollar. "Before I drink that, you might tell me who you are." The man hands Foster a card that reads, "Nicholas Beal, Agent," and he asks, "Agent for what?" "That depends," Beal responds. "Perhaps for you." He offers to recover the missing Hanson books. They strike an agreement, and Beal leads Foster into a dingy warehouse

Audrey Totter's characer, Donna Allen, has her first encounter with the sinister Nick Beal (Ray Milland).

where he uncovers a ledger tucked away in an old file cabinet. Foster is amazed as he pages through it but concedes it would be illegal for him to take the ledger without a warrant. "Didn't you say you would give, I believe it was your soul, to nail Hanson?" Beal asks. Foster looks at the ledger carefully and finally tucks it under his arm. He turns to talk to Beal, but he has vanished. He searches for him but only encounters a large grey rat. The music on the soundtrack plays Beal's theme, suggesting the rat is actually Beal. Foster turns out the light and leaves the warehouse.

A newspaper headline proclaims, "FOSTER TRIUMPHS, HANSON GUILTY!" At his home, Joseph and his wife are having a celebration over his success. Foster sheepishly admits to her that he stole the decisive evidence. Martha is stunned at first and then tells her husband to make sure he never does anything like that again. Rev. Garfield drops by with two leaders of the Reform party, Judge Hobson and Paul Norton. They have come to urge him to run as their candidate for governor. Foster steps into the next room to make himself a drink, when Nick Beal suddenly appears seated in an easy chair. When Martha enters the room, she takes an instant dislike to Beal, who asks for and then rejects "payment" for his services. Instead he offers Foster a cash donation of $25,000 for his gubernatorial campaign. He leaves the money on Foster's desk and goes into the room where Rev. Garfield and his friends are waiting. Foster follows Beal, but he has vanished. He questions Garfield, who replies that he saw no one. The Reform leaders press the DA to consider becoming their candidate.

Outside the China Coast Cafe, Beal recruits Donna Allen, a downtrodden young lady who has been ejected from the bar. She is intrigued and lets Beal lead her to an elegant hotel room. Donna becomes puzzled and frightened when Beal recounts her personal history, including her involvement with an actor who died mysteriously. "Accident, they called it," Beal sneers, and Donna starts to flee in panic. As she opens the door, a delivery man arrives with a large number of boxes. They contain a selection of luxurious clothes, including a sable coat embroidered with her name and a cigarette case encrusted with sapphires. "What do I gotta do, murder?" she asks hesitantly. "Just the opposite … reform work in a boys' club." Soon, Donna is a staple at the Garfield Boys' Club, and Foster compliments her for bringing order to the establishment. She asks Foster if she can adjust his tie. She says it is too drab and offers to help him select ties the next time he goes shopping. Beal appears mysteriously from the back of the office and persuades Foster to retain his campaign donation. Foster introduces Beal to Donna Allen, who pretends not to know him, and Rev. Garfield. The minister becomes intrigued by Beal and asks him to help lead the evening's Bible reading for the boys. Startled, Beal declines, "No, it's your book, read it yourself." The sinister figure slips away as Garfield starts to recite one of the psalms, and all of the boys lower their heads.

Back at home, Foster has difficulty selecting a tie and claims that his selection is only appropriate for a retired undertaker. His wife offers to buy him some new ones, but Foster says he would prefer to make his own purchases from now on. Martha seems puzzled by this exchange. A stranger comes to Foster's house and demands to speak with him. The man is nervous and introduces himself as Henry Finch, Hanson's bookkeeper. He claims the mob is after him because they believe he turned the books over to Foster. Finch insists he burned the books, and he implores Foster to provide some funds to allow him to escape the mob and leave town. Foster agrees to meet Finch at his office at 10 PM. While the lawyer's back is turned, Finch steals one of his pipes from a custommade holder in his study. Later, Finch arrives at the China Coast Cafe, and he tells Beal that he carried out his instructions. After Beal verifies that Finch took one of Foster's pipes, he tells the nervous bookkeeper to follow him outside so he can pay him off. Again, it is a very foggy night. Beal starts to whistle his tune. Finch has trouble seeing, and Beal urges him to the end of the dock. Finch lets out a yelp in the dark, and moments later a loud splash is heard.

Foster, pacing in his office when Beal arrives, blurts out his concerns about Finch. Beal dismisses the approach as a shakedown and tells Foster to ignore it. Foster is upset by Finch's claim that the ledger used at the trial was a fake. At this moment, Hobson telephones Foster, who agrees to accept the Reform party's nomination. A smirk crosses Beal's face as he hears Foster's decision. Donna Allen now has a key post in Foster's election campaign. Foster and Beal enter the headquarters after a campaign appearance. At a meeting of his election committee, Foster learns that he is trailing his rival, a corrupt politician named Kennedy. Beal advises making a political deal for Faulkner's support. Hobson says he would prefer defeat to any deals. In private, Beal reveals that he has already set up an arrangement with Faulkner, but Foster is free to repudiate it. The lawyer, upset by this news, steps close to Beal, who dislikes being touched. He warns Foster to keep his distance and then persuades him to make a realistic decision: either deal with Faulkner or watch Kennedy win. After leaving the inner office, Beal alerts Donna that Foster will visit her that evening. Rev. Garfield approaches Beal, saying his face seems familiar to him. He asks, "Did anyone ever paint your portrait?" Beal sarcastically replies, "Yes, Rembrandt in 1655."

When Foster explains the Faulkner plan to his wife over dinner, she demands that he reject it. She would prefer to see Kennedy elected than have her husband make such a compromise. Foster becomes indignant when she starts to compare him to Hitler and Mussolini, and he storms out of the house. At Donna's apartment, Beal coaches her closely, predicting what Foster will say to her to the exact word. She doubts that Beal can forecast what Foster will say, but she agrees to follow his script. Foster shows up at her apartment moments later, and their conversation proceeds exactly as Beal predicted. Donna becomes terrified by Beal's powers as she echoes his words. She urges Foster to accept the Faulkner deal and hustles him out. She then tries to locate Beal, who was eavesdropping on the conversation from her bedroom, but he has completely vanished. In a panic, Donna decides to run away and heads to the train station. She stops in a bar for a drink, but Beal suddenly appears, fully aware of her planned escape.

On election night, Foster is running slightly behind Kennedy, with only a handful of districts, including the two controlled by Faulkner, still not reporting. Surprisingly, Foster swamps Kennedy when the results are announced. Hobson is furious, realizing that a deal with Faulkner must have been made. This is confirmed when Faulkner shows up at campaign headquarters, and Hobson leads a walkout of Reform party members when it is announced that Kennedy has conceded the election.

A few weeks later, Foster is being fitted for a new inauguration suit when Beal arrives with the morning papers. The independent Reform party has disassociated itself from Governor-Elect Joseph Foster. Outraged, the lawyer flings the paper aside, calling the Reformers hypocrites who only know how to lose. He hastens off to visit Garfield. The minister tells Foster that he has changed, and the rumors about him and Donna Allen will ruin his marriage. He also warns Foster about Nick Beal, claiming there is something strange, almost supernatural about his reclusive advisor. Garfield is trying to locate a medieval woodcut of Lucifer that is the exact image of Beal. Foster is flabbergasted by this suggestion. "Where is the tail and the horns? Where is the smell of sulphur and brimstone? And where is the contract?" Garfield replies that maybe the Devil has adjusted to the twentieth century.

At Donna's apartment, Foster is pouring out his troubles to the young woman, who listens sympathetically to his every word. After Foster departs, Donna pleads with Beal, who has made one of his mysterious appearances. She asks him to leave Foster alone. For a moment, she tries to seduce Beal, who snarls, "Don't you ever touch me!" and slaps her.

At Foster's home, Martha informs her husband that she will not attend his inauguration. She begs him one last time to reject Beal and never see him again. Foster agrees, but as soon as Martha exits the room, Beal appears. He warns Foster that he is the target of a murder investigation in the case of Henry Finch. The police were tipped (apparently by Beal himself) that Foster was involved. One of Foster's distinctive pipes was found in the murdered man's pocket. Foster notices that one of his pipes is missing from his set. Beal says the police are planning to arrest him at any minute. He promises to save Foster if he signs a document promising to make Beal the keeper of the state seal when he becomes governor. Since this position is only a ceremonial post with no power, Foster sees no harm in granting it. There is also a forfeit clause, however. If Foster doesn't make this appointment, the contract binds him to accompany Beal to the island of Almas Perdidas.

Foster consents to the deal just as the police arrive at his home. The detectives question Foster about the pipe found on Finch's body, and he says it resembles one of his own. His set of pipes, however, now appears to be complete, and the police seem pleased that their lead was a false one. Beal takes his contract, commenting on Foster's legible handwriting. The next day, Foster is dejected as he prepares his inaugural address. Beal comes in and hands him a prepared speech. He also discusses which state positions should go to Faulkner's control. Foster yields to each of Beal's requests.

A downpour greets Foster as he mounts the steps of the state capitol. He spots Donna Allen by one of the columns, and she calls to him. She is dressed in a plain coat, the same one she wore when she first met Beal. She admits her previous appearance was all a pose designed by Beal. She starts to warn him about Beal being the Devil, when the man himself appears and tells Foster it is time to go inside. Beal now seems unconcerned about Donna and allows her to escape.

Foster is troubled as he waits to take his oath of office. Beal urges him to study a scrapbook recounting the events of the past eight months. As he turns the pages, Foster appears to come to a decision. He is then sworn into office before a small crowd and immediately resigns, allowing Paul Norton, his reform-minded lieutenant governor, to succeed him. Moments later, Foster leaves the building and confronts Beal on the front steps. Beal appears strangely pleased, saying, "Fine gesture. Virtue triumphant." "But your plans didn't work out," Foster stammers. "Just the opposite. They worked out exactly as scheduled," Beal gloats.

Arriving home, Foster learns that Martha has left him. He receives a phone call from Beal stating he will enforce the forfeit clause in their contract, since he wasn't appointed keeper of the state seal, and he instructs Foster to meet him at eleven that night at the China Coast Cafe for their voyage to Almas Perdidas. Foster turns to Garfield for help. At the boys' club, he searches the almanac and finds no island listed with that name. Garfield insists the contract is invalid if the island does not exist. He also reveals that the name of the place in Spanish translates as the Island of Lost Souls. The minister urges Foster to talk with Martha and says she is staying at his house. Foster takes a taxi to go to her. Larry Price enters the boys' club to drop off a package for the minister. He remarks that he was surprised to see that Nick Beal had become a cab driver and explains that he saw him driving off with Foster. Garfield is startled, and he decides to go with Martha to the China Coast to see if they can rescue Foster. Outside the China Coast, a preacher is holding a street service. Beal and Foster listen for a moment and then enter the cafe. Several individuals, other lost souls, come in and rendezvous with Beal for their journey to Almas Perdidas. One of them recognizes Foster and greets him. Beal starts to outline what Foster's duties will be as one of his agents of darkness: "You will be a valuable addition. You have a good front, you inspire confidence, and people will trust you."

As they proceed to the end of the wharf, Beal reminisces about the night when the city had a huge fire: "We picked up quite a lot of recruits that night. It made quite a transportation problem." Martha and Garfield finally arrive, and the minister asks Beal if he can see the contract. "Take a look," Beal boasts. "Good clear signature. You will find everything else in order too." The minister drops the contract and as he bends to pick it up, his

Bible falls on top of it. "Pick it up!" Beal demands.

Foster, who has been in a daze, suddenly seems to revive. "Suppose you pick it up, Mr. Beal. It's right at your feet." Beal suddenly realizes he has been defeated. "You've jockeyed me into sort of a morality play, haven't you? Only we've a pier instead of the nave of a cathedral, but the props are the same. It's always been bell or candle or that worn-out book of yours." Foster bends down to retrieve the contract, tucking it inside the Bible. He offers it to Beal, who refuses to accept it. Beal comments about Foster's luck and forlornly wishes he had some luck when he fell. He vanishes into the darkness as he speaks. Relieved, Foster embraces his wife and turns the Bible with the contract over to Garfield. The minister proclaims, "You've won. That's the important thing. Forget him. Go home." The theme of "A Mighty Fortress Is Our God" blares triumphant on the soundtrack as the end credits roll.

Performances

Ray Milland is superb as the Devil, being both suave and sinister. His basic approach is to portray Lucifer as a cunning con man, a minor hood loath to openly display his powers, but who becomes more lackadaisical about protecting his identity as he narrows in on his prey. There are many excellent touches to his portrayal, such as paying his debts with silver coins rather than cash. At all times, his appearance is ordinary; his clothing consists of a dark business suit with a dark tie and a fedora hat. His manner of speech is in the vernacular of the day, sounding most like a streetwise salesman, persuasive but with little sophistication. Milland also manages to bring a sinister air to the most ordinary expressions or comments. His flawless performance completes one of the most convincing portrayals of the Devil in the history of the screen. Milland is ably supported by the rest of the cast, particularly Audrey Totter. In the sequence where Foster first appears at her apartment, her multilayered performance is breathtaking: her facial expressions reflect her actual thoughts, which are completely different than her rehearsed dialogue with Foster. Her acting in this complex role is of the highest order. Thomas Mitchell, while convincing, is somewhat bland, and his reading lacks the depth of the other characters. He seems to be excruciatingly slow in his thinking at times, and he is too easily manipulated by the Devil. Perhaps a younger, less world-weary performer might have been better as a naive but ambitious Foster. On the other hand, George Macready hits the right note as the minister who is perplexed about Beal. Although suspicious of him, Macready's character never fully believes that Beal is the Devil. This hesitancy renders his performance more believable. Geraldine Wall is fine as Martha Foster, and she conveys the fact that Martha is good-hearted but not the intellectual equal of Foster. At one point, she foolishly compares her husband to Hitler and Mussolini, suggesting that they wanted to do good but were corrupted by "downstate" political machines. This is probably the only American film where any character attributes noble motives to Adolf Hitler.

In an interview for this book, Audrey Totter informed me that the atmosphere on the set while making this picture was an extraordinarily happy one, thanks largely to the personalities of Ray Milland, Thomas Mitchell, and director John Farrow. She also reports that Mia Farrow, age four, was often brought to the set by her mother, Maureen O'Sullivan. The working title for the picture was *Dark Circle*, and Totter reports that most of the cast were disappointed by the later title change. At least it was better than *The Contact Man*, another title that was briefly considered. While making the film, everyone felt it was going to be a huge hit, but the picture never found its audience. Totter felt it was poorly and inaccurately promoted by Paramount, which sold it as straight *film noir*. The publicity featured such silly tag lines as "the shock-filled story of a man whose love was more dangerous than a loaded gun." Someone in the bureaucracy of Paramount must have taken a dislike to the film, and it was simply dumped on the market. It was somewhat more successful overseas. In Italy, the film scored well using the title *La Sconfitta di Satana*. Many critics and fans have praised the film over the years, and it has been shown frequently on television, particularly during the 1960s and 1970s. *Alias Nick Beal* is an exceptional and compelling film that merits a major rediscovery.

Notable Quotes

- I'm just a humble follower of your work ... wayward boys set straight, criminals successfully prosecuted, and I [dramatic pause] admire you, incorruptible enemy of the legions of evil. (**Beal to Foster at their first meeting**)
- How do we know you are not some sort of racketeer? (**Martha to Beal**)

My racket concerns good government. (**Beal**)
- I've walked in the darkness. I've wrestled the Devil and thrown him. I've pinned his shoulders to the mat. Yes, I've pinned his shoulders to the mat. (**preacher at street service**)

I wonder if he knows it is two falls out of three? (**Beal, commenting to Foster**)
- You've saved yourself just in time, didn't you? But there will be others who won't ... a lot of others. And I will tell you why. In everyone there is a seed of destruction ... a fatal weakness. You know that now, Foster. You are lucky. You are luckier than I when I fell, but that was a long time ago. (**Beal's farewell to Foster**)

Angel Heart

1987   Rating: ***   Robert De Niro as the Devil

Carolco. Written by Alan Parker, based on the novel *Falling Angel* by William Hjortsberg; Photographed by Michael Serversin; Edited by Gerry Hambling; Special Effects by J. C. Brotherhood and William Trent; Music by Trevor Jones; Produced by Alan Marshall and Elliott Kastner; Directed by Alan Parker. Color, 113 minutes.

Annotated Cast List

Mickey Rourke (*Harry Angel*, private detective and *Johnny Favorite*, missing crooner); Robert De Niro (*Louis Cyphre*, the Devil); Lisa Bonet (*Epiphany Proudfoot*, teenage voodoo priestess); Charlotte Rampling (*Margaret Krusemark*, fortune teller; also known as Madame Zora); Stocker Fontelieu (*Ethan Krusemark*, her wealthy father); Brownie McGhee (*Edison "Toots" Sweet*, blues guitarist); Michael Higgins (*Fowler*, doctor); Charles Gordone (*Spider Simpson*, jazz band leader); Elizabeth Whitcraft (*Connie*, Harry's girlfriend); Eliott Keener (*Sterne*, police detective); Pruitt Taylor Vince (*Deimos*,

18 • *Angel Heart*

Robert De Niro as the elegant Louis Cyphre in Angel Heart. ***Note how his polished nails come to a sharp point.***

Sterne's partner); Dann Florek (*Herman Winesap*, Cyphre's lawyer); Kathleen Wilhoite (nurse); George Buck (*Izzy*, man at Coney Island beach); Judith Drake (his wife); Gerald Orange (*Pastor John*, Harlem evangelist); Peggy Severe (*Mammy Carter*, herbalist); Jarret Narcisse (Epiphany's son).

Appraisal and Synopsis

The novel upon which this film was based, *Falling Angel* by William Hjortsberg, is magnificent. It presents the story of a seedy private eye, Harry Angel, who is hired by an enigmatic figure named Louis

Cyphre to find the whereabouts of Johnny Favorite, a forgotten crooner who had a momentary burst of fame a decade earlier. The book proceeds like a typical *noir* novel, becoming darker as it continues until the plot is revealed as a clever Devil story, with Angel discovering that Johnny Favorite actually murdered him and absorbed his soul in an effort to outwit Satan. The Devil is now ready to collect. The unaltered original story would have made a terrific film, perhaps done in black and white and in genuine *film noir* style. Unfortunately, Alan Parker did a pedestrian job with his screenplay, muddying the plot and altering a number of characters. Epiphany Proudfoot, for example, is changed from a prosperous young pharmaceutical store owner to an impoverished waif with a young child. The director/writer's worst idea was transferring the bulk of the action from New York City to New Orleans, which completely changed the dynamic from a hard-boiled detective story to a sleazy southern Gothic, weakening it considerably. Parker's tinkering deprived *Angel Heart* of much of the extraordinary atmosphere of the book, although he included a few interesting visual touches, such as a recurring fan motif (in the first scene with the Devil, there are two ceiling fans, but the one pointed at the Devil hardly rotates at all) and heart imagery.

The credits appear over a cryptic scene as a figure with a cane (probably the Devil) is seen walking down a gloomy alley. A dog and a cat later appear in the same alley, and the dog discovers a dead body. The story proper never refers back to this sequence. A different Manhattan street appears in daylight with a title card reading, "New York 1955." The plot is set up rather quickly as private eye Harry Angel is summoned by attorney Herman Winesap to meet with his client Louis Cyphre at an evangelical revival hall in Harlem. Hired to locate Jonathan Liebling, who became a pop sensation known as Johnny Favorite, Angel travels to a private sanitarium outside Poughkeepsie, where the singer has supposedly been a patient for the past twelve years, a victim of injuries received in the Second World War. Angel tracks down Fowler, Favorite's doctor, a narcotics addict, and learns that the singer was spirited away by a man and woman twelve years earlier. Fowler was paid $25,000 by the pair to send an annual report to Winesap that Favorite remained a comatose patient at the sanitarium. When Fowler passes out, Harry goes to a local diner to pick up some cheeseburgers for the doctor. Returning to Fowler's apartment, Angel finds him murdered, and he flees the scene.

Cyphre gives Angel $5,000 to pursue, saying slugs always leave slime in their tracks. The detective researches Favorite's old associates, which lead him to New Orleans. He contacts "Toots" Sweet, a blues guitarist, and Madame Zora, Johnny's old flame, a fortune teller who is actually the daughter of Ethan Krusemark, the shipping magnate. He learns that Johnny had an affair with a beautiful West Indian woman named Evangeline Proudfoot, since deceased. Johnny is also reported to be the father of Epiphany Proudfoot, Evangeline's daughter. Angel feels sorry for the poor teenager, who already has a child of her own. He discovers that she is a voodoo practitioner. Epiphany later visits his hotel room, and they make love.

"Toots" Sweet and Madame Zora are horribly murdered. The New Orleans police consider Angel a suspect because he was the last one to see both of them alive. Louis Cyphre also turns up in New Orleans for a report on Angel's progress on the case, and Harry suspects his employer may be involved in the murders. Harry also is beginning to have flashes of images that he cannot explain, some of Times Square and another of himself descending in a rickety elevator. Finally, Harry tracks down Ethan Krusemark and forces him to tell what he knows about Johnny Favorite. The old man spins a wild tale that Favorite sold his soul to the Devil in exchange for his success as a singer. He planned to trick Satan by utilizing an obscure ritual to switch souls with another individual. Johnny picked up an ex-soldier in Times Square on New Year's Eve, drugged him in a bar, and brought him to his hotel where Krusemark, his daughter, and Johnny performed their ceremony. They killed the soldier, and Johnny cut out his heart and ate it. Johnny planned to assume the soldier's identity, but then he himself was drafted and assigned to the Entertainment Division. He was seriously wounded during a show when a Luftwaffe attack strafed the stage. He was brought home in a comatose state. A year passed, and on New Year's Eve, Ethan and his daughter bribed Fowler and smuggled Johnny out of the hospital. Johnny's face had been reconstructed through plastic surgery, and he lost the memory of being Johnny Favorite, only recalling the memories of the murdered soldier. Ethan's daughter simply released him in Times Square, since that was the last locale the soldier remembered.

Harry becomes more and more disturbed listening to this story, for he himself had a memory gap after receiving a medical discharge during the war. He asks Ethan the name of the soldier killed by Johnny. All Ethan can report is that the dead man's dog tags were sealed in an urn kept by his daughter. Feeling sick, Harry runs to the bathroom, and when he returns, he finds that Ethan has been murdered. Frantic, Harry drives to Zora's apartment, sealed by the police as a crime scene. He breaks in and locates the urn, smashing it open. The name on the dog tags reads "HAROLD ANGEL."

Stunned, Harry turns to see Louis Cyphre sitting on Zora's sofa. Harry finally realizes his employer's identity. The Devil says, "For twelve years you've been living on borrowed time on another man's memories, Johnny." He also reveals that Harry/Johnny committed the murders of Fowler, Sweet, Krusemark and his daughter under the Devil's direction. The wily Satan was merely toying with his victim, whose pride led him to believe that the Devil could be outwitted. Finally, the Devil allows Harry to recall the murders. Satan becomes more demonic in his appearance, and his eyes transform into those of a snake. Stunned, Harry also realizes that he killed Epiphany, his daughter. He races back to his hotel room to find her body, as well as the police. They arrest him, and as he is taken away, Epiphany's son glares at him, and the boy's eyes are inhuman, just like those of Satan.

The end is fascinating, depicting Harry/Johnny as he descends into hell in a shadowy antique elevator. The scene cuts back and forth between the somber Mickey Rourke and a black screen with end credits. The final shot, as the credits end, shows the elevator reaching the bottom level. It is a shame that the rest of the film lacked the imaginative power of this remarkable finish. *Angel Heart* wound up as a good film, but it could have been a great one.

Performances

Robert De Niro provides a quiet, subtly shaded reading as the Devil, who approaches his victim in the same methodical manner with which he peels and consumes an egg. Also unusual is his preference for setting meetings in religious or semireligious locations, such as the evangelical center in Harlem or an ornate New Orleans church. Louis Cyphre is an intriguing pseudonym for Lucifer, and when Harry Angel finally figures it out (Harry is slow on the uptake), De Niro gives one of his few smiles in the picture. As the Devil,

De Niro speaks softly and wears a well-trimmed beard. He wears an ordinary, dark, three-piece suit, carries a cane, and has an oversized ring on the fourth finger of his right hand. He has a number of nervous hand gestures, such as continually stretching his fingers or spinning his cane. The only indication of his supernatural origin is that his fingernails and hair grow at an extraordinary rate. In his opening scene, his hair is rather closely cropped, but it appears longer and wilder in each succeeding scene. Likewise, his highly polished fingernails grow to Fu Manchu length as the film progresses. During his last words to Angel, the Devil's eyes change color and shape, becoming serpentlike, as he points to Angel and proclaims in a whisper that his soul belongs to him. Mickey Rourke is fair to good as Harry. Better casting would have been to choose a more sympathetic performer, perhaps someone more in the style of the classic shamus stars of the 1940s and 1950s. Other cast members who stand out include Charlotte Rampling as the fortune teller, Brownie McGhee as Toots, and Gerald Orange as the sleazy Harlem preacher.

Notable Quotes

- I don't like messy accounts. (**Cyphre to Harry Angel while peeling an egg**)
- They say there is just enough religion in the world to make men hate one another, but not enough to make them love. (**Cyphre to Harry Angel, meeting him in a New Orleans church**)
- Alas, how terrible is wisdom when it brings no profit to the wise, Johnny. (**the Devil to Harry Angel, quoting *Oedipus Rex* by Sophocles**)
- Mephistopheles is such a mouthful in Manhattan. (**the Devil to Angel, after Harry has figured out Cyphre's pseudonym**)

Angel on My Shoulder

1946   Rating: ****   Claude Rains as the Devil

United Artists. Written by Roland Kibbee and Harry Segall; Photographed by James Van Trees; Special Effects by Harry Redmond, Jr.; Edited by Asa Clark; Music by Dimitri Tiomkin; Produced by Charles R. Rogers and David W. Siegal; Directed by Archie Mayo. B&W, 100 minutes.

Annotated Cast List

Paul Muni (*Eddie Kagle*, gangster, and *Judge Frederick Parker*, reform candidate for governor); Claude Rains (*Nick*, the Devil); Anne Baxter (*Barbara Foster*, Parker's fiancée); Onslow Stephens (*Matt Higgins*, Parker's doctor); George Cleveland (*Albert*, Parker's valet); Hardie Albright (*Smiley Williams*, henchman who kills Kagle); Erskin Sanford (minister); Sarah Padden (*Agathe*, minister's wife) George Meeker (*Bentley*, man on trial for murder); Marion Martin (*Rosie Bentley*, his wife and codefendant); Addison Richards (*Big Harry*, Bentley's crooked lawyer); Archie Twitchell (police sergeant who sees Eddie refuse a bribe); James Flavin (*Bellamy*, mob boss out to discredit Parker); Joan Blair (woman who arrives in hell); Noble Johnson (trusty in hell); Kurt Katch (warden in hell); Jonathan Hale (committee chairman in Parker's campaign); Fritz Leiber (chemist in hell who poisoned his wife); Ben Weldon (*Shaggsy*, hood who leads vegetable attack); Edward Keane (prison official who oversees Kagle's release); Murray Alper (*Jim*, hood who poses as cabbie); Lee Shumway (court bailiff); Russ Whiteman (intern in judge's chambers); Chester Clute (stage manager at rally); Saul Gorss (henchman and stuntman for Muni); Jimmy Dundee, Mike Lally, Duke Taylor (henchmen); Frank Hagney, Jack Roper, Gil Perkins (guards in hell).

Appraisal and Synopsis

Writer Harry Segall won an Academy Award for his original story for *Here Comes Mr. Jordan* (1941), a fantasy about a prizefighter (Robert Montgomery) whose soul is prematurely removed from his body by a bumbling angel. Mr. Jordan, a heavenly messenger played by Claude Rains, tries to put matters right by finding a new body for the soul to inhabit. Several years later, Segall developed the concept of *Angel on My Shoulder*, a sort of diabolic counterpart to the earlier fantasy. This time the Devil transplants the soul of a murdered gangster into the body of a reform candidate for governor in an attempt to ruin the reputation of this champion of virtue. Rains was recruited to play the Devil, but instead of the smooth confidence of Mr. Jordan, Rains portrays the Devil on a losing streak; his most elaborate plans always seem to backfire. Good performances and strong production values, including a powerful score by Dimitri Tiomkin, make the film a worthy effort, although it never rivaled the success of *Here Comes Mr. Jordan*. A few years later, Segall developed a third picture depicting unearthly visitors called *For Heaven's Sake* (1950), in which angels Clifton Webb and Edmund Gwenn come to the aid of a married couple played by Joan Bennett and Robert Cummings. These three films are similar in nature; they are basically well-constructed comedies with interesting characters thrown into extremely odd and colorful scenarios. All three derive their humor from the fact that the earthly cast is unaware of the supernatural intervention operating in its midst.

Angel on My Shoulder opens with mob boss Eddie Kagle just released from a stretch in the penitentiary and being killed by his second-in-command, Smiley Williams, who enjoyed running the gang himself. Eddie descends to hell, imaginatively rendered as a demonic prison, with a warden, trusties, and general prison population. He meets a confused woman who was killed crossing the street and a scientist who was hanged for killing his wife. At first, Eddie cannot accept his fate, and he runs wild, breaking into Satan's office while leading trusties on a reckless chase. After he is dragged off, the warden of hell apologizes to the Devil for allowing the new arrival to get out of hand. The Devil has been cranky, upset by labor shortages in hell and the overall decline in temperature to below 180°. He is discouraged that he has been losing recent skirmishes with the Almighty, and he is determined to best him in the situation involving Judge Parker, a leading force for righteousness who is running for governor in a major state. But seeing Eddie Kagle, the spitting image of Parker, gives Satan an idea. He can discredit Parker by placing Kagle's soul in his body and allowing Kagle's worst instincts to take charge.

Satan poses as a trusty in the demonic boiler room and makes friends with Kagle. He strikes a deal with the hood, offering to help him escape and kill Smiley Williams in exchange for discrediting Judge Parker. The Devil leads Eddie through the flames inside the furnace to a hidden freight elevator, which surfaces in front of Schmalhausen's Bakery in Judge Parker's home town. Eddie asks his new friend if he uses an alias. "I have a long record under the name of Mephistopheles," the Devil replies and asks that Eddie call him Nick. Eddie thinks he is just a lowly con man and insists that in their collaboration, he is the boss. Coyly, the Devil agrees, deferring to Eddie whenever possible. He explains that they are invisible on Earth until they inhabit some bodies. He takes Eddie to Judge Parker's chambers, where the judge is resting after having fainted in the courtroom. Nick works a spell to infuse Eddie's soul into Parker's body, and when he awakens, Eddie is in control. After a hilarious encounter with Parker's manservant, Eddie charters a plane to St. Louis where he intends to bump off Smiley. When the Devil suddenly appears, he forces Eddie to turn back by causing engine trouble, promising that he'll be able to take care of Smiley later.

Barbara, Parker's fiancée, is upset by the sudden change in the judge's personality, but Higgins, Parker's doctor, advises her to play along with him, saying Parker is exhausted from working too hard. When Eddie interacts with others, the Devil, invisible to everyone but Eddie, keeps advising him on what to say and how to behave. But instead of ruining the judge, Eddie's actions make Parker more popular. During a political speech, for example, when Eddie is pelted with vegetables by a bunch of local hoods, he goes after them, fists flying. His actions make Parker a hero. The Devil organizes a bribe scheme for the judge, which also backfires. Bellamy, the local mob boss, calls Smiley Williams and sends him after Parker. Barbara is encouraged to take Eddie away to relax, and he starts to grow fond of her. At her insistence, they stop by a minister's house to get married. Eddie overhears the preacher preparing his sermon about Lucifer, and he is startled to learn that the Devil is also known as Mephistopheles. He goes to Nick and rejects him now that he knows his true identity. He also refuses to marry Barbara, telling her the time is not right.

Returning to his apartment, Eddie finds Smiley asleep on a couch, just as if he were a sacrificial offering presented to him by the Devil. A changed man, Eddie refuses to take advantage of his sleeping enemy. Instead he wakes him, and Smiley is frightened by Parker's resemblance to Eddie. Backing away, he falls out the window. The Devil no longer has any claim on Eddie and is forced to appeal to God to reclaim the gangster's soul. Eddie agrees to return to hell if Satan agrees not to interfere at any time in the future with Judge Parker and Barbara. Eddie vacates Parker's body, and as he descends to hell, he wrings one final concession from Satan, who agrees to make Eddie a trusty in return for his silence about the Devil's failure in his latest escapade.

This film was remade as a TV movie for ABC in 1980. George Kirgo updated the original script but kept most of it intact. Richard Kiley took the role of the Devil, playing Nick as more exasperated and with less finesse than Rains. Peter Strauss played the role of Eddie, Seymour Cassel performed as Smiley, and Barbara Hershey assumed Anne Baxter's role, called Julie in this version. Critical reaction was mixed, with most commentators considering it a lightweight variation of the original classic.

Performances

The danger with the Devil's part in this screenplay is that he can easily appear too effete or foolish. Claude Rains has to walk a fine line to avoid these pitfalls and be both charming and crafty. He could have been a remarkably nasty Devil if he played him as he played Alexander Hollenius, the egotistical and dominating composer who tormented Bette Davis and Paul Henreid in *Deception* (1946). Instead, we have a smug, self-satisfied Devil whose plans simply never work out and who in essence is a bit of a wimp. According to the warden, hell is a rundown prison, beset with many administrative problems. The Devil himself is not doing much better. With all the resources at his command, he is unable to sidetrack even one virtuous official, Judge Parker. In one fascinating scene at the end of the film, this downtrodden Satan is forced to appeal to God Himself in his attempt to maintain a shred of dignity. At this point, he is even on the verge of eliciting sympathy from the audience for his recurring humiliations. All these elements make quite a different characterization than the hell administered by Laird Cregar, for example, in another comedic fantasy, *Heaven Can Wait* (1943).

The conception of hell in this film is quite dismal and striking. Even the Devil's office is barren, consisting of stone pillars and lintels, with flames visible in the distance through his doorway. For most of the film, Nick, as he prefers to be called, is dressed in the plain garb of a prison trusty. Rains wears no special makeup and is mild-mannered throughout, as if in his heart he anticipates every setback that comes his way. At one point, when he spots a group of clergymen who are supporting Parker at a rally, he slinks backward to avoid being in the presence of virtuous men. By the end of the picture, even slow-witted Eddie is able to get the better of him, blackmailing Satan as they return to the fiery pit at the final fadeout. Satan faces a prison riot in hell of unprecedented dimensions unless he submits to Eddie's request. The picture ends as almost a parody of *Casablanca* (1942) with Paul Muni in place of Humphrey Bogart as Eddie and Nick look forward to a "beautiful friendship." That scene is just one example of how Rains plays Nick with understated humor throughout. Even at his most blatant, Rains is subtle. For instance, instead of exclaiming, "What the hell is that?" he uses the phrase, "What in my domain is that?" Rains interacts exceptionally well with Paul Muni, whose deadpan reactions add immeasurably to the film's success. At the end of the film, Muni returns to hell almost in triumph, having gained a measure of redemption by sacrificing his eternity unselfishly for Judge Parker and Barbara, the woman he had come to love. Anne Baxter carries off the role of Parker's fiancée with elegance and class. This was director Archie Mayo's last picture, and it was a stylish close to a career which included such memorable efforts as *Svengali* (1931) and *The Petrified Forest* (1936).

Notable Quotes

• Gosh, it's hot here. It gets like this in Florida sometimes. (**confused woman in hell**)

Florida? Naw, Florida never smelt like this. (**Eddie's reply**)

• I have lately been beset by great problems. My adversary is working overtime, but superior though He may be, and though He set up a thousand Judge Parkers to thwart me, He must recognize that I am still master ... of my own sphere. (**the Devil to his helper, the warden of hell**)

• Being up so high makes me uncomfortable. I'm much happier down below. (**the Devil's comment to Eddie while in the airplane**)

• My children, my children, you would be lost without me. (**the Devil's reflections after eavesdropping on the local gangsters**)

• No soul has ever escaped from my domain before. I've got to get you back, or I'll be jeered at and derided. Why, the upheaval would be cataclysmic in its proportions. (**the Devil, asking Eddie to return to hell**)

Autopsia de un Fantasma
AKA Autopsy of a Ghost

1967   Rating: *   John Carradine as the Devil

Azteca Films. Written by Lucio Battistrada and Armando Crispino; Photographed by Carlos Carbajal; Edited by Fernando Martinez; Music by Raul Lavista; Produced and Directed by Ismael Rodriguez. Color, 108 minutes.

Annotated Cast List

Basil Rathbone (*Canuto Perez*, spirit unable to rest in his crypt); John Carradine (the Devil); Cameron Mitchell (*Molecolo Pulido*, a crazy inventor); Amadee Chabot (*Dr. Galina Pulido*, his daughter); Ahui Camacho (*Electron*, his grandson); Susana Cabrera (*Susana*, his housekeeper); Pompin Iglesias (*Pompin*); Delia Magana (beggar); Javiern Lopez (*Chabelo*); Nacho Contla (Chabelo's father); Manuel Palacios (*Manolin*); Carlos Pinar (*Jaime Blondo*, secret agent 07½); Mario Garcia Haropos (secret agent 0); Arturo Castro (judge); Famie Kaufman (*Vitolo*); Estanislao Schilinsky, Jorge Delong, Hermanes Tejada, Manuel Trejo Morales.

Appraisal and Synopsis

This picture is legendary for being rock-bottom awful, and for once the rumored evaluation of a seldom-seen film is completely accurate. Originally this Mexican film was made with an eye toward an English-language release, since whenever a sign is seen in the film, it appears in both Spanish and English. The producer/director, Ismael Rodriguez, had success in placing his previous works in the American market, such as *Beast of Hollow Mountain* (1956) and the television series *Sheena, Queen of the Jungle* (1955–1956) with Irish McCalla. The quality of this bizarre fantasy was so poor, however, that no American distributor would touch it with a ten-foot pole, so only the Spanish version was ever released. It would have been interesting to actually hear Carradine, Rathbone, and Mitchell doing their roles in English. Of the film's three stars, only Mitchell was fluent in Spanish. An English-language version, however, would probably have been as awful, confusing, and inept as the original.

The picture opens with a paraphrase of Socrates by Rodriguez, who states, "The healthiest diversion is what children enjoy. He who is ashamed of laughing at simple things is a cretin." After this challenge to viewers not to enjoy his accomplishment, Rodriguez sets the credits on placards carried by skeleton puppets, devil puppets, and ghosts, all accompanied with mouselike squeaks. The primary plot begins with the 400-year-old ghost of Canuto Perez being unable to find peace in his underground crypt. He has a conversation with his alter ego, who appears in the shape of a talking skeleton, and when Satan arrives, Canuto hears a proclamation, apparently from God. Because Canuto treated women in such a disparaging manner during his life, he will be sent to hell unless he can gain the love of a woman within four days. The Devil is assigned both to monitor and assist Canuto in this endeavor. Needless to say, this plot gets buried and trampled on by a series of subplots centering on the laboratory of a crazy scientist, Molecolo, and the robbery of a large sum of money from the bank. The Devil proceeds to line up candidates for Canuto to woo, which he does in various guises, such as a beatnik, Cyrano de Bergerac, and an Apache dancer. In one scene, Rathbone gets to recite Hamlet's "to be or not to be" soliloquy to a skull. The only conquest Canuto makes is the love of Robotina, the robot invented by Molecolo, whose other ideas include an odorless, tasteless cigarette and a rotating chair. Zany slapstick abounds from beginning to end. When two passersby comment on the odor of the Devil, he turns them into goats. Robotina periodically flips her lid and wrestles every member of the household, from the inventor's bikini-clad daughter to his dumpy housekeeper. There is a James Bond subplot with secret agent 07½. Toward the finish, Canuto is seen heading down a dark staircase to the nether regions when Robotina sacrifices herself for him, assuring his salvation. The entire plot then is revealed as a mad entertainment concocted by the Devil, who concludes the picture inside a giant television on the stage of a theater. After delivering an obscene gesture to the audience, the Devil reaches down and turns the set off, ending the most mindless and fatuous series of escapades ever shown onscreen. Bad-movie fanatics should be obligated to watch this entire effort before declaring which film rates as the worst ever made.

Performances

This film is frequently considered to be the nadir of John Carradine's illustrious career. Yet, according to most sources, the arthritic actor had a marvelous time making the picture. His performance is simply the hammiest, most farcical, and absurd burlesque of the Devil on film. His costume is a travesty of the standard operatic get-up used in Gounod's *Faust*, including tights, large white Elizabethan ruffled collar, short black caped coat, and a red skullcap with curved horns emerging from the side of his head. He has a long retractable tail with a forked point which he constantly uses as a prop, twirling or flipping it, and at the end of the film he even tries to strangle himself with it. In his Devil costume, Carradine is invisible to everyone but Rathbone, and while unseen he comments directly to the audience about the people he observes. When the Devil wishes to be seen, such as when he appears as landlord to his tenant, the daffy scientist Molecolo, he appears as an undertaker. Too bad Carradine was unable to imbue the role with some of the macabre charm he used as the mortician in "The Munsters," but there is no room for any whimsy in this extravaganza. His makeup includes slightly slanted eyebrows, two wispy mustache fragments about two inches apart, and a flat-ended paintbrush beard, but his makeup varies when he assumes different disguises. His facial expressions are similarly exaggerated and at times moronic. His performance is painful to watch because it is so vulgar and embarrassing. His slapstick bits are forced and awful and no doubt caused astonishment to anyone familiar with the usual caliber of Carradine's work. His Spanish dubbing is poorly done, and even those fluent in the language find his dialogue difficult to understand and often not suited to the action of the moment. The last shot of the film features a close-up of Carradine pulling his thumb away from his teeth in the classic gesture of contempt for the audience, both those seen on the screen as well as, one assumes, those watching the film at the cinema. Basil Rathbone and Cameron Mitchell also offer buffoonish performances, yet their readings do have flashes of humor and interest. Rathbone is exceptionally active in his part, and some

John Carradine's Satan finds baby milk to be too sour in Autopsia de un Fantasma.

film historians have commented that his activity in the high altitude of Mexico City may have contributed to his death twelve weeks after completing his role, a sad finish to a great career.

Notable Quotes

- You think *I'm* cruel? (**the Devil to the audience, before being sprayed by a water pistol**)
- Why are we endlessly waiting for women? (**Canuto to the Devil**)
- It's simply because of your knack of belittling women. (**the Devil's reply**)
- Why do I get my tail caught in an electric fan just when I'm on my way to a funeral? (**the Devil's rhetorical question**)
- A woman will fall in love with any man but not with a set of marimbas. (**the Devil to Canuto's skeleton, which he earlier tried to play like a musical instrument**)

Bait

1954   Rating: **   Cedric Hardwicke as the Devil

Columbia. Written by Samuel W. Taylor with additional dialogue by Hugo Haas; Photographed by Edward F. Fitzgerald; Special Effects by Lee Zavitz; Edited by Robert S. Eisen; Music by Vaclav Divina and Martin Schwab; Produced and Directed by Hugo Haas. B&W, 79 minutes.

Annotated Cast List

Hugo Haas (*Marko*, old prospector); John Agar (*Ray Brighton*, his new partner); Cleo Moore (*Peggy*, woman Marko marries); Emmett Lynn (*Foley*, general store owner); Bruno Ve Sota (*Jackie Webb*, owner of diner); Jan Englund (*Annie*, diner waitress); George Keymas (*Chuck*, Foley's customer); Cedric Hardwicke (the Devil).

Appraisal and Synopsis

Bait is one of a series of low-budget melodramas that Hugo Haas directed and in which he starred. Unlike most of his other vehicles, he did not write this one as well but relied upon a somewhat seedy script by Samuel W. Taylor, writer of *The Absent-Minded Professor* (1961). As a melodrama, it is neither better nor worse than the other Haas pictures, such as *Pickup* (1950) and *Strange Fascination* (1952), and one should note that they were so cheaply made that they were profitable. The plots of these pictures were often cast from the same mold: Haas plays an older man inappropriately married to a younger woman, played either by Cleo Moore or Beverly Michaels. These marriages usually disintegrate, and Haas is either ruined or saved.

Realizing that the completed film was rather humdrum, a prologue was added with Cedric Hardwicke as the Devil, and his voice is heard planting ideas in Haas' mind as the film progresses. The Devil is shown ascending a long staircase while two spotlights are focused on him. At the top of the stairs, he signs a number of autographs and then talks directly into the camera, explaining that he is the Devil who has come to speak with us in the guise of a well-known individual. He escorts the audience into a screening room where he shows a motion picture which illustrates his usual working methods. The story unfolds of Marko, a burly old prospector who found a gold mine fifteen years earlier. Marko and his partner were trapped in an unexpected blizzard while returning to file a claim for the mine. The partner froze to death, and Marko has been unable to locate the mine ever since. He persuades Ray, a young farmer, to join him in another hunt for the mine, promising him half of the gold if they locate it. Together with Ray's dog, Mike, they set off by jeep. They load up supplies at Foley's general store, where Ray meets Peggy, an attractive young widow. Marko insults Peggy and warns Ray that she is a bad woman.

After many weeks of hunting, Ray locates the boarded-over entrance to the lost mine within a short distance of the squatter's cabin which they use as a base. The Devil then whispers to Marko, suggesting he find a way to avoid sharing the gold with his partner. When Marko returns to the general store to obtain supplies and file his claim, he treats Peggy kindly and unexpectedly asks her to marry him. She agrees, and Ray is stunned when Marko returns with her to the cabin. Marko treats his new wife with complete indifference. The prospector notices the strong attraction between Peggy and Ray, and he encourages their closeness in many ways, such as suggesting that they dance to the radio playing in the cabin.

They agree to spend the winter at the cabin, continuing to mine the gold as best they can. When Peggy and Ray go out to cut down a Christmas tree, Marko poisons Ray's dog, making it appear to be an accident. The wily prospector then claims he forgot to purchase salt, an essential commodity. Since their dirt road is buried in snow, Marko plans to hike to the main highway where he can flag down the daily bus that heads to town. This trip will take overnight, but he tells Ray and Peggy that he is not concerned about them spending the night alone together in the cabin.

That night, Ray finds a package of salt hidden in the cabin, and he spots Marko peeking through a window. He understands that Marko was planning to find Ray and Peggy in a compromising position so that he could kill his partner with impunity, relying on the unwritten law excusing murder when a husband discovers someone molesting his wife. Ray instructs Peggy to feign inviting him into her bed, and he turns out the light. When Marko barges into the cabin, Ray is hiding behind the door, and he disarms the prospector. Ray accuses him of marrying Peggy simply to use her as bait in his deadly scheme. He killed Mike so he couldn't bark while Marko spied on them from outside the cabin. Peggy and Ray decide to leave the cabin, and they toss Marko aside when he tries to stop them. After they leave, Marko discovers that his leg is broken. He tries to crawl after them, but a violent snowstorm starts. Peggy and Ray manage to reach the main highway, but Marko freezes to death and becomes buried in the snow.

Performances

At first, Sir Cedric Hardwicke gives the impression that the Devil is an English gentleman who wears glasses and carries an umbrella, until he finally explains, "I never show my face," and that he is appearing in the guise of an actor, "rather a good one in my opinion." This line is richly ironic, since we have Hardwicke praising his own acting abilities using the Devil as his spokesman. There is an additional irony in that the Devil has a private screening room where he likes to view movies from Columbia Pictures. One wonders what other films he watches in his spare time besides those by Hugo Haas. He then refers to his projectionist as Lucifer, making this one of the rare films that attempts to distinguish the Devil from Lucifer. It is unfortunate that Hardwicke's appearance is so brief, since his sinister smile and snide tone of voice makes him a particularly effective Satan, filled with an abundance of sinister charm. Hardwicke's voice appears three times in the picture, twice encouraging Marko to develop his greedy plans and finally in uproarious laughter as the prospector freezes to death. It can be assumed that the death of Marko's first partner was also murder, although this is never clearly verified in the story. This would perhaps provide the Devil's motivation for wanting to land this particular sinner. Hugo Haas portrays Marko as a greedy hypocrite with his head always buried in the Bible, obviously ignoring whatever moral guidance it contains but always ready to lecture others about its wisdom. None of the other characters interacts with the Devil in any way. John Agar is likable as Ray, although he lacks credibility. Cleo Moore is restrained in her role, but the motivation for her character is a mystery to the audience. The film could have used additional commentary by the Devil after the conclusion of his screening of the picture.

Notable Quotes

• I personally appear only in your thoughts, as a little germ inside your brain, infiltrating your ideas, whispering into your ears, getting into your blood, penetrating. Would you like to see how I operate? (**the Devil to the audience**)

• Ask the Devil to forgive you. Nobody else would listen to your prayers. (**Ray to Marko**)

Beast of the Yellow Night

1971   Rating: *   Vic Diaz as the Devil

New World. Written by Eddie Romero; Photographed by Justo Paulino; Edited by Ben Barcelon; Special Effects by Teofilo Hilario; Music by Nestor Robles; Produced by John Ashley and Eddie Romero; Directed by Eddie Romero. Color, 86 minutes.

Annotated Cast List

John Ashley (*Joseph Langdon*, American soldier who deserted in the Philippines, and *Philip Rogers*, American businessman possessed by Langdon); Vic Diaz (the Devil); Mary Wilcox (*Julia Rogers*, Philip's wife); Ken Metcalfe (*Earl Rogers*, Philip's brother); Leopoldo Salcedo (*Santos*, police inspector); Eddie Garcia (*Campos*, police detective); Andres Centenera (blind man who befriends Langdon).

Appraisal and Synopsis

John Ashley started his career in teenage delinquent films, such as *Dragstrip Girl* (1957) and *Motorcycle Gang* (1957), and horror films, such as *Frankenstein's Daughter* (1959). He later was lured to the Philippines, where he became a minor mogul of Philippine exploitation films with writer/director Eddie Romero, who cut his teeth on such decent efforts as *Terror Is a Man* (1959) with Francis Lederer and Richard Derr. The heyday of this effort was in the 1970s, when performers such as Pam Grier, Sid Haig, and George Nader appeared in numerous features ground out in the Philippines. Eventually, Ashley returned to America where he continued as a producer of television shows and feature films up until his death in 1997 at the age of sixty-two while working on a film. *Beast of the Yellow Night* was the first film in which he served as producer with Romero. It is a muddled effort that is not as clearcut as the following synopsis.

The picture opens toward the end of World War II in the Philippine jungle, where military convict Joseph Langdon, an American deserter and enemy collaborator, is attempting to escape. Starving and wounded, he collapses, and a mysterious individual in tribal dress speaks to him. Langdon pleads for help and agrees to serve the stranger, who is the Devil. He comments that even though Langdon will soon be dead, he will still be useful to him. The credits follow, and the scene shifts to a funeral twenty-four years later. The Devil has been using Langdon's soul, transferring it from body to body, in order to carry out his will and bring out the evil in the people he meets. Langdon's spirit asks if he might be allowed to rest for a while, but the Devil replies that he is needed at once and that he will find his new body particularly interesting. American businessman Philip Rogers has just died in the hospital, mangled in an industrial accident. His wife and brother are summoned to his bedside before his body is moved to the morgue. Langdon's soul is placed in Roger's body, and it starts to move. His doctor, witnessing this event, collapses and dies of shock. Philip's bandages are removed, and his face is unharmed and is identical to Langdon's original face. After Rogers is discharged, he goes to his luxurious home where he makes love to Julia, his wife. Returning to work, Rogers discharges his board of directors and reorganizes his company so that he has sole control.

The Devil meets with Langdon, concerned that he is becoming too independent since he has become Rogers, perhaps due to the fact that he has his original face again in this incarnation. The Devil warns him that he is his servant and must carry out his duties or face the consequences. Nevertheless, as Rogers, Langdon continues to resist evil. While walking one evening in front of a church, he is attracted by the organ music. He suddenly doubles over in pain, and the Devil transforms him into a monster, a grotesque creature similar to a werewolf. He kills a passerby and wanders about in a fury. The next morning, waking in a field, he is restored to normal.

The police investigate the savage murder. That night, when Julia tries to kiss her husband, he pushes her away, runs off, and is again transformed into a monster. He rushes out of the house and goes on a killing spree throughout the city. As the police track him down, he finds refuge in a garage where an old, blind man gives him shelter. Sleeping, Langdon again changes back to himself.

The police are informed that Philip Rogers has disappeared under strange circumstances, and he becomes a suspect in the series of killings. He turns himself in, and Inspector Santos recognizes him as the murderous American deserter, Joseph Langdon. Of course, Rogers is only thirty-five years old, and Langdon, if alive, would be an old man. Nevertheless, Santos arrests him. The Devil visits him in jail and tells him that he can avoid future transformations by ending his resistance. Released from jail, Langdon is attacked by a mob and stabbed, but he is completely unharmed by the knife wound. The police put him under surveillance. That evening, he begins to make love to Julia, but when he says he loves her, he transforms again into the monster. He heads to the garage to find the old man but mauls the man's nephew when he tries to drive Langdon away. The next day, the old man plans to help Langdon escape from the city, but they are cornered by the police in a field, which the police set on fire. The old man is shot and wounded, and Langdon turns into the beast again, this time in broad daylight. The old man calls out to him, and Langdon meekly goes to his side, then allows the inspector to shoot him in the head. The Devil's voice is heard on the soundtrack, denouncing Langdon as a sniveling fool. He proclaims that he will continue to do evil.

This story is presented in a rambling, almost incoherent manner. Every time the Devil appears, Romero uses a fog machine, which churns out an overabundance of smoke in a ludicrous fashion. Perhaps this is what "yellow night" means in the otherwise senseless title. John Ashley's makeup is not bad, but his performance as the beast is rather inconsistent. As a second feature at a 1970s drive-in, *Beast of the Yellow Night* might pass muster, but it is a rather weak entry as a Devil movie.

Performances

Vic Diaz is one of the most recognizable of Filipino actors, since he appeared in over forty movies before his death in 1995, usually as a police detective or a gang lord. The chubby-faced actor puts little effort into this role as the Devil, endowing the part with neither mystery nor color. It is only during the closing narration that he gives his lines any emotion. For the most part, he simply speaks his lines plainly, as if he were performing his standard crime lord role. John Ashley has solid screen charisma, but he also is unusually sluggish and empty as Langdon/Rogers. Mary Wilcox is attractive to watch, but her performance is totally vapid. Ken Metcalfe is adequate, and he bears a marked resemblance to Roger Corman, whose New World company released the film.

Notable Quotes

- It isn't as easy as it might seem to find qualified agents.... There's been a good deal said about the scarcity of truly good men. Why? Truly evil men are just as hard to find. (**the Devil to Langdon**)
- I am a man, damned maybe, but still a man. (**Langdon to the Devil**)
- I accept forgiveness from no one! No one! I alone am answerable for what I am. I will not serve ... I will not be overcome. (**closing narration by the Devil**)

La Beauté du Diable
AKA Beauty and the Devil *and* Beauty of the Devil

1950   Rating: *****
Michel Simon and Gérard Philipe as the Devil

Enic Universalia and Franco London Films. Written by René Clair and Armand Salacrou, based upon the legend of *Faust*; Photographed by Michel Kelber; Edited by James Cuenet; Music by Román Vlad; Produced by Salvo D'Angelo; Directed by René Clair. Color, 97 minutes.

Annotated Cast List

Michel Simon (*Dr. Faust*, old scholar, and *Mephistopheles*, the Devil); Gérard Philipe (*Henri*, Faust restored to his youth and *Mephistopheles* at his first appearance); Nicole Bresnard (*Marguerite*, gypsy girl with a trained-dog act); Simone Valére (princess); Carlo Ninchi (prince); Raymond Cordy (*Antoine*, Faust's servant); Tullio Carminati (prince's diplomat); Paolo Stoppa (official of the prince); Gaston Modot (gypsy).

Appraisal and Synopsis

One of the undisputed geniuses of French cinema, René Clair also created several quality American films in Hollywood during the Second World War. Among his masterpieces are *The Italian Straw Hat* (1927), *Le Million* (1931), *A Nous la Liberté* (1931), and *Quatorze Juillet* (1934). His notable American films include *I Married a Witch* (1942) with Frederic March and Veronica Lake, *It Happened*

Tomorrow (1944) with Dick Powell, and *And Then There Were None* (1945), the first screen adaptation of Agatha Christie's *Ten Little Indians*. Clair was a master of the light touch, and his 1950 film of the Faust legend is the most charming, suave, and delectable version possible. It absolutely brims with good humor and energy, largely due to the incredible performance of Michel Simon as Faust and Mephistopheles. His physical humor and infectious charm are a sheer delight, and Gérard Philipe also holds his own in their comic duel. Cowritten by Clair, this adaptation concentrates entirely on grotesque characters and situations rather than the diabolical, and the Devil himself seems nothing but a humbug in this endeavor. The plot veers considerably from the usually tragic story. The picture was made in Italy at the Cinecitta Studio in Rome where Clair took advantage of lavish sets with ornate palaces and busy streets in a ninteenth-century period setting. The film ranks among Clair's best, and it is somewhat surprising that it is not better known since it succeeds on every level, except for a rather lengthy dull patch about two-thirds of the way through the story.

The picture opens in the musty laboratory of the elderly Dr. Faust. His servant, Antoine, tries to straighten up, but he is frightened by the illustration of a horrifying Devil in an old book. Faust is being honored at a ceremony for his fifty years of service as a professor at the local university, but the cranky professor is preoccupied with his dark thoughts. The Devil, appearing as a young man, chuckles while observing him, and the scholar wanders out of the auditorium halfway through the event. The Devil speaks to him on the street as the scholar heads home to his lab. Faust tries to ignore him, but the Devil's voice continues to tempt him, mocking his scientific failures and offering him a fresh start and success with his experiments to fabricate gold. Faust finally challenges him to show himself, but he loses heart, afraid of what terrible form Satan might assume. He is flabbergasted when the Devil appears as a mirror image of himself. When addressed as Lucifer, the Devil replies that he is Mephistopheles instead. Mephistopheles transforms his appearance from a youthful Faust to an aged one. Faust refuses to sign the pact until the Devil offers him his youth unconditionally, and Mephistopheles then transforms him into a young man. Amazed, the young Faust heads out for a night on the town to recapture the joys of youth. Calling himself only by his first name, Henri, he gets into a series of misadventures after attending the gypsy circus and meeting the lovely Marguerite, who performs an act with trained dogs. After running up a large tab in the tavern, he realizes he has no money and slips home to pick up a stash of bills. Antoine sees him and assumes he is a thief. Henri is eventually arrested and accused of murdering Faust. At his trial, Henri is about to reveal that he himself is Faust restored to youth, when Mephistopheles shows up as old Faust and clears Henri of any wrongdoing.

Mephistopheles permanently assumes his impersonation of the aged Faust, and he and Henri engage in a prolonged cat-and-mouse game revolving around Henri's access to money. Henri is forced to live hand to mouth as a vagabond. Mephistopheles, meanwhile, begins to enjoy his masquerade as Faust, indulging in earthly pleasures. Faust is summoned by the prince, who is concerned that his treasury is empty. He asks if the scholar has had any success in making gold. Mephistopheles, as old Faust, promises to help. After failing to get Henri to sign his pact, Mephistopheles consults with Lucifer, who inspires him to try a new approach and grant all of Henri's wishes automatically, starting with his desire to create gold. Henri moves back to his mansion with the Devil, who continues to pose as Faust. They create gold out of sand and bring the wealth to the prince. The entire city becomes awash in wealth, and Henri, considered to be Faust's assistant, is made a chevalier by the prince. Mephistopheles and Henri attend a royal ball where the Devil dances enthusiastically. Henri also becomes enamored of the princess, the ruler's wife. Henri is overjoyed when he gains her affection and becomes her favorite, but Mephistopheles transports Henri back to the streets where he has to sleep in an alley with rats. Now Henri is hooked, and he sells his soul to Mephistopheles and signs his pact in blood. The Devil is ecstatic at having attained the slippery soul of Henri, which he has sought for so long. Having lost his soul, Henri becomes depressed and asks the Devil to show him the events of the future year. In a mirror, Mephistopheles casts a vision in which Henri becomes the lover of the princess, causes the prince to be poisoned, and becomes the most important man in the land. Eventually, he seeks out a series of new mistresses, and he invents terrible new weapons as he sets out on world conquest. Eventually, he foresees his death.

This vision both horrifies and discourages Henri, and he runs off to see Marguerite, who has fallen in love with him. Unknown to Henri, Mephistopheles, as the aged Faust, approaches Marguerite and tries to entice her to sell her soul. Henri returns to his laboratory and starts to burn all his papers. When Mephistopheles shows up, Henri commands the Devil to destroy all traces of his work. All the gold created by him crumbles back into sand, and the country goes wild with riots when they discover that all their gold has vanished. The prince orders the arrest of Marguerite. The palace is stormed by a mob carrying pitchforks and scythes, and Mephistopheles joins them. The prince issues a statement blaming the crisis on witchcraft practiced by Marguerite. The crowd demands that she be turned over to them, and Henri orders Mephistopheles to save her. The Devil goes to her prison cell, but she refuses to sign his pact. When he shows her his signed pact with Henri, she snatches it and tosses it out the window. It falls into the hands of the crowd, and after reading it, they turn their fury against the aged Faust, who manages to recover the document. They chase Mephistopheles to a balcony, and he falls to the pavement below. His pact with Henri dissolves into a giant cloud of black smoke which spreads throughout the city. A chorus sings a hymn of praise as the smoke dissipates before the religious statues decorating the cathedral. When the last of the smoke clears, Henri discovers he is free of the Devil's pact, and he still has his youth as well. Victorious, Henri embraces the liberated Marguerite, and they leave together with the circus.

The defeat and overthrow of Mephistopheles is a shock, and the swiftness of it comes as a complete surprise. Mephistopheles calls upon Lucifer to save him, but nothing happens. The onslaught of the crowd is so rapid, it seems that this turn of events must have happened while Lucifer was temporarily distracted by God, who saves Henri and Marguerite in this expedient manner.

Performances

Michel Simon received his training on the stage as a music hall clown and acrobat, which is well put to use, particularly in his enthusiastic dancing scenes. He uses his heavy-set physique with extraordinary grace, and he became a major character actor, a Gallic combination of Sebastian Cabot, Charles Laughton, and Jackie Gleason. His performances on film range from tragic to slapstick in *La Chienne* (1931), as Scarpia in *La Tosca* (1940), and as Shylock in *The Merchant of Venice* (1952). American audiences probably recognize him best as Papa Boulle, the elderly train engineer and saboteur in *The Train* (1964) with Burt Lancaster, or as the anti-Semitic peasant who cares for a Jewish boy in the memorable film *The Two of Us* (1967). In real life, Simon was a bit of a recluse, who reportedly kept four apes as pets on his country estate. Simon brings *La Beauté du Diable* to life with his boisterous reading as Mephistopheles, who in this film is portrayed as a rather clumsy emissary of Lucifer. As in the Christopher Marlowe play *Dr. Faustus*, Lucifer and Mephistopheles are different personalities. Simon is also excellent as the original Henri Faust, moody, frustrated, and fearful of his approaching death. As Mephistopheles posing as Faust, Simon is an energetic whirlwind, like a kid in a candy shop, experiencing all of the delights of life for the first time. His glee is positively infectious. When events turn against him, he beseeches Lucifer with a humble anxiety that is amazing to watch. Simon's every gesture, grimace, and misstep combine to make this one of the all-time great readings of Mephistopheles. Gérard Philipe also pursues his role with subtlety and delight, and it is easy to forget that he also appears as the Devil in brief glimpses at the beginning of the film before Faust begins his negotiations with Mephistopheles. Philipe was a popular leading man in many French films in the late 1940s and early 1950s, and he died of a heart attack at the early age of thirty-eight. The other characters are also well played, particularly Raymond Cordy as Antoine, Faust's befuddled servant.

Notable Quotes

- I'm not afraid, not of you, nor of your ridiculous disguises ... large horns, coarse hair, cloven feet, bat's wings. Poor Devil. You think I'm afraid? I am Faust, your equal! Your future master! I bid you show yourself. (**Faust in response to the Devil's endless taunts**)
- You are the winner, I concede. Now you are free to enjoy the delights of youth while I must look after my rheumatism. No hard feelings. You know where to find me if you want me. (**Mephistopheles to Faust, after arranging for his freedom by assuming the identity of the aged Faust**)
- In the name of Lucifer, the said Mephistopheles, on my last day, shall have my soul. Signed Faust. It is quite in order. Master, I am now your faithful servant. (**Mephistopheles, reading his newly signed arrangement with Faust**)
- We can settle things nicely. You have a choice little soul, quite a collector's piece. (**Mephistopheles to Marguerite**)

Bedazzled

1967   Rating: ***   Peter Cook as the Devil

20th Century–Fox. Written by Peter Cook, based on a story by Dudley Moore and Peter Cook; Photographed by Austin Dempster; Edited by Richard Marden; Music by Dudley Moore; Produced and Directed by Stanley Donen. Color, 104 minutes.

Annotated Cast List

Dudley Moore (*Stanley Moon*, short-order cook); Peter Cook (*George Spiggott*, the Devil); Eleanor Bron (*Margaret Spencer*, waitress); Raquel Welch (*Lust*, Satan's helper); Robert Russell (*Anger*); Alba (*Vanity*); Barry Humphries (*Envy*); Daniele Noel (*Avarice*); Howard Gourney (*Sloth*); Parnell McGarry (*Gluttony*); Lockwood West (*St. Peter*, God's attendant); Michael Bates (*Inspector Clarke*, investigator of Moon's disappearance); Bernard Spear (*Irving Moses*); Robin Hawdon (*Randolph*, harp teacher); Erik Chitty (*Seed*, butler); Michael Trubshawe (*Lord Dowdy*, pool player); Evelyn Moore (*Mrs. Wisby*, tricked by Satan into buying ten bottles of eyewash); Charles Lloyd (vicar); Max Faulkner (priest); Betty Cooper (*Sister Phoebe*); John Steiner (TV announcer); Anna Turner (shop assistant).

Appraisal and Synopsis

Irreverent, mod, and fairly amusing, *Bedazzled* well sums up British humor in the 1960s. The film is the brainchild of Peter Cook and Dudley Moore, who teamed together as cabaret entertainers early in their careers. Much of the humor of this movie has dated, but much of it is still rather funny. The picture is basically a collection of skits stitched together about tongue-tied short-order hamburger cook Stanley Moon, who is so bedazzled by waitress Margaret Spencer that he is becoming desperate to win her over. While praying to God for courage to approach her, Stanley actually attracts the attention of Satan, who passes himself off as George Spiggott, a Carnaby Street hipster. He interrupts Stanley as he is about to commit suicide and tries to convince him he is the Devil. He offers him seven wishes in exchange for his soul. Stanley is dubious, so the Devil offers him a free wish. Stanley chooses a popsicle, expecting the Devil to materialize one out of thin air. Instead, he escorts Stanley to an ice cream parlor and buys him one. Actually, he has to borrow the money from Stanley to pay for it. Unconvinced, Stanley asks for a miracle, so the Devil flies him through the air at supersonic speed.

The Devil finally brings Stanley to his rundown headquarters, where he complains about his seven helpers, who personify the seven deadly sins. Stanley signs the Devil's contract as the rules are explained to him. He must outline each wish to the Devil in as specific terms as possible, and the Devil will fulfill his wish, using the magic words "Julie Andrews." Whenever Stanley desires to terminate a wish, he can cancel it by blowing a raspberry, which will return him to the Devil's presence. Of course, the Devil doesn't explain that he actually intends to subvert each wish so that Stanley fails to achieve what he really wants, the love of Margaret Spencer. Meanwhile, in the real world, Stanley is reported missing. Inspector Clarke finds a possible suicide note addressed to Margaret, and since he fancies the girl, he drags out his investigation as long as possible so he can be close to the cute waitress.

Most of the humor of the picture revolves around Stanley's elaborate wishes for winning Margaret and the clever ways the Devil subverts each wish. First, feeling inarticulate, Stanley wishes to become an intellectual with a special talent for communicating with Margaret. At first, everything seems to be wonderful, as Stanley escorts his fantasy Margaret to the zoo and then back to his apartment. He uses his gift of gab to discuss everything from animal behavior to Johannes Brahms. Despite the fact that Margaret seems completely responsive to him, when he tries to kiss her, she screams, "Rape!" As his neighbors start to bash down his door, the frustrated Stanley blows a raspberry to terminate the wish.

His first experience sets the pattern for the remaining wishes, where Stanley becomes a multimillionaire, a rock star, and the illicit boyfriend to a married Margaret. The Devil, without fail, finds a loophole that undermines each wish so Stanley never wins Margaret. He also tricks Stanley into wasting a wish when he idly comments that he would like to be a fly on the wall to hear what Inspector Clarke and Margaret are saying about him. As a fly, Stanley finds it almost impossible to blow a raspberry, and he barely manages to approximate the sound after Clarke douses him with bug spray. The Devil even tries to cheer Stanley up when he becomes depressed at the way his wishes turn out, taking him on a double date to the amusement park with Avarice and Gluttony. Stanley spends time with the other sins as well, including Lust, played in genuine camp style by Raquel Welch. Despite his devious nature, Stanley begins to enjoy the Devil's company, because he always takes time to talk with him, and he even encourages Stanley to call him George as he accompanies him while he engages in his diabolical pranks.

Stanley finally thinks he has devised a foolproof wish to enable him to triumph with Margaret. He wishes they are both good quiet people, in love together, with no other men in her life, far away from the hubbub of the modern world. When the Devil enacts it, Stanley finds himself transformed into a nun, Sister Luna. Together with Margaret, he is cloistered in a remote convent devoted to Beryl of Sussex, a shepherdess who disappeared after leaping into the sky to follow a vision. Each member of the order is obligated to maintain silence until Beryl is canonized as a saint. This time, nothing happens when Stanley blows a raspberry, so "she" leaves the convent to track Satan down. When "she" finally confronts the Devil, he refuses to turn Stanley back, saying the last wish is permanent. Stanley insists he has another wish but learns the Devil cheated on the contract and included his demonstration wish for a popsicle. The Devil relents, however, saying that he has won his long-standing bet with God, being the first to win 100 billion souls. According to their wager, God must restore Lucifer to His right hand in heaven. No longer needing Stanley's soul, he gives it back to him as a good deed. He asks only one favor, to watch over a party for his helpers to make sure they have a good time.

The Devil heads to heaven, where St. Peter acts huffy, wanting Lucifer to grovel. God remains invisible as Satan enters His arboretum to apply for readmission. The Devil insists he has carried out God's dictum to tempt man without wavering. But when he tells of his good deed in returning Stanley's soul, God reneges on His promise to restore him. St. Peter informs him that he did his good deed for the wrong reason, in order for himself to feel good. The Devil vows to get back Stanley's soul and return it for the right reason. He speeds back down to Earth, but when Stanley hears him coming, he sets fire to his contract and vanishes, returning to the real world at the point he left it. The next day, back at work cooking hamburgers, Stanley works up his courage to ask Margaret to have dinner with him that evening. She turns him down, saying she's busy, but suggests he ask her another night. The Devil shows up, saying he has a new deal for him to win Margaret. This time, Stanley turns him down, saying he would prefer to try it his own way. The sound of God's laughter fills the room. The Devil heads outside and raises his voice in defiance, saying he'll make the world so noisy, rotten, and disgusting that even God would be ashamed. God continues to roar with laughter as the end credits roll.

Bedazzled is at its best during the rambling conversations between Stanley and the Devil, which sound at times like brilliant improvisations. Four of these routines stand out. The first is when the Devil introduces himself to Stanley, handing him his calling card and introducing himself as

"Beelzebub, Mephistopheles, the horned one." Next is the Devil's impersonation of God while sitting atop a mailbox in the street. Then there is his bewildering double talk about the nature of truth and lies. Lastly, and funniest of all, is the Devil's lament about last-minute repentance, bemoaning how he can toil for sixty years with a mean, nasty, old skinflint, only to have him repent on his deathbed. He is particularly galled by Benito Mussolini who, just before he was killed, looked up to heaven and said, "Scusa," and the Devil lost the rights to his miserable soul. Curiously, a novel written about a decade after this film, *Inferno* by Larry Niven and Jerry Pournelle, portrays Mussolini as an agent of redemption who serves as a guide out of hell, leading souls directly past Satan.

Other clever bits involve the Devil's endless petty antics, setting wasps on picnickers, making prank phone calls, scratching phonograph records, and causing parking meters to expire early. These vignettes are clever essentially because they are so measly and niggling, wrongs that one would consider far beneath the personal attention of the Devil. The wish fantasies, however, are letdowns by comparison. They are too artificial, becoming stale quickly. Stanley gives up far too easily whenever he encounters any resistance, such as when he is a pop singer, and simply gives up when a rival, played by Satan, shows up to sway the crowd. Stanley also doesn't seem to care that it is not really Margaret in these scenarios, only a substitute developed by the Devil for each new setting. The most colorful and entertaining wishes are those involving the fly and the leaping nuns, who have a trampoline ritual that is simply hilarious.

The production values of the film are excellent throughout. The script by Peter Cook is quite lively, and Dudley Moore's music score is more than adequate. The most intriguing thing about this script is that God acts in the same way as the Devil. Satan never intends to allow Stanley to have a successful wish in which he scores with Margaret. Similarly, God never intends to let the Devil back into heaven. Both fall back on an endless supply of loopholes, so there is some sense of equity as the Devil receives the same treatment that he gives to Stanley. The original film had enough of a following that Harold Ramis of "SCTV" fame decided to remake *Bedazzled* for release in 2000 as a Brendan Fraser vehicle, with Elizabeth Hurley as the Devil.

Performances

Peter Cook is very likable and witty, but he makes a rather weak Devil, mired in trivialities. Never once does he exude any sense of real evil. He is just an inconsequential, two-bit trickster. His interpretation, clever as a stage bit, is simply not convincing. Even George Burns in *Oh, God! You Devil* was able to provide the right aura when needed, which Cook seems incapable of doing. Dudley Moore is far more successful as Stanley, and their give-and-take is marvelous. Eleanor Bron grows rather tiring as Margaret, and about halfway through the film you pull for Stanley to find someone else instead. Raquel Welch is excellent as Lust, and it is too bad her appearance is more of a cameo than a full-fledged part.

Notable Quotes

- In order for people to be really good, they have to make a free choice between good and evil, and choose good. I'm a vital part of His plan. I provide the evil. (**the Devil to Stanley**)
- Come on, Vanity, you worthless old sin, stop preening and tidy up the Mens' Room.... What rotten sins I've got working for me. (**the Devil to Vanity**)

- Everything I've ever told you has been a lie, including that. (**the Devil**)
Including what? (**Stanley**)
That everything I ever told you has been a lie. That's not true. (**the Devil**)
- If I were you wanting to get in, I should try being a bit more humble. (**St. Peter to the Devil**)

Oh, would you really? Yes, woo hoo, I dare say you would. You're quite right, of course. I know. I'll throw a bit of filth over meself. That should please him. (**the Devil**)

Bedazzled

2000   Rating **   Elizabeth Hurley and the Devil

20th Century–Fox/Regency. Written by Harold Ramis, Larry Gelbart, and Peter Tolan, based on a screenplay and story by Dudley Moore and Peter Cook; Photographed by Bill Pope; Special Effects by Richard Edlund and Alan E. Lorimer (co-ordinator); Edited by Craig Herring; Music by David Newman; Produced by Trevor Alpert and Harold Ramis; Directed by Harold Ramis. Color, 94 minutes.

Annotated Cast List

Brendan Fraser (*Elliot Richards*, customer service representative for Synedyne); Elizabeth Hurley (the Devil); Frances O'Connor (*Allison*, woman whom Elliot loves, and *Nicole*, Elliot's new neighbor); Gabriel Casseus (God, posing as Elliot's jail cellmate); Orlando Jones (*Dan*, Elliot's coworker and wish characters *Esteban*, beach jock, sportscaster, party guest); Toby Huss (*Jerry*, Elliot's coworker and wish characters *Alejandro*, beach jock, sportscaster, *Lance*); Paul Adelsten (*Bob*, Elliot's coworker and wish characters *Roberto*, beach jock, sportscaster, aide to President Lincoln); Miriam Shur (*Carol*, Elliot's coworker and wish character in penthouse); Brian Doyle (priest); Rudolf Martin (*Raoul*, wish character who seduces Allison); Aaron Lustig (Elliot's supervisor at Synedyne); Jeff Doucette (*Murray*, desk sergeant who books Elliot); Julian Firth (*John Wilkes Booth*, assassin in Lincoln wish sequence).

Appraisal and Synopsis

When news spread that Harold Ramis, the brilliant writer/director/actor best remembered for *Groundhog Day* (1993), as well as his work on *Ghostbusters* (1984) and the "SCTV" series, was planning to revamp the old Dudley Moore/Peter Cook vehicle, hopes were high for a new comedy masterpiece. Unfortunately, the completed film fails to live up to its potential. Cowritten with Larry Gelbart and Peter Tolan, the screenplay streamlined and clarified the original plot, but it also made several choices that eviscerated the entire concept. Most of these changes involve the Devil, who was transformed from a stumbling but hard-working trickster, working out of a rundown clubhouse in London assisted by seven loony helpmates representing the seven deadly sins, into an elegant, high-powered woman (Elizabeth Hurley), operating out of a massive underground discotheque in Oakland, California. Where Moore's Devil labored in a ramshackle back office and concentrated on such trivial tasks as scratching phonograph records, Hurley's Devil works out of a large, fashionable suite with tapestries of the Garden of Evil and high-tech, wall-sized televisions. The altering of the Devil's status (and sex) robs the story of much of its sparkle.

The basic plot remains the same. In both films the Devil selects a lowly nerd and offers him seven wishes in exchange for his soul. In both pictures, the protagonist is smitten with a female coworker. Oddly, in the remake, Elliot, the main character, calls out not to the Devil but to God for help to win over his love. (In a way, this negates the entire plot.) Elliot works for a San Francisco computer firm as a technical support representative and is infatuated with Allison, who he has loved for years. Elliot is disliked by his fellow employees, who make him the butt of their jokes. When the Devil appears, she offers Elliot seven chances to "score" with his adored. Of course, Elliot doubts the beautiful woman is the Devil, and she offers him a free wish. He asks for a Big Mac, expecting her to materialize one out of thin air, but instead she takes him to a McDonald's restaurant and orders him one. When Elliot mocks this effort, the Devil takes him for a ride in her car, bringing him to her discotheque where she briefly transforms into a traditional male Devil in red tights with a pointy beard. Finally, Elliott is convinced, and he signs her contract. The rest of the plot swirls around how each wish fails because of tricks by the Devil which undermine each request. These elaborate wish sequences are basically imaginary, and the Allison who appears in them is as unreal as the fantasy scenarios themselves. However, the fact that these episodes are totally outside of reality never seems to occur to Elliot (or to Dudley Moore in the original). The wishes are merely humorous skits for the entertainment of the audience, and they are largely constructed as pure satire, such as the hilarious basketball episode.

For his first wish, Elliot tells the Devil that he wants to be rich, powerful, and married to Allison. She turns him into a Columbian drug lord. This becomes the funniest skit in the movie, as Brendan Fraser goes over the top in this Spanish-language satire. It turns out that his wife does not love him, and her lover, Raoul, is planning a coup to topple Elliot. (Elliot can terminate each wish by pushing 666 on a pager. In the original film, all Moore had to do was blow a raspberry.) For his second wish, Elliot learns that Allison desires a "sensitive" man, so he asks the Devil to turn him into the most sensitive man on Earth. The wish is fulfilled as Allison and Elliot are having a picnic on the beach, and Elliot weeps at the beauty of the sunset. He is so sensitive that he drives Allison crazy, and she runs off with some beach jocks who kick sand in Elliot's face. It suddenly dawns on him that the Devil plans to subvert each wish, so he tries to be quite specific with his requests to plus any loopholes. A rabid basketball fan, Elliot wishes to become the greatest basketball player of his time. The devil turns him into a 7'6" giant, lead player of a team called the Diablos. He dominates the game, scoring almost every point in the contest. However, he also finds himself unable to speak except in dumb clichés. Allison, a sportswriter in this wish, approaches Elliot in his locker room and flirts unabashedly with him. She teases him into lowering the towel around his waist and is startled to discover that he is drastically undersized. Elliot is likewise stunned, and he pushes 666 on the pager to end the wish. In his fourth wish, Elliot specifically proposes that he be well endowed. He also wants to be wealthy, intellectual, respected, and a

Elizabeth Hurley in Bedazzled *was the loveliest image of the Devil to appear on screen.*

celebrity. The Devil delivers Elliott to an exclusive penthouse cocktail party, where Elliot dazzles the guests with his wit and charm. He meets Allison, another guest, and they discuss why existentialism need not be bleak. His charisma wins Allison over, and they head to his apartment for a night of lovemaking. But when Elliot brings her to his bedroom, they find a man there named Lance who claims to be Elliot's lover. Allison heads off, and Elliot ends the wish, disappointed that the Devil made him a homosexual this time.

Temporarily abandoning his quest for Allison, Elliot now wishes instead to do something important for mankind, and he asks the Devil to make him president of the United States. She transforms him into Abraham Lincoln on the night of his assassination. As John Wilkes Booth aims his gun, Elliot asks him to pause, and he pushes the Devil's pager to end the wish.

Elliot delays making another wish when the Devil claims that he has only one wish remaining. She now counts the Big Mac wish in her calculations. Elliot visits a church where he tells a priest that he needs to talk to God because he signed a deal with the Devil. Thinking him a nut, the priest calls the police who put him in jail for observation. He is thrown into a cell with an easygoing, insightful black man who calmly talks with Elliot, encouraging him. When Elliot asks the man's identity, he replies that he is just a good friend.

After his release, Elliot confronts the Devil, saying he does not intend to make another wish. The Devil throws him into hell, showing her dark side as she transforms into a huge demon with a pitchfork. As she thrusts the giant pitchfork against him, Elliot wishes "that Allison has a happy life." Everything changes, and Elliot learns that a benevolent, unselfish wish voids the contract. The Devil, now dressed as a businesswoman and lawyer, tells him that the battle between good and evil takes place inside every human being, and she helps individuals by forcing them to choose. She wishes Elliot well as they part, and the Devil heads to a courtroom to settle a legal case in which she has an interest.

Now a changed man, Elliot returns to his life, and his coworkers are surprised by the differences in him. He finally approaches the real Allison, and they chat amiably, but she declines Elliot's offer of a date because she is seeing someone else. Going home, Elliot meets Nicole, a new neighbor. He helps her move in, and they hit it off. As they go out later, Elliot sees the Devil and his cellmate (presumably God) playing a game of chess in the park.

Unlike the conclusion of the original *Bedazzled*, the remake seems to suggest that God and the Devil are actually cooperating, providing tests for mankind to prove its worthiness. This is quite different from the Cook version, where Satan wants a reconciliation with the Almighty but is clearly rebuffed. In the Ramis view, the conflict of the Devil and God over human souls is merely a big show hiding their basic collaboration. In the Cook view, the arbitrary God is as big a trickster as the Devil, using loopholes to make His victim, the Devil, suffer in an endless fight against hopeless odds. Considering the fact that these are both comedies, the philosophical backdrop of both films suggests that humanity serves merely as pawns and playthings in the overall scheme of existence.

Performances

By making the devil a woman, the *Bedazzled* remake alters the dynamics, which in turn considerably alter the relationship between the lead character and the Devil. Much of the witty banter, clever byplay, the camaraderie are lost, replaced instead by bland innuendo. Brendan Fraser and Elizabeth Hurley never develop the relationship that Dudley Moore and Peter

Cook do in the original. When Cook tricks Moore, he leaves the impression that he is sorry that his nature requires him to act in such a fashion. This is lacking in the Fraser-Hurley association, so much so that when the remake repeats the line from the original film, "You are my best friend," it seems completely wrong. Hurley's Devil hardly appears in the wish sequences, unlike Cook who figured quite prominently in them. Hurley merely has brief and pointless cameos as a beach bunny or a cheerleader. There is no equivalent to the "double date" sequence in the original nor the hilarious shenanigans in the convent sequence. On the other hand, Hurley does get to show the Devil's dark side, and when she transforms into the monstrous demon in the spectacular sequence in hell, it is the highlight of the film. Otherwise, Hurley seems more like a Bond girl than the Devil for most of the film. The problem lies in the script, not in her performance, however, and she comes across as well as any other contemporary actress could, given the limitations of the part. Brendan Fraser's performance has its highs and lows, and it is unfortunate that his first ten minutes in the film are his weakest. His nerd Elliot is so unlikable and irritating that many filmgoers will be turned off. He gets better as the film goes along, however, and his satirical bent really shines in the basketball and suave author sequences. His transformation at the end of the film is also well handled. He never seems quite as smitten with his dream girl, Allison, as Moore did with Margaret. Frances O'Connor outperforms Eleanor Bron as the wish girl, showing far greater versatility and range in the part. She seems totally believable in each incarnation. The four actors playing Elliot's coworkers also do a splendid job as the different characters in Elliot's wishes. It also would have been nice if Harold Ramis himself had performed a cameo as he did in *As Good as It Gets* (1997). Back in a hilarious "SCTV" skit called "Dante's Inferno," Ramis played a hapless game show victim who gets tossed into hell for not confessing to his sins fast enough. Too bad more of the wild humor in that skit was not present in the remake of *Bedazzled*.

Notable Quotes

- I think you're hot! (**Elliot to the Devil, thinking she is a mortal woman**)

  Baby, you have no idea. (**the Devil's reply**)

- Do you have $3.47? I left my purse in the underworld. (**the Devil to Elliot after ordering a Big Mac for him**)

- It's not easy being the Barbra Streisand of evil. (**the Devil to Elliot between wishes two and three**)

Cabin in the Sky

1943   Rating: ***   Rex Ingram as the Devil

MGM. Written by Joseph Schrank, based on the musical by John Latouche and Lynn Root; Photographed by Sidney Wagner; Edited by Harold F. Kress; Music by Harold Arlen, Vernon Duke, and Duke Ellington; Produced by Arthur Freed; Directed by Vincent Minnelli. B&W, 98 minutes.

Annotated Cast List

Eddie Anderson (*Little Joe Jackson*, repentant sinner); Ethel Waters (*Petunia Jackson*, his wife, who devotedly prays for him); Lena Horne (*Georgia Brown*, beautiful singer and temptress); Rex Ingram (*Lucifer Jr.*, the Devil and *Lucius*, gambler); Kenneth Spencer (*General*, God's representative, and *Rev. Greene*, minister); Oscar Polk (*Fleetfoot*, General's messenger, and the deacon, Rev. Greene's assistant); John William Sublett (*Domino Johnson*, gambler and gunman); Louis Armstrong (Lucifer's helper with trumpet); Mantan Moreland (Lucifer's top idea man); Willie Best (Lucifer's sleepy idea man); Fletcher Rivers (Lucifer's team member); William Bailey (*Bill*); Butterfly McQueen (*Lily*, Petunia's friend); Ruby Daindridge (*Mrs. Kelso*); Ernest Whitman (*Jim Henry*, nightclub owner); Nicodemus (*Dude*, Jim's sidekick); Duke Ellington (himself).

Appraisal and Synopsis

Cabin in the Sky was the directorial debut of Vincent Minnelli, who was brought to Hollywood by Arthur Freed due to his success as a polished director of Broadway musicals. The all-black cast made this an unusual venture for MGM, which hired Duke Ellington and Louis Armstrong to flesh out the cast and broaden its appeal. Minnelli retained Ethel Waters from the original Broadway production but replaced the male lead, Dooley Wilson, who played Sam in *Casablanca* (1942), with Eddie Anderson, who was probably the best known and most popular black actor in the country due to his radio work as Rochester on "The Jack Benny Program". Another brilliant stroke of casting was the magnificent Lena Horne as Georgia Brown. Although modern viewers can easily detect the racial stereotypes, it was a successful and well-intentioned effort for its day and showcased many black performers in a quality production.

On the day Little Joe Jackson is going to declare his repentance at his local church, he backslides when Lucius and his other gambling cronies lure him out of church. His loving wife, Petunia, tracks him down to the night spot and finds that he has been shot in a gambling dispute. He is taken home where he lingers in a coma between life and death while Petunia continues to pray for him. The rest of the film can be regarded as true or merely as Joe's delirium.

Lucifer Jr. and a team of demons appear to claim his soul. Petunia fervently appeals to God, who responds by sending the General, His representative, to deny the Devil from claiming Joe and to extend his life for six additional months so that he can genuinely reform. Back in hell, Lucifer Jr. and his team of idea men devise a surefire scheme to corrupt Joe. He asks Pappy Lucifer to arrange for Joe to win the Irish Sweepstakes. He feels certain that, with all the extra cash, Joe will fall for the temptations of Georgia Brown, the irresistible daughter of Satan who lives in the same town as Joe. While her husband recovers, Petunia sings several songs, including "Happiness is a Thing Called Joe" and the musical's showstopper, "Takin' a Chance on Love."

Georgia stops by to visit Little Joe. Lucifer Jr. and the General watch as she does her best to seduce him, but Little Joe resists, singing "Life's Full o'Consequences." As a last resort, Georgia reads to Little Joe the cablegram he received that proclaims him a finalist in the Irish Sweepstakes. Filled with excitement, Joe hugs Georgia, which is observed by Petunia, who doesn't realize that Joe has actually resisted Georgia's temptation. She kicks him out of the house. Crestfallen, the General notes that she didn't even give him a chance to explain.

As time passes, Petunia has second thoughts and plans to win her husband back. Little Joe spends most of his time living it up at Paradise, Jim Henry's nightclub. Because of Joe's bankroll, the club is now able to feature headliners such as Duke Ellington. Domino Johnson, the gambler who shot Little Joe earlier, arrives in town, singing a sassy number, "What Is There About Me?" Decked out in her most elegant clothes, Petunia shows up at the club just in time to catch Joe and Domino fighting over Georgia Brown, the club's singer. Using reverse psychology, Petunia flirts with Domino to make her husband jealous. Things quickly get out of hand as Domino and Joe start to brawl, and a desperate Petunia calls up to God to destroy the wicked club. A tornado strikes, tearing the Paradise club to pieces. Unfortunately, Domino shoots and kills both Petunia and Joe at the same time.

The General tallies up Joe's ledger and finds that he has come up short in gaining entrance to heaven. Lucifer Jr. is about to claim him when it is learned that Georgia Brown has repented and has given the money she obtained from Joe to charity. The General recalculates his books and proclaims that the new figures just barely allow Joe to enter heaven. Lucifer Jr. is demoted by his father for his failure. As Little Joe and Petunia climb the heavenly stairway, he begins to grow weary and cannot reach the top step. He suddenly finds himself back in bed, coming out of his delirium. Petunia, waiting by his bedside, is overjoyed to see him recover, and she reprises "Takin' a Chance on Love" as the picture concludes.

Performances

Rex Ingram played the Devil in the original stage production of *Cabin in the Sky*. Some people confuse him with the producer and director with the same name who helmed such important films as *The Four Horsemen of the Apocalypse* (1921) and *The Magician* (1926). Actor Rex Ingram was born in 1895 on a Mississippi riverboat, and he studied to become a doctor before the performing bug bit. He scored a huge triumph playing God in *Green Mansions* (1937), the retelling of Bible stories with a black cast. He also was impressive as the genie in *The Thief of Baghdad* (1940). Like Max von Sydow and George Burns, Ingram has the distinction of playing both the Almighty as well as his counterpart. As Lucifer Jr., Ingram is the chief administrator of hell, answerable only to his father, Satan. The best scene in the film is the conference chaired by Ingram in the Hades Hotel, as he brainstorms with his lackeys on the best way to trap Joe. Louis Armstrong and Mantan Moreland, Birmingham from the Charlie Chan film series, are superb as they trade quips and jibes. Lucifer Jr. and all his men are dressed in elegant uniforms, featuring an impressive assortment of brass buttons. They all sport horns on their heads, but Mantan's horns are only waxed hair shaped to resemble horns. Ingram has a distinct air of authority in all of his scenes. He and Kenneth Spencer, who plays God's representative, have a number of sparkling scenes together while they observe Joe. Of course, no one on Earth can hear their voices, but both have the ability to project thoughts into the brains of mortals. The scene where Ingram transmits his suggestions to Lena Horne is another outstanding one. Unfortunately, Ingram didn't sing in the film; his imposing voice would have been equally impressive in song.

Notable Quotes

• Sometime when you fight the Devil, you got to jab him with his own pitchfork. (**Petunia to God**)

- Pappy has got to make a test case out of this one. He ain't going to let the Lord get away with breaking all the rules by giving Little Joe another chance. (**Lucifer Jr. to his team**)

- Give a man money, watch him act funny. (**trumpet devil Louis Armstrong to Lucifer Jr.**)

Cataclysm
AKA The Nightmare Never Ends *and* Satan's Supper

1980   Rating: ***   Robert Bristol as the Devil

Genesis. Written by Philip Yordan; Photographed by Art Fitzsimmons and Bruce Markoe; Edited by Bruce Markoe; Music by Steven Arthur Yeaman, Casey Young, and Gustav Holst; Produced by Daryl A. Marshak; Directed by Tom McGowan, Greg Tallas, and Philip Marshak. Color, 92 minutes.

Annotated Cast List

Cameron Mitchell (*Lt. Sterne*, police detective); Robert Bristol (*Olivier*, the Devil); Marc Lawrence (*Abraham Weiss*, elderly Nazi hunter, and *Lt. Dieter*, police detective); Richard Moll (*James Hansen*, antireligious author); Faith Clift (*Dr. Claire Hansen*, his wife, a surgeon); Maurice Grandmaison (*Papini*, defrocked monk fighting against Satan); Juan Luis Curiel (psychic); Christie Wagner (*Ann*, victim of Satan); Klint Stevenson, Elizabeth Martin, Robyn Russell, Georgia Geerling, T. J. Savage, Lou Edwards, Richard Bulik, Phil Yordan, Jr.

Appraisal and Synopsis

This is a true low-budget oddity, made with undeniable style and flashes of brilliance. The bold technique allows viewers to ignore the poor film stock, the mediocre acting, and the inconsistent storyline. Eventually, the film was released under three different titles, with slightly different cuts. The original, *Cataclysm*, has the longest running time, with the other prints running six to ten minutes shorter. A long segment was later added to an anthology film entitled *Night Train to Terror* (1985) in which God and Satan argue over the fate of three souls. In that cut, the material from *Cataclysm* is altered to seem like a comedy, with sequences of stop-motion monsters added to provide a humorous touch. *Night Train to Terror* is almost unwatchable and even inexplicable as the three directors— Marshak, McGowan, and Tallas— hack and trash their earlier superior footage. It is difficult to detect which of these three is responsible for the quality moments in the original *Cataclysm*. There is a moodiness and genuine flair for cinematic horror at work in stretches of the film, with a dash of surrealism. If only this talent could have been distilled and some of the rubbish removed, *Cataclysm* could have had the same impact as underground classics such as *Phantasm* (1979) or *The Evil Dead* (1982). Instead, it is a flawed but quite interesting also-ran.

The film begins with just a quick title card, as it launches into a depiction of Dr. Claire Hansen's nightmare of Nazi war atrocities. At the same time, elderly concentration camp survivor Abraham Weiss spots at a ballet premiere on television the Nazi responsible for the murder of his family. He persuades his neighbor, Lt. Sterne, to drive him to the theater to track and identify the individual, who turns out to be a wealthy playboy named Olivier. Sterne doubts he is the Nazi for whom Weiss is searching because Olivier is too young, a man in his twenties. Dr. Hansen continues to be plagued by bad dreams that feature Olivier. Her husband, James Hansen, is the author of the controversial book *God Is Dead*, which critiques belief in any religion. Claire, a devout Catholic, is at odds with James over his theories.

Weiss is brutally murdered, attacked by an inhuman beast, and his dying words to a cop are "Look on the wall." Sterne inspects his neighbor's apartment, which is plastered with historic photographs and newspaper articles. Olivier's face, always the same age, appears again and again in these documents which date back to the Franco-Prussian War of 1870. Sterne decides to investigate. James is approached by Papini, a strange-looking holy man who resembles Rasputin. He warns the author that the Devil exists and that he will be targeted by him shortly.

The Hansens are visiting a discotheque when Olivier shows up, tailed by Sterne and his partner, Dieter. Claire's nephew Jim introduces his girlfriend, Ann, an employee of the disco. Olivier casts a spell on Ann, and she leaves with him. Upon bringing her to his apartment, Olivier removes his shoes, and Ann screams when she sees that he has hooves instead of feet. Later, senseless and confused, Ann is dumped from a car into the street in front of the disco. Sterne questions Olivier, who is mocking and evasive in his replies. Jim attempts to confront Olivier with a gun, and afterward his body is found torn to pieces like Weiss. Claire consults a psychic, who warns her that her husband is in danger. James is approached by a foundation that wishes to fund his work. He attends a meeting with the head of this organization, who turns out to be Olivier. He praises the author's writings, particularly when he denies the existence of God. Olivier is taken aback, however, when Hansen also denies the existence of Satan. Infuriated, the Devil slays him and returns to the discotheque, where Ann attends to him devotedly.

Papini presents Claire with evidence that Olivier murdered her husband. Papini intends to confront Olivier, and if he fails, he implores Claire to carry on his work opposing the Devil. When he breaks into Olivier's house that evening, Papini encounters a beautiful woman, who taunts him for his beliefs. He demands to know her identity, and she replies, "My name is Legion," the same response given to Christ by a possessed man in Luke 8:30. Papini is knocked over by howling wind, tossed out of the house, and destroyed.

Claire is informed by Sterne about the death of Papini. She meets Olivier at police headquarters when he is brought in and accused by Sterne of responsibility for five murders. Sterne, however, is forced to release him since he lacks evidence, and that evening, he and Dieter are killed when their car bursts into flames. *Mars* from Holst's *The Planets* starts to play on the soundtrack as Claire tries to kill Olivier, running him down with her car while he walks with Ann. At first he continues to cackle after being sprawled out over her hood, but he then passes out. Claire throttles Ann, who comes to her senses, and they drag Olivier to the hospital where Claire tries to cut out his heart. She removes it, but Olivier revives, kills Ann and Claire, and stomps out of the operating room as the pounding chords from *Mars* brings the film to a conclusion. The Devil has vanquished all of his opponents, and he emerges as the only character left alive. The Holst music is quite effective and helps the film to end with a rather impressive final shot.

Performances

This is the only significant part ever played onscreen by Robert Bristol; his other film appearances are brief bit parts. His features are androgynous, and he speaks with a pronounced English accent, which doesn't sound genuine. Bristol vaguely reminds one of British actor Shane Briant, star of *Straight on 'til Morning* (1972) and *Frankenstein and the Monster from Hell* (1974). Bristol lacks any screen charisma and makes little impression. His characterization is as a hip, mod Devil, always accompanied by at least two female attendants. Except for his eyes, he wears little makeup, and the only diabolical thing about his appearance is his feet, which are cloven hooves. The Devil is a trickster and enjoys pseudonyms. In this picture he uses Olivier, which is the name accorded in mythology to Lucifer's lieutenant in charge of cruelty and mercilessness to the poor. Since the poor are not among his targets, Olivier is no doubt the Devil himself. Although he does refer to himself in the third person Olivier becomes incensed whenever the existence of the Devil is doubted. The Devil's plans in this picture are undefined, except that he enjoys inflicting suffering through the ages and particularly enjoys impersonating German officers. It is not entirely clear, but the female demon encountered by Papini could be yet another manifestation of Satan. The plot has nowhere to go except to show the Devil triumphant again and again over each of his opponents. The rest of the cast ranges from adequate to awful. Cameron Mitchell walks through his part halfheartedly, but screen veteran Marc Lawrence, whose career dates back to the 1930s, is remarkably effective in his two roles as the elderly Nazi hunter and as Mitchell's sidekick. His makeup as Abraham Weiss is convincing, and he is almost unrecognizable. Almost twenty years later, Lawrence appeared in another Devil film, *End of Days* (1999). Richard Moll, later famous as Bull Shannon in the television series "Night Court," makes his screen debut billed as Charles Moll. His hairpiece is particularly unconvincing, and the grey fringe to his sideburns changes from scene to scene. His dramatic delivery while appearing on a talk show attacking the "myth" of God is one of the picture's highlights, but he is weak in his encounter with the Devil. Faith Clift is particularly bad as Claire Hansen, which is unfortunate because she has more screen time than any other character.

Notable Quotes

- Thanks to contemporary research, that imaginary being, Satan, has completely disappeared. His place has been taken by scientific reality. (**James Hansen to Papini**)
- Satan was God's favorite angel.... Though a fallen angel, Satan is still an angel, and if he can show God that man was a mistake, not worth creating or saving, perhaps God will forgive him and give him his place back in heaven. (**Papini to James**)
- Be careful, Mr. Olivier. Don't step on me or you will never get rid of the smell. (**Sterne to Olivier**)

The Company of Wolves

1984   Rating: **   Terence Stamp as the Devil

Cannon Films. Written by Neil Jordan and Angela Carter, based on her book *The Bloody Chamber and Other Stories*; Photographed by Bryan Loftus; Edited by Rodney Holland; Special Effects by Peter MacDonald; Music by George Fenton; Produced by Chris Brown and Stephen Woolley; Directed by Neil Jordan. Color, 95 minutes.

Annotated Cast List

Sarah Patterson (*Rosaleen*, young girl troubled by disturbing dreams); David Warner (her father); Tussie Silberg (her mother); Georgia Slowe (*Alice,* her sister); Angela Lansbury (her grandmother); Graham Crowden (priest); Micha Bergese (huntsman and werewolf); Shane Johnstone (amorous teenage boy); Brian Glover (his father); Susan Porrett (his mother); Dawn Archibald (witch woman); Katharyn Pogson (young bride); Stephen Rea (young groom); Terence Stamp (the Devil); Vincent McClaren (boy approached by the Devil); Danielle Dax (wolfgirl); Ruby Buchanan (dowager); Jimmy Gardner, Roy Evans, Edward Marsen, Jimmy Brown.

Appraisal and Synopsis

The Company of Wolves is basically a rambling series of episodes dreamed by Rosaleen, a young girl who is sick in bed with a stomachache. Her parents are concerned about her, but Alice, her older sister, thinks that she is merely milking a minor ailment. In her dreams, Rosaleen imagines herself living in a primitive rural village in a nebulous period of time that combines elements of the Middle Ages and the eighteenth century. In her fantasies, Alice has been killed by a wolf, and Rosaleen spends most of her time with her grandmother, who recounts many stories, usually about wolves and men who are wolves in spirit. The older woman is basically hostile to all men and warns Rosaleen about the beast in man. Her folktales are bloody ones in which the characters usually come to unpleasant ends. One of her tales involves the Devil, which she tells after the local priest passes by. The worst werewolves are bastard sons of priests, she relates, particularly if the child is born feet first on Christmas day. Such a person is destined to meet the Devil in the woods. The scene then shifts to a dark evening in the woods as a young man appears lost in a thick fog. Suddenly, a white Rolls Royce appears before him, driven by a young girl with golden hair, dressed in an elegant white chauffeur's uniform. She opens the passenger door for the young man, and the Devil, seated in the rear, beckons him closer. Clothed in a black suit, the Devil reaches into a box and removes a small vial of liquid which he hands to the young man, urging him to use it wisely. He then dismisses him with a wave of his hand. The Devil returns to examining a small skull which he was holding when the driver stopped the car. The Rolls then drives off. This car, incidentally, is the only modern element in the dream portion of the picture, suggesting the Devil's timelessness. The young man dabs some of the liquid on his chest, and hair starts to sprout forth. Vines start to twine around his legs, and he starts to scream. Rosaleen sees the man's image in an oval mirror; as the sequence ends, she comments, "That is a horrid story."

The main section of her dream is an elaborate variation on "Little Red Riding Hood." Rosaleen encounters and chats with a handsome young huntsman in the forest while on her way to visit her grandmother. After their flirtatious meeting, the huntsman bets he can beat her to her destination by cutting across country. He then bounds off and when he reaches the hut, kills her grandmother, slicing off her head with a single blow of his open hand. When Rosaleen appears at the door, she seems only mildly surprised to find the huntsman in place of her grandmother. She seems to realize that her new companion is a werewolf, and their conversation begins to take on a double meaning. He coaxes her to kiss him. Finally the huntsman starts to transform when Rosaleen comments, "What large teeth you have," and he replies, "All the better to eat you with!" At the surreal climax, various images from different segments of the story combine as the villagers hunt the wolf, who Rosaleen now tries to protect. The final scene is back in her modern-day bedroom. A wolf breaks through her window, no doubt symbolizing the awakening of her own sexual desires.

Most of Angela Carter's work combines feminism, folklore, and Freudian analysis, and this unorthodox and ethereal fantasy blends together bits and pieces from her various stories in a sometimes confusing but nevertheless stimulating concoction. The Devil figures only marginally in the images, so *The Company of Wolves* receives a modest evaluation for this volume.

Performances

Terence Stamp appears as the suave, elegant, but disengaged Devil, who apparently travels in opulent style as he dispenses his evil wares in *The Company of Wolves*. Stamp has been cast in a wide range of films since his Oscar-nominated debut in *Billy Budd* (1961), including *The Collector* (1965), *Superman II* (1980), and *Wall Street* (1987). He had an earlier run-in with the Devil on-screen in *Spirits of the Dead* (1968), originally called *Histoires Extraordinaires* and based upon three stories by Edgar Allan Poe. The third segment, directed by Federico Fellini, was called "Toby Dammit," a lively and wild piece of surrealism loosely drawn from Poe's "Never Bet the Devil Your Head." As Dammit, Stamp portrays a dissipated and arrogant British Shakespearean actor who comes to Rome to act in a spaghetti Western that will depict the life of Christ. Dammit's fee is a Ferrari. He gets drunk at a film award ceremony and heads off in his car for a wild, midnight ride. Dammit is haunted by the image of the Devil, only fleetingly seen as a young girl (Marina Yaru) with a peek-a-boo hairdo and a rather silly smirk. Dammit gets stuck on an unfinished bridge, but when he spots the child bouncing a large white ball on the other side of the span, he decides to race his Ferrari across the open span to reach her. His head is lopped off by a wire strung across the road, and the final scene of the segment shows the child taking Dammit's head in place of her ball. So it is rather appropriate that Stamp was used as the unbilled Devil who rides in a luxury car in *The Company of Wolves*.

Notable Quotes

• Waste not, want not. (**the Devil to the young man while handing him the vial**)

• If you should spot a naked man in the woods, run as if the Devil himself were after you. (**grandmother to Rosaleen**)

• They say the prince of darkness is a gentleman, and as it turns out, they are right, a fine gentleman. (**Rosaleen to the huntsman**)

Crossroads

1986   Rating: ***   Robert Judd as the Devil

Columbia. Written by John Fusco; Photographed by John Bailey; Special Effects by Lawrence J. Cavanaugh; Edited by Freeman A. Davies; Music by Ry Cooder; Produced by Mark Carliner and Tim Zinnemann; Directed by Walter Hill. Color, 96 minutes.

Annotated Cast List

Ralph Machio (*Eugene "Lightning" Martone*, young guitarist fascinated with the blues); Joe Seneca (*Willie Brown*, elderly blues musician); Guy Killum (Willie at seventeen); Jami Gertz (*Frances*, teenage runaway); Tim Russ (*Robert Johnson*, blues guitarist who sold his soul to the Devil); Robert Judd (*Scratch*, the Devil); Joe Morton (Scratch's assistant); Steve Vai (*Jack Butler*, the Devil's top blues guitarist); Dennis Lipscomb (*Lloyd*, bar owner who propositions Frances); Harry Carey, Jr. (bartender in Weevil); John Hancock (*Tilford*, corrupt sheriff); Allan Arbus (*Dr. Santis*, Juilliard music professor); Gretchen Parker (dancer in the club in hell); Al Fann (pawnbroker); Wally Taylor (*O.Z.*); Tex Donaldson (*John McGraw*); Akosoa Rusia (girl at boardinghouse); Edward Walsh (*Harley Terhume*, man whose wallet was stolen); Alan Graff (*Alvin*, barroom brawler); Diana Bellamy (nursing home supervisor); Natasha Pearl (young girl at crossroads who calls Willie "Four Eyes").

Appraisal and Synopsis

Although deserving of a five-star rating as a blues film, *Crossroads* rates a borderline three stars as a Devil film. The plot involves musicians who sell their souls in exchange for their musical talent at a mysterious crossroads in rural Mississippi. The story likely evolves from the myth of the extraordinary violinist Nicolo Paganini, who reportedly bartered his soul to the Devil for his prodigious talent. Paganini even encouraged the myth as he became the first musical showman of the nineteenth century, blazing the trail for Franz Liszt and other Romantic-era virtuosos. Indeed, there is a legend about the true-life blues master Robert Johnson selling his soul to the Devil after meeting him at a crossroads at night. This story became part of the folk history of the blues after Johnson died mysteriously in 1938, and people claimed that the Devil came to collect his dues. The original concept of meeting the Devil at a crossroads dates far back into legend, and the earliest version of Faust in the sixteenth century includes an initial meeting at a crossroads between Faust and Mephistopheles. The metaphor of the crossroads is a powerful and dramatic one. Oddly, there also was a television anthology series called "Crossroads" which ran from 1955 to 1957 and illustrated crises faced by members of the clergy.

The premise of this motion picture is excellent, and the cinematography, particularly of the vista at the crossroads, is magnificent, but the plot about the Devil gets sidetracked. This happens particularly in the road segment of the picture, which bogs down when the protagonists get involved in a series of misadventures in various motels, bars, and roadhouses. The film is a fresh and interesting hybrid even if the story never truly gels.

The picture opens in the 1930s with bluesman Robert Johnson waiting with his guitar at a lonely dirt crossroads. The scene fades out and shifts to a recording session where Johnson is singing and playing a song he composed called "Crossroads Blues." Many years later, young Juilliard School musician Eugene Martone is fascinated as he listens to Johnson's recording. Eugene is a musical prodigy who finds his interest drawn to the blues. His classical teachers warn him that he needs to make a decision about which musical path he wishes to pursue, especially since the classics require a special intense dedication. Eugene tracks down "Blind Dog" Fulton, a famous blues harmonica player who was an old friend of Robert Johnson. The musician, now using the name Willie Brown, is confined to a security nursing home, having been convicted years earlier on a manslaughter charge. Brown refuses to see any visitors, so Martone gets a job as a janitor at the nursing home and strikes up an acquaintance with the crotchety old musician. When he tells Willie that he is also a bluesman, the old man mocks him, saying it is impossible for a white boy from Long Island to be a bluesman. Eugene begs Willie to teach him the lost song of Robert Johnson, which he never recorded. Willie promises to teach it to him if he breaks him out of the security facility and takes him back to Mississippi. Reluctantly, Eugene agrees to the old man's terms. Willie's real intention is to return to the mysterious crossroads and see if he can convince the Devil to cancel the contract he signed with him many years earlier.

Eugene whisks Willie out of the facility at 5 AM, and they hop a bus heading down south. When they run out of money, they start to hitchhike, eventually teaming up with Frances, a teenage runaway heading for Los Angeles. They get into a series of misadventures, including robbery, panhandling, and playing music to raise cash. Willie dubs Eugene "Lightning," and he teaches him genuine delta blues techniques, including the use of a slide. Eugene starts to fall in love with Frances.

The three travelers are broke when they reach the town of Weevil. Willie tells Eugene and Frances to hustle some dough in the bars on the white side of the main street, and he'll try to raise cash on the black side. Frances lifts a man's wallet but is caught, and she and Eugene are kicked out by the bartender. They find Willie, and they are a big hit when they perform for the crowd in the black bar. Frances decides to leave, and she slips out of Eugene's room early the next morning. Willie sees her and gives her some of the money they earned from their gig.

Eugene is deeply depressed by her departure, and Willie tells him the secret of the blues is simply "a good man feeling bad about the woman he once was with." Willie also tells Eugene that the missing song of Robert Johnson is only a myth. Eugene sits down and records his own blues number.

Willie stops by a boardinghouse and speaks with the granddaughter of a woman who once ran a whorehouse. He describes the crossroads, and the woman arranges for them to be driven there. Willie instructs Eugene to play his blues tune, and moments later the Devil's assistant shows up in a stylish car. He tells Willie that the Devil now uses the name of Scratch. He offers Willie a ride, but he declines, saying he will wait for Scratch. The Devil then arrives on foot, dressed dapperly in black. Willie tells him that he wants out of their deal, but the Devil refuses. Eugene then offers his own soul to save Willie in a blues contest that the Devil proposes. If Eugene can outplay Jack Butler, the Devil's bluesman, then he will tear up Willie's contract. If Eugene loses, then the Devil will claim both their souls. The Devil whisks them instantly to the blues showdown at a crowded club in hell. Eugene and Jack Butler challenge each other with wilder and wilder blues licks. Eugene finally wins when he mixes in some of his classical training, crossing the blues with Bach. Jack Butler tries but fails to match the innovation, and he drops his guitar. The Devil tears up Willie's contract, and Eugene and Willie find themselves back at the crossroads. Willie offers to help Eugene get started as "Lightning Boy" in blues clubs in Chicago, but then he must go his own way, perhaps to Los Angeles where he might find Frances.

Performances

Robert Judd made only one other screen appearance besides *Crossroads*, and his performance is stylish and far too brief. Dressed in a black, three-piece suit with string tie and hat, Judd oozes personality, reminding viewers of the smooth and beguiling style of Scatman Crothers. It is a shame that he is wasted with only a few lines of dialogue at the crossroads. He has no lines in the scene at the club in hell. He just smiles approvingly when his guitarist, Jack Butler, plays an impressive lick. His expression when he tears up Willie's contract is one of disappointment but not fury. It is ironic that in the climactic showdown, Eugene succeeds not from his virtuosity in the blues but by reaching into his own musical soul where his love of the classics saves him from losing to the Devil's protegé. This calls to mind another fable that jazz and rhythm and blues are the Devil's music; Eugene would fail if he did not reach beyond the scope of that style. It is also interesting to note that the audience in hell was a fair one, which responded on strictly musical terms and wasn't stacked by the Devil to ensure a victory for Butler.

The major reason for the success of the picture is the masterful performance by Joe Seneca, whose background included being a member of a musical group known as the Three Riffs. Seneca steals the film without trying. Ralph Machio, best known for the *Karate Kid* film series, is good but not exceptional. His guitar fingering is genuine and impressive, although musician Ry Cooder provided the actual performances heard on the soundtrack. Some of the other cast members had later success. Tim Russ, who plays Robert Johnson, found fame as Tuvoc, the black Vulcan on the series "Star Trek Voyager." Joe Morton went on to a formidable screen career, including an impressive job as the scientific genius Miles Dyson, who sacrifices himself to save mankind in *Terminator II: Judgment Day* (1991).

Notable Quotes

- You looking for me, Willie Brown? It's been a long time, hasn't it, Willie? ... You were about seventeen the last time we saw each other, right on this old crossroads, wasn't it? (**the Devil's overly friendly greeting to Willie**)
- You got what you were supposed to get, bluesman. Ain't nothin' ever as good as we want it to be, but that ain't no reason to break a deal. (**the Devil to Willie, who complained that the Devil let him down**)

Damn Yankees

1958   Rating: ***   Ray Walston as the Devil

Warner Brothers. Written by George Abbott and Douglass Wallopp, based on Wallopp's novel *The Year the Yankees Lost the Pennant*; Photographed by Harold Lipstein; Choreography by Bob Fosse; Edited by Frank Bracht; Music and Lyrics by Richard Adler and Jerry Ross; Produced by George Abbott, Frederick Brisson, and Stanley Donen; Directed by George Abbott and Stanley Donen. Color, 110 minutes.

Annotated Cast List

Tab Hunter (*Joe Hardy*, star baseball player created by the Devil); Robert Shafer (*Joe Boyd*, middle-aged baseball fan transformed into Joe Hardy); Ray Walston (*Applegate*, the Devil); Gwen Verdon (*Lola*, the Devil's assistant); Shannon Bolin (*Meg Boyd*, Joe's wife); Russ Brown (*Benny Van Buren*, Washington Senators' manager); Nathaniel Frey (*Smokey*, veteran ballplayer); James Komack (*Rocky*, young ballplayer); Rae Allen (*Gloria Thorpe*, sports reporter); Elizabeth Howell (*Doris Miller*, Meg's friend); Jean Stapleton (*Sister Miller*, Meg's friend); Albert Linville (*Vernon Welch*, owner of the Senators); Bob Fosse (Lola's dancing partner in mambo skit).

Appraisal and Synopsis

The basic idea of the novel *The Year the Yankees Lost the Pennant* is quite clever, combining the *Faust* story with America's national pastime (and the general frustration of American League fans outside of New York). This is the glue which holds the project together. The story of Faust, of course, has received numerous operatic treatments by Charles Gounod, Arrigo Boito, Ferrucio Busoni, and others. The 1955 Broadway musical became a blockbuster, highlighted by two dynamite songs, "You Got to Have Heart" and "Whatever Lola Wants," which kept the audience humming. The original show provided the theatrical high point of Gwen Vernon's career and in addition brought accolades to Ray Walston and Jean Stapleton. These principals recreated their roles for the 1958 film, which was a disappointment on many levels compared to the original show. It was plagued with static dance numbers, as well as overall cinematic stodginess and mediocre editing. A number of songs were cut and replaced by inferior numbers. Compared to the other classic musicals of the 1950s and 1960s this picture has not worn well on the whole and seems dated, although the revival of the stage version on Broadway and on tour during the 1990s, often headlined by Jerry Lewis in the role of the Devil, bolstered the reputation of the show as a theatrical triumph. The picture, although flawed, still furnishes an abundance of entertaining moments that makes it quite worthwhile and deserving of multiple viewings.

The film opens with middle-aged, diehard Washington Senators fan Joe Boyd rooting with all his heart in front of the television for his favorite team. Joe (who reminds one of Rodney Dangerfield) is frustrated as the Senators blow another game. Joe's wife, Meg, a baseball widow, sings a song about her six-month ordeal every season from opening day to the World Series. Joe steps onto his porch and mutters that he would sell his soul if the

Senators could sign a home run-hitter, their greatest need. The Devil materializes behind Joe, and he introduces himself as Applegate, a baseball fan. He speaks of Joe's former longing to have played ball. Applegate produces fire from his fingers to light his cigarette, and he says, "I'm handy with fire" when Joe asks how he managed the trick. When two passersby, the Miller sisters, are unable to see Applegate, Joe realizes the identity of his visitor. The Devil states his proposition. He will transform Joe into a twenty-two-year-old baseball titan named Joe Hardy, who can lead his team to the World Series. Joe asks many questions, refusing to sell his soul unless the Devil provides an escape clause. Joe will be given a chance to back out of this deal at the stroke of midnight on September 24. With that concession, Joe shakes Applegate's hand, agreeing to the deal. Joe leaves a note to his wife to explain his absence, and when he finishes his letter (and song), Applegate transforms him into young, handsome Joe Hardy.

The next day at the ballpark, the Senators' manager, Benny Van Buren, sings "Heart" to his players to buck up their lagging spirits. Applegate approaches the manager on the field and persuades him to allow his client, Joe Hardy, to take a few swings at batting practice. Joe manages to hit each pitch out of the park. Amazed, Benny asks Joe to field a few balls. Benny decides to sign Joe, who that afternoon hits two home runs, winning the game for the Senators. Sports reporter Gloria Thorpe is annoyed that the Senators' new star avoids giving interviews and is secretive about his past. She decides to dub him "Shoeless Joe," which becomes the basis of an elaborate production number performed with the other ballplayers. Joe misses his wife, goes home, and asks Meg if he can rent a room. The Miller sisters recognize the new tenant as Joe Hardy, the baseball sensation. Applegate is furious with Joe, and he calls his sultry assistant, Lola, to keep Joe from missing his wife. After a victory over the Yankees, Applegate introduces her to Joe as Lolita Hernando, a beauty queen who is Miss West Indies. Using a thick accent, she sings "Whatever Lola Wants" in an attempt to seduce him, but Joe resists her, to Applegate's astonishment. He decides to sow seeds of scandal in Meg's neighborhood to force Joe out, and his scheme works. In triumph, Applegate sings a devilish number, "Those Were the Good Old Days," recalling his past triumphs including Nero, Jack the Ripper, and the guillotine.

September 24 is approaching, and Applegate is worried about the escape clause in his agreement with Joe. He plants a rumor with Gloria Thorpe that Joe is actually Shifty McCoy, who was ejected from the Mexican League for taking a bribe. She prints the story, and the baseball commissioner calls a hearing for the night of September 24 to determine the truth of the allegation. Joe is cleared of the charge, but the hour of his escape clause passes while he is busy at the hearing. Depressed at being damned, Joe goes to a nightclub with Lola and they sing "Two Lost Souls." The Senators have to win the final game of the season to clinch the pennant. Lola learns the Devil actually intends to help the Yankees win, as he always does, and she drugs his drink of rum so he can't interfere with the outcome of the game. Applegate revives while the game is in the seventh inning with Washington leading 1–0. He rushes to the ballpark with Lola, changing her into an old hag. They arrive during the ninth inning. The Yankees have two out, and Micky Mantle is at bat. He hits a long fly ball to center field, and Applegate changes Joe Hardy back into Joe Boyd. He stumbles but manages to catch the ball nonetheless, and the Senators win the pennant. The Washington players go wild with joy while the middle-aged Joe Boyd runs off

Gwen Verdon as the temptress Lola prepares to strut her stuff for Joe (Tab Hunter) as Applegate (Ray Walston) looks on approvingly. Moments later she sings the showstopper "Whatever Lola Wants."

through a doorway at the back of the outfield wall. Some time passes before the players realize that Joe Hardy is missing. The newspapers that evening blame his disappearance on kidnapping by New York gangsters, gamblers who back the Yankees.

By transforming Joe moments before the end of the season, Applegate has presumably violated his contract. He goes to Joe's home, where the Boyds are celebrating their reunion. He tries to tempt Joe to become Joe Hardy again and help the Senators win the World Series. Joe ignores Applegate, however, and joins Meg in song. The Devil jumps up and down in rage and dematerializes as the film ends.

The abrupt, anticlimactic end of the film is one of its weakest moments, especially since it leaves the plotline in shambles. The Devil's agreement with Joe was that he would lead the Senators to the championship. However, since the Devil never intended to let the Yankees lose, his agreement with Joe was faulty, even without the escape clause. These plot elements are never really examined nor resolved. Of course, Applegate is actually playing for bigger game, hoping to plunge the Senators' fans into total despair so they will be easy prey for him. A clean resolution to the film would have improved it greatly, but as it stands, almost everyone is perplexed at the end.

Performances

Ray Walston was a highly regarded character actor with extensive stage experience before breaking into films in his midforties, largely on the basis of his stage triumph on Broadway in *Damn Yankees*. Although he appeared in numerous films later in his career, his main success was on television as the whimsical alien visitor in "My Favorite Martian." Applegate is somewhat of a hybrid characterization of the Devil, largely dependent on his function as the play's comic villain, a standard ingredient of the American musical. He appears with little makeup except for the creation of a widow's peak in his hairline. There are many facets to Applegate's character that are never clearly explained. His powers seem very limited at times, as if he were bound by a number of unspecified rules. For example, he is forced to use a pay telephone to call Lola, apparently unable to summon her at will. He uses his powers to get his coins back, but his abilities certainly seem minimal since he was required to use coins in the first place. He is also affected by sleeping pills when Lola drugs his drink. When he finally awakens, he moves at super speed getting dressed, but then he is forced to take a slow taxi to get to the ballpark. Why couldn't he just materialize at the ballpark in the same fashion he materialized on Joe's porch at the beginning of the film? In one cryptic line, when Joe questions him about his powers, he notes that he has to do things the hard way. Why is this so? Some attention to this issue would have made Applegate even more intriguing. Instead we are merely puzzled by his arbitrary limitations. His pseudonym, Applegate, apparently comes from Celtic mythology, where the entrance to the "other world," Avalon, is known as the Isle of Apples. There are a number of interesting details relating to Applegate. The decor in his apartment, for example, has a repetitive motif of arabesques in flame-like designs. He sleeps in red silk pajamas that are patterned with tiny pitchforks. The Devil's best moment in the film is his song "Those Were the Good Old Days," and Walston sings it with relish, mimicking both Al Jolson and Ted Lewis, altering his catch phrase "Is everybody happy?" to "Was anybody happy?" His utter delight while recalling the rack and the plague is priceless. The rest of the cast also does a fine job. Jean Stapleton's role is a precursor of her classic "dingbat" portrayal of Edith Bunker in "All in the Family." Tab Hunter is a trifle bland, but his enthusiasm and wide-eyed innocence are completely appropriate. Gwen Verdon is great, especially in her trademark song and in the mambo number with choreographer Bob Fosse, who she married in 1960.

Notable Quotes

- That amusing little stunt, it was all the rage during the Middle Ages. (**Applegate, discussing his ability to make himself invisible**)

- No, Joe, I have to do most things the hard way. The only thing that comes really easy is the cigarette trick [lighting one up], and now I am trying to break myself of the filthy habit. (**Applegate, explaining his earthly limitations**)

- This is a mass torture deal, like the Thirty Years' War. I've got thousands of Washington fans drooling under the illusion that the Senators are going to win the pennant. (**Applegate, explaining his scheme to Lola**)

- I see cannibals munchin' a missionary luncheon. The years may have flown, but the memory stays, like the hopes that were dashed when the stock market crashed. Yah ha ha ha, those were the good old days. I walk a million miles or more for some of the gore of the good, old days. (**ending of Applegate's song**)

Dante's Inferno

1924   Rating: ***   Unknown as the Devil

Fox Films. Written by Cyrus Wood and Edmund Goulding, based on *The Inferno* from *The Divine Comedy* by Dante Alighieri; Photographed by Joseph August; Produced by William Fox; Directed by Henry Otto. B&W silent, 60 minutes.

Annotated Cast List

Ralph Lewis (*Mortimer Judd*, wealthy and cold-hearted miser); Winifred Landis (his wife); William Scott (*Ernest*, their son); Pauline Starke (*Marjorie Vernon*, Mrs. Judd's nurse); Josef Swickert (*Eugene Craig*, neighbor facing bankruptcy); Gloria Gray (Craig's daughter); Lorimer Johnson (*Dr. Josephs*, Judd family physician); Lon Poff (Judd's secretary); Bud Jamison (Judd's butler); Lawson Butt (*Dante Alighieri*, medieval poet who tours hell); Howard Gaye (*Virgil*, classical Roman poet who escorts Dante through hell); Robert Klein.

Appraisal and Synopsis

Dante's epic poem describing his tour of hell, purgatory, and heaven is one of the masterpieces of Western literature, but it has never been seriously portrayed on film. The first and only legitimate venture was a two-reel Italian short by Giuseppe de Liguoro made in 1911. This film was quite impressive and bold, with dramatic scenes of crowds of the damned suffering the various torments outlined by Dante. This short is often cited as the first film to include frontal male nudity, but at such a distance little can be actually distinguished. Scenes from this film were acquired by William Fox for this 1924 attempt. In 1935, Spencer Tracy starred in another version about an ambitious carnival barker who rises to own an amusement park featuring an elaborate exhibit based on Dante's poem. When adversity strikes, Tracy has a dream which again recycles footage from the silent Italian short; the brief sequence recreates the horrors of hell as described by Dante, but Satan never appears in Tracy's reverie. The first eight cantos of *The Inferno* are read in a 1989 telefilm known as *TV Dante*, but nothing is portrayed except the talking heads of the performers, including John Gielgud as Virgil and Bob Peck as Dante. Ken Russell also made a picture entitled *Dante's Inferno* (1987), but it is actually a biopic of the nineteenth-century Pre-Raphaelite artist Dante Gabriel Rossetti, played by Oliver Reed.

The Henry Otto version uses Dante's poem as a gimmick which frightens a wealthy miser into becoming a compassionate human being. The story is actually a variant on *A Christmas Carol* by Charles Dickens with Dante and Virgil substituting for Jacob Marley and the Christmas ghosts. The major difference between Ebenezer Scrooge and Mortimer Judd is that Judd is a married man with a family while Scrooge is a bachelor. The picture opens with a series of title cards describing Judd as a man capable of creating a veritable hell on Earth. Judd berates his secretary for bothering him with mail for charitable requests. He receives a phone call from Eugene Craig, his neighbor, asking his help in avoiding bankruptcy, but Judd rejects him, hanging up the phone during his plea.

Craig sends him his copy of *The Inferno* with illustrations by Gustave Doré, writing on the flyleaf, "If there is a Hell, then my curse will take you there!"

Judd continues to demonstrate his skinflint reputation by commenting to his sick wife, "Only the wives of rich men can afford to be ill." He then berates Ernest, his son, who is concerned about the hazardous and inadequate living conditions in the tenement apartments owned by his father. When Craig's book arrives, Judd tears out the title page, crumples it, and tosses it to the floor. The figure of the Devil appears in Craig's study and picks up the page. He stares at Judd and compels him to read the book. The scene shifts to the opening of *The Divine Comedy*, as the poet Dante is lost in the woods, and the image of his beloved Beatrice conjures up the classical writer Virgil, asking him to be Dante's guide. Virgil appears to Dante and offers to lead him through a tour never before undertaken by mortal man. He then takes him through the entrance to hell.

The scenes in the inferno are tinted red, both to enhance the image of the abyss and to disguise the change in film stock from the Italian footage. Virgil and Dante pass lower and lower through the various circles of hell, observing the cruel torments and sufferings of the damned. Sections of Dante's cantos appear as title cards on-screen, describing the horrifying journey. At one point a winged angel with a sword appears and rescues Dante when a group of demons try to block his way. Hellish tormentors with pitchforks are observed torturing the liars and the deceitful. Violent offenders are tossed into a flaming river of blood. Heretics are entombed in fiery crypts. Hoarders and spendthrifts engage in an eternal struggle. Suicides are transformed into trees and eternally pecked by demonic birds. Historic victims, such as Cleopatra, are pointed out by Virgil on their tour.

In Judd's study, the Devil watches as the miser continues to read. He withdraws, however, when Judd's butler enters to announce dinner. Next door, Craig, in despair, commits suicide. The Devil then announces himself to Judd and leads him to an adjoining room where his son and his wife's nurse are having a tryst. Enraged, Mortimer tosses his son out of his mansion. When his wife tries to interfere, he tells her that she can leave as well. The Devil then alerts Judd about Craig's suicide attempt and urges him to go next door to try to save him. He is too late and finds Craig hanging in his cellar. Craig's daughter accuses Mortimer of being responsible for her father's death. The Devil summons his demons to take Craig's soul to hell. Returning home, Judd finds his wife has died as well. The Devil mocks Judd for being too late. Ernest comes at him, blaming him for her death. They struggle, and Mortimer shoots him by accident. The Devil urges him to flee when the police are summoned, and he suggests that he hide out in the basement of one of his tenement buildings. When he reaches them, however, all his tenements are ablaze, and many of the residents are being burned alive. The survivors spot Judd, and they hold him for the law. Paying for his crimes with the death penalty, Judd is captured by Satan, who orders him transported to hell, where he is tossed into a pit of molten gold for eternity.

The next morning, Judd's secretary finds him asleep in his study. His wife and son are alive and well, and Eugene Craig has arrived to make one final plea to Mortimer. Waking from his horrible nightmare, Judd says, that, like Dante, he has been lost in the dark woods of ignorance, but now he has seen the light. Mortimer greets his family joyfully and promises to reform and become a new man. Like Scrooge, his redemption appears to be genuine, but the story ends before the audience can judge the extent to which he helps Eugene Craig or improves his rundown fire-trap tenements. His enthusiasm, however, suggests that he will follow through.

Performances

The Devil has a major role in this version of *Dante's Inferno*, but the name of the actor who plays the role is uncredited. The actor is tall, angular, and thin, and he appears almost naked, wearing only a leopard skin around his midriff. His hair is short and combed forward, but no horns appear on his head. He has a shadowy beard that is probably makeup. The actor moves with grace and frequently gesticulates with his arms. His performance is very accomplished, and he makes an impressive Devil. A French actor sometimes billed as Robert Klein is listed in some sources as appearing in the film as "a friend." Since no friend of Judd appears in the film, this could be a reference to the manager of Judd's tenements, who was a friend of the son. Since Klein played the role of Death in another film entitled *The Ancient Mariner* (1925), he possibly could have portrayed the uncredited Devil in *Dante's Inferno*. Most of the other players seem less polished by comparison, except for Ralph Lewis and Howard Gaye. Both Lewis and Gaye had key roles in *The Birth of a Nation* (1915), Lewis as Senator Austin Stoneman and Gaye as Robert E. Lee. Bud Jamison plays the butler in obvious blackface. Lon Poff, Judd's austere secretary, had a long career, appearing in films and serials, including *Flash Gordon* (1936), until his death in the early 1950s.

Notable Quotes

- I am the curse sent by Craig to torment you. (**the Devil, presenting himself to Judd**)
- Go to his house. Perhaps you can save him, and perhaps you will be too late. (**Satan, challenging Judd to save Craig**)
- Take him away to the pit of molten wealth, wherein he may gratify his desire for money and power which ne'er enough could satisfy him. (**the judgment upon Judd in hell**)

Deconstructing Harry

1997   Rating: **   Billy Crystal as the Devil

Sweetland Films. Written by Woody Allen; Photographed by Carlo DiPalma; Special Effects by Thomas Rosseter, John Ottensen, Greg Hyman, and Camille Geier; Edited by Susan E. Morse; Produced by Jean Doumanian; Directed by Woody Allen. Color, 96 minutes.

Annotated Cast List

Woody Allen (*Harry Block*, neurotic novelist); Kirstie Alley (*Joan Block*, Harry's second wife, a psychiatrist); Eric Lloyd (*Hiliard Block*, Harry's ten-year-old son); Amy Irving (*Jane Block*, Harry's third wife); Judy Davis (*Lucy*, Jane's sister); Elizabeth Shue (*Fay*, Harry's girlfriend); Billy Crystal (the Devil and *Larry*, Harry's romantic rival); Gene Saks (Harry's father in hell); David Moran (the Devil guarding his father); Robert Pope (*Death*); Bob Balaban (*Richard*, Harry's friend who dies in his car); Hazelle Goodman (*Cookie Williams*, hooker); Caroline Aaron (*Doris*, Harry's sister); Eric Bogosian (*Bert*, her husband); Mariel Hemingway (*Beth Kramer*, Joan's friend); Howard Spiegel (*Farber*, Joan's patient); Eugene Troobnick (*Wiggins*, college professor). **Imaginary characters invented by Harry:** Richard Benjamin (*Ken*); Stephanie Roth (*Janet*); Joel Leffert (*Norman*); Julia Louis-Dreyfus (*Leslie*); Jane Hoffman (Leslie's blind grandma); Tobey Maguire (*Harvey Stern*); Sunny Chae (*Lily Chang*); Julie Kavner (*Grace*); Robin Williams (out-of-focus man); Stanley Tucci (*Paul Epstein*); Demi Moore (*Helen Epstein*); Peter Jacobson (*Goldberg*); Hy Anzel (*Max Pincus*); Shifra Lerer (*Dolly Pincus*); Violas Harris (*Elsie*); Si Picker (*Wolf Fishbein*).

Appraisal and Synopsis

Although diehard Woody Allen enthusiasts may revel in *Deconstructing Harry*, it is a rather difficult and unlikable picture for general audiences and occasional Allen fans. It is one of his most self-indulgent works, filled with foul language and unresolved vignettes. His writing contains genuine flashes of genius and a number of brilliant one-liners, but the style of the film as a whole is disconcerting and nihilistic. The film is filled with endless jump-cuts in scene after scene, which become irritating quickly. The storyline is fragmented, and there are many bits and pieces illustrating Harry's stories which are abandoned or cut off just as they start to get interesting. For example, Harry launches into a tale of an actor (Robin Williams) who simply goes out of focus one day, and everyone sees him as a mere blur. This fascinating escapade is simply dropped after five minutes, giving the impression that Allen is simply airing undeveloped ideas from his notebook, and this frustrates rather than entertains many viewers.

Woody plays a Philip Roth–like novelist with writer's block (a pun on his character's name, Harry Block), and he drifts in and out of his memories, fantasies and stories as he considers his life. Harry is a miserable soul, a sex-obsessed neurotic whose love life is in shambles with three failed marriages. His new girlfriend, who he truly loves, has decided to marry his best friend. He winds up squandering all of his money on psychiatrists, lawyers, and whores. In the central event of the film, Harry receives a writing award from the college that expelled him years earlier. He drives to the ceremony with a hooker, his friend Richard (who dies on the way), and his young son, Hiliard. When he gets to the college, he is arrested for kidnapping since he didn't obtain his ex-wife's permission to bring his son to the ceremony. He is bailed out of jail by his girlfriend and her new husband, who rush over from their wedding reception when they hear of Harry's troubles. Harry is cleared of his writer's block when he imagines that all of his fictional characters hold a reception for him, thanking him for bringing them to life in his work.

The scene in which Harry visits hell is undoubtedly the highlight of the picture. He descends to the inferno in an elevator, as a computer voice ticks off the inhabitants of each floor, such as lawyers who appear on television and aggressive panhandlers. Amid the steaming sulphur pits, he encounters various damned souls, including the inventor of aluminum siding and his own father. He is shown into Satan's office where Harry tries to impress the Devil with his own misdeeds. In fact, Harry and the Devil get along rather well, comparing notes on the sexual proclivities of various women. The Devil reveals that he used to take jobs on earth, such as running a film studio, but that he could never trust the people around him. Harry paraphrases John Milton, saying it is better for the Devil to rule in hell than to serve elsewhere. This scene abruptly ends just after it really starts to cook. Like much of the

Performances

Billy Crystal is superb as the wry Devil, and he is a perfect counterpoint to Woody Allen in both delivery and style. Crystal also appears as Larry, Harry's best friend, who steals Fay, the only woman in the film who Harry really appears to love. It is Harry's sense of outrage and jealousy that casts the Devil in Larry's image. Crystal grew up in a show business family and started quite young as a stand-up comic. His depiction of the Devil is as a modern-day yuppie. He compares notes with Harry and trades quips with him as if they were equals. Their smooth cameraderie is one reason the scene seems so sharp. The only disappointing element is that it is so brief. The scene really starts to build and the creative sparks start to fly, when (poof!) the film shifts to another sequence in which Harry is arrested for kidnapping his son. Allen's sense of cinematic timing was never before or after as off stride as it is in *Deconstructing Harry*.

Notable Quotes

• I'm more powerful than you because I'm a bigger sinner. You're a fallen angel, and I never believed in God or heaven or any of that stuff.... Also, I do terrible things. I've cheated on all my wives, and none of them deserved it. I sleep with whores. I drink too much. I take pills. I lie, and I'm vain and cowardly. And I'm prone to violence. (**Harry to the Devil**)

Violence? (**the Devil, astonished**)

I once almost ran over a book critic with my car, but I swerved at the last second. (**Harry's reply**)

• Do you want me to turn on the air conditioner? (**the Devil to Harry, trying to accommodate him**)

• To evil. It keeps things humming. (**the Devil's toast**)

The Devil and Daniel Webster
AKA All That Money Can Buy

1941   Rating: *****   Walter Huston as the Devil

RKO. Written by Dan Totheroh and Stephen Vincent Benét, based upon his short story; Photographed by Joseph August; Edited by Robert Wise; Special Effects by Vernon L. Walker; Music by Bernard Herrmann; Produced and Directed by William Dieterle. B&W, 107 minutes (original version), 85 minutes (revised version).

Annotated Cast List

Edward Arnold (*Daniel Webster*, U.S. senator); Walter Huston (*Mr. Scratch*, the Devil); James Craig (*Jabez Stone*, farmer who sells his soul to the Devil); Jane Darwell (*Ma Stone*, his mother); Anne Shirley (*Mary Stone*, his wife); Lindy Wade (*Daniel Stone*, their son, named after Daniel Webster); Simone Simon (*Belle*, the Devil's envoy who serves as nursemaid); H. B. Warner (*Justice Hathorne*, judge from hell); Gene Lockhart (*Slossom*, Cross Corners squire); Sarah Edwards (*Lucy Slossom*, his wife); George Cleveland (*Cy Bibber*, tavern owner); John Qualen (*Miser Stevens*, moneylender);

Frank Conlan (Cross Corners sheriff); Walter Baldwin (*Hank*, neighbor who borrows seed from Jabez); Sonny Bupp (*Martin Van Buren Aldrich*, son of only Democrat in Cross Corners); Jeff Corey (*Tom Sharp*, Cross Corners grange enthusiast); Carl Stockdale (*Van Brooks*, grange supporter from Massachusetts); Alec Craig (*Eli Higgins*, grange supporter); Robert Dudley (*Lem*); Patsy Doyle (servant); Harry Hood (tailor); Harry Humphrey (minister); Stewart Richards (doctor); Sherman Sanders (square dance caller); Robert Strange (court clerk from hell); Jim Farley (*Benedict Arnold*, foreman of the jury from hell); Charles Herzinger (old farmhand); Eddie Dew, Jim Toney, Hazel Boyne (farmers); Ferris Taylor, Frank Austin, Robert Emmett Keane, Fern Emmett, Robert Pittard.

Appraisal and Synopsis

The Devil and Daniel Webster is the quintessential American Devil story, written by Stephen Vincent Benét (1898-1943) in 1936. Many people mistakenly assume it was written far earlier because of the mythic quality of the original tale. The story compares favorably with *Faust*, since Jabez Stone is more of an Everyman than the bookworm scholar of Germanic legend. More important, the American story offers a genuine contest, with the Devil's real aim being to capture the soul of Daniel Webster, arguably the finest American of his age. Webster's clash with the Devil also

Publicity for the original run of The Devil and Daniel Webster *when it was known as* All That Money Can Buy.

brings in other unforgettable figures from American history, from Benedict Arnold to John Hathorne, the notorious judge from the Salem witch trials. Hathorne's great-great-grandson was the brilliant Nathaniel Hawthorne, author of *The House of the Seven Gables* and "Young Goodman Brown," a memorable short story about the Devil. The novelist changed his name from Hathorne to Hawthorne to disassociate himself from his ancestor. The film version of *The Devil and Daniel Webster*, originally titled *All That Money Can Buy*, expanded and developed the original story, which is only fifteen pages long. The added material only enriched the story, making it more effective and dramatic, raising the level of the picture to a genuine classic.

The picture opens with the Devil in the guise of a crafty rustic sporting an Alpine hat. Walking the dusty back roads of New Hampshire, he pages through his black book of prospects, stopping at the name of Jabez Stone, married farmer, aged 27 years. The Devil arranges a string of misfortunes to plague Jabez, including a persistent fox who raids the hen house (likely Satan himself in disguise), a pig who breaks its leg, and finally an accident that injures Mary, Jabez's wife. Meanwhile in Washington, Senator Daniel Webster composes a speech in support of a bill to protect the assets of bankrupt farmers. The shadow of the Devil appears behind the senator, whispering in his ear that he will never become president if he continues to support such causes. Webster pounds his fist on the table, urging his unseen tormentor to stop pestering him.

After tearing a sack of seed with which he intended to make his mortgage payment, Jabez mutters in total frustration that he would sell his soul to the Devil for two cents. A rumble of thunder is heard in the distance, and the animals start to whinny as the Devil appears before Jabez in the barn. He hands him a card that gives his name as Mr. Scratch, adding that he often goes by that name while in New England. Jabez recognizes the stranger's identity immediately, and being a stubborn New Hampshire man, the farmer will not retract his offer. He signs a contract in blood with Mr. Scratch, selling his soul in exchange for seven years of good luck. The Devil pokes at the floorboards of the barn, uncovering a sack of gold which he claims to be Hessian gold from a wagon train shipment hijacked at the time of the American Revolution. As he leaves, the Devil burns the due date of his contract into a tree outside the barn: April 7, 1847.

As Jabez explains his good fortune in finding the gold to his wife, she seems overwhelmed, while his mother is outright skeptical about the gold's origins. The next day, Jabez goes to town to pay off his mortgage and buy a new plow. While at the blacksmith shop, he meets Daniel Webster, who is pitching horseshoes with the store owner. Jabez also plays and impresses the senator while beating him at the game. Later Jabez and Webster go to the center of Cross Corners, where Jabez makes an impromptu speech about Webster's efforts to help the common man. Mary Stone is proud as she listens to her husband and Daniel Webster. Mr. Scratch is also in the crowd that gathers, and he gently taunts Webster, offering him his assistance.

As time passes, Jabez prospers. At first he is generous to the other farmers, offering to loan them seed and money to help them out. The Devil, however, brings a terrible hailstorm before harvest time which ruins all of the crops except for those of Jabez. The Devil arranges for the other farmers to work for Jabez, and they fall deeply into his debt. Mary gives birth to a son, who they name after Daniel Webster. The Devil sends his envoy, Belle, to act as nursemaid to the child as well as to keep an eye on Jabez.

At a celebratory barn dance, Mr. Scratch grabs a fiddle and plays a madcap rendition of "Pop Goes the Weasel." As the music becomes wilder and wilder, Jabez falls into a spell, becoming enchanted by Belle as she participates in a square dance. Time passes, and Mary stoically watches as her husband ignores her and becomes deeply infatuated with Belle. He also becomes more hard-hearted, thinking only about acquiring more and more money. Finally, Mary goes to visit Daniel Webster to tell him about the strange changes that have come over Jabez. He advises her to be patient and promises to try and help her, intending to visit Cross Corners as soon as possible.

Jabez has overseen the construction of a large new mansion, and he plans a housewarming party to which he invites Daniel Webster as guest of honor. En route to the party, Webster stops and talks with the town folk, and he discovers that Jabez has treated them as harshly as any loan-shark. Meanwhile, Jabez is disturbed that no one has shown up for his party but Miser Stevens, the money lender who held his mortgage years earlier. Stevens is depressed, fretting over the state of his soul. Suddenly, the house is filled with guests invited by Belle, shadowy figures who have come from "the other side of the hill." Belle drags Stevens off to join her in the ballroom, and he collapses dead at the end of their *danse macabre*.

When Senator Webster arrives, he tries to talk to Jabez about his neighbors and why they have refused to come to his party. He criticizes him for not paying attention to his wife and child. This enrages Jabez, who instantly turns his wife out of the mansion, and Daniel Webster escorts her away. Mr. Scratch shows up to talk with Jabez, suggesting the possibility of a contract extension. A moth escapes from under his coat, and it speaks to Jabez in the voice of Miser Stevens. The Devil says that he has just regretfully closed an old account. Jabez asks if most souls are so small, and the Devil replies that the ones he takes usually are, but that the wingspan of the soul of Daniel Webster, for example, would be astonishing.

In a panic, Jabez tries to cut down the tree bearing the date on which his contract expires. The Devil appears, saying that this action is a contract violation, but that he would give him seven more years in trade for the soul of his son. When Jabez refuses, Mr. Scratch says that he will return at midnight to claim his soul. Jabez mounts a horse and rides in pursuit of his wife and Daniel Webster. Upon learning the particulars, Webster offers to help Jabez and to represent him. They go to the barn, the site where the contract was signed, and await the Devil's appearance.

Mr. Scratch appears delighted when he sees Webster with Jabez. Webster demands a jury trial to determine the fate of Jabez, because any contract that binds an American to a foreign prince is invalid. The Devil replies that he has been in America since its earliest days. Webster offers the Devil his own soul if he loses the case with any American jury, "be it the quick or the dead." Mr. Scratch accepts and summons up a jury from the bowels of hell. The infernal jury consists of damned souls: Captain Kidd, the pirate; Simon Girney, who encouraged the Indians to war against the patriots; Governor Thomas Dale of the colony of Virginia, who broke men on the wheel; Asa, known as "Black Monk"; Floyd Iverson; Steve Bonny; Captain Walter Butler, the Loyalist fighter behind the Cherry Valley massacre; Micajah and Wiley Harpe, the frontier serial killers called Big and Little Harpe; Pete the Cutthroat; Thomas Morton of Merry Mount, the enemy of the Puritans; and General Benedict Arnold. The presiding judge is John Hathorne, the only one of the Salem witch trial judges who didn't recant after the period of hysteria had passed.

Daniel Webster protests the inclusion of Benedict Arnold, but Hathorne denies his objection. Mr. Scratch calls one witness, Jabez Stone, who admits he signed the contract. Hathorne refuses to let Webster cross-examine him. When Webster demands to speak, Hathorne warns him that if he fails to convince the jury, he too will be damned. After pausing, Webster delivers a powerful summation about freedom and what it means to be an American. He ends his plea by urging, "Don't let this country go to the Devil!" Scratch is astounded when the jury decides to deliberate, and Benedict Arnold tears up the contract signed by Jabez Stone. Hathorne announces the verdict in favor of the defense. The Devil offers his hand to Webster in congratulations but instead Webster boots him out of the barn, demanding that he never return to New Hampshire. The Devil sticks his head in the window, however, proclaiming that Daniel Webster will never become president.

The new mansion goes up in flames, and all the neighbors turn out to help Jabez, but he tells them to let it burn, adding that he also plans to burn all the unfair contracts he made with them. Ma Stone prepares a country breakfast for everyone. She had cooked a special peach pie for Daniel Webster, but when she lifts the lid, the pie is missing. The scene shifts to the Devil, who is gobbling down the pie on the outskirts of Jabez's property, the same locale where the picture began. After finishing the pie, the Devil begins to page again through his black book. He looks around and finally points his finger directly at the screen, indicating that his next victim will be a member of the audience watching the film. As a close-up of Mr. Scratch's grinning face fills the screen, the picture comes to an end, and the credits roll.

The technical aspects of *The Devil and Daniel Webster* are tremendously impressive. William Dieterle's direction is flawless, providing the film with an extraordinary, creepy mood and a sense of timelessness. The editing by Robert Wise, who later became a great director, is exceptional. The cinematography is haunting and moody. The magnificent musical score earned an Oscar for composer Bernard Herrmann. One of Herrmann's favorite anecdotes in later years described his playing a tape of the "Pop Goes the Weasel" violin solo for Jascha Heifetz, who gaped in astonishment at the near-impossible dexterity. Finally, Herrmann revealed that it was a doctored tape created by layering various tracks together. Heifetz was so impressed that he later recorded Bach's *Concerto for Two Violins* the same way, playing both parts.

The film was not a great success upon initial release, and the title *All That Money Can Buy* was later changed to the instantly recognizable name *The Devil and Daniel Webster*. Some rerelease prints also featured the title *Daniel and the Devil*. Although released at 107 minutes in length, the picture was trimmed down to 85 minutes in the 1950s, and the original footage was not restored until the film appeared on video. The truncated version cut the entire opening of the film, eliminating the introduction of Mr. Scratch, Jabez, his wife, and his mother. Other scenes cut included brief meetings between Jabez and the Devil, the winter sleigh ride with Belle and Jabez, and the scene where Daniel Webster gives a ride in his buggy to his godson, Daniel. Another oddity of the film is that Thomas Mitchell was initially cast as Daniel Webster, but he broke his leg and was replaced by Edward Arnold. If you look closely, in the distant shot of the horseshoe game, you can make out Thomas Mitchell in the role of Daniel Webster. Incidentally, the time frame of the film is 1840 through 1847. Webster resigned from the senate to become

A superbly lit character portrait of Walter Huston as Mr. Scratch.

secretary of State after the election of William Henry Harrison, "Tippecanoe." When Harrison died after one month in office in 1841, Webster found himself frequently at odds with his successor, John Tyler. After two years, he resigned and was reelected to the Senate. He died in 1852, and it is generally considered a lost opportunity for the nation that Daniel Webster was never elected president.

Performances

Walter Huston is simply amazing in the role of the Devil, easily equalling his Academy Award performance in *The Treasure of Sierra Madre* (1947). Nothing is wasted in his delivery, and every gesture, grimace, and grin adds to the characterization, be it a scratching of his stubbly beard or his leer as he plays the fiddle. Huston literally spent days synchronizing his fingering and bowing in this sequence to create a perfect illusion onscreen. Mr. Scratch is always able to blend in with the crowd, whispering suggestions in someone's ear or taking a more active role, such as when he recruits the other farmers to toil for Jabez Stone. His soft-spoken cackle is infectious as he spreads his diabolical charm equally to his friends and adversaries. The highlight of the film is probably his perplexed series of facial reactions after Daniel Webster's speech to the infernal jury, when he is amazed that the great orator has moved the stone hearts of this ultimate hand-picked jury. Likewise, Edward Arnold is exceptional as Webster, no doubt turning in a stronger and more forceful presentation than Thomas Mitchell. Interestingly, Arnold himself played the Devil in a film short made the following year entitled *Inflation* (1942), in which the Devil tries to undermine the war effort in America by unleashing a round of inflation. Other great performances in the film are turned in by Simone Simon as the otherworldly Belle, Jane Darwell as the down-to-earth Ma Stone and H. B. Warner as Judge Hathorne (whose name is misspelled in the end credits but not in the original short story). James Craig and Anne Shirley are credible as Jabez and Mary Stone, although not on the same level as their exceptional costars. Sonny Bupp, who played Martin Van Buren Aldritch, also played Charles Foster Kane, Jr., in *Citizen Kane* (1941).

Notable Quotes

• Do you deny that you called me? I've known people in other states who went back on their word, but I didn't expect it in New Hampshire. (**the Devil to Jabez**)

• I thought with the presidential election coming up, you might need some help, Mr. Webster, sir. (**the Devil**)
I'd rather see you on the side of the opposition. (**Daniel Webster**)
Oh, I'll be there too. (**the Devil**)

• Oh, come, come now. Just because you sold your soul to the Devil, that needn't make you a teetotaler. (**Webster to Jabez when he refuses to join him in a drink of rum**)

• General Arnold, you fought so gallantly for the American cause until, let me see, what was the date? 1779, a date burned in your heart. The lure of gold made you betray that cause. And you, Simon Girney, now known to all as Renegade, a loathsome word, you also took that other way. And you, Walter Butler, what would you give to see the grasses grow in Cherry Valley without the stain of blood? I could go on and on and name you all, but there is no need of that. Why stir the wounds? I know they pain enough. (**Webster to the infernal jury**)

The Devil and Max Devlin

1981   Rating: **   Reggie Nalder and Bill Cosby as the Devil

Buena Vista. Written by Mary Rogers and Jimmy Sangster (story); Photographed by Howard Schwartz; Edited by Raymond A. de Leuw; Special Effects by Mike Reedy; Music by Buddy Baker and Marvin Hamlisch (songs); Produced by Jerome Courtland; Directed by Stephen Hilliard Stern. Color, 96 minutes.

Annotated Cast List

Elliot Gould (*Max Devlin*, owner and operator of an apartment building); Bill Cosby (*Barney Satin*, manager of souls); Reggie Nalder (*Lucifer*, chairman of the Devil's Council); Julie Budd (*Stella Summers*, aspiring singer); David Knell (*Nerve Nordlinger*, aspiring dirt biker); Adam Rich (*Toby Hart*, youngster who wants a new father); Susan Anspach (*Penny Hart*, Toby's mother); Sonny Schroyer (*Big Billy Hunniker*, champion dirt bike racer); Jeannie Wilson (*Laverne Hunniker*, his wife); Chuck Shamata (*Jerry Nadler*, record company executive); Deborah Baltzell (*Heidi*, Stella's friend); Ronnie Schell (*Greg Weems*, concert tour promoter); Ted Ziegler (*Billings*); Vic Dunlop (*Brian*); Stanley Brook (diner operator); Julie Parrish (*Sheila*, Nerve's girlfriend); Susan Tolsky (Nerve's mom); Sally Marr (*Mrs. Gromlev*, tenant); Madelyn Gates (*Mrs. Trent*, tenant); Ruth Manning (*Mrs. Davis*, tenant); Sheila Rogers (Stella's mother); Robert Baron (Stella's father); Vernon Weddle (justice of the peace); Helene Winston (*Agent Hargraves*, the Devil's emissary); Bartine Zane (God's emissary); Army Archerd (himself); Lilian Muller, Gustav Unger, Bertil Unger, Joseph Burke, Tak Kobota (Devil's Council members).

Appraisal and Synopsis

A second-rate Disney comedy, *The Devil and Max Devlin* is a film with many opportunities, which simply fails to deliver. The basic plot is sound enough, but the denouement is a mess that contradicts the premise of the film. This is sheer laziness on the part of the filmmakers in order to crank out a happy ending without explaining how it came about. A line or two earlier in the film, perhaps an aside between Bill Cosby and the Devil's Council could have provided a logical framework. This sloppy approach spoils the modest entertainment the rest of the film provides. This is a shame, since the first fifteen minutes of the picture are really quite good.

Max Devlin is the owner of a seedy apartment building in L.A. He tells his tenants he is only the manager, so that he can deny any reasonable request or repair they might need. While chasing one tenant late with his rent, Devlin is tripped by a blind woman and falls in front of a bus. Moments later, his soul falls down an enormous fiery pit, hurtling toward hell. The impressive panorama of hell was apparently designed for an earlier Disney film, *The Black Hole* (1979). Devlin is brought before the Devil's Council to determine his punishment. As his sins are recounted, a member of the council complains that they are only trivial misdemeanors. Barney Satin, the manager of souls, explains this is part of a new policy related to recruitment. Max learns that the blind woman who tripped him was Agent Hargraves, an emissary of the Devil. "That's entrapment!" Max protests. He is then given a choice. If he returns to Earth for two months and is able to sign up three souls, then the Devil will release him. Max starts to name several bad people he knows, but the chairman of the council, Lucifer himself, makes it clear he wants only innocent souls. Barney projects the image of three young people as his quarry. Max agrees, and he is returned to his body. A group of Hari Krishna, passengers on the bus, are chanting over him as he revives. Barney shows up to explain the rules to Max. He now has special powers, such as the ability to travel anywhere instantly through mere concentration. He can also use magic properties on others, as long as they remain in his direct line of vision. On the other hand, Max no longer casts a reflection in the mirror. He begins his mission to round up the three souls for Satan.

The first individual is Stella Summers, a young woman whose dream is to become a popular singer. Max endows her with a powerful singing voice during her audition. His second target is Nerve Nordlinger, a high school nerd whose dearest wish is to become a first-class motorbike rider. Max poses as a dirt bike instructor and uses his powers so Nerve can ride expertly on his first test run on a dirt bike. Max's third prospect is Toby, a bright ten-year-old who takes a liking to Max when they meet at an amusement park. However, Toby has no special aspirations, so Max is stumped as to how to tempt him. Finally, Toby reveals that his only genuine want is for a new father, someone like Max, and he hopes that he will marry his mother.

Max negotiates a major record deal for Stella and helps Nerve win his first dirt bike race, but Penny, Toby's mom, seems resistant at first to Max's charms as he tries to court her. His perseverance finally wears her down. She teases him about the frequent nicks on his face from shaving (since he lacks a mirror image), and she buys him an electric razor. As the end of the two months approaches, Barney starts to pressure Max to get signed contracts. Max tricks Stella and Nerve into signing documents that contain hidden clauses selling their souls. Their personalities turn nasty after they sign. Max fails to get Toby to sign anything until he marries his mother, so he devises a contract for Toby to give him a set of baseball cards, the *Guinness Book of World Records*, his soul, and two packages of red-hot cinnamon candies. Toby agrees to sign but only after the wedding ceremony. Max proposes to Penny, and their wedding day is set for the day of the Devil's deadline. After Toby signs, his sunny demeanor suddenly turns dour.

Barney informs Max that he intends to take possession of his three victims at midnight, and Max himself will be free. Earlier, Max was told that the signers would be allowed to live out their natural life spans. Max decides to forfeit his own soul and burns the contracts. He has a vision of Barney warning him that eternal damnation awaits him. No longer endowed with special powers, Max rushes to the site of Nerve's race to warn him not to ride. He arrives after the start of the race but learns that Nerve missed the race, injured when he was tripped by a blind old lady. Max confronts her and discovers she is an angel, sent to protect Nerve by preventing him from racing.

Expecting to be dragged to hell at midnight, Max says goodbye to Penny and Toby. He then notices that his reflection has returned in the mirror, and he assumes somehow Barney lost the rights to his soul. Max takes his wife and Toby to Stella's farewell concert, which she performs successfully without benefit of any magic.

The plot completely unravels towards the end, as the loopholes simply become

Reggie Nalder in a characteristic pose, surrounded by a cloud of smoke.

too enormous to overlook, but the film ends by pretending they aren't even there. Did God intervene in Max's behalf? Did Barney violate some essential principle? Was this all only a charade to make Max a better person, or were the souls of his three targets ever really in danger? It seems that all three signed without realizing that their souls were at stake, making the documents invalid. The film makes no effort to resolve any of this. Every film has minor inconsistencies, but *The Devil and Max Devlin* excels in loose ends, and the entire story is sloppy. The time frame, for example, is unrealistic, since Stella is transformed from a complete unknown to a Grammy Award winner in only two months. Except for the final concert, Stella only seems to manage to sing one song, "Any Fool Can See," which she belts out again and again. Since Max has the ability to go anywhere in an instant, why does he wish himself onto a plane en route to his destination instead of to his actual destination? Max is still technically dead as the film ends. Another misstep is the failure to provide a closing scene for Barney. Many films fail to resolve a subplot, but *The Devil and Max Devlin* fails to resolve the main plot.

his accent, it is also quite amusing. Nalder is sometimes overlooked for his body of work, which stretches from an Apache dancer in Paris in the 1930s to numerous TV appearances in "Thriller," "Fantasy Island," "The Wild Wild West" and "Star Trek," where he played the Andorian ambassador in the key episode "Journey to Babel." If Nalder is one of the best features of *The Devil and Max Devlin*, the other Devil in the story, Barney Satin, played by Bill Cosby, is one of the most disappointing. Cos is one of the great comedians, but he is flat, bland, and a complete letdown in this film. The only segment where he shows any flair is the brief bit when he appears in horns and tail to rant against Max for burning the contracts. Other than that, Cosby's performance is simply dead weight in the story. The entire film could have been lifted an entire notch if one last scene had been added at the end. Barney could have appeared before Lucifer to offer a halting explanation of how he bungled the operation. This scene would have offered Cosby a chance to provide a memorable exit for Barney, it would have clarified the story, and it would have brought back Nalder, the most striking character in the film.

Performances

Reggie Nalder is magnificent in his brief appearance as Lucifer. Nalder is best remembered as the assassin in Albert Hall during Bernard Herrmann's concert in Hitchcock's *The Man Who Knew Too Much* (1956). He also played Barlow the vampire in Stephen King's *Salem's Lot* (1979) which was released in two forms, as a miniseries and as a feature film overseas and on video. Nalder sits magnificently on a throne in hell. His stare and the otherworldly tone of his voice are the high points of the film. When Elliott Gould repeats Nalder's line, trying to approximate

Notable Quotes

• Maxwell Hardy Devlin, for cheating on a 4th-grade spelling test, for misrepresenting his age at the local movie house, prank phone calls, stealing bubble gum at the local supermarket, ditching an ugly blind date ... (**recitation of Max's sins**)

• No good. Sooner or later we'll get those people anyways. (**Lucifer, chairman of the council, rejecting the candidates Max mentions as potential soul sellers**)

• Eat first and corrupt later, that's what I always say. (**Max to Barney**)

The Devil in Love
AKA L'Arcidiavolo (The Archdevil)

1966   Rating: **   Vittorio Gassman as the Devil

Warner Brothers. Written by Ruggero Maccari and Ettore Scola, inspired by *Belfagor* by Niccolo Machiavelli; Photographed by Aldo Tonti; Edited by Carcello Valvestito and Tatiana Casini; Music by Armondo Trovaioli; Produced by Mario Cecchi Gori; Directed by Ettore Scola. B&W, 96 minutes.

Annotated Cast List

Vittorio Gassman (*Belfagor*, the Devil); Mickey Rooney (*Adramalek*, imp who serves Belfagor); Claudine Auger (*Magdalena*, daughter of Lorenzo de Medici); Luigi Vannucchi (*Prince Franceschetto*, son of Pope Innocent VIII); Gabriele Ferzetti (*Lorenzo the Magnificent*, prince of Florence); Annabella Incontrera (*Lucrezia*, Lorenzo's mistress); Ettore Manni (*Gianfigliazzo*, Captain of Lorenzo's guards); Liani Orfei (innkeeper's wife); Giorgia Moll (aristocrat's wife); Paolo Di Credico (*Cardinal Giovanni*); Helene Chanel (*Clarice*); Sherill Morgan.

Appraisal and Synopsis

Niccolo Machiavelli (1469–1527) was one of the most resourceful writers of the Italian Renaissance. Many people are unaware that he also wrote fiction. *Belfagor: the Devil Who Took a Wife* was a novella composed around 1518, several years after his memorable treatise on power, *The Prince*. When most new souls in hell blame their wives for their corruption, Belfagor the archdevil is sent by the Council of Hell to Earth to research this situation. He is instructed to marry and live as an ordinary mortal for ten years, then return to hell and make a report. Belfagor settles in Florence and marries Madonna Onesta, who is endowed with "more pride than Lucifer ever had." Soon, even the devils Belfagor brought with him as retainers prefer to return to the fires of hell rather than live in the world under Onesta's authority. Eventually Belfagor is led into poverty and degradation by her, and he is forced to resort to extraordinary means to pay off his creditors. Returning to hell, Belfagor lives in fear that Onesta will appear and claim him.

Screenwriter Ruggero Maccari adapted Machiavelli's satirical story by concentrating on the madcap courtship of Belfagor, who actually is on a completely different mission. In *The Devil in Love*, the Council of Hell wants to discredit the peace treaty of 1478 between Florence and Rome and instigate war instead. The archdevil, Belfagor, is sent to earth to carry out this mission, accompanied by the imp Adramalek as his retainer. Arriving on earth, Belfagor finds himself irresistibly drawn to women. Belfagor plans to break up the arranged marriage between Magdalena, daughter of Lorenzo de Medici, the ruler of Florence, and Prince Franceschetto, the son of Pope Innocent VIII. Belfagor lures Franceschetto into playing cards with him in a high-stakes contest. Franceschetto gambles his life and loses, and Belfagor then assumes his identity. He then rejects Magdalena at their wedding ceremony, proclaiming a desire for war instead.

Lorenzo orders his troops, led by Gianfigliazzo, to capture the prince.

Adramalek helps Belfagor to escape, leading him to Leonardo da Vinci's workshop where he confiscates some of his inventions, including his experimental helicopter and hygroscope, to effect his escape. At the same time, Belfagor also has a number of encounters with women, which incurs the wrath of their husbands and fathers. Lucrezia, Lorenzo's own mistress, helps to hide him. Becoming enamored of Magdalena, Belfagor meets with her secretly to elicit her forgiveness. But he tricks her to appear naked on her balcony, further enraging the Florentines in their desire to punish him. Belfagor's most spectacular episode is his escape using Leonardo's flying machine with two large canvas wings, which he uses to fly away from his pursuers.

Out of the city, Belfagor becomes embroiled in a sword fight with an opponent he believes is Gianfigliazzo, but when he lifts the helmet of his defeated opponent, he discovers it is Magdalena in disguise. Adramalek urges the archdevil to kill her. Instead, Belfagor releases her and orders Adramalek back to hell. After his aide vanishes, Belfagor is captured by the Florentines. He is ordered to be burned at the stake. Adramalek appears to tell him that the Council of Hell has ordered his devilish powers removed because of his erratic behavior. Belfagor now feels the flames like an ordinary mortal. Magdalena threatens to jump in the fire with him. Lorenzo orders the execution halted, but Gianfigliazzo thrusts at him with his sword. Belfagor steps aside, and his opponent falls into the flames. Belfagor and Magdalena embrace as the film concludes.

Originally filmed in color, the English-language version was released only in black and white. The best feature of the production is the location footage in Florence, including the Piazza della Signoria, the Palazzo Vecchio, and the famous church San Miniato al Monte. But these features cannot make up for pedestrian and clumsy storytelling. The comedy is forced, and except for a few clever scenes with Mickey Rooney, there is barely a smile in the entire film. It would have been far better if Machiavelli's original story had been followed more closely. At least they could have added an epilogue, ten years later, with Belfagor appealing to be let back into hell to escape from his wife. This would have worked, recalling Buster Keaton who threw ice water on a traditional romantic ending at the conclusion of *College* (1927), showing the couple proceeding from their wedding to old age and the grave. Unfortunately, Scola wanted to make a light romantic adventure, and the hard edge of Machiavellian satire, which the film desperately needs, was avoided.

Performances

Vittorio Gassman was a popular actor in Italian cinema, and he had also appeared in a number of American films. Briefly married to Shelley Winters, Gassman handled almost every part with casual ease and charm. As a Don Juan caricature, Gassman is convincing, but the diabolical side of Belfagor is too frequently overlooked. Mickey Rooney shines as his impish sidekick, however, although his screen time is limited. Claudine Auger, the Bond girl from *Thunderball* (1965), is good but never really given a chance by the clumsy script.

Notable Quotes

- No, I'll take war! (**Belfagor's reply at his marriage ceremony when asked if he will marry Magdalena**)
- Andramalek ... go to hell! (**Belfagor's dismissal of his aide when Andramalek suggests he kill Magdalena, who is posing as a man in their duel**)

The Devil Rides Out
AKA The Devil's Bride

1968   Rating: ****   Eddie Powell as the Devil

Hammer Films. Written by Richard Matheson based on the novel by Dennis Wheatley; Photographed by Arthur Grant; Special Effects by Michael Staiver-Hutchins; Edited by Spencer Reeve; Music by James Bernard; Produced by Anthony Nelson Keyes; Directed by Terence Fisher. Color, 96 minutes.

Annotated Cast List

Christopher Lee (*Duc Nicholas de Richleau*, esoteric scholar); Charles Gray (*Mocata*, coven leader); Niké Arrighi (*Tanith Carlisle*, psychic and companion to the countess); Leon Greene (*Rex Van Rjin*, Richleau's friend); Patrick Mower (*Simon Aram*, Mocata's newest recruit); Gwen Ffrangcon-Davies (countess, member of Mocata's coven); Sarah Lawson (*Marie Eaton*, Richleau's niece); Paul Eddington (*Richard Eaton*, her husband); Rosalyn Landor (*Peggy*, their young daughter); Russell Waters (*Malin*, their butler); Eddie Powell (the Devil).

Appraisal and Synopsis

Christopher Lee himself lobbied Hammer Films to undertake this adaptation of Dennis Wheatley's classic occult novel *The Devil Rides Out*. The film, however, was poorly marketed when released in the United States, and the title was changed to *The Devil's Bride* because the American distributor, 20th Century–Fox, feared that the original title might cause the film to be mistaken for a Western. The film represents Hammer at its finest, with superb cinematography, a brilliant musical score, and exceptional pacing. It is a fascinating period piece set in the 1920s with clearly drawn and evenly matched protagonists steeped in arcane knowledge. The battlefield is for the soul of wealthy young Simon, unofficial ward of Rex Van Rjin and Nicholas, the Duc de Richleau. Their battle makes an intriguing story, and the Devil himself briefly appears at one of Mocata's rituals. Unfortunately, the film was not a box office success, and plans to make the adventures of the Duc de Richleau another Christopher Lee series to rival his Fu Manchu and Dracula endeavors were dropped.

After an impressive credit sequence featuring occult symbols and images of the Devil, the story launches immediately with Nicholas and Rex disturbed that Simon missed their annual reunion. They go to Simon's mansion where they interrupt a strange gathering. Nicholas quickly discovers that Simon's new companions are Satanists, led by a sinister figure named Mocata. They knock Simon out and whisk him away in their car. Nicholas hypnotizes him, and they return to spy on the coven, which has dispersed for the evening. When they get home, however, they find that Simon has vanished.

Rex is acquainted with Tanith Carlisle, traveling companion of the countess, a member of Mocata's coven. Rex learns she is terrified of Mocata. He also learns that she and Simon are to be baptized as Satanists at an elaborate outdoor black mass

Eddie Powell as Baphomet, the goat of Mendes, the form taken by the Devil during the black mass in The Devil Rides Out.

to be held that evening. Hundreds of Devil worshipers attend the dark ritual in which Satan himself is summoned from hell in the form of Baphomet, the goat of Mendes, a hideous being that is half goat with humanoid features. Nicholas positions Rex on the running board of his car and hands him a blessed cross to throw at the Devil. He then drives into the crowd. The Devil appears startled when the headlights shine in his eyes, and moments later he vanishes in a puff of smoke when his body comes in contact with the cross hurled by Rex. Simon and Tanith are rescued in the confusion, and Nicholas brings them to the Eaton estate, the home of his niece Marie, her husband, Richard, and daughter, Peggy.

The second half of the film is an elaborate duel between Mocata and Nicholas, as the Satanist conducts a campaign of black magic, attempting to destroy Nicholas and his friends. Tanith runs away, Rex chases after her, and they hide out in a barn. The climax of the battle occurs as Nicholas, Rex, and the Eatons take refuge in a charmed circle drawn on the floor of the living room by Nicholas. Mocata conjures a series of illusions and demons against them. One vision, a giant spider, almost causes Marie to break the circle. Finally, Mocata summons the Angel of Death, the Infernal Horseman who, once summoned, cannot return to the nether regions without the soul of a victim.

Nicholas invokes a dangerous spell, and the assault of the horseman is repelled.

The next morning, Tanith is killed, claimed by the Horseman of Death, and Rex carries her body back to the house. Peggy is kidnapped, and Nicholas and the others track her down to Mocata's hideout. The spirit of Tanith intervenes and confronts Mocata as he attempts to sacrifice Peggy's life. In an unexpected twist, the defeat of Mocata has shifted time. Tanith is now alive and unharmed, and we learn that the Angel of Death has claimed Mocata in place of Tanith. Peggy is unharmed as well, and Nicholas explains the development to his puzzled friends. Rex and Tanith have fallen in love, and Simon has returned to his normal self. The weakest point of the production is this rather abrupt wrap-up, where Nicholas has to explain what happened. It would have been far better if the audience had been able to see the Dark Horseman galloping off with Mocata instead of just hearing it described. Except for this lapse, *The Devil Rides Out* remains one of Hammer's most remarkable and impressive efforts, one that easily could have been developed into a successful new series.

Performances

Eddie Powell is one of the unsung heroes of horror and science fiction. In addition to appearing in numerous scenes as the title character in *Alien* (1979), Powell has also appeared onscreen as the Mummy and Dracula. The 6'3" Powell served as Christopher Lee's stunt double in many films. When Kharis sank into the swamp in *The Mummy* (1959), Eddie Powell was in the wrappings for the long shots. As Dracula, he doubled for Lee in *Dracula: Prince of Darkness* (1966) and for Jack Palance in *Dracula* (1974). Powell also stunted for Gregory Peck in *The Omen* (1976) in the scene where he is attacked by wild dogs in the cemetery, as well as for Clint Eastwood in *Where Eagles Dare* (1968). On occasion, Powell was cast in specific roles, such as the inquisitor in *The Lost Continent* (1968) and as Satan in *The Devil Rides Out*. As Baphomet, the goat of Mendes, Powell looks impressive, but unfortunately he is banished back to hell when Rex tosses a cross at him a few minutes after his arrival. In addition to the Devil, Powell doubled for Lee in several sequences of the picture. Charles Gray is magnificent, underplaying the role of Mocata. Leon Greene, however, is a disappointment as the Watson-like Rex, and another actor, Patrick Allen, was later employed to redub Greene's dialogue. Niké Arrighi is splendid as Tanith, but Patrick Mower's Simon is merely run-of-the-mill. Christopher Lee provides the cerebral but dynamic hero at the center of the story. One jarring distraction is that Lee's moustache seems inconsistent from scene to scene. Years later, Christopher Lee played Lucifer in a pilot for a television comedy series, which was never picked up, called "Poor Devil" (1973). Sammy Davis, Jr., played a demonic emissary who had failed to capture a soul for Satan in over 1,400 years. The projected series would have featured his bumbling exploits week after week, sort of a "Touched by an Angel" in reverse. Lee's cameo as the Devil was too downplayed to be successful, and as a whole the pilot was a rather weak and pedestrian effort.

Notable Quotes

- When we get to the bottom, throw that straight in the face of that damned monstrosity. God help us then. (**Richleau's instructions to Rex as he hands him a cross, and prepares to drive toward Satan**)
- Time itself has been reversed for us. Tanith's death, Peggy's abduction, the ritual in the cellar, all these things happened, but now they have not happened. We are back, and we are all safe again. (**Richleau's explanation of their shift in time**)

Devil Souls

1997   Rating: **   Kory L. Andrew as the Devil

Horror International. Written by Kory L. Andrew and Jeffrey Scott Buckles; Photographed by Tod Curtis Riddle; Edited by Charlie McCracken; Music by Gateway Broadcasting; Produced by Kory L. Andrew; Directed by Jeffrey Scott Buckles. Color, 85 minutes.

Annotated Cast List

Kory L. Andrew (the Devil); Curtis Huskins (*Alex Storm*, teacher and psychic); Jeff Buckles (*Wayne*, his friend, a disgraced cop); Denise Gross (*Casey Waite*, housewife who obtains the wishing stone from the Devil); David Webb (*Raymond Jasper Waite*, her redneck husband); Roman White (*Steve Dunn*, Ray's friend); Ron Ellis (archaeologist); Steve Pilkington (mummy and *Alan Arbis*, werewolf); Jerry Crosswhite (*Jerry*, hiker); Dennis Rash (*Dennis*, his companion); Tricia M. Riddle (*Marcy*, woman who becomes a vampire); Tod Curtis Riddle (*Dan*, her husband); Misty Crumb (woman in TV movie); Debbie Cable (*Lisa*, Alex's friend); David Daniel, Sr. (*Terry*, martial arts expert aiding Alex); Jonvon Barnes (*Tim*, hunter); Kevin Overbeck (*Frank*, hunter); Chrissy West (victim at train station).

Appraisal and Synopsis

Two enthusiastic young filmmakers, Kory Andrew and Jeff Buckles, shot this semiprofessional effort in various locations in Tennessee and Virginia. In their enthusiasm, they produced a decent film, rough in many spots, but with a naiveté and vitality that raise it over many other polished, professional efforts. Some of the scenes in the woods clearly foreshadow the wildly successful *Blair Witch Project* (1999). The editing of the picture is atrocious, with long static shots and jumpcuts. The awkwardness could easily have been rectified with a few insert shots between the jumps. The sound is poor and difficult to understand at times. But the picture has a quirky sense of fun and avoids gore effects and nudity (except for one quick shower scene in a video watched by Marcy). The picture is both a homage and a spoof of older traditional monster films, with its use of a vampire, a mummy, and a werewolf. It also gently satirizes the southern drive-in flick, with goofy rednecks, hunters, and ex-cops woven into the plot. The form of the picture also has a different slant. At first, the plot seems to be leading to a standard, sketch-based horror film, however, the vignettes are brief and to the point. Then, these elements are tied together into an overall pattern for the final half of the picture. *Devil Souls* had some sporadic showings at local theaters and colleges and eventually had decent distribution on video.

The film starts with a bang, as the Devil, prowling the woods at night, leaps upon a rock and issues a direct challenge to God that he intends to claim every soul on Earth. Alex Storm, a teacher, has a terrible dream. He is taken to a spot in the woods at dawn the next morning by his friend Wayne; they find evidence that the Devil has emerged from hell and is walking the Earth. A short time later the Devil, using the name Tom Highway, appears at the home of Casey and Ray Waite and places in their hands a wishing stone, which could grant their every desire. There are three absolute conditions regarding the stone. First, the owner can't wish for a long life; second, he cannot wish harm upon others; finally, he cannot wish the dead back to life. The Devil tells them three stories to illustrate the importance of these rules.

The first tale involves the discovery of an unmarked tomb in Egypt by a solitary archaeologist. The amazed explorer opens the tomb to discover the remains of a mummy clutching an object. The archaeologist removes and examines it, but it appears to be only a simple stone. Aloud, the man mutters that he wishes the mummy were alive so he could explain the significance of his discovery. Moments later, the mummy revives and slays the dumbfounded explorer. The second story involves Jerry, a hiker who stumbles across a wishing stone in the woods. He later has an argument with his companion, Dennis, and wishes that he would drop dead. His friend immediately collapses, but his enraged ghost revives moments later and takes his revenge on the hapless Jerry. The third tale involves a young woman, Marcy, who came into possession of the wishing stone. Watching a horror film on television, she wishes she could live forever like the vampires in the movie. Marcy is instantly transformed into a vampire, and when her husband comes home she drains him of his blood.

The Devil offers to leave the wishing stone with the Waites for two weeks, to see if they can obey the rules. One night, after they invite their friend Steve Dunn for dinner, Ray and Steve get into an argument, and Ray wishes that his friend would become a demon from hell. Transformed into a beast, Steve kills the Waites. Steve is later revived by the Devil, who recruits him into his service. Alex and Wayne investigate the Waite killings, and they conclude that it is the Devil's work. They fear he is organizing an all-out assault against mankind. Alex recruits two friends, Lisa and Terry, to investigate the woods where he believes the Devil is hiding. In a remote cave, Satan has gathered the monsters from his stories, including Marcy, Dennis, the mummy, Demon Steve, and Alan Arbis, a hunter who he turned into a werewolf. These creatures attack Alex's group as they wander through the dark forest. Karate expert Terry battles Demon Steve, and they kill each other. Marcy kidnaps Lisa. Wayne destroys the mummy but is killed by Marcy. Alan steals the Devil's wishing stone and gives it to Alex. The Devil kills Alan when he learns of his treachery. Thanks to the wishing stone, Alex is able to fend off the Devil, sending him back to hell. As Lisa and Alex leave the woods, they hear the Devil's manic laughter in the distance.

Performances

The famous American storyteller and humorist Jean Shepherd had a PBS series called "Jean Shepherd's America" in which he played the Devil in one memorable episode. Dressed entirely in black, with dark glasses and a sinister beard, Shepherd depicted Satan on holiday, visiting New Orleans. In terms of sheer style, Shepherd's rendition was one of the most effective Devils ever portrayed, and to a large extent, Kory Andrew's appearance and performance as the Devil seems patterned on Shepherd's scintillating example. Of course, he lacks Shepherd's commanding personality, but he does an effective job recreating Satan in the Shepherd mold: diabolical but with a touch of whimsy. Andrew's performance is the only credible one in the picture, with the remaining players seeming earnest but crude.

Notable Quotes

- Be sober, be vigilant, because your adversary, the Devil, is a roaring lion, walking about, seeking whom he may devour. (**opening title card, paraphrasing I Peter 5:8**)
- Playtime is over. Do you hear me, God? This is my time, and I shall be the victor. No more vying over individual souls. I want them all! Consider this fair warning, Yahweh. The game is afoot. (**the Devil's brazen challenge to the Almighty**)
- Do you mean to tell me that you haven't enjoyed my company all this time? Frankly, I'm hurt. (**the Devil to Alan**)
- Don't patronize me. I was a good man 'til you turned me into this monster. (**Alan**)
- No, Alan, you were a monster already. I merely gave you a look to match your attitude. (**the Devil**)

The Devil with Hitler

1942/1943   Rating: **   Alan Mowbray as the Devil

Hal Roach Productions. Written by Cortland Fitzsimmons and Al Martin; Photographed by Robert Pittack; Edited by Bert Jordan; Special Effects by Roy Seawright; Music by Edward Ward; Produced by Glenn Tryon and Hal Roach (executive); Directed by Gordon Douglas. B&W, 87 minutes.

Annotated Cast List

Bobby Watson (*Adolf Hitler*, German dictator); Joe Devlin (*Benito Mussolini, Il Duce*, Italian dictator); Rex Evans (*Hermann Göring*, Reich Marshall); Charles Rogers (*Joseph Goebbels*, minister of propaganda); Wedgwood Nowell (*Heinrich Himmler*, Gestapo chief). **Island Plot:** Johnny Arthur (*Sukiyaki*, Japanese general); Henry Victor (*Von Popoff*, Nazi foreign minister); Ian Keith (island chief); Jean Porter (*Kula*, island beauty); Frank Faylen (*Benson*, American seaman); Emory Parnell (*Spencer*, seaman). **Devil Plot:** Alan Mowbray (the Devil); George E. Stone (*Sukiyaki*, Japanese diplomat); Sig Arno (*Julius*, Hitler's valet); Herman Bing (*Louis*, Hitler's astrologer); Douglas Fowley (*Walter Hill*, insurance salesman); Marjorie Woodworth (*Linda Krauss*, failed spy).

Appraisal and Synopsis

The Three Stooges made two short Hitler parodies called *I'll Never Heil Again* (1941) and *You Nazty Spy* (1939). Taking note of a good thing, Hal Roach released two Hitler shorts of his own, *The Devil with Hitler* (1942) and *That Nazty Nuisance* (1943). At the time, Roach was experimenting with extended shorts called "streamliners," which ran about forty-two minutes in length. When the streamliners proved awkward to distribute, Roach recut *The Devil with Hitler* to feature-length by combining both pictures, and this is the best-known version. As a short subject, *The Devil with Hitler* would not qualify for inclusion in this book, but the feature version, despite being awkwardly stitched together, certainly qualifies.

The spoof opens with a Hitler speech, no doubt inspired by a similar scene in

Charlie Chaplin's *The Great Dictator* (1940). The scene switches to hell, which is run along the lines of a large corporation. The board of directors is dissatisfied with the latest statistical reports about sin, and the directors consider replacing the Devil with Hitler as the new chairman of the board. Hearing of the board's concerns, the Devil tells of a recent escapade of *Der Führer* in which he performed poorly. At this point, *The Devil with Hitler* splices in the plot of *That Nazty Nuisance*. Hitler concludes that he needs a treaty with the mythical island nation of Nuram, and he goes on a secret mission to confer with the island chieftain, who will only sign an alliance with the head man of the Axis. Mussolini and Japanese General Sukiyaki get wind of Hilter's mission and accompany him on his submarine. When they arrive, their plans are foiled by a group of American merchant marine sailors whose ship was torpedoed and who are stranded on the island. They capture Hitler and make him look foolish, finally shooting him out of the torpedo tube of his own sub.

Returning to the original *Devil with Hitler* footage, Satan claims he can trick Hitler into doing a good deed within forty-eight hours, and the board of directors of hell agrees that if he can do this, he can keep his job. The Devil travels to Hitler's private quarters, where *Der Führer* is giving a speech from his tub. Making himself invisible, the Devil trips up the valet, Julius, which ruins the speech and gets Julius fired. The Devil then steps into the valet job, handing Hitler his robe. Using the name Gesatan, the Devil worms his way into Hitler's confidence by showing up Louis, his astrologer. Try as he may, however, the Devil finds it impossible to trick *Der Führer* into doing a good deed. Hitler confers with Mussolini and Japanese diplomat Sukiyaki. When an insurance salesman approaches Hitler, *Der Führer* decides to take a policy out on Mussolini with himself as beneficiary. Mussolini and Sukiyaki get the same idea, however, and all three men plant bombs that evening in an extended routine. They all manage to escape the blast, however, and Hitler orders the arrest of the insurance salesman. Growing desperate, the Devil decides to impersonate Hitler and do the good deed himself. He orders the release of the salesman as well as Linda Krauss, a failed spy. *Der Führer* himself is arrested as an impostor, and when he straightens matters out, he commands that the two prisoners be immediately executed. In his Hitler guise, the Devil lures *Der Führer*, Mussolini, and Sukiyaki into chasing him into a munitions warehouse, where he locks them in. Threatening to blow him sky high, he forces Hitler to set free the prisoners. He gives Hitler the key to the door, but *Der Führer* fumbles with the lock and is blown up. The board of directors in hell gives the Devil a standing ovation as he returns with Hitler as his prisoner. Members of the board grab their pitchforks and start jabbing at *Der Führer*, as the Devil orders them to "give him the works."

As a whole, *The Devil with Hitler* is a mixed bag, but the idea of ridiculing the leaders of the Axis during the traumatic early days of the war permits one to overlook a multitude of weaknesses. The threading of the two plots is awkward, and no explanation is given how Hitler, Mussolini, and Sukiyaki got back from the island of Nuram. Who is Sukiyaki anyway? He goes from being a general to a diplomat, but the real puzzle is why they didn't use the figure of Tojo, the wartime leader of Japan, instead of this fictitious substitute. Both Johnny Arthur and George E. Stone are terrible in the role. Arthur played a similar role more effectively as the spy Sakima in the serial *The Masked Marvel*. Both Mowbray and Watson are diverting in their satirical roles, and as a curiosity item the film is amusing. Of course,

82 • The Devil with Hitler

Satan (Alan Mowbray) orders his cohorts to begin the torture of Hitler (Bobby Watson).

this type of humor dates quickly, and the jokes about concentration camps would never have been made if the full extent of that horror had been known. Likewise the racist remarks about the Japanese are regrettable, but understandable as a symptom of the hysteria following the attack on Pearl Harbor. Some of the slapstick is hilarious, but most of it is downright idiotic. The humor in the island subplot is far less funny than in the Devil sequences. The highlight of the physical humor is the moment when Hitler's hand gets stuck on the handle of a pull-down wall map. The invisible Devil cuts the cord, and Hitler falls through several floors where people stop and "Heil" him as he crashes through. Another high point is a silly song warbled by Hitler as he paints a wall mural for relaxation. The Devil's scenes with Hitler are fairly good, although here too there are inconsistencies. At some points, the Devil has to rely on a pill to make himself invisible, but at other times, he fades in and out of view at will. Members of the board of directors also appear to warn Satan that doing a good deed while posing as Hitler does not count, yet they accept his equally phony solution by forcing *Der Führer* to release the prisoners due to a threat on his life. It is ironic to note that hell is managed like a business corporation, where the head can be ousted by the rest of the board. It seems Satan is far less authoritarian in hell than Hitler was on Earth.

Performances

Alan Mowbray was one of the most successful character actors of the 1930s and 1940s. Born and raised in England, he became an American citizen shortly after launching his film career. Although usually cast as a British aristocrat or spy, Mowbray tackled a variety of parts, ranging from George Washington in three films to Prince Metternich in *The House of Roth-*

schild (1934). He played a murderer in *Charlie Chan in London* (1934) and a hilarious scoundrel, Cribbs, in the comic melodrama *The Villain Still Pursued Her* (1940). W. C. Fields earlier played Cribbs in *The Old-Fashioned Way* (1934). To a certain extent, Mowbray undertakes his role of the Devil as a more sophisticated version of Cribbs. He goes about his devilish chores with a twinkle in his eye and tosses off clever quips *sotto voce*. He uses no makeup as Satan, but in the scenes in hell, both he and the board of directors sport skullcaps with the phoniest-looking horns ever used onscreen, resembling the cardboard cores from rolls of toilet paper. In a way, it seems that the Devil has met his match in Hitler because he fails to induce him to do a good deed. Nevertheless, Hitler winds up as a prisoner in Hades at the final fadeout, and the Devil's final remark, directed at the audience, suggests that he has many special tortures in mind for *Der Führer*.

Closely resembling Hitler, Bobby Watson is fairly amusing as the dictator. Born Robert Watson Kuecher in Evanston, Illinois, one year before the birth of Adolf Hitler in 1889, Watson was the most remarkable of the screen Hitlers, appearing in at least nine films as *Der Führer*, including a straightforward performance in *The Hitler Gang* (1944). Watson started as a vaudeville dancer, appearing in such silent films as *The Song and Dance Man* (1926). He was also the lead in Republic's first musical, *Syncopation* (1930). Later Watson had a memorable routine with Donald O'Connor and Gene Kelly as their elocution teacher in *Singin' in the Rain* (1952). Invariably, most listings of Watson's screen credits confuse him with a child actor with the same name who appeared in the *Boys Town* films and alternatively used the billing "Bobs" Watson. Joe Devlin does a good job as the comic Mussolini, only a few pegs weaker than Jack Oakie's masterful rendition of *Il Duce* in *The Great Dictator*.

Notable Quotes

- Give me forty-eight hours on Earth with that little Schicklgruber and I'll prove no one can replace the Devil himself. (**Satan to his board of directors**)
- So you found his soft spot, his Achilles' heel? (**board member to the Devil, mockingly**)

That particular Achilles is all heel. (**the Devil**)

- Look, Gesatan, I can change hands without missing a stroke. (**Hitler to the Devil, displaying his prowess with a paintbrush**)
- You don't think that I look like the Devil? (**Satan disguised as Hitler**)

Oh no, *Mein Führer*! (**Nazi aide**)

So easy it makes me feel a little ashamed. (**Satan to himself**)

The Devil's Advocate

1997   Rating: ****   Al Pacino as the Devil

Warner Brothers. Written by Jonathan Lemkin and Tony Gilroy, based on the novel by Andrew Neiderman; Photographed by Andrzej Bartkowiak; Edited by Mark Warner; Special Effects by Rick Baker, Richard Greenberg, Stephanie Powell, CFC, and Cinesite; Music by James Newton Howard; Produced by Arnold and

Anne Kopelson, Arnon Milchan, and Taylor Hackford (executive); Directed by Taylor Hackford. Color, 144 minutes.

Annotated Cast List

Keanu Reeves (*Kevin Lomax*, successful attorney); Al Pacino (*John Milton*, head of top law firm, actually the Devil); Charlize Theron (*Mary Ann Lomax*, Kevin's wife); Jeffrey Jones (*Eddie Barzoon*, managing director of Milton's law firm); Pamela Gray (*Diana Barzoon*, his wife); Judith Ivey (*Alice Lomax*, Kevin's mother); Connie Nielsen (*Christabella Andriotti*, the Devil's daughter); Wei Mei (*Giselle*, Christabella's friend from Paris); Craig T. Nelson (*Alexander Cullen*, wife killer defended by Kevin); Ruben Santiago-Hudson (*Leamon Heath*, associate in Milton's law firm); Tamara Tunie (*Jackie Heath*, his wife); Laura Harrington (*Melissa Black*, Cullen's mistress); Debra Monk (*Pam Garrity*, Kevin's advisor in Milton's firm); Vyto Ruginis (*Mitch Weaver*, Justice Department investigator); George Wynter (*Meisel*, criminal lawyer); James Saito (*Taksori Osumi*, media specialist); Christopher Bauer (*Gettys*, teacher and child molester defended by Kevin): Heather Matarazzo (*Barbara*, Gettys' young victim); Murphy Guyer (her father); Neal Jones (*Larry*, Florida reporter); Delroy Lindo (*Philippe Moyez*, voodoo priest defended by Kevin); Daniel Orestes (*Murtaugh*, prosecutor cursed by Moyez); Don King, Senator Alfonse D'Amato, Ambassador Charles Gagano, Lou Rudin, Ernie Grunseld, Alan Grubman, Kim Chan.

Appraisal and Synopsis

The Devil's Advocate is a major film, lengthy, substantial, and entertaining. It can best be described as a wild mixture combining elements of *The Firm* (1993) with *Rosemary's Baby* (1968) and *Paradise Lost*. The film also serves as a showcase for Al Pacino as the Devil and Keanu Reeves, who discovers that he is his son. The only drawback is that there is no real dramatic conflict in the story. Merely a process of self-discovery for Reeves, the film really has nowhere to go. The production is first class, however, and it has many satirical moments although it never develops into a black comedy.

The story starts off in a Florida courtroom where attorney Kevin Lomax is defending a math teacher who molested one of his students. Ruthlessly, Kevin destroys the young woman on the witness stand, despite knowing that her testimony is true. After this sleazy courtroom victory, Kevin, who has never lost a case, is approached by a prestigious New York law firm to serve as a consultant in jury selection. Kevin meets the dynamic and strange head of the firm, John Milton, who offers him a permanent position. Mary Ann, Kevin's wife, is overwhelmed by the perks, including a luxury apartment and an astronomical salary. Soon, Kevin becomes Milton's favorite, and Milton takes him under his wing. The young lawyer finds himself attracted to Christabella Andriotti, the international customs expert. Kevin's first case is that of a voodoo chieftain arrested for violating the health code. Kevin easily wins the case, and Milton assigns him to the high-profile case of millionaire Alexander Cullen accused of murdering his wife. Eddie Barzoon, the managing director of the firm, becomes suspicious of the favoritism accorded to the new arrival. Mary Ann becomes friends with Jackie Heath, the wife of one of the firm's attorneys. Mary Ann seems to fit in until she becomes terrified when she believes that she has seen Jackie's face transform into that of a demon, and she becomes more and more isolated, neglected by her husband, who spends most of his time on the Cullen case.

Kevin's mother, Alice, visits New York but becomes upset and evasive after meeting John Milton. Eddie Barzoon is murdered by vagrants in the park. Mary Ann has a breakdown and tells her husband that Milton raped her. Kevin doesn't believe her, since Milton was in the courtroom with him at the time of the reported rape. Kevin wins the Cullen case, but Mary Ann kills herself after being confined to a mental hospital. Alice confesses to Kevin that she met Milton decades earlier when she visited New York and that in fact he is Kevin's father.

Going to his executive office, Kevin has a showdown with Milton, who admits that he is actually the Devil. He has always watched over Kevin, which is why he has never lost a case. Milton has grandiose plans and finds his law firm an ideal position from which to dominate Earth. The Devil reveals that Christabella is his daughter and Kevin's half sister. If they mate, their offspring will become the Antichrist. Christabella appears and removes her clothes, attempting to seduce Kevin. After learning the full extent of his father's plans, Kevin grabs a gun and shoots himself in the head. The Devil is momentarily stunned by this turn of events.

Kevin finds himself back in time, in Florida at the trial of the math teacher, the point at which the film began. Instead of choosing to grill the teacher's accuser, Kevin asks to withdraw from the case. The judge threatens to recommend he be disbarred. Larry, a reporter, approaches Kevin for an interview, claiming this story could become a feature segment on "Sixty Minutes." At first reluctant, Kevin agrees to participate in Larry's plans. After Kevin and his wife leave, Larry transforms into the image of John Milton. The Devil is launching another scheme to ensnare Kevin.

The Devil's Advocate was fairly well received critically, and it won the Saturn Award as best horror film. A minor

The Devil (Al Pacino) introduces his daughter (Connie Nielsen) to her half brother (Keanu Reeves, back to camera) in The Devil's Advocate.

controversy developed concerning the frieze that appears in John Milton's office. Sculptor Frederick Hart sued, claiming that the frieze resembled his work situated above the entrance to the Episcopal National Cathedral in Washington, D.C. When the film was initially released on video, a special disclaimer preceded the film, noting that any resemblance to Hart's sculpture was coincidental and unintentional. Later versions of the film used special effects to alter and obscure the frieze in scenes in which it appears. At the end of the film, when Christabella attempts to seduce Kevin, the figures in the sculpture come to life and begin to embrace each other, recalling a similar effect in the film *The Loved One* (1964).

Performances

Al Pacino creates a brash, earthy, arrogant Devil, a consummate New Yorker who combines the instincts of a cutthroat executive with the tenacity of an aggressive cabbie. Symbolizing the worst imaginable characteristics of a lawyer with infernal cunning, Pacino seems totally unbeatable, able to defeat anyone on any level from pure logic to licentious temptation. If anything, he seems too powerful since nothing seems able to defeat him. *The Devil's Advocate* is handicapped as a drama because there is no opposition to the Devil. God and the force of goodness seem totally invisible or, as the Devil describes him, as "an absentee landlord." The film is slightly diminished because the Devil faces no credible opposition. Pacino uses no blatant makeup in the role, yet his face seems altered, perhaps by a dental appliance which helps create the expansive and ugly grin which is his trademark in the role. His Devil has the ability to morph into any disguise, which we see when he changes into Larry, Kevin's reporter friend. He also has the ability to mimic any voice. In the office climax, the Devil repeats Kevin's words using Kevin's voice. The Devil also does a song and dance, singing with the voice of Frank Sinatra. On the whole, Pacino gives a spellbinding performance, making the part totally his own, equaling his work in the *Godfather* trilogy and his magnificent personal film essay, *Looking for Richard* (1996). Naming the Devil John Milton is an interesting touch, somewhat obvious but it also beautifully sets up the reference to *Paradise Lost* that it is better to reign in hell than serve in heaven. Keanu Reeves does a decent job, but it is a problematic role because Kevin Lomax is not a sympathetic part. He is a scheming, immoral wolf from his initial appearance. His suicide at the climax of the film is an unconvincing gimmick, one that fails to signify any redemption for Kevin, but is only a lawyer's trick to outfox his father, the Devil, with whom he is angry over the death of his wife. This act is the only scene in the film where Pacino appears to suffer a defeat. He recovers swiftly, calling a "do-over," and steps back in time to try a different approach with Kevin. No matter what happens, therefore, the Devil can never lose because he is able to negate the setback by jumping back in time. The rest of the characters are also well played, but the subplot with Jeffrey Jones seems fragmented and disjointed. The picture also contains an unusually large number of cameos, including New York Senator Alfonse D'Amato, a good sport for appearing in a film as an associate of the Devil. On the other hand, he lost his next election. Boxing promoter Don King shot his cameo during a genuine Madison Square Garden fight card in October 1996.

Notable Quotes

• Don't ever let them see you coming! That's the gaff, my friend. You've got to keep yourself small, innocuous. Be the little guy. (**the Devil, as John Milton, giving advice**)

- I've had so many children. I've had so many disappointments, mistake after mistake, and then there's you, the two of you. (**the Devil to Kevin and Christabella**)
- Let me give you a little inside information about God. God likes to watch. He's a prankster. He gives man instincts.... He sets the rules in opposition. It's the goof of all time. Look, but don't touch. Touch, but don't taste. Taste, don't swallow. And while you're jumping from one foot to the next, what is He doing? (**the Devil to Kevin**)
- In the Bible, you lose. We're destined to lose, Dad. (**Kevin**)

Consider the source, son. Besides, we're gonna write our own book! (**the Devil**)

- Vanity, definitely my favorite sin. (**the Devil to the audience, the last line in the film**)

The Devil's Daughter

1972   Rating: ***   Joseph Cotten as the Devil

Paramount. Written by Colin Higgins; Photographed by J. J. Jones; Edited by Rita Roland; Special Effects by Robert C. Petersen; Music by Laurence Rosenthal; Produced by Thomas L. Miller and Edward K. Milkis; Directed by Jeannot Szwarc. Color, 76 minutes.

Annotated Cast List

Shelley Winters (*Lilith Malone*, Satanist); Belinda J. Montgomery (*Diane Shaw*, the Devil's daughter); Joseph Cotten (*Judge Weatherby*, the Devil); Jonathan Frid (*Mr. Howard*, Lilith's mute servant); Robert Foxworth (*Steve Stone*, Diane's fiancé); Martha Scott (*Mrs. Stone*, Steve's mother); Diane Ladd (*Alice Shaw*, Diane's mother); Ian Wolfe (*Fr. MacHugh*, Alice's priest); Barbara Sammeth (*Susan Sanford*, Diane's roommate); Lillian Bronson (landlady); Abe Vigota (*Alikine*, anthropologist and Satanist); Sharon Barr (*Kitty*, his wife); Lucille Benson (*Janet Poole*, Satanist and black woman); Thelma Carpenter (*Margaret Poole*, her sister, a white woman); Robert Cornthwaite (wedding minister); Nick Bolin (*Turk*, Satanist); Rozelle Gayle (*Fedora*); Mark Thomas (*Julio*).

Appraisal and Synopsis

This telefilm is a decent variant of *Rosemary's Baby* (1967) that is both modest and well handled. The picture was the directorial debut of Parisian-born Jeannot Szwarc, who went on to helm such films as *Jaws II* (1978) and *Somewhere in Time* (1980). *The Devil's Daughter* is well paced, featuring a cast with far greater depth than a run-of-the-mill TV movie. Although somewhat predictable, the film has a genuine style, and at its conclusion one wishes that it had been longer and extended the storyline beyond the abrupt finish, which leaves matters somewhat unresolved. The film debuted on ABC on January 9, 1973.

The pre-credit sequence focuses on a troubled woman, Alice Shaw, who is confronted by her daughter's father, who walks on crutches. She attempts to shoot him but instead collapses and dies. Diane, her daughter, attends her funeral, sorrowful that she never really knew her mother since she spent most of her life at boarding school. She decides to stay in Los Angeles and attempt to become a commercial artist. She is befriended by Lilith Malone, a friend of her mother, who puts her up at her rooming house. Diane is uncomfortable staying with Lilith, but she forms a bond with Howard, Lilith's mute servant. Fr. MacHugh finds a roommate for Diane, and Lilith organizes a party for her with her mother's old friends, including the anthropologist Alikine and the dressed-alike sisters, Margaret and Janet Poole, who belong to different races. Diane makes a stunning discovery, learning that all of her mother's old associates are Satanists who proclaim her "the Princess of Darkness" and the literal daughter of Satan. In addition, they want to arrange her marriage to the Demon of Endor and prepare her to rule the coven.

Diane knows nothing about her father, and she is contacted by Judge Weatherby, who informs her that he is the administrator of a legacy created for her by her father shortly after her birth. Diane feels drawn to the kindly old lawyer and confides in him about her misgivings and problems with Lilith. Her roommate dates their new neighbor, Steve Stone, but she is killed in a strange accident when her horse goes wild and tramples her. Diane and Steve have a whirlwind affair. They plan to marry, and Judge Weatherby agrees to give the bride away. Diane goes to Lilith's house and defies the coven, saying that if any of them try to interfere with her marriage, she will use the power they believe she has to destroy them. Lilith appears frazzled, but Alikine tries to placate Diane, who throws a drink at the Devil's portrait and stomps off.

Steve and Diane arrange a low-key wedding at a private chapel. When Judge Weatherby arrives, he is on crutches, claiming to have sprained his leg in a fall. The ceremony goes off without a hitch, but after taking her vows, Diane turns to discover that all of Lilith's coven have slipped into the chapel, and all of the attendees have donned black robes. The minister himself is a Satanist, and her husband's eyes glow, the trademark of the Demon of Endor. Judge Weatherby has vanished, but he reemerges behind the altar as the Devil, with cloven hooves and Satanic regalia. The Devil speaks reassuringly to Diane, announcing that he is her father. Screaming, Diane spins around in total shock, but the only sympathetic face she sees is Howard's, whose eyes well up with tears for the girl.

Performances

The director cheats in the early scene in the film where the Devil confronts Alice, Diane's mother. The camera pans down to show his shoes and crutches as he enters the room, but a different voice is heard instead of the familiar tones of Joseph Cotten. Astute viewers, however, noting that Cotten is always seated or positioned behind his desk, assume that he is the unseen Devil. By the time he appears at the wedding in crutches, only the most naive viewer will have failed to penetrate his actual identity. When Cotten finally emerges as the undisguised Devil, we see he has goat legs and cloven hooves, which account for his inability to walk easily while wearing shoes. He vaguely resembles the portrait of the Devil worshiped by the coven, and he wears a dark, flowing cape and holds a scepter topped with a Satanic symbol, which appears throughout the film on cuff links and rings. Cotten is excellent as the Devil, but his appearance is far too brief. Incidentally, a number of published reviews of the film incorrectly identify Shelley Winters as playing Satan. Winters is superb in the film, but she is only the coven's den mother. Jonathan Frid, Barnabas Collins from the television series "Dark Shadows" has genuine screen charisma, but his role is mere window dressing in the story. Unfortunately, Frid's talents were never properly utilized onscreen, except as the lead in *Seizure* (1974), Oliver Stone's directorial debut. Almost all of the cast perform well, with special praise reserved for Abe Vigota and his Karloff-like reading of Alikine, and Ian Wolfe, who appeared with Boris Karloff and Bela Lugosi in the 1935 classic about Devil worshipers, *The Black Cat* (1934).

Notable Quotes

- You are your father's daughter. He is the evil one. (**Alikine to Diane**)
  The all-seeing one! (**Janet Poole**)
  He is Samhain! (**Turk**)
  He is Lucifer! (**Kitty**)
  He is Satan! (**Lilith**)
  And you are his daughter, the Princess of Darkness! (**Alikine**)
- I'll be at the wedding come hell or high water! (**Judge Weatherby to Diane on the telephone**)
- Arise, my daughter, and take thy father's hand! (**the Devil to Diane, the last words in the film**)

The Devil's Eye
AKA Djävulens Öga

1960   Rating: ****   Stig Järrel as the Devil

Svensk. Written by Ingmar Bergman; Photographed by Gunnar Fischer; Edited by Oscar Rosander; Music by Domenico Scarlatti; Produced by Allan Eklund; Directed by Ingmar Bergman. B&W, 86 minutes.

Annotated Cast List

Gunnar Björnstand (onscreen narrator); Stig Järrel (the Devil); Jarl Kulle (*Don Juan*, famed ladies' man, a subject of hell); Bibi Andersson (*Britt-Marie*, beautiful young woman who Satan tries to corrupt); Nils Poppe (the vicar, her father); Gertrud Fridh (*Renata*, her mother); Axel Düberg (*Jonas*, Britt-Marie's fiance); Sture Lagerwall (*Pablo*, Don Juan's servant); Ragnar Arvedson (guardian demon); Allan Edwall (ear demon); Georg Fundquist (*Count Armand de Rochefoucald*, advisor in hell); Gunnar Sjöberg (*Marquis Giuseppe Maria de Macopanza*, advisor in hell); Kristina Adolphson, Torsten Winge.

Appraisal and Synopsis

Ingmar Bergman's delightful fantasy depicts a weakened, troubled, and defensive Devil, far different from the triumphant Satan envisioned in *The Devil's Wanton* (1949), a dark Bergman film which suggests a world entirely subject to the Devil's rule. Although central to the story, Satan does not actually appear in *The Devil's Wanton* as he does in *The Devil's Eye*. Whereas the earlier picture is lugubrious, *The Devil's Eye* is light, deft, and fascinating. In the opening credits, Bergman himself calls the film a *rondo capriccioso*, and he uses a rondo by Scarlatti in the soundtrack.

The film opens with a shot of the keyboard of a harpsichord, as a title scrawl relates an old Irish proverb, "A woman's chastity is a sty in the Devil's eye." A narrator appears and speaks directly to the audience, preparing them to watch a comedy. He introduces the characters and interrupts the action with observations and commentary throughout the story. He talks about hell and its ruler, the Devil, who is troubled by a sty in his eye. He sends for two advisors, Count Armand and Marquis Giuseppe, and they identify the earthly cause of his continuous discomfort, the beautiful daughter of a vicar whose maidenly virtue is so resolute that it affects the Devil himself. Considering this a challenge, the Devil summons Don Juan, another of his subjects in hell, and offers him a 300-year mitigation of his punishment if he returns to Earth for one day and seduces Britt-Marie. He also grants him permission to bring along Pablo, his servant. At first the pair seem perplexed by modern-day clothes, and a demon is assigned to them as assistant, guide, and observer. He changes later into the guise of a cat.

The vicar drives by the spot where Don Juan and Pablo emerge from hell, and his car breaks down. The demon arranges its repair, and the vicar invites Don Juan and Pablo to be his guests for dinner. He introduces them to his wife and daughter. When left alone with Britt-Marie, Don Juan has a frank conversation with her, and she kisses him, claiming she wants to kiss fifty men before marrying Jonas, her fiancé. Pablo feels drawn to Renata, the vicar's sickly wife. A violent rainstorm breaks out (caused by Satan), and the vicar invites his guests to stay the night. Jonas also joins the family for dinner. Don Juan entertains them after dinner, relating the story of the downfall of Don Juan and his meeting with the stone guest who dragged him to hell. The evening ends with a nasty fight between Britt-Marie and her intended. Using this as an opening, Don Juan tries to move in and use his talents to deflower Britt-Marie.

The night passes with many clandestine meetings and conversations. As dawn breaks, a number of unexpected developments have occurred. Don Juan has fallen in love with Britt-Marie, and due to this emotion, he is unable to seduce her. Renata has taken pity on Pablo, who has touched her heart, and has passed the night with him. When the vicar learns about this, it merely serves to reawaken their love for each other. The vicar also manages to trap the demon, locking him in his cupboard and extracting numerous secrets from him.

The Devil is bitterly disappointed by these failures when his unsuccessful emissaries return. Depressed, he threatens to close down hell just to see how God would cope with that situation. He devises a modest torture for Don Juan, summoning an ear demon who can report any conversation heard on Earth. He forces Don Juan to listen to the wedding night chatter of Jonas and Britt-Marie. The Devil's sty goes away, not when she loses her virginity but when she tells her first lie to Jonas, claiming she has never been kissed. As the film concludes, the Devil takes comfort in his token victory since the married Britt-Marie has already resorted to deceit.

This film could serve as an excellent introduction to Bergman for anyone who has not yet approached his work. Its structure, with the all-knowing and friendly narrator, works well indeed, and the humor is both universal and timeless. The use of the Don Juan legend is extraordinarily well handled. It is interesting to note that the same year this film appeared, George C. Scott appeared as the Devil in a television version of George Bernard Shaw's play *Don Juan in Hell*, which is actually the third act of *Man and Superman* (see appendix 2). In comparison, Bergman's version comes off as both more perceptive and more human.

Performances

Stig Järrel was one of Sweden's most prolific actors, appearing in a 150 films from

1935 until his death in 1998. His concept of the Devil shows him at low ebb, discouraged, glum, and troubled by his painful eye. Järrel uses little makeup, appearing in a drab business suit and spending much of his time staring at his eye in a mirror. He is soft-spoken, somber, and derives little enjoyment from any of his diabolical activities. His victims, such as Don Juan, find his tortures monotonous rather than frightening. It is interesting to compare the decor of his office to Claude Rains' office in *Angel on My Shoulder* or Laird Cregar's in *Heaven Can Wait*. Järrel's quarters are cozier, less regal, and more homelike than the others. The flames appearing outside his window seem almost elegant compared to the roaring fire that Rains' Devil sees from his desk. Järrel's desk seems far less cluttered than Cregar's as well. Järrel's Satan seems to have little to do; no wonder he dreams of retirement like any mortal, shopworn executive. It is his very *Weltschmertz* that makes his conception so unique, and one wonders, with the distraction over his eye resolved, will he delve back into his work with renewed zest, or will he continue to languish?

Notable Quotes

- Only hell seriously practices free will. (**the Devil to Don Juan, making him a proposal**)
- I am weary and fed up. I think I'll retire. Heaven will have to manage without hell. That will teach Him up there a lesson. (**the Devil's soliloquy**)
- I remain Don Juan, despiser of God and the Devil, and I permit myself to spit at your feet. Good night, sire. I wish you and He up there success in your mean little profession. (**Don Juan to Satan**)
- A tiny victory in hell is often more fateful than a great success in heaven. (**narrator to the audience**)

The Devil's Hand
AKA La Main du Diable *and* Carnival of Sinners

1942   Rating: ****   Pierre Palau as the Devil

Distinguished Films. Written by Jean-Paul Le Chanois, based on the novel *La Main du Diable* by Gerard de Nerval; Photographed by Armand Thirard; Edited by Christian Gaudin; Music by Roger Dumas; Produced and Directed by Maurice Tourneau. B&W, 78 minutes.

Annotated Cast List

Pierre Fresnay (*Roland Brissot*, artist); Pierre Palau (the Devil); Josseline Gael (*Irene*, Brissot's wife); Noel Roquevert (*Melisse*, seller of the talisman); Guillaume de Sax (*Charles Gibelin*, art dealer); Jean Despeaux (*Angel*, man who warns Brissot); Antoine Balpetre (*Auguste Denis*, owner of Hotel L'Abbaye); Rexiane (his wife); Andre Varennes (colonel, guest at the hotel); George Charmarat (*Duval*); Jean Coquelin (*Maximus Leo*, medieval monk); Andre Bacque, Pierre Larquey, Rene Blanchard, Andre Gabriello, Georges Douking, Garzoni, Robert Vattier (ghosts of previous owners of the talisman).

Appraisal and Synopsis

Maurice Tourneau (1876–1961) had a lengthy and distinguished career, both in the United States and France, dating back to 1911. His son, Jacques Tourneau, became another outstanding director, who helmed such classics as *Out of the Past* (1947) and *Curse of the Demon* (1957). During the early 1940s, Jacques was in America making films for producer Val Lewton, while his father was in occupied France, struggling to make films under the censorship of the Nazi overseers. In 1942, the same year that Marcel Carne depicted the Devil in *Les Visiteurs du Soir*, Tourneau tackled the same theme in *La Main du Diable*, based on the nineteenth-century novel by Gerard de Nerval. Tourneau's film is a grim masterpiece, and like Carne's film, viewers can detect a hidden message reflecting the contemporary situation. As the characters in the film find themselves grafted with an appendage controlled by a creature of evil, the Devil, France is grafted with an evil appendage, the Vichy government essentially controlled by Hitler. Tourneau's disguised message of hope is that the soul of France will be eventually freed, even if it comes at great cost. *La Main du Diable* was distributed in the United States with subtitles in 1947. In 1948, the British dubbed the film with an all-star cast, promoting it as *The Devil's Hand*, and this is the version that is most commonly seen today. The problem with this version is that it alters the flavor of the film far too much, providing most of the characters with stuffy British accents and English colloquialisms. Brissot's charwoman sounds Cockney, for example, using terms like "bloke." This distraction makes the subtitled version preferable to the dubbed one.

The story, similar in part to "The Bottle Imp" by Robert Louis Stevenson, begins in an isolated mountainous region on the border between France and Italy that has been cut off due to an avalanche. Tourists stranded at the Hotel L'Abbaye are intrigued by another guest, a moody man with one hand who carries a small wooden chest around with him. When the power fails at the hotel, this small chest is stolen in the dark, and the stranger becomes hysterical. The others try to calm him down and ask about the contents of his missing parcel. The man introduces himself as Roland Brissot, an artist, and he begins the uncanny story of his desperate situation.

A year ago he was an unsuccessful painter. When his girlfriend, Irene, turned down his marriage proposal while dining at Melisse's restaurant, the owner of the establishment approached him with a strange offer. He promised him fame, fortune, and love if he purchased a talisman, a severed left hand kept in a small chest. Another man called Angel warned Brissot to reject the offer. Melisse informed him that the talisman must be sold before he dies for a lower price than he paid for it, otherwise he will be condemned to hell. Thinking his tale to be a joke, Brissot gives Melisse one sou, the coin of lowest denomination. The moment he hands the money over, Melisse winces in pain, and his left hand vanishes, leaving only a stump. Immediately, he encourages Brissot to leave. That night, Brissot paints two canvases with his left hand. The artist has no memory of painting the pictures, which he signed with the pseudonym Maximus Leo. Irene is instantly impressed by them and sells them at once to Gibelin, owner of a prestigious art gallery. Brissot examines his left hand, which seems changed. He asks Irene again to marry him, and this time she accepts.

A year later, Brissot is a tremendous success as an artist, living with Irene in a large mansion. A strange little man wearing a bowler hat is always following him. Finally, the man comes to visit him. He claims to be the Devil, and he is preparing to claim Brissot's soul since he is unable to sell the talisman. When the artist asserts he can sell it for a centime, the Devil, who is also a lawyer, reminds the artist that use of the centime is no longer legal, so he is out of luck. He then makes an unusual offer to Brissot. He will sell him his soul back for one sou in exchange for the talisman. Of course, all his success will vanish and his wife will leave him if he does. Brissot intends to pay the sou, but when Irene enters the room, he hesitates, unable to bear the thought of losing her. The Devil promises Brissot time to consider the offer, but the selling price for his soul will double every day.

Three weeks later, Brissot is frantic. The purchase price of his soul has risen to a large sum, and he finally decides to pay. He summons the Devil, who magically makes the selling price dance on a piece of paper. As Brissot gathers his cash, he discovers he is short by several hundred francs. He discovers that Irene has borrowed the money for some of her expenses. The Devil chuckles that he is willing to wait until the next day, but of course the price will again double. Brissot goes to see Melisse for advice but learns that the man has died. Irene manages to gather a large sum of money for her husband, but she is murdered and the fortune stolen. Angel recommends that Brissot travel to Monte Carlo, telling him of a friend with a foolproof system to win at roulette.

At first, Brissot wins a fortune, but on the verge of obtaining enough money, he starts to lose after the appearance of a stranger at the casino. He returns to his hotel a broken man, and is visited by the spirits of all of the individuals who had bought the talisman since the fifteenth century. Each of these spirits is missing his left hand. The first one to own it was a musketeer, who purchased it from an alchemist the night before he was to fight a duel. In fact, the alchemist was the Devil. Other souls who owned the talisman included a magician, a juggler, a surgeon, and a prizefighter. The last ghost to appear is Melisse, and they all express a desire to help Brissot. The Devil appears and mocks their offer. Brissot asks about the original owner of the hand, Maximus Leo. He tries to summon him. When his spirit appears, he explains that he was a monk who was given a special gift by God, who endowed his left hand with amazing abilities. The Devil kept harassing Leo all his life, and after his death, the Devil cut off his hand and stole it. Maximus Leo proclaims that each deal made by the Devil involving the hand is invalid, since it was stolen property. He implores Brissot to bring his hand back to his tomb. Brissot passes out, and when he awakens, his left hand is a stump. He sets out to find the cemetery where Leo is buried.

Brissot finishes his narrative to the travelers at the Hotel L'Abbaye, the site of the monastery where Maximus Leo was cloistered. He explains that he is pursued by the Devil, since he is the only living man who has outwitted him. He knows the Devil has stolen the talisman from him, and he must get it back to complete his restitution. There is a pounding at the door. The hotel owner opens it, and discovers the dark outline of a hand imprinted on the door. Brissot dashes outside, and the others follow, watching him wrestle with a dark figure in the ruins of the abbey. Brissot falls, and the figure vanishes. The chest is beside Brissot on the ground, but when they open it, they find it is empty. They move Brissot's body and discover it is lying on top of the grave of Maximus Leo. In death, Brissot has completed his mission and restored the hand to its original owner.

The Devil's Hand is an extraordinarily dark film in which all of the major characters wind up dead by the conclusion. There is little humor in the story, except for the Devil himself, who in his initial appearance behaves like an eccentric figure of comic relief, lulling the audience into underestimating his capacity for evil. This too may be considered a parallel to Hitler, who initially seemed to be a figure of ridicule with a Charlie Chaplin mustache who thought he could topple the government in his beer hall *Putsch*. The first half of *The Devil's Hand* is a trifle rambling, up until the point when the Devil identifies himself. Then the picture gains in intensity and tragedy until the finale at the Hotel L'Abbaye. The long sequence with the victims of the Devil's scheme is one of the most outstanding in all Devil films. Each shade initially appears in a colorful carnival mask, which he removes before he narrates his own experience. Expressionistic sets are used to illustrate the individual adventures, and these vignettes are highly creative and extraordinary, including the appearance of Maximus Leo himself. It is a unique phenomenon that, at the same time that Maurice Tourneau was generating these extraordinary images, his son, Jacques, was developing equally memorable scenes for *The Cat People* (1942).

Performances

Pierre Palau, sometimes billed as just Palau, appears to American viewers as almost a double for Cecil Kellaway, the charming character actor. Indeed, they could easily be mistaken for one another. Palau plays the Devil as a fussy and outlandish little oddball, dressed in a black suit and wearing a bowler hat, which he uses frequently as a prop as he exaggeratedly tips his hat. In this film, the Devil is a consummate schemer who never plays fair and always has a trick up his sleeve. His transformation from a seemingly harmless mountebank into the essence of evil is done gradually, as one comes to appreciate the depths of his plans. The real turning point is the murder of Irene, an unexpected development which dramatically alters the character of the picture. In the English-language rendition, Palau is expertly dubbed by David Kier, one of the few voices that is perfect in the British version. Palau remained active in films for many years, up until his death in the mid-sixties.

Notable Quotes

• All I'm after in this life is to be proclaimed as a genius. (**Brissot to Irene while courting her**)

• Today I've come to inspect the soul that you've bartered just as any wise farmer assesses his harvest when he is about to reap it. (**the Devil**)

Then you are ... (**Brissot**)

Yes, I am. I hope you will not be too disappointed in me. (**the Devil**)

• The pact he cunningly induced all of you to make with him was invalid. Therefore, he deceived you all. No one can sell that which is not his own, not even the Devil himself. (**Maximus Leo to the other spirits**)

• Why, sir, I'm the only living person who has outwitted the Devil. He never pardons anyone who has incurred his wrath. Why, yes, my soul is saved, it's true, but my body is not. (**Brissot to the colonel**)

The Devil's Messenger

1960/1962   Rating: **   Lon Chaney as the Devil

Herts-Lion Films. Written by Leo Guild and Curt Siodmak; Photographed by William G. Trioano and Max Wilen; Edited by Lennart Wallen and Carl-Olaf Skeppstedt; Music by Alfred Gwynn and Len Fors; Produced by Kenneth Herts, Leo Guild, and Gustav Unger; Directed by Herbert L. Strock and Curt Siodmak. B&W, 71 minutes.

Annotated Cast List

Lon Chaney (the Devil); Karen Kadler (*Satanya*, the Devil's messenger); Michael Hinn (*John Radian*, Satanya's former lover and man slain in third tale); John Crawford (*Don Powell*, photographer, first tale); Ralph Brown (*Charlie*, Don's agent, first tale); Inga Botorf (woman in the photograph, first tale); Eva Hassner (*Dixie*, Don's model, first tale); Edward Maze (*Gerard*, magazine publisher, first tale); Frank Taylor (*Sven Sjöstöm*, scientist who is spellbound by the woman in the glacier, second tale); Sara Harts (*Angelica*, woman in the glacier, second tale) Jason Lindsey (*Dr. Olsen*, anthropologist murdered by Sven, second tale); Lee Melin (*Dr. Holt*, museum curator, second tale); Tor Steen (*Dr. Lund*, museum staff member, second tale); Gordon Adler (police inspector, second tale); Ann Catherin Widlund (*Inga*, Sven's wife, second tale); Gunnel Broström (*Madame Germaine*, fortune teller, third tale); Chalmers Goodin (*Dr. Humes*, John Radian's analyst, third tale); Gita Alm (woman on street, third tale); Len Cooper (policeman, third tale); Jan Blomberg (street vendor, third tale); Tammy Newmara, Ingrid Bedoya.

Appraisal and Synopsis

The Devil's Messenger has a rather involved background. In 1960, Curt Siodmak, scriptwriter of *Frankenstein Meets the Wolfman* (1943), *Donovan's Brain* (1953), and other classic projects, wrote and directed a horror anthology series shot in Sweden called "13 Demon Street." Lon Chaney played the narrator/host for the program, as a cursed soul who could not die because of the gravity of his sin. Although not fully developed, his character was probably intended to be Kartaphilos, the Roman soldier who served as doorkeeper for Pilate's tribunal. After brutally striking Jesus Christ, Kartaphilos was cursed to eternal life as punishment for his crime. A complete version of this story appeared in *The Chronicle of St. Albin* in 1228. This was the earliest version of the story later transformed into *The Wandering Jew*, the human cursed to remain on Earth until the final judgment. In "13 Demon Street," the premise of the show was that Chaney would be released from his curse if he could find a crime worse than his own. Thirteen episodes were shot in the series, and each of them portrays the downfall of an individual, usually through greed, lust, or jealousy. The supernatural figures in each episode, but the stories are so constructed that a viewer could interpret that all of the unnatural events occur only in the mind of the doomed protagonist. As a whole, the episodes are far below the caliber of "The Twilight Zone" or "Alfred Hitchcock Presents," but several of them might equal an average entry of "One Step Beyond." In most cases the original concept of each entry has some merit, but the production is dull, stodgy, and not very imaginative. The producers were unable to find a market for it in the United States, so the program only aired in Sweden. In an attempt to recoup some of his investment, producer Ken Herts persuaded Herbert L. Strock to create a feature film by stitching together three episodes from the series, "The Photograph," "The Girl in the Glacier" and "Condemned in the Crystal." Herts wanted Strock to develop a new framework for the stories using Chaney and Karen Kadler, Herts' wife. Leo Guild wrote the new framework, casting Chaney as the Devil, who recruits Kadler to serve as his messenger, delivering items to Earth which are elements in each of the three episodes. When released, *The Devil's Messenger* only credited the crew who made the framework story, but the credits above include the names of those responsible for the three tales which make up the bulk of the screen time. In all honesty, the footage of the framework is far more interesting than the three rather uninspiring episodes from "13 Demon Street."

The picture opens with the Los Angeles skyline, and the camera pans down through endless layers of soil to the vestibule of hell where the Devil sits at a desk with a rolodex, evaluating all the new arrivals to his domain. After consigning one woman to the pit, the Devil takes an interest in another woman because he likes her name, Satanya. Since she was a suicide, the Devil promises her special treatment if she agrees to serve as his messenger, noting that his special tribunal can alter her sentence. Hesitant to return to the land of the living but fearful of the torments of hell, Satanya reluctantly agrees to the mission, and the Devil gives her a camera to deliver to Don Powell, a professional photographer in New York City.

The first tale begins as Powell travels to Maine to take photographs of the country in winter for his portfolio. He takes a photo of a farmhouse, and a mysterious, elegant woman emerges from the building. Don asks if he can photograph her, but she ignores him. He follows her into the woods, growing suddenly angry at her indifference. After catching her, he kills her in a fit of madness. When he returns to his studio in New York, his agent is thrilled by the quality of his work. He places the photos in a gallery where the picture of the farmhouse garners critical attention. When a magazine publisher asks to use it for the cover of his next issue, Don takes the photo out of the exhibit. He is stunned that the photo was there because he didn't give the item to his agent. Don becomes obsessed by the picture, because the image changes, and the woman he murdered now appears emerging from the house. He begins to crack up, and when he destroys the painting, the woman appears in his studio and starts to strangle him. His agent eventually finds Don's body, and he decides that the photographer frightened himself to death with his overactive imagination.

The Devil next gives Satanya a pick to deliver to a mine in Sweden. This story opens with a scene reminiscent of *Frankenstein Meets the Wolfman* when Larry Talbot finds the frozen body of the Frankenstein monster in an underground glacier. In this film, miners discover the body of a naked woman in a glacier. A large block of ice is cut out and delivered to a museum in Stockholm where scientist Sven Sjöstöm becomes enamored with her image. He asks the curator to put him in charge of the new exhibit, which is stored in the museum icehouse. Instead, she is assigned to the care of his rival, Dr. Olsen. Sven is upset that anyone else will see her nakedness. Unable to keep away, Sven finally murders Olsen so he will be placed in charge. As he watches her, he becomes convinced that the girl is still alive. He names her Angelica and buys clothes for her, and when he shows them to the figure, she opens her eyes. He tries to thaw her out, but the melting water inside the cav-

Lon Chaney as Satan instructs his messenger. Does he really have all the damned listed in that single rolodex file?

ity of ice threatens to drown her. Sven goes mad, desperately trying to break through the ice to try to rescue her, and he collapses in madness before his museum colleagues. Again, the ending suggests that Sven only imagined that the girl had returned to life.

The Devil overcomes Satanya's reluctance to resume her work by announcing that the next victim will be John Radian, the boyfriend who jilted her. He gives her a crystal ball to deliver to Madame Germaine, a fortune teller in the Limehouse District of London. It turns out that Satanya's old flame is having recurrent nightmares about a building in Limehouse. His psychiatrist tells him to go to the actual house, ending his nightmares by confronting his fear. Radian discovers a fortune teller living in the old structure. He asks for a reading in her crystal ball and learns that he will die at midnight, killed by the soothsayer herself. Radian storms out, but when other things she told him comes true, he returns to the woman's apartment and waits for midnight. He telephones his doctor and explains what has happened. As midnight approaches, Radian starts to threaten the fortune teller and eventually pushes her out the window. As he goes down to the back alley to examine her body, a life-sized statue of Madame Germaine topples from the building and kills him. When his doctor arrives at the scene, he learns that the building was vacant and condemned and that Radian's body is alone in the alley. Again, the supernatural events seemed to occur only in the imagination of the victim. This story is undermined by the framing device, because Satanya could not have delivered a crystal ball to the fortune teller if she did not exist and was only an old figurehead attached to the building.

Now in hell, Radian and Satanya bicker over her suicide. The indignant Radian is not impressed with the Devil and threatens to leave when he suddenly realizes he is dead. The Devil now reveals his plans. He needed a pair of former lovers to carry out his ultimate mission: to bring to mankind a new super-weapon, a 500-megaton bomb, which will lead to the devastation of the planet and permit hell to annex the charred remains of the surface. The Devil conjures up the image of an exploding bomb as the film concludes.

Unfortunely, none of the episodes fit well into the scenario, unlike other anthology efforts such as *Tales from the Crypt* (1972). The loopholes and pointlessness of much of the film is overpowering. Why would Satan bother with the activities of a New York photographer or a Stockholm museum specialist when he is about to unleash world destruction? Why does he need an alienated couple to deliver the formula for the bomb? If this last mission is the crux of the Devil's entire plan, why isn't any of that story shown?

even to the reluctant Satanya, who initially has no sympathy for the Devil's schemes despite her diabolical-sounding name. Noting this, the Devil invokes her enthusiasm by targeting her cold-hearted lover who drove her to suicide. Even with minimal sets and unexceptional dialogue, Chaney's reading is masterful, and his concept of a sly, wicked, but good-natured Satan is a joy to behold.

Performances

Lon Chaney's performance is the only reason for tracking down or watching this rare title. Even if his segment were filmed in a single day, Chaney plays the part with charm, style, and a sense of delight. The force of his personality alone makes his scenes worth watching. He uses no makeup and is outfitted in a simple, black, short-sleeved shirt with a black, polka-dot tie. He sits at a desk with several rolodexes, and one wonders exactly what these rolodexes contain. Is it the souls to be collected that particular day, or a list of souls the Devil most desires to capture? He complains that hell is overcrowded, so surely his daily quotient must exceed the capacity of these files. Chaney's Devil is happy with his work and the success of his endeavors. He appears to be a positive thinker (perhaps he read Norman Vincent Peale), and his enthusiasm eventually spreads

Notable Quotes

• Love is such a stupid emotion. I hate to see such a pretty girl go down *there*, at least not yet. I'd like to help you. I have an idea. You could be my messenger. (**the Devil to Satanya**)

• Actually what you'll be doing is delivering to your society up there a passport, a ticket, one way of course, for them to join our society down here. We try very hard to make it easy for them to join us. [chuckles] It's like a big country club. (**the Devil to Satanya**)

• I've come up with a diabolical idea. (**the Devil**)

Is there any other kind of idea in a place like this? (**Satanya**)

Ha, ha, hey, that's a pun, though. I'm not much for puns but that's a good one. You know, my plan may be sort of a pun too. (**the Devil**)

The Devil's Nightmare
AKA Plus Longues Nuit du Diable

1971   Rating: ***   Daniel Emilfork as the Devil

Hemisphere. Written by Patrice Rhomm and Charles Lecocq; Photographed by Andre Goeffers; Edited by P. Panos and Pierre Jorssin; Special Effects by Paul Defru; Music by Allesandro Allesandroni; Produced by Charles Lecocq; Directed by Jean Brismee. B&W, 93 minutes.

Annotated Cast List

Erika Blanc (*Lisa Muller*, succubus); Daniel Emilfork (the Devil); Jean Servais (*Baron von Rhoneberg*, last member of ancient family); Lucien Raimbourg (*Hans*, butler); Jacques Monseu (*Alban Sorrell*, seminary student); Ivana Novak, Lorenzo Terzon, Shirley Corrigan, Christian Maillet, Frederique Hender, Maurice DeGroot, Yvonne Garden, Colette Emmanuelle.

Appraisal and Synopsis

Many films are issued and reissued under various titles, but *The Devil's Nightmare* comes close to setting a record for alternate titles used over the years and on video, not even counting the numerous foreign-language titles. At various times, this film was issued as *Castle of Death*, *The Devil Walks at Midnight*, *The Devil's Longest Night*, *In Service to the Devil*, *Nightmare of Terror*, *Succubus* and *Vampire Playgirls*. This picture was made in Belgium, was coproduced with Delfino Films in Rome, and features Erika Blanc, one of the most alluring divas of the European screen. The plot is a variation on the theme of a lost traveler stranded in a haunted house or castle.

The picture opens in Berlin in 1945 during an air raid. A woman dies giving birth, and when her husband, General von Rhoneberg, learns the child is a girl, he baptizes her and kills her with a knife thrust through the heart. The scene shifts to twenty-five years later as Baron von Rhoneberg refuses to grant an interview to a young woman writer who wants to do a feature article about his ancestral castle, which dates back to the eleventh century. While returning to her car, she is attacked and killed by an unseen assailant.

A small tour bus is lost. The group consists of Max Ducot, tour guide; Alban Sorrell, a seminary student; Howard Foster and his wife; a grumpy old-timer named Mason; and two young ladies, Corinne and Regina. Max stops the bus and asks directions from a man in black standing by the roadside. The tourists don't realize that this stranger is the Devil, lying in wait for them. He advises them to head to Rhoneberg Castle for overnight lodgings. As they arrive, a terrible storm breaks out, and they are surprised to learn that the baron had received a mysterious phone call informing him to prepare to receive guests.

At dinner, the baron is questioned about his family curse. He reveals that in the twelveth century, his ancestor Siegfried von Rhoneberg supposedly signed a pact with the Devil. It designated the eldest daughter of each generation to be in service to Satan as a succubus, seducing men and leading them into perdition. Hans, the butler, adds that this evening is the anniversary date of the pact. Another visitor arrives, Lisa Muller, a beautiful young woman also stranded in the storm. Martha, the elderly servant who is also the baron's sister-in-law, recognizes her and denies her entrance, but Hans overrules her, citing the baron's policy of hospitality. After she joins the other guests, the harmonium is heard playing, a warning, according to Hans, that the succubus is due to strike.

That night, the guests are upset when tour guide Max is unable to open the front door. They are further disturbed when Regina discovers blood seeping through the ceiling of her room. They investigate and uncover a medieval torture chamber in the attic, with the blood coming from a cat that got caught in one of the torture implements. Each of the seven guests personifies one of the seven deadly sins. Lisa stalks and kills the tourists one by one, playing upon their weaknesses. Mrs. Foster sets out to steal the baron's treasure. Lisa leads her to a dungeon chamber filled with gold and, screaming, the greedy woman sinks in it as if it were quicksand. Max is taken by Lisa to a room adjacent to the kitchen that is filled with a feast. The gluttonous Max chokes to death after drinking wine poured by Lisa. Corinne seduces Howard Foster, and they slip off to make love in the torture chamber. Lisa intervenes, locking the lustful Corinne in the iron maiden and lopping off the head of the envious Howard. Her next victim is Mason. She provokes his anger by disturbing his sleep, and while he chases after her in a rage, she shoves him out a window to his death impaled on spikes. Lisa is unable to awaken the slothful Regina, so she murders her by placing a deadly snake in her bed.

The only survivor is Alban, but as hard as she tries, Lisa is unable to seduce him. The Devil arrives and tells her that he will take care of Alban, who flees to the chapel. The Devil taunts him from outside the doorway. Finally, Alban's pride gets the better of him, and he offers to make a deal with Satan. If he will restore the six murdered guests to life, Alban will agree to serve Satan. The Devil hands him a parchment. Alban scratches at the vein in his wrist and uses his blood to sign the document, which immediately bursts into flames.

The next morning, Alban awakens and believes the events of the previous evening were only a dream. The other tourists, alive and well, prepare to leave on their tour. The baron and Hans are having a mock duel, but an accident occurs and the Baron is wounded. Alban leaves the tour to remain with the dying man, who confesses before he dies that he murdered his own daughter at birth so she wouldn't become a succubus. This deed has weighed upon his conscience for the past twenty-five years. Martha then informs Alban that Lisa is her daughter. Her father was the baron's brother, killed at Stalingrad. She confirms that Lisa is possessed by the Rhoneberg curse, and she is a succubus. The tour bus goes over a cliff and bursts into flames. The Devil, driving a rickety horse cart, watches in delight as fire consumes the vehicle.

The Devil's Nightmare is a better-than-average horror film due to the allegorical cleverness of the plot, although the revelations in the last two minutes of the story are a bit confusing unless viewers pay the closest attention. The baron is unaware that his brother had a daughter. It is she, Lisa, who inherited the curse. His own baby, who he murdered, would have been free of the taint. *The Devil's Nightmare* is far more complex than it first appears. The subtleties of the film only become apparent after a second or third viewing. The picture does excel in terms of Gothic mood and atmosphere. The main problem is that the dialogue in the English version is often garbled, and it undermines the plot. At one point, the image of Lisa keeps appearing and disappearing in Alban's room. Is this due to her supernatural powers, or is this image only Alban's imagination, since he is captivated by Lisa's beauty? The answer only becomes apparent through later dialogue, which can be easily overlooked. The fact that Martha is the baron's sister-in-law is also tucked into a throwaway line early on and can be easily missed. Most of the loopholes in the plot are plugged, but it requires close concentration. Another drawback is that there is not a single appealing character in the entire story. The tourists are crude, vulgar, and unlikable, and Alban, the supposed hero of the film, is smug, arrogant, and insufferable. The audience may find it easy to root for the Devil to sweep away this unpleasant bunch as soon as possible.

Performances

Daniel Emilfork is perfect as the gaunt and skeletal Devil, seeming like a medieval woodcut come to life. He brings a vitality to each of his brief appearances, a relief from the bickering and backbiting of the guests, which wears quickly. Emilfork made his screen debut in the Anthony Quinn version of *The Hunchback of Notre Dame* (1959), and he was also memorable in Federico Fellini's *Casanova* (1976) and the masterful and evocative French fantasy *The City of Lost Children* (1995). In *The Devil's Nightmare*, he is dressed in a flowing black robe with a hood. He speaks distinctly, with careful enunciation that seems other worldly. In terms of storyline, it seems unfair that a twelveth-century ancestor should have the authority to seal the fate of family members for centuries to come. The Devil's soul of choice, his intended prey, is Alban, not because he is of value himself, but because he will become influential and save many souls, who will fall victim to Satan once Alban is removed from the scene. Emilfork depicts the Devil as a master chess player, with the other tourists, the baron, Hans, Martha, and Lisa mere pawns in his game to vanquish Alban. *The Devil's Nightmare* is also an impressive *tour de force* for Erika Blanc as Lisa. The actress is bewitching as well as frightening in her subtle transformations as she carries out her murderous deeds. She manages to rivet the audience's attention in every scene. The remaining cast members are adequate but far beneath the level of Emilfork and Blanc. Many of them appeared in only one or two other films, and cast lists for this picture fail to match up the performers with the roles they play.

Notable Quotes

- When I'm hungry, I'd even eat with the Devil. (**Max Ducot at dinner**)
- I'm an atheist, thank God for that. (**Mason when asked if he believes in the Devil**)
- You speak defiantly because your body is protected, but admit your thoughts are troubled.... the night will be long. (**the Devil to Sorrell**)

The Devil's Rain

1975   Rating: **   Ernest Borgnine as the Devil

Bryanston. Written by James Ashton, Gabe Essoe, and Gerald Hopman; Photographed by Alex Phillips, Jr.; Special Effects by Carol and Chris Wenger, Frederico Farfan, and Thomas L. Fischer; Edited by Michael Kahn; Music by Al DeLory; Produced by James V. Cullen, Michael S. Glick, and Sandy Howard (executive); Directed by Robert Fuest. Color, 85 minutes.

Annotated Cast List

Ernest Borgnine (*Jonathan Corbis*, warlock and host body for the Devil); William Shatner (*Mark Preston*, rancher whose family possesses the *Book of Lost Souls*, and *Martin Fyffe*, his ancestor); Tom Skerrit (*Tom Preston*, his younger brother); Joan Prather (*Julie*, his wife, a psychic); Ida Lupino (*Mrs. Preston*, his mother); Eddie Albert (*Sam Richards*, medical doctor and paranormal investigator); John Travolta (*Danny*, devil worshiper); Woody Chambliss (*John*, Preston family handyman); Keenan Wynn (*Sheriff Owen*); Erika Carlsson (*Aaronessa Fyffe*, woman who betrayed Corbis in colonial times); Claudio Brook

(*Rev. Blythe*, preacher who burns Corbis); George Sawaya (*Steve Preston*, Mark and Tom's father); Lisa Todd (*Lilith*, queen of delights, follower of Corbis); Tony Cortex (first captor); Robert Wallace (*Matthew*, the warlock's son); Diane LaVey (*Priscilla*, the warlock's wife); Anton Sandor LaVey (Satanic high priest).

Appraisal and Synopsis

This film has a somewhat surprising cult following, due in part to the well-known performers appearing in it, including John Travolta in his screen debut. Other unusual elements include the participation of avowed Satanist Anton Sandor LaVey, who acted as the film's technical advisor. Then there is the crazy denouement of the picture when the cast melts away in a gooey mess, with hilarious makeup effects. Other than the salaries of the name performers and the cost of makeup, the budget for this shoestring film, shot in Mexico, was minimal. The plot is difficult to follow, making little sense as if key scenes are missing from the final print.

The credit sequence features the artwork of the fifteenth-century Dutch painter Hieronymus Bosch, particularly his vision of hell as portrayed in the right panel of *The Garden of Delights*. During a night of violent thunderstorms, Mark Preston is upset when his father disappears from his ranch. A figure resembling him finally appears, saying Corbis is waiting in Redstone for the return of his *Book of Lost Souls*, which was stolen from him back in colonial times. The messenger then dissolves in the rain. When his mother retrieves the book from its hiding place, Mark refuses to return it: "I won't give the Devil's man what he wants!" Moments later, while he is outside, Mark's mother is kidnapped and John, their elderly helper, is hung upside down from the ceiling. After tending to John's wounds, Mark heads off to Redstone, a ghost town in the desert.

He confronts Corbis and challenges him to a duel of faith, pitting his family's safety against the surrender of the book. The warlock accepts and brings Mark into an old wooden church that has been reconsecrated to Satan. The followers of Corbis, dressed in black robes, are chanting their dark prayers. Mark kneels down and starts to recite the Apostle's Creed. Corbis summons the spirit of Martin Fyffe, Mark's lookalike ancestor. When Mark discovers his mother, her eyes are two black, unseeing cavities. Mark shoots one of the Devil worshipers and runs outside, but he collapses as he reaches his car and Corbis towers over him, saying that the Preston family name will soon be extinct. They bind him and start an interrogation, seeking his hiding place for the book.

The next day, medical researcher Tom Preston is notified about the disappearance of his family. The local sheriff seems unconcerned, being preoccupied with the damage resulting from the heavy storm. Tom and his wife, Julie, head to Redstone to conduct their own search. Danny, a disciple of Corbis, attacks Tom as he searches through the ghost town. After Tom overpowers Danny, the psychic Julie has a vision from 1680 when Corbis led a coven in New England. He was betrayed by Aaronessa Fyffe, who stole his *Book of Lost Souls*, which contains the signatures in blood of people he converted to Satanism. Corbis and his followers were captured and burned alive at the stake, at which time the warlock placed a curse on the Fyffe family and its descendants until the book is restored to him. Now, Corbis and his followers exist in an eternal limbo, unable to enter hell until Corbis regains his book. Meanwhile, their souls are stored in a large glass container in which they experience the Devil's rain, a never-ending shower which sustains them.

Ernest Borgnine as Satan in The Devil's Rain.

After dark, an unholy ceremony is held by the Satanists in which Mark's soul is imprisoned in the Devil's rain, and his body is possessed by Martin Fyffe after his eyes are turned into black sockets. The Devil himself is summoned from hell and inhabits the body of Corbis, which becomes half human and half ram. Danny spots Tom, and the followers capture Julie and chase Tom, who escapes.

Dr. Richards arrives to assist Tom in his battle against Corbis. He has with him Corbis' book, given to him by John. Richards goes to the church and uncovers the vessel bearing the souls and the Devil's rain. Sheriff Owen arrives and attacks the pair with an ax. Observing his black eyes, Tom realizes that the lawman is possessed. Richards pushes him through a hole in the church floor, which leads to a flaming pit. Richards drops the book, and it is recovered by Danny, who takes it to Corbis. The warlock is overjoyed, and he returns to the church with his followers, who are carrying the unconscious body of Julie. Richards attempts to stop the ceremony, threatening to destroy the glass container holding the Devil's rain, but Mark, possessed by Martin Fyffe, seizes the vessel. Richards tells him that if he destroys the container, his soul will be free and he will be able to rejoin Aaronessa. Upon hearing his wife's name, Martin smashes the vessel and releases the Devil's rain, which overwhelms Corbis and his followers, who begin to melt like wax. Satan again assumes control of the body of Corbis, but it is too late and his body continues to deteriorate as he fights with Tom. All the Satanists dissolve into a gooey mess, and their church catches fire and burns to the ground. When all of their opponents are destroyed, Tom embraces his newly freed wife. The camera reveals, however, that Julie is now possessed by Corbis, who plans to continue his evil campaign. The soul of Julie is shown imprisoned in a new vessel with the Devil's rain. The film ends with many matters unresolved. Why does the Devil's rain sustain the souls in the jar but destroy them when it is unleashed? Are the followers of Corbis actually set free as announced by Richards? Or have they been sent to hell since the book was recovered by Corbis? Where is the second container in which the soul of Julie is imprisoned? Only a single vessel was ever shown in the film up to this point. Is Julie alone in her prison with the Devil's rain? Does Corbis have to start again from scratch to gain new souls for Satan? Or will the released souls migrate out of force of habit to this second vessel? Due to these numerous loose ends, the picture finishes in an unresolved muddle.

Performances

Ernest Borgnine was one of the busiest character actors in films during the last half of the twentieth century, playing everything from a Roman gladiator to a Viking to a cowboy. He is best remembered for his Academy Award–winning role as *Marty* (1955) and as Skipper Quentin McHale in TV's "McHale's Navy." Few parts gave him the opportunity to milk a role as broadly as he plays Corbis in *The Devil's Rain*, and his histrionics are perhaps the most enjoyable element in the film. In the traditional black mass, a composite human/goat is supposed to appear, and this figure is called Baphomet, or the goat of Mendes. This being can also be a form of Satan himself, as portrayed by Borgnine, although in this film he assumes a more ramlike than goatlike appearance. His makeup is effective, and it is a convincing transformation. When Satan assumes the body of Corbis, he develops two large, curved horns, his nose flattens, and he grows a shaggy grey mane and goatee. He speaks with a raspy, deeper voice, which sounds more commanding than Corbis'. After an impressive introduction, the lines become blurred between Corbis and the Devil, especially when he mouths a blasphemous prayer to Satan. It would seem pointless for Satan to pray to himself, but then this sequence is supposed to be part of a ritual where William Shatner's character is transformed into his ancestor, who originally signed Corbis' book. The dramatic clashes between Borgnine and Shatner are ripe with scenery chewing and some entertaining overacting. Eddie Albert and Tom Skerrit, by comparison, seem too tame in their confrontations with Corbis. It is unclear why the Devil reappears at the climax of the film since Corbis hadn't summoned him. But seeing Corbis melt in his Satanic makeup is far more impressive than if he dissolved as plain old Corbis. One is supposed to assume, perhaps, that his body was melting anyway due to contact with the Devil's rain, and perhaps Satan's assumption of his body allowed Corbis to possess the body of Julie. Since neither Tom, Julie, nor Dr. Richards had signed the book, their bodies were not affected by the release of the Devil's rain. The Devil's actions allow Corbis the opportunity to wreak his revenge on Tom after the film is over. Many prize this film for its camp value, and watching the heavily disguised John Travolta stumble around the ghost town set is one of the definite highlights. Ida Lupino's part is somewhat demeaning, given her prestigious background as both a director and actress, but on the other hand she seems to be having fun. Watching this film in the right frame of mind can be amusing, as long as you don't try to make much sense of the outlandish turn of events.

Notable Quotes

- In the name of Satan, ruler of the Earth, king of the world, I command the forces of darkness to bestow their infernal power upon my limbs. Come forth from the abyss, open wide the gates of hell.... you have bestowed upon us a vessel for the sacred rite of the holy water. For this, we thank thee and summon the soul of Martin Fyffe. (Corbis' appeal during his battle of wills with Mark)
- The book is gone, but I am not. (**Corbis to his followers in 1680**)
- Who calls me from out of the pit? What is thy purpose? (**the Devil after assuming the body of Corbis**)

Doctor Faustus

1967   Rating: ****

Andreas Teuber and Elizabeth Taylor as the Devil

Columbia. Written by Neville Coghill, adapted from the play *The Tragical History of the Life and Death of Doctor Faustus* by Christopher Marlowe; Photographed by Gabor Pogany; Edited by John Shirley; Special Effects by Peter Harman; Music by Mario Nascimbene; Produced by Richard Burton and Richard McWhorter; Directed by Richard Burton and Neville Coghill. Color, 93 minutes.

Annotated Cast List

Richard Burton (*Dr. John Faustus*, professor at the University of Wittenberg); Andreas Teuber (*Mephistopheles*, the Devil); Elizabeth Taylor (multiple roles as *Roxanne*, paramour of Alexander the Great; *Helen of Troy*; Faust's idealized woman; and *Mephistopheles*, the Devil in female guise); Ian Marter (*Charles V,* Holy Roman emperor); Elizabeth O'Donovan (empress); David McIntosh (voice of *Lucifer*, Prince of Devils); Jeremy Eccles (voice of *Beelzebub*, Chief Devil after Lucifer); Ram Chopra (*Valdes,* magician and friend of Faustus); Richard Carwardine (*Cornelius,* magician and friend of Faustus); Patrick Barwise (*Wagner,* servant); Adrian Benjamin (pope); Richard Durden-Smith (*Benvolio*, knight given horns by Faustus, and voice of the skull, evil angel); Michael Menaugh (bishop and voice of Sebastian, good angel); Angus McIntosh (Rector); Ambrose Coghill, Neville Coghill, Richard Harrison (professors); members of the Oxford University Drama Society.

Appraisal and Synopsis

Christopher Marlowe was born the same year as Shakespeare, 1564, and was stabbed to death with a knife at an inn on May 30, 1593, nine months short of his thirtieth birthday. In that brief span, he wrote seven major plays that ensured his immortality, including *Doctor Faustus* shortly before his death. He was inspired by a German narrative of the Faust story, which first started to appear in the early sixteenth century. Marlowe's play was a milestone in English literature, yet the piece presents a distinct challenge to modern audiences. Marlowe's own name now has diabolical connotations. A recent film, *A Murder of Crows* (1998), featured a neo-Faustian plot in which a disbarred lawyer, played by Cuba Gooding, Jr., is seduced into plagiarism by a serial killer who poses as an elderly English teacher named Chris Marlowe.

The film of *Doctor Faustus* was a labor of love for Richard Burton, the only film for which he served as director. Burton actively disliked watching himself on the screen, and he never saw most of his own films. The major exception was *Doctor Faustus*, since he was intimately involved in every step of the production. Reaction to this film varies widely, from those who find it a vivid and sensitive rendition of Elizabethan drama to those who regard it as bewildering claptrap. The more one is familiar with the original play, the more appreciative one is of the film. Neville Coghill, who penned this screen adaptation, originally helped Burton to launch his career as an actor in the 1940s. Burton used many unknowns in this film, mostly drawn from the Drama Society of Oxford University, his old school. *Doctor Faustus* was filmed in Rome at the studios of Dino de Laurentiis.

The tragedy centers on John Faustus, renowned and honored scholar at the University of Wittenberg, the same school attended by Hamlet in Shakespeare's famous play. Driven by a desire for power and knowledge, Faustus seeks to strive beyond the boundaries of normal human endeavor. Therefore, he conjures up the Devil and offers to sell his soul to Satan in exchange for twenty-four years of service by Mephistopheles. When Mephistopheles first appears, he takes the form of a maggot-ridden skeleton. In the original play, he comes as a dragon. Faustus entreats him to appear in the guise of a Franciscan friar, which he maintains for the remainder of the film, except when he changes into the form of a woman. In Marlowe's conception, Mephistopheles, Lucifer, and Beelzebub are separate personalities, unlike more recent concepts which consider them different names of the same Devil. Lucifer is foremost, the prince of Darkness, Satan, while Beelzebub and Mephistopheles are his chief lieutenants. Faustus is not tricked into selling his soul, which he does with his eyes wide open, although he starts having misgivings early on until Lucifer himself visits him, warning him never to pray or call upon Christ, or he will send demons to tear his body to pieces. Faustus is then entertained by the appearance of the seven deadly sins.

With restored youth, Faustus attends the court of Emperor Charles V, who asks Faustus to conjure up the spirits of Alexander the Great and his paramour, Roxanne. One of the knights mocks Faustus, who makes him a target of his humor by causing horns to grow on his head. Later, Faustus visits the pope, after being made invisible by Mephistopheles. Faustus engages in some low humor by imitating farting sounds among the group of bishops attending the holy father. Then he levitates dishes and throws cake at the face of the pope.

The years pass, and the hour when Faustus must surrender his soul finally approaches. Visiting scholars request that Faustus summon the spirit of Helen of Troy, and they are bewitched by her beauty. Faustus admits to his friends that he has sold his soul to the Devil, and he soon must forfeit it. They offer to pray for him and leave him alone for his last hour, as Faustus regretfully considers his terrible decision to have bargained with the Devil. As midnight approaches, Mephistopheles, in the form of a woman, drags Faustus screaming down to hell. The story ends with the admonition that the reward of sin is death.

The atmosphere of *Doctor Faustus* is extraordinarily moody. Much of the film is shot in shadows and semidarkness. The picture uses the device of having images appear in the primitive eyeglasses worn by Faustus. The characters of the good angel and bad angel are personified in the film by a statue of St. Sebastian and a human skull. The music by Mario Nascimbene is

Mephistopheles (Andreas Teuber) guides a rejuvenated Faustus (Richard Burton) to the court of the Holy Roman emperor in Doctor Faustus.

powerful and effective, making frequent use of tolling bells and the voice of a wordless soprano. Some of the images are less imaginative. Lucifer and Beelzebub, for example, do not actually appear but are represented by statues. The last fifteen minutes are the most successful moments of the picture, as the distress of Faustus grows as his doom approaches. The final scene when he is dragged off to hell is magnificent. The music blends with vocal excerpts from the drama and wailing screams in the background, and Faustus whirls in the arms of his captor. The conclusion of the film is simply unforgettable.

Performances

Andreas Teuber was a professor of philosophy at Brandeis University when Burton approached him to play Mephistopheles, first at a benefit theatrical performance and later on film. His reading is one of quiet, eerie understatement. As requested by Faustus, Mephistopheles appears as a simple friar with shaven head throughout the story, except when he transforms himself into the image of a cat or a woman. His eyes seem to convey a poignant sadness, particularly when discussing the loss of paradise, which pains him greatly. Teuber's reading is a deliberate contrast to Richard Burton's flamboyant, larger-than-life rendition, which is at first mocking and overconfident and later tinged with hysteria. After *Doctor Faustus*, Teuber concentrated on his teaching although he did work on an occasional film script and appeared sporadically in various roles. Elizabeth Taylor is often mentioned in reviews as appearing only briefly as Helen of Troy. In fact, her image haunts the screen in various guises from Alexander the Great's paramour with gold-painted skin to a cackling female Mephistopheles in the final scene as Faustus is taken to hell. Of course, her cameo as Helen is striking, particularly with Burton's poetic delivery of the tribute to Helen by Faustus. Although she has no dialogue, Taylor has a beguiling impact on the entire film. As for Burton himself, his reading does go over the top at times, but his overacting is entirely in character, particularly at the climax. For the most part, his uses his electrifying voice to great advantage throughout the picture.

Notable Quotes

- I charge thee to return and change thy shape. Thou art too ugly to attend on me. (**Faustus to Mephistopheles, who is appearing as a hideous skeleton**)
- When all the world dissolves, and every creature shall be purified, all places shall be hell that is not heaven. (**Mephistopheles, answering Faustus on the nature of hell**)
- Faustus, we are come from hell to show thee some pastime. Thou shall see all the seven deadly sins appear in their proper shapes. (**Beelzebub**)

That sight will be as pleasing unto me as paradise was to Adam the first day of his creation. (**Faustus**)

Talk not of paradise nor creation but mark the show. Talk of the Devil and nothing else. (**Lucifer**)

- The stars move still, time runs, the clock will strike. The Devil will come and Faustus must be damned! Oh, I leap up to my God. Who pulls me down? See, see where Christ's blood streams in the firmament. One drop would save my soul! Half a drop! Ah, my Christ. Yet will I call on Him. Oh, spare me, Lucifer! (**Faustus as his time expires**)

End of Days

1999 Rating: ***
Gabriel Byrne and Arnold Schwarzenegger as the Devil

Universal. Written by Andrew W. Marlowe; Photographed by Peter Hyams; Special Effects by Eric Durst and John Des Jardin; Edited by Jeff Gullo and Steven Kemper; Music by John Debney; Produced by Marc Abraham and Thomas Bliss; Directed by Peter Hyams. Color, 123 minutes.

Annotated Cast List

Arnold Schwarzenegger (*Jericho Cane*, security expert); Gabriel Byrne (the Devil); Kevin Pollak (*Chicago*, Jericho's sidekick); Robin Tunney (*Christine York*, the Devil's intended mate); C. C. H. Pounder (*Margie Francis*, police detective who is resurrected by Satan); Rod Steiger (*Fr. Kovac*, priest working against the Devil); Derrick O'Connor (*Fr. Thomas Aquinas*, priest who tries to assassinate the Devil's host body); Miriam Margolyes (*Mabel*, Christine's stepmother and Satan worshiper); Victor Varnado (albino demon who turns into porcelain); Michael O'Hagan (cardinal); Mark Margolis (pope); Luciano Miele (pope's advisor); Rainer Judd (Christine's mother); David Weisenberg (her doctor); Udo Kier (*Dr. Able*, Christine's doctor and Satanist); Lynn Marie Sager (Able's wife); Linda Pine (*Evie Able*, their daughter); Yannis Bogris (skateboarder); Eve Siegel (old woman); Lloyd Garroway (Con Ed worker); Gary Anthony

Williams (*Charlie*, utility worker); John C. Nielson (hospital cop); Elliot Goldwag (doctor attending Fr. Aquinas); Elaine Corall Kendall (TV newscaster); Denise D. Lewis (*Emily*); Rebecca Renee Olstead (*Amy*); Matt Gallini (monk); Marc Lawrence (old man); Van Qualtro (Satanic priest); Jack Shearer (*Kellogg*); Robert Lesser (*Carson*); Charles A. Tamburro (helicopter pilot); David Franco (assistant priest); Steve Kramer (businessman at restaurant with the Devil); Melissa Mascara (his wife, kissed by the Devil); Walter von Huene (subway motorman); Fr. Michael Rocha (*Fr. Mike*); Kassandra Kay (nun); Frankie Ray (squatter).

Appraisal and Synopsis

End of Days can be regarded as a typical Arnold Schwarzenegger action flick with an apocalyptic and demonic twist, with plenty of razzle-dazzle but not much substance. It retreads sequences reminiscent of *Gremlins* (1984), *Predator 2* (1990), *Speed* (1994), *Eraser* (1996), and *Stigmata* (1999), which also starred Gabriel Byrne as a priest and hero of the story. Even the credit sequence seems derivative of other recent films. At other moments, the picture comes close to becoming pure camp, such as when Arnold is crucified in a back alley. Nevertheless, it provides a colorful two hours of entertainment and even contains a few clever lines and incidents that will manage to linger in the memory of viewers. That is a modest achievement in spite of the panning of the picture by numerous critics. Having Satan himself as Arnold's adversary casts a surreal aspect to the story, which screenwriter Andrew Marlowe (whose last name appropriately matches one of the greatest writers about the Devil, Christopher Marlowe) deliberately utilizes at key moments of the film. It is one of the few films where Arnold (playing a human being) dies onscreen. The underlying premise, that the Devil has an opportunity every thousand years to end the world and bring about his kingdom, is never adequately explained. At one point it is mentioned that he must conceive a son at this precise moment, but on other occasions it is suggested that the union in and of itself will engender the so-called End of Days. Rod Steiger attempts to outline the plot fundamentals in *Cliffs Notes* fashion. The picture does leave itself open for a quip, when the Devil's appointed hour passes, and he is consigned back to hell for another thousand years; audience members may be tempted to repeat Arnold's trademark line from many films, "I'll be back!"

The plot begins in 1979, when prophecy scholars in Rome inform the pope about the birth of Satan's appointed mate, whose physical union with the Devil during the last hour of the old millennium will bring about the End of Days. Some around the pope urge him to order her murder, which he refuses to do and instead assigns one of his advisors, Fr. Thomas Aquinas, to locate the girl and protect her.

The scene shifts twenty years later to the last three days of December 1999. On the evening of December 28, the Devil rises to Earth, bursting out of an exploding sewer in New York City. He flies, almost invisible, to capture his preselected host body, a wealthy Wall Street banker who is dining at an exclusive restaurant. He enters the body when the man visits the lavatory. After gaining complete control, the Devil lasciviously kisses the wife of his dinner partner and leaves the restaurant, which erupts in a fiery explosion moments later.

Jericho Cane heads a security team serving as bodyguards for the banker possessed by Satan. He saves him from an assassination attempt, and he tracks down and wounds the sniper, who turns out to be Fr. Aquinas. Cane and his partner locate the priest's hideout, which is filled with manuscripts about the Devil and the Apocalypse. The walls are scrawled in blood with a biblical verse, Revelation 20:7, concerning Satan. They find a photograph of a young woman, and the scene shifts to Christine York, a troubled twenty-year-old plagued by disturbing visions, who doesn't know that she is the Devil's intended nor that her doctor and wealthy stepmother are Satanists.

At St. Thomas Church, Cane meets Fr. Kovac, who explains that Fr. Aquinas was a visionary who had disappeared a few months earlier. The priest tells Jericho that he couldn't possibly understand the forces at work behind these events. Meanwhile, the Devil, walking the streets, bumps into a skateboarder who wears a shirt proclaiming, "Satan Rules!" He compliments him on his shirt, but after the skateboarder replies, "Screw you," Satan arranges for him to get hit by a bus. Cane eventually learns the girl's name through a message carved into the flesh of Fr. Aquinas, who was killed and mutilated in his hospital room. As he and his partner arrive at her home, Christine is being attacked by a group of intruders, who are trying to kill her. Cane fights them off and rescues her. He rips an amulet from one of her assailants, which he later identifies as the emblem of the Knights of the Holy Seal, a secret order whose mission is to oppose Satan. He returns at night to question the girl. Moments later the Devil arrives, killing Christine's police bodyguards and Cane's partner by causing their vehicles to burst into flames. Cane and the girl escape after battling off her stepmother, who has superhuman strength. In the street, they are attacked by Cane's police friends, and Jericho is forced to kill them. The Devil resurrects one of them, Margie Francis, and assigns her the task of tracking the the girl down.

Cane brings Christine to Fr. Kovac, who explains Satan's plans to mate with Christine during the last hour of New Year's Eve, which would bring about the eclipse of mankind. Christine decides to accept Kovac's offer to hide her, but Jericho considers Kovac's tale to be religious nonsense. Upon returning to his apartment, Cane is visited by Satan, who tries to learn where he has hidden Christine. Jericho is stunned to learn that the banker whose life he saved is indeed the Devil. Satan tempts Jericho by offering to resurrect his wife and child, who were killed the previous year. This loss is what has turned Jericho into an embittered man, but he resists the Devil's offer. When he makes no headway with his persuasive logic, the Devil pushes Cane out the window onto the ledge of the building, but Cane manages to cause Satan to fall instead. He crashes into a parked car on the street below but is unharmed. Later Cane's partner shows up at his apartment, claiming he escaped the burning van.

Members of the Knights of the Holy Seal arrive at St. Thomas Church and offer to help Fr. Kovac, but Christine recognizes some of the men as those who previously attacked her. When they attempt to kill her, Cane shows up to save her, but he is followed moments later by the Devil, who kills most of them. At first, Jericho and Christine escape, but his partner betrays Cane and turns the girl over to Satan, who orders his followers to crucify Cane. Hours later, Fr. Kovac finds him, takes him down, and tends to his wounds.

The next evening, New Year's Eve, Cane revives and sets out to locate Christine and free her. Alone, but heavily armed, he sets out to find the secret meeting place where the Satanists are gathered to watch their master launch his reign on Earth with his union with Christine. He locates an underground chamber adjacent to a subway tunnel and tries to break up the meeting with machine gun fire. Satan orders Cane's former partner to kill him, but he refuses and the Devil causes him to go up in flames. Cane snatches Christine and escapes with her onto a subway train. The Devil follows, and his body is destroyed when it is struck by a train. Returning to his natural form, Satan emerges as a ferocious and horrifying presence as he pursues Cane and Christine into a church. The hour of midnight is approaching, and the Devil possesses the body of Cane. He is about to overcome the prone Christine when Jericho regains momentary control and hurls himself onto a statue of an angel holding a sword. Midnight passes, and the enraged Devil leaves Cane's body and returns to hell. Mortally wounded, Jericho sees a vision of his wife and daughter coming to greet him, and he dies peacefully as Christine watches. She kneels beside his still body and whispers, "Thank you."

Performances

Born in Dublin, Gabriel Byrne's original career was as an archaeologist. Among his early roles was a rather sinister portrayal of Lord Byron in Ken Russell's *Gothic* (1986). Unfortunately, he didn't match this rather successful outing in his conception of Satan, but instead plays him as if he were a slick Mafia chieftain. Although he shows a few quick flashes of humor, he seems bitter, impatient, and without any charisma. The heart of the film, and the only scene where he shows any charm, is the long battle of wits as he tempts Jericho in his apartment. For a few moments, he appears convincing, shrewd, and logical, and he comes close to persuading Jericho to fall in with his plans. It is the best-written and best-acted scene in the film as well. In it, Byrne seems a bit reminiscent of Al Pacino in *The Godfather Part II* (1974), but it is the only episode that crackles with vitality and ardor. His Devil seems particularly quick-witted when Jericho questions him about the End of Days. "Think of it as a new beginning," he snaps back, "and you'll be in on the ground floor." In scenes with his followers, Byrne comes across as particularly flat, and he disposes of them at the slightest hint of failure. The script also fails to give him enough time to interact with Robin Tunney as Christine. In the apartment, he tells Jericho, "I'll treat her like a queen," but he is never given an opportunity to work his charm on her, and this is a shortcoming.

It should be noted that Schwarzenegger himself plays the Devil briefly in the climax of the picture when Jericho is possessed by Satan, and Arnold carries this out rather well. The name of his character has scriptural overtones, with Jericho derived from the biblical city that was besieged by Joshua and Cane derived from the jealous and wicked son of Adam and Eve. This is also balanced out by Christine's Satanic doctor, whose name is Able, reminding us of the good brother killed by biblical Cane. There are a number of other significant characters' names including Thomas Aquinas, a reference to the noted thirteenth-century scholar and saint.

Jericho Cane is perhaps the most flawed hero that Schwarzenegger has ever played. He is angry, bitter, alcoholic, and generally unpleasant, and Arnold is convincing in his portrayal. In his opening scene, he even toys with the idea of suicide. The Devil relates to Jericho's dark side, which explains why he spends so much time trying to win him over in the apartment scene. Schwarzenegger's acting in this scene is quite good, except for one hilarious outburst when he calls the Devil a choir boy compared to himself. In other moments of the story, Schwarzenegger resorts to his typical schtick, which simply doesn't work in this film. Many of the other supporting players do a fine job. Miriam Margolyes, star of the underappreciated satire *Ed and His Dead Mother*

(1992), does a wonderful job as Christine's demonic stepmother. Rod Steiger is credible as the only sensible cleric in the story, and C. C. H. Pounder is terrific as Jericho's police ally who is controlled by Satan. Finally, Robin Tunney is splendid as Christine, and she displays more depth than any of the other principals.

Notable Quotes

- Every thousand years on the eve of the millennium, the dark angel comes and takes a body and then he walks the Earth looking for a woman to bear his child.... If he consummates your flesh with his human body, he unlocks the gate of hell, and everything as we know it ceases to exist. (**Kovac to Christine, about Satan's intent**)
- Satan's greatest trick was convincing man he didn't exist. (**Kovac to Cane**)
- Let me tell you something about Him. He is the biggest underachiever of all time. He's just got a good publicist, that's all. If something good happens, it's His will. If something bad happens, He moves in mysterious ways. (**the Devil to Cane, talking about God**)
- Jericho, how can you expect to defeat me when you are but a man, and I am forever? (**the Devil upon leaving his host body**)

Equinox
AKA The Beast

1967/1971   Rating: ***   Jack Woods as the Devil

Visto International. Written by Jack Woods and Mark Thomas McGee; Photographed by Mike Hoover; Edited by John Joyce; Music by John Caper; Produced by Jack H. Harris and Dennis Muerin; Directed by Jack Woods. Color, 80 minutes.

Annotated Cast List

Edward Connell (*David Fielding*, student who survives an ordeal in the woods); Barbara Hewitt (*Susan Turner*, his picnic date); Frank Bonner (*Jim Hudson*, student); Robin Christopher (*Vicki*, student and Jim's girlfriend); Jack Woods (*Asmodeus*, the Devil posing as a forest ranger); Fritz Leiber (*Dr. Waterman*, University professor with a cabin in the woods); James Phillips (*Sloan*, reporter); Patrick Burke (*Johanson*, psychiatrist); Jim Duran (orderly); Norville Brooks (*Harrison*, police detective); Irving L. Litchenstein (crazy old man in the cave); Jim Danforth (orderly with syringe); Forrest J Ackerman.

Appraisal and Synopsis

Equinox was originally an amateur 16mm effort made in 1967, which was about forty minutes in length. It included a number of primitive but nevertheless fascinating special effects created by Jim Danforth and David Allen. When film producer Jack Harris viewed the footage a year later, he felt it had potential and decided to finance an expansion of the picture to feature length for theatrical distribution. Several years later, Harris reunited the principal players and shot additional scenes. The end result is somewhat disjointed but compelling, a genuine cult film. At times, it reminds the viewer of *The Blair Witch Project* (1999), since the plot depicts four young people who get lost on a field trip to the woods, with three of them winding up dead and the last survivor insane. The story is a rather unique blend of a traditional Devil tale folded into an H. P. Lovecraft story. The cosmology of these two approaches do not easily mesh, and the film makes no real effort to reconcile them. Although a stretch, the plot is intriguing if erratic. The story unfolds in a rather complicated fashion, involving multiple flashbacks. This synopsis is repackaged in linear fashion.

Dr. Waterman, a university professor and geologist, comes across a strange, ancient book that corresponds to the key ingredient of Lovecraft's Cthulhu Mythos, the *Necronomicon* by the mad Arab, Abdul Alhazred, which contains formulas to contact and summon the Old Ones, a race of ancient beings, dark gods, who once ruled the Earth and most of the universe. The Old Ones are now dormant, sleeping in a different dimension, but awaiting a summons to return and overtake the Earth. Waterman becomes fascinated with the book and tries to employ some of the incantations, unleashing some horrors, including a beast with many tentacles that destroys his cabin in the woods.

Earlier, the professor had contacted his top student, David Fielding, and asked him to come to his cabin. David asks his friend Jim Hudson to take him, and Jim decides to turn it into an outing. His girlfriend, Vicki, prepares a picnic, and they invite a visitor from New York, Susan Turner, to be David's blind date. They drive out to the woods but find Dr. Waterman's cabin a complete wreck. A park ranger introduces himself as Asmodeus and suggests that Dr. Waterman must have returned to the city. The young people hear some strange laughter in a cave, which they investigate. They meet a crazy old man who gives them an ancient book. They open it and find notes from Dr. Waterman describing the book as a bible of evil. The group also catches sight of a medieval castle on top of a nearby hill. They decide to explore it, when an apparently demented Dr. Waterman appears and snatches the book. The boys chase him, and the old professor appears to fall into a stream, hitting his head on a rock. He seems to be dead, but his body disappears moments later. The boys wonder if he has somehow recovered and wandered off while they were distracted. Asmodeus shows up, but David prevents Jim from telling the ranger about Dr. Waterman.

They find some additional notes tucked in the book written by Dr. Waterman in which he further describes the meaning and significance of the text. Using the book, the group prepares some protective amulets to ward off evil. When they separate, Susan is attacked by Asmodeus, who starts to kiss her until he is frightened off by her crucifix pendant. The old man from the cave is pursued and killed by a giant ape-like creature. The creature next attacks the group, but when the boys jab it with a wooden spear, the creature collapses, and its body dematerializes.

The castle on the hill also vanishes, and the group discovers it has slipped into another dimension. Asmodeus questions Jim, asking about the book. When Jim uses his amulet to hold him at bay, Asmodeus offers him a deal, tempting him with wealth, power, or anything he wants in return for the book. Jim runs off, and the four friends join up. It suddenly dawns on them that Asmodeus is one of the names used by the Devil.

The Devil begins a new assault, first creating an eight-foot-tall, dark, primitive man to attack them. When Jim gets trapped in the alternate dimension, David goes in to fetch him, but he is fooled by Asmodeus, who impersonates Jim. One by one, members of the group are killed by Asmodeus when he turns into a flying demon. Finally, David alone escapes, and the Devil warns him that he will be dead "in one year and one day." David reaches the main highway but is struck down by a mysterious car with an invisible driver. Another car stops and transports the injured student to the hospital.

The police and doctors are perplexed by David's story. After telling all he knows, David lapses into a catatonic state, only interested in clinging to Susan's cross for protection. A full year passes, and a reporter speaks with David's psychiatrist at the asylum. The doctor plays the tape of David's initial interview. The reporter finds his story useless, the ramblings of a madman. The asylum orderlies take David's cross away from him, and he cries out in panic. Meanwhile, the image of Susan, presumably the Devil in disguise, approaches the hospital to carry out the death threat against David, and the film ends.

The confusing presentation actually works in the film's favor, giving it a surreal atmosphere. Some scenes are repeated. The scene with David being struck down by the driverless car is shown twice, at the film's beginning and again at the end. Most of the narrative is related through the tape recording played for the reporter by David's doctor. The real bewilderment for the audience is the Devil's motivation. He learns that Dr. Waterman has located the *Necronomicon*, and he wants to obtain it. He poses as the park ranger to achieve his purpose. The identity of the old man in the cave is a complete mystery. This madman somehow retrieved the book from the ruins of Waterman's cabin, only to surrender it to the first people he encounters, David and Jim. The Devil conjures up one of the Old Ones to destroy the old man and then sets about obtaining the book for himself. His motivation is unknown. He seems already able to summon up the Old Ones without the aid of the *Necronomicon*. Why does he want it? If anything, the book would seem to suit his purposes more if it fell into the hands of an amateur enthusiast of black magic, who could cause unlimited mischief with its incantations. Perhaps the Devil's real purpose is to hide the book, leaving his possible rivals, the Old Ones, undisturbed. Possibly the Devil's plans are meant to be indecipherable to mankind. In any case, the film, although very low budget, is extraordinarily fascinating and imaginative, a mad puzzle with no real denouement except that David, like the rest of his friends, is doomed, and the Devil is working on some scheme beyond human understanding. *Equinox* is simultaneously provocative, audacious, inept, clever, intriguing, and just plain fun. That in itself is a pretty impressive accomplishment for any film, not to mention a fringe production shot in two segments four years apart.

Performances

Since *Equinox* is only a semiprofessional film, the standard of the performances is somewhat below par. Fritz Leiber, the famous horror and science fiction writer, appears briefly as Dr. Waterman. His most famous work is *Conjure Wife*, filmed in 1944 as *Weird Woman* (with Anne Gwynne, Evelyn Ankers, and Lon Chaney) and in 1962 as *Burn, Witch, Burn!* (with Janet Blair and Peter Wyngarde). Leiber's father, also named Fritz, was a well-known character actor in the 1930s and 1940s, appearing in such films as *A Tale of Two Cities* (1935), *The Phantom of the Opera* (1943) and *Monsieur Verdoux* (1947). Forrest J Ackerman, editor of *Famous Monsters of Filmland*, served as literary agent for the younger Leiber, and he reportedly provided one of the voices heard on the tape recorder when the film was redubbed. One cast member, Frank Bonner, billed as Frank Boers, Jr., went on to success in television, appearing as advertising salesman Herb Tarlek on "WKRP in Cincinnati" (1978–1982) and as Father Hargis, the head of a Catholic boys' school in "Just the Ten of Us" (1988–1990).

Jack Woods as Asmodeus, the Devil, probably delivers the best performance in the film. Slightly resembling Robert Ryan, Woods effectively projects the cold brutality that is a Ryan trademark. It is quite intriguing to watch Satan wander around in the guise of a park ranger. At one point, the Devil transforms into Jim, and Frank Bonner conveys Satan's icy demeanor quite well. The Devil's most spectacular transformation is into a winged demon, reminiscent of a Doré print. Watching the Devil swoop down on his helpless victims is one of the highlights of the picture and one of the finest moments in all Devil movies. Woods' weakest moment, however, is the scene in which he kisses Susan. The image of his drooling, open mouth approaching the camera is absurd, and it is foolishly repeated several times. Woods' Satan derives some of his powers from his silver ring, and the actor/director uses the prop well. The Devil's final appearance is as a huge, menacing shadow, reminiscent of a scene from the 1926 *Faust*. Everything considered, *Equinox* is a most impressive and imaginative minor effort produced on a minuscule budget.

Notable Quotes

• This is some piece of literature, only it is going to be a little difficult to follow without a translation. (**Jim to his friends, while examining the *Necronomicon***)

• So we'll make a deal. Let me tell you, I can make a deal like nobody you ever saw. (**the Devil to Jim**)

• You will not escape. In one year and one day, you will be dead (**the Devil, in the form of a huge shadow, to the fleeing David**)

The Evil
AKA House of Evil

1978   Rating: *   Victor Buono as the Devil

New World Pictures. Written by Galen Thompson; Photographed by Mario Di Leo; Edited by Jack Kirschner; Music by John Fresco and Johnny Harris; Produced by Ed Carlin, Paul A. Joseph and Malcolm Levinthal; Directed by Gus Trikonis. Color, 88 minutes.

Annotated Cast List

Richard Crenna (*C. J. Arnold*, psychologist); Joanna Pettet (*Caroline Arnold*, his wife, a medical doctor); Andrew Prine (*Raymond Guy*, Professor helping the Arnolds); Mary Louise Weller (*Laurie Belman*, student and Guy's girlfriend); Cassie Yates (*Mary Harper*, drug rehabilitation staff member); George O'Hanlon (*Pete Brooks*, cook); Lynne Moody (*Felicia Allen*, former addict and program assistant); George Viharo (*Dwight*, Arnold's handyman); Ed Bakey (*Sam*, caretaker of the Vargas estate); Milton Selzer (*Decker*, realtor); Galen Thompson (*Emilio Vargas*, ghost of the original owner of the house); Emory Souza (demon); Victor Buono (the Devil).

Appraisal and Synopsis

This is a rather unimaginative, by-the-numbers horror film that is unable to either terrify or even hold the interest of its audience. A large isolated mansion, the Vargas House, is purchased by the Arnolds, who intend to run it as a medical retreat and center for drug rehabilitation patients. When they and a group of their friends and work/study students arrive to clean up and prepare the facility, which was uninhabited for many years, they find themselves locked in and subject to a series of supernatural attacks. The plot borrows bits and pieces from *The Haunting* (1963), *The House on Haunted Hill* (1958), *The Legend of Hell House* (1973), and other films but lacks any of the style, flair, or Gothic poetry of these classics. This independently financed picture was intended as an advance rip-off of *The Amityville Horror* (1979), beating it to the theaters by many months. Unfortunately, *The Evil* turned out to be so flat and dull that the Devil was drafted into the story to liven it up, but obviously the producers were of two minds because some prints were released without the Devil's sequence in it. As it stands, the scene with the Devil near the end of the film is the most interesting part, although it comes too late in the story to save the picture.

The Evil opens with the caretaker of Vargas House being mysteriously burned to death as he inspects the structure. Psychologist C. J. Arnold and his wife, Caroline, a physician, arrive to take charge of the place. Professor Raymond Guy brings along his girlfriend, work/study student Laurie. Other staff for their rehabilitation center include handyman Dwight, cook Pete, and program assistants Mary and Felicia. Shortly after their arrival, Mary's dog heads down to the cellar, becomes frightened, and disappears. Caroline, a psychic, repeatedly sees the ghost of Emilio Vargas, the original owner of the mansion. He leads her to find his diary, but all the pages are blank except for one with biblical verse. She takes it as a warning that they should leave, but C. J. dismisses it as simply an interesting old book. Mary and Felicia find the charred remains of the caretaker while searching for Mary's dog. C. J., searching through the cellar, finds a trap door sealed with a crucifix. He opens the locked door and leaves, after which an earthquake occurs and a mysterious force rises from the depths. Dwight is electrocuted by a loose generator cable, and all the doors and windows in the house slam shut and lock by themselves. The Arnolds and the others find themselves unable to leave as the house has sealed itself tight.

One by one, the occupants are killed by a supernatural force. C. J. locates an open window in the tower room, and Pete is killed by a lightning strike when he tries to shimmy to the ground on a rope. Mary is knocked over the banister at the top of a stairway by her dog who had suddenly reappeared. Professor Guy cuts off his hand with a rotary blade while trying to cut through the front door, but Caroline seals the wound and saves his life. Laurie is devoured by an unseen demon. Felicia is shocked to death when she backs into an electrical grid when the dead body of Mary comes at her. Guy crashes through a window but then vanishes in a patch of quicksand. Unbelievable death scenes like these were satirized in the silly but occasionally witty *Bloodbath at the House of Death* (1983).

C. J. and Caroline reread Vargas' book and identify the verse as Revelation 20:1–3, which describes the binding of Satan in a pit for a thousand years. Vargas takes control of Caroline's body and reveals that he had issued numerous warnings to frighten them away, but C. J. released "the evil" when he removed the crucifix that sealed the pit. He instructs him to reseal the trap door before it is too late. They head to the cellar and try to close the door but instead are pulled into the opening. C. J. wanders into a glowing, luminous chamber where the Devil sits cackling in an enormous chair. He orders C. J. to destroy the crucifix and mentally projects pain at C. J. when he refuses. Caroline rushes into the room and uses the cross as a weapon to stab the Devil in his chest. He topples backward, and the Arnolds escape, climb out of the pit, and reseal the trap door with the crucifix. The mansion returns to normal, and the Arnolds leave by the front door and drive off as the end credits roll.

Performances

Victor Buono was only forty years old when he made his brief appearance in *The Evil*, but he seems far older, and he died only a few years after completing the film. He was often compared to Laird Cregar, another heavy-set actor who played the Devil and had a brief but meteoric career. Buono was far more obese than Cregar, and he made an immediate impact in film, being nominated for an Academy Award as best supporting actor for his role in *Whatever Happened to Baby Jane?* (1962). He also starred in a decent thriller, *The Strangler* (1964), as a sympathetic murderer. Buono's contribution is the highlight of the film, and he plays a bemused Satan dressed all in white. He wears no makeup at first, but as he becomes enraged at Richard Crenna's lack of cooperation, he sprouts thick, short horns on his head, and his white hair and beard darken. His performance displays a considerable range for such a brief part, revealing charm, humor, and a distinct streak of sadism. If Buono's role had been expanded and had he entered the film at an earlier point, he definitely would have improved its quality. As it is, only Joanna Pettet delivers a first-rate performance. Richard Crenna is fine in his earlier scenes, but his characterization suffers as the story enters its supernatural phase, and he is simply awful in the scenes where C. J. becomes possessed. Fortunately, his performance recovers, so his confrontation with Buono comes off in grand style.

Notable Quotes

• I sealed the pit, and you released the evil.... The key is in your hands. Seal the pit. Return the beast. Do not disturb this place again. (**ghost of Vargas to C. J., speaking through Caroline**)

• I feed on terror, Mr. Arnold. Your puny fears give birth to it and you suckle it like swine 'til it overcomes you. (**the Devil to C. J.**)

• This can last an eternity. It drains nothing from me, causes me no discomfort. I expend nothing to hold you here and place you in pain far greater than anything you can imagine possible. I'll snap your stubborn will.... Defy me, you insignificant speck of vomit. (**the Devil, as he inflicts his mental torture on C. J.**)

Fame and the Devil
AKA Al Diavolo la Celebrita

1949   Rating: ****   Aldo Silvani as the Devil

Scaleria Films. Written by Mario Monicelli, Steno, and Edmund Legiardi (English dialogue); Photographed by Leonida Barboni; Edited by Renzo Lucidi; Music by Carlo Franci, Mario Funaro, and Arrigo Boito; Produced by Herman Cohen and Maleno Malenotti; Directed by Mario Monicelli and Steno. B&W, 90 minutes (original version), 80 minutes (English-language version).

Annotated Cast List

Leonardo Cortese (*Franco Bresci*, language scholar); Aldo Silvani (the Devil); Ferruccio Tagliavini (*Gino Marini*, opera singer possessed by Bresci); Marcel Cerdan (*Maurice Cardan*, prizefighter possessed by Bresci); Mischa Auer (*Bernard Stork*, diplomat possessed by Bresci); Marilyn Buferd (*Ellen Rawlins*, Stork's secretary); Carlo Campani (*Amilio Pugliachi*, Bresci's best friend and Stork's cook); William Tubbs (*Antonio*, Cardan's trainer); Franca Marzi (*Flora*, Cardan's girlfriend); Alba Arnova, Folco Lulli, Giuseppe Pierozzi, Caesare Polacco, Gianni Rizzo.

Appraisal and Synopsis

This little-known but delightful fantasy has many elements in common with *Here Comes Mr. Jordan* (1941). Both films feature an individual who is transferred from body to body in pursuit of a specific goal. Both involve professional boxers and feature extensive ring action in the course of the story. A supernatural being assists the main character in both films. In *Here Comes Mr. Jordan*, it is an angel played by Claude Rains. In *Fame and the Devil*, it is Satan who performs this function. Most unusually, the Devil is given a rather sympathetic treatment. Another unusual feature is the casting, which used an actual boxer, the middleweight champ Marcel Cerdan, and a genuine opera star, Ferruccio Tagliavini, to portray the prizefighter and the tenor in the film.

The picture opens at a news conference in Rome held by Bernard Stork, spokesman for the Universal Relief Commission, known as the URC. Stork asks his secretary, Ellen Rawlins, to locate an interpreter for that evening's banquet in honor of the prince of Lower Tibet, who is considering joining the URC. She is unable to track one down until Amilio, Stork's chef, informs her that his best friend in Rome is Professor Bresci, an expert in Asian languages. She visits Bresci, a shy young scholar, to recruit him. The professor becomes infatuated with Ellen and mistakenly provides Stork with a mistranslation for his toast. Thinking Stork has called his wife a cow, the prince and his entourage storm out of the banquet, colliding with Amilio, who spills a tray of food all over the prince.

Ellen drives home the tongue-tied professor, who is unable to express his feelings for her. Alone in his room, the depressed Bresci takes an amulet of the Devil, one of his many artifacts, and tosses it out of the window. Moments later, the Devil pays him a visit, returning the amulet. He offers to make the professor a celebrity, so he can pursue Ellen. He tells Bresci that the famous opera star Gino Marini has just committed suicide, and he could transfer his soul immediately to the tenor's body, and he would be an instant celebrity. The Devil works his magic, and Bresci vanishes into thin air, awakening moments later in the body of Marini. He telephones Amilio to explain his strange experience. The chef is convinced by the strange tale after meeting Marini face to face. He agrees to help his friend in his quest to win Ellen.

Stork and his party are invited to the opera. They arrive to hear Marini sing a selection from Boito's *Mefistofele*. He sends an invitation through Amilio for Ellen and Stork to visit his apartment. As Marini, Bresci talks quietly but confidently to the girl he loves. Unfortunately, Marini's wife comes roaring in and kicks the guests out. Marini, unaware he is married, flees to his bedroom and invokes the Devil. At first, Satan suggests he could murder his wife, but he then offers to transfer him into the body of another notable man to try again with Ellen, who is heading to Mexico with Stork and the URC delegation.

Preparing for a championship fight in Mexico City, the boxer Maurice Cardan has a fatal car crash, and the Devil transfers Bresci to his dead body just as help reaches the scene. Bresci soon learns that boxing promoter Ramirez is a crook who wants Cardan to take a dive in his next bout. Bresci befriends Antonio, his trainer, who fills him in on the situation. Cardan is pursued by Flora, an unscrupulous woman who intends to use him. Cardan slips away to the hotel where the URC group is staying. He meets up with Amilio, who was fired by Stork, and tells him he is now Cardan. Two men get fresh with Ellen in the hotel bar, and he rescues her. In the turmoil, Amilio accidentally knocks Stork over with a tray of food. Ellen promises Cardan that she will attend his championship fight. Ramirez orders Cardan to throw the bout since he has wagered a huge sum that he will lose. Unwilling to take a beating in front of Ellen and wishing to help Antonio, who bet on him to win, Cardan battles hard and manages to win the fight. Outraged, Ramirez ties up the boxer and plans to kill him. Bresci summons the Devil, who agrees to help him again, this time placing his soul inside the body of someone very near to Ellen. He explains that Stork was just assassinated, and using his body Bresci could devote his full attention to winning Ellen.

As Stork, Bresci has to address a conference in Paris. He rehires Amilio and tells him about his latest transference. He attempts to woo Ellen, who rejects his advances. She tells him that she is actually in love with Professor Bresci. Stunned, Stork wants to return to his original body. At the Paris conference, Stork and the entire audience are attacked by an assassin with an "atomic pill" who blows up the hall.

Bresci awakens back in his original body in Rome and learns that it is actually the day following the fiasco with the Tibetan prince. Amilio tells him that Stork wants to hire him permanently as a URC staff member. It appears the prince has been overthrown during the night by a coup, and since Stork had insulted the fallen leader, the new government plans to join the URC. When Bresci meets Ellen, he grabs her and kisses her passionately. They declare their love for each other. While being driven to URC headquarters, Bresci spots the Devil posing as a traffic cop. He smiles and winks at Bresci, apparently pleased that the professor has finally won the girl of his dreams.

Although the plot moves swiftly, it is difficult to conceive what audience the filmmakers had in mind. The first half features operatic aria and sophisticated comedy. The second half blends slapstick and a rather brutal and convincingly staged boxing match. Many viewers would love the first half and hate the second or vice versa. The two segments don't blend easily. At the end, the film makes a gesture of stitching them together by having the driver of the car turn on the radio, which features the news of Cardan's triumph in the ring followed by an aria sung by Marini. It is uncertain if the body shifts had actually occurred (followed by a shift in time) or were merely a vision projected by the Devil so that Bresci would gain confidence to approach Ellen as himself. The latter seems the most likely interpretation since there is no indication that Marini had committed suicide nor that Cardan was involved in a car accident. In any case, the picture was promoted in an awkward fashion that completely distorted the plot, suggesting that three different men sold their souls to the Devil competing over a beautiful woman. The film involved no soul bartering, and the three men were the same person inhabiting three different bodies. Many critics were equally confused in their reviews, which no doubt hurt the film's box office. The tragic death of Cerdan in a plane crash in October 1949 also cast a pall over the picture, as did the unexpected serious illness of Tagliavini at the time of the film's release. Fortunately, Tagliavini made a full recovery and lived into the mid-nineties. Mischa Auer, however, avoided the film's curse and suffered no misfortune.

Most scenes in the film were shot twice, in both English and Italian, although several dubbed scenes are also present in the English version, which is ten minutes shorter, mostly due to the elimination of two additional arias by Tagliavini. *Fame and the Devil* was also the first screen credit for Steno, who later wrote, directed, and acted in over sixty films, including *Nero's Mistress* (1956), *Flatfoot* (1973), and *Dr. Jekyll Jr.* (1979). Steno's actual name was Stefano Vanzina. His son, Carlo Vanzina, is an extremely productive director in the Italian film industry.

Performances

Aldo Silvani (1891–1964) was a veteran of scores of Italian films. American audiences might recognize him best as Mr. Giraffe in *La Strada* (1954) or as Charles in the Humphrey Bogart film *Beat the Devil* (1954), which was lensed in Italy. Silvani's most memorable role was the lead in *Rigoletto* (1954) for which opera star Tito Gobbi provided the singing voice. Silvani plays a most atypical Devil, rather bohemian in appearance, as if he were an eccentric art critic. He usually wears a flashy scarf In his initial appearance before the professor, he claims that Bresci tossed the amulet at precisely the right hour, the stroke of midnight while invoking the Devil's name, which fulfilled the ancient purpose of the talisman. The Devil never presses any claim on Bresci's soul. He seems to feel sorry for the gentle scholar and simply tries to help him in his love life without any recompense. At one point in midstory, he remarks that it would be nice if Bresci would commit murder, but he gently sighs that the professor is not "the sort" to do it. Silvani's quiet, dry humor presents a side of the Devil seldom seen, a good-natured meddler who decides to do a good deed in Bresci's case as a change of pace. Leonardo Cortese is excellent as the professor, but large credit must also go to Tagliavini, Cerdan, and Auer, who effectively create the illusion to maintain Bresci's personality. Marilyn Buferd is also stunning and appealing as Ellen, his Dulcinea.

Notable Quotes

• You've dreamed of wealth, fame, power? Well then, I'm in a position to make all of your fondest dreams come true right away. You want to become famous, become a great man, a celebrity, so as to overcome your shyness and be able to win the heart of a girl named Ellen. (**the Devil to Bresci**)

• You must have been watched over by some angel. (**Antonio to Cardan at the scene of his car accident**)

Or some Devil. (**Bresci, as Cardan, in reply**)

• The Devil is very powerful. If you are nice to him, he will help you, but if you are not, it is just too bad. (**Bresci to Ellen**)

Faust

1926   Rating: *****   Emil Jannings as the Devil

UFA. Written by Hans Kyser, based on the *Faust* plays by Goethe and Marlowe and German legend; Photographed by Carl Hoffmann; Edited by F. W. Murnau; Special Effects by Robert Herlth and Walter Röhrig; Produced by Erich Pommer; Directed by F. W. Murnau. B&W, silent, 116 minutes (original version), 89 minutes (standard version).

Annotated Cast List

Gösta Ekman (*Johannes Faust*, elderly professor); Emil Jannings (*Mephistopheles*, the Devil); Camilla Horn (*Gretchen*, Faust's lover); Werner Fütterer (*Archangel Michael*, wagers with Mephistopheles over Faust); Frieda Richard (Gretchen's mother); Yvette Guilbert (*Martha Scherdtlein*, Gretchen's aunt); William Dieterle (*Valentine*, Gretchen's brother); Eric Barclay (count of Parma); Hanna Ralph (duchess of Parma); Hans Rameau (farmhand); Lothar Muthel (monk); Hertha von Walther, Emmy Wyda.

Appraisal and Synopsis

The *Faust* legend was a favorite subject of early filmmakers, dating back to the French cinema pioneer Georges Méliès, who made three *Faust* films starting in 1898. Over a dozen of these pictures were made, and many of them are now lost. These films are enumerated in the first appendix. Friedrich Wilhelm Murnau, director of the classics *Nosferatu* (1922) and *The Last Laugh* (1924), helmed the most prestigious and famous screen version of *Faust*, the yardstick against which all other versions are measured. The technique of German expressionism is fully utilized in this picture, and critics have rated it as the finest use of chiaroscuro in film history. Frequent smoke, diffuse lighting, masterful sets, and miniatures are expertly used to create unforgettable screen magic. Unfortunately, most of the film's brilliance occurs in the first half, and interest starts to drag when the focus switches from Faust and Mephistopheles to Gretchen in the second half. The same criticism, however, holds true of Goethe's original drama. Also in this version, Lucifer and Mephistopheles are one being as opposed to the version by Christopher Marlowe, who casts them as two separate personalities. Nevertheless, the screenplay by Hans Kyser relies on Marlowe as well as on elements of the original legend.

The picture opens with a verbal confrontation between Lucifer and Archangel

Michael over possession of the Earth. They place a wager on the soul of Faust. If Lucifer can turn Faust away from God, then Michael will acknowledge the Devil's sovereignty over the Earth. The archangel's challenge, resembling God's earlier joust with Satan in the Old Testament over Job, is perplexing, because there is no downside for the Devil. He has nothing to lose by participating and working his worst mischief upon the unfortunate victim chosen by heaven. All the adversity and misery unleashed by this bet could rightly be attributed to the archangel, who provoked the contest. Murnau stages this encounter with extraordinary style and atmosphere.

The Devil sweeps down to Earth, his cloak covering the land like a black cloud. Lucifer initiates a terrible plague over the city inhabited by the aged Faust. The people appeal to the scholar for help in saving them. With the existence of his entire community at stake, Faust summons Mephistopheles to ask his help in ending the pestilence. Disguised as an old monk, the Devil appears and offers Faust a contract. When the scholar hesitates, the Devil offers him a twenty-four-hour trial offer. Faust signs the pact in blood with the stipulation that he can back out of the deal after one day. As depicted by Goethe, Faust's deal commits Mephistopheles to be his servant until Faust experiences one moment of perfect contentment.

Faust ends the deadly plague, but the crowd of supplicants becomes enraged when they notice that Faust is no longer able to look at the crucifix. They attack the scholar for consorting with the Devil, and Faust falls into despair. Mephistopheles brings back Faust's youth and assumes a more youthful appearance as well, as he leads Faust in a quest for pleasure. He calls up the image of the most beautiful woman in Italy, the duchess of Parma, and Faust orders the Devil to bring him to her. Mephistopheles flies him on his billowing cloak, passing an entire flock of winged devils. He intends to dazzle Faust with such splendors that he will forget about the twenty-four-hour deadline to cancel their agreement. When the moment of opportunity arrives, Faust is on the verge of seducing the beauty, and he decides to retain his youth and pledge his soul permanently to Satan.

As time passes, Mephistopheles is bewildered by Faust's insatiability. Faust catches a glimpse of the modest and lovely Gretchen, and he asks Mephistopheles to plot out his campaign to win her. An extended courtship follows, during which time Mephistopheles courts Martha, Gretchen's aunt. After Faust wins Gretchen's love, the Devil maneuvers to allow Valentine, Gretchen's brother, to stumble across the lovers. Mephistopheles kills Valentine as he fights with Faust, forcing the scholar to flee. At this point, Faust abandons Gretchen, who is seen as a fallen woman by the community. She offers public penance by standing at the pillory in the town square. Later, Gretchen has a baby, who perishes from exposure during a snowstorm when Gretchen is unable to find anyone who will grant her shelter. She is arrested and charged with infanticide. When news of this reaches Faust, who is in another part of the country, he orders Mephistopheles to bring him to Gretchen at once. The Devil deliberately tries to delay carrying out this order, but Faust insists.

Horrified that Gretchen is condemned to death, Faust curses youth as an illusion, and Mephistopheles turns him back into an old man. Faust goes to Gretchen's execution, and she recognizes the old man as her lover. Faust joins her as she is burned at the stake, and the archangel proclaims that this act has redeemed Faust, and the Devil loses his wager. Mephistopheles withdraws and the film ends.

Faust received instant recognition as one of the masterpieces of world cinema, although in Germany itself the picture was not the towering financially success that it was in the rest of the world. A shortened version that was produced initially for Canada became the standard version in later releases. The original version was recently revived. The most powerful aspect of *Faust* is its compelling mastery of visual storytelling. On the large screen, the film must have been breathtakingly stunning. One weakness that stands out in the last half of the film is the rather poor job Faust does in using the powers of Mephistopheles. When Valentine is wounded, for example, Faust could have ordered Mephistopheles to save him, but he doesn't. He also could have ordered the Devil to free Gretchen and transport both of them to safety far away.

After completing *Faust*, Murnau moved to America, where he directed *Sunrise* (1927), perhaps the greatest film cinemagraphically of the silent era. Unfortunately, Murnau died in an automobile accident four years after moving to Hollywood, an irrevocable loss to world cinema. He was only forty-three years old at the time of his death.

Performances

The leading star of the German silent cinema, Emil Jannings, believed he had been born in Brooklyn, but later records showed that his parents had moved to Switzerland by the time of his birth. Among his famous screen roles were those of King Louis XV, Danton, King Henry VIII, Othello, Peter the Great, and the tragic doorman in *The Last Laugh* (1924). In sound films he made a big splash with Marlene Dietrich in *The Blue Angel* (1930), but his association with the Nazi film industry overshadowed the later years of his career. His performance a Mephistopheles is regarded as one of the highlights of his career, although several critics have blamed him for excessive scene stealing and overacting, particularly in his scenes with Yvette Guilbert as Martha. On the other hand, his early scenes with Archangel Michael and the elderly Faust are simply magnificent. His appearance goes through several transformations. With Michael, he is Lucifer the fallen angel, hairless with horns and massive black wings. With old Faust, he is a grizzled monk, but when Faust regains his youth, Mephistopheles likewise assumes a younger appearance, and he dresses in the traditional black costume with a feathered skullcap that is associated with the operatic *Faust* by Charles Gounod. Jannings milks his role as a crafty schemer, always several steps ahead of Faust, who never figures out how to command the Devil to be his servant. Gösta Ekman is an intriguing Faust, basically tricked into turning to the Devil for the purest motives: saving his community from the plague. The transition from the compassionate Faust to the insatiable pleasure seeker is never fully satisfactory, but he is able to match Jannings in their scenes together, and their onscreen chemistry is one of the strengths of the film. He does not have a similar chemistry with Camilla Horn as Gretchen, a role originally intended for Lillian Gish. William Dieterle, who played Gretchen's doomed brother, Valentine, soon after abandoned acting for directing, eventually helming another diabolical masterpiece, *The Devil and Daniel Webster* (1942).

Notable Quotes

• Withdraw! Stop! Why dost thou scourge mankind with war, plague, and famine? (**Archangel Michael to Satan**)

The Earth is mine. (**the Devil's response**)

• Blood is a juice of rarest quality. (**Satan's comment as Faust signs his pact**)

• Thou hast darted from pleasure to pleasure, experienced raptures untested before, but nothing satisfies you. (**the Devil to Faust, remarking on his insatiable nature**)

• One word makes thy agreement null and void—love! (**Archangel Michael to the Devil**)

Faust

1994   Rating: ****   Petr Cepek as the Devil

Anthanor. Written by Jan Svankmajer and George Roublcek, using excerpts from the *Faust* plays by Marlowe, Goethe, and Grabbe; Photographed by Svatopluk Maly; Edited by Marle Zemanova and Alan Brett; Special Effects by Bedrich Glaser; Music by Charles Gounod and Johann Sebastian Bach; Produced by Jaromir Kallista and Colin Rose (English version); Directed by Jan Svankmajer and Matt McCarthy (English version). Color, 97 minutes.

Annotated Cast List

Petr Cepek (*Faust*, scholar who signs a pact with the Devil, and *Mephistopheles*, the Devil); Andrew Sachs (all character voices, English version); Jan Kraus, Vladimir Kudla, Antonin Zacpal, Jiri Suchy.

Appraisal and Synopsis

Czech filmmaker Jan Svankmajer gained much of his expertise during a twenty-year stint as a theatrical designer and director, and this mastery is clearly evident throughout *Faust*. His 1988 rendition of *Alice in Wonderland* created an international sensation for its ingenuity and brilliance. *Faust* is similar in many ways, combining an array of techniques such as animation, claymation, puppetry, and live action in a dazzling display. The result is not a literal retelling of the *Faust* legend, but a phantasmagoria, a free-flowing impression of elements of the story, a blend of everyday reality with outrageous flights of fancy. For his text, Svankmajer selected various fragments of the well-known *Faust* dramas, principally those by Christopher Marlowe and Goethe to a lesser extent, as well as the lesser known *Don Juan und Faust* by Christian Dietrich Grabbe, a colorful 1829 drama. Elements of Gounod's opera *Faust*, Weber's *Der Freischütz*, and puppet theatricals are also employed. Linear plot development is meaningless in this surreal adventure, but several guideposts to the production will be noted.

The film begins in modern-day Prague, where an ordinary Everyman, Faust, is handed a flyer by two pamphleteers outside a subway station. At his drab apartment, the man cracks open a magical egg while eating supper, and this somehow inspires him to puzzle out the elusive pictorial directions printed on the flyer. It eventually leads him to an underground labyrinth beneath a theater where he finds an ancient manuscript, perhaps Marlowe's play. Faust dresses in a medieval costume from the theater's stockroom, puts on makeup, and enacts the scene from *Doctor Faustus* in which Mephistopheles is summoned. Fairly traditional up until this point, the plot jumps wildly between a puppet farce set in the underground chambers while intermingling live action and theatrics performed on the stage of the playhouse above. Fragments of the story are always being presented, whether in a grassy meadow or on a mountaintop in the real world or in the dressing room where Faust, as performer, relaxes between scenes. At times, life-sized marionettes break out of the theater and run around the streets of Prague. In another sequence, Faust goes to a sidewalk cafe where he uses a drill to tap into a geyser of wine, which emerges from the wooden top of his table. In between, we hear segments from Marlowe, Goethe, Grabbe, and the Gounod opera. The theater audience pays rapt attention to most of the action, and Faust himself is transformed into a puppet in several scenes. When Faust attempts to repent, the Devil adopts the disguise of a woman to seduce Faust and prevent his reconciliation with God. Faust's twenty-four-year deal with the Devil passes in a twinkling. Faust hires two thugs to ward off the Devil when he approaches to claim his soul, but these wooden puppets are set aflame by Lucifer and Mephistopheles. Faust runs out of the theater into the street where he is run over by a car and killed. The pamphleteers from the start of the picture smile at each other as they watch his demise, and an old man pulls Faust's leg from underneath the car, wraps it in newspaper, and runs off with it. A policeman opens the door of the car, but no one is there, and the shot of the empty interior of the vehicle is the last one in the picture, followed by the credits.

Svankmajer's film is an exhilarating experience, but a thorough knowledge of Faust and the various dramas is really needed to fully appreciate the production. One disappointment is that many visuals concentrate on the unseen puppeteer's hands, which are continually manipulating the figures or rattling a metal sheet to simulate thunder whenever Mephistopheles is about to appear. Since Svankmajer drew special attention to these hands, did he intend for them to represent God, Goethe, or himself? By the conclusion, he has provided no hint whatsoever of his intent.

Performances

Petr Cepek is one of the best-known Czech actors, and he appears in almost every scene of this film as Faust. Mephistopheles' scenes are relatively brief, but Cepek is wonderful in both roles. Whenever Mephistopheles appears, his presence begins as a claymation head that protrudes up from the floor in front of Faust, and his face slowly transforms and starts to take on the features of Faust himself, except for his eyebrows, which are thicker, wider, and flared upward. The lighting of his face is from beneath, which enhances his sinister look. If angered, he bears exaggerated fangs. As he talks, Mephistopheles' facial movements are never smooth but electronically altered with static blips like the computer generated-character from the old ABC television series "Max Headroom." His voice, provided by Andrew Sachs, is flat and hollow, with echo-chamber reverberations. Mephisto, as he sometimes refers to himself, also appears in other forms, but he always assumes the features of Faust for any extended conversation. The visual of Faust conversing with a talking head-duplicate of himself is striking and among the most memorable images of the film. The character of the evil angel from Marlowe's text appears in the film in the form of a Devil marionette. Sachs uses an exaggerated accent, reminiscent of Bela Lugosi or, more precisely, of Joe Flaherty as Count Floyd from "SCTV" doing a bad Lugosi accent with babbling moans. These moments are rather corny but fit in entirely with the zany nature of this production. Lucifer later appears in marionette form, notably in the final scene to collect the soul of Faust, but his countenance is a disappointment compared to many others seen during the story. On the whole, Sachs' mastery of voices is amazing, and it is startling to hear the great variety he creates in the film.

Notable Quotes

- I am but a humble follower of great Lucifer, and may not follow thee without his leave. (**Mephistopheles to Faust when summoned by him**)
- How comes it then that thou are now out of hell with me? (**Faust to Mephistopheles**)

Why, this is hell, nor am I out of it. (**Mephistopheles**)

- I'm learning the Devil knows no more than we poor fools. (**Faust during his intermission break**)
- If you wish to catch a bird, do not throw a stone at it. (**Lucifer to Faust**)

Fear No Evil

1981   Rating: **   Stefan Arngrim and
Richard J. Silverthorn as the Devil

Avco Embassy. Written by Frank LaLoggia; Photographed by Fred Goodich; Edited by Edna Ruth Paul; Special Effects by Peter Kuran and John Seay; Music by Frank LaLoggia; Produced by Frank LaLoggia and Charles M. LaLoggia; Directed by Frank LaLoggia. Color, 99 minutes.

Annotated Cast List

Richard J. Silverthorn (*Rosario Bonamo*, eccentric architect, actually Lucifer); Stefan Arngrim (*Andrew Williams*, teenage reincarnation of Lucifer); Elizabeth Hoffman (*Margaret*, earthly disguise of Archangel Michael); Jack Holland (*Fr. Thomas Damon*, earthly disguise of Archangel Raphael); Kathleen Rowe McAllen (*Julie Fanshaw*, earthly form of Archangel Gabriel); Frank Birney (*Fr. Arthur Daly*, church pastor); Barry Cooper (*Barry Williams*, Andrew's father); Alice Sachs (*Marion Williams*, Andrew's mother); Paul Haber (*Mark Landers*, Julie's boyfriend); Mari Anne Simpson (*Brenda*, student); Joyce Bumpus (*Susan*, student); Patricia Decillis (*Bette*, student); Daniel Eden (*Tony*, leader of school clique); Roslyn Gugino (*Marie*, Tony's girlfriend); Chris Devincentis (*Richard*, student); Malcolm Hegge (*Tommy*, student); Robert Kuhn (*Steve*, student); Don O'Neil (*Mr. Altman*, teacher); Philip E. Roy (gym teacher); Jeff Richter (Christ in Passion play); Pam Morris (Mary in Passion play); Toby Gold (reporter); Dick Burt (mayor); Frank Montesanto (hermit); Joe LaLoggia (drunk).

Appraisal and Synopsis

Fear No Evil is regarded as a minor cult film in some circles. No doubt there is much to admire in the fortitude and ingenuity of young filmmaker Frank LaLoggia in raising the funds and creating this film in and around Rochester, New York. There are a number of excellent moments in terms of style and vision. Unfortunately, the picture ultimately fails to hang together. This becomes even more apparent upon watching the film a second or third time, when the inconsistencies and lapses render the picture incomprehensible. Some reviewers mistakenly refer to young Andrew Williams as the Antichrist, a mistake engendered by LaLoggia himself, who uses a punk song, "I Am the Antichrist," on his chaotic soundtrack. In the script, however, he clearly indicates that Andrew is the Devil himself reincarnated. Much of the confusion is also due to poor exposition in the script. The self-awareness of Satan and Archangels Michael, Gabriel, and Raphael, is never clarified, which undermines the plot throughout the story. Most of LaLoggia's characters are inadequately developed. The major disappointment with *Fear No Evil* is that the young filmmaker came very close to accomplishing a major feat. Up until the high school scenes, the picture is masterful, with brilliant touches such as the montage of the front yard of the Williams house, which calls to mind the breakfast montage in *Citizen Kane* (1941). Unfortunately, the level of excellence quickly dissipates.

The film opens with a superb prologue, relying on a series of religious artworks illustrating the basic premise of the conflict between good and evil. This was no doubt added at the last minute to try to bring some coherence to the plot, revealing that God assigned three warrior archangels to be born on Earth to track down and outwit Lucifer when he is incarnated in human form. As the narration concludes, the scene shifts to a figure in a small boat approaching an island in Lake Erie off the coast of New York. The opening shot is reminiscent of Arnold Böcklin's famous painting *The Island of the Dead*, which also inspired a Val Lewton film in 1945. This classy opening quickly dissipates into a rambling battle between Fr. Thomas Damon, actually Archangel Raphael, and the Devil, masquerading as Rosario Bonamo, an eccentric wealthy architect with the ability to transform himself into a beautiful woman. The Devil leads the priest on a wild chase through a half-built, labyrinthian castle. Finally, Bonamo kills himself by causing the metal crozier carried by the priest to fly through the air and pierce him through the chest. He announces, "I will be reborn" before collapsing. Lightning strikes the ground, and the opening credits roll. Later in the film we learn that the priest is tried for the murder of Bonamo, and he passes away in prison. Before he dies, he summons his sister, Margaret, who is actually the reincarnation of Archangel Michael. Raphael promises to look after Michael in his angelic form and to seek out Archangel Gabriel, who was also supposed to be born as a human but who has not yet appeared.

Lucifer is reborn as Andrew Williams (with that name one keeps expecting him to start a crooning career). While a baby, he is brought to church to be baptized, but the ceremony is interrupted by unseen forces, which cause the baptismal water to turn into blood. Marion, Andrew's mother, runs off with the child before the sacrament can be completed. A montage follows showing the outside of the Williams house as the years pass. Marion and Barry Williams grow increasingly hostile to each other, seemingly dominated by their quietly assertive son. On his eighteenth birthday, his mother is crippled in a bizarre accident while his parents are arguing.

At high school, Andrew is a loner, an unpopular straight-A student who appears to be the only good kid in a rough and unruly lot. The top dog of the school gang, Tony, dislikes him and targets him for harassment. Andrew likes Julie, a quiet girl who seems perplexed around him, since he resembles the phantom lover who inhabits her dreams. Julie is secretly engaged to Mark, who is mysteriously killed during a volleyball game in the gym, an accident that Andrew apparently wills to happen. During his free time, Andrew visits the unfinished castle, which he designed years earlier as Bonamo and which he vows to restore.

Julie is visited in her sleep by Archangel Raphael, who inspires her to visit Margaret. After seeking out the kindly old woman, Julie realizes that she herself is the incarnation of Archangel Gabriel, and together with Margaret/Michael, they prepare for their coming battle with the Devil. Margaret approaches Fr. Daly, asking him to cancel his annual Passion play since she has a premonition of disaster, but the priest refuses to listen to her.

Andrew enacts a ritual at the castle and summons the dead bodies of Bonamo's victims, killed and secretly buried on the grounds of the estate, sending them to break up the Passion play, which he finds offensive. The actor playing Christ, during the crucifixion scene, begins to suffer the actual wounds of Christ and dies. The audience starts to flee in panic. Lightning bolts from the sky start to rain down on the panicked crowd. Margaret approaches the corpse of the actor playing Christ, still hanging on the cross. The figure speaks to her with the voice of Raphael, instructing her and Gabriel to take action against Lucifer. The body then bursts into flames, struck by lightning. The two archangels head to the island, bringing the crozier with which Lucifer was killed when he was Bonamo. They pursue Lucifer in a roundabout chase. After trapping him, in an absurd scene they force him to recite the Lord's Prayer. The Devil strikes back, killing Margaret, but he cannot resist the power of the crozier, which starts to glow and becomes transformed into a pillar of pure energy. The spirits of the three archangels appear in this pillar. The Devil shouts his defiance at God, complaining that He broke the promise made to the Devil at the beginning of time. He then vanishes in an explosion of light, and the story concludes.

The final scenes are clumsy, illogical, and the weakest in the film. The resurrection-of-the-dead sequence starts quite promisingly but then goes nowhere as the minions of the dead seem to drop out of the plot and never reach the site of the Passion play, which is instead broken up by a thunderstorm. The cause of the stigmata appearing on the actor playing Christ is not explained and seems to occur with no reference to the rest of the plot. Up until the very end, Julie/Gabriel appears uncertain whether to fight Andrew or embrace him. The conclusion appears empty and unresolved, since there seems to be no reason why the cycle would not continue all over again. The unexplained issues pile up until the story collapses in a complete muddle. The picture as it stands could have been dubbed *I Was a Teenage Satan*, as LaLoggia wastes most of his footage on the dumb antics of the local punk, Tony, and his gang, who target Andrew as an object of ridicule. The subplot with Tony eats up a lot of time, but it is never cleanly integrated into the overall story. Tony and some of his friends coincidentally decide to party on the island when Andrew stages his big show. Andrew finally cuts the arrogant thug down to size, something he could have done sooner instead of using it as a throwaway during the awkward finale. For the most part, the film's technical aspects are fairly good. The cinematography and editing are commendable. The music in the opening scenes is excellent, until the picture bogs down in high school at which point it too becomes a total mess. With so many promising opportunities entirely wasted as the picture unwinds, the primary impact on the audience is one of total frustration.

Performances

The two Devils in the film, played by Richard J. Silverthorn as Bonamo and Stefan Arngrim as Andrew, are not bad but inconsistent. Arngrim, noted principally for his role as young Barry Lockridge in the television series "Land of the Giants," seems rather unsatanic for the most part, a virtual goody two-shoes. The Devil would have had the teenage clique eating out of his hand and at his beck and call, instead of finding himself a target of their teasing. Arngrim seems more like a male counterpart to *Carrie* (1976) rather than the Devil. The only time he shows any powers is the scene in the gym, when he is angered by being required to do extra push-ups, and he takes out his annoyance by staging the deadly volleyball contest. At this point, his eyes take on a serpentlike appearance, as he provokes the gym instructor to sink into temporary madness. The various transformations of the Devil at the end of the picture are too little, too late to have any real import. Arngrim's concept of the Devil as a cool, refined, lonely figure just doesn't pan out with the story. Silverthorn's roaring, aggressive reading seems more in line with the overall film, but ultimately his performance also goes nowhere. Some cast members acquit themselves rather well, including Elizabeth Hoffman, who later played the grandmother who refuses to come down from the mountain in *Dante's Peak* (1997), and Barry Cooper, who steals the film as Andrew's bewildered father who finally accepts the fact that his son is actually Satan.

Notable Quotes

• And God endowed one specific archangel with striking beauty, wisdom, and power. He named him Lucifer, promised him eternal life in heaven. But Lucifer asserted independence and proclaimed himself to be like the Most High. The promise broken and driven from heaven, Lucifer vowed to bring vengeance and suffering on mankind. (**opening narration spoken by Archangel Raphael**)

• Its goal is slavery of all mankind. It's Lucifer, the Devil incarnate. (**Margaret to Fr. Daly**)

• Through I, Lucifer, and the power of the Unholy Trinity, with my brothers Beelzebub and Leviathan, the stay-behind spirits, take these, the flesh of your earthbound servants, and rise, rise, rise! (**the Devil,s summoning the dead to carry out his commands**)

Forbidden Zone

1980   Rating: ***   Danny Elfman as the Devil

Hercules Films. Written by Matthew Bright, Richard Elfman, Mark James, and Mark L. Martinson, based on a story by Richard Elfman; Photographed by Gregory Sandor; Edited by Martin Nicholson; Special Effects by John Nelson; Music by

Danny Elfman; Produced and Directed by Richard Elfman. B&W, 73 minutes.

Annotated Cast List

Hervé Villechaize (*Fausto*, king of the Sixth Dimension); Danny Elfman (the Devil); Susan Tyrrell (*Doris*, queen); Marie-Pascale Elfman (*Susan "Frenchie" Hercules*, first intruder into the Sixth Dimension); Virginia Rose (*Ma Hercules*); Ugh-Fudge Bwana (*Pa Hercules* and *Huckleberry P. Jones,* original owner of the Hercules home); Phil Gordon (*Flash Hercules*, eldest son); Hyman Diamon (*Grandpa Hercules*); Matthew Bright (*Squeezit* and *Rene Henderson,* twins who are friends of Flash); Joe Spinell (Squeezit's father); Giselle Lindley (*Princess*, daughter of Fausto); Viva (ex-queen); Jan Stuart Schwartz (*Busto Rod*, giant frog servant of Fausto); Nicholas James (pope); Albert Brokhim (trumpeter); Dennis Olivier (stuttering student); Kedric Wolfe (schoolteacher); Herman Bernstein (old Yiddish man); Richard Elfman (*Masseuse*, prisoner); the Kipper Kids.

Appraisal and Synopsis

Although not to everyone's taste, *Forbidden Zone* is one of the wildest movies ever made, a genuine cult film that combines surrealism, guerrilla theater, parody, improvisation, rock video, cartoon satire, street dance, and drama of the absurd. The madcap adventure might drive conventional audiences crazy, but it is so audacious, creative, energetic, and enthusiastic that it may be among the most unique seventy-three minutes ever recorded on film. It is a tribute to the Mystic Knights of the Oingo Boingo, an amateur theater ensemble combining diverse elements of Spike Jones, Ernie Kovacs, and Kabuki theater. Excerpts of the group in performance can be found on the video of Danny Elfman's farewell concert with *Oingo Boingo* (Halloween 1995). Richard Elfman, best known as a theatrical director, founded the original group, and his brother Danny Elfman was its musical leader. Later, Danny created his own band, known simply as Oingo Boingo, from the original group.

Filmed in black and white, *Forbidden Zone* employs minimal sets and often uses painted backdrops. It frequently switches to cartoon animation that recalls the heyday of Max Fleisher. *Forbidden Zone* visually references many films and television, from *The Cabinet of Dr. Caligari* (1919) to "The Outer Limits," from jazz short subjects to Charlie Chaplin's *Modern Times* (1936), particularly the scene where Chaplin gets drawn into the innards of the giant machine in the factory. The picture can be seen as primarily a musical, although the music is split between original songs and adaptations, such as "Some of These Days" and "The Alphabet Song" ("B-A Bay, B-E Bee, B-I Bicky-bi, B-O Bo Bicky bi bo, B-U bu, Bicky bi bo bu"). Of course, their lyrics for the letter *f* deviate considerably. The film is defiantly *not* politically correct. The picture spins through many moods: raucous, vulgar, tender, sassy, poignant, ugly, and sublime. It naturally defies conventional synopsis.

Loosely, the action of the film takes place in a strange, ramshackle house where a doorway in the basement is a portal to the Forbidden Zone, another dimension. The original owner of the home, Huckleberry P. Jones, is terrified after finding this doorway, and he sells the place to the Hercules family, consisting of Ma and Pa Hercules; their son, Flash; their daughter, Frenchie; and Gramps. The Henderson twins, Squeezit and Rene, are their frequent guests. Rene is a crossdresser who is so serious about the illusion that he regularly suffers from pseudomenstrual cramps. The youngsters attend a wacky school filled with fellow students as weird and wild as the denizens of the Forbidden Zone. Adventurous Frenchie wanders into the Forbidden Zone, and other family members venture in to rescue her. Frenchie arouses the interest of diminutive King Fausto, ruler of the Sixth Dimension, and Queen Doris imprisons her.

When Squeezit enters the Forbidden Zone, he gets sidetracked to hell. He helps Satan capture Princess, the daughter of Fausto. Nevertheless, the Devil orders his head chopped off, and it flies around and makes strange observations for the rest of the picture. Queen Doris is finally shot to death by Pa Hercules, and King Fausto installs Frenchie as his new consort in a grand ceremonial finale.

Many members of the multitalented Elfman family are present in the film, including Richard's wife, Marie-Pasquale Elfman as Frenchie, and Richard's grandfather, Norman Bernstein, in a small role. Marie also doubled as production designer, and it is interesting to note that the giant dice motif from the film seemed to inspire the lair of Oogie Boogie in *The Nightmare Before Christmas* (1993), for which Danny Elfman served as lead singer, composer, and associate producer.

Performances

Danny Elfman, born in 1952, is one of the outstanding creative talents of our time. First recognized as a singer and pop star with Oingo Boingo, Elfman's fame shifted to his impressive work as a film composer; his major scores, such as *Edward Scissorhands* (1990), *Nightbreed* (1990), and *Dolores Claiborne* (1995), rate among the best soundtracks ever composed. He has been justly recognized as a worthy successor to such giants as Max Steiner, Miklos Rosza, and Bernard Herrmann. If you add to this his popular scores, such as *Batman* (1989), *To Die For* (1995), and *The Nightmare Before Christmas*, the range of his talents grows even more impressive. *Forbidden Zone* offers us a glimpse of Elfman as performer, and his skit as the Devil is also unique, being an enthusiastic parody of Cab Calloway doing "Minnie the Moocher." Our first glimpse of Elfman is as a conductor, when Squeezit is led into a cavern with the traditional message "abandon hope all ye who enter here" overhead. Elfman mimics Calloway's stage antics perfectly. He is dressed in a white suit with white gloves and shoes but black socks. He has a wispy beard extending from his chin, two shiny white horns sticking out of his forehead, two sets of eyebrows, and red lipstick. His song lasts only a few minutes, climaxing in the removal of Squeezit's head at the chopping block. The best moment is when Princess screams, and a cartoonlike insert displays the Devil's head singing within her throat. His demon band marches around, and Elfman's bit ends at the keyboard, as he flashes a sinister and maniacal smile.

Notable Quotes

• Well, sir, let me tell you, I'm so pleased to meet you. The boys and I have been expecting to greet you. I'm just the father of the house of the dead. Now just relax and lay yourself down and say goodbye to your head. Hidee hidee hidee hi! Hodee hodee hodee ho! (**the Devil's song to Squeezit**)

• Why does it feel so good to be so bad? (**Queen Doris' dying words**)

The Greatest Story Ever Told

1965   Rating: ***   Donald Pleasence as the Devil

United Artists. Written by George Stevens and James Lee Barrett in association with Carl Sandberg, from radio scripts and a book by Fulton Oursler and Henry Denker, based on the Bible and other ancient writings; Photographed by William C. Mellor and Loyal Griggs; Special Effects by J. Macmillian Johnson, Clarence Slifer, A. Arnold Gillespie, and Robert Hoag; Edited by Harold F. Kress, Argyle Nelson, Jr., and Frank O'Neill; Music by Alfred Newman, based on selections by George Frederick Handel, Samuel Barber, and Giuseppe Verdi; Produced and Directed by George Stevens. Color, 260 minutes (original version), 199 minutes with overture, intermission, and exit music (standard version).

Annotated Cast List

Max von Sydow (*Jesus Christ*); Dorothy McGuire (*Mary*); Robert Loggia (*Joseph*); Claude Rains (*Herod the Great*, king of Judea); Jose Ferrer (*Herod Antipas*, his son and successor); Marian Seldes (*Herodias*, his wife); Charlton Heston (*John the Baptist*); Donald Pleasence (the Devil); Martin Landau (*Caiaphas*, high priest); Victor Buono (*Sorak*, associate of Caiaphas); David McCallum (*Judas Iscariot*); Gary Raymond (*Peter*, formerly Simon, foremost apostle); Burt Brinckerhoff (*Andrew*, Peter's brother and apostle); Roddy McDowall (*Matthew*, tax collector who becomes an apostle); Robert Blake (*Simon the Zealot*, apostle); David Hedison (*Philip*, apostle); Peter Mann (*Nathaniel*, apostle also known as Bartholomew); Tom Reese (*Thomas*, apostle); David Sheiner (*James the Elder*, apostle); Michael Anderson, Jr. (*James the Younger*, apostle); Jamie Farr (*Thaddeus*, apostle); John Considine (*John*, the Beloved Disciple); Joanna Dunham (*Mary Magdalene*); Michael Tolan (*Lazarus*); Janet Margolen (*Mary of Bethany*, sister of Lazarus); Ina Balin (*Martha of Bethany*, sister of Lazarus); Telly Savalas (*Pontius Pilate*, Roman governor); Johnny Seven (Pilate's aide); Harold J. Stone (*Varus*, Roman general); Paul Stewart (*Questor*); Michael Ansara (Herod's commander); Sal Mineo (*Uriah*, cripple healed by Jesus); Ed Wynn (*Aram*, blind man cured by Jesus); Van Heflin (*Bar Armand*, witness to resurrection of Lazarus); Joseph Schildkraut (*Nicodemus*, righteous council elder); Abraham Sofaer (*Joseph of Aramathea*, righteous council elder); Richard Conte (*Barabbas*, criminal freed in place of Jesus); Sidney Poitier (*Simon of Cyrene*, man who helps Christ carry the cross); Carroll Baker (*Veronica*, woman who wipes the face of Jesus with a cloth); Celia Lovsky (sorrowful woman at Christ's trial); John Wayne (centurion who oversees crucifixion); Richard Bakalyan (repentant thief); Marc Cavell (unrepentant thief); Nehemiah Persoff (*Shemiah*); John Abbott (*Aben*); Cyril Delavanti (*Melchior*, first wise man); Mark Lenard (*Balthazar*, second wise man); Frank Silvera (*Caspar*, third wise man); Angela Lansbury (Pilate's wife); Shelley Winters (woman of no name); Russell Johnson (scribe); John Crawford (*Alexander*); Joe Perry (*Archelaus*); Joseph Sirola (*Dumah*); Philip Coolidge (*Chuza*); Pat Boone (angel in tomb).

Appraisal and Synopsis

Stately, reverent, and sometimes leaden, *The Greatest Story Ever Told* presents the story of Christ largely from a Protestant point of view. While for the most part the depiction is traditional, at times the film takes an idiosyncratic turn that is both puzzling and frustrating. When Jesus raises Lazarus from the tomb (a high point of any cinematic portrayal of Christ), the viewpoint of the camera totally avoids Lazarus and instead switches to Sal Mineo, Van Hefflin, and Ed Wynn, who begin an impromptu foot race from Bethany to Jerusalem to see who can break the news first to the Roman guards atop the city gates. Pushing the scene entirely over to kitsch, the soundtrack plays an extended portion of the "Hallelujah Chorus" from Handel's *Messiah*, as the editor switches from Van to Sal to Ed and back again to Van. Despite the difference in their ages, the race is a virtual tie, but then Mineo's character was a cured cripple, which might have slowed him down. This utter squandering of film time is presented as the climax of the film's first half as the picture breaks for intermission.

Other distractions abound, such as the scenery of Monument Valley, familiar to filmgoers as the setting of countless Westerns, being used as the backdrop for Stevens' biblical epic. Then there is the sea of familiar faces in the cameo-laden story. I usually enjoy star cameos, but this film has so many that it detracts from the story. Many of these stars, it is said, directly called George Stevens and volunteered to accept any role without consideration of pay so they could be in the picture. Stevens didn't seek them out, but he was happy to accommodate them. In addition, many of the actors in the cast later became familiar faces in noteworthy television roles. We find Klinger from "M*A*S*H" (Jamie Farr) and Captain Crane from "Voyage to the Bottom of the Sea" (David Hedison) along with Roddy McDowall and David McCallum among the apostles. The final major problem is the pacing. Max Von Sydow delivers many of Christ's pronouncements with extended pauses between each phrase. While filming, Stevens called for endless retakes, asking for a more deliberate pace. If von Sydow had been allowed to speak more naturally, the initial cut of the picture probably would have been reduced by minutes.

On the positive side, most of the film's technical credits are outstanding. The cinematography is magnificent, although William C. Mellor died while working on the film, he was seamlessly replaced by the talented Loyal Griggs. Each large scene seems to rely on the work of a famous artist, such as Breughel, El Greco, da Vinci, Alma Tedema, Giotto and others. Over 300 original oil paintings were commissioned in place of storyboards by Stevens in preparation for the film. The influence of this clearly shows, as the film has remarkable, intriguing vistas, brilliant use of light and shadows, and technical excellence on every level with the exception of the music where Alfred Newman provided a half-hearted, derivative score largely based on Samuel Barber's *Adagio for Strings*.

A traditional synopsis is unnecessary, but the presentation does contain several unconventional features. For instance, Judas commits suicide not by hanging, as is tradition, but by leaping into the sacrificial fire that burns continuously outside the temple. This also varies from the Bible, Acts 1:16–19, where Judas dies in a field when his stomach ruptures after a fall. Perhaps the most interesting feature is the prominence accorded to the Devil, who weaves through the entire film like a thread through fabric. After his initial appearance, Satan continuously reappears as an observer in the crowds following Christ. Sometimes he is silent, but often he participates in events, taunting Jesus and, on another occasion, urging a hostile assemblage to stone Christ. In two of the gospels, John 13:27 and Luke 22:3, Satan is specifically described as "entering into" Judas and bringing about Christ's betrayal. In the film, Judas bumps into the Devil on the street and then meets with Caiaphas and offers to betray Jesus. When Peter follows Jesus after his arrest, it is Satan who accuses Peter of being a disciple, bringing about the apostle's denial of Christ. Finally, the Devil is most prominent during Christ's appearance before Pilate, where he initiates the call for his crucifixion. The Devil also utters the scriptural response to Pilate, "We have no king but Caesar," which is attributed in John 19:15 to one of the chief priests. The film's interpretation of the Devil as an active participant working against Jesus is one of its most successful innovations.

Performances

Starting with his appearance in a mountaintop cave, which Jesus enters during his forty-day fast in the wilderness, Satan, also called the Dark Hermit, is virtually omnipresent in all succeeding events; this was even more pronounced in the original cut. The selection of Donald Pleasence was an inspired one. The diminutive character actor had just completed two brilliant screen roles, as the title characters in *Dr. Crippen* (1962) and *The Caretaker* (1964), as well as a key appearance in *The Great Escape* (1963). The British actor was already well established, but still not overly familiar to film audiences, but that was soon to change with his appearance as the quintessential Bond villain Blofeld in *You Only Live Twice* (1967). Donald Pleasence is masterful as the Devil, delivering a vibrant, fascinating performance, which has far greater depth than the typical interpretation. His countenance is plain and unassuming, and he comes across as crafty and a trifle coarse, but on a deeper level he acts with a sense of melancholy and resignation. The Devil takes little pleasure in tormenting his adversary. When Peter denies Christ, there is no triumph shown by Satan but almost a sense of disappointment. Similarly, when he encounters Judas approaching the abode of Caiaphas, he shows little satisfaction.

The intention behind Pleasence's interpretation is somewhat complex. The Devil knows that Christ is on Earth to bring salvation to mankind, but in actuality he has no idea how this will be accomplished. This leads to an issue that is a theological quandary; that is, if Christ wasn't betrayed, then He wouldn't have been able to atone for the sins of man. Therefore, Judas and Satan, ironically and without intent, serve the divine plan with their actions. Satan's sorrow, therefore, is either that he realizes that he is himself nothing but a pawn in the grand scheme, or it is genuine regret for what he is doing. There is even the possibility that the Devil is disappointed because mankind is so corrupt that he can manipulate them far too easily. The richness of Pleasence's approach is that it is able to accommodate these different assessments simultaneously. That is one of the hallmarks of genuine greatness in a performance.

Von Sydow, having made his mark in Europe in a series of Ingmar Bergman films, was still relatively unknown to English-speaking audiences when he starred in this production. His austere Jesus is the undeniable highlight of the epic. He also shows Christ's militant side, not often shown in most depictions of Jesus which prefer to concentrate on His humility. Years later, von Sydow gained the unique distinction of playing both Christ and Satan when he starred as the Prince of Darkness in *Needful Things* (1993). Other players whose work in *The Greatest Story Ever Told* merit commendation include Claude Rains, Jose Ferrer, Victor Buono, and Gary Raymond. The weaker performances are by Martin Landau, Carroll Baker, and Dorothy McGuire. Joseph Schildkraut died during production, and some of the lines in his unfinished scenes were transferred to Abraham Sofaer. The uncredited actress who performs Salome does an incredible job. Richard Bakalyan as the good thief and Celia Lovsky (Peter Lorre's first wife) provide the most effective cameos, while those by Pat Boone and John Wayne are often cited as the most absurd in the picture.

Notable Quotes

• [cackling laughter] Long, hard climb, wasn't it? Come on in, if You like. Some think the whole of life should be hard like that. An easy life is a sinful life. That's what they think. Not so, life should be as easy as a man could make it. And it can be easy, friend, if a man knows the way to power and glory in this world. (**the Devil, greeting Christ as he enters a cave after struggling to the top of a mountain**)

• How would You like to be the ruler of all of this? Hmm? All of the power and the glory of these kingdoms? I can give them to You, if You do me homage. (**the Devil, pointing out the vista below to Christ as he continues munching on some cooked meat**)

• It is written He shall put His angels in charge to keep thee from harm, and they shall hold up their hands lest You dash your foot against a stone. (**the Devil then kicks a rock down the side of the cliff, and Jesus watches it fall**)

If you are the Son of God, throw Yourself down from here. (**the Devil, refining his temptation**)

Hammersmith Is Out

1972   Rating: *   Richard Burton as the Devil

Crean Films. Written by Stanford Whitmore; Photographed by Richard H. Kline; Edited by David E. Blewitt; Music by Dominic Frontiere; Produced by Alex Lucas; Directed by Peter Ustinov. Color, 108 minutes.

Annotated Cast List

Richard Burton (*Hammersmith*, asylum patient and the Devil); Elizabeth Taylor (*Jimmie Jean Jackson*, waitress); Peter Ustinov (doctor who runs asylum and narrator); Beau Bridges (*Billy Breedlove*, asylum attendant who makes a deal with Hammersmith); Leon Ames (*Gen. Pembroke*, castle guest); Leon Askin (*Dr. Krodt*, castle guest); Anthony Holland (*Oldham*, nervous asylum attendant); George Raft (*Guido Scartucci*, nightclub owner); John Schuck (*Henry Joe Fisk, Jr.*, Texas oil tycoon); Marjorie Eaton (princess, castle guest); Joe Espinoza (duke, castle guest); Linda Gaye Scott (*Miss Quim*, realtor); Mel Berger (fat man who hassles Jimmie at the diner); Brook Williams (*Pete Rutter*, new man hired at the asylum); Carl Down (*Cleopatra*, asylum patient); Lisa Jak (*Kiddo*, Billy's secretary).

Appraisal and Synopsis

Intended as a modern-day satire of *Faust*, this film is a colossal disappointment given the caliber of the talent involved. Peter Ustinov, usually a perceptive and extraordinary director, here falls flat on his face. The only amusing moments in the picture are provided by Ustinov's appearances as actor. Other than that, *Hammersmith Is Out* is a complete misfire on all levels, including a hokey music score, sloppy editing, and a weak script. The basic concept—casting Faust as a poor southern drifter and Marguerite as a diner waitress—has potential, but it just never develops.

The film opens in a sanitarium at night. Oldham, a psychiatric aide, becomes frightened when one of his patients, a man called Cleopatra, keeps repeating, "Hammersmith is out!" No doubt the name Cleopatra is an inside joke referring to the extravagant Burton/Taylor Egyptian epic. Oldham checks Hammersmith's isolation cell, where the madman keeps repeating calmly, "Let me out of here." After the credits, the focus shifts to Billy Breedlove, a drifter who recently joined the staff of the asylum. Breedlove heads off to a local hash house where he flirts with Jimmie Jean Jackson, the sexy waitress. He seduces her and urges her to run off with him the following night. She agrees to meet him at midnight under the bridge at the forked road.

Billy makes a deal with Hammersmith, who appears to possess supernatural powers. He casually removes his straitjacket and promises Billy wealth and power if he allows him to escape. Billy leaves his cell unlocked as Hammersmith requests. The asylum director fires Billy for negligence after the madman is discovered to be missing. After their rendezvous, Billy, Jimmie and Hammersmith walk over to a drive-in theater. Hammersmith steals a car and disposes of the owner, dumping his body in the trunk, and the trio speed off and check into a motel. Hammersmith kills another man at a night spot and steals his suit for his protegé. They drive to the next state where Hammersmith arranges for Billy to take over a nightclub.

The doctor decides to track the Devil, leaving Oldham in charge of the asylum. He says that if he fails to capture Hammersmith, the world could end. Meanwhile, Hammersmith arranges with cutthroat efficiency for Billy to rise fast in the business world, taking over an important firm. Jimmie Jean and Billy live an ever more affluent lifestyle, but Billy begins to tire of her. She falls in love with Henry Joe, an oil tycoon with whom Hammersmith is negotiating. She warns Henry Joe that Hammersmith is a murderer, but he mocks her. The next day, Hammersmith wipes out Henry Joe and his board of directors, claiming they all drowned in a swimming pool accident. Billy's next move, as prompted by Hammersmith, is to finance and help elect a presidential candidate. He wins and appoints Billy as his international ambassador-at-large. Billy meets the pope and treats him as if he were a two-bit union boss. Billy soon tires of the diplomacy and moves to Spain, purchasing a castle. Hammersmith arranges for Billy and Jimmie to mingle with a class of jet-setters, who become guests at his estate.

Completely bored with Jimmie Jean, Billy asks the Devil to kill her. As he leads her away, Hammersmith offers her a pact. If she will bear his child, Hammersmith will allow her to survive. The next day, Hammersmith arranges for Billy to have an accident while water skiing, which leaves him a cripple. Depressed, he shuts himself away in an isolated estate and finds himself completely at the mercy of Jimmie Jean. After she announces her pregnancy and liaison with Hammersmith, Billy tries to kill her, but Hammersmith intervenes.

Richard Burton assumes a deadpan look as Hammersmith, despite the allure of Jimmie Jean (Elizabeth Taylor) and the quick wit of Billy Breedlove (Beau Bridges) in Hammersmith Is Out.

He encourages Billy to kill himself, offering him a revolver. The doctor arrives in a helicopter, convincing Hammersmith to return to the asylum. Billy shoots himself, and Hammersmith and the doctor depart, leaving Jimmie Jean alone as they take off.

Back at the asylum, Oldham has cracked up, becoming one of the patients. The doctor interviews a job applicant, Peter Rutter, a former boxer with a dishonorable discharge from the marine corps. Reviewing his spotty work history, the doctor considers him a perfect candidate to be his new aide and gives him a telegram to bring to Hammersmith. The message reveals that Jimmie Jean has given birth to a baby girl. "As usual," Hammersmith comments as he sizes up his new prospect. "Get me out of here," he whispers. "I'll make you rich and strong." The picture ends as the cycle begins to repeat itself yet again.

Perhaps *Hammersmith Is Out* was intended to serve as an allegory, with Ustinov representing God, who allows his mental patient, Hammersmith, the Devil, to escape time and again to test the moral shortcomings of mankind. It seems clear they are working in cooperation, otherwise why would the doctor hire such obvious losers to watch over his prize patient? Also, the doctor, supposedly in pursuit of Hammersmith, makes no effort to close in even though Billy's location is no secret but a matter of public record. No doubt, the doctor is merely biding his time until Hammersmith is finished with Billy.

Hammersmith's motivation, on the other hand, seems simply to refine his techniques of corruption and to experiment with various types of individuals to test the limits of their depravity. Once he finishes toying with his guinea pig, the Devil abandons the person to his fate and allows himself to be recaptured. During each escape, Hammersmith sires a child, always a girl. It is unclear if he seeking a male heir, as he seems completely indifferent when news of the birth arrives. No underlying meaning to this unending cycle seems evident, and nothing in the pattern reflects any deeper significance. There are no insights, comic or otherwise, into the basic *Faust* legend, and it is difficult to understand exactly what Stanford Whitmore, one of the principal writers for the TV series "The Wild, Wild West," actually had in mind with his spoof. Neither he nor director Ustinov nor any of the performers really bring anything worthwhile to this empty bag of tricks.

Performances

It has been said that Richard Burton could read the telephone book and make it sound interesting. But in one of the most intriguing roles for any actor, that of the Devil, he makes very little impression other than ennui. It is a hollow, halfhearted reading, as if Burton were sleepwalking through the film. His continuous monotone and unchanging expression make Hammersmith seem empty, a void, a complete blank. No doubt this is what was intended, but it is a thankless, boring interpretation. At least Burton doesn't embarrass himself, unlike Elizabeth Taylor, whose performance is one of unending kitsch. Her accent shifts from scene to scene, and her characterization is equally inconsistent. Her long bedroom scene with John Schuck is downright awful. The amazing thing, however, is that she won the Silver Bear as best actress for this performance at the 1972 International Berlin Film Festival. Peter Ustinov was nominated for a Golden Bear as well. The only explanation for this must be that the Devil cast a spell over the festival judges. The talented Beau Bridges also does a miserable job, with only his endless nose picking being memorable. One cannot tell if Billy ever realizes that Hammersmith is the Devil. The only bright spots are Ustinov's exchanges with Anthony Holland as Oldham and Linda Gaye Scott as Miss Quim. One would have expected some sparks when Ustinov and Burton finally appear together, but Burton's lack of response renders this scene a washout as well.

Notable Quotes

- Again, the Devil taketh him and showeth him all the kingdoms of the world and the glory of them, and said unto him, "All these things will I give thee if thou wilt fall down and worship me." Then sayeth he unto Satan, "It's a deal." (**opening narration**)
- No member of the syndicate has ever jumped out of a gentlemen's toilet on the fourteenth floor of a building and lands in the back seat of his own car. He was not pushed by a member of the syndicate. He was pushed by someone with a sense of humor... Hammersmith has a vast and terrible sense of humor. (**the doctor, commenting on a reported suicide in the newspaper**)
- Come on, Hammersmith. It is too easy for you out here. As a consequence, you tire yourself and people don't understand you. They haven't your intelligence. (**the doctor to Hammersmith, urging his return to the asylum**)

Haunts of the Very Rich

1972   Rating: ***   Moses Gunn as the Devil

ABC Circle Films. Written by William Wood, based on a short story by T. K. Brown; Photographed by Ben Colman; Edited by Frederic Steinkamp; Music by Dominic Frontiere; Produced by Lillian Gallo; Directed by Paul Wendkos. Color, 76 minutes.

Annotated Cast List

Lloyd Bridges (*David Woodrough*, businessman); Cloris Leachman (*Ellen Blunt*, secretary); Anne Francis (*Annette Larrier*, housewife); Edward Asner (*Albert Hunsicker*, arrogant salesman for the Space Age Trucking Company); Robert Reed (*Rev. John Fellows*, minister and anthropologist); Tony Bill (*Lyle Dugan*, newlywed); Donna Mills (*Laurie*, his bride); Moses Gunn (*Seacrist*, administrator of the Portals of Eden, actually the Devil); Phyllis Hill (*Rita Woodrough*, Dave's wife); Michael Lembeck (*Johnny Delmonico*, pop singer); Todd Martin (*Roger Harris*, pilot); Susan Foster (*Upton*, stewardess); Beverly Gill (*Miss Vick*, beautician).

Appraisal and Synopsis

Haunts of the Very Rich is a telefilm that seems like an extended episode of "Night Gallery" or "Tales of the Unexpected" or even a diabolical offshoot of "Fantasy Island." It is a pleasant, mildly enjoyable film, perhaps worth a second viewing to see how well the various hints are presented and to observe the subtleties in the portrayals of the characters. It is definitely an above-average example of early 1970s made-for-television fare.

The story begins on a private jet carrying seven passengers en route to an unknown destination, an exclusive resort called the Portals of Eden. The windows of the plane are painted over, so the location of the site remains a mystery. Each vacationer was contacted in a different manner to visit this luxury facility. While comparing notes, they discover that they each received a completely different brochure describing the place alternately as a health spa, a sports retreat, a swingers' club, or a honeymoon resort. Each has a different reason for coming. Rev. Fellows wants to study the religious practices of the primitive Indian tribe living near the Portals of Eden. David Woodrough is seeking a good time, escaping from his possessive wife. Lyle and Laurie Dugan are on their honeymoon. Annette Larrier wants to relax and recover from a recent illness. Ellen Blunt came expecting to receive a beauty makeover. The last individual, pushy salesman Albert Hunsicker, awakens in midflight, expecting to be landing in Dallas on a business trip. He loudly complains but is told by the stewardess that his company made the arrangements for his visit as a surprise holiday. Lyle and Laurie dance in the aisle to the music of their favorite performer, Johnny Delmonico. They sadly note that they heard a news bulletin reporting his death while they were on their way to the airport.

The jet lands at a remote airstrip in a lush and beautiful tropical valley surrounded by mountains. The last leg of their journey is by boat, and all are impressed with the exotic wonders of the locale. The hotel, which resembles an elaborate European chateau, becomes visible as their boat slips underneath a stone gateway. Their host is a tall, exceedingly courteous black man named Seacrist, who explains that all of the help in the hotel understand English but are unable to speak it. He tells them they are the first guests at the Portals of Eden for the new season, and additional groups will arrive shortly. Their individual quarters are opulent and luxurious, except for Hunsicker's room, which reminds him of a seedy motel in Schenectady. The salesman later makes a racist observation that none of the help is white. The tourists unwind after their journey. Ellen Blunt is attended to by Miss Vick, who gives her a beauty treatment. Lyle and Laurie make an unexpected discovery when they turn down the blanket on their bed and find a writhing snake. Laurie screams, and the other guests rush into their room. Seacrist arrives and removes the snake, claiming it is nonpoisonous. At dinner, David dines with Ellen, who looks stunning in her new hairdo and outfit. They are attracted to each other, and David reveals that he is married but plans to divorce his possessive and clinging wife as soon as possible.

In the middle of the night, a violent thunderstorm strikes the resort, knocking out power and damaging many windows. The next morning, Seacrist explains that the tropical downpour destroyed the airfield, and the electric generator, which was struck by lightning. He estimates that help will take several days to arrive. Hunsicker offers to work on the shortwave radio, also damaged by lightning. He manages to pick up transmissions but is unable to send any. The guests become restless and argumentative. David discovers that each of the guests had a recent close call with death. He just recovered from a heart attack, Rev. Fellows almost drowned, and the honeymooners totaled their car after leaving their wedding. Miss Vick, the beautician, collapses and dies in the lounge. Seacrist claims she ate a can of spoiled food, and they place her body in a storeroom.

The native staff flee the resort, leaving the seven guests and Seacrist stranded. The administrator offers to hike out of the valley through a dangerous trail, promising to return with help in four days. After his departure, David tries to organize the others. Annette cuts her wrists in a suicide attempt but quickly recovers. Ellen is certain that no one could survive after the loss of so much blood. She asks David to show her the body of Miss Vick, but it is missing from the storeroom. The realization strikes her that they may all be dead. David discusses the idea with the other guests, who first are doubtful, but then confess their own unsettling suspicions, all of which support Ellen's outlandish theory. Annette fears that her husband, Alan, poisoned her the night before her trip.

A mini-seaplane splashes down in the lagoon near the hotel. The pilot emerges briefly to reassure the guests, telling them he will send help as soon as possible, then takes off. At first everyone is thrilled, but when the Dugans realize that the pilot was Johnny Delmonico, the singer who was killed in a plane crash, a sense of depression sweeps over them. That evening, Rev. Fellows returns to the hotel. He reveals that the native tribe, which greeted him warmly, has vanished completely after their religious ceremony, as if they were unreal and had never existed. Fellows searched carefully and discovered that there is no way out of the valley. The group opens up about their private fears and losses. Despite their gloomy situation, David and Ellen feel blessed because they have found each other and are in love. Fellows predicts that something will happen to shatter their happiness.

The next day, Seacrist returns with a large seaplane. He tells the guests to gather their belongings, but by the time they return with their luggage, the plane is gone, responding to an emergency call, according to Seacrist. Dave makes the observation that it would be impossible for the plane to leave without anyone hearing it. Ellen says Seacrist is merely toying with them, that he is really the Devil. As if to verify this, Seacrist introduces a new guest: Rita, David's wife. As Rita reaches out to him, David runs off with Ellen, bounding headlong into the jungle. Seacrist's image is superimposed over them as they wander aimlessly, and a montage of voices is heard, repeating phrases uttered by the travelers over the past week, ending with the shout, "Go to hell!"

Haunts of the Very Rich is a diverting presentation that expertly teases the audience before confirming the idea that the Portals of Eden is actually the Portals of Hell. The picture manages its clues quite skillfully, and Edward Asner is convincing as the skeptic who up until the end mocks the concept that they are dead. Each of the seven guests is given fairly balanced attention, except that none of Rev. Fellows' experiences with the natives is shown on-screen. Lloyd Bridges' character becomes the center of attention as he assumes the role of leader after the departure of Seacrist. The dialogue, which could easily have become silly or trite, remains natural and believable. The film parallels earlier classics, such as *Outward Bound* (1930) and *Between Two Worlds* (1944), where travelers on a cruise slowly learn that they have died and are being transported to another realm. *Haunts of the Very Rich* blends this concept with that of the Devil, who playfully torments the new arrivals in hell, giving them logical excuses while the situation grows worse and worse. When they are about to sink into despair, he again provides momentary hope before beginning the process anew. The Devil soaks up everyone's distress as they are broken down and stripped of their hopes and dreams. The newlyweds lose their illusion of married bliss, Annette her illusion of family life, Hunsicker his illusion of success, and Rev. Fellows his quest for spiritual renewal. Seacrist allows David and Ellen a momentary glimpse of happiness, before adding David's wife to the mix to form an eternal triangle of misery. What is unclear is whether the travelers will face eternity in this deteriorating jungle resort, or whether this is merely their first stop in a descent to the torments of hell. The latter seems the more likely course, although these individuals for the most part do not appear to be wicked people who merit the torments of hell. After the Devil consigns them to the lower reaches, he probably begins his game all over again with a fresh group of arrivals.

Performances

Moses Gunn gives an exceptional reading as the unctuous and self-assured administrator of the Portals of Eden. His very name has a blasphemous connotation, "See Christ," when the one we see is the Devil. He speaks in an elegant British accent, with flowery phrases that become more and more transparent to his victims. The refined torture he inflicts is certainly as traumatic as the medieval tortures envisioned by Bosch in his art. Gunn endows Seacrist with a regal coolness, while giving the impression that he is savoring every moment of his charade. Moses Gunn, who passed away in 1993, was a magnificent actor who was never fully utilized in films compared to the equally talented James Earl Jones, with whom he appeared in *The Great White Hope* (1970). Gunn did have outstanding moments in *The Hot Rock* (1972), *Ragtime* (1981), and *Heartbreak Ridge* (1986). Even though *Haunts of the Very Rich* is a minor film, Gunn raises the quality of the picture with his performance. The other players are also quite good, and it is an unusually strong cast for a telefilm. Lloyd Bridges, Anne Francis, Cloris Leachman, Robert Reed, and especially Ed Asner lend credibility to a production which easily could have become ludicrous in lesser hands.

Notable Quotes

• I am your host here at the Portals of Eden. I trust you all had a very smooth flight. Anything you need during your stay here, anything at all, come to me. Our aim here is to provide a unique recreative experience at all times. (**Seacrist to his guests**)

• Well, I suppose every Eden has its serpent. (**Rev. Fellows' remark after Laurie is startled by a snake in her bed**)

• I've had enough darkness for a while. (**Annette after her suicide attempt**)

• I don't think she died. How can there be death in hell? (**Ellen to David, referring to the missing body of Miss Vick**)

Heaven Can Wait

1943   Rating: ****   Laird Cregar as the Devil

20th Century–Fox. Written by Samson Raphaelson, based on the play *Birthday* by Laszlo Bus-Fekete; Photographed by Edward Cronjager; Special Effects by Fred Sersen; Edited by Dorothy Spencer; Music by Alfred Newman; Produced and Directed by Ernst Lubitsch. Color, 112 minutes.

Annotated Cast List

Don Ameche (*Henry Van Cleave*, distinguished gentleman who requests admission to hell); Gene Tierney (*Martha*, his wife); Charles Coburn (*Hugo Van Cleave*, his grandfather); Spring Byington (*Bertha*, his mother); Louis Calhern (*Randolph*, his father); Laird Cregar (the Devil); Florence Bates (*Edna Craig*, woman who barges in to see the Devil); Allyn Joslyn (*Albert Van Cleave*, Henry's cousin); Alfred Hall (Albert's father); Grayce Hampton (Albert's mother); Michael McLean (Henry as a baby); Scotty Beckett (Henry as a young boy); Marlene Mains (*Mary*, Henry's childhood girlfriend); Dicky Moore (Henry as a teenager); Dicky Jones (Albert as a teenager); Eugene Palette (*E. F. Strabel*, Martha's father); Marjorie Main (Martha's mother); Signe Hasso (*Yvette Blanchard*, French maid in Van Cleave household); Helene Reynolds (*Peggy Nash*, showgirl); Michael Ames (*Jack Van Cleave*, Henry's son); Nino Pipitine, Jr. (Jack as a child); Leonard Carey (*Flugdell*, Van Cleave butler); Aubrey Mather (*James*, Van Cleave butler in later scenes); Clarence Muse (*Jasper*, Strabel butler); Trudy Marshall (*Jane*, Jack's wife); Clara Blandick (Henry's grandmother); Anita Sharp-Bolster (*Mrs. Cooper-Cooper*, warbling singer); Claire DuBrey (*Miss Ralston*, Jack's secretary); James Flavin (policeman); Edwin Maxwell (Henry's doctor); Doris Merrick (daytime nurse); Maureen Rodis-Ryan (*Nellie Brown*, night nurse); Gerald Oliver Smith (*Smith*).

Appraisal and Synopsis

Heaven Can Wait is a delightful romantic comedy, a model example of the "Lubitsch touch," a unique style which combines wit, subtlety, and sophistication,

The elderly Henry Van Cleave (Don Ameche) finds his interview with the Devil (Laird Cregar) interrupted by Edna Craig (Florence Bates). Cregar activates a trap door moments later, dumping the woman into the fiery pit.

particularly in dealing with the relations between the sexes. Lubitsch's cinematic magic makes this picture an unusually rich and alluring production. It was the third and most popular Lubitsch film to be nominated for an Academy Award as Best Picture. It represented the old-fashioned type of film that people loved to watch to simply feel good. The picture excels in conveying the flavor of the early years of the century with nostalgia but without an excess of sentimentality. The color photography is sumptuous. The editing is deft, and the plot never lags despite its episodic nature. The soundtrack is filled with old favorites such as "The Merry Widow Waltz" and "By the Light of the Silvery Moon." Quite appropriately, *Heaven Can Wait* has the friendliest, most reassuring Devil to appear onscreen.

The story begins with the recently deceased Henry Van Cleave entering the luxurious office of his excellency, Satan, who receives him in a most dignified and cordial manner. As Henry starts to explain why he belongs in hell, their meeting is interrupted by an arrogant older woman who demands to speak with the Devil at once. He disposes of her by means of a trap door, but the Devil is intrigued with Henry's suave and mellow reaction to the intruder, a slight acquaintance he met only once at a party in his youth. He decides to take the time to listen to Henry's reminiscences. Henry tells him that the easiest way to relate his life of "one continuous misdemeanor" would be to talk about the women he knew.

Henry's reflections always center around his birthday. He was born with numerous advantages, a member of the New York aristocracy. As a young lad, Henry flirts with a girl in the park, who asks him to part with his prized possession, his favorite beetle. Quickly, the boy learns that if he wants to be successful with women, he will need to have "lots of beetles." The sixteen-year-old Henry is introduced to another level of female companionship through Mademoiselle Yvette, the French maid in the wealthy Van Cleave household. With her, he samples his first champagne, as well as his first hangover. Henry is developing into a charming rogue, an image of his old grandfather Hugo and unlike his stuffy parents. At twenty-six, Henry meets and falls in love with Martha, a girl he meets while shopping. The next day, he learns that Martha is actually the fiancée of his straitlaced cousin, Albert. At a family party, he learns that Martha had accepted Albert's proposal simply because he was the only person upon whom both her continually bickering parents could agree. Impulsively, Henry kisses her, and she admits to him that he is the person she really loves. They rush out of the party and elope, to the consternation of the entire household except Hugo, who sends the butler after them with a fistful of money to pay for their honeymoon. On his thirty-sixth birthday, Martha leaves Henry and returns to stay with her parents in their mansion in Kansas. She is suspicious about Henry's fascinating ways with attractive women. They have a young son named Jack, the spitting image of his father, a charming finagler. Henry pursues Martha, slipping into her room in her parents' mansion at midnight and persuading her to run off with him again. They sneak off in the dead of night, assisted by the elderly Hugo. When he turns fifty, Henry and Martha go to the *Follies* where one of the headliners is Peggy Nash, a glamorous showgirl. Henry later hears that his son is smitten with the woman, and he pays her to break up with his son. It turns out that Jack had tired of her on his own and has switched to a different showgirl. Martha tells Henry not to worry, that Jack is going through a Casanova stage just like he did himself. On his following birthday, their silver anniversary, Henry becomes jealous because of Martha's frequent unexplained absences. He learns, however, that she is seeing a doctor; this anniversary is their last, since she dies a few months later. After his sixtieth birthday, Henry has resumed his roguish ways. Jack, now in charge of the family's affairs, criticizes him for going out every night with younger women. At seventy, Henry is bedridden, but his interest is still piqued by the nurses who attend him, and when the new, beautiful night nurse arrives, Henry passes away quite contentedly.

After Henry concludes his story, the Devil smiles broadly and says, "Sorry, Mr. Van Cleave, we don't cater to your class of people here." He then advises Henry to apply to heaven. He believes they will have a small room in an annex for him, and with residents such as Hugo and especially Martha pleading for him, he will eventually be granted entrance. The Devil escorts Henry to an elevator, shakes his hand, and instructs the operator to transport him up. The film ends with the Devil's good-natured smile.

Years later, Warren Beatty remade *Heaven Can Wait* (1978), but the only thing he used from the original film was the title. Beatty actually took his plot from *Here Comes Mr. Jordan* (1941) with Robert Montgomery and Claude Rains, altering the main character from a prizefighter to a football player. It is not clear why he used this title for his version, and it confused a lot of people who were expecting to see an update of the Lubitsch film.

Performances

Laird Cregar's screen career only lasted five years, cut short by his tragic death at the age of twenty-eight, yet he made a lasting impression in a handful of notable roles, including the obsessive police detective in *I Wake Up Screaming* (1941), Jack the Ripper in *The Lodger* (1944), the doomed composer George Harvey Bone in *Hangover Square* (1945), and the soft-spoken Devil in *Heaven Can Wait*. Cregar certainly has a completely fresh and different approach as Lucifer. He wears a neatly trimmed beard and dresses in a most dapper fashion. The only diabolical touch about his appearance is his widow's peak. His elegant Devil is not angry or upset to lose Henry Van Cleave as a resident of hell but is openly delighted to steer him in the right direction, because heaven is where Henry genuinely belongs. In displaying detailed knowledge of the ways of heaven, Cregar's performance reminds us that Lucifer was at one time the foremost angel in heaven, and it is distinctive of this picture that this aspect of the Devil is emphasized. Indeed, the Devil displays a number of uncharacteristic virtues during his visit with Henry, being considerate, graceful, courteous, and sympathetic. This is not to say he isn't dangerous, as the pesky Mrs. Craig discovers when he pushes the button to drop her into the fiery pit. But for the most part, only the velvet glove rather than the iron fist is on display in this film. This role is one of the most warm-hearted in the career of the usually villainous Laird Cregar. The other cast members are also excellent. Don Ameche delivers the finest performance of his career as Henry, and he is completely credible for each of the character's various ages. Gene Tierney and Charles Coburn are magical, endowing their parts with considerable depth as well. Michael Ames, who plays Henry's son, became better known in films later as Tod Andrews.

Notable Quotes

- As Henry Van Cleave's soul passed over the Great Divide, he realized that it was extremely unlikely that his next stop could be Heaven. And so philosophically he presented himself where innumerable people had so often told him to go. (**opening title card**)
- I hope you will forgive me, but we are so busy down here. Really, sometimes it looks like the whole world is coming to hell. (**the Devil to Henry upon greeting him**)
- A passport to hell is not issued on generalities. (**the Devil to Henry, wanting to hear his story**)
- The bed may be hard and you might have to wait a few hundred years until they move you into the main building. Well, it doesn't hurt to try. After all, they may inquire about you among the residents of the main building. I think you will find a lot of people who will give you a good reference. That always helps. (**the Devil to Henry, telling him how he can get accepted into heaven**)

Highway to Hell

1990   Rating: ***   Patrick Bergin as the Devil

Hemdale Films. Written by Brian Helgeland; Photographed by Robin Vidgeon; Edited by Todd Ramsay and Randy Thornton; Special Effects by Steve Johnson and Randall William Cook; Music by Hidden Faces; Produced by Mary Anne Page and John Byers; Directed by Ate de Jong. Color, 93 minutes.

Annotated Cast List

Chad Lowe (*Charlie Sykes*, young man who storms hell to find his girlfriend); Patrick Bergin (*Beezle*, the Devil); Kristy Swanson (*Rachel Clark*, Charlie's fiancée); Adam Stroke (*Royce*, leader of bikers in hell); Richard Farnsworth (*Sam*, gas station owner who guards the road to hell); Pamela Gidley (*Clara*, Sam's love, kidnapped by hell cop); C. J. Graham (*Bedlam*, hell cop); Jarrett Lennon (*Adam*, child apprenticed to Beezle); Kevin Peter Hall (*Charon*, ferryman across River Styx); Lita Ford (hitchhiker); Gilbert Gottfried (*Adolf Hitler*); Amy Stiller (*Cleopatra*); Ben Stiller (*Attila the Hun)*; Jerry Stiller (desk cop); Ann Meara (*Medea*, waitress); Be Deckard (dentist); Julian Charles Wright (doctor); Darren Mark Edwards (clown); Troy Tempest (exterminator); Buddy Douglas (page); Doug Harriman (bartender); Michael Dellafemina (woodsman); Gregory Mars Martin (state policeman); Michael Reid McKay (demon posing as Rachel); Michael Waxman (beer pitchman); Paul MacKey (palace guard); Helen Bradley, Kenneth Bridges, Marina Palmer (victims of Good Intentions pavers); Das Psycho Rangers (Royce's gang).

Appraisal and Synopsis

A resourceful and clever fantasy that was largely ignored or underrated by critics, *Highway to Hell* is filled with delightful surprises and an imaginative reworking of the myth of Orpheus in the Underworld. Although a few ideas flop, the level of creativity in this modestly budgeted endeavor is quite high.

The story opens with a nervous young couple, Charlie Sykes and Rachel Clark, who are eloping. En route to Las Vegas, they take a back road in case Rachel's mother has called the authorities. They stop at a remote gas station whose owner alerts them that the road is dangerous and in need of repair. They ignore his dark warning and head off into the night. A police car pulls them over, but the officer who emerges from the vehicle is a demonic figure with messages of hate carved in his flesh, and his uniform is inscribed "Hades." He knocks Charlie out and drags off Rachel, using two severed but living hands as handcuffs to bind her. They drive off, and regaining his senses, Charlie returns to the gas station for help. Sam, the proprietor, informs him that many young women have been captured and taken to hell by Sergeant Bedlam, the hell cop, including Clara, his own fiancée, fifty years earlier. Sam explains that there is only one chance to save Rachel, that is by catching the hell cop before he reaches Hell City. Providing Charlie with a new car and a special sawed-off shotgun, Sam instructs him how to reach hell by slipping into another dimension in the stretch of road between two old juniper trees.

Charlie gets stopped by an actual Nevada highway patrolman as he speeds back and forth down the road. As the trooper chases him, Charlie escapes through a dimensional rift and emerges in the hellish counterpart of the road. Meanwhile, the hell cop stops at Pluto's, a roadside greasy spoon frequented by the animated corpses of cops in various states of decay, most of them gnawing on stale doughnuts. Rachel breaks away from Bedlam briefly but is captured and returned to him by Royce, leader of an infernal motorcycle gang. Charlie almost catches the hell cop's patrol car, but his vehicle breaks down and is salvaged by Beezle, a helpful repair man. Charlie chats with Adam, a youngster whose family was killed by Bedlam and who now is apprenticed to Beezle. Charlie learns that he has twenty-four hours to accomplish his mission or he will be trapped in hell forever. He tracks Bedlam and Rachel to Hoffa's, a truck stop founded by Jimmy Hoffa. Attila the Hun, Cleopatra, and Adolf Hitler are among its clientele. He gets into a shootout with the hell cop, who blasts him in the chest. Beezle shows up and manages to revive Charlie, explaining that it was possible only because his soul is still uncorrupted. Charlie sets off again and is shown a shortcut to Hell City by Beezle. Passing through a cave, he meets Clara, who is as youthful as she was while engaged to Sam. She tries to help him with her best advice. He next encounters a demon posing as Rachel, but her mirror image reveals her true identity. Bribing Charon, the ferryman, Charlie is transported to Hell City. As the boat slips into a dark cave, a neon sign proclaims, "Abandon all hope ye who enter here."

After a long search, he locates the real Rachel, who has been given a violin by the Devil. He has also endowed her with prodigious talent. Charlie pleads with Satan to permit them to leave. Surprisingly, the Devil agrees, on condition they don't look back as they leave. After they depart, the Devil looks in the mirror and transforms into Beezle, his alter ego. "Now we'll have some fun," he chuckles. Charlie and Rachel are followed by a crowd of demons, and they make their escape by stealing the hell cop's car.

They head toward Beezle's repair shop, which now has become a mansion. Beezle acts amazed to see them. Charlie asks Adam if he wishes to leave hell with them, and he eagerly agrees. Disappointed, Beezle reveals that he is the Devil. Stunned, Rachel exclaims that she has already met the Devil. "Just one of my many manifestations," Beezle replies. He was just toying with them, and he will not allow them to take Adam. Charlie suggests a wager, offering their souls in a race with Bedlamo. Sportingly, Beezle agrees. "I don't always get what I want," he says, but he would like to have children with Rachel.

The Devil brings them to a desert strip, pointing out an exit point. If they can reach it before Sergeant Bedlam catches them, they will be free. Charlie, Rachel, and Adam take off in Sam's car, immediately pursued by the hell cop. Royce and Clara also decide to race for the exit, but they crash in their attempt. Unknown to the Devil, Sam had equipped Charlie's car with a rocket booster, giving them a sudden burst of speed to explode through the exit. As they emerge back on the highway in Nevada, the trooper arrests Charlie. Moments later, the hell cop's patrol car comes through as well. He stalks and overpowers the trooper and Charlie. Rachel shoots Bedlam, targeting his dark glasses as advised by Adam. The hell cop blows apart. Back in hell, Beezle watches these events impassively. The closing scrawl describes the happy life in store for Charlie, Rachel, and Adam.

Highway to Hell has a pedestrian opening, seemingly just another teenage comedy, but as the scene shifts to hell, the film comes to life with many interesting ideas. Not all of them work, such as Gilbert Gottfried's miserable cameo as Hitler, but enough of them do to make the film worthwhile and a pleasant surprise. In one scene, the Good Intentions pavers are shown in operation, interviewing victims. If they feel their intentions were good enough, they grind up their bodies to pave the road to hell. The scene with Cerberus, the three-headed guard dog of hell, is another great example. Up to this point, the inclusion of Charlie's dog, Ben, on the trip seemed a pointless idea. But Ben distracts Cerberus, justifying his presence in a clever sequence. The other scene, of the bumper-to-bumper traffic with nothing but Volkswagen Beetles is a visual delight. Almost every scene has an ingenious little kicker. The picture's resourceful mixture of elements from *Back to the Future* (1985), *Mad Max* (1979), and Dante provides for an entertaining narrative. The only disappointment is the failure to extend the Orpheus parallel to the last quarter of the film.

Performances

Patrick Bergin, the memorable villain from *Sleeping with the Enemy* (1991), does an excellent job. As the Devil, he has an enlarged forehead with three small horns emerging from each temple. He has catlike eyes and wears a stylish medieval costume. His voice is electronically altered to give it an appropriately eerie tone. As Beezle, he first comes across as a simple, good-natured handyman. Of course, the name Beezle would tip off astute viewers as a nickname for Beelzebub. Beezle is quietly self-assured and sees his domain of hell as a vast laboratory with endless levels of torment. Most of all, he loves being a trickster and a games player. He can even afford to be generous and play fair, as he seems to do with Charlie and Rachel. Note that before the race, he shakes Charlie's hand and compliments him for his gutsy determination to win back Rachel. Watching Bergin's performance carefully, it becomes apparent that he extends magnanimous gestures only because that's his mood for today. Tomorrow, he may choose instead to be ruthless, savage, or brutal. This ambivalence is what makes Bergin's performance special and a worthy addition to the gallery of celluloid Devils. Kristy Swanson also delivers a fine performance, but Chad Lowe is humdrum and merely adequate. The film also contains some interesting cameos from Ann Meara and Jerry Stiller, as well as two of their children.

Notable Quotes

• There is nothing I would rather reach for than a fire-brewed bottle of Styx Beer, made from the filthiest waters of our own River Styx. Styx Beer is a third more toxic than any other regular beer. (**television commercial in hell**)

• I am darkness made visible. I am the prince of princes. I once basked in the light of God's love.... I know how everyone feels. (**the Devil to Charlie and Rachel**)

• I may not be carrying a pitchfork, Charlie, but I think you know who I am. Don't make me lose my temper. (**Beezle, revealing his true identity as the Devil**)

• Hey, Charlie, suppose I made you quarterback of the Rams, would you give me Rachel and Adam? (**Beezle's last words just before the race**)

You know, if you said the 'Niners, I might have said, "Yeah." (**Charlie's reply**)

Howl of the Devil
AKA El Aullido del Diablo

1988   Rating: **   Paul Naschy as the Devil

Heraldo Films. Written by Jacinto Molina; Photographed by Julio Burgos; Edited by Jose Antonio Rojo; Special Effects by Francisco Garcia San Jose; Music by Fernando Lopez; Produced and Directed by Jacinto Molina. Color, 93 minutes.

Annotated Cast List

Paul Naschy (*Alex Dorlani Kerensky*, horror film star; *Hector Dorlani*, his twin brother; and ten other characters, including the Devil); Howard Vernon (*Eric*, Hector's butler); Sergio Molina (*Adrian Dorlani*, Alex's son); Caroline Munro (*Carmen*, Hector's housekeeper); Fernando Hilbeck (*Fr. Damien*, priest obsessed with Carmen); Chris Huerta (*Zachary*, town drunk who spies on Hector for Fr. Damien); Roberta Kuhn, Chema Gomez, Tamara Greys, Isabel Prinz.

Appraisal and Synopsis

The cinema of Paul Naschy basically follows the same formula: a heaping dollop of sadism, a smattering of gore, and a dash of female nudity added to a genuine throwback to the classic monsters from the heyday of Universal films. His biggest success has been as Waldemar Daninsky, a Polish werewolf conceived as a tribute to Lon Chaney. In fact, Chaney's photograph is displayed on the cover of a monster magazine shown onscreen. Naschy made a dozen films in which his version of the werewolf appears, from *La Marca del Hombre Lobo* (1967) to *Lycanthropus: The Moonlight Murders* (1996). *Howl of the Devil* also includes a brief cameo of his werewolf. *Howl of the Devil* was intended by Naschy to be his breakthrough film to the English-speaking market, as it was the only one of his pictures that was simultaneously shot in English and Spanish, and it costarred English screen siren Caroline Munro. Unfortunately, this idea came rather late in his cycle of films. *Howl of the Devil* is more of a swan song than a fresh start.

The complicated plot has a number of different strands that don't actually entwine until the end of the film. The backdrop to the plot is the mysterious death of actor Alex Dorlani, who under the pseudonym Kerensky was a major star of horror films. His death two years earlier was listed as suicide, but many believe he was murdered. He was survived by his wife, Lorena, who died inexplicably a year later, his brother Hector, and his son, Adrian. Hector is in charge of the Dorlani estate and resides in a large mansion. Hector is also an actor, but his stage career is undistinguished. Hector sends Eric, the family butler, out to recruit prostitutes for him. He dresses in elaborate disguises, such as Rasputin, when he sleeps with these women. Hector does not get along well with his twelve-year-old nephew, Adrian, who adores his father's horror films. Adrian is lonely, and his imaginary playmates are the monsters his father enacted on the screen, such as Quasimodo and Mr. Hyde. Adrian is on good terms with Eric, who practices the black arts and holds seances to contact the spirit of Alex. Lovely Carmen serves as housekeeper to the Dorlani household. The local priest, Fr. Damien, is in love with Carmen, and he hires Zachary, the town drunk, to keep an eye on her and to spy on Hector. At the same time, a series of murders is happening in the area, and a number of young women have been killed.

Events come to a head when Hector fires Eric and plans to ship Adrian off to boarding school. When Zachary trespasses onto the grounds of the Dorlani estate, he is slain with an ax. Hector makes amorous advances toward Carmen, tempting her with valuable jewels, which she politely declines. But when Fr. Damien tries to rape her, she turns to Hector for comfort. As they make love in bed, they are killed by a sword wielded by Adrian. A flashback reveals that Lorena and Hector faked Alex's suicide and that Adrian is behind the series of murders, which began after he killed Lorena. Eric attempts to conjure up Alex's spirit but winds up invoking Satan instead. Fr. Damien breaks into the Dorlani mansion and is killed by the Devil, who also blinds Eric. In the last scene, the Devil proclaims Adrian as the future Antichrist and plots to rule the world.

In summary, *Howl of the Devil* is an ambitious attempt that is unsuccessful due to a cluttered and confusing plot that has too many dead ends and is almost impossible to follow. Some of the extraneous scenes include a chainsaw massacre nightmare of Carmen's and a break-in at the Dorlani estate by two hoods. The nudity is unnecessary and detracts from the essence of the story: the developing madness of Adrian. The Devil element of the story is introduced too late in the film and is unconvincing, seemingly tacked on to an already overplotted tale. It is impossible, however, to deny the genuine Gothic poetry in the scenes between Adrian and the monsters. The poignant scene in which the boy convinces the Phantom of the Opera to let him remove his mask is sensational, as is his earlier encounter with the Frankenstein monster. If Naschy had downplayed the sleaze and concentrated instead on the psychological aspects of the story, it might have become a bona fide masterpiece.

Performances

As Paul Naschy, Jacinto Molina Alvarez, a former circus strongman, has become the leading horror star in continental Europe during the last half of the twentieth century. Indeed, he has a genuine cult following in both Europe and the Orient, but in America his work is little known in comparison. He has starred in over fifty horror movies, many of which he also wrote and directed. *El Aullido del Diablo* in many ways is the ultimate Naschy film, allowing him to portray an incredible array of characters in the course of the story, including the Frankenstein monster, Fu Manchu, Quasimodo, Mr. Hyde, the Wolfman, Bluebeard, Rasputin, and the Devil himself. His actual son, Sergio, plays Adrian, his son (and nephew) in the movie. Naschy's depiction of Satan comes only in the last two minutes of the film, and although it is the dramatic highlight of the picture, it is far from Naschy's best moment in the film. Since his Devil is in the guise of a rotting corpse, he seems rather artificial, lacking the power and personality of the other monsters in the film. Because those creatures appeared in atypical circumstances, as playmates and companions to his son, they seemed more real and had genuine charm. The Devil, on the other hand, is largely static with an immobile face. After the colorful parade of ogres and creatures, Naschy's Devil is a bland disappointment.

Notable Quotes

- Don't go in there. It's the Devil's house. (**Zachary to Brigitte, a beautiful hiker**)
- Have you seen Larry Talbot? He suffers like you. (**Adrian to werewolf Waldemar**)
- I, the Fallen Angel, the emperor of thunderstorms, have won once again and will forever rule the human race. (**the Devil to Adrian**)

Hunk

1987   Rating: *   James Coco as the Devil

Crown International. Written by Lawrence Bassoff; Photographed by Bryan England; Edited by Richard E. Westover; Special Effects by Thomas Wayne Schwartz; Music by David Kurtz; Produced by Marilyn Jacobs Tenser; Directed by Lawrence Bassoff. Color, 102 minutes.

Annotated Cast List

Steve Levitt (*Bradley Brinkman,* computer programmer); John Allen Nelson (*Hunk Golden,* Bradley's alter ego); James Coco (*Dr. D,* the Devil); Deborah Shelton (*O'Brien,* the Devil's emissary); Rebeccah Bush (*Dr. Susan "Sunny" Graves,* Hunk's analyst, actually O'Brien in disguise); Avery Schreiber (*Constantine Constapopolis,* computer software manufacturer); Cynthia Szigetti (*Polly "Chachka" Claudia,* matronly beach buff); Coaster Royce (Wall Street wiz and beach clique leader); Hilary Shepard (*Alexis Cash,* his rich girlfriend); Melanie Vincz (*Laurel Springs,* cheerleader and beach bunny); Doug Shanklin (*Skeet Mecklenburger,* pro football player); Robert Morse (*Garrison Gaylord,* TV celebrity); J. Jay Saunders (Gaylord's director); Charles Dougherty (Gaylord's cameraman).

Appraisal and Synopsis

Lightweight and almost inconsequential, *Hunk* basically seems improvised and merely patched together into a feature film. Running 102 very slow minutes, it uses an endless stream of obvious sight gags and innuendoes, making even a single viewing seem like a repeat performance. The plot is inconsistent and filled with enormous loopholes, and few of the characters are likable or even tolerable. The few times an interesting idea pops up, it is quickly abandoned, and the film trundles on to its obvious conclusion.

The film starts as good-looking ladies' man Hunk Golden implores analyst Dr. Susan Graves to listen to his story. He then explains that six weeks previously, he was another person entirely named Bradley Brinkman, a computer wiz who had sunk into an unproductive funk since his girlfriend dumped him. His boss demanded that he come up with a productive idea for a software program in one week or be terminated. Bradley, desperate, typed into the computer that he would sell his soul for a money-making idea. His computer came to life and spewed out a detailed program designed as a guide to the yuppie lifestyle. His boss was so pleased that he gave Bradley the summer off with pay, so he left L.A. and rented a rundown beach house in trendy Sea Spray. Chachka, a transplanted New Yorker, introduced him around to the local beach gentry, who rejected Bradley as a total nerd. Bradley became enchanted by a beautiful girl on the beach but was surprised to learn that he was the only one who could see her. When Bradley held an open house, stocked with good food, nobody showed up, not even Chachka. Finally, the beautiful girl materialized and revealed that she is an agent of the Devil. She offered Bradley a free trial offer to become a "hunk" for the summer. After Labor Day, if he so chooses, he could sign a contract for his soul and be permanently transformed into his new identity.

The next morning, Bradley awakened as a sexy, muscle-bound stud named Hunk Golden, who quickly became the favorite Adonis on the beach. All the nubile women madly pursued him, and he found that he was a master sportsman as well. The bullies who picked on him as Bradley found they were unable to compete with him. One night, O'Brien brought the Devil, dressed as Attila the Hun, to chat with him. The Devil outlined his plans for Bradley once he signed up: to become a recruitment officer for him and to time travel to sign up souls from different eras of history. The Devil talked about his busy weekly schedule, including visits to the sacking of Rome by the Huns, the San Francisco earthquake, and the sinking of Atlantis. After Satan left, Bradley had second thoughts.

Hunk finishes his narrative to Dr. Graves, who insists that he forget all about Bradley and concentrate purely on being Hunk Golden and accepting himself in that role alone. She sets up their next session at his beach house. They go for a walk on the local pier where a segment of "Filthy Rich", a clone of "Lifestyles of the Rich and Famous" is being shot. The star, Garrison Gaylord, is trapped in a runaway jeep, which Hunk stops with his bare hands. The incident is captured on camera, and Hunk becomes an instant celebrity. Soon his face adorns the covers of *Time* and *Newsweek*. Hunk's relationship with Dr. Graves, who he calls Sunny, becomes romantic. After Hunk leaves her office, the Devil shows up dressed as a Nazi general, and the audience learns that Sunny is actually O'Brien. He reminds her that her own demonic deal is due to expire unless she obtains a contract from Bradley by Labor Day.

Hunk is getting a swelled head from his publicity. In his sleep, he is visited by his original body warning him not to sign the infernal deal. On Labor Day at midnight, when the Devil presents Hunk with the contract, he refuses it, saying he prefers to become Bradley again. The Devil also changes Sunny back into O'Brien and finally to her original self, a plain-looking princess from the tenth century who was sold to the Vikings by her father. He offers them a six-month extension, a Hitler's birthday offer, which they refuse. The Devil then dismisses O'Brien from his service since she has failed to sign a soul since that of Otto von Bismarck in 1887, and he returns her to Earth to live out her normal life span. The next day, the beach crowd is surprised to see Bradley walking hand in hand on the beach with a girl, and the end credits roll.

Besides its feeble humor, the major drawback to the story is the sloppy writing. For example, Hitler's birthday is in April, not September, but screenwriter Bassoff throws it in, thinking it sounds cute. More seriously, he misuses the entire concept of soul selling. The way this film operates, hell must be virtually empty, since everyone manages to escape as if it were a sieve or a revolving door. If the princess sold her soul in the Middle Ages, how does she get it back at the end of the picture as if nothing ever happened? She is free to return to Earth without any consequences. At the start of the film, Bradley promises to surrender his soul for a successful program.

He gets his program, but no bill ever comes due. Apparently, these deals casually come and go without anyone ever losing his or her soul. This undercuts the premise of any deal-with-the-Devil story, comedy or drama, and makes it completely pointless and without purpose.

Performances

James Coco died of a heart attack shortly after making this film in February 1987, and most of his scenes are drained of their humor because he looks so unwell. Coco was a wonderfully charming performer, and even a dismal film such as *Man of LaMancha* (1972) benefited from his whimsical performance as Sancho Panza. Here, he comes across as listless and dull. Normally, he would have endowed the material with some pep, but he merely walks through the role. Other cast members try earnestly, particularly John Allen Nelson, who eventually wound up on "Baywatch." Deborah Shelton, a former Miss USA and cast member on "Dallas," adds no luster to her resume with her appearance in *Hunk*.

Notable Quotes

• The Devil is a doctor? (**Hunk**)
A doctor of death, sworn to the hypocrite oath, to take life, whenever possible. (**the Devil**)
• This is beginning to sound like a horror film. (**Hunk**)
I always say, art imitates death. (**the Devil**)
• I finally meet a beautiful woman, and she wants me to bomb Pearl Harbor. (**Hunk to Dr. Graves**)
• To heaven with both of you! There are plenty of takers throughout the centuries to carry out my master plan, to make all the happy endings in history evil ones, like all those *Lassie* movies. (**the Devil to Bradley and O'Brien**)

Invitation to Hell

1984   Rating: ***   Susan Lucci as the Devil

Moonlight Productions. Written by Richard Rothstein; Photographed by Dean Cundy; Special Effects by Introvision; Edited by Gregory Prange and Ann Mills; Music by Sylvester Levay; Produced by Robert M. Sertner and Frank von Zerneck (executive); Directed by Wes Craven. Color, 98 minutes.

Annotated Cast List

Robert Urich (*Matthew Winslow*, scientist); Joanna Cassidy (*Patricia Winslow*, his wife); Barret Oliver (*Robbie*, their son); Soleil Moon Frye (*Chrissie*, their daughter); Susan Lucci (*Jessica Jones*, the Devil, posing as the director of Steaming Springs); Kevin McCarthy (*Harry Thompson*, president of Micro-Digitech); Joe Regalbuto (*Tom Peterson*, Matt's best friend); Patty McCormack (*Mary Peterson*, Tom's wife); Gino DeMauro (*Jimmy Peterson*, their son); Anne Marie McEvoy (*Janie*, their daughter); Virginia Vincent (*Grace Henderson*, Matt's secretary at Micro-Digitech); Bill Erwin (*Walt Henderson*, veterinarian and Grace's husband); Lois Hamilton (*Tracy Winters*, Grace's replacement);

Nicholas Worth (sheriff and doorkeeper to hell); Bruce Gray (*Larry Ferris*, Tom's supervisor); Jason Presson (*Billy Ferris*, Larry's son); John Zenda (doorman at Steaming Springs); Billy Beck (mover who snitches candy bar); Greg Monahan (*Pete*); Michael Berryman (valet); Frank von Zerneck, Jr. (newsboy).

Appraisal and Synopsis

This modest but intriguing telefilm was mounted by Wes Craven the same year as his breakthrough film, *Nightmare on Elm Street* (1984). The picture cleverly mixes elements of *The Mephisto Waltz* (1971), *Necromancy* (1972), *The Stepford Wives* (1975), *The Sentinel* (1977), and *Halloween 3* (1983), and it foreshadows some of the ideas from *The Firm* (1993). The basic premise is that the entrance to hell is in the Silicon Valley area of California, and the Devil has disguised it as a country club resort, which enables her (in this case) to capture the souls and control the activities of the up-and-coming giants of the computer industry. No doubt the Devil also plans to influence the entire world with this maneuver, but a brilliant inventor stumbles onto her evil scheme. Although the picture has a few tedious and predictable stretches, the concept of exploring hell in a space suit capable of withstanding intense heat is quite distinctive.

The telefilm starts with an awkward teaser that doesn't quite fit the flavor of the rest of the story. A chauffeur from Steaming Springs is distracted by two girls in bikinis, and his vehicle runs over the Devil in the guise of Jessica Jones. Levitating to her feet unharmed, the Devil gestures at the unfortunate driver, whose body erupts in flames. After the credits, the plot shifts to scientist Matthew Winslow, his wife, Pat, and children, Robbie and Chrissie, who are moving to California where he has just been put in charge of special projects at Micro-Digitech. His first assignment is to perfect a space suit commissioned by NASA for a future space mission to Venus. Matt's friend, Tom Peterson, is an executive at Micro-Digitech, and he helps Matt to get started in his new position.

Matt's car is sideswiped by a limousine near the entrance of Steaming Springs while he is taking his family to buy new furniture. Jessica Jones, the occupant of the vehicle, tries to placate the upset Matt, and when the sheriff arrives, he is condescending toward Matt. Meanwhile, Tom, his wife Mary, and their children go through an initiation ritual to become members of Steaming Springs, which involves entering through the special doorway in the basement of the club, supposedly to bathe in the thermally heated underground springs.

Several weeks pass, and Matt's improvements on the space helmet endow it with sophisticated sensors that can give temperature readings to the wearer, as well as the ability to detect the presence of other life forms and determine if they are benign or hostile. Grace, Matt's secretary, tries to give him a secret report, but she is interrupted by Harry Thompson, president of the corporation, who instructs Matt to give Jessica a private tour of his lab and to show her the classified improvements that he has made on the space suit. Unseen by Matt, his helmet evaluates Jessica as "nonhuman and malignant." Tom is given a promotion at the corporation and offers to sponsor Matt and his family at the club, telling him that all the important people in the area are members.

The following day, Matt is upset to learn that his secretary was fired by Harry Thompson. Pat also urges her husband to apply for membership at Steaming Springs. He finally accepts Jessica's invitation to tour the country club with Pat. Matt wanders off and locates the elaborate doorway leading to the sulphur springs and is startled by the surface heat of the metal door.

Jessica shows up and distracts him by flirting with him, which frightens the scientist. Matt locates his wife and asks her to leave with him at once, but she decides to stay and have lunch with Jessica instead. Jessica informs Pat that she and the children will be permitted to join the club without Matt.

Several days later, Matt is shocked when the family dog seems frightened of his wife and kids. He learns from Walt Henderson, the local vet, that Pat tried to have the dog put to sleep. Walt is the husband of Matt's former secretary, and Matt is saddened to hear that she was killed in a mysterious car accident. Matt becomes increasingly estranged from his family, whose behavior is growing more bizarre. Jessica gives Pat a grand piano as an apology for their recent auto accident, and she helps her redecorate their home in a dark and somber fashion. Matt researches the employment records and discovers that all of the executives in Micro-Digitech were promoted after joining the club.

Steaming Springs is holding a masked Halloween ball. Matt sneaks in while they are decorating, and using a special gauge, he discovers that the temperature behind the metal door is in excess of 800°. The sheriff attacks Matt after he takes his reading, and he is killed by Matt during their fight. Returning home, Matt learns that his entire family is demonically possessed; as they turn against him, he has to battle them one by one. The evil Chrissie reveals that their normal counterparts are trapped in the vestibule of hell by the Devil. He sets out to rescue them using the heat-resistant space suit. Tom tries to murder him when he takes the suit from the company lab, but Matt kills him with a special weapon built into the suit.

When he arrives at the party at Steaming Springs, Matt keeps his visor down and pretends that he is Tom. His helmet sensors detect that all the party guests are nonhuman. He sneaks down and passes through the doorway, but Jessica notices his movements and follows him. Matt blasts her with the suit's flamethrower, but she is unharmed. Descending, Matt discovers that the doorway leads to a vast cavern that heads downward through tremendous heat, and his electronic listening device picks up screams and cries in the distance. He continues on until he comes to a bottomless shaft. Jessica appears and taunts him, but when he hears his children's cries, he leaps down the shaft. After blacking out, Matt awakens in a bizarre equivalent of his home street (shot using negative footage). He enters his house and finds his family, each imprisoned by a beam of light. Pat is imprisoned with her piano, which she plays endlessly. The Devil appears and tries to prevent him from interfering, but Matt rebuffs her. He talks to Pat, and she breaks out of her invisible prison and embraces Matt. Together they free their children, and as they do this, the illusion of their house turns against the Devil. The keys of the piano fly at her like projectiles, and the Devil twirls around and disappears in a burst of flames. Matt and his family awaken in their own home as it originally appeared with their old furniture. He steps outside, and all of the neighbors are staring in the direction of Steaming Springs. "It erupted in flames last night and they can't put it out," somebody shouts at him. His family joins him, staring at the billowing smoke on the horizon.

Performances

Susan Lucci is best known for her role as Erica Kane on "All My Children", and she is considered one of the all-time greatest divas of soap operas. She finally won an Emmy for her part in 1999, after having been nominated twenty times. She was cast as Satan in this telefilm in tribute no doubt to her renown as the devious Erica. As the Devil, she uses different approaches with men and women to entice them to join her club. She appeals to the men by dangling the possibility of increased power, and if that fails she tries to seduce them with sex appeal. For the women, she portrays the club as an essential step to gaining prestige and to being a success in this exclusive community. As a woman, she is able to adapt and control her prospects far easier than if she were a man. On the whole, Lucci's performance is adequate, but it becomes somewhat weak during the climax. This is not principally her fault as the script makes the Devil seem rather inept and powerless at the finish, where all she can do is pout and scream Matt's name over and over, warning him not to free his family. How and why the house itself turns against her is unclear. It is also unclear exactly what happens at the end of the story. Did everyone die at the party, or did their good halves return to Earth like Pat, Robbie, and Chrissie? The Devil points out that everyone who joined Steaming Springs did so voluntarily, but that is not the case since the sheriff intercedes to force Chrissie though the doorway. It would seem logical that all the other members of the club remained damned and were victims of the destruction of Steaming Springs, which would no doubt leave a major vacuum at Micro-Digitech and the other nearby corporations. The writing is vague as to the Devil's eventual plans, which suggests that Richard Rothstein might have originally intended his script to be a pilot for a series. Rothstein helped to develop "The Hitchhiker" as an HBO series in 1983. This would explain several of the story's gaps, which could have been intended for development in later episodes. The conclusion of the film as it stands, however, seems decisive rather than open-ended.

Robert Urich delivers a smooth performance, but his character's acceptance of the supernatural comes too abruptly. A scientist would apply some empirical thought, especially when his only evidence is one abnormal reading from a temperature gauge. It is also unclear why he is so afraid of Susan Lucci when she tries to seduce him. All of these elements bring a lack of credibility to the roles played by both Urich and Lucci. Additional character development is sorely missed. On the other hand, a number of innovative ideas rescues the film from becoming either boring or silly. The picture is also aided by some fine work by the remainder of the cast, including nice bits from Patty McCormack, the original evil child, Rhoda, in *The Bad Seed* (1956), and veterans Bill Erwin, Kevin McCarthy, and Virginia Vincent. The actors playing the Winslow children both deserve special mention for their work: Barret Oliver, who won the starring part in *The Neverending Story* (1984), and Soleil Moon Frye, who was shortly to gain fame as Punky Brewster in her own television series. Together with Joanna Cassidy, they create a sense of believability, which Urich and Lucci fail to maintain. It is appropriate that young Frye has the last line in the picture, chirping, "All gone!" as the last vestige of Steaming Springs vanishes in flame and smoke.

Notable Quotes

- You don't care that much about money, I can tell, but you care about power and you care about pleasure.... Trust me, Matthew. I like you, and I will personally see to it that your membership here is as pleasurable as possible. (**Jessica to Matt, while she distracts him from the door to hell**)

- Do you think you can run from me? Do you think your weapons can touch me? (**Jessica to Matthew after he enters hell**)

- All you can do is lie and tease and tempt, but the choice is up to us. (**Matt to the Devil in defiance**)

Jesus

2000   Rating: **
Jeroen Krabbé and Manuela Ruggeri as the Devil

Trimark. Written by Suzette Couture; Photographed by Raffaele Mertes; Special Effects by the Interactive Group; Edited by Benjamin Weissman; Music by Patrick Williams; Produced by Paolo Piria and Russell Ragan; Directed by Roger Young. Color, 175 minutes.

Annotated Cast List

Jeremy Sisto (*Jesus Christ*); Jacqueline Bisset (*Mary*); Armin Müller-Stahl (*Joseph*); David O'Hara (*John the Baptist*); Luca Barbareschi (*Herod Antipas*, Tetrarch of Galilee); Elena Sofia Ricci (*Herodias*, his wife); Gabriella Pession (*Salome*, her daughter and Herod's stepdaughter); G. W. Bailey (*Livio*, advisor to Pilate); Jeroen Krabbé (the Devil in male form); Manuela Ruggeri (the Devil in female form); Christian Kohlund (*Caiaphas*, high priest); Tom Lockyear (*Judas Iscariot*); Luca Zingaretti (*Peter*, formerly Simon, foremost apostle); Gilly Gilchrist (*Andrew*, Peter's brother and apostle); Sebastian Knapp (*Matthew*, tax collector who becomes an apostle); El Housseine Dejjiti (*Simon the Zealot*, apostle); Karim Doukkali (*Philip*, apostle); Mohammed Taleb (*Bartholomew*, apostle); Sean Harris (*Thomas*, apostle); Fabio Sartor (*James the Elder*, apostle); Abedelouhahad Novaddine (*James the Younger*, apostle); Said Bey (*Taddeus*, apostle); Ian Duncan (*John*, the Beloved Disciple); Debra Messing (*Mary Magdalene*); Jerry Zimmerman (Wealthy client of Mary Magdalene); Peter Gevisser (*Lazarus*); Stefania Rocca (*Mary of Bethany*, sister of Lazarus); Mary Cristina Heller (*Martha of Bethany*, sister of Lazarus); Gary Oldman (*Pontius Pilate*, Roman governor); Claudio Amendola (*Barabbas*, criminal freed in place of Jesus); Roger Hammond (*Mordecai*); Omar Lahlou (*Nathaniel*); Rick Warden (*Jared*); Iddo Goldberg (*Seth*); Ichrak Berraoui (woman accused of adultery); Elaine English (Canaanite woman with sick daughter); Elliott Levy (tax collector); John Francis (*Zerah*); Tony Vogel (farmer); Carl Pizzie, Nicholas Sidi (zealots); Zach McGuire (*John the Baptist*, age twelve); Josh McGuire (*Jesus*, age twelve); Miles C. Hobson (*Jesus*, age six).

Appraisal and Synopsis

Jesus was first shown in the United States in two parts on television in May 2000 and was lambasted by most critics. It is a curious and offbeat effort, mixing various elements. In essence, the picture infuses the Bible with the atmosphere of "Xena the Warrior Princess." Some segments are fresh and innovative and work well. Many of the biblical scenes are beautifully rendered. But then, other sections are corny and stumble along in a feeble manner. The best sequences include the relationship between Jesus and Joseph (the concept that the public life of Jesus was triggered by the death of Joseph is unique), the easygoing charm of Jesus as he wins the confidence of his followers, and the unpretentious portrayal of many well-known incidents from the gospels. The Lazarus sequence is a highlight, as is the wedding feast in Cana, the many miracles, the

Sermon on the Mount, and the cleansing of the money changers at the temple. On the other hand, the numerous flashbacks are awkward and artificial. The scene in which Mary breaks the news of the annunciation is a good example, as is the scene where the six-year-old Jesus brings a dead bird back to life. The most dynamic and innovative scenes are those with the Devil. Consider the temptation sequence, quite static in many other films, but dynamic and imaginative in *Jesus*. The biggest letdown is the crucifixion. Golgotha is set under an aqueduct, which cracks with the death of Jesus. As Christ is hung on the cross (a disturbing moment as Christ screams when the nails are hammered into his wrists), Mary is told he is positioned in such a way so as to prolong his agony. He dies, however, about forty-five seconds later, with no cinematic indications that a longer period of time has passed. This editing miscue is repeated at several other moments. Pilate's scenes are overlong, largely because major star Gary Oldman is cast in the part. The script goes out of the way to make Pilate seem like a weasel and smart aleck, and while Oldman is excellent in the role, it throws off the balance and emphasis of the film. Other key roles, including most of the apostles, are weakly written and poorly portrayed. The mixing of accents in the film is unfathomable. Many characters sound as if they are from the American Midwest (including Jesus), others from England, and yet others speak with thick, almost indecipherable accents. The picture was shot in Malta and Morocco, so no doubt the use of local talent led to some of this confusion.

Performances

Two different performers play Satan, Jeroen Krabbé and Manuela Ruggeri, and the two sequences with the Devil are perhaps the most interesting in the film. The Devil is first seen during the temptation in the desert while Christ is fasting, appearing first in female form and wearing a red cloak. She is young and lovely, but her form is transparent, and appears and disappears as she speaks. She asks Jesus to give up his shield, the power that abides in him, so he can be tested as a mere mortal. After he agrees, Jesus lets out a scream as the protection of God the Father is ripped away from Him. "Welcome to life, Jesus," the Devil whispers as Christ appears before her fully mortal. She passes her cloak over his face. The cloak is then carried off in the wind and when it touches the ground, Satan emerges as a middle-aged man. He is dressed in a modern black suit and a black mock turtleneck shirt. His hair is quite unusual, resembling the hairstyle worn by Boris Karloff when he played a Satanist in *The Black Cat* (1934) combined with a touch of a mohawk. He first tempts Jesus to turn stone into bread. When Jesus refuses, Satan produces a group of starving children, and he asks Jesus again to turn the stone into bread for their sake. Again, Christ refuses. The Devil then conjures up the great temple in Jerusalem, suggesting that if Jesus wants the people to listen to Him, He should throw himself down from the heights of the temple. God will send His angels to catch Him, and the people will know he is the Messiah. "It is not my Father's will," Christ replies. The Devil waves his arms and brings Christ deep into space where they can see the entire planet. He tempts Jesus a final time, describing unlimited power. Transforming back into a woman, the Devil describes the limits of power. Christ finally rejects the temptation, and He is whisked back to the desert. From a distance, the Devil, now a male, calls out, "See you again, Jesus. It has only just begun."

The Devil's second appearance occurs on the Mount of Olives, where Christ prays before being delivered to the soldiers of the temple by Judas. In Luke 22:43, Christ is comforted by an angel at this point. The script, however, inserts the Devil as a substitute. Appearing only in male form, the Devil tries to convince Jesus not to allow Himself to be crucified. He claims that his sacrifice will be in vain. To prove his point, he takes Jesus forward in time to the period of the Crusades. He shows Jesus how warriors will kill their enemies using the name of Jesus Christ as their rallying cry. The Messiah is horrified, and the Devil then transports Him to a raging night battle during World War I. With bombs and mortar shells exploding around them, the Devil revels in the concept of war on such a scale. He then urges Christ to intervene and end the conflict, but Jesus refuses, saying man is endowed with free will. Returning to the garden of Gethsemane, Christ tells the Devil that He forgives him. "I don't want your forgiveness," the Devil exclaims, and he passionately begs Him to forsake His future agony. "No," Christ insists. "I am in the hearts of men. I will die for the everlasting kindness of the human heart created by the Father." Satan backs away into the shadows.

The Dutch actor Jeroen Krabbé is extraordinary as Satan, vibrant and effective. He is crafty, passionate, and logical but totally lacking in charm. His modern-day garb at first seems silly, but the incongruity fades away as the scene continues. When he later escorts Christ through the trench warfare of the First World War, the scene is riveting and dramatic. It also calls to mind *Civilization* (1916), the Thomas Ince film in which Christ returns to Earth in the guise of a German officer to end the conflict. Krabbé has been a major star in European films since the 1970s, and he is perhaps best known in American films as the villainous doctor in *The Fugitive* (1993) who frames Harrison Ford for the death of his wife. Manuela Ruggeri is a less-threatening presence than Krabbé, but it is fascinating to watch the Devil switch identities as casually as one changes hats.

One could also make a case that the Devil appears in yet another guise in the film as Livio, the character who is the Roman advisor to Herod Antipas and Pilate. Livio seems to have knowledge beyond the capacity of an ordinary man. His advice is always detrimental to Christ, attempting to frustrate His mission. When Christ is on the cross and cries out, "Father, forgive them, for they know not what they do," Livio replies softly, "We know exactly what we are doing, Messiah." G. W. Bailey, the actor who plays Livio, seems to base his speech pattern at times after that of Krabbé. Although it seems likely that Livio is another incarnation of Satan, this is never actually confirmed in the script. Jeremy Sisto makes a friendly, approachable Jesus, and he is effective in the intimate moments with Joseph, Mary, his mother, and Mary of Bethany. He is particularly good in the lighter moments, showing the charisma of Jesus and His natural sense of humor. He does seem outclassed, however, in his scenes with Gary Oldman as Pilate. Sisto's efforts fall a bit short in the "big moments," but on the whole he makes a refreshing and rather appealing Jesus. Sisto previously appeared as Elton in *Clueless* (1995), T. K. in *Suicide Kings* (1998), and Sonny in *This Space between Us* (1999).

Notable Quotes

• Power is what every man wants more than anything else in the world. They kill for it. There is nothing more precious, and it is yours to have. (**the Devil in female form, showing Jesus the entire planet from outer space**)

How? (**Jesus, very softly**)

Bow down to me, Jesus, just once. In all of existence, in before and after time, just once, Jesus. It is a small price. Consider the reward. (**the Devil, morphing back to a male form**)

Away with you, Satan! (**Jesus, yelling**)

• Killing for Christ will be a big business through the centuries, Christ Jesus. [chuckling] And this is what You're dying for. This is what your agony will give them, another reason to kill and torture each other. (**the Devil to Jesus, showing him an army of Crusaders launching an attack**)

• Make the earth a paradise. End poverty and hunger and war. You can do it! It is within your power right now! (**The Devil to Jesus, showing him a World War I battlefield at night**)

No, I cannot. It is not God's will. (**Christ's reply**)

It is not God's will to end a war? What kind of God is that? (**the Devil**)

One who loves mankind so much that He gives them freedom of choice. (**Jesus**)

• You don't know the plan. I do. I've seen it. Nothing changes. They don't have the capacity to love like you want them to. (**the Devil's final appeal to Jesus as Judas approaches to betray him**)

Judgment Day

1988   Rating: ****   Peter Mark Richman as the Devil

Rockport Films. Written by Ferde Grofé, Jr.; Photographed by Peter Warrilow; Special Effects by Romeo and Alberto Mabitol; Edited by Joe Zucchero and William Schlueter; Music by Lucas Richman; Produced by Ferde Grofé, Jr. and Keith Lawrence; Directed by Ferde Grofé, Jr. Color, 89 minutes.

Annotated Cast List

Kenneth McLeod (*Pete Johnson*, American tourist); David Anthony Smith (*Charlie Manners*, his companion); Monte Markham (*Sam Flarity*, Satana Cantina owner); Cesar Romero (*Octavio*, seventeenth-century nobleman who made a deal with the Devil); Gloria Hayes (*Maria*, his lovely daughter and ancient woman on road); Peter Mark Richman (*Fr. Dominic*, Satana village priest who becomes transformed into the Devil); Jennifer Perez (*Angela Flarity*, Sam's daughter); Brett Sergeant (*Frank Henry*, representative from American embassy in Manila); Joko Diaz (bus driver); Soji Sodeke, Joe Mar Avellana, Nigel Hogge, Edmundo Gaerlan, Tita Munoz, Jenny Andrada.

Appraisal and Synopsis

Judgment Day is an unpretentious but well-conceived film that works well within the modest limits of its storyline. It functions as a fable, a morality play, and a horror film. The story centers on Charlie and Pete, two American tourists in the Philippines, who decide to leave their bus when it breaks down, and on the advice of an elderly woman dressed entirely in black, who they encounter on the road, they follow her to Satana, a nearby town. The woman mysteriously vanishes as they approach the outskirts of Satana. They strike up the acquaintance of Sam Flarity, the American proprietor of the local cantina. He informs them of an unusual tradition of the town. One day each year, the entire populace abandons the town because of an old legend. Three hundred years earlier, the nobleman who founded Satana made a deal with the Devil to spare the town from an outbreak of the plague. The Devil's price was that he be permitted to take over the town as an outpost of hell for one day each year. No one dares to remain on that day, lest they be imprisoned in hell. Sam offers to drive them to San Marcos, the next village, when his daughter returns from school, and he locks up his cantina.

At first, the tourists mock the concept, but when they see all the citizens leaving in cars, carts, and wagons, they decide to join Sam, who becomes concerned when his daughter, Angela, fails to come home. She has become trapped in the bell tower during a game of hide-and-seek. As evening descends, her friends head off to join their families. Soon, Satana is abandoned as everyone has left. Sam begins a frantic search. He asks help from Fr. Dominic, the village priest, who helped to rescue his late wife, Teresa, twelve years earlier when she was trapped in the town during the time of the Devil. This time, the priest absolutely refuses to help Sam.

Charlie and Pete try to walk out of town, but they get trapped in a torrential downpour and return. At midnight, a procession of dark, cloaked figures enters the town. A distinguished-looking gentleman offers Charlie and Pete refuge in his luxurious pueblo. Introducing himself as Octavio, the man presents Maria, his daughter, who seems immediately drawn to Pete. Bit by bit, Charlie learns that Octavio is the founder of the town who bargained with Satan. Part of the deal was that he and his daughter are forced to live for eternity in exile in their house in the midst of the twilight world of Satana, which the Devil rules one day a year. The nobleman and his daughter are ageless, and the Devil and his horde of demons leave them entirely in peace in their pueblo. Octavio further explains that the Devil maintains his control over Satana through his third hand, a three-fingered claw. During the rest of the year, a resident of the town, someone who made a deal with the Devil, carefully stores and guards the hand. During the day of the Devil, this person is transformed into the Devil himself, and the third hand comes alive and becomes part of his body. Charlie tries to convince Pete to flee with him, but his companion refuses, and Charlie heads off on his own. Angela quietly approaches Pete as he rests in his room. They make love. She tells him that she fell in love with him when she first saw him on the road, but Pete cannot believe that Maria was the elderly cloaked figure.

The Devil arrives at the bell tower and captures Angela. Charlie encounters a terrified Sam in the street. Moments later, Sam is seized by cloaked demons, who scourge him with a whip. Charlie returns to the pueblo to talk with the kindly Octavio. This time Pete is convinced to attempt an escape when Octavio confirms that if they don't escape the Devil's domain that day, it will be a full year before they will have another opportunity.

Charlie and Pete sneak through the streets of the town, which remain in total darkness during the day of the Devil. They see Sam being tortured, and he is placed on a cross and brought before the Devil, who imprints his third hand on Sam's chest, searing his flesh. His body is later discarded, and Charlie and Pete try to rescue him. It is too late, since Sam is dying, and he says that he made a bargain with Satan to save Angela. He then whispers something privately to Charlie before dying. The two friends race off after battling with some cloaked demons. Running desperately, they get separated after Pete sprains his leg. Charlie races off as the hour tolls, signaling the end of the Devil's day. He passes out and revives next to the sleeping Angela. The young girl is confused, explaining that she experienced terrible dreams and then awoke next to Charlie on the side of the hill just outside of town.

The next day, the people of Satana return. Charlie goes to see Fr. Dominic to seek his advice. He tells him about Sam's death and his special message of forgiveness for the priest. Charlie accuses him of being the protector of the Devil's third hand. The priest reveals that he agreed to accept the hand in exchange for saving his sister, Sam's wife, when she was trapped in Satana during the Devil's day. Fr. Dominic shows Charlie the hand, which resembles a three-fingered glove. The priest says that he prays to be permitted to die before the next day of the Devil when he must wear the hand and be transformed into Satan. He tells Charlie that Sam has given his life to save Angela and that Pete will remain unharmed if he reached the safety of Octavio's house.

A year passes. Charlie stays in Satana to care for Angela and to operate Sam's cantina, planning to rescue Pete during the Devil's day. Frank Henry, the American Consul in Manila, arrives in search of Pete, who was reported missing by his parents. Charlie explains that he should be returning shortly. They observe the funeral procession of the late Fr. Dominic.

During the Devil's night, Charlie waits in town until the tolling of the midnight bell. He then goes to seek out his friend, only to discover too late that Pete had made a diabolical deal. Charlie screams as two demons grab him and drag him before Pete, who now has the third hand and who has been transformed into the Devil.

Ferde Grofé, Jr., son of the composer of the ever-popular *Grand Canyon Suite*, developed the film from start to finish, doing an excellent job on all counts. The portrayal of hell is unembellished but excellent, with a convincing mood and atmosphere that even conjures up images of the art of Hieronymus Bosch. Grofé is able to achieve this infernal ambience on a skimpy budget but without ever making the film look cheap. The writing and characters manage to remain credible, never becoming parodies such as in *Bill and Ted's Bogus Journey* (1991). The only serious drawbacks are a number of unresolved plot loopholes. Satana, the village to which the Devil brings hell on Earth once a year, is a compelling idea, although the name of the town is a little too transparent. It is unclear, however, exactly how this concept operates. Are there actually two Satanas, one in hell and one on Earth, and they merge once a year? This might explain the haven of Don Octavio's abode, which is in ruins on Earth but completely intact in hell. We never learn if this house is surrounded by demons continuously or only during the Devil's day. The idea of the third hand is also a good one, but it would have been far more impressive if its use were demonstrated at the film's conclusion. Charlie could have found Pete as himself and then be forced to witness him transform into the Devil when he attaches the third hand. It is also never explained how Maria was able to leave her home to seek out Charlie and Pete. Could both Octavio and Maria return to Earth for brief periods? If a few of these loopholes were explained, it really might have improved *Judgment Day* from the level of an interesting curio to that of a minor masterpiece. Oddly, most reviewers of this picture mistakenly place its locale in Mexico instead of the Philippines, despite the presence of the American Consul from Manila in the story.

Performances

Peter Mark Richman, a fine actor, gives a superb reading as the angst-ridden Fr. Dominic. He appears all too briefly as the Devil in a superb, flamboyant vignette which calls to mind Tim Curry's elaborate demon, Darkness, from the film *Legend* (1985). This Devil is ruthless, calculating, and totally malevolent. He is also a Devil who can be defeated, although Fr. Dominic, Sam, Charlie, and Pete fail in their efforts. But the good-hearted Don Octavio made a deal with Satan in which he got the better of the Prince of Darkness. Cesar Romero is superb as Octavio, teasing the audience at first into thinking that he may be the Devil in disguise. Romero plays his part with an avuncular charm that is hard to resist, and it is a shame that the film's budget couldn't permit a flashback to show how Octavio bested Satan in their initial encounter.

Notable Quotes

• Think about it, Pete, if you could spend a night in an honest-to-God haunted house, that would be the biggest kick in your whole life.... Think about it, you, me, the Devil, and the whole town deserted. (**Charlie to Pete**)

• Imagine Hades is a comet traveling through the universe. Once, only once in a year, it pauses close to Earth, attaching itself like a parasite for twenty-four hours on this valley, and then races off on its journey. (**Octavio to Charlie**)

What if we can't get out during the twenty-four-hour period? (**Charlie**)

You must wait another year for your chance. (**Octavio**)

• Satan is clever, so very clever. There is no pleading, no mercy. Only if you want something, you pay for it. (**Fr. Dominic to Charlie**)

• I don't care who you are, Devil, priest, whatever. To hell with your bargains. I will face you, and I'm going to beat you at your own game. (**Charlie to Fr. Dominic**)

The Killing of Satan

1983   Rating: *   Charlie Davao as the Devil

Puzon Film Enterprises. Written by Joe Mari Avellana; Photographed by Ricardo Herrera; Edited by Boy Vinarao; Special Effects by Un Gapo Marvella; Music by Ernani Cuenco; Produced by Pio C. Lee; Directed by Efren C. Pinon. Color, 93 minutes.

Annotated Cast List

Ramon Rivilla (*Orlando San Miguel*, new village leader); Elizabeth Oropesa (*Laura San Miguel*, his wife); Charlie Davao (the Devil); George Estgregan, Paquito Diaz, Cecile Castillo, Erlyn Umall.

Appraisal and Synopsis

A completely bizarre and mind-blowing Filipino escapade whose scenario is a jumble of martial arts, fairy tales, sorcery, and science fiction. The picture is practically incomprehensible, yet if you stick with it there are brief moments of interest that save it from being a total wipe-out. In essence, a remote village is plagued by a supernatural being known as the Prince of Magic. He kills the town elder by spinning him like a top until his insides become homogenized. On his deathbed, the old man names his nephew, Orlando San Miguel, a mustachioed former convict, as his successor. The villagers summon him by psychic means, and he soon arrives by canoe with his wife, Laura, and daughter, Betty. They fled their former home after gangsters killed their son, David. Nicknamed Lando (just like Billy Dee Williams in the *Star Wars* saga), the new leader is undergoing a ritualistic experience at sea when his daughter is kidnapped by the Prince of Magic, who intends to offer her as a virgin sacrifice to Satan, his master. Heir to his uncle's supernatural powers, Lando sets off on a quest to free Betty. He is led to a dark cavern known to be the entrance to the Prince of Magic's dark realm. He fights off snakes and various demons who seem like rejects from the World Wrestling Federation. The Prince of Magic himself, decked out in snappy red tights, overpowers him with a wave of his hand, and Lando's body is tossed off a cliff back into the sea. He washes up in a lagoon where he is pulled out of the water by a small mute child, who may be the reincarnation of Jesus Christ. Lando is given a magic cane to fight evil by the boy's parent, a venerable greybeard who claims to be the great "father" of all. He tells Lando that his opponent is Satan himself and that he can be defeated with the cane. Meanwhile, the Prince of Magic summons Satan, who first appears as a wimpy figure in red tights carrying a pitchfork. Later, his figure seems to bulk up as he changes threads to a dark suit with a cape. Lando encounters the Prince of Magic and defeats him with a combination of punches, jabs with his stick, and waves of power emanating from his hands. He shouts out to Satan, challenging him to single combat in order to free Betty. Giggling wildly, the Devil appears before Lando, then tosses him aside with a series of wrestling holds. They confront each other with bolts of fire emerging from their extended hands. After the appearance of the mute boy, Lando gains new strength and engages Satan in a stick fight with his magic cane against the Devil's pitchfork. He finds he can wound Satan, who screams in pain when the cane touches his body. Demon women join the fight, but Lando disintegrates them with a ray blast from his cane. Stripped of his defenses, Satan is finally overcome, as he shouts, "Drat!" and some garbled curses before he disappears. Lando retrieves Betty, who is in a daze, and tries to revive her. Meanwhile, back at the village, a demonic windstorm suddenly arises, which threatens to destroy them. Laura's clothes are blown off down to her black underwear. Lando finds a figurine of the infant Jesus on the spot where the mute boy last appeared, and as he lifts it from the ground, the storm back at the village dissipates. Lando and Betty then sail back to the village, where they are given a hero's reception.

The Killing of Satan is alternately a surreal drama, a crime story, an absurd fantasy, a religious allegory, a wrestling adventure, and a kung fu flick. It changes its focus so quickly that it numbs the audience with its preposterous narrative. It is impossible to determine why Lando, for example, uses magic force fields one minute and his fists the next. Likewise, Lando trudges through a cave one minute and an open field the next, that is, when he is not being lured into an underground drawing room populated by snake women. Despite the low budget, this film has a few decent qualities. The cinematography isn't bad, and the music score is actually quite good at times. The acting is non-existent, however, and the special effects are ludicrous. Nevertheless, it is fun watching the Devil being forced to use his pitchfork as if he were a gladiator in the arena.

Performances

Charlie Davao is a ridiculous and pathetic Devil, particularly in his initial appearance with his spindly arms and legs and a skinny, ratlike tail dangling down to the ground. He is slightly more impressive when he switches to a suit and cape, but he still seems more loony and laughable than menacing. His voice is a scratchy, snarling whisper, and his madcap cackle renders this Satan as perhaps the most ludicrous one ever to appear onscreen.

Notable Quotes

- Satan! Where are you? Come out and fight! You're yellow, Satan! (**Lando's shouted challenge**)

The King of Kings

1926   Rating: ****   Alan Brooks as the Devil

Pathé. Written by Jeannie MacPherson; Photographed by Peverell Marley, Fred Westerberg, and Jacob A. Badaraco; Special Effects by Paul Sprunck and Norman Osunn; Edited by Anne Bauchens, Harold McLernon, and Clifford Howard; Music by Hugo Reisenfeld; Produced and Directed by Cecil B. DeMille. B&W with color sequence, silent with synchronized sound and music, 115 minutes.

Annotated Cast List

H. B. Warner (*Jesus Christ*); Dorothy Cumming (*Mary*, his mother); Joseph Schildkraut (*Judas Iscariot*); Ernest Torrence (*Peter*, formerly Simon, foremost apostle); David Imboden (*Andrew*, apostle); Robert Edesen (*Matthew*, apostle); Robert Ellsworth (*Simon the Zealot*, apostle); Charles Belcher (*Philip*, apostle); Clayton Packard (*Bartholomew*, apostle); Sidney D'Albrook (*Thomas*, apostle); James Neill (*James the Elder*, apostle); Charles Requa (*James the Younger*, apostle); John T. Prince (*Thaddeus*, apostle); Joseph Striker (*John, the Beloved Disciple*); Jacqueline Logan (*Mary Magdalene*, rich courtesan later cleansed by Jesus); Sally Rand (her slave); Alan Brooks (the Devil); Rudolf Schildkraut (*Caiaphas*, high priest); Dot Farley (servant to Caiaphas); Theodore Kosloff (*Malchus*, head of high priest's guard); Sam De Grasse (pharisee); Otto Lederer (*Eber*, pharisee); Cason Ferguson (scribe); Kenneth Thomson (*Lazarus*); Josephine Norman (*Mary of Bethany*, sister of Lazarus); Julia Faye (*Martha of Bethany*, sister of Lazarus); Victor Varconi (*Pontius Pilate*, Roman governor); Majel Coleman (Pilate's wife); George Siegmann (*Barabbas*, criminal freed in place of Jesus); William Boyd (*Simon of Cyrene*, man who helps Christ carry the cross); Clarence Burton (repentant thief); James Mason (unrepentant thief); Viola Louie (woman accused of adultery); Muriel McCormack (blind girl cured by Jesus); Bryant Washburn (young Roman); Lionel Belmore (Roman nobleman); Leon Holmes (imbecile boy); Monte Collins (rich Judean); Soijin (Persian prince); William Costello (Babylonian nobleman); Nobel Johnson (zebra charioteer); Richard Alexander, Tom London, Robert McKee, Peter Norris, Dick Richards (soldiers).

Appraisal and Synopsis

Cecil B. DeMille became established as the master of the religious epic in 1923 with his production of *The Ten Commandments*, even though only a portion of that film was set in ancient Egypt. Actually billed as *Cecil B. DeMille's The King of Kings*, this picture was highly successful both financially and in the opinion of countless filmgoers for whom it represented the finest religious picture of its day. For the most part, the film sticks closely to the text of the four gospels, and almost all of the title cards cite chapter and verse for their content. However, it should be noted that the opening is extraordinarily decadent and camp, straying considerably from the Bible. The film opens at a wild and lavish party thrown by the wealthy courtesan Mary Magdalene. The scantily clad trollop becomes outraged when some of her guests taunt her that her favorite lover, Judas, has left her to follow a lowly preacher from Nazareth. Judas is a Romanized Jew in this film, who avoids wearing a beard or following other Jewish traditions. Outraged, Mary orders her chariot, drawn by a team of zebras, and she heads off to reclaim Judas and embarrass Jesus. After this perfectly awful introduction in which Mary seems like a modern-day flapper, the film switches to a truly magnificent introduction of H. B. Warner as Jesus. A blind girl is brought before Jesus, and as He cures her, the audience is given the viewpoint of this sightless child, whose vision is slowly restored; the first image she sees is the face of Jesus. In one fell swoop, DeMille goes from the ridiculous to the sublime, and this particular scene is masterful, handled with wonderful sensitivity. When Mary Magdalene shows up, Jesus casts out her seven deadly sins, and this scene also reeks of kitsch, as the sins appear as phantoms trying to lure Mary back into evil with their pleasures. After this scene, the film finally settles down to a traditional story of Jesus. There are many superb moments, but the film has momentary stumbles and a few awkward touches. It never sinks as low as the vulgar level of the opening, however, nor does it ever surpass the excellence of Christ's introduction.

The highlights include the wondrous revival of Lazarus, an excellent depiction of the Last Supper, a powerful and visually impressive rendering of the crucifixion, and a spectacular resurrection sequence filmed in two-strip technicolor. The musical soundtrack is synchronized to the film, and there are also occasional sound effects, which are well handled and never intrusive. For many, no doubt, this version served as the yardstick by which future religious epics were measured, and despite its numerous lapses, it is one of DeMille's finest endeavors. In 1961, the film was remade under the helm of Nicholas Ray. Dropping the initial "*The*" from the title, this remake was one of the finest of the later biblical epics, marred only by an artificial subplot with Harry Guardino as Barabbas, raising this character to the status of an underground rebel leader. The cast had many first-rate performances, including Jeffrey Hunter as Jesus, Royal Dano as Peter, Rip Torn as Judas, Robert Ryan as John the Baptist, and Orson Welles providing the superb narration. The Devil did not appear in this version of *King of Kings*, and the temptation in the wilderness occurred only as thoughts in the mind of Christ.

Performances

Alan Brooks was a journeyman actor who appeared in a handful of pictures starting with *Red Dust* in 1926. His best part was as John Krenton in the melodrama *Pals in Paradise*, also 1926. He appeared sporadically in films up to his death a few days after Irving Thalberg's passing in September 1936. *The King of Kings* is the only prestigious entry in his filmography. His scene, set against the pillars of the temple in Jerusalem, is a variant of Christ's temptation by Satan during his forty-day fast. In Mark 1:13 and Luke 4:1–13, this occurs in the wilderness, but Matthew 4:1–11 also has the Devil take Christ to the pinnacle of the temple in Jerusalem during his temptation and then later to a mountaintop. The gospel also implies that these travels, which normally would have taken days, occurred instantaneously. Therefore, DeMille's temple setting for this encounter is biblically accurate. Brooks is clothed in an elaborate, flowing black garment trimmed in gold braid and wears a flamboyant black headdress. He points out the crowded street before the temple and in a vision transforms the crowd into a marching legion of Roman soldiers. As He watches this, Christ strikes His breast repeatedly with His clenched left hand. The Devil dismisses the vision rather hastily and withdraws after this rather half-hearted effort. The timing of this enticement seems ill chosen on the Devil's part, because Christ had just rejected the crown of Israel, which was offered to Him by an adoring crowd outside the temple. Since Christ had just demonstrated that worldly power meant nothing to Him, this lure proposed by the Devil was not only futile but unintelligent. Overall, Brooks makes little impact, and his time on screen lasts less than a minute.

H. B. Warner basically carries the entire film, and his believable interpretation of Jesus is the finest element in the production. Rudolf and Joseph Schildkraut, father and son, are both superb, particularly in their scene together. Few of the other actors leave much of an impression, except for young Muriel McCormack, who is so natural as the young blind girl. Also excellent are the youngsters in the scene where Jesus puts his carpentry skills to work when He mends a child's broken doll. A poignant moment such as this illustrates the film's positive reputation.

Notable Quotes

- Behold the kingdoms of the world—and the glory of them. All this power will I give Thee—if Thou will fall down and worship me! (**the Devil, as noted in Matthew 4:8–9**)
- Get thee behind Me, Satan! It is written, "Thou shall worship the Lord, thy God, and Him only shalt thou serve." (**Jesus, as noted in Luke 4:8**)

The Last Temptation of Christ

1988   Rating: ***   Juliette Caton as the Devil

Universal. Written by Paul Schrader, based on the novel by Nikos Kazantzakis; Photographed by Michael Ballhaus; Special Effects by Dino Galliano and Iginio Fiorentini; Edited by Thelma Schoonmaker; Music by Peter Gabriel; Produced by Barbara De Fina and Harry Ufland (executive); Directed by Martin Scorsese. Color, 164 minutes.

Annotated Cast List

Willem Dafoe (*Jesus Christ*); Harvey Keitel (*Judas Iscariot*); Barbara Hershey (*Mary Magdalene*); Verna Bloom (*Mary*); David Bowie (*Pontius Pilate*, Roman governor); Andre Gregory (*John the Baptist*); Harry Dean Stanton (*Paul of Tarsus*, formerly Saul); Juliette Caton (Satan in the guise of a young angel); Leo Marks (Satan's voice as a pillar of fire); Roberts Blossom (spirit of dead religious leader); Victor Argo (*Peter*, formerly Simon); Gary Barsaraba (*Andrew*, apostle); Michael Been (*John*, apostle); Paul Herman (*Philip*, apostle); Leo Burmeister (*Nathaniel*, apostle also known as Bartholomew); Alan Rosenberg (*Thomas*, apostle); John Lurie (*James*, apostle); Irvin Kershner (*Zebedee*, father of James); Nehemiah Persoff (temple rabbi); Tomas Arana (*Lazarus*); Randy Danson (*Mary of Bethany*, sister of Lazarus); Peggy Gormley (*Martha of Bethany*, sister of Lazarus); Paul Greco (zealot); Barry Miller (*Jeroboam*); Robert Spafford (steward of wedding in Cana); Del Russel (money changer who claims to be fair); Donald Hodson (Saducee).

Appraisal and Synopsis

Martin Scorsese's controversial project offers one of the freshest and most unique studies of Jesus Christ and His importance. The picture can be troubling for viewers for whom the portrayal of Jesus is a sacred matter, for the Savior revealed in this film is filled with doubts and uncertainties, an image as far from the traditional image of Jesus as possible. This turns out to be both a strength and a weakness. The main brouhaha engendered by the story is somewhat of a red herring, since the image of a married Christ with a family is only an illusion created by Satan to tempt Jesus to disavow His sacrifice on the cross for the redemption of mankind. This sequence as presented in the film would probably cause little distress to devout filmgoers because it is consistent with the biblical depiction of the Devil as tempter. What would trouble them far greater, however, is the overall character of Jesus in the film. He is ambivalent and indecisive, lacks clarity of vision, and is somewhat of a wimp. At other times, when delivering a fiery tirade, He appears only to be putting on a theatrical performance for His audience. These elements, of course, derive from the disquieting and masterful novel by Nikos Kazantzakis. Finally, Jesus is too thoroughly decived by Satan in his disguise. If the Devil can hoodwink Jesus so completely, what chance would the ordinary individual have in resisting him?

Putting all of these theological considerations aside, *The Last Temptation of Christ* is flawed as a film for many technical reasons, including a meandering script and the presence of a number of extraneous elements, such as the frequency of bare-breasted women onscreen and the use of language that makes most characters sound as if they are from the Lower East Side of Manhattan. The employment of modern slang is also disruptive and annoying. Scorsese bends over backward to present a Judea as far removed as possible from the sugar-coated Hollywood conception, but in doing so he creates an image of biblical times that is just as distorted. On the one hand he tries to make Jesus seem more immediate by using modern vernacular, but he then places Him in a setting more strange, exotic, and alien than ever previously shown. These elements work against each other continually, so it never really gels.

The picture is divided into three sections. In the first third, Jesus is shown resisting the call from God and trying to avoid His mission. He uses His carpentry skills to build crosses for the Romans, hoping this will make God consider Him unworthy. His only genuine friend is Judas, who berates Him and calls Him a collaborator. He visits a religious community, only to learn that their leader, with whom He had spoken, is dead, and He was talking with a spirit. He goes to see John the Baptist, who recognizes Him as God's chosen, and then Jesus heads out to the desert. In the wilderness, He draws a circle in the sand and insists that God tell Him in plain words what He wishes Him to do. Instead, Jesus is visited by three images of Satan, first as a serpent, then as a lion, and last as a pillar of fire. Jesus rejects His temptations, and as He departs, the Devil warns Jesus that they will meet again. A vision of John the Baptist appears with a message from God for Jesus to bring His word to everyone.

The middle portion of the film more or less conforms with the biblical story of Christ, except that Judas is His staunchest supporter instead of Peter, who is somewhat plodding and dull. After Jesus raises Lazarus from the dead (an excellent sequence), the Pharisees send assassins to murder the resurrected man, destroying proof of the miracle. When He brings His crusade to Jerusalem, Jesus asks Judas to betray Him so He can fulfill the prophecy and bring redemption to mankind. His suffering is portrayed in great detail.

The last third of the film occurs as Jesus is in agony on the cross. A beautiful young angel appears, who informs Jesus that God has relented and sent her to save Him. Taking Him down from the cross, she tells Jesus that He is really not the Messiah, and they slip away from the crucifixion scene, ignored by all of the other figures, who seem to be in a trance, gesturing at and mocking the empty cross as if Christ were still on it. She tends to His wounds and prepares Him for His marriage to Mary Magdalene, who dies after their wedding night. The angel tells the outraged Jesus that there is only one woman in the world who wears many different masks, and she brings Jesus to live with Mary and Martha, the sisters of Lazarus. Years pass, Jesus lives an idyllic life, and Mary bears Him many children. One day, he meets Paul of Tarsus, who preaches about the resurrected Christ. Jesus tells him that it is a lie, that He is Christ, and that He escaped the cross. More years pass until the year 70, when Jerusalem is burned by Roman troops. The elderly Jesus falls ill, and on His deathbed He is visited by Peter and a bitter Judas, who berates Jesus for not fulfilling His purpose designed by God. Jesus replies that He was rescued by an angel, but Judas identifies the being as Satan, who transforms at once into a pillar of fire. The elderly Jesus crawls to Golgotha and implores God the Father that He indeed wants to redeem mankind and fulfill the scriptures. Suddenly, Christ is back on the cross, and the entire episode is exposed as an illusion by the Devil to have Christ renounce His mission. Having resisted His last temptation, Jesus surrenders His life, saying, "It is accomplished!" and the film ends, stressing the image of light. Beyond any doubt, the final third of the film is its most successful segment. It is the only section in which Jesus seems genuine rather than stilted and where He displays a degree of humanity. This section also contains some of the film's finest moments of acting, editing, and cinematography.

Interestingly, the device employed in the final third of the film was borrowed by "Star Trek: The Next Generation" for an episode first shown in 1992 called "Inner Light." Captain Picard is zapped by an unknown probe in deep space and winds up living an entire alternate lifetime on a small, alien planet where he marries and has children. Only at the end of this life span does Picard learn that it was an illusion created by this alien world, which was facing extinction, so that its culture and heritage could be passed on. In both "Star Trek" and *The Last Temptation of Christ*, this complicated plot gimmick succeeds exceptionally well. In the former, it serves as a final legacy of hope and love for a dying civilization. In the latter, it serves as a well-baited trap to dissuade Christ from His purpose. In both cases, these pastoral reveries provide ample food for thought and represent high points of filmmaking.

Performances

It is the Devil who is at the heart of *The Last Temptation of Christ*, and it is his scenario which is presented on the screen, a desperate and all out-assault to prevent the redemption of mankind. Satan employs four different disguises while tempting Christ. First he appears as a serpent who speaks with the voice of Mary Magdalene. "I feel sorry for you. You are lonely," the serpent says, claiming to be Christ's spirit. He employs the concept of human love and sex as his bait, but Jesus rejects the appeal, and the serpent vanishes. The Devil reappears as a lion and speaks with the voice of Judas. He claims to be Jesus' heart and offers Him worldly power. After Jesus dismisses him, he returns as a pillar of fire and taunts Jesus, who had prayed as a small child to be transformed into God. Christ finally names His tempter as Satan, who promises to return. Each of these masquerades has scriptural significance: the serpent is the form in which the Devil appeared to Eve in the Garden of Eden, the lion is from the Book of Daniel, when the prophet was tossed into the lion's den, and the pillar of fire appeared in Exodus to guide the Israelis out of Egypt. The scene illustrates a passage in Mark 1:13, "And He was in the wilderness forty days, tempted by Satan, and He was with the wild beasts." But the Devil's most astounding disguise is during the final third of the picture, when he appears as a beautiful angel. Could this triumphant deception be a reflection of how Lucifer may have originally appeared when he was an archangel in heaven who sat at the right hand of God? Is this why the deception completely fooled Jesus, because Lucifer reverted to an appearance close to his original form? In other words, it was a natural form for him to take, except his angelic form seemed to be female. Astute viewers may penetrate the disguise when the Devil belittles God by implication after the death of Mary Magdalene. For the most part, however, this angel seems pure, holy, and unspoiled.

Juliette Caton does a magnificent job as Satan. Her attitude is straightforward and simple, and her clothing is plain, just an ordinary robe. Her appearance has a Pre-Raphaelite beauty, with long, flowing, curly hair. This was the first film for the young actress, whose next role was as Heidi in *Courage Mountain* (1992) with many other films to follow. Her refined English accent is in marked contrast to the rather brusque New York dialect spoken by the others in the cast, except for David Bowie as Pilate and Leo Marks as the voice of Satan in the pillar of fire. She never lets her mask drop for an instant, as she guides and advises Jesus in his haven of bliss.

Willem Dafoe was an unusual choice to play Jesus. Unlike many actors who have an immediate charm and appeal, Dafoe projects a rather negative aura, which makes him ideal when he is cast as a villain. He is definitely cast against type, and the audience does not naturally bond with him. During the first half of the film, his Jesus is irritating and somewhat abrasive. It is difficult to accept him in the role until the Last Supper, which Scorsese also portrays quite differently, with more women in attendance than men. During the passion and the alternate life vision, Dafoe is magnificent. Harry Dean Stanton and Harvey Keitel are also excellent, after one adjusts to their inappropriate speech patterns. Irvin Kershner, director of *A Fine Madness* (1966), *The Empire Strikes Back* (1980), and many other films, appears briefly and effectively in the role of Zebedee. The ultimate measure of success or failure of this film is the personal reaction of each viewer. One needs to reach out and overlook the film's many flaws, distractions, and pretensions, however, to consider one's personal interpretation and reaction.

Notable Quotes

- To love and care for a woman? To have a family? This is a trick? Why are You trying to save the world?... The world doesn't have to be saved. Save Yourself. Find love. (**Satan as the serpent to Jesus in the desert**)
- When You were making crosses for the Romans in Nazareth, your head was exploding with dreams of power, power over everyone. You said it was God, but You really wanted power. (**Satan as the lion to Jesus**)
- You are God! The Baptist knew it. Now it's time you admit it. You are His Son, the only Son of God. Join me, and together we'll rule the living and the dead. (**Satan as the pillar of fire**)
- I'm the angel who guards you. Your father is the God of mercy, not punishment. He saw you and said, "Aren't you His guardian angel? Well, go down and save Him. He suffered enough." Remember when He taught Abraham to sacrifice his son? Abraham was just about to kill the boy with his knife when God stopped him. So if He saved Abraham's son, don't you think He would want to save His own? (**Satan as the Angel of Light**)

Leaves from Satan's Book
AKA Blade af Satans Bog

1918/1921   Rating: ****   Helge Nissen as the Devil

Nordisk Films. Written by Edgar Hoyer and Carl Theodor Dreyer, inspired by a novel by Marie Corelli; Photographed by George Schnéevoigt; Produced and Directed by Carl Theodor Dreyer. B&W, silent, 132 minutes.

Annotated Cast List

Helge Nissen (the Devil). **First Story:** Halvard Hoff (*Jesus Christ*); Jacob Texiere (*Judas*, the betrayer); Erling Hansson (*John*, the beloved disciple). **Second Story:** Hallander Helleman (*Don Gomez de Castro*, famous scholar); Ebon Strandin (*Isabella*, his daughter); Johnnes Meyer (*Don Fernandez y Argote*, monk who instructs Isabella); Hugo Bruun (*Count Manuel de Herrera*, Isabella's cousin); Nolle Holden (*Jose*, butler). **Third Story:** Viggo Wiehe (*Count de Chambord*, provincial aristocrat); Emma Wiehe (*Countess de Chambord*, his wife); Jeanne Tramcourt (*Genevieve*, their daughter); Elith Pio (*Joseph*, their servant); Emil Helsengreen (provincial commissar); Vilhelm Petersen (*Quentin Fouquier-Tinville*, public prosecutor); Tenna Kraft (*Marie Antoinette*, deposed queen of France); Viggo Lindstrom (*Pitou*); Sven Scholander (*Michonnet*). **Fourth Story:** Clara Wieth (*Siri*, White partisan); Carlo Wieth (*Paavo*, her husband, another White supporter); Karina Bell (*Naima*, woman whose father is murdered by the Red tribunal); Carl Hillebrandt (*Rautaniemi*, Red supporter with designs on Siri); Christian Nielsen (*Motti*, White corporal).

Appraisal and Synopsis

Visionary film genius Carl Theodor Dreyer started this episodic film in 1918 before finishing his first film, *The President*

(1919). Without doubt this movie was inspired by *Intolerance* (1916), D. W. Griffith's ambitious, multi-story presentation. Oddly, Griffith also made a film, *The Sorrows of Satan* (1926), based on the same Marie Corelli novel as *Leaves from Satan's Book*. Actually, little of Corelli's novel is used in this film, except for the sympathetic premise that God is compelling Satan to perform his evil deeds and that the Devil benefits when someone resists his temptations. This picture clearly reveals Dreyer's stylistic flair, which he fully demonstrated in later films such as *The Passion of Joan of Arc* (1928) and *Vampyr* (1932). In terms of drama, this picture has a sophistication surprising for its day. The plots move at a stately pace, and the composition of each scene is beautifully laid out, reflecting at times the influence of Pre-Raphaelite art, particularly in the depiction of women such as Mary Magdalene. Recent editions of the film, with the added classical soundtrack featuring music by de Falla, Tchaikovsky, Gustav Holst, and others, help to present Dreyer's work in the best possible light.

The picture begins with lengthy title cards which present the basic premise: the Devil, after his fall from paradise, is ordered by God to walk the Earth in the form of a man and to continually tempt and test mankind. For each person who succumbs to his temptation, Satan's exile from heaven is extended another hundred years, but when anyone resists him, then his sentence is reduced by a thousand years. With this judgment in place, it seems that the Devil is clearly not motivated to do an effective job corrupting mankind, so God has to keep reminding him to continue with his assignment. In this scenario, the Devil is a reluctant pawn in God's grand design who is forced into doing a disagreeable task in which his every success condemns him to a lengthier sentence. Satan's lot is a miserable one, since his deepest wish is to find favor again in the eyes of God. Now his only triumph occurs when he fails in his endless labors.

The initial story is one of the Devil's most bitter assignments, to tempt Judas to betray Christ. To achieve his goal, Satan assumes the persona of a Pharisee and advisor to Caiaphas, high priest of Israel. He finds it easy work to turn the scribes and other priests against Jesus, playing on their hubris. Judas, sulking over a rebuke from Christ when He complained about the cost of oils used to anoint the Lord's feet, is also readily manipulated. The scenario depicts the Last Supper and Christ's agony in the garden of Gethsemane. Satan engineers Judas' betrayal of Christ with a kiss. After Jesus is led away, the Devil pays off the crestfallen Judas with thirty pieces of silver. Judas then falls to his knees in despair. Suffering profound grief, the Devil hears God's voice, urging him to continue his work.

The second story is set in sixteenth-century Spain during the Inquisition. The Devil has assumed the role of the grand inquisitor, and his target is Don Gomez de Castro, a noted scholar, and his daughter, Isabella. The instrument of his assault is Don Fernandez, a young monk who has fallen deeply in love with Isabella while instructing her in mathematics. When Isabella's cousin, Count Manuel, a military officer, pays the Gomez family a visit, Fernandez becomes more obsessed. Satan recruits Fernandez to work for the Inquisition, suggesting it would enable him to obtain everything he desires. Jose, the butler in the Gomez household, reports to the grand inquisitor that he observed his employer casting horoscopes. The Devil assigns Fernandez to pursue the accusation. When ordered to torture Isabella, Fernandez instead brings her to his own room and gazes at her longingly until the Devil arrives with instructions for Isabella to be burned at the stake. Fernandez collapses,

Satan with a widow's peak (Helge Nissen) masquerading as the grand inquisitor in the Spanish story in Leaves from Satan's Book. *Johnnes Meyer plays the monk who falls victim to the Devil's temptations.*

and his figure is regarded by the melancholy Satan, who regrets that he has no time for contemplation but must continue to carry out his campaign of corruption.

The next story is set in France in 1793 after the overthrow of the monarchy and the establishment of the republic. Louis XVI had been executed in January after a trial before the convention. His widow, Marie Antoinette, is in prison awaiting her own trial in the fall. Apparently, the revolution had bypassed the aristocratic Chambord family at their castle in the backwoods of the provinces. Satan's mission is to destroy this family, as well as to hasten the execution of Marie Antoinette. He assumes the role of Erneste Durond, a member of the Jacobin Club. The pawn of his schemes is Joseph, a servant of the Chambord family. When a local tribunal convicts and beheads Count de Chambord, his last request to Joseph is for him to lead his wife and Genevieve, his daughter, to safety and to remain loyal to them. Joseph conceals their identities and brings them to Paris. Erneste befriends Joseph and gets him an important position in the Jacobin Club.

With his new importance, Joseph decides to announce his love to Genevieve, but she rejects him as anything but a friend, feeling he is too far beneath an aristocrat of her station. The Devil assumes a new role, as a deaf cripple who brings a note that throws suspicion on the incognito mother and daughter to Fouquier-Tinville, the public prosecutor. He orders their detention for questioning. Countess de Chambord, too proud to lie even to save her daughter, reveals their actual identities. Joseph is then questioned as their protector, but the Devil, still disguised as the cripple, indicates that it was Joseph who wrote the note to implicate the pair. The startled Joseph falls to temptation and pretends this is true. The Chambords are sentenced to death, and Joseph is congratulated by the tribunal for his diligence. As the cripple leaves the trial, he dematerializes in front of one of Fouquier-Tinville's men, who is ordered to tail him.

Marie Antoinette's trial occurs on October 14 and 15, and she is condemned to death. Joseph has an opportunity to rescue her but changes his mind at the last minute. As he leaves the prison, the Devil heaps his scorn upon him, revealing himself as Satan and claiming that Joseph betrayed not one, but three women to death. The Devil wants to pause in his work but God shows no mercy, and again orders him to continue.

The fourth story is contemporaneous to its day, using the 1918 Finnish Civil War as a backdrop. In 1917, Finland declared its independence from Russia at the time of the Russian Revolution. The new government quickly faced its own revolt when communist "Reds" tried to seize control and replace the republican "Whites" who wanted to maintain a constitutional republic. The Devil takes on the character of Ivan, a monk who acts as a judge for the Red tribunal in Hirola, a Finnish city. His objective is to undermine the White cause, in particular the married couple Paavo and Siri, dedicated White partisans. They are simple farmers with two small children. Their only helper is Rautaniemi, who becomes a convert to the Red side after attending a lecture by Ivan. He threatens to denounce Paavo unless Siri yields to his advances, but she refuses. Siri is captured and falls into the hands of Ivan, who attempts to persuade her to betray the White cause. He offers to spare her husband, who is supposedly entering a Red ambush. When she refuses, Ivan threatens to kill her children. The Red troops are distracted by a surprise White attack, and Siri grabs a knife and stabs herself rather than yield to Ivan. Paavo arrives with the victorious White troops and comforts Siri as she dies. Her heroic sacrifice provides the Devil with a thousand-year reprieve from his sentence. The picture ends as the camera focuses on the heart-shaped pendulum of a clock.

Each of these four leaves from Satan's book is more complicated than it initially appears. What originally seems superficial is actually a moral quagmire, filled with unusual ironies. For example, in the first story, if Christ is not betrayed, then the salvation of mankind will not follow. Judas and the Devil provide a vital function in the divine plan, a function which casts Judas as the lowest, most treacherous, and unredeemable individual who ever lived. But if Judas had resisted Satan, then Christ's mission on Earth would not have been fulfilled. The second story is the most compelling episode, magnificently photographed, and the depiction of the Inquisition is stunning if overly melodramatic. The delineations of the various strata of society, as much as the Inquisition itself, seem to drive the destinies of the characters. Why does Jose betray his master? Was Fernandez driven to join the Inquisition by his jealousy of Count Manuel, who performs an ambiguous function in the story? The third story rambles too much and is weakened by the maudlin portrayal of Marie Antoinette, which diverts from the main thrust of the episode. In this segment, Dreyer errs in other ways. It seems unbelievable that the Chambords behave as if the revolution had never occurred. Their aristocratic airs pave the way for their own doom. For example, Countess de Chambord considers herself too important to maintain the image that she is a commoner, even if it costs her daughter's life. Genevieve considers herself so far above Joseph that she seems insulted by the thought of him as her equal. In the last story, Siri is portrayed as the only victim of Satan who resists evil, although she dies by suicide, usually considered an unforgivable sin. The rich tapestry of these issues, many deliberately unresolved, helps to make the film fascinating, powerful, and thought provoking.

Performances

Helge Nissen's depiction of the Devil has many nuances. Its scope goes far beyond the usual screen rendition, endowing Satan with a nobility beyond that suggested by John Milton in *Paradise Lost*. This Devil is God's reluctant tool, pressed into service as the corruptor. Unfortunately, the film offers Nissen no opportunity to be seen as purely the Devil. The prologue shows no visuals of Lucifer as he receives his judgment. Instead, we are provided with five different Satanic disguises in four stories. We first encounter him as a Pharisee, with grey beard and penetrating gaze. In this role, he seems most recalcitrant, continually disappointed by the nature of man and by the quickness with which his seeds of treachery take root. He appears most diabolical in the second episode, as the grand inquisitor with an exaggerated widow's peak, dark piercing eyes, and wrapped in ecclesiastical robes. This is the only time in which his countenance seems somewhat diabolical. He uses sex as the lure to corrupt Fernandez, after which he pulls his strings like a puppet. In the French installment, he is dapper yet ordinary as Erneste, but as the cripple he is grotesque, with heavy makeup. He seems incensed when Joseph yields to his temptations, and it is likely that the Devil had hopes that Joseph would resist him. At the very end, again as Erneste, the Devil turns on Joseph with genuine rage, and for the only time in the story, reveals his real identity. In the final segment, Satan resembles Rasputin, with a thick black beard and a simple black robe. In some ways, this is his poorest incarnation, and he seems to lack the subtleties shown in the earlier episodes. He seems far less tormented by his evil doing, and he never lets his persona drop for a moment as he does in his other personalities. At the end, the script goes astray, and instead of showing Satan's reaction to Siri's act of sacrifice, we are left only with Paavo and his dying wife to wind up the film. The picture definitely should have concluded with Satan instead of a mere title card stating that further misadventures are in store for the Devil.

Notable Quotes

- Thou shalt continue thy evil doings against man. Go among men in [the] fashion of a man and tempt them to do against My will. (**God's command to the Devil after his fall from heaven**)
- Why do you believe in Him? God's Son is what He calls himself. The Devil's son is what He is, and you have been snared by the power of the Devil. (**the Devil in disguise to Judas**)
- What is the body of a heretic to me as long as the soul be saved? (**the Devil as the grand inquisitor to Don Fernandez**)
- Murderer is your name as Satan is mine. Eternal damnation to you who dragged me into your ruin. (**the Devil as Erneste to Joseph**)

Legend of Hillbilly John
AKA Who Fears the Devil?

1973   Rating: ***   Severn Darden as the Devil

Jack H. Harris Enterprises. Written by Melvin P. Levy, based on a cycle of short stories by Manly Wade Wellman; Photographed by Flemming Olsen; Edited by Russell Schoengarth and Barton Hayes; Special Effects by Gene Warren; Music by Roger Kellaway; Additional songs by Hoyt Axton and Hedges Capers; Produced by Barney Rosenzweig; Directed by John Newland. Color, 86 minutes.

Annotated Cast List

Hedges Capers (*Hillbilly John*, traveling minstrel and fighter for virtue); Severn Darden (*Marduke*, the Devil); Denver Pyle (*Grandpappy John*, killed while defying the Devil); Sharon Henesy (*Lily*, John's beloved); Sidney Clute (*Clem*, still owner); William Traylor (minister); Harris Yulin (*Zebulon Yandro*, undertaker and evildoer); Susan Strasberg (*Polly Wilkes*, witch); Alfred Ryder (*O. J. Onselm*, evil magician who controls Ugly Bird); R. G. Armstrong (*Bristowe*, farmer bullied by Onselm); Percy Rodriguez (*Captain Lajoie*, voodoo master at plantation); Val Avery (plantation overseer); Chester Jones (*Uncle Adanasi*, cotton picker who confronts Lajoie).

Appraisal and Synopsis

Manley Wade Wellman, the well-known fantasy writer, created the character of Silver John, a shaman and minstrel who traveled the backwoods of Appalachia helping people who were troubled by supernatural forces. One of his first Silver John stories, from the early 1950s, was "O Ugly Bird." The renowned publisher Arkham House, originally established by August Derlith to print hardcover editions of the writings of H. P. Lovecraft, published a collection of Wellman's stories as *Who Fears the Devil?* This same collection was later reprinted as *Silver John the Balladeer*, and this film was a sincere attempt to bring Silver John to the screen, even though these fantasy tales do not seem to be well suited for a feature film. Originally titled *Who Fears the Devil?* the picture was later marketed as *Legend of Hillbilly John* and *Ballad of Hillbilly John*, an odd choice since Silver John is never called by that name. It just sounds wrong as a moniker for Wellman's unique hero. The project was filmed almost entirely in Appalachia and directed by John Newland, actor and familiar host of the ABC television series "Alcoa Presents," which became better known in syndication as "One Step Beyond." The film has a number of unusual features for a low-budget endeavors including a strong cast of supporting players such as Susan Strasberg, Alfred Ryder, and Denver Pyle. Stylistically, the picture has a number of clever techniques. Grandpappy John's death, for instance, is depicted with an interesting effect, making it seems as if the film breaks at that very moment. The stop-motion animation of Ugly Bird, while not on a level with Ray Harryhausen's work, is nevertheless fun and entertaining. The musical aspects are both a plus and a minus. The "Devil Defying" song, composed and sung by Hoyt Axton, is raw, earthy, and impressive. John's "Nebuchadnezzar" song drags on, however, until viewers feel like shouting, "Enough already, get on with the plot!" When John breaks his guitar fighting Ugly Bird, many viewers consider it a double blessing. The picture is also sprinkled with subtle humor. For example, when farmer Bristowe, who boasts that he visited Frankfurt, Kentucky, twice, hears John's tales of wild goings-on in Nashville, his reaction is simply priceless. One plantation worker is called "Manley Wade" in tribute to author Wellman. There is much to admire overall in this offbeat effort.

The Devil directly addresses the audience to open the film, explaining how he is a tangible presence in Appalachia, where he is blamed for everything, including pollution and superhighways. He transforms himself into the persona of Mr. Marduke, an amiable dowser on good terms with almost everyone. Reminding the audience that the Devil is a joker, he tells several tales of the legend of Hillbilly John and how he set out to become a defyer, a modern-day Don Quixote who seeks to right wrongs and to help innocent victims of the Devil's cohorts.

John receives his calling after his Grandpappy John announces that he plans to sing the "Devil Defying" song to challenge Satan. The elder thinks he will be safe because he has cast his guitar strings from Kennedy half dollars, unaware that the government no longer uses pure silver in its coins. Everyone in town gathers to witness the event, and the mysterious Marduke and his mule, Asmodeus (the Devil's name in Jewish mythology), arrive as well. Grandpappy is struck dead the moment he finishes his song, and Silver John vows to carry on in his footsteps. His girlfriend, Lily, is afraid she will lose him. Marduke befriends John and promises to help him locate true silver in exchange for a meal of salt pork. Using a dousing stick, Marduke leads John directly to a buried treasure of Spanish pieces of eight "419 years old this spring," according to Marduke's reckoning. He tells John where an entire chest can be found, but it will take a long time to dig out. John isn't tempted, however, as he is anxious to set out as a Defyer. Out of John's earshot, the Devil surmises to his mule that John is his mother's son after all. They share a meal of salt pork, and Marduke assures John that he is a friend.

John uses his coins to cast true silver strings for his guitar. The local minister advises John that Zebulon Yandro, an undertaker who frequents the community, is a servant of the Devil. That evening, Yandro interrupts the local hoedown with his ominous presence. John sings a song about Yandro's grandfather who made a deal with an alluring witch named Polly Wilkes. He promised to spend a year in her loving embrace in exchange for a treasure of gold, but he ran out on her instead. It is rumored that Polly has raised up an even greater treasure to be claimed by Yandro if he dares to approach it. John offers to guide Zebulon to the place. The evildoer's greed exceeds his common sense, and he asks John to show him the gold. As they approach the haunted locale, the beautiful witch appears and claims Yandro. She shows him the gold but insists he must fulfill his grandfather's pledge and spend a year in her arms. Dazzled by her beauty, he agrees. Polly advises Silver John to seek out Harp Mountain where he can test if his strings are indeed true silver. Polly and Zebulon withdraw to her private chamber, and she transforms into a hideous hag who embraces the undertaker while he shrieks in terror.

Silver John wanders through the woods in search of Harp Mountain with his dog, Honor Hound. The dog is unable to keep up with him due to the presence of evil. John sends him home, and a huge vulture-like creature known as Ugly Bird swoops down from the sky and attacks John. He holds up his guitar, and the creature swerves to avoid it. A feather from Ugly Bird falls onto his guitar, and the black plume melts and dissolves, proving the strings are indeed true silver. Ugly Bird flies away. John then comes across Bristowe, a farmer who is being ordered about by O. J. Onselm, a backwoods magician. Onselm is demanding an immediate meal of cooked meat. John starts to sing, and his music makes Onselm twitch. He orders John to be gone, but when John raises his guitar, Onselm cowers in fear. Bristowe tells John how Onselm terrorizes the inhabitants of the area. John theorizes that Ugly Bird is a formless spirit called into existence by Onselm, and if the monster is killed, Onselm will also die. Onselm returns with three strong men who try to threaten John. Ugly Bird returns, the Defyer clobbers him with his guitar, and both the monster and Onselm dissolve into lumps of clay. However, John's guitar is also destroyed. He removes the silver strings and continues on his way.

He is picked up by Marduke, now driving a truck. He encourages John to give up defying and settle down. When John insists he has to continue, Marduke reluctantly gives him a new guitar after John talks about refashioning his strings into silver bullets. Eventually, Marduke reaches a crossroads and tells John that their paths must diverge for a while. The road brings John back to his home town, where his girlfriend and dog rejoice at his return. They settle in a small cabin selected by Lily. Eventually, John's guitar strings emit a strange tone, and John interprets it to mean that it is time for them to move on. Together they travel down some new roads until they encounter a strange plantation that seems as if it belongs to an earlier era. The workers appear to be enslaved. John and Lily watch as one old-timer talks back to the overseer and demands to confront Captain Lajoie, the voodoo master. John interferes in the encounter, allowing the oldtimer to destroy Captain Lajoie with his silver-stringed guitar.

Lily wants to return home as John sets off again. She encounters Marduke, now without his truck. The Devil explains that defying is solitary work. She asks him about his name, and he mentions the proper pronunciation is Merodach. When Lily recognizes it as an evil name from the scriptures, the Devil replies, "That was a mix-up. I was long gone from Babylon by then." She asks him to take her home, and he offers her a ride on Asmodeus. Meanwhile, John heads off to Washington D.C., where he sets out to defy the evildoers on Capitol Hill as the end credits appear. The second half of the film seems to lose its focus, and the last story involving the plantation is weak and anticlimactic. Wellman's concept, understandably, is a difficult one to bring to the screen, but the film could have used a startling or dramatic conclusion instead of an inconclusive non-ending. Was a confrontation at Capitol Hill actually considered, or was it just a throwaway tucked into the end credits? There are a large number of loose ends as the picture concludes. The blend of story and folksong wears thin by the second half as well, but the film is still a respectable effort, worth seeking out.

Performances

Severn Darden's Devil is a bit of a paradox, since he seems to be assisting John in his efforts as a defyer for most of the film. As Marduke, the Devil appears harmless and merely an observer to any evil being done. But as he says in his opening line, the Devil is a joker, and it is far more subtle and clever for him to be a trusted friend to John, who he respects, than to confront him as an enemy. It is easy to forget that the Devil shows up to strike down Grandpappy, even though John doesn't realize it. John remains a wide-eyed innocent in the presence of Marduke and never comes to suspect that he is the Devil. As Marduke, the Devil watches over him, gently dissuading him from continuing on his course of action. There also is a suggestion that Marduke, in an earlier guise, is actually John's father, which is why he tolerates his defying. Darden is extraordinarily good in this part. In his first appearance, he is decked out in robes, which he discards as he becomes Marduke, a colorful dresser who seems a cross between W. C. Fields and Hoss Cartwright. His vivid, entertaining performance is the best thing in the entire picture, since Hedges Capers lacks the essential fire to really bring Silver John to life.

Notable Quotes

- The Devil is a joker, and he don't want you alive. (**Lyric from the "Devil Defying" song**)
- Here in the hills of Appalachia, the Devil or the stranger, Old Nick, or the Corps of Army Engineers or Satan or Beelzebub or his majesty or what you will is as familiar and more fearsome than old age or smog. He turns true lovers against one another. He dams up streams and fills their courses with silt, and he destroys God's green earth with great eight-lane superhighways. The Devil is just as real here as I am. (**the Devil, addressing the audience, as he transforms himself into Marduke**)
- People cling to the evil they know, fearing what's to come may be even worse. (**Marduke to John**)

Lisa and the Devil
AKA House of Exorcism *and* The Devil and the Dead

1972   Rating: ****   Telly Savalas as the Devil

Leone International Films. Written by Mario Bava and Alfredo Leone; Photographed by Cecilio Paniagua; Edited by Carlo Reali; Special Effects by Franco Tocci; Music by Carlo Savina and Joaquin Rodrigo; Produced by Alfredo Leone; Directed by Mario Bava. Color, 95 minutes.

Annotated Cast List

Telly Savalas (*Leandre*, the Devil, who poses as a butler); Elke Sommer (*Lisa Reiner*, tourist who gets lost, and *Eleonore*, Maximilien's lost love); Alessio Orano (*Maximilien*, melancholy young man in the villa); Alida Valli (blind countess, Maximilien's mother); Eduardo Fajardo (*Carlos*, Maximilien's stepfather); Franz von Treuberg (*Francis Lehar*, wealthy traveler); Silvia Koscina (*Sofia Lehar*, his young wife); Gabriel Tinti (*George*, their chauffeur); Kathy Leone (Lisa's friend); Espartaco Santoni (antique dealer).

Appraisal and Synopsis

In its original form, *Lisa and the Devil* is an extraordinarily rich and hypnotic film, both subtle and elaborately detailed. Producer Alfredo Leone tried to provide director Mario Bava funding for an A-level picture without his usual budgetary restrictions. The film was critically praised and received multiple-showings at the Cannes Film Festival. Unfortunately, distributors considered it to be too elegant and classy to be marketed as a horror film. It wasn't released in America until 1976, when Leone recut it, tacking on added gore as well as a new finale in which Elke Sommer becomes possessed and undergoes an exorcism in a hospital room by a priest played by Robert Alda. Now marketed as *House of Exorcism* to capitalize on the success of *The Exorcist* (1973), the new footage butchered the film, and all the Bava-directed scenes were structured as flashbacks. Mario Bava insisted his name be dropped, and the fictitious Mickey Lion was inserted as director, since the use of the name Alan Smithee in such cases was still not commonplace. Leone was able to salvage his losses, but years later he continued to promote the original film. He eventually completely restored *Lisa and the Devil*, considering it as the only legitimate version of the picture.

The story begins in a small town in Italy, where a tour bus stops to examine an unusual medieval fresco that portrays the Devil carrying off the dead. After closely studying the fresco, one tourist, Lisa Reiner, wanders off from her girlfriend to look at some of the stores in the town square. She is drawn into an antique store, attracted by the sound of an elaborate music box. She offers to buy it but is told that it already belongs to another customer. Lisa is startled when she sees the owner, who is the spitting image of the Devil in the fresco. She is frightened and leaves by a side door. Finding herself in a narrow alley, she tries to reenter the shop, but a stone wall has replaced the doorway through which she has just passed. She finds herself hopelessly lost in the labyrinth of narrow passageways and back streets. The man resembling the Devil, carrying a life-sized mannequin, approaches her, offering directions. His instructions lead her nowhere. She then encounters a second man, who appears as if he is the mannequin come to life. He acts as if he knows her, calling her Eleonore. Lisa pushes him away and runs off, while the man falls down a stairway and appears to be injured.

Evening falls, and Lisa implores the occupants of a passing car to give her a ride. An elderly, dapper man, Francis Lehar, instructs his chauffeur, George, to pick her up. Moments later the car breaks down in front of a secluded villa. The door opens and again Lisa encounters the Devil, who is serving as majordomo of a large and luxurious estate. A young man, Maximilien, after catching a glimpse of Lisa, persuades his mother, the countess, to allow the stranded travelers to spend the night. The Devil, using the name Leandre, shows them to their rooms. Sofia Lehar, as soon as she is away from her husband, corrals George and induces him to make love to her.

At dinner, the autocratic countess interrogates her guests. Ambiguously, the old woman announces that another person yet unseen has arrived at the villa that evening. Lisa learns that the countess is blind when her hostess asks if she can touch her face. Outside, George works to repair the car. Maximilien brings a slice of pie to his room and offers it to the mummified corpse of a woman who lies beside him in his bed. He annouces to the body that Carlos, his stepfather, has returned, but he will not let him come between them again. He then burns a photograph of a woman who looks exactly like Lisa. Meanwhile, Lisa plays the music box which originally attracted her to the antique shop. Six figures spin around and around on it, and one of the figures, Death, appears to stop and stare directly at her. She has a vision of herself dressed in nineteenth-century clothes, embracing a man resembling the mannequin.

George completes his repair of the car and honks the horn to signal the Lehars. When they reach the car, however, they find George's body stabbed to death. Leandre urges them to leave at once and let him dispose of the body. Maximilien takes Lisa for a midnight walk and tells her he loves her. His mother finds them and leads Maximilien away, saying that such a love can only end badly. Again Lisa sees Carlos, the same man who resembles the mannequin. She follows him to a cemetery plot, where Leandre is laying out a corpse in a casket, snapping off its legs in order to make the body fit. When Lisa sees the corpse's face, it seems to be Carlos, who suddenly appears behind her. Screaming, she dashes off as Carlos cries out, "Eleonore." Following, he startles her in a large chamber in the villa, which now is filled with life-size figurines. Lisa faints.

Francis Lehar starts his car as he and his wife prepare to leave. When he goes to open the gate at the end of the driveway, Sofia runs him down with the vehicle, killing him. The Devil appears amused as he watches this murder from a window. Carlos places the unconscious Lisa on a bed, unaware that Maximilien is stalking him from behind, finally striking him on the head with an ax. Sofia enters the room at this moment, and Maximilien pursues her through the villa, hacking her to pieces after he catches her.

The Devil lifts the figure of Carlos and places it in a chair. It is not a body, however, but a mannequin again. He repairs the damage caused by Maximilien's blow. Observing the dormant figure of Lisa, the Devil talks aloud of his plans to create a new mannequin in her image. He wakes her with a kiss, asking, "Did you sleep well?" Groggy, she walks over to the dummy of Carlos, but Leandre warns her not to touch it since the glue is still wet. She dashes off confused and runs into Maximilien, who leads her to his room. After showing her the body of Eleonore, Maximilien chloroforms Lisa, removing her clothes and positioning her body beside the corpse on his bed. He then attempts to make love to her but fails, while in his mind he hears the sound of Eleonore's laughter. The countess finally tracks down Maximilien, berating him for his murderous spree. When she embraces him, Maximilien stabs her to death. Leandre arranges all of the corpses sitting at a table as if they are awaiting supper. When Maximilien enters, he believes the corpse of his mother has awakened and is approaching him. He tumbles backward out a window. The Devil, who was carrying the body of the countess, puts it down and looks pitifully at the dead figure of Maximilien on the ground below.

It is daylight when Lisa finally awakens. She gets dressed and hears voices coming from outside the villa. She observes children at play, but as she emerges from the villa, they run off. "She's a ghost," one of them screams. "No one has lived there for a hundred years." Lisa makes her way back to the center of town. Leandre follows her, accompanied by the antique dealer who is holding a life-sized mannequin of Lisa. Eventually, Lisa makes her way to the airport. After boarding a plane, she closes her eyes as the jet takes off. When she opens her eyes, the aircraft is deserted. She looks around and finally sees the bodies of the countess, George, the Lehars, Carlos, and Maximilien. She rushes to the cockpit and, opening the door, finds Leandre at the controls. He doffs his hat to her, and she crumples to the floor. "Eleonore," the Devil whispers and chuckles to himself as the end credits roll.

This detailed synopsis cannot begin to convey the otherworldly mood which permeates the entire film. The cinematography is magnificent, with masterful use of shadows. The musical score is lush and romantic, making exceptional use of Joaquin Roderigo's *Concierto de Aran-guez*. The plot unfolds in a compelling manner, making the surreal elements seem totally logical. The intricate plot can be analyzed in various ways. A basic interpretation would be that the wealthy inhabitants of the villa faced tragedy in the distant past when Carlos, the husband of the countess, planned to run off with his stepson's fiancée, Eleonore. Maximilien, in a rage, responded by killing everyone. The Devil, in charge of collecting the dead, was unable to obtain the soul of Eleonore, who was reincarnated a hundred years later as Lisa. The Devil lures her into a fantasy world through the antique shop, much like Alice through the looking glass. He also entraps the Lehars and their chauffeur in the same nightmare. The dead figures in the villa, revived as living mannequins, do not realize they are dead and relive their tragic fate with the newcomers. The Devil, in the role of their butler, has a ringside seat to this event, which he staged for his own amusement and the capture of Lisa. In the end, the Devil succeeds in carrying off his dead not in a hearse but in a jumbo jet. The complex plot calls to mind "The Twilight Zone," with its bizarre use of mannequins, people unaware that they are dead, back streets from which there is no escape, and necrophilia. In addition, the script is filled with fascinating references, sometimes even in the names of the characters. Francis Lehar, for example, is no doubt inspired by the composer Franz Lehar, whose operettas *Paganini* and *Der Zarewitsch* have diabolical connotations. Maximilien and Eleonore could perhaps be an allusion to Maximilien Robespierre and his fiancée, Eleonore Duplay, who he never lived to wed. Each new viewing of the film can bring about additional insights. In any case, the availability of the restored print is most welcome, making it easy to appreciate the dramatic intensity and imagination of Mario Bava's masterful achievement.

Performances

As the Devil, Telly Savalas is charming and malevolent in equal parts. He uses no special make up, appearing at all times as an elegantly attired butler. Savalas uses his voice magnificently, endowing each phrase with a sinister undertone. In this rendition, the Devil enjoys his elaborate charade, referring to the residents of the villa as his puppets with whom he toys for his own pleasure and enjoyment. As in his depiction in the ancient fresco, the Devil is in complete control of the entire situation. Even in the credits, the Devil is portrayed dealing cards, controlling the destiny of the ensemble. Satan is also having fun throughout, even in his mock complaints to himself about his demonic work load. His use of a lollipop as a prop, a later trademark in Savalas' television series "Kojack," is witty and clever. He sneaks a smoke, borrowing a cigarette from Lehar, only to berate him for smoking without permission when the countess complains. The other performers in the film are also well cast. Elke Sommer is dazzling as Lisa. She conveys a special magic, even when her role has her running in endless circles or passing out. Alessio Orano is exceptional as the sympathetic child/man whose delicate madness is at the heart of the story. Alida Valli is effective as the countess, whose blindness extends far beyond her loss of sight. Silvia Koscina, as the thoroughly rotten Sofia, is an excellent counterpoint to Elke Sommer. Franz von Treuberg, as Sofia's long-suffering husband, gives a superb reading in his relatively brief appearance, as does Eduardo Fajarado. The original love-making scenes with Silvia Koscina and Gabriel Tinti were shot by Bava with varying degrees of erotic intensity. Bava eventually chose one of the less-revealing takes, since he felt that more explicitness ultimately would detract from the overall mood of the film.

Notable Quotes

- This representation of the Devil carrying off the dead goes far beyond the formalized art of its day. Look closely. The face of Satan expresses a quality which reflects the very soul of pleasure in evil. The Devil seems a presence so strong and overpowering that this painting has led to a local superstition. The people of this region believe that it is only the power of the Devil himself which has kept this fresco from ruin. (**tour guide**)

- It's not always wise to stir up the past. We all have some unforgivable secret. (**the Devil to Lehar**)

- What does tradition mean to a poor Devil like me? More work and fatigue. (**the Devil, complaining to himself during his labors**)

Little Nicky

2000   Rating: ***   Harvey Keitel and Rodney Dangerfield as the Devil

New Line Cinema. Written by Tim Herlihy, Adam Sandler, and Stephen Brill; Photographed by Theodore Van De Sande; Edited by Jeff Gourson; Special Effects by Terry D. Frazee (coordinator), Howard Berger (supervisor), and Robert Kurtzman (supervisor); Music by Teddy Castellucci; Produced by Robert Simons, Jack Giarraputo, Adam Sandler (executive), Michael De Luca (executive), and Brian Witten (executive); Directed by Stephen Brill. Color, 90 minutes.

Annotated Cast List

Adam Sandler (*Nicky*, third son of the Devil); Harvey Keitel (the Devil); Rodney Dangerfield (*Lucifer*, the retired original Devil and father of the current Devil); Rhys Ifans (*Adrian*, first son of the Devil); Tom "Tiny" Lister, Jr. (*Cassius*, second son of the Devil); Patricia Arquette (*Valerie*, artist who becomes Nicky's girlfriend); Allan Covert (*Todd*, Nicky's roommate); Peter Dante (*Peter*, hippie fan of Nicky); Jonathan Loughran (*John*, hippie fan of Nicky); Reese Witherspoon (*Holly*, angel and mother of Nicky); Blake Clark (*Jimmy*, the Devil's chief assistant); Salvatore Cavaliere (*Sal*, demon); Kevin Nealon (gatekeeper to hell); Jon Lovitz (Peeping Tom who falls out of a tree and goes to hell); Dana Carvey (basketball referee possessed by Cassius); Lewis Arquette (cardinal possessed by Adrian); George Wallace (New York mayor possessed by Cassius); Michael McKean (New York police chief possessed by Adrian); Quentin Tarantino (blind holy man); John Witherspoon (street vendor who steals Nicky's flask); Clint Howard (transvestite); Brandon Rosenberg (*Zachariah*, Nicky's son in epilogue); Sylvia Lopez (TV newscaster); Henry Winkler (himself); Regis Philbin (himself); Bill Walton (himself); Ozzy Osborne (himself); Dan Marino (himself); Carl Weathers (*Chubbs Peterson*, dictator in heaven); Christopher Carroll (*Adolf Hitler*, dictator tortured in hell); Robert Smigel (voice of Mr. Beefy, the bulldog); Jana Sandler, Kalie Stewart-Conner, Tracey Ostrand, Kimberly Velez, Stephanie Chao (angels); Harlem Globetrotters.

Appraisal and Synopsis

"Saturday Night Live" alumnus Adam Sandler played the Devil in a cameo for *Dirty Work* (1998). Perhaps the experience gave him the idea for this full-length comic fantasy about a family feud in hell. On the whole, the humor of the film is geared toward teenagers, and it heavily relies upon scatological humor, topical jokes, and product placement such as Popeye's fast food items. If the viewer is able to get beyond these weak points, *Little Nicky* is a rather effective picture. The scenes in hell are impressive, with mesmerizing art direction and a spectacular infernal vista. The overall look of the film is first rate, and there is some satire beyond the obvious gross jibes. One of Nicky's hippie followers does a subtle impersonation of Peter Sellers as Dr. Strangelove. The picture is fast paced, and the jokes, slapstick, and puns come at a rapid clip, some good, some bad, and a few hilarious. The production has an imaginative cast, including many witty cameos. It is undoubtedly Adam Sandler's finest film, although not as high grossing as *The Waterboy* (1998).

The action of *Little Nicky* begins when a peeping tom is killed falling out of a tree and winds up in hell. He eavesdrops on the Devil and learns that the infernal kingdom is in turmoil. The Devil is due to retire after ruling hell for 10,000 years, just as his father, Lucifer, had done before him. He must choose his successor from his three children: the unscrupulous Adrian, the power-hungry Cassius, and the gentle Nicky, whose features are deformed from being hit with a shovel by Adrian. The Devil, fearing that Adrian is not ready to rule since he does not understand the balance of power between good and evil, elects to serve another 10,000-year term himself. Adrian and Cassius are outraged, and they set off for Earth, obstructing the gates to hell. This disruption will cause the Devil to totally disintegrate within two days. The only one left who has the ability to pass back and forth between heaven and hell is Nicky, and his father sends him on a mission to trap the spirits of his two brothers in a magic flask and return them to hell. Only this will save his father.

A complete klutz, Nicky travels to Earth, emerging on the subway tracks outside a station at 42nd Street and Grand Central Station in New York City. He is killed after getting hit by a train, returns to hell, and then sets off again on his mission. This time he is met by a demon in the form of a talking bulldog named Mr. Beefy, who tries to help Nicky, teaching him about eating, drinking, sleeping, and the other human functions that Nicky must learn to operate on Earth. The dog sets him up with Todd, who is looking for a roommate. Meanwhile Adrian has possessed the cardinal of New York, who now proclaims, "Let the sin begin!" Cassius possesses the mayor, who lowers the legal drinking age to ten and changes the motto of the city from "I love New York" to "I love hookers."

Nicky meets Valerie, a design artist who helps him retrieve his magic flask after a street vendor snatches it. Nicky also meets Peter and John, two Satanic hippies who realize that Nicky is a devil. Adrian learns that Nicky has pursued him to Earth, and he uses his powers to force Nicky to insult Valerie. Cassius attends a

Harlem Globetrotters game and possesses the referee, who penalizes the Globetrotters. Between quarters, Nicky arrives, and he and Cassius engage in a one-on-one challenge which Nicky wins. He tells Cassius that he has gained additional powers from the liquid in the flask. When Cassius snatches the flask and drinks from it, his spirit is trapped in it. Nicky then parties with Peter, John, and Todd, telling them about his mission.

Valerie is visited by Nicky, and she pushes him off her fire escape. He falls to the street but floats back up to her window. He reveals his true identity, and she joins him in a flight over Manhattan, paralleling a similar scene from *Superman* (1978). Meanwhile, Adrian, disguised as the police chief, announces that Nicky is a serial killer and issues an all-points alert to apprehend him. A mob tracks down Nicky, and he turns into a legion of spiders to frighten them off. He asks Todd to kill him so he can consult with his father, but when he gets to hell, he finds that the Devil is falling apart and only his mouth is left.

Nicky lays an elaborate trap to hoodwink Adrian into drinking from the flask, but at the last moment his brother sees through his trick. Adrian seizes Valerie, Nicky battles his brother in the 42nd Street subway station, and they are hit by a train. Nicky is stunned to find himself in heaven. He learns that he is half divine, and his mother, Holly, is an angel. In hell, however, Adrian tries to take over, and his grandfather, Lucifer, is unable to stop him. Adrian arranges to have a segment of hell rise in the middle of Central Park in a plan to take over Earth. Holly gives Nicky a small, glowing globe, a special weapon that God has permitted Holly to give to her son.

Adrian is awaiting midnight, at which time his father will completely vanish, and he will take over. For entertainment, Adrian tortures Peter, John, and Valerie. He also produces Henry Winkler and sets a swarm of bees upon him. Nicky arrives, and he and Adrian engage in an epic battle using their supernatural powers. Eventually, Nicky unleashes his glowing globe, out of which Ozzy Osborne emerges and forces Adrian into the flask. Nicky brings it back to hell, and his father, the Devil, is instantly restored. Lucifer takes the magic flask with Adrian and Cassius and shoves it up the backside of Adolf Hitler. The Devil gives his blessing to Nicky to return to Earth and marry Valerie. In a brief epilogue, Nicky and Valerie are shown with Zachariah, their newborn baby, in a perambulator. The film ends as subtitles reveal the eventual fate of the various people who appeared in the story.

Performances

Harvey Keitel is most entertaining as the principal Devil in *Little Nicky*. He wears a neatly trimmed beard and has two tiny upturned horns protruding from his forehead. If anything, he is a well-meaning Devil, interested in maintaining the balance between good and evil. He responds warmly to the open admiration and love of his son Nicky, the product of his romance with the angel Holly, who he met at a heaven/hell mixer. Keitel never plays the Devil as frightening, and his reading is light and whimsical. His humor becomes broader as his body disintegrates. In one hilarious scene, his ear falls off, and he is no longer able to hear the words of his advisor. Rodney Dangerfield is equally humorous as Lucifer, the original Devil, who decided to retire after ruling for 10,000 years. The former master, Lucifer now finds himself largely ignored, especially by his grandchildren Adrian and Cassius. He delivers his one-liners with genuine style. He even recycles his trademark quip about getting no respect. Dangerfield is a magnificent comic Devil. Rhys Ifans, as Adrian, the presumptive successor, is the only Devil onscreen who seems to be openly evil. He tackles his part with unrestrained glee, and he makes an excellent counterpart to Sandler. Tom "Tiny" Lister is somewhat less impressive as Cassius, who seems more a strong arm for his brother than anything else. Finally, there is Sandler himself, and Nicky is a rather odd character, part Quasimodo, part Richard III and part Little Engine that Could. He is sweet-tempered rather than evil, and it isn't until well into the film that the audience learns he is half angel. He is a complete innocent, and much of the humor derives from his naivete. He has a rather strange appearance, with half his face obscured by his stringy black hair, and he speaks in a raspy whisper, with his mouth twisted to one side.

That Sandler manages to make Nicky at first tolerable and finally appealing is a genuine accomplishment, although the demonic side of Nicky is never credible.

Notable Quotes

- Even the voice inside your head has a speech impediment. (**Adrian to Nicky**)
- I command you in the name of Lucifer to spill the blood of the innocent. (**voice heard when a song on a Chicago album is played backward**)
- Even in hell I get no respect. (**Lucifer to himself**)
- God is so smart! (**first angel to Nicky**)
   Like "Jeopardy" smart! (**second angel**)

Lost Souls

2000   Rating: *   Ben Chaplin as the Devil

Castle Rock. Written by Pierce Gardner, based on a story by Pierce Gardner and Betsy Stahl; Photographed by Mauro Fiore; Edited by Anne Goursaud; Special Effects by Cinesite Hollywood, Clay Pinney, and Jay Riddle; Music by Jan A. P. Kaczmarek; Produced by Meg Ryan and Nina R. Sadowsky; Directed by Janusz Kaminski. Color, 97 minutes.

Annotated Cast List

Winona Ryder (*Maya Larkin*, French teacher in a Newark school and lay assistant to Fr. Lareaux); Ben Chaplin (*Peter Kelson*, True-crime writer who becomes transformed into the Devil); John Hurt (*Fr. Lareaux*, exorcist); Philip Baker Hall (*Fr. James*, Kelson's uncle); Sarah Wynter (*Claire Van Owen*, Kelson's fiancée); Elias Koteas (*John Townsend*, deacon who attempts to kill Kelson); John Diehl (*Henry Birdson*, possessed criminal who requests an exorcism); Alfre Woodard (Birdson's psychiatrist); Kim Ornitz (*Joe*, Birdson's orderly); Brad Greenquist (*George Viznik*, Serial killer studied by Kelson); W. Earl Brown (*William*, Peter's brother); Victor Slezak (*Fr. Thomas*, Lareaux's associate); Daniele Jones (demonic girl in diner); Brian Reddy (*Fr. Frank*); James Lancaster (*Fr. Jeremy*); John Beasley (*Mike Smythe*).

Appraisal and Synopsis

Lost Souls was originally scheduled for release in October 1999 but was shelved instead until October 2000, reportedly to avoid competition with *End of Days*. Ironically, it was eventually released at the same time as the re-release of *The Exorcist* (1973) with additional footage. *Lost Souls* starts with a good deal of potential that is almost entirely squandered despite an interesting premise, a capable cast, and masterful but low-key cinematography. The director, Janusz Kaminski, an Academy Award–winning cinematographer, simply fails to bring cohesion to the ill-conceived plot, which builds to a nonclimax that is a total letdown. The film is all window dressing without any window, and it seldom clarifies the Byzantine nature of the plot.

The picture begins with a quote: "A man born of incest will become Satan and the world we now know will exist no more." It is cited as being from Deuteronomy 17, but the translation seems quite unlike the actual biblical verse. Nonetheless, it sets up the story, which centers on Peter Kelson, who is intended to serve as the host for Satan when he appears on Earth. Kelson is a New York writer in the Ann Rule mold, whose books concentrate exclusively on serial killers. He is approached in his office by Maya Larkin, a strange young woman, who gives him a tape recording of a recent exorcism attempted on Henry Birdson, an insane killer in a Brooklyn asylum. During this exorcism, Birdson boasted that the Devil himself is planning to emerge on Earth to transform it into a Satanic realm. The exorcism failed and the exorcist, Fr. Lareaux, collapsed, falling into a semiconscious state. Among Birdson's papers is an enigmatic code which reveals the name of the Devil's intended host — Peter Kelson. The writer believes this is all nonsense. He is an atheist who theorizes that what we call evil is only "malignant narcissism." Maya persuades Kelson to visit Birdson in the asylum, but the madman has now lapsed into a coma.

Another participant in the exorcism, Deacon John Townsend, is convinced that the Devil will soon possess Kelson and makes a failed attempt to assassinate the writer at a cocktail party. After this incident, Kelson starts to investigate Maya and learns that she had been possessed as a child but was saved by Fr. Lareaux. She is now a visionary, and she sees many frightening illusions about both Birdson and Satan. Kelson has a recurring dream in which he sees a book with the title "XES." His fiancée jokes that it is merely sex spelled backward. Later, with Maya, Kelson learns that "XES" means "666" in a number system used in ancient Greece. Kelson and Maya break into Townsend's apartment and find a note explaining that Kelson will be transformed into Satan at the precise moment of his thirty-third birthday, which is fast approaching. Kelson also sees a terrifying vision of Birdson which convinces him to probe further. Maya tells him to check the blood types of his parents, and he discovers that it is impossible for his late father to have been his biological father. He learns he is actually the offspring of his mother and her brother, Fr. James. Maya brings Kelson to the bedside of Fr. Lareaux, who has made a remarkable recovery. When Maya talks with her mentor, she finds that his beliefs have drastically changed. When she starts to ridicule Satan, she discovers that Lareaux has become demonically possessed. The priest's associates perform an exorcism, which succeeds, but Lareaux collapses. With his dying words, he urges Maya to track down Kelson's uncle (and father), Fr. James.

Maya and Kelson go to the church pastored by James and discover it is actually a cult of Devil worshipers. Desperate, Kelson shoots James when he confirms all of his suspicions. Kelson and Maya park their car underneath the Williamsburg Bridge on the Brooklyn side and wait for the clock to reach 4:55 P.M., the time when his transformation is supposed to occur. He instructs Maya to shoot and kill him if he changes. 4:55 P.M. arrives, and Kelson tries to convince Maya that nothing has occurred. She hesitates since nothing at all has happened, but when the dashboard clock changes to 666, the sign of Satan, Maya shoots Kelson in the head, and the film abruptly ends.

During the last fifteen minutes of *Lost Souls*, the plot seems to disintegrate. Bodies are left all over the place, as Kelson kills his fiancée, his uncle, and some of the Satanic congregation. However, when the moment of transformation arrives, it is a total cop-out, that almost negates the entire film in which the supernatural elements are presented as genuine and terrifying. The basis of the entire plot was to lay the groundwork for the Devil's arrival. But when he gets there, the Devil merely pretends his arrival hasn't happened, and he is blown away. This resolution is almost as bad as if they chose to make the entire plot a nightmare from which Maya (or Kelson) awakened at the end. The Devil is indeed weak if all his cosmic plans can be toppled so easily. It makes the entire film rather pointless.

There is a good deal of genuine creepiness in many sequences, but they seem somewhat derivative of films such as *The Omega Code* (1999), *Stigmata* (1999), in which the spirit of a saintly priest possesses a young woman, or the original *Exorcist* (1973). The main problem with *Lost Souls* is simply that it is a dreary film, without any moments of wit or levity to relieve the deadening presentation. Even its best feature, the moody cinematography drenched in sepia tones, becomes tedious by the end of the picture. At one point, the plot changes to suggest that Kelson is actually to become the Antichrist, who, according to the Book of Revelation, is distinct from the Devil. *The Omega Code* makes the same assumption, but then justifies it in its plotline. *Lost Souls*, on the other hand, just tosses in the Antichrist reference haphazardly and then drops it again. Of course, there are so many different demonic possessions in the film, from Birdson to Lareaux, that events become blurred and confusing. At one point, Maya has a vision of a young girl, who seems to be a demon as well. The story has no real logic or cohesiveness but is just a random gathering of shock sequences that become gradually less impressive. Winona Ryder, in particular, seems unable to get a handle on her role. Ben Chaplin, as Peter Kelson, also fails to connect as the protagonist, and John Hurt spends most of the film on his back in a stupor. In the final analysis, *Lost Souls* is misconceived, although a number of individual scenes are modestly impressive, including location footage in the Williamsburg section of Brooklyn. One of the film's producers is Meg Ryan, who has produced a handful of pictures in addition to her career as an actress.

Performances

In *Lost Souls*, Ben Chaplin appears for roughly thirty seconds as the Devil. This is the moment toward which the entire film has been building. What does the Devil do? Why, he pretends to be Peter Kelson, the downbeat, bland character that Chaplin has been playing for the past ninety minutes. The transformation goes by without any outward indication, as the Devil tries to convince Winona Ryder that he is still Peter Kelson. It should be an easy task, but the Devil is foiled by the car clock. The Devil assumes control of Peter at 4:55 P.M. At 4:56, the clock flickers and displays 666 instead, the sign of the Devil. Taking this as confirmation, Ryder pumps a bullet through Chaplin's forehead, and his performance as Satan concludes, certainly the briefest, most nondescript, and disappointing appearance of the Devil in film history.

Notable Quotes

• Good and evil are illusions. ... There is no evil with a capital *E*. (**Peter during his television interview**)

• Satan is not what you think he is. (**Maya to Peter**)

• If you die, then Satan can't stay. (**Maya to Peter**)

• I'm giving you a gift, absolute power, absolute knowledge. (**James to Peter**)

Maciste in Hell
AKA Maciste all'Inferno

1926   Rating: ****   Umberto Guarracino (and others) as the Devil

Italia Films. Written by Riccardo Artuffo, based on a character created by Titus Livus; Photographed by Ubaldo Arata and Massimo Terzano; Produced and Directed by Guido Bregnone. B&W, silent, 66 minutes.

Annotated Cast List

Bartolomeo Pagano (*Maciste*, strongest and most virtuous man on Earth); Umberto Guarracino (*Barbariccia*, leading warlord Devil who visits Earth to trap Maciste); Elena Sangra (*Persephone*, Maciste's wily enemy); Franz Sala (*Pluto*, infernal administrator); Pauline Polaire (*Rosabel*, Maciste's cousin); Domenicco Serra, Lucia Zanussi, Mario Salo, Antonio Grimaldi, Nicolo Torre.

Appraisal and Synopsis

Most Italian Hercules movies from the 1960s and 1970s are not about the demigod from Greek mythology but actually about a character named Maciste in their original-language film versions. At other times, his name was changed to Samson for English language prints. This legendary muscle man dates back to an early film epic called *Cabiria* (1914) in which the prototype for the legendary muscle man was a Roman slave named Maciste who undertook many heroic deeds. This early sword-and-sandal extravaganza was a two-hour saga set in the days of the Punic Wars against Hannibal. Maciste's owner was a Roman spy in Carthage, and in this film Maciste was portrayed as a black man. The character proved so popular that a sequel was made the following year simply called *Maciste* (1915). The actor who played the part was a hefty longshoreman from Genoa named Bartolomeo Pagano, and he proved so popular in the part that a long series of films was launched based on the character. He no longer was portrayed as dark-skinned, however, and he seemed to appear in various eras throughout history. The most elaborate of these films is *Maciste in Hell*.

In some ways, Maciste is a far more interesting character than Hercules. For one thing, he seems to be timeless, and *Maciste in Hell*, for example, is set contemporaneously in the early twentieth century; Maciste wears a suit in most of his scenes. The picture opens in hell, where the top Devil, named Barbariccia, leads a band of demons on a raid to the world of men. Barbariccia decides to confront Maciste, the strongest and most virtuous man alive, and win him over to the Devil's side. Maciste spurns him, and Barbariccia gets revenge by stealing a baby belonging to Maciste's cousin, Rosabel. In her desperation, she blasphemes God, and this lapse enables Barbariccia to seize her. Maciste intervenes, and the demon takes him straight to hell where the rest of the film takes place. The infernal scenes are lively, imaginative, corny, and impressive, all at the same time. It is a dazzling display of filmmaking, and even the most absurd and silly moments retain a curious vitality. At times one expects Olsen and Johnson to turn up with some jokes from *Hellzapoppin'* (1941). The film's depiction of hell combines elements of Dante and Milton with vaudeville. For example, when the demons want to adopt human form, they resemble lawyers with frock coats, top hats, and exaggerated Victorian mustaches. Some devils play catch using their own heads during a rather goofy sequence. Then there are the scenes of the victims of eternal torture, such as those endlessly assigned to push large stones up an incline; they always roll back again. These scenes are heavily stylized but sinister nonetheless. The scenes of the demons swirling in the air are magnificent, seeming like a print by Gustave Doré come to life. This hell combines elements of classical Hades with Christian depictions. Lucifer is there, performing an endless torture. Pluto is there, endlessly strutting as if leading a bacchanalia. Charon is there, ferrying souls to the nether regions. The giant Minos is there, guarding an escape route from the lower depths. Everything considered, these scenes are stunning and breathtaking, a most impressive achievement. Living human beings, we learn, have to be returned to Earth within three days, unless they kiss one of the alluring female demons. If they do, then they become slaves in hell indefinitely. Maciste is given a tour, flying around hell on a fire-breathing dragon. He watches events surrounding Rosabel back on Earth via television! When he is attacked, Maciste battles all the devils, until they realize they cannot overpower him. Then the female devils try to tempt the virtuous Maciste. Persephone, portrayed in mythology as Pluto's concubine, here transfers allegiance to Barbariccia. Persephone manages to lure Maciste into kissing her. The virtuous strongman is then transformed into a demon himself. He decides to become a warlord and overthrows King Barbariccia who had brought him into the underworld. Pluto grants Maciste his freedom to return to Earth, but Persephone tricks the strongman yet again. Brains are definitely not one of Maciste's strong points. This time, years pass while he is chained to a rock. Finally, back on Earth, the child of Rosabel makes a special prayer on Christmas Eve that is so powerful that it frees Maciste, and he returns to Earth to share Christmas with his relatives.

Maciste in Hell is a compelling, bizarre, and thoroughly enjoyable excursion into fantasy. Incidentally, in the early 1960s, a semi-remake was attempted also called *Maciste in Hell*, but the English version is known under the more prosaic title *The Witch's Curse* (1962). In this version, Maciste, played by Kirk Morris, winds up in Scotland where he goes to hell to lift a curse on a remote village. This film also stands above many other of the later Maciste films in interest, but for sheer absurd melodrama, nothing can compete with the 1926 original.

Performances

The multiple devils presented in this film make it difficult to resolve exactly which character is the Devil. The closest appears to be Lucifer, described as Emperor of the Kingdom Dolorous. He is observed in one scene only, taken directly from Dante, where he is shown eternally munching on a victim, presumably Judas. Lucifer resembles a wild Neanderthal, with a mane of woolly hair and two rather dainty horns just above his hairline. He has a mangy beard and is dressed only in a leopard skin. Pluto seems to be the chief day-to-day organizer and administrator of the nether regions. He dresses in a fancy embroidered cape, carries an elaborate scepter, and wears an absurd crown with seven six-inch spikes. He makes the decisions which affect Maciste, and his rule actually seems to be fair to a certain degree. King Barbariccia is the most prominent and active Devil; he pits himself against Maciste and tricks him into descending into hell, but is overthrown as chief warlord when Maciste defeats him in battle. Umberto Guarracino is very stylized as the Devil Barbariccia, swaggering and theatrical in his various guises. Guarracino's only other major film credit is as the Frankenstein monster in the little-known *Il Mostro di Frankenstein* (1920). The performances by these players are all broad yet effective. The supporting players and their various roles are not specified. Bartolomeo Pagano, well versed as Maciste, the role in which he specialized for over twenty-two years, is an impressive screen presence. He appeared in two more Maciste films and retired from the screen at the end of the silent era. Pauline Polaire appeared as Rosabel in an earlier epic called *Maciste e il Nipote d'America* (1924) or *Maciste's American Relative*. Director Guido Bregnone helmed over seventy films, remaining active in Italy through the war years and afterward. His final picture was *Sheba and the Gladiators* (1958).

Notable Quotes

• Get thee behind me, Satan! This does not tempt me. I only want you to go away. Otherwise, I will throw you out of the window. (**Maciste to Barbariccia, after the Devil offers him supreme power on Earth, showing him a vision of the New York skyline**)

• With the verse of the famous poet, Dante, I answer you, "Abandon hope all ye who enter here!" (**Barbariccia's response when Maciste asks how he may be freed**)

Meet Mr. Lucifer

1953   Rating: *   Stanley Holloway as the Devil

Ealing Studios. Written by Monja Danischewsky, based on the play *Beggar My Neighbor* by Arnold Ridley; Photographed by Desmond Dickinson; Edited by Bernard Gribble; Special Effects by Sydney Pearson; Music by Eric Rodgers; Produced by Monja Danischewsky; Directed by Anthony Pelissier. B&W, 83 minutes.

Annotated Cast List

Stanley Holloway (*Sam Hollingsworth*, music hall entertainer, and *Mr. Lucifer*, the Devil); Geoffrey Keen (voice of Mr. Lucifer); Jack Watling (*Jim Norton*, drug store clerk); Peggy Cummins (*Kitty Norton*, his wife); Joseph Tomelty (*Pedelty*, their neighbor, recently retired); Barbara

Murray (*Pat Pedelty*, his daughter, an airline stewardess); Humphrey Lestocq (*Arthur Simmons*, Pat's boyfriend); Gordon Jackson (*Hector McPhee*, pharmacist); Ernest Thesiger (*Euan MacDonald*, drugstore owner); Jean Cadell (*Mrs. MacDonald*, his wife); Kay Kendall (*Miss Lonely Hearts*, TV singer); Charles Victor (*Elder*, neighbor who intrudes on Pedelty and the Nortons to watch television); Olive Sloane (*Mrs. Stannard*, his companion, another neighbor); Frank Pettingell (*Albert Roberts*, pub owner); Roddy Hughes (*Billings*, office manager); Eliot Makeham (*Edwards*, his assistant); Raymond Huntley (*Patterson*, new head of firm); Toke Townley (street musician); Dandy Nichols (*Mrs. Clark*, drugstore patron); Molly Hamley-Clifford (*Mrs. Ensor*, landlady of boardinghouse); Edie Martin (her deaf lodger); Gilbert Harding, Philip Harben, MacDonald Hobley, David Miller (television personalities); Olga Gwynne, Joan Sims, Ian Carmichael (music hall performers); Irene Handl, Gladys Hensen, Bill Fraser, Fred Griffiths, Herbert C. Walton.

Appraisal and Synopsis

Meet Mr. Lucifer is a rambling and often irritating comedy, which may have been mildly amusing in the early 1950s as a satire on the medium of television. Shallow, ill-conceived, and rather pointless, the picture wastes Holloway whose appearances function as mere bookends to open and close the picture, with only momentary bits in the main story. The Devil is presented merely as a framing device, and he takes no part in the main plot. The film makes a few mild and clever points, then quickly runs out of ideas and just trudges on. Jackie Gleason and Art Carney probably could have worked this material up to a classic "Honeymooners" episode, but this film is simply wearying and threadbare.

Stanley Holloway plays Sam Hollingsworth, an alcoholic music hall performer who plays a mock Devil in a dreadful stage musical of *Robinson Crusoe*, complete with an embarrassing black-face minstrel as Friday, an uncoordinated chorus, and a miserable subplot about fairies. The cast members outnumber the audience. No wonder Sam drinks. He hits his head while making an entrance using a trick stage elevator, and the Devil takes advantage of his unconscious state to seek his assistance to make television a tool of misfortune. Of course, the film forgets this subplot, and the help Hollingsworth renders the Devil is to make three extraordinarily brief appearances as a TV installer, a policeman, and a pub patron in the main story. Since these bits are largely peripheral, the entire purpose of the Devil's presence in the story is of minor impact.

The main body of the film traces the history of a television set that is given to Mr. Pedelty upon his retirement. He becomes a TV addict, running up a large tab at the local pub buying liquor and refreshments for the guests who come to watch his television. To get out of debt, he is forced to sell the set to his upstairs neighbors, Jim and Kitty Norton. Jim works as a clerk in MacDonald's drugstore, and after the death of the owner, he is made manager of the place by MacDonald's widow. Her nephew, Hector McPhee, is a licensed pharmacist who tries to undermine Norton's position by continually complaining to his aunt. Norton, studying to pass the pharmacist's examination, is continually distracted at home by the television blaring in the next room and by his neighbors, who always hang out in his flat to watch the latest shows. Instead of using earplugs, Jim goes to pieces when a misunderstanding makes it appear to Mrs. MacDonald and his nosy neighbors that he is having an affair with Pat Pedelty. Jim abandons both wife and job, stomps off, and gets drunk. Considering the television to be bad luck, he decides to give it to his rival, Hector McPhee. Hector, a reclusive and unlikable young stick-in-the-mud, falls in love with Miss Lonely Hearts, an attractive television singer who tailors her program to charm an audience of shy introverts. Hector bases his entire life around her show. When Miss Lonely Hearts quits her job, he sinks into a deep funk. Worse yet, when her program returns to the air, Hector finds the show is continually disrupted by his boardinghouse neighbors who make noise during the course of the program. He swipes the noise-making items, such as his landlady's vacuum cleaner, his neighbor's hammer, and a street musician's trumpet, arousing their ire until they start pounding on McPhee's door demanding the return of their possessions. Hector is then crushed to hear that the Lonely Hearts singer is moving to America where she has just signed a new contract. Finally, his aunt shows up and scolds him for his antisocial behavior. She rehires Jim, who becomes reconciled with his wife.

The Devil is quite pleased with the misery this TV set has caused, and he sends Hollingsworth back in time to the moment just before he got knocked out. Now Hollingsworth makes his entrance cue on time, and the film ends as he struts his stuff onstage. Meanwhile, Lucifer, perhaps to demonstrate that the story was not just a dream, appears in a 3-D movie for his next experiment, so that he can spring out directly into the audience and sit on their laps.

Performances

Stanley Holloway is rightly remembered for his exuberant and dynamic reading as Alfred Doolittle in *My Fair Lady* (1964). He played in over fifty films from 1921, ranging from the gravedigger in Laurence Olivier's *Hamlet* (1948) to a colorful spy reporting Japanese troop movements in Otto Preminger's *In Harm's Way* (1965). Knowing his capable talents, *Meet Mr. Lucifer* seems even more of a misfire. Since most of the Devil's banter occurs offscreen between Hollingsworth and Lucifer, the Devil's voice is rendered by Geoffrey Keen instead of Holloway himself, further undermining the effectiveness of his portrayal. As both Hollingsworth, costumed as the Devil for his theatrical turn, and as Lucifer, Holloway dresses almost the same, with tights, cape, and tail. The only difference is that the Devil has genuine horns sprouting out of his bare head while Hollingsworth wears a cheap hood with flaplike horns. Lucifer also complains that his tail style is out-of-date. The banter between them is trite, stale, and not funny. They appear only on one set, which is really just a backdrop displaying flames and shadows. Most of their time is spent spying on people through a submarine periscope which descends when bidden from the top of the screen. Their commentary on their observations is plain and matter of fact, not fleshed out with any humorous quips. Holloway is simply not given the opportunity to add any color, style, or satire to either part. Some of the other cast members are excellent. Ernest Thesiger shines as the dour drugstore owner with a puritanical bent. It is interesting to remember that in Thesiger's most famous screen role, Dr. Pretorius in *The Bride of Frankenstein* (1935), he grew miniature men and women, one of whom he dressed as the Devil. In the film, Pretorius notes that he believes he himself resembles the Devil. Peter Shaw is the six-inch Devil who does this brief cameo, a weird detail sometimes overlooked in the 1935 classic.

Joseph Tomelty has a few good scenes as Pedelty, the first victim of the unlucky TV set. Kay Kendall is also exceptional as the television singer who appeals to lonely hearts. Her radiant charm makes this subplot the most entertaining and amusing passage of this film, which falls flat at almost every other turn. Kendall married Rex Harrison in 1957, two years before her unfortunate death at a rather early age.

Notable Quotes

- I suppose you brought me here to bargain for me soul? Well, I'm not having any. (**Hollingsworth to the Devil**)

My dear fellow, I've had your soul for years and years, ever since that regrettable incident with the Fairy Queen. (**Lucifer's reply, referring to one of Hollingsworth's indiscretions**)

- There are lots of people waiting to be made miserable. (**the Devil's motto**)
- I'm telling you, Mrs. Clarke, a sprained ankle obtained while playing football on the Sabbath is not an illness, it's a judgment. (**stern and intolerant druggist Euan MacDonald to a patron**)

The Milky Way
AKA La Voie Lactée

1969   Rating: ***   Pierre Clementi as the Devil

Greenwich-Fraia. Written by Luis Buñuel and Jean-Claude Carriere; Photographed by Christian Matras; Edited by Louisette Hautecoeur; Music by Luis Buñuel; Produced by Serge Silberman; Directed by Luis Buñuel. Color, 105 minutes.

Annotated Cast List

Paul Frankeur (*Pierre Dupont*, older hobo); Laurent Terzieff (*Jean Duval*, younger hobo); Pierre Clementi (the Devil); Delphine Seyrig (prostitute); Bernard Verley (*Jesus Christ*); Edith Scob (*Virgin Mary*); Jean Clarieux (*Peter*, apostle); Christian Van Cau (*Andrew*, apostle); Francois Maistre (French priest); Claude Cerval (brigadier); Muni (mother superior who is crucified); Augusta Carriere (Sister Francoise); Julien Bertheau (maitre d'hotel); Jacqueline Rouillard (hotel maid); Michel Daquin (*Garnier*, diner in hotel); Ellen Bahl (his wife); Michel Piccoli (*Marquis de Sade*, man who denies God); Christine Simon (*Therese*, de Sade's companion); Bernard Musson (French innkeeper); Agnes Capri (head of Lamartine Institute); Michel Etcheverry (inquisitor); Jean-David Erhmann (condemned man); Pierre Lary (young monk); Georges Marchal (Jesuit, duelist); Jean Piat (Jansenist, duelist); Denis Manuel (*Rodolphe*, medieval heretic); Daniel Pilon (*Francois*, medieval heretic); Claudio Brook (bishop); Julien Guliomar (Spanish priest); Marcel Peres (Spanish innkeeper); Jean-Claude Carriere (*Priscillian*, medieval cleric); Jose Bergosa (Priscillian's deacon); Georges Douking (shepherd); Pierre Maguelon (civil guard corporal); Claude Jetter (virgin in Spanish inn); Maurius Laurey (blind man); Alain Cuny (man with cape).

Appraisal and Synopsis

A rather difficult film to approach, particularly for casual viewers, *The Milky*

Way seems like a dizzying mixture of *A Pilgrim's Progress*, "The Twilight Zone," and a Jacques Tati comedy, but is entirely grounded in the dogmas and heresies of the religious philosophers of history. Two hobos, Pierre and Jean, are wandering through southern France, heading toward the shrine of the Apostle James in Santiago, called Compostela, or Field of Stars, which has been the focal point of pilgrimages dating back many centuries. The route traveled by these pilgrims is commonly referred to as "the Milky Way."

While en route, the travelers meander in and out of various time periods, a phenomenon they accept without question. Jesus Christ and his disciples appear along the route, as do historical personages such as saints, bishops, and proponents of various beliefs such as the Jansenists and Albigensians. The duo also crosses paths with the Devil himself. The camera wanders further afield from its two main characters for numerous episodes as their journey proceeds. Structured similarly to Tati's *Playtime* (1967) or *Traffic* (1972), they never actually reach the shrine.

At the start, while strolling down a highway, the two hobos encounter a mysterious man with a cape, from whom they beg alms. The man gives nothing to Jean, who is penniless, but then gives a large bill to Pierre, who had a handful of change. He asks if they are on pilgrimage to Santiago de Compostela and then provides them with a cryptic instructions "Find a harlot and have children by her. Name the first *You Are Not Thy People* and the second *No More Mercy*." The man continues to walk down the road, now unexpectedly accompanied by a dwarf or small child. The scene shifts suddenly to a barn, where Christ is preparing to shave when his mother Mary says she prefers Him with a beard. Back on the road, Pierre and Jean are unable to obtain a ride. Farther down the highway, they meet a mute child, who seems to bear signs of the stigmata.

The youngster stops a car, and the pilgrims are offered a ride all the way to Spain, but then the driver kicks them out of the vehicle when Jean takes the name of God in vain. These early moments set the surreal tone of the film, open to various allegorical interpretations. For instance, the actor playing the man with a cape is Alain Cuny, who starred as the Devil's envoy in *Les Visiteurs du Soir* (1942). By casting him, Buñuel appears to be indicating that this stranger is also an envoy of the Devil. Likewise, the child who grants them an unexpected boon seems to be Christ in another guise.

The film is not only highly symbolic but has unexpected scenes of humor. Everyone, for example, is discussing subtle points of dogma. While preparing to receive guests at a restaurant, the maitre d'hotel discusses the nature of Christ as God and man with his staff as casually as if they were discussing the weather or sports scores. It is all very incongruous. In another cut-away scene, the Marquis de Sade is observed denying the existence of God to a young girl named Therese, possibly a reference to the legend that de Sade resurrected St. Teresa to escort her on a tour of hell. There are numerous inexplicable among between the various scenes. Christ throws away a bowl of water with a sweeping gesture that is repeated moments later by an insane priest tossing his drink at a policeman. Also, a program at the Lamartine Institute is contrasted with an interrogation during the Inquisition.

The pilgrims encounter the Devil about halfway through the film. Jean, frustrated at being passed by a motorist who refuses to give them a lift, wishes the car would crash and burn. This occurs as soon as he says it, and the two hobos rush to the wreck to see if they can help. The driver is dead, crushed behind the wheel. Pierre suggests they notify the police when the Devil, sniffing a rose and dressed entirely in white, materializes in the back seat of the vehicle. He instructs them not to bother the police. When asked his identity, the Devil replies, "a laborer who is never out of work." He tells Jean that he made his wish come true. He takes a St. Christopher medal from the car and stamps it into the mud. He turns on the car radio and translates the messages being broadcast, a reference to Jean Cocteau's *Orpheus* (1949), when Jean Marais hears radio broadcasts from the land of the dead. As the two vagabonds leave, the Devil calls Pierre back and offers him the shoes of the dead driver, since he will no longer be needing them. He also expresses hope that at the Final Judgment, God will show mercy to all.

Other events witnessed by the two travelers include a sword duel between a Jesuit and a Jansenist and a mother superior at a convent who is willingly crucified by her order. Toward the end of the film, two blind men in modern dress come across Christ and his apostles in the woods. Jesus cures their blindness with his spittle and then launches into his proclamation recorded in Matthew 10:34 that he comes not to bring peace into the world but a sword.

A whore in a white car beckons to Pierre and Jean as they enter Santiago. She explains that it has been determined that the body at the shrine is not the apostle James, but the headless body of Priscillian, the same bishop who held a medieval prayer service along the road earlier in the film. She offers to sleep with the pair, and if they have children, she says she will name the first *You Are Not Thy People* and the second *No More Mercy*. They go off with the woman, who is likely another envoy of the Devil. The circle complete, the picture ends.

Buñuel's film is brilliant, provocative, but also at times confusing. A friend of artist Salvador Dali, Buñuel created some of the most fascinating films ever made, including *The Golden Age* (1930), *Los Olvidados* (1950), and *The Discrete Charm of the Bourgeoisie* (1972). This picture is not Buñuel's only depiction of the Devil. In the extended short *Simon of the Desert* (1965), Buñuel cast a woman, Silvia Pinal, as the Devil, who tempts the holy man Simon, who is meditating atop a pillar in the desert during the early Middle Ages. Pinal, sometimes wearing a beard, tries to dissuade Simon from his prayerful endeavors. The film ends in a bizarre fashion, as the Devil whisks Simon centuries into the future where she entertains him in a discotheque in New York City.

Performances

Pierre Clementi is a youthful Devil, soft-spoken and wearing a wispy beard. Apparently he was spurred into action by Jean's evil wish upon the passing motorist. As the Devil converses with the two pilgrims, he disappears and reappears in different locations around the car, sometimes wearing a black cape and other times without. His tone is somber and gentle with them, even melancholy as he expresses his hope that there will be a general amnesty at the Final Judgment. Known for his usually fierce performances, Clementi was also associated with the underground film movement in France. He also appeared in another Buñuel classic, *Belle du Jour* (1967).

Notable Quotes

• What happens to the body of Christ inside your stomach? (**Pierre to priest, discussing whether the host is literally or symbolically the body of Christ**)

• This God of yours is a chimera that is found only in the minds of madmen. (**Marquis de Sade to Therese**)

• Down there, where tears are of no avail, where repentance is useless, where prayers go unanswered, where good solutions are rejected, where there is no time given to penitence, since beyond the point of life, there is no more time for penitence. (**the Devil, replying to Jean's question about his place of origin**)

Mr. Frost

1990 Rating: ***
Jeff Goldblum and Kathy Baker as the Devil

AAA/Hugo Films. Written by Philip Setbon and Brad Lynch; Photographed by Dominique Brenguier; Edited by Ray Lovejoy; Special Effects by Georges Demetrau; Music by Steve Levine; Produced by Xavier Gelin; Directed by Philip Setbon. Color, 92 minutes.

Annotated Cast List

Jeff Goldblum (*Mr. Frost*, the Devil); Alan Bates (*Felix Detweiler*, British homicide inspector); Kathy Baker (*Dr. Sarah Day*, Frost's psychiatrist at St. Clair); Roland Giraud (*Dr. Raymond Reynhardt*, head of the Hospital of St. Clair); Jean-Pierre Cassel (*Corelli*, French police inspector); Vincent Schiavelli (hotel manager); Daniel Gelin (*Simon Scolavi*, Detweiler's father-in-law); Francois Negret (*Christopher Kovac*, patient possessed by Frost); Henri Serre (*Andre Kovac*, Chris's father); Maxime Leroux (*Dr. Frank Larscher*, St. Clair psychiatrist in love with Sarah); Mike Marshall (*Dr. Patrick Hollander*, member of St. Clair staff); Charley Boorman (car thief); Boris Bergman (*Dr. Victor Sabowsky*, member of St. Clair staff); Herve Lavdiere (*Joseph*, hospital orderly); Philippe Polet (*Roland Day*, Sarah's crippled brother); Catherine Allegret (*Dr. Corbin*, Roland's doctor); Louise Vincent (*Louise*, Roland's nurse); Aina Wall (*Carole*, Detweiler's wife); Patrice Melennec (*Phil*, bartender); Jo Sherridan (jogger); Raymond Aquilon (*Dr. Elias*, member of St. Clair staff); Herve Langlouis (*Racket*, mental patient who pantomimes a tennis game); Catherine Cyler (*Christy*); Steve Gadler (archery instructor).

Appraisal and Synopsis

Largely ignored by the critics, *Mr. Frost* is a grim, deliberately paced story of the Devil quietly at work with his elaborate but oblique agenda. It is a disturbing film calculated to stimulate thought. A somber fable, *Mr. Frost* begins in darkness and grows continually blacker as the picture unfolds. For brief moments, there is a glimmer that it may become a black comedy, but these embers never develop and are quickly stamped out.

Mr. Frost opens in England as two car thieves break into the garage of a large estate and attempt to steal a sporty Astin-Martin, but they flee in horror when they discover a dead body in the vehicle. When they are later captured, they report this incident to the police, and Inspector Detweiler is sent to investigate. He is stunned when the charming occupant of the house, a man named Frost, openly admits the existence of the body, which he claims to have just buried. Detweiler then stumbles across another corpse in Frost's living room, and the scene shifts to a news broadcast, announcing the discovery of two dozen mutilated bodies of men, women, and children on the estate. As he is led away, Frost gives the inspector a videotape, a documentary record of his crimes.

Years later, Frost is transferred to St. Clair, a special mental hospital in France. Frost hasn't spoken a word for two years, except for a prison interview with Detweiler. Five of Europe's best psychiatrists have failed in their attempts to analyze him, and the authorities have been unable to learn his first name, his nationality, or any trace of his existence prior to his crimes. Professor Reynhardt, the pompous head of the facility, introduces his new patient to his staff, and Frost immediately addresses Dr. Sarah Day, saying that when he chooses to speak, it will be with her alone. Detweiler, no longer a policeman, approaches Reynhardt, seeking an interview. When rebuffed, he warns him that Frost is actually the Devil and should not be treated as if he were an ordinary patient.

During their first meeting, Frost examine's Sarah's ring, and holding it in his hand, he melts it into molten silver. Christopher Kovac, Sarah's favorite patient, is about to be released as cured. She then interviews Detweiler, who describes his final meeting with Frost, who detailed for him the last moments in the life of his wife, Carole, who was murdered during a burglary attempt while the inspector was having a drink at his local pub. "She hated you for not being there to save her life." This encounter led to Detweiler's breakdown. The troubled man gives Sarah a copy of the videotape Frost recorded when he tortured his victims. Sarah feels sickened when she watches the tape. Before Christopher is released from the hospital, he has an encounter with Frost who stares at him intently.

In a crucial session, Sarah asks Frost why would the Devil pose as a mental patient. He replies that psychiatrists have undone years of Satanic effort, muddying the waters of the differences between good and evil. So he has decided to confront the practitioners with his own presence, something they cannot explain away. Ultimately, he wants to expose the impotence of science by persuading his own analyst to murder him. That act would reveal the complete bankruptcy of psychiatry and rational thought. To demonstrate his power, he tells Sarah to follow what happens to her favorite patient.

Back at home, when Christopher is reunited with his father, he kills him with a hunting rifle. He then goes on a shooting spree, sniping and killing priests, seemingly at random. Sarah is informed that her crippled brother, Roland, has experienced a miraculous cure and is now able to walk. When the psychiatrist visits Frost, he says that he can affect both good and evil events. When Sarah mocks the entire concept of the Devil, her patient loses his cool for the first and only time. That evening Frost possesses Dr. Larscher, Sarah's occasional boyfriend, forcing her to knock him out with a vase when he assaults her. Sarah finally admits to Frost that she is convinced that he is the Devil. She implores him to save Christopher, and Frost calmly replies that she knows there is only one way to do that, by killing him. Sarah consults Detweiler, who has been having visions of his wife returning from the dead and attacking him.

Inspector Corelli, assigned to track down Christopher, asks Sarah for her help, but she refuses. Frost plays a game of chess with Professor Reynhardt, provoking him into a nosebleed after toppling over the chess pieces. Sarah confronts Frost, saying she wishes to understand and learn from him. He dismisses her, saying she is still at the stage of words when he insists upon action. In her apartment building as Sarah enters the elevator, she is confronted by a vision of Frost, who embraces and kisses her, then smashes her head against a mirrored wall. Christopher continues his killing spree. He goes to a sleazy hotel to rent a room, but the hotel manager recognizes him and summons Corelli. Reynhardt, under Frost's influence, steps out onto the ledge outside his office and threatens to jump. The police are called, and Sarah goes to Frost, begging him not to kill Reynhardt. As a gesture of good faith, he releases his hold on the professor and Christopher, but he insists that Sarah must follow through with his request to be murdered.

Corelli arrests the subdued Christopher, who claims he was compelled to commit the killings against his will. The young man kills himself by breaking away from Corelli and running headlong into a truck. Detweiler prepares a gun for Sarah to use on Frost. The Devil is ecstatic when Sarah enters his cell: "Together, we are obliterating centuries of civilization!" Sarah insists that he remain silent, but Frost babbles on. She shoots while he continues to talk, and after his body falls, Sarah completes the sentence he was speaking, indicating that Frost has now taken over her body. The last scene jumps ahead in time. Sarah is now committed to an asylum, and Sarah/Satan is refusing to speak. Her psychiatrist tries to elicit a response but instead his patient passes the time catching flies. The Devil is biding her time, waiting to choose the next victim.

There are a number of parallels between *Mr. Frost* and several other pictures, such as *Hammersmith Is Out* (1972). Both films portray the Devil as an inmate in an asylum. Both films are cyclical in nature, with the Devil as a mental patient pausing before starting another cycle in his demonic scheme. But whereas Hammersmith, played by Richard Burton, selects easy targets as his victims, Frost seeks more challenging ones. Hammersmith likes to work his mischief after escaping the hospital, but Frost prefers to conduct his campaign of destruction from his cell. Both are cool, arrogant, and seemingly unstoppable. *Hammersmith Is Out*, however, is a misfire, a directionless and vulgar comedy. *Mr. Frost*, on the other hand, is a deadly serious film, with the Devil's sarcastic and mean-spirited

Dr. Reynhardt (Roland Giraud) encounters difficulty in his game with the Devil, Mr. Frost (Jeff Goldblum). Actually, the position of the pieces make no sense, since only one king is shown on the chessboard.

wit providing the only comic relief, except for a brief cameo by Vincent Schiavelli as the colorful operator of a Parisian flophouse. *The Medusa Touch* (1978) is another Burton film that resembles *Mr. Frost* in odd and interesting ways. In it, Burton plays a brooding writer who convinces his psychiatrist, Lee Remick, that he has the power to will catastrophes, such as airplane disasters and nuclear reactor meltdowns. She then attempts to kill him. Remick is practically identical to Kathy Baker in portraying a cool and rational doctor pushed to the edge of madness by a patient with inexplicable powers. In other ways, *Mr. Frost* also resembles *The Silence of the Lambs* (1991), with a number of similarities between Hannibal Lecter and the Devil. Both prefer interacting with women. Both show extreme intelligence, a fascination for cooking, and an outwardly gentle and courteous manner. Finally, they are both incredibly dangerous, capable of playing mind games that can easily destroy their opponents at will. In these two films, Jeff Goldblum and Anthony Hopkins completely dominate the action with the force of their personalities. Also, both pictures have an outside series of murders that serves as a counterpoint to the asylum scenes. In *The Silence of the Lambs*, Lecter is actually assisting, to a degree, in the capture of the outside killer. In *Mr. Frost*, the Devil is controlling the outside killer like a puppet on a string. *The Silence of the Lambs* is by far the better film. *Mr. Frost*, by contrast, is more distasteful even though little gore or violence is portrayed on camera. There is simply no relief in the film from the overwhelming power of Satan. There is no way to fight him, to resist him, or to bargain with him. He also has a coherent plan, one destined to promote misery and despair, although on a small scale. God does not figure in the story at all, and Sarah never has a shred of hope from the moment Frost sets eyes on her. This unequal struggle and the lack of any relief from the Devil's loathsomeness makes *Mr. Frost* a difficult film to watch, much less enjoy. Nevertheless, it is a powerful film, well thought out and made with great style.

Performances

Jeff Goldblum, one of the screen's most popular actors, stretches the envelope as the malevolent, repulsive Devil using the pseudonym Frost. Goldblum uses no special makeup as the Devil, although in one scene his stringy hair is tied in a pony tail, symbolic, perhaps of his unseen Devil's tail. Neither are any special effects used to show his powers. Goldblum manages to portray pure evil through his acting skills alone, with expert control of his voice, facial muscles, and personality. There are moments when he can be charming and persuasive, as when he describes the battle between good and evil as a vital and productive force. But, like Hitler, Frost's fervor is directed toward an evil end. Goldblum's Devil is also cerebral. His schemes involve a subtle and tricky attack upon the cold logic of science, figuring that if he can discredit this discipline, it will leave mankind with no foundation, with nothing to be relied upon. Goldblum conveys this intellectual campaign most convincingly. When he discusses chaos, it may remind many viewers that the same actor played an expert in chaos theory in *Jurassic Park* (1993), three years after his largely unheralded performance in *Mr. Frost*. There are fleeting moments of wit, such as when the Devil claims to have invented language so that it could frequently hide rather than reveal the truth. When Goldblum plays the silent Frost, he uses his body effectively, including his elaborate technique of catching flies and shaking them in his fist, a gesture later repeated by Kathy Baker when she plays Sarah after her possession by the Devil. In every respect, Goldblum is as convincing a Devil as possible, unrivaled in his ability to distill the essence of evil in his depiction. The supporting players, Kathy Baker, Alan Bates, and Jean-Pierre Cassel, are all excellent, although they seem overshadowed by Goldblum because of the layout of the script. Vincent Schiavelli also stands out, making a memorable impression in his two short scenes.

Notable Quotes

• I am the extreme case. I'm darkness.... All fanatics know something about me. They have a greater fear of me than love of their God. (**Frost to Sarah**)

• If the Lord moves in mysterious ways, then the Devil moves in mysterious ways as well. (**Detweiler to Sarah**)

• I'm chaos. It's my destiny to destroy. (**Frost to Sarah, after his chess game with Reynhardt**)

• You believed in me, and now I know that nothing and no one will ever resist me. (**Frost to Sarah, just before she shoots him**)

National Lampoon's Favorite Deadly Sins
AKA Favorite Deadly Sins

1995   Rating: ***   Gerrit Graham as the Devil

Showtime Original Films. Written by Ann Lembeck (*Greed*), Michael Barrie, Jim Mulholland (*Anger*) and Lee Biondi (*Lust*); Photographed by Jamie Thompson and Tony Janelli (*Lust*); Edited by Christopher Ellis and Michelle Gorchow (*Lust*); Special Effects by Joshua Rose; Music by Christopher Tyng and Adam Roth (*Lust*); Produced by Peter Moanoogian; Directed by Denis Leary and David Jablin (*Lust*). Color, 99 minutes.

Annotated Cast List

Greed: Joe Mantegna (*Frank Musso*, TV producer); Cassidy Rae (*Norma Jean Hazelrigg*, waitress who murders her family); Brian Keith (himself and *Noble Hart*, lawyer); William Ragsdale (*Todd Farrit*, rival producer); Dale Raoul (*Allison Shoop*, woman who sells her children); Lois Foraker (*Charlotte*, Norma's stepmother); Lee Everett (*Freda*, Norma's stepsister); Carolyn Key Johnson (*Diane*, Norma's stepsister); Allan Rich (*Ziggy Brillman*, Musso's friend); Kristopher Logan, Steven M. Porter (reporters); Mark Blankfield (*Sheik Abdul Achmed*, blind Muslim cleric on trial); Eleanor Mondale (trial TV reporter); Gloria Allred, Robert Philibosian (TV attorneys); Tanya Roberts, Morgan Brittany, Charlene Tilton, Ed Marinaro, Robert Culp, Pia Zadora (television performers). **Anger:** Andrew Dice Clay (*Richard Spencer*, angry man); Farrah Forke (his wife); Ted Davis (Seven-Eleven cashier); David Harris, Robert LaSardo (store robbers); Clyde Kusatsu (*St. Peter*, heavenly gatekeeper); Gerrit Graham (the Devil); Bee-Be Smith, Susan Barnes,

Kenneth Randale (Seven-Eleven customers). **Lust:** Denis Leary (*Jake*, security guard); Annabella Sciorra (*Brenda*, his wife); Tanya Pohlkotte (*Sara*, his beautiful neighbor); Saverio Guerra (*Eddie*, Jake's coworker).

Appraisal and Synopsis

National Lampoon sponsored a series of satirical movies dating back to *Animal House* (1978) and including such top-notch entries as *Christmas Vacation* (1989) and *Loaded Weapon* (1993). This cable telefilm is a mixed effort, but the first section is such a powerful and hilarious one, it carries along its two lesser brothers fairly well. It seems the initial idea was for a series of seven episodes, but energy seemed to run out after the first three. The initial chapter, "Greed," must be seen to be believed. It skewers everything from *film noir* plots like *The Postman Always Rings Twice* (1946) to sleazy TV docudramas, celebrity show trials, and the media in general. Joe Mantegna is splendid as slimy TV producer Frank Musso who aids an oversexed waitress in killing her stepfamily, which he considers the ideal plot for a "based on fact" TV movie. He stimulates nationwide publicity by billing his protegé, Norma Jean, as the Cinderella Killer. Musso hires writers to script the testimony for the trial and hires folksy attorney Noble Hart, played by Brian Keith doing a dead-on impersonation of Gerry Spence. Things backfire when a rival producer induces Norma Jean to change her testimony, accusing Musso as the mastermind of the plot. Convicted and sentenced to death, Musso stages his execution as a TV special and winds up being buried with a coffin filled with cash.

The central story, "Anger," features raunchy comedian Andrew Dice Clay as Richard Spencer, a man with a monster temper who engages in nonstop, bullying rage with everyone he meets. Asked by his wife to go to the Seven-Eleven to pick up a package of tampons, Spencer weaves a nonstop tapestry of four-letter obscenities directed at anybody who crosses his path. The only exception is a young kid, paging through an issue of *National Lampoon* by the magazine rack. Spencer's temper subsides briefly as he is delighted to find the latest issue of his favorite girlie magazine. A gang of thugs holding up the store draws his ire. They shoot him, and as he dies he continues to rant and rave. He arrives at the pearly gates in a foul mood. When St. Peter judges him to be a basically good man with a temper problem, Spencer explodes until the gentle saint pushes a button that opens a trap door that drops him down to hell while still clinging to his girlie magazine. Spencer's rage, however, has just gotten started, and next he rips into the Devil, making fun of his breath, his appearance, and his pet demons. Satan starts to wilt under Spencer's barrage, especially when he calls him a pitiful excuse of a Devil. Satan pushes a button, and Spencer disappears, sent back to Earth. His dead body revives en route to the hospital morgue. Spencer's wife is there, and she starts to rage when she sees the brand of tampons he purchased. "Soon as you are out of here, I'm going to make your life a living hell!" The image of St. Peter and the Devil appear over her shoulder agreeing with each other: she is the only one equipped to handle her husband.

The final episode, "Lust," is a complete letdown after the great opening and its good follow-up. It is insipid and boring, as security guard Jake, tired of his wife, Brenda, develops a passion for Sara, his beautiful neighbor across the courtyard, who he spies on constantly. He manages to meet her when they both bring their children to the local playground. She invites him to bring his kids to her apartment on the next day so they can play. Jake imagines all sorts of scenarios in which he seduces her. When he arranges to visits her, he learns that she has jilted her husband because she has discovered she is a lesbian. In fact, she always spies on Jake's wife. In the meantime, Brenda herself stares longingly at a male neighbor in another apartment. Not only are there no chuckles in the finale, there is not even a smile, and it ends the film on a lackluster note. There is another film called *The Seven Deadly Sins* (1952) in French, Italian, and English, which explores all the sins in witty vignettes. Gérard Philipe stars as a carnival barker with an exhibit illustrating the sins. This picture is both clever and outstanding, ending with the revelation of an eighth deadly sin, the willingness to read evil in the action of others.

Performances

Gerrit Graham is a busy comic character actor who has appeared in over a hundred films and television shows, including the starring role in *C. H. U. D. II: Bud the Chud* (1989) and as Dr. Frankenstein in an episode of TV's "Weird Science." Graham is heavily made up as a reptilian Lucifer, similar in appearance to G'Kar the Narn ambassador in "Babylon Five." In his performance, he displays a quick variety of emotions, a difficult accomplishment given the heavy makeup. He plays his scene perfectly. In the end credits, Graham has an additional bit, as Satan is seen enjoying himself as he pages through Spencer's girlie magazine. Andrew Dice Clay basically parodies himself throughout the episode, combining the insult bullying of Jack E. Leonard and Don Rickles with the foul-mouthed vocabulary of B. S. Pulley. In this sequence, it works perfectly.

Notable Quotes

• With all due respect to your assholiness, with your big desk and your major connections, I'm a little goddamned sick and tired of always hearing about my problems! (**Spencer, blowing his top at St. Peter**)

• Richard Spencer, your life has been weighed and found wanting. You are hereby condemned to an eternity in hell. (**the Devil**)

That's very good, and you did that all by yourself. Did you see that everybody? He did it all by himself, and tomorrow we are going to teach you to shit fire out of your asshole. (**Spencer's response**)

• I've got two words for you, Lucy Fur: breath mints! Talk about your hellitosis.... You think that scares me? Trick or treat, trick or treat, smell my feet! (**Spencer, reacting to Satan's roar**)

Needful Things

1993   Rating ****   Max von Sydow as the Devil

Columbia. Written by W. D. Richter, based on the novel *Needful Things* by Stephen King; Photographed by Tony Westman; Edited by Rob Kobrin; Special Effects by Gary Paller; Music by Patrick Doyle; Produced by Jack Cummins and Peter Yates (executive); Directed by Fraser C. Heston. Color, 120 minutes; extended television print, 185 minutes.

Annotated Cast List

Ed Harris (*Alan Pangborn*, sheriff); Max von Sydow (*Leland Gaunt*, the Devil); Bonnie Bedelia (*Polly Chalmers*, cafe owner and Alan's fiancée); Amanda Plummer (*Nettie Cobb*, waitress); J. T. Walsh (*Danforth Keeton III*, Marina owner and head selectman); Gillian Barber (*Myrtle Keeton*, his wife); Ray McKinnon (*Norris Ridgewick*, deputy sheriff); Duncan Fraser (*Hugh Priest*, public works handyman); Frank C. Turner (*Peter Jerzyk*, turkey farmer); Valri Bromfield (*Wilma Jerzyk*, his wife); Shane Meier (*Brian Rusk*, kid who collects baseball cards); Lisa Blount (*Cora Rusk*, his mother); Don S. Davis (*Rev. Willie Rose*, Baptist minister); William Morgan Sheppard (*Fr. Meehan*, Catholic priest); Campbell Lane (*Frank Jewett*, school principal); Eric Schneider (*Henry Beaufort*, bartender); Tamsin Kelsey (*Sheila Ratcliffe*, police dispatcher); Lochlyn Munro (*John LaPointe*, cop); Bill Croft (*Andy Clutterbuck*, cop); Dee Jay Jackson (*Eddie Warburton*, custodian); Robert Easton (*Lester Pratt*, physical-education teacher); Debra Wakeham (*Myra Evans*); Ann Warn Pegg (*Ruth Roberts*); Gary Paller (*George Cobb*, Nettie's husband, who she murdered seven years earlier); Trevor Denman (race track voice); Mel Allen (baseball announcer).

Appraisal and Synopsis

Needful Things is considered by many to be one of the crowning jewels of Stephen King's work. It is the ultimate novel of his various works set in Castle Rock, a fictional town having many similarities to Bridgton, Maine. In this film, Castle Rock is changed into a coastal town along Route 1, instead of in the lake country interior as is the actual Bridgton. In the novel, King weaves a masterful spell of the Devil setting up an antique business in town and slowly but inexorably destroying the fabric of the community and the lives of its citizens. Structurally, his book resembles the novels of Ray Bradbury, such as *Dandelion Wine* and *Something Wicked This Way Comes*, weaving many stories and incidents around a central hub. Stylistically, the novel is pure King, perhaps with a dash of Goethe. Such a book, however, is extraordinarily difficult to translate to the screen. In essence, *Needful Things* is a splendid dramatization of the novel, far better than various assessments that criticized the film as confusing with too many plot strands. Only those who have read the book will appreciate the integrity of this adaptation, both in the original version and the expanded television print, which runs over an hour longer. The longer version, although awkward in its editing, is even better at depicting the total chaos that the Devil provokes in Castle Rock.

The film begins as the Devil's car, a black Mercedes, is shown approaching Castle Rock behind the opening credits. Soon the appearance of a new business called Needful Things begins to whet the curiosity of the town's residents. Brian Rusk, an inquisitive ten-year-old, is the first to enter the store, where he meets the mysterious but amiable Leland Gaunt, the Devil's current pseudonym. His encounter sets the pattern for the rest of the town, as Gaunt offers each of his customers an item so special that they can't resist, an article that summarizes their lost hopes or dreams. The Devil then suggests a modest price for the item but also requires a secret deed to be done by the buyer. The pranks suggested by Gaunt become more and more provocative until the entire community is divided into bitter rivalries that erupt into violence. Gaunt offers Brian a 1956 Topps baseball card autographed by Mickey Mantle "to my good friend Brian." For this priceless collector's item, Gaunt asks ninety-five cents and induces Brian

Max von Sydow as the Devil, Mr. Gaunt, in Needful Things.

to pull a practical joke on Wilma Jerzyk, a local turkey farmer, by splattering her laundry with turkey dung.

The sheriff of Castle Rock is Alan Pangborn, who has just become engaged to Polly Chalmers, owner of the local cafe. Most of the events that unfold are seen through his eyes. The leading citizen of Castle Rock is Danforth Keeton III, an arrogant and pushy man who offends most people who come in contact with him. Behind his back, people call him "Buster," a nickname derived from the great silent film comedian. Keeton explodes in anger when anyone calls him that to his face. Keeton is feuding with deputy sheriff Norris Ridgewick for ticketing his car while he was illegally parked in a handicapped zone.

The Devil's antique store starts to do a booming business. Hugh Priest buys a high school jacket similar to one he owned in his youth. Polly Chalmers buys a charm which relieves her painful arthritis. Frank Jewett buys an autographed first edition of *Treasure Island*. Each new patron is entered into the Devil's black book as he seeks to inflame natural rivalries, while pretending to be friendly to all parties. He sets waitress Nettie Cobb against Wilma Jerzyk, Norris Ridgewick against Danforth Keeton, the Baptist minister, Willie Rose, against Fr. Meehan, the Catholic priest, bar owner Henry Beaufort against his bad tempered-patron Hugh Priest, and so on.

Sheriff Pangborn discovers that Danforth Keeton has been dipping into town funds to cover his gambling losses. Keeton promises to pay back the shortage before the state auditors arrive. The head selectman visits Needful Things where he buys a toy horse race set, which Gaunt guarantees can pick the winners in advance of actual horse races. Gaunt forces Brian to break all the windows at the Jerzyk home, and he solicits Hugh Priest to kill Nettie Cobb's dog. Wilma and Nettie blame each other for these escalating crimes and, in uncontrollable rages, kill each other. Brian Rusk, overwhelmed by guilt over these deaths, tries to commit suicide, after telling the sheriff that Mr. Gaunt is not human. Pangborn breaks into Needful Things and discovers a carton of newspaper clippings proclaiming disasters, wars, and assassinations going back indefinitely, and the sheriff reaches the conclusion that Gaunt was there in each case, instigating the trouble.

As night falls, Castle Rock starts to go to pieces. Danforth Keeton has a total breakdown after killing his wife. Gaunt provides him with enough explosives to blow up the entire town, starting with the Catholic church. Fights, looting, and rioting break out, and as the chaos escalates, Pangborn fires his rifle into the air at the main crossroads of the town, trying to get everyone's attention so he can explain what Gaunt is doing. He asks the townspeople to confess what crimes they committed at Gaunt's urging. Sheepishly, a young girl admits that he made her steal Jewett's copy of *Treasure Island*. Fr. Meehan admits to slashing Hugh Priest's tires. One by one, all of the incidents that uncorked the violence are brought to light. At this point, Keeton shoots Pangborn in the leg from inside Gaunt's store. Then, walking into the street, he reveals himself as a human bomb wired with dynamite. At first, the citizens are stunned by this development, and the enraged Keeton vents his spleen against everyone. The wounded sheriff tries to reason with him, blaming Gaunt for the trouble. The Devil becomes more and more impatient as Keeton raves on, and he finally yells at him, "For Christ's sake, put this town out of its misery, Buster!" Keeton turns and charges at Gaunt, knocking him back into his store as the dynamite explodes. The building goes up in an enormous fireball. When the debris settles, Ridgewick comments, "Shouldn't have called him Buster."

The Devil emerges from the flaming rubble unscathed, dusts off his coat, and says to Pangborn that this wasn't his finest effort. He predicts that Pangborn and Polly will have a wonderful family, but that he plans to meet up with his grandson, Bob, in Jakarta on August 14, 2053 at 10 AM. Gaunt then gets into his Mercedes and drives off. As it leaves town, the vehicle disappears into thin air.

In almost all regards, *Needful Things* is a most satisfactory film, a marvelous black comedy, expertly photographed with strong production values. Although filmed in British Columbia, the film has an authentic Maine atmosphere that is usually lacking in movies done in western Canada that try to approximate New England. The excellent music score by Patrick Doyle frequently uses classical selections by Franz Schubert, Johann Strauss, and Edvard Grieg. His quoting of *In the Hall of the Mountain King* is the cleverest use of the melody since Fritz Lang used it in *M* (1931). W. D. Richter's script stays fairly close to King's storyline, with a few interesting alterations. For example, in the novel, Brian wants a Sandy Koufax baseball card, not Mickey Mantle. There always seems to be a diabolical atmosphere surrounding the New York Yankees, but it also allows the familiar voice of Mel Allen to be used in the film. The reasons for other minor changes are less apparent, such as substituting Meehan for Brigham as the name of the town priest. The expanded version includes more detailed plot development, such as Brian's mother, who becomes obsessed with a bust of Elvis which she purchases from Gaunt. There is also greater focus on Hugh Priest, as well as a scene in which Pangborn completely loses his temper and starts to beat Gaunt, who offers no resistance but also seems incapable of being hurt. The alternate opening of the longer version features a wild car chase, ending in the wreck of the Devil's Mercedes. Although not bad, it is extraneous, as the Devil reappears in another vehicle moments later.

The major running gag in the film is the continuing tribute to the great Buster Keaton. Unfortunately, there may be many younger viewers who don't understand the reference (such as the character of Nettie Cobb), so it might have been wise if someone, such as one of the characters in the bar, tuned in an old Keaton film on TV and made a wisecrack about Danforth Keeton. The cast does a fine, ensemble acting job, and fledgling director Fraser Heston, son of Charlton Heston, handles the project well. There is a cute anecdote concerning his involvement. One day he was in conference with Max von Sydow, who made his American debut playing Christ in *The Greatest Story Ever Told* (1964). Fraser Heston made his own screen debut as baby Moses in *The Ten Commandments* (1954). Someone watching their conversation quipped, "Look, there's Moses telling Christ how to play the Devil."

Performances

In *Needful Things*, Max von Sydow plays the Devil as a shrewd businessman, a master psychologist who knows all the appropriate buttons to push with each person. His cleverness enables him to deal with each individual on a personal level, so he is equally at home interacting with one person as with another. In a discourse in the longer version, the Devil details his long experience as a traveling peddler dating back to Mesopotamia and the dawn of civilization. His astuteness makes it almost impossible to thwart him. On the other hand, he has a healthy respect and even a liking for Sheriff Pangborn, as opposed to his personal distaste for Danforth Keeton. Von Sydow plays Gaunt exceedingly well, with calculated ease and assurance. No special makeup is used, but the actor employs an occasional sinister expression that works extraordinarily well. Gaunt is such a meaty part that it is fascinating to consider alternate approaches to the role, with offbeat casting such as someone like Jimmy Stewart. The other cast members are excellent in their parts, particularly Ed Harris, whose work over the years has resulted in performances of the highest caliber. Don Davis, memorable as Harlan Briggs in "Twin Peaks," and Amanda Plummer bring a special vitality to their roles. Oddly though, only Frank C. Turner as Peter Jerzyk brings a true Down East flair to his performance.

Notable Quotes

- I'm afraid I have a tendency to turn up the heat. (**Gaunt to Frank Jewett**)
- Oh, Jesus! (**Hugh Priest, examining a gun in Gaunt's store**)

The young carpenter from Nazareth? I knew Him well, a promising young man. He died badly. (**the Devil's reply**)

- You can't win. I've got God on my side.... So in His infinite wisdom, He tolerates my little shenanigans, a famine here, a flood there, a little bloodlust, a broken heart. So get off my case, I'm just a fall guy. (**the Devil to Pangborn in the extended version**)
- Kill them all. Let God sort them out! (**the Devil, urging Pangborn to use his gun on the rioters**)
- Hey, don't blame me. Blame it on the bossa nova, but how about you take some responsibility for once in your life, Buster? (**the Devil to Keeton at the climax**)

The Ninth Gate

1999   Rating: *****   Emmanuelle Seigner as the Devil

Artisan Entertainment. Written by Enrique Urbiz, Roman Polanski, and John Brownjohn, based on the novel *El Club Dumas* by Arturo Perez-Reverte; Photographed by Darius Khondji; Special Effects by Sony Pictures Imageworks, Duboi Digital Effects, Eclair Numerique, and Mikros Images; Edited by Herve de Luze; Music by Wojciech Kilar; Produced and Directed by Roman Polanski. Color, 132 minutes.

Annotated Cast List

Johnny Depp (*Dean Corso*, rare book dealer); Frank Langella (*Boris Balkan*, wealthy publisher and collector of demonic literature); Emmanuelle Seigner (*Green Eyes,* the Devil masquerading as a student); Barbara Jefford (*Frieda Kessler*, baroness obsessed with the Devil); Lena Olin (*Liana Telfer*, head of the Order of the Silver Serpent); Tony Amoni (Liana's bodyguard); Willy Holt (*Andrew Telfer*, Liana's husband, a suicide); Jack Taylor (*Victor Fargas*, refined Portuguese book antiquarian); James Russo (*Bernie Ornstein*, bookshop owner); Jose Lopez Rodero (*Pablo* and *Pedro Ceniza*, Spanish book merchants, and *Pepe Lopez* and *Ricardo Herrera*, Spanish tradesmen); Bernard and Marrinette Richter (cafe owners); Jacques Dacomine (elderly man forced to sell his book collection); Joe Sheridan (his son); Rebecca Pauley (His daughter-in-law); Allen Garfield (*Witkin*, book dealer, Corso's rival); Maria Ducceshi (Kessler's secretary); Catherine Benguigui (concierge); Jacques Collard (*Gruber*, Parisian hotel manager); Dominique Pozzetto (desk clerk); Lino Ribeiro De Sousa (head porter); Emmanuel Booz (baker); Asil Rais (New York cab driver).

Appraisal and Synopsis

A number of critics dismissed or misunderstood this remarkable film, one of the most brilliant of Roman Polanski's career. Part of the reason is that it requires genuine concentration. To penetrate the actual story is as challenging a puzzle as the one faced by the protagonist in the film. Much of the enigma hinges on the identity of the character played by Emmanuelle Seigner, called Green Eyes. Only when one deduces that she is the incarnation of the Devil does the scope and significance of the story take shape. Polanski keeps this point vague and only implies it, letting the viewer reach his own conclusion. In fact, several lines from the original script were cut in which Green Eyes talks with Corso about whether he would realize it if he met the Devil. At the end, many have assumed that she is merely an emissary of the Devil, missing the final intuitive leap that solves the riddle which is the entire thrust of the film. Clear verification of the identity of the mysterious girl can be found in the source novel, *El Club Dumas* by Arturo Perez-Reverte. In chapter 9, the girl gives Corso a present, Jacques Cazotte's novella *Le Diable Amoureau* (1776) or *The Devil in Love*. The plot of this Gothic romance involves the Devil assuming the form of a woman, Biondetta, who falls in love and has an affair with Captain Alvaro, the hero of the story. Biondetta conceals that she is the

Devil, instead allowing her lover to think she is only a sylph until after they mate. *Le Diable Amoureau*, therefore, provides Corso with the key to the actual identity of Green Eyes. In chapter 10, when Corso asks her point-blank, she replies, "The Devil." By chapter 13, Corso accepts this, commenting to his friend, "The Devil has fallen in love with me and been incarnated as a twenty-year-old girl who now acts as my bodyguard." In the last line of *El Club Dumas*, Perez-Reverte notes, "Everyone gets the Devil he deserves." Green Eyes' demeanor and appearance is precisely tailored to Corso. Dressed as a tomboy with dirty sneakers and a baggy anorak, she is the ideal counterpart to Corso. The gist of *The Ninth Gate* is that she is the Devil he deserves. The revelation of the Devil also provides a coherent explanation of the entire plot, why the events of the film occur and what they actually mean. This analysis will follow the synopsis.

The picture opens as book collector Andrew Telfer scribbles a note in his library chamber and hangs himself from a chandelier. A dreamlike credits sequence follows in which the viewer is led through a series of elaborate doorways. Dean Corso, an unscrupulous rare book expert, is summoned by Boris Balkan, the wealthy owner of the Balkan Press. When the book dealer arrives for his meeting, Balkan is giving a lecture on demonic literature. The book dealer notices an attractive, casually dressed blonde girl listening to Balkan's remarks. Corso falls asleep, and Balkan wakes him at the conclusion of his talk and escorts him to his private library in the penthouse, which is totally devoted to works about the Devil. He is most puzzled about his latest acquisition, a seventeenth-century work entitled *The Nine Gates of the Kingdom of Shadows*, a book with a notorious reputation. The author of the volume, Aristede Torchia, was a bookbinder from Venice who was inspired to write it after uncovering a copy of *The Delomelanicon*, or *Invocation of Darkness*, a text purportedly written by the Devil himself. Torchia published his book in 1666 (note the "666" significance) and the following year was burned as a heretic by the Holy Inquisition, and all but three copies of *The Nine Gates* were destroyed. Balkan suspects something is amiss with his copy, and he commissions Corso to take his book and compare it with the other two editions held in private collections in Europe. While doing research in the public library, Corso again encounters the mysterious girl who vanishes when Corso tries to approach her.

Corso interviews Liana Telfer, the widow of the collector who sold Balkan his copy of *The Nine Gates* the day before he committed suicide. At first, Liana seems indifferent when she learns that her husband had sold the book. Later, however, she seduces Corso in an attempt to regain the rare volume. Corso asks his friend Bernie Ornstein to store the book for him. When Corso goes to retrieve the book, he finds Bernie murdered, his body suspended upside down in a pose identical to an illustration in *The Nine Gates*. He telephones Balkan and attempts to withdraw from the project, but Balkan offers him ten times his already substantial fee to continue his research. Corso goes to Toledo, Spain, to question Pablo and Pedro Ceniza, the eccentric book dealers who originally sold Telfer his copy of *The Nine Gates*. The identical twins draw Corso's attention to the nine engravings in the book. Six are inscribed "AT" by Aristede Torchia, but the remaining three are labeled "LCF" and were drawn by Lucifer himself. Corso studies one of these engravings, in which a traveler is threatened by danger from above by a figure resembling the Ceniza brothers. After Corso leaves their shop, he is almost killed by metal scaffolding in the street, which collapses as he passes by. Corso encounters the blonde girl in the train en route to Portugal. She gives the impression of being a student. They finally speak, and Corso calls her Green Eyes when she asks him to guess her name.

The book dealer's next stop is the Fargas estate. Victor Fargas is a kind and gentle scholar whose family fortune has dissipated, and his large house is practically empty of furnishings. Of his rare book collection, only 800 of his original 5,000 books remain. He freely shows his copy of *The Nine Gates* to Corso, who is stunned to discover that the illustrations in Fargas' copy differ from Balkan's copy. Three different ones are labeled "LCF," and there are subtle differences in the details. For example, in one illustration, the keys are held in a different hand of an elderly gentleman approaching a doorway. The man in the illustration resembles Victor Fargas. After leaving the Fargas estate, Corso is almost run down by a car. Corso recognizes the driver as Telfer's servant. The man stops his car and approaches him threateningly when a motorcyclist arrives and frightens off the driver. Back at his hotel, the book dealer receives a call from Balkan, and he explains about the alternate engravings labeled "LCF." Corso discovers that the helpful motorcyclist is none other than Green Eyes. In the middle of the night, the girl knocks at his door, urging him to return to the Fargas estate at once. There they find the old man murdered, drowned in a water fountain. Corso finds Fargas' copy of *The Nine Gates* has been burned, but by examining the remnants, he determines that the "LCF" engravings were removed.

Corso accepts Green Eyes as his companion, and they catch a flight to Paris. Corso has a fruitless meeting with Baroness Kessler, an eminent author who has devoted her life to the study of Lucifer. Corso is followed and attacked by Liana's bodyguard, but Green Eyes overpowers the assailant with an exotic fighting technique. She brings Corso back to his hotel room and smears her blood on his forehead as if she were baptizing him. Balkan calls to hear his latest report. At his employer's insistence, Corso returns to see Baroness Kessler, finally persuading her to show him her copy of *The Nine Gates*. He learns from the baroness about a secret cult called the Order of the Silver Serpent, which tries to raise the spirit of the Devil by invoking a ritual from *The Nine Gates*. Liana, originally a French noblewoman named St. Martin, now heads this group, and the baroness surmises that Liana's husband killed himself after learning about the extent of her Satan worship. Corso is attacked from behind as he examines the copy of *The Nine Gates* owned by the baroness. When he awakens, he finds the baroness strangled to death and her library in flames. He has no doubt that the three "LCF" engravings were stolen from her copy of the book.

When Corso returns to his room, he finds his copy of *The Nine Gates* has been stolen. Balkan, calling from a nearby hotel, is outraged when Corso tells him it is missing. Corso quickly learns that Liana Telfer stole it, and Green Eyes steals a car so they can track Liana as she and her bodyguard drive out of Paris. They find she is heading to the village of St. Martin, where she owns a chateau.

That evening, the Order of the Silver Serpent is holding its annual meeting. Green Eyes and Corso sneak into the estate, attempting to take back the book. They are captured, and Liana orders her servant to kill them. They overcome him, however, as he leads them to the cellar. They eavesdrop on the ceremony of the black-robed members of the cult. Liana is attempting an incantation from *The Nine Gates* when Boris Balkan interrupts the assemblage, declaring, "Mumbo jumbo!" He seizes his copy of *The Nine Gates*, choking Liana to death when she tries to stop him.

The Order of the Silver Serpent convenes in The Ninth Gate *moments before Boris Balkan (Frank Langella) crashes the ceremony. They intend to summon Satan, unaware that the Devil is already there in the guise of a beautiful female observer.*

Corso tries to interfere but is stopped by Green Eyes, who flies through the air to restrain him. The meeting disperses in panic, and Green Eyes comments that Balkan's act has cleared Corso of any suspicion in the previous murders. Corso steals Liana's car and chases after Balkan, who heads to the remote ruins of a Cathar castle which he owns. There he arranges the nine "LCF" engravings and starts to invoke the ritual. Corso tries to stop him, but he falls through the weakened floor. As he hangs on, Balkan urges him to watch as he completes his ritual, translating the hidden message of the engravings. Believing himself immortal, Balkan sets himself on fire to demonstrate his new power. Too late, he realizes his error, and he is burned alive. Corso climbs up and retrieves the engravings. As he leaves the castle, he encounters Green Eyes, who appears as if by magic. She kisses Corso passionately, and they make love on the ground as Balkan's castle goes up in flames behind them.

Green Eyes reveals, as they drive away, that the ninth engraving is a forgery. She then vanishes when Corso stops the car at a gas station, leaving him a message on the forged engraving with the name "Ceniza." Corso heads back to Toledo, but Ceniza's bookstore has been vacated. Two workmen are removing the furniture. A single page flutters down when they tilt a large bookcase. Corso picks it up, and it is the ninth engraving, in which the image of Green Eyes is riding the Beast of the Apocalypse. As he studies it, Corso dematerializes, finding himself before the Ninth Gate, which is portrayed in the engraving. The Ninth Gate opens as he approaches it, and he disappears into the blinding light beyond the entrance. A white light fills the screen, and the film ends.

The motivation for the Devil's grand scheme in *The Ninth Gate* is open to various interpretations. The most intriguing one cleverly ties up the various threads of the plot. If we consider that Dean Corso himself is actually a fallen angel who has blotted out the painful memory of his downfall and loss of heaven, then all of the elements of the story fall into place. The Devil's plan is to gather his defeated comrades and make one last try to reconcile with God and regain heaven. The Devil could have foreseen Corso's incarnation at the end of the twentieth century and inspired the publication of *The Nine Gates* specifically with Corso in mind, to reunite him with his destiny. That is why the illustrations refer directly to events which happen in the film and why the figures in the engravings resemble Corso and the individuals he encounters. The Devil prepared for Corso's journey of discovery 300 years earlier. Boris Balkan was just a puppet in the Satanic plan to launch Corso on his quest. This interpretation fits in with Corso's personality, a loner without attachments, a mercenary, a "wolf in sheep's clothing," who is not really of his time. The book makes his otherworldliness quite plain, and Johnny Depp certainly endows Corso with all these characteristics in his portrayal. With this assessment, the action of the film can be seen as a rescue mission by the Devil of a beloved lost comrade. The Devil, in this view, is not the roaring lion seeking to devour souls but the courageous antihero of John Milton's *Paradise Lost* fused with the passionate and androgynous Devil from Jacques Cazotte's *Le Diable Amoureau*. *The Ninth Gate* is a rare, sympathetic depiction of the Devil as a noble and defeated figure who rose up against unquestioned obedience to the rule of God and engendered the ruination of his comrades and allies.

The screenplay of *The Ninth Gate* does a masterful job of adapting *El Club Dumas* by eliminating an entwined subplot involving *The Three Musketeers* and Alexandre Dumas, which in essence is a red herring. For instance, in the novel, there is no Order of the Silver Serpent, instead it is the Club Dumas. Liana is obsessed with *The Three Musketeers*, not *The Nine Gates*. By discarding the red herring, the film loses some of the novel's humor but gains greater substance. The other qualities of the film are of the highest order. Much attention was given to the creation of the volume of *The Nine Gates*, one of the most significant props ever developed for a film. Artist Francisco Sole, who illustrated the original novel, carefully developed and adapted the engravings, casting the figures in the illustrations with the images of the actors in the picture. The cinematography by Darius Khondji is stunning, particularly with his use of color where red tones are highlighted as the film progresses. The musical score by Polish composer Wojciech Kilar is magnificent, surpassing his earlier score to *Bram Stoker's Dracula* (1992). Like Danny Elfman, Kilar raises the musical score to new heights in the creation of mood and atmosphere. Roman Polanski's direction is that of a master at the height of his creativity. His stylistic competence is unique, making the film a rich and luxurious tapestry. Even his decision to be ambiguous has its merits, allowing the audience to come to its own conclusions or to investigate the original novel and discover the underlying meanings. In time, this film may even be regarded as the pinnacle of his career.

Performances

Emmanuelle Seigner is enthralling as the beguiling and mysterious Green Eyes. Her appearance is completely ordinary, and she is dressed in drab, baggy clothes. She wears no special makeup, but her eyes are optically enhanced to make them glow with an otherworldly light, a subtle but most effective touch. Hailing from a renowned French family of actors, Seigner became a fashion model at the age of fourteen and soon gained international fame. She broke into films in the mideighties, gaining notice for her work in *Detective* (1985) by Jean-Luc Godard and *Frantic* (1988) by Roman Polanski. She married Polanski in 1989. Seigner walks a fine line throughout *The Ninth Gate*, keeping the audience guessing as to whether she is another agent of Boris Balkan or someone of far greater significance. She has tremendous screen charisma, most evident in the scene where she marks Corso's forehead with her blood. On repeated viewings, the supernatural aspects of her character are more noticeable. She can appear and disappear at will, and she can float through the air as if on a cloud. It also seems likely that she can transform herself into other guises. When Corso emerges from Baroness Kessler's burning apartment, a Great Dane appears to be guarding him. This animal, undoubtedly, is Green Eyes. The Devil often appears as a dog in folklore. On the whole, her character is fully consistent as a feminine incarnation of the Devil. This adds a special irony to the film. For example, she crashes the secret ceremony of the Order of the Silver Serpent, whose purpose is to raise the Devil. It would have been admirable if more of her original dialogue from the novel could have been included, such as her wistful observations about her downfall as Satan, "After the battle, I walked across a plain as desolate and lonely as eternity is cold." Seigner could have made this line sound quite poignant. Frank Langella and Johnny Depp are also both terrific in their roles. Langella, cool, arrogant, and ruthlessly determined to reach his goal, is masterful as Boris Balkan. Depp's role is even more challenging, and he intuitively underplays the role with subtle shadings. As Dean Corso, his character slowly evolves from a cynical mercenary and nonbeliever in the supernatural to an obsessed zealot and the Devil's mate. His impressive performance has rich undertones and can be interpreted in different ways and on different levels, even being consistent with the conception that Corso himself could be a fallen angel. The other supporting cast members are likewise excellent, particularly Barbara Jefford as the wheelchair-bound Countess Kessler. Jose Lopez Rodero also deserves to be singled out for special merit, appearing in four different roles in his first appearance as an actor. Previously, Rodero always worked behind the camera as an assistant director or producer on such films as *Spartacus* (1960), *King of Kings* (1961), and *Dune* (1984).

Notable Quotes

- The engravings.... form a kind of Satanic riddle. Correctly interpreted with the aid of the original text and sufficient inside information, they are reputed to conjure up the Prince of Darkness in person. (**Boris Balkan to Corso**)
- Why the Devil? (**Corso to Baroness Kessler**)

I saw him one day. I was fifteen years old, and I saw him as plain as I see you now. It was love at first sight. (**her reply**)

- To travel in silence by a long and circuitous route, to brave the arrows of misfortune and fear, neither noose nor fire, to play the greatest of all games and win, forgoing no expense, is to mock the vicissitudes of fate and gain at last the key that will unlock the Ninth Gate. (**Balkan's translation of the hidden message of the engravings**)

Oh, God! You Devil

1984   Rating: ***   George Burns as the Devil

Paramount. Written by Andrew Bergman; Photographed by King Baggot; Special Effects by Tim Donahue and William Mesa; Edited by Andy Zall and Randy Roberts; Music by David Shire; Produced by Robert M. Sherman and Irving Fein (executive); Directed by Paul Bogart. Color, 96 minutes.

Annotated Cast List

George Burns (God and *Harry O. Tophet*, the Devil); Ted Wass (*Bobby Shelton*, musician in dead-end career); Roxanne Hart (*Wendy Shelton*, his wife, a social worker); Robert Desiderio (*Billy Wayne*, celebrity who contracted with the Devil); Eugene Roche (*Charlie Grey*, Bobby's agent); Ron Silver (*Gary Frantz*, Astral Records executive); Robert Picardo (*Joe Ortiz*, his associate); Cynthia Tarr (their receptionist); John Doolittle (*Arthur Shelton*, Bobby's father); Julie Lloyd (*Bea Shelton*, Bobby's mother); Ian Giatti (*Bobby* as a child); Belita Moreno (*Mrs. Vega*, Wendy's client); Luis Daniel Ponce (her son); Jason Wingreen (*Dave*, hotel manager in Miami); Danny Mora (hotel attendant); Jane Dulo (widow plagued by Tophet during the wedding reception); Stephen Dunaway (waiter at reception whose pants fall down); Susan Peretz (*Louise*, hostess at Gennaro's restaurant); Arthur Malet (*Wilson*, butler); James Cromwell (priest consulted by Bobby); Arnold Johnson (sidewalk preacher); Martin Garner (rabbi); Buddy Powell (Caesar's Palace stage manager); Jim Hodge (doctor who attends Billy Wayne); Brandy Gold (Bobby's young daughter).

Appraisal and Synopsis

Oh, God! You Devil is the third film in a series where George Burns plays the Almighty. The first film, *Oh, God!* (1977) was directed by Carl Reiner and was a huge hit. The sequel, however, was a disappointment. For the third film, Burns is cast as both God and the Devil, with most of his screen time devoted to the latter. While not as excellent as the original, this film is quite good and provides one of the most entertaining of all screen Devils. The story begins in 1960, when young Bobby Shelton is seriously ill with scarlet fever. His father offers a heartfelt prayer to God to watch over his son, and he then entertains the boy by singing "Can Do" from *Guys and Dolls*. Attracted by either the prayer or the song (we are never quite sure which), God appears in the street below and enters Bobby's name in his book of people to whom he gives special attention.

Twenty-four years later, Bobby is a frustrated composer and musician whose career is stuck in limbo, and he has to depend on his wife's earnings as a social worker. His agent, Charlie Grey, is unable to sell any of his music and can only get him temporary gigs such as entertaining at wedding receptions. Confronted with his failure, Bobby says he would sell his soul to the Devil if he could be a success. In Miami, Harry Tophet checks out of his hotel in the midst of a hurricane. "Nice weather," he tells the hotel manager. As he drives to California, Tophet's onboard computer alerts him to Bobby's comment. Even though he is watched over by God, since Bobby asked for the Devil's help,

Tophet is now free to deal with him. Tophet approaches Bobby as he entertains at a wedding at an estate in Brentwood. He gives Bobby his business card as a theatrical agent and promises him great success if he becomes his client. That evening, Tophet takes possession of singer Billy Wayne whose seven-year contract has expired.

The next day, Astral Records calls Charlie Grey to bring Bobby to a meeting. They intend to buy one of Bobby's songs outright and use it for one of their other stars. Harry Tophet also turns up at the office and convinces Bobby to become his client. Bobby agrees and drops Charlie. When Harry meets with the recording executives, he offers them a proposal for a multimillion-dollar deal for two record albums. Bobby is startled and hesitates to sign Tophet's seven-year contract. The Devil then crosses out the time clause and says the contract will just be for a trial period. As soon as Bobby signs, he becomes transformed into Billy Wayne, and the executives accept Tophet's deal. Bobby is stunned, and he finally realizes that Tophet is the Devil when he lights his cigar with his fingertips. Even though he still looks like himself, everyone else sees him as Billy Wayne, and Bobby steps into his superstar lifestyle, including private jets, beautiful women, and a luxury mansion. At the same time, Billy Wayne is now seen as Bobby Shelton, and Tophet arranges for Wayne to actually believe he is Shelton. All of the success Tophet has promised Bobby comes true, but Bobby feels empty because

George Burns as both God (standing in white) and the Devil (seated in black). God bluffs Satan in a poker game to win back the soul of Bobby Shelton.

his fame is in the guise of another person, and he is only going through the motions. Most of all, he misses his wife, Wendy, who he truly loves. He asks Tophet if he can return to his previous existence because the contract was only for a trial period. Tophet puffs on his cigar and tells him that he lied, and the contract stands.

On the date of his anniversary to Wendy, Bobby goes to Gennaro's restaurant, their traditional meeting place. Wendy is there with the phony Bobby, and he speaks with her. She believes he is Billy Wayne, and he learns she is pregnant and that the baby was conceived before his deal with Tophet. Learning this, Bobby is determined to seek out God, hoping he can get him out of his contract. He visits a priest and a rabbi, asking how to reach God, but they think he is loony. He finally encounters a grizzly street preacher, a modern-day John the Baptist with a van. He tells Bobby, "Look for Him in the desert."

Performing at Caesar's Palace, Bobby leaves a message for the hotel loudspeaker to page "the Lord" and have Him call his room. Time passes, and when God does call, He advises Bobby to praise Him and hangs up. Bobby prays and asks for a sign that He will help him. After waiting for hours, Bobby leaves to prepare for his stage show, and he misses seeing God's reply to his prayer, a rainbow in the sky at night. Depressed, Bobby attempts suicide. Meanwhile, God and Harry meet in the Casino and play poker with Bobby's soul as the stakes. Tophet has a full house, but he folds when God raises the stakes to include all of the select souls that He watches over. God wins, but when He shows Trophet His hand, He was only bluffing. Bobby is himself again, and the body of the actual Billy Wayne is lying dead. God comes to see Bobby and tells him, "There's no unknown. There's Me, and everything unknown I know." He tells him to be a loving father and resist temptation, because He won't bail him out again.

An epilogue is dated five years later. Bobby's daughter is ill, and he slips into her room at night. He starts to sing "Can Do" to cheer her up, and he hears God's voice singing along with him.

Performances

George Burns plays the Devil as a foxy old scoundrel, a shrewd and mischievous manipulator of human weakness who amuses himself with his antics. "It's the little things I enjoy," he chortles to himself after pulling a devious prank. This Devil has adopted the appearance and speech patterns of God because deep down he can't help trying to imitate him. The name he uses, Harry O. Tophet, has a number of interesting connotations. First, it provides him with the initials HOT, which he uses as a monogram and as a vanity plate for his car. Second, the Bible describes Topheth as a valley where children were burned alive as human sacrifices to Moloch, a pagan sun god (Jeremiah 7:31). The place was regarded as a locale of terrible evil, and it was also referred to as Gehenna, another name for hell. Finally, the name sounds similar to *Teufel*, the German word for Devil. Tophet usually displays a pleasant disposition, but if he is challenged, he grows quiet and serious while his eyes glow red. He likes to smoke cigars simply because he enjoys the appearance of smoke. He is a storyteller who likes to hear himself talk, and he frequently casts aspersions on God, who he calls "a very disappointed man, bitter." As God, Burns is a bit more remote than in his two previous outings, and he actually interacts only briefly with Ted Wass. God's best scene is His poker confrontation with the Devil, and this remarkable moment is unique in film history, because it actually shows a comedian stealing scenes from himself. The sense of timing shown by Burns is impeccable, both as God and Tophet. In many ways, his performance is a *tour de force* unequaled by any other demonic portrayal in this book. The remaining players are adequate but somewhat out of their depth. Eugene Roche is best remembered from commercials as a dishwasher with a missing tooth. Robert Picardo later landed the role of the holographic doctor in "Star Trek: Voyager." Ron Silver grew into a leading actor, but he is unimpressive here. Ted Wass is another disappointment; he is simply bland and uninteresting compared to George Burns, who was eighty-eight years old when he made this film, a remarkable achievement.

Notable Quotes

- I haven't met a cop yet who couldn't use an extra twenty dollars. (**Tophet to the hotel manager**)
- I love to scare the hell out of people. (**Tophet, muttering to himself**)
- Listen, if I didn't exist, God would have had to make me up. I make Him look good. (**Tophet to Bobby**)
- I'm on my way to New Hampshire. The leaves are changing. (**God to the Devil**)

Good time to go. Next year I'm bringing back the gypsy moth. (**Tophet's reply**)

The Omega Code

1999   Rating: **   Michael York as the Devil

TBN Films. Written by Stephen Blinn and Hollis Barton; Photographed by Carlos Gonzalez; Special Effects by Ron Trost and Vision Art; Edited by Peter Zinner; Music by Harry Manfredini; Produced by Matthew Crouch, Lawrence Mortorff and Robert Marcarelli; Directed by Robert Marcarelli. Color, 99 minutes.

Annotated Cast List

Casper Van Dien (*Dr. Gillen Lane*, scholar of mythology and religion); Michael York (*Stone Alexander*, millionaire raised from the dead and possessed by Satan); Catherine Oxenberg (*Cassandra Barashe*, television reporter); Michael Ironside (*Dominic*, assassin employed by Alexander); Jan Triska (prophet #1); Gregory Wagrowski (prophet #2); William Hootkins (*Sir Percival Lloyd*, World Council member and Alexander's major supporter); Robert Ito (*Shimoro Lin Che*, World Council member); Devon Odessa (*Jennifer*, Lane's estranged wife); Ayla Kell (*Maddie*, Lane's young daughter); George Coe (*Senator Jack Thompson*, Lane's friend and father-in-law); Janet Carroll (*Dorothy Thompson*, Jack's wife and Jennifer's mother); Ravil Issyanov (*Rykoff*, World Council member); Yehuda Efroni (*Rostenberg*, Jewish scholar who discovers the Omega Code); Oded Teomi (Israeli prime minister); Stella Voedemann (*Princess Gabrielle*, presenter of Alexander's UN award); Robert O'Reilly (Omega Code technician); Walter Williamson (Orthodox archbishop); Ross McKerras (*Ferguson*); Steve Franken (*Jeffries*).

Appraisal and Synopsis

The Omega Code is an apocalyptic drama in the mode of *The Seventh Sign*

(1988) and *Holocaust 2000* (1978). The basic premise is that a hidden code is discovered within the text of the Torah, the collected writings of Jewish religious literature including the Old Testament. The problem is that after introducing this concept, the script never develops it properly and fumbles its way through a rather muddled plot, wasting an excellent conceptual opportunity. The film hired popular writer Hal Lindsey as a scriptural advisor, but his suggestions were either ignored or merely added to the confusion. The most important character in the film is Stone Alexander, a media mogul who becomes involved in politics, where he has remarkable success on the world stage, but who in actuality is the Antichrist. In biblical prophecy, the Antichrist is not the Devil, but in this film, Satan possesses Alexander after bringing him back from the dead, and so Alexander is simultaneously the Beast and the Devil.

The story begins with the murder of Rostenberg, a Jewish biblical scholar, and the theft of his computer disk containing a program to interpret the Omega Code. The assassin and thief is Dominic, a former priest and the right-hand man of wealthy Stone Alexander, current chairman of the European Economic Council, who uses his castle in Rome as his headquarters. The program is incomplete, because the final segment of the code is missing, which has been retrieved by two mysterious prophets. Alexander installs the Omega Code in his super computer, and it periodically spits out vague pronouncements that sound like fortune cookie messages. Alexander uses these dictums to determine his course of action. The Omega Code becomes the linchpin of the story, but the prophecies are so vague and random that the audience is never impressed by them. At one point, it prints, "Rebirth of Empire begins." What is the connection between the date the computer prints the message and the event to which it refers? Sometimes the message seems to be in advance, but usually it is simultaneous with the event, which makes it almost useless as prophecy. This is never explained, so these prophecies seem rather pointless. Nevertheless, Alexander uses them to consolidate world power. One message, "Single Lane leads the way," prompts Alexander to hire mythology professor and motivational speaker Gillen Lane to become his spokesman. Lane, however, is not privy to Alexander's secret computer revelations. Alexander clandestinely arranges to blow up the Muslim holy site the Dome of the Rock in Jerusalem. When the Middle East erupts in violence, Alexander hosts a peace conference at which he personally offers to finance the rebuilding of the Dome of the Rock and the Temple of King Solomon (destroyed by the Romans in the first century) if the Israelis and Arabs make peace. He is triumphant, and a peace treaty is signed which guarantees the borders of Israel and the formation of an independent Palestine. Alexander garners tremendous prestige, and he proposes a world union of nations. To the countries that join, he gives priceless formulas to desalinate ocean water and to neutralize atomic weaponry. Alexander becomes chairman of the new World Council, and an era of unprecedented peace and prosperity begins. Three years pass.

The mysterious prophets preach that the end time is approaching. Lane stumbles across Alexander's secret computer room. Alexander tries to placate him, making excuses for Rostenberg's murder and the sabotage of the Dome of the Rock, in light of the good he has done. He implores Lane to stand by him and be his prophet. Dominic, overhearing this, is filled with rage, and he shoots at Lane, but misses and instead hits Alexander in the head. At that exact moment, the Omega Code spouts out, "Blood pours from

Stone — World wonders." As usual, these prophecies seem to arrive too late to be acted upon. Lane runs, and Dominic sets the police after him, claiming that Lane assassinated Alexander.

The next message of the code reads, "The Sepulchre re-occupied," and Stone Alexander's body becomes reanimated at the hospital. Rising from the dead, Alexander grabs Dominic by his wrist and almost breaks it. He relents and demands complete obedience from his treacherous assistant. The world, meanwhile, is astounded at Alexander's resurrection, and he is named chancellor of the United Earth. He will be coronated during the dedication of Solomon's temple in Jerusalem. The prophets, meanwhile, approach Lane through Cassandra Barashe, a television reporter who is helping him elude the police. Lane goes to a clandestine meeting to speak with them. They give him an envelope with the completion of the code, warning that Alexander is now possessed by Satan himself. They explain that he soon will proclaim himself God, after which he will embark on a reign of terror. They also reveal that Lane will play a key factor in these upcoming events.

Alexander admits to Dominic that he has greatly changed. He no longer needs sleep and feels a new presence in his mind, as if some force has him under total control. Meanwhile, Lane finds himself being hunted, and people he trusts have turned against him. When he gives his copy of the code to Cassandra for safekeeping, she draws a gun on him and takes him prisoner. When Alexander dedicates the rebuilt temple in Jerusalem, he dedicates it to himself, claiming to be both king and God over all mankind. The large audience falls silent, totally stunned. The two prophets appear and denounce Alexander as Lucifer in person. They offer their own lives as proof of their words. They challenge the Devil to kill them, saying they will rise from the dead in three days. Alexander signals Dominic to shoot them, and the crowd flees the temple, screaming. Catastrophes occur around the world. Millions are killed in a meteor shower, and even the molecular structure of the ocean becomes toxic due to mutation. The entire world becomes divided into two camps, for and against Alexander.

Returning to his castle in Rome, Alexander opens the envelope containing the code completion, but it appears to him to be a denunciation written by the dead prophets. He has Lane brought before him, but the beaten man knows nothing about the completion of the code. Alexander tells him that he will launch a nuclear strike against the nations that have turned against him, starting with Israel.

The bodies of the dead prophets resurrect in Jerusalem, and they appear miraculously in Lane's prison cell at Alexander's castle, freeing Lane and killing Dominic with a gesture when he tries to interfere. They return to Lane the completion of the Omega Code, which the Devil discarded. Lane confronts Alexander, asking him to call off his planned attacks. Instead, Alexander drops his pretense and admits he is Satan, who previously possessed Judas and others in history and now possesses Stone Alexander. Lane enters the final code into Alexander's computer. This act somehow creates a miraculous ripple of light, which spreads around the Earth. The gargoyle-like figure of the Devil is blasted out of Alexander's body, and he roars as he tries to hang on, but the force against him is too strong and Satan is swept away. The body of Alexander, deprived of its demonic inhabitant, collapses dead. Lane observes the final message of the code, "Dawn of New Millennium."

Performances

Almost all of the characters in this film are unsympathetic, and most of the actors deliver less-than-adequate performances. Casper Van Dien is insufferable as the ambitious, cheeky, and cold Gillen Lane. Shallow acting also mars the work of Catherine Oxenberg and Michael Ironside. A few of the minor players are good, such as William Hootkins, the rebel Porkins from *Star Wars* (1977) and Lt. Eckhard from *Batman* (1989). The film is marred by constant amateurish errors, such as the appearance of Lane's young daughter, whose age remains unchanged throughout the four-year time span of the film. This leaves Michael York, who delivers a polished, clever, and thoughtful performance as Stone Alexander, both as a man and as the Devil. His powerful and subtle reading is largely spoiled because he is acting in a vacuum, delivering a masterful performance without anyone to respond or react to his work on the same level. York, born Michael Johnson, has had an impressive career. He broke into films with Franco Zeffirelli in *Taming of the Shrew* (1967) and had various admirable roles in *Cabaret* (1972), *The Three Musketeers* (1973), and *The Riddle of the Sands* (1979). He even made an exceptional John the Baptist in Zeffirelli's *Jesus of Nazareth* (1977). York makes a credible Stone Alexander, an idealist who actually believes he is doing good but who has a dark, ruthless past. Dominic, his aide, was originally a priest who Alexander had visited as a young man to confess that he murdered his father and that he is troubled by preternatural voices. These voices continue to plague Alexander until he is shot, and when he is revived, he is totally possessed by the Devil. York renders his gradual transformation with poise and conviction. At the end of the film, when he is fully Satan, his character reveals that the Devil has possessed many characters throughout history, from Adolf Hitler back to Judas, as suggested by John 13:27 and Luke 22:3. York's Devil is a tinkerer, involving himself relentlessly in the affairs of mankind. The true form of the Devil is glimpsed only once, a large, terrifying apparition that roars like a wounded lion. The Devil also has large, flapping wings like a dragon. The major problem with this conception is that in Scripture, the Devil is never portrayed as the Antichrist. In Revelation 20:10, the Devil, the Beast (or Antichrist), and his false prophet are clearly delineated as distinct and separate. This is why films such as *The Omen* (1976) and *Rosemary's Baby* (1968) are not included in this book. Dramatically, York makes a powerful case for the possessed Antichrist even if the concept is faulty. His impressive performance would have carried far greater weight had the rest of the film not been so poorly made.

Notable Quotes

- If fate assigns us our roles and we don't fulfill them, are we damned for it? If Adolf Hitler was assigned his role and he played it out perfectly until the end, was he damned for his obedience? When we took Rostenberg's program, none of us could dream that following the prophecies would bring all this about.... Is it of my own free will, or have I become the Beast, a pawn in something? (**Alexander to Dominic, questioning his destiny**)
- You should know by now, Gillen, even Satan comes as an angel of light. (**Cassandra to Lane as she betrays him**)
- I am the one who controls the outcome of history. I'm the one who calls the shots, who tells people what to think. I was Judas, betraying Christ to be crucified. I was Hitler leading millions to be slaughtered, and I was the drunken driver who killed your mother. (**the Devil to Lane, detailing his various roles in history**)

Petey Wheatstraw
AKA The Devil's Son-in-Law

1977   Rating: *   G. Tito Shaw as the Devil

Generation International. Written by Cliff Roquemore, based on the character created by Rudy Ray Moore; Photographed by Nicholas Joseph von Sternberg; Edited by Cecelia Hall and Jack Tucker; Special Effects by Conrad Jimmy Lynch; Produced by Theodore Toney; Directed by Cliff Roquemore. Color, 95 minutes.

Annotated Cast List

Rudy Ray Moore (*Petey Wheatstraw*, stand-up comic); G. Tito Shaw (the Devil); Ebony White (*Nell*, Petey's girlfriend, and *Pet*, the Devil's daughter); Wildman Steve (*Steve*, owner of club headlining Petey); Jimmy Lynch (*Jimmy*, Petey's friend); Leroy Daniels (*Leroy*, comic); Ernest Mayhand (*Skillet,* comic); Ted Clemmons (*Ted*, Petey's helper); Bryan L. Roquemore (*Larry*, Ted's teenage brother); Marvin Jones (*Scarface Willie*, thug hired by Leroy); George Mireless (*Mr. White*, producer who backs Leroy and Skillet); Clifford Roquemore II (*Baby Petey*); Danny Poinson (*Young Petey*); Rose Jewel Williams (Petey's mother); Sy Richardson (Petey's father); A. Jay Malone (pastor); Joe Williams (D.J.); Randy Williams (*Castro*, Scarface's associate); Brian Breye (*Bantu*); Audubon Walls (*Dago*); J. B. Baron (doctor); Brenda Humbard, Julie Martin, Deborah Guidry, Deranne Keni, Gail Womack, Conchita Guiterrez, Princess Annette (the Devil's girls).

Appraisal and Synopsis

The 1970s were the heyday of blaxploitation films, from the original *Shaft* (1971) to *Black Fist* (1976). Many of these pictures were based on horror classics, such as the classy *Blacula* (1972), the wry *Blackenstein* (1973), and *Dr. Black and Mr. Hyde* (1975). Even the last of these titles was moderately entertaining, at least as a parody. On the other hand, *Petey Wheatstraw* represents the dregs of the genre, a vulgar, ragged entry with no redeeming features. The humor is so forced and ineptly handled that sitting through the entire film is a painful ordeal. This is one title definitely worth avoiding except for diehard lovers of blaxploitation.

The story opens with Petey Wheatstraw addressing the audience in rather flat rhyming verse, totally lacking the wit of Muhammad Ali. A flashback takes us to Petey's birth, where he emerges from the womb as large as a three-year-old and talks sassily to those in attendance. We cut to a few years later when Petey is taught kung fu by a mysterious old man who may or may not have been the Devil in disguise. After becoming a master of the martial arts, Petey declares his actual ambition is to become a stand-up comic. Again we jump ahead a few years and catch a few minutes of Petey's act, which is awful. The high point of his obscene comedy routine is a commentary on the large backside of one of the members of the audience.

In another city, the comedy team of Leroy and Skillet (L & S) borrows a hundred grand from a loan shark named Mr. White, the token white member of the cast. L & S own a club and plan to promote a new act, expecting to be the only show in town. Later they discover a rival club is planning to put on a revue headlined by Petey Wheatstraw. In fact, both shows plan to open the same night. L & S try to persude Petey to delay his opening. Failing that, they hire Scarface Willie to harass Petey and his troupe. They try to intimidate Ted, who is hanging posters for Petey's show, A scuffle breaks out, and Larry, Ted's teenage brother, is shot to death. Fearing reprisals, L & S order a hit on Petey. Scarface mows down the entire procession outside the church during Larry's funeral, the best and most outrageous scene in the movie. The Devil appears and walks around dead bodies until he reaches Petey. He calls him back to life and offers him a deal, promising him anything he wants in exchange for marrying his daughter, the incredibly ugly Pet. Petey accepts and asks the Devil to restore to life all of the people killed at Larry's funeral. Satan erases the massacre from history, and Petey and all of his friends are brought back to life. The Devil gives Petey his magic walking stick, a device so powerful it can grant any wish.

Petey delays his show and attends the opening debut of L & S. He uses his magic cane to ruin each act, finally making the theater go up in flames. When the Devil approaches Petey about his upcoming wedding ceremony, the comedian plans to outwit Satan by substituting a drunken wino in his place after creating a mask that is a perfect likeness of himself. The Devil provides Petey with a bachelor party with eight gorgeous female demons. Satan's men arrive to escort Petey to hell, but as they take the wino away, he comes to his senses and rips off his mask.

The Devil launches an assault against Petey while he attempts to flee out of town. Their confrontation occurs on the roof of his club, and at first it appears that Petey is triumphant, using the Devil's magic cane to vanquish him and his henchmen. But as he enters his car to escape, he finds the Devil and his daughter in the vehicle along with L & S, the Devil's new recruits. Petey screams as they drive off to hell for his wedding.

The basic story is filled with countless inconsistencies, particularly Petey's belief that he can elude the Devil by simply leaving town. As a comedian, Petey is completely unfunny. His rivals, Leroy and Skillet, are equally bad, on a level far below the humor of Amos and Andy. Blaxploitation films usually can get away with foul language if it is used in a stylish manner, but the dialogue in *Petey Wheatstraw* is simply degrading. This film appeared toward the tail end of the blaxploitation craze, and no doubt it helped to put a few nails in its coffin.

Performances

The opening credits proclaim, "Introducing G. Tito Shaw as Lucifer." They could have added, "and farewell performance," since this is Shaw's only film. In fact, Shaw is the best performer in the film. He uses his voice well and has a good sense of timing. Shaw shows up in various distinguished and well-tailored guises throughout the film, including a silken red jogging suit, but he usually appears as a middle-aged man with salt-and-pepper hair and a beard. He appears with Devil's horns in only one scene, otherwise there is nothing diabolic about his countenance. During his encounter with Petey on the roof, he appears aged, with a long white beard, but otherwise there is nothing to distinguish him from a well-dressed businessman going about his daily routine. Shaw's precise diction suggests he had considerable stage experience, and he plays his role with style, dignity, and a modest degree of flair. Unfortunately, his work is completely buried by the low quality of the other performers and the miserable script.

Notable Quotes

• Romance without finance is a damned nuisance. (**Petey to Nell, his girlfriend**)

• You know how powerful the Devil is, and if you cross him, he is going to be as mad as hell, I mean heaven. (**Nell to Petey**)

• You will marry my daughter, and I will see to it that she makes every breath you draw a prayer for death. (**the Devil, confronting Petey on the roof**)

• You can't trust the Devil. Any fool knows that. Daniel Webster tricked you, but you still brought your little ol' ass back. The time is over, no more heartache and pain. I'm going to destroy your ass with your own walkin' cane. (**Petey, as he turns the magic cane against Lucifer**)

Prince of Darkness

1987   Rating: *   Susan Blanchard as the Devil

Universal. Written by John Carpenter as Martin Quatermass; Photographed by Gary B. Kibbe; Special Effects by Kevin Quibell; Edited by Steve Mirkovich; Music by John Carpenter and Alan Howarth; Produced by Larry J. Franco; Directed by John Carpenter. Color, 102 minutes.

Annotated Cast List

Donald Pleasence (*Fr. Loomis*, priest opposing Satan); Victor Wong (*Howard Birack*, professor helping Loomis); Jameson Parker (*Brian Marsh*, theoretical physics student); Lisa Blount (*Catherine Danforth*, applied physics and mathematics student); Susan Blanchard (*Kelly*, student who metamorphises into Satan); Dennis Dun (*Walter*, student who witnesses the transformation); Anne Marie Howard (*Susan Cabot*, radiologist and first person possessed); Ann Yen (*Lisa*, specialist in theology and ancient scriptures); Ken Wright (*Albert Lomax*, engineering student); Dirk Blocker (*Frank Mullins*, physics student); Jessie Lawrence Ferguson (*Calder*, microbiologist); Peter Jason (*Dr. Paul Leahy*, biochemist); Robert Grasmere (*Frank Wyndham*, biochemistry student); Thom Bray (*Etchinson*, Leahy's assistant); Betty Ramey (nun who finds Fr. Carlton's body); Joanna Merlin (bag lady); Alice Cooper (street people leader); Jessie Ferguson (dark figure in the dream).

Appraisal and Synopsis

Although a number of individual scenes are creepy, frightening, and effective, as a whole *Prince of Darkness* is a complete muddle, particularly for viewers who try to follow plot. The dialogue is burdened with pseudo-scientific mumbo jumbo, including a long lecture on the nature of reality by Victor Wong as a scholarly college professor. Fragments of the background storyline are handed out piecemeal until Carpenter gives up and concentrates on gory effects instead.

Essentially, the plot combines religious theology with quantum physics. Every element has a corresponding negative twin in an alternate universe. There is, therefore, an anti-God, who is an evil counterpart to God. This evil being, described as the "Father of Satan," broke through to our universe seven million years ago, and he deposited the Devil, his son, in a sealed container which he buried. It was later dug up during the time of Christ who warned man about the evil trapped in the container. Finally, a secret religious sect known as the Brotherhood of Sleep uncovered and guarded the capsule, depositing it in the sixteenth-century Spanish catacomb located beneath St. Godards, a church in Los Angeles. They kept daily vigil over the container and a sacred book of commentary about the capsule through the centuries by using a series of guardian priests. When each guardian became too ill to continue, he informed the Vatican to appoint another designee. Other than this, the sect never kept the Vatican informed of its mission. In the story proper, Fr. Loomis learns of the existence of the sect when the most recent guardian priest, Fr. Carlton, dies unexpectedly. He also discovers that the container, dormant for millennia, is showing signs of activity. Loomis contacts Professor Birack of the Doppler Institute of Physics, one of the nation's most brilliant scientists, to determine exactly what is happening within the capsule. Birack recruits a large team of scientists and a number of specialist students to undertake an evaluation of the object. Too late they discover that Satan is preparing to emerge and is arranging for his father, the anti-God, to return to our universe and envelop it in evil and darkness.

The team secretes itself in the church to study the capsule, which resembles a cross between Houdini's water torture tank and a giant mixmaster in which green goop is endlessly rotating. Lisa, an expert on ancient texts, starts to translate the book kept with the capsule. While no one else is looking, a bit of the goop squirts out of the capsule into the mouth of Susan (who is continually described by the other team members by two words: "radiologist, glasses"). One by one the members of the team are possessed as Susan squirts some of the goop into the mouths of others. Meanwhile, street people become mentally possessed by the Devil, and they surround the church and kill any of the group who try to leave the building.

Finally, Satan finds a host body in Kelly, one of the students, and she transforms into the Prince of Darkness. Satan/Kelly discovers that mirrors provide a doorway to the alternate universe and tries to summon her father by reaching into the alternate universe and physically pulling the anti-God into our world. Catherine, another student, sacrifices herself by pushing Satan/Kelly and herself through the mirror into the alternate universe. All the possessions cease, and the possessed members of the group die. Outside, the street people return to their own lives, and the police arrive to clean up the mess. Survivors Loomis and Birack congratulate themselves for saving the world, although for the most part they only cowered and hid while the Devil was active.

Prince of Darkness has neither style nor vitality. It squanders a host of interesting undeveloped ideas and concepts. For example, anyone who sleeps in the church shares the same dream, a vision of a dark figure emerging triumphant from the church. This vision is never really explained, although some of the scientists speculate that it is a warning sent back from the future. More likely, it is a transmission from the alternate universe, because at the end of the film the vision now includes Catherine, who vanished into the mirror with Satan/Kelly. This, however, is just another loose end which litters the poorly related story. Other loose ends include a massive number of candles that are endlessly burning in the chamber beneath the church which are never maintained nor replaced, yet always lit. John Carpenter's thuddingly dull score is irritating. The entire production is pretentious and lacks humor for the most part. On all counts, this entry is one of the most disappointing of all Devil films since it completely fritters away its potential.

Performances

Some commentators mistake the being in the capsule as the son of Satan, but it is supposed to be Satan himself. In the hierarchy of this story, however, Satan is subservient to his father, which is a feature unique to this production. Susan Blanchard plays this most unconventional Devil, who was never before portrayed as a willowy blonde with a pony tail and a face festering with oozing red pus. Besides leering and grimacing, Satan has little to do except for one unique encounter with Donald Pleasence. Fr. Loomis spends most of the latter half of the story hiding in a closet reading his breviary, but when he notices Satan/Kelly up and about, he grabs an ax and has at her. First he chops off her arm, but a new arm just sprouts back. Then he gets serious and hacks off her head. Satan/Kelly just bends down, picks up her head, and places it back atop her shoulders. This brief sequence is clever and the highlight of the picture. When Blanchard reaches into the glass to the alternate universe, she says her only lines as the Devil, whispering, "Father." This bit falls flat, as her tone of voice sounds exactly like Linda Blair calling for Richard Burton in *Exorcist II: The Heretic* (1977). Otherwise, Susan Blanchard makes little impression in her part except as a curiosity. The rest of the cast is likewise bland or ineffective. The usually wonderful Donald Pleasence is rather lifeless in this outing. The name of the priest he plays is not spoken during the course of the picture, but according to most cast lists his name is Loomis, the identical name that Pleasence is called in Carpenter's most memorable and brilliant effort, *Halloween* (1978). Victor Wong is colorful as the noted physicist, and is one of the few costars who is shorter than Pleasence. But Wong showed far more sparkle in *Tremors* (1990) as the crafty store owner who named the Graboids. Among the students, Dennis Dun gives the most interesting performance as the quick-witted Walter, particularly in the scenes where he is locked in a closet while he describes the transformation of Kelly into Satan. Peter Jason is outstanding as a wacky professor, particularly in the improvised bit when he imitates a jazz trombone. The cast lists two individuals with almost identical names, Jessie Lawrence Ferguson and Jessie Ferguson, who appears as the Dark Figure. Finally, the colorful cult rocker Alice Cooper has a nice cameo as one of the street people who is controlled by the Devil.

Notable Quotes

• And the Prince of Darkness was himself sealed, that old life called the Devil and Satan, which deceiveth the whole world. (**translation of ancient text describing the contents of the capsule**)

• The father of Satan, a God who once walked the Earth before man, was somehow banished to the dark side. Apparently the father buried his son inside the container.... Now later on here, Christ comes to warn us. He was of extraterrestrial ancestry, but a humanlike race. (**Lisa, summarizing her translation of the text**)

• You will not be saved by the Holy Ghost. You will not be saved by the god plutonium. In fact, you will not be saved. (**message relayed by Satan on the computer**)

The Private Lives of Adam and Eve

1959   Rating: *   Mickey Rooney as the Devil

Universal. Written by Robert Hill, based on a story by George Kennett; Photographed by Philip Lathrop; Edited by Eddie Broussard; Music by Van Alexander with title song composed by Paul Anka; Produced by Red Doff; Directed by Albert Zugsmith and Mickey Rooney. B&W with color sequence, 87 minutes.

Annotated Cast List

Mickey Rooney (*Nick Lewis* and the Devil); Martin Milner (*Ad Simms*, mechanic, and biblical *Adam*); Mamie Van Doren (*Evie Simms,* Ad's wife and biblical *Eve*); Fay Spain (*Lil Lewis*, wife being dumped by Nick, and *Lilith*, temptress in Garden of Eden); Cecil Kellaway (*Doc Bayles*, bus driver); Paul Anka (*Pinkie Parker*, hot rod owner); Mel Tormé (*Hal Sanders*, lingerie salesman); Tuesday Weld (*Vangie Harper*, runaway teenager); Ziva Rodann (*Passiona*, the Devil's familiar); June Wilkinson (*Saturday*, Satan's bathtub beauty); Leonora Bryant, Phillipa Fallon, Barbara Walden, Toni Covington (the Devil's companions); Nancy Root, Donna Lynne, Sharon Wiley, Seiko Kato, Andrea Smith, Toni Bacon, Stella Garcia (Satan's sinners).

Appraisal and Synopsis

Undoubtedly, *The Private Lives of Adam and Eve* is one of the all-time oddest concepts: the opening chapters of Genesis as interpreted by Mickey Rooney with a home-movie budget and a fascinating cast. The heart of the film, the Garden of Eden story, is tucked around a modern-day plot, the same technique used by Cecil B. DeMille in his silent version of *The Ten Commandments* (1923) and by Darryl F. Zanuck in *Noah's Ark* (1929). Here, the wraparound sequence was no doubt developed because the central parody of Adam and Eve was too brief and sketchy to stand on its own as a feature, and the additional material was needed to pad it. Rooney's codirector, Albert Zugsmith, served as producer on major classics such as *The Incredible Shrinking Man* (1958) and Orson Welles' *Touch of Evil* (1958). As director, however, his field was exploitation movies. No doubt the original idea for this picture was the concept of seeing Mamie Van Doren as the biblical Eve. This is illustrated by posters for the film highlighting Mamie waist deep in a pond in slick exploitation fashion, letting the viewer imagine he will see far more of her in the film. Her breasts, however, are always neatly covered by her long blonde wig, and both she and Adam, Martin Milner, wear leaf-patterned underwear from the moment of their creation. The main interest in the film then becomes Mickey Rooney in his broad, scenery-chewing gig as Satan, which has the undeniable flavor of a burlesque review. Noting all of these elements, the film is worth at least a single viewing, during which it will no doubt produce many groans of disbelief and, possibly, a rare smile.

The film begins when the local bus stops at Paradise, Nevada (Population 7). Nick Lewis, owner of the one-horse town's living room casino, is heading to Reno, where he plans to dump one wife, Lil, and acquire a new wife, Evie, who is also running off to get a divorce. Evie's husband, auto mechanic Ad Simms, chases after her but misses the bus. When he hears that the bridge is flooded out due to torrential rains in the mountains, he borrows the jalopy brought to him for repair by Pinkie Parker, who is also on his way to Reno. Others on the bus include lovely teenage runaway Vangie Harper and traveling salesman Hal Sanders. When Nick sees that Ad is catching up with them, he shoves driver Doc Bayles out of his seat and takes over the bus himself. After Ad drives over a cliff, Nick is forced to stop while Pinkie is shattered by the loss of his jalopy. Ad is unhurt, having jumped out of the vehicle before the plunge, and he explains about the washout ahead. The bus tries to head back, but it gets caught in the storm, and everyone is forced to flee the bus when it becomes trapped on a bridge that is being swept away by the flood. The survivors take refuge in a local church, and Doc brings up the topic of the Bible to comfort the others. Nick mocks the Bible, and Evie and Ad become reconciled. The group then settles down to get some sleep.

A collective dream begins, and the biblical story of the creation unfolds. Adam awakens in the Garden of Eden, and the picture switches to color. The first man curiously explores his surroundings. God, unheard by the audience, speaks to Adam and assigns him the task of naming the animals. He starts inventing names in alphabetical order. In hell, Satan starts naming his beautiful group of familiars, calling

Mickey Rooney as the burlesque Satan of The Private Lives of Adam and Eve. *The bathing beauty receiving his attention is June Wilkinson.*

them by the days of the week. The most beautiful one is taking a bath, and she throws a handful of suds in his face when he names her Saturday. He sends Lilith, a dark haired beauty, to visit Adam to tempt him. The Devil shouts instructions to her, telling her to put "a little Marilyn Monroe wiggle" in her walk. Adam explains how lonely he is as Lilith guides him over to the tree with the forbidden fruit and urges him to try it. The Devil, playing a baseball game with his familiars, urges Lilith to act more quickly. Just as Adam is about to succumb, a peal of thunder is heard, and Adam is summoned by God. He puts him to sleep, and when Adam awakens, he sees Eve who calls to him, urging him to join her for a swim. She explains she is his wife, and Adam teaches her how to eat and then how to kiss.

The Devil organizes a hot jazz band with his sinners, and he explains to them how he will move in on Eve once the honeymoon is over. His prediction comes true, as Eve feels neglected when Adam resumes his animal-naming assignment. Left alone, Eve is approached by Satan in the guise of a snake. She quickly falls for his temptation and eats an apple from the tree of forbidden knowledge. Adam returns, catching her with the fruit in hand. She is broken-hearted, and he quickly takes a bite of the apple to ease her misery. The film color disappears, and the picture returns to black and white. A windstorm develops, and the Devil chortles in triumph. Forced to leave the garden, Adam and Eve move into a cave. They quickly start to bicker over the loss of paradise. When they make up, the Devil comments, "I hate the mushy parts." Satan and Lilith build a nearby house, and Lilith resumes her advances on Adam, who tells her, "I'm only a week old, and already I am a failure!" She gets him drunk, and at the same time the Devil keeps filling Eve with bad advice, such as cutting her hair. Satan engineers a major fight between Adam and Eve, and she runs off and becomes lost. She prays to God for help, and He informs her she will have a child. Adam rejects Lilith and seeks out Eve, and the dream ends as he finds her and they embrace. When they awaken, the storm is over and the danger has passed. Evie suggests to Ad that they read the Bible and learn the true story. As the survivors vacate the church, Evie has some odd food cravings. Suddenly, Ad realizes she is pregnant, and they walk off joyfully as the film ends.

The scenes after the expulsion from the Garden of Eden are particularly weak and threadbare. Most of the humor derives from Eve's endless attempts to improve their cave dwelling by having a boulder repositioned whenever Adam or the Devil are available to do the chore. Lilith keeps trying to impress Adam with her special invention called a bed. Much of the strained humor derives from irrelevant and anachronistic quips about people such as Nero or Marilyn Monroe or events such as the backyard barbecue or contributing to the Community Chest. Another unclear point is why Eve is never named by Adam until the very end of the flashback. This is supposed to have some significance, because the plot keeps emphasizing it, but after he starts to call her Eve, the importance of this becomes pointless. Most of the audience, no doubt, express a sigh of relief when Evie and Ad awaken from their slumbers.

A number of other films depict the Garden of Eden story from Genesis, although the Devil only appears as the serpent. In Genesis, of course, the serpent is never specifically revealed as the Devil. One of the most interesting of these other films is *Adan y Eva* (1956), a Mexican film made by Alberto Gout, which judiciously employed nudity in its portrayal of the first couple.

Performances

Mickey Rooney's Devil is truly painful to behold at times. He spends most of the film engaging in silly skits with his familiars, which are continually intercut with the activities of Adam and Eve. At various times, he is getting a manicure, playing cards, umpiring a baseball game, or preparing for a dinosaur rotisserie. His initial contact with Eve while he is disguised as a snake is practically without any humor or irony, and the script continually fails to come up with anything genuinely funny. His serpent costume is merely foolish, with Mickey's face appearing inside the open mouth of the serpent wading along the edge of the pond. Rooney is far more effective as Nick Lewis, and the opening sequence in which the jalopy tries to catch up with the bus is excellent filmmaking. Rooney's demonic glances at Milner from the bus window are far more impressive, creepy, and even cynical than anything else he does in the picture. As the Devil, Rooney is negligible and silly, missing the mark with almost all of his comments. The film also completely wastes Mel Tormé, Cecil Kellaway, Paul Anka, and Tuesday Weld. Was the scene in which the Devil names his familiars with days of the week a satire about her name? If so, it would have only worked if she were the familiar dubbed Tuesday by the Devil, but she doesn't appear at all in the Garden of Eden sequence, and neither do the others except for Fay Spain, who steals most of the scenes in which she appears. The Lilith story, incidentally, is not in the Bible but derives from Jewish folklore in which Adam has a different wife prior to Eve. Later, Lilith became a succubus or vampire who lived in desolate places and preyed upon children. The use of Lilith is quite interesting, and Fay Spain delivers one of the best performances in the film. Mamie Van Doren is fetching and fairly good as Eve, but she is given little worthwhile material in the script. Martin Milner isn't bad either, but he maintains his wide-eyed naivete even after eating of the fruit of forbidden knowledge. He seems to be the same Adam both before and after, unlike Mamie who develops a harder edge after their banishment. The satire could definitely have used another element, perhaps Cecil Kellaway as God, who could have provided some clever exchanges with Rooney's Devil.

Notable Quotes

• Oh, you can't see him, that's his charm. Evil is always invisible. (**Lilith, explaining to Adam about the Devil**)

• Would you like a taste of this fruit? (**the Devil, tempting Eve**)

I can't. (**her reply**)

Oh, you have an allergy? Do you get a strawberry rash or something like that? (**the Devil, playing dumb**)

• Now that Adam has eaten of the forbidden fruit, he's going to see women in a, shall we say, much different light.... and I want his children, one way or another. (**the Devil to his familiars**)

• If he's the mold for husbands to come, I'm going to coin a new word, "divorce." (**the Devil, sowing dissension with Eve**)

The Prophecy
AKA Seraphim *and* God's Army

1995   Rating: ****   Viggo Mortensen as the Devil

Miramax. Written by Gregory Widen; Photographed by Richard Clabaugh and Bruce Douglas Johnson; Edited by Sonny Baskin; Special Effects by Joe Van Kline, Douglas Johnson, and David Gallion; Music by David C. Williams; Produced by W. K. Border and Don Phillips; Directed by Gregory Widen. Color, 98 minutes.

Annotated Cast List

Christopher Walken (*Gabriel*, archangel leading a revolt in heaven); Viggo Mortensen (*Lucifer*, the Devil); Elias Koteas (*Thomas Daggat*, failed priest turned police detective); Clark Smithson (*Thomas Daggat*, age seven); Eric Stoltz (*Simon*, Loyalist angel); Jeff Cadiente (*Uziel*, Rebel angel); Virginia Madsen (*Katherine Hendly*, teacher); J. C. Quinn (*Arnold Hawthorne*, man who possesses the Dark Soul); Moriah Shining Dove Snyder (*Mary*, young girl serving as host for Hawthorne's soul); Emma Shenah (Mary's grandmother); Adam Goldberg (*Jerry*, corpse revived by Gabriel); Amanda Plummer (*Rachel*, second corpse revived by Gabriel); Steve Hytner (*Joseph*, coroner); Albert Nelson (*Grey Horse*); Shawn Nelson (Indian healer); Sandra Lafferty (*Madge*, waitress); William "Buck" Hart (graveyard attendant); Emily Conforto (*Sandra*, schoolgirl); Christina Holmes (*Allison*, schoolgirl); Nicholas Gomez (*Jason*); Jeremy Williams-Hurner (*Brian*); Sioux-z Jessup (nurse); Thomas "Doc" Boguski (security guard); Bobby Lee Hayes (*Bob*, deputy); John Sandkovich (*Jack*, deputy).

Appraisal and Synopsis

This picture is not to be confused with the John Frankenheimer film *Prophecy* (1979) about a mutant bear set in the Mount Katahdin region of Maine near Millinocket. Instead, this entry is a sleeper, a modestly budgeted effort containing an innovative script, snappy performances, and taut direction. The storyline is a brilliant antidote to the saccharine and schmaltzy portrayal of the heavenly hosts from *Highway to Heaven* to *Touched by an Angel*. Here we have a rather different portrayal of angels with one wing dipped in blood, recalling passages of the Bible where angels were dispatched by God on missions of violence such as the destruction of Sodom and Gomorrah. Based partially upon a theme from the nineteenth-century poet William Blake, this film envisions a second war in heaven. While not a revolt against God himself, a group of angels led by Archangel Gabriel seeks to destroy mankind, who they believe has displaced them in God's plan. Michael leads the Loyalist angels, and God has apparently withdrawn from the conflict. This second war began shortly after the time of Christ, and it is still in progress. The story of this celestial uprising is told in the twenty-third chapter of Revelation, a passage of the Bible unknown to humans.

The story proper of *The Prophecy* starts with the ordination of Thomas Daggat to the priesthood. In the middle of the ceremony, the novice collapses screaming, seized by a powerful vision of angels in conflict. The scene switches to ten years later, and Thomas, who has lost his faith, is now a homicide detective. He is approached in his apartment by Simon, an angel in disguise, who suggests to him that he will play a significant role in God's plan.

Later Uziel, Gabriel's chief lieutenant, is killed after assaulting Simon. When Thomas is assigned to the case, he is startled to learn from the coroner that Uziel was not fully human, having the genetic makeup of an aborted fetus. Uziel's only possession was a handwritten Bible dating back to the first century. Thomas takes the book to translate the mysterious twenty-third chapter of Revelation, learning about the second war in heaven.

Simon, wounded during his encounter with Uziel, takes refuge in an abandoned school building. Simon's mission is to prevent the Rebel angels from obtaining the Dark Soul, which was possessed by the late Colonel Hawthorne, a war criminal who committed acts of cannibalism during the Korean War. Simon removes the Dark Soul from the colonel's body. Mary, a young Indian girl playing hide-and-seek with her friends, discovers Simon during their game. She agrees to keep his presence a secret. Simon deposits the Dark Soul in Mary. Meanwhile, Archangel Gabriel comes to Earth and locates the body of Uziel in the morgue and incinerates it. Gabriel is assisted by Jerry, a reanimated corpse who serves as his lackey and chauffeur. Together they track down Simon, and Gabriel tries to convince him to join the Rebel side. When he refuses, Gabriel tortures him to learn the location of the Dark Soul, which the Rebels believe will help them win their war. He finally kills Simon by ripping out his heart, the only method of killing an angel.

Katherine, Mary's teacher, is concerned by the sudden change in her behavior. When doctors seem unable to help, her grandmother turns to tribal healers who claim she is possessed. Katherine comes across Gabriel talking with some school kids, showing them his horn. One of them toots on it, and windows in the school shatter. The archangel learns that Mary crossed paths with Simon, and he plans to hunt her down. Thomas and Katherine catch Gabriel in the process of retrieving the Dark Soul. A scuffle breaks out, and Jerry is shot. As he collapses, he thanks Thomas for putting him out of his misery. Mary grabs Thomas' gun and shoots at Gabriel. Katherine and Mary flee the home, and it explodes when a stray bullet hits a gas tank.

The police arrive and remove Gabriel's body, but Mary tells them that he cannot be killed unless his heart is ripped out. Thomas drives the young girl to the Indian reservation, and they pass the wrecked police car, verifying that Gabriel has escaped. The archangel heads to a hospital and waits for the next patient to die, who turns out to be a young woman named Rachel. He revives her and forces her to replace Jerry. She drives him to the reservation.

That evening, Katherine takes a walk and encounters a mysterious intruder, who reveals himself to be the Devil. He tells her that half the angels are rebelling because they hate man. He explains about the Dark Soul and why Gabriel is trying to secure it. He offers to save Mary and help mankind, because if Gabriel wins, he will create a second hell, something the Devil will not tolerate. Later, the Devil appears to Thomas, telling him how Gabriel can be thwarted. An ambush is set up that evening at the tribal ceremony for Mary. When Gabriel shows up, Thomas challenges him, saying that his rebellion is actually based solely on jealousy and why won't he simply ask God about his purpose in creating man. They battle until the Devil intervenes, capturing Gabriel and carrying him off to hell. Mary is liberated from the Dark Soul, which also descends to hell. After a few words to Katherine and Thomas to keep him in mind, the Devil transforms into a flock of bats and flies away. As dawn breaks, Thomas and Katherine head off, and the end credits roll.

The Prophecy was followed by two sequels. In *Prophecy II*, the Devil releases Gabriel from hell. The actor remains in shadows, so it is a stand-in for Viggo Mortensen. Gabriel seeks to prevent the birth of a child resulting from the union of a mortal woman, Valerie, and a Loyalist angel. At the climax of this picture, Gabriel and Valerie are suspended high above the ground in Archangel Michael's stronghold when they receive a message from God, "Jump!" They do so, and Valerie lands completely unharmed on top of Gabriel, who is rendered unconscious. Valerie survives to give birth to her child, and Gabriel becomes a vagabond. In the last film, *Prophecy III*, Gabriel has undergone a transformation. He has lived as a hobo for many years, becoming reconciled with man. Raphael now leads the Rebel angels, attempting to kill Danyael, Valerie's grown son, who Gabriel watches over. Eventually, the second war in heaven ends when Pyriel, the new hope of the Rebel angels, is defeated by Danyael. Presumably Gabriel returns to heaven to lead a reconciliation. In quality terms, the second film is repetitive and dull, but the third film recovers and is clever and entertaining, with Christopher Walken stealing the show as the flaky but rehabilitated Gabriel.

Performances

Viggo Mortensen's Devil is the unlikely, reluctant hero of the film. Sitting on the sidelines and observing the tide of battle, Lucifer finds himself in the curious position of saving mankind by ensuring that the Rebel angels fail to capture the Dark Soul, which would have tipped the scales in their celestial stalemate. He has one demon at his side, and he occasionally roars at him to keep him under control. Mortensen portrays the Devil as both laid back and cocky, and he vaguely resembles a long-haired, bearded beatnik, a relic from a past age not quite in sync with current trends. The sparks really fly in his short exchange with Gabriel at the close of the film, and one wishes the Devil's role had been larger since he brings a cutting edge to all of his scenes. He manages to convey a remarkably complex character in a few concise scenes, showing arrogance, pride, envy, remorse, longing, humor, despair, and even compassion. Mortensen has an impressive resume as an actor dating back to the prestigious mini-series *George Washington*, and his screen appearances include *Prison* (1988), *Young Americans* (1993), and the remake of *Psycho* (1998). He also landed the plum role of Aragorn in the new *Lord of the Rings* trilogy.

The rest of the cast is adequate, with Amanda Plummer and Adam Goldberg both particularly good as Gabriel's unwilling helpers. Christopher Walken's part is a showcase for his talent. His colorful reading incorporates angelic lore about Gabriel, not only with his trademark trumpet of destruction but with the imagery that he created the dent on humans' upper lips by telling unborn babies about the wonders of heaven and then touching their lips with his finger, shushing them to forget. Walken retains the shushing as a continuing trait of his character. Gabriel and the other Rebel angels refer to humans as "talking monkeys," but by the third film, he has become quite fond of man, buying a small stuffed monkey to decorate his car. The only drawback to Walken's bravura performance is his accent, which leaves an impression that the denizens of heaven talk with a New York dialect.

Notable Quotes

- Are you an angel? (**Katherine to Lucifer**) I am the first angel, loved once above all others, a perfect love, but like all true love, one day it withered on the vine. (**his reply, half sung and half spoken**)

- While heaven may be closed, I am always open for business, even on Christmas. (**the Devil**)
- Little Tommy Daggat, how I loved listening to your sweet prayers every night. Then you would jump in your bed, so afraid I was under there, and I was! (**the Devil's greeting to Thomas**)
- Lucifer, sitting in your basement, sulking over your breakup with the boss, you're nothing! (**Gabriel**)

Repossessed

1990   Rating: *   Linda Blair as the Devil

Carolco. Written by Bob Logan; Photographed by Michael D. Margulles; Edited by Jeff Freeman; Special Effects by Reel EFX and Special Effects Unlimited; Music by Charles Fox; Produced by Steve Wizan; Directed by Bob Logan. Color, 84 minutes.

Annotated Cast List

Linda Blair (*Nancy Aglet*, housewife possessed by the Devil); Leslie Nielsen (*Fr. Jedediah Mayii*, priest who exorcised Nancy seventeen years earlier); Ned Beatty (*Ernest Waller*, televangelist); Lana Schwab (*Fanny Mae Waller*, his wife); Robert Fuller (*Dr. Hackett*, Nancy's doctor); Anthony Starke (*Fr. Luke Brophy*, Nancy's priest); Thom J. Sharpe (*Braydon Aglet*, Nancy's husband); Willie Garson (student who nags Fr. Mayii); John H. Ingle (*Fr. Crosby*); Bryan O'Bryne (*Fr. Stills*); Ben Kronen (*Fr. Nash*); Frederick Daniel Scott (*Fr. Young*); Johnny Dark (*Aaron Kurtz*); Eugene Graytak (pope); Jacquelyn Masche (Nancy's mother); Benj Thall, Dave Dellas (Aglet children); Jake Steinfeld, Jack LaLanne, Army Archerd, Wally George, Gene Okerlund, Jesse Ventura (themselves).

Appraisal and Synopsis

In general, films about possession don't usually involve the actual Devil but rather a demon or some other lower surrogate. In *The Exorcist* (1973) and its first sequel, for example, Regan MacNeil is not possessed by Satan but by Pazuzu, a relatively minor Sumerian demon. *Repossessed*, a wild burlesque filmed seventeen years after the original film, employs the actual Devil, thereby qualifying it for inclusion in this book. The film is patterned after *Airplane* (1980), *Spaceballs* (1987), *Hot Shots* (1990), and many other no-holds-barred parodies. Much of the humor is crude, silly, or just plain stupid, but there are so many jokes, wisecracks, and sight gags that a few manage to provoke a chuckle or a downright guffaw. One visual gag about Senator Ted Kennedy is a classic. Most of the antics produce far more groans than laughs, and enjoyment of this film depends on a willingness to overlook nine bad jokes to enjoy one good one.

The plot, of course, does not stand up to close examination, nor does it need to in this type of film. Basically, the storyline involves Nancy Aglet, a woman who was possessed seventeen years earlier by the Devil. She was exorcised by Fr. Jedediah Mayii, a priest who was shattered by the experience. The picture is narrated by Mayii during a college lecture series called Champions of Humanity, in which he presents the case of Nancy's recent repossession by Satan. The details involve much vomiting, head twirling, and levitation, as Fr. Luke Brophy, a rookie priest, is called upon to handle the case. He brings the facts to the Supreme Council on Exorcism Grantings. New church policy involves interfaith participation, and televangelist Ernest Waller and his wife, Fanny Mae, clones of Jim and Tammy Bakker, seize the opportunity to stage the exorcism as a live TV event and fundraiser. They are assisted by the dubious Fr. Brophy, who foresees disaster. Due to the wild nature of the stunt, the exorcism garners the largest television audience in history. The Devil then transforms Ernest and Fanny Mae into jackasses and sets out to convert the entire audience into devil worshipers. Brophy broadcasts an SOS for all men of God to come to the studio and challenges the Devil to face his old adversary, Fr. Mayii, in a showdown. Mayii and Brophy try their best to conquer the Devil, and their efforts are described by wrestling announcers "Mean" Gene Okerlund and Jesse "the Body" Ventura. The Devil changes Mayii into different people, including a rabbi, the Singing Nun, Rambo, and a witch doctor. As a last resort, the priest tries to drive the Devil out of Nancy using music, creating a rock band with the pope, the Dali Lama, and the Greek Orthodox patriarch. They sing "Devil in a Blue Dress," and the ferocity of their rendition sends the Devil screaming back to hell. Concluding the university lecture, Fr. Mayii brings out Nancy Aglet to answer student questions. When a nerd berates them as phonies, both Nancy and Fr. Mayii drown him in vomit as this entry comes to a close.

The main target of the satire, besides *The Exorcist*, is *Star Wars* (1977) with Leslie Nielsen playing Obi-Wan to Anthony Starke's Luke Skywalker. Television preachers, organized religion, and politicians receive their share of jibes, as well as exercise gyms and the broadcast media. Four-letter words are less abundant than in the original *Exorcist*, but the scatological comments are done to excess. In addition, there are a number of women who flash their breasts for Leslie Nielsen, who then sheepishly mugs for the screen. Although far below the laugh quotient of other similar pictures, one or two genuine belly laughs save the film from being a total debacle.

Performances

At first it would seem that the role of a woman possessed by the Devil would be demeaning for Linda Blair, but she tackles the part with such enthusiasm and verve that this does not seem to be the case. In fact, she seems to be enjoying herself. Her makeup is similar to the possessed Regan from *The Exorcist*, except now she is able to use her own voice for the Devil's raspy comments. The film is quite insistent that she is possessed by the actual Devil, and in terms of plot, the whole possession is a Satanic scheme to reach the largest audience possible to demonstrate the power of evil. Blair's sense of comic timing is good, and she is able to trade quips and hold her own with Nielsen, the master of parody humor. On the whole, Nielsen is good but not in top form as he was in *Spy Hard* (1996) and the *Naked Gun* trilogy. Ned Beatty, a veteran of *Exorcist II* (1977), is adequate as the smarmy preacher, but his part is somewhat one-note. It is an added bonus to watch Jesse Ventura in his prime as a wrestling commentator, and it is even more amazing when you consider his future political career.

Notable Quotes

• Did you know the Christian religion has over a billion followers? (**Fr. Brophy to the Devil**)

Big deal, so does the "Wheel of Fortune." (**the Devil's reply**)
- And Luke, may the faith be with you. (**Fr. Mayii to Fr. Brophy**)
- This is the craziest exorcism I ever performed. (**Fr. Mayii upon being transformed into Groucho Marx by the Devil**)
- Satan, you've got him on the run. What move are you going to use next? (**Jesse Ventura to the Devil**)

Santa Claus

1959   Rating: *   Trotsky as the Devil

Churubusco-Azteca. Written by Adolfo Torres Portillo and Rene Cardona; Photographed by Raul Martinez Solares; Edited by Jorge Bustos; Music by Antonio Diaz Conde; Produced by William Calderon Stell and K. Gordon Murray (English-language version); Directed by Rene Cardona and Ken Smith (English-language version). Color, 90 minutes (original version); 93 minutes (English-language version).

Annotated Cast List

Jose Elias Moreno (*Santa Claus*); Trotsky (*Pitch*, the Devil); Armando Arriola (*Merlin*, ancient magician helping Santa); Angel Di Stefani (*Llavon*, Santa's blacksmith and keymaker); Lupita Quezadas (*Lupita*, poor child who wants a doll); Nora Veryan (Lupita's mother); Cesareo Quezadas (*Pedro*, Santa's young helper); Antonio Diaz Conde, Jr. (neglected boy in Mexico City); Manolo Calvo (his father); Graciela Lara (his mother); Jose Carlos Mendez, Jesus Brook, Ruben Ramirez (wicked boys controlled by Pitch); Guillermo Bravo Sosa, Polo Ortin, Queta Lavat, Rosa Maria Aguilar.

Appraisal and Synopsis

Five years before Nicholas Webster filmed his kitsch extravaganza *Santa Claus Conquers the Martians* (1964) on Long Island, Mexico's Rene Cardona uncorked his own eccentric Christmas fantasy, *Santa Claus*, in which jolly old Saint Nick fights a running battle with the Devil, who is trying to ruin Christmas. K. Gordon Murray released an English-language version, and this bizarre holiday yarn became a regular feature at special kiddie matinees during Christmas week. Both productions are prized by bad cinema aficionados, but for regular film lovers over the age of seven, these films are ordeals to sit through.

The story begins in the skies far above Earth where Santa has a flying palace made of crystal and gold. From here, he employs his special eavesdropping devices to keep tabs on all of the world's children. In hell, Lucifer plots to ruin Christmas and turn all the kids against Santa. Apparently he chooses Mexico City as the best place to make a stand, and he assigns his top Devil, Pitch, to carry out his plans. Frustrated, Santa spies on Pitch with his super telescope as he sets out to corrupt Lupita, a sweet young child, into stealing a doll she badly wants. However, Lupita resists the temptation and Santa celebrates. In fact, Pitch is rather unsuccessful in his efforts and manages only to recruit three wild youngsters to his cause.

On Christmas Eve, Santa takes off on

his rounds equipped with a special powder prepared by Merlin the magician, who moved to Santa's palace after tiring of Camelot. Llavon, Santa's blacksmith, builds him a magic golden key which can open all doors. He also brings with him a special rose, which renders him invisible. Santa decides to make Mexico City his first stop, but he spends so much time there, it appears to be his only stop. Pitch pulls many little pranks on Santa, such as moving the location of chimneys and heating up doorknobs so Santa will burn his fingers. Saint Nick, however, gives as good as he gets, firing a toy cannon with a dart into Pitch's rear end. Finally, Pitch uses his three young henchkids to kidnap Santa, but he outwits them by sending a meteor down to the rooftop site of their intended ambush.

Meanwhile, Santa grants a special gift for the neglected son of rich parents who left him at home alone to go to a party. Santa permits the young man to see him, and he tells him that in fact his parents love him very much. Santa then visits the party and poses as a waiter. He prepares two smoking, bubbling cocktails which he gives to the parents. When they drink it, they get an uncontrollable urge to return home and bring cheer to their son.

Pitch manages to tear the pouch in which Santa carries Merlin's magic powder, and it all spills out. Santa then loses his magic rose which falls into Lupita's house. Pitch tricks Santa by setting Dante, a watchdog, after him, forcing him to climb a tree where he is trapped. Pitch rouses the entire neighborhood, suggesting that Santa is a burglar, and he also summons the police and fire departments. Santa cries out for help to Merlin, who

Jose Elias Moreno as Santa Claus confronts his nemesis, Trotsky, as the Devil, Pitch.

conjures up a cat. The dog runs off in pursuit of it, allowing Santa to escape moments before a crowd of the various neighbors and the police arrives intending to nab the intruder.

It is almost dawn by the time Santa stops at Lupita's house, and he rewards the poor girl with a doll almost as big as herself. He retrieves his rose and speeds on his way as the film comes to an abrupt end, leaving the fate of Pitch unresolved. In some aspects, the Mexican film is superior to its American counterpart. The massive sets at Churubusco Studios are transformed into an impressive palace for Santa. His scientific equipment is kooky and outlandish. Unfortunately, Santa is given little to do in his baronial surroundings. He spends the first fifteen minutes of the film at his organ laboriously cranking out holiday music for the children of the world, whose representatives are visiting his toyland, from African kids with bones in their hair (a scene snipped out of some prints), to those of Spain, England, Italy, China, the Caribbean, South America, Central America, the United States, and, of course, Mexico. It is a deadeningly clumsy way to open the film, boring all but the youngest members of the audience. The soundtrack of the film basically plays "Jingle Bells" and "Silent Night" to death. Unexpectedly, the tune "Fascination" is employed extensively as well. The reindeer special effects are pathetic. The initial presentation of hell is excellent, featuring a ballet sequence with a company of red devils. The accompanying music, *Danza del Infierno,* by composer Conde, is superb. Most of the scenes on Earth, both with the Devil and Santa, are clumsy and poorly staged. A narrator chatters nonstop, prompting the kiddies to worry that Pitch might take Santa's sleigh or that Lupita might be tempted to steal. The meeting between Santa and Lupita takes place entirely offscreen, robbing the film of any sort of climax, since the plot with the Devil is also dropped after Santa escapes from the tree. The English-language version runs three minutes longer than the Spanish, including a closing narration with Christmas greetings. Curiously, in one scene the film prefigures Tim Burton's masterful *The Nightmare before Christmas* (1993), in which Oogie Boogie plans for his three small henchmen, Lock (Paul Rubens), Shock (Catherine O'Hara), and Barrel (Danny Elfman), to kidnap Santa Claus.

Performances

Trotsky is the stage name of eccentric Mexican dancer Jose Luis Aguirre, and his physical antics make him quite entertaining to watch. His opening dance is colorful and lively, and while not of the same caliber as Robert Helpmann in *The Soldier's Tale*, it nevertheless provides the highlight of the film. Trotsky is dressed entirely in red, including tights, shorts, and cowl with horns. His face is painted red as well, and he has two grotesque ears twice as large as those of Mr. Spock. Throughout the picture, Trotsky uses his thin frame to great advantage. He has the ability to lean far forward while seemingly impervious to gravity, a screen trick originally developed by Buster Keaton. Trotsky employs this clever visual gimmick constantly, and it is effective when he appears to be leaning off the ledge of a building. As Lucifer's representative on Earth, Pitch is invisible to everyone except the audience and Santa Claus. Nor can anyone hear his voice, though he can project suggestions into anyone's mind. He can appear and disappear at will. Despite these talents, Pitch is no match for St. Nicholas, and one of the weakest points of the film is that Pitch is simply dropped from the last few minutes of the movie without explanation. Lucifer is not seen in the film, only heard. For the original Spanish version, one source suggests that Guillermo Bravo Sosa dubbed the voice of Lucifer, but the actor performing his voice in English is uncredited.

Notable Quotes

- You must not be defeated by that bearded old goat, Santa Claus. If you do not succeed in making all the children of the Earth do evil, you shall be punished, and instead of red-hot coals, you will eat chocolate ice cream. (**Lucifer to Pitch**)
- Blast it! Darn that Devil! I'm sorry, but that old Devil is always annoying me with his mischief. If I could only go down there now, I'd put him in his place. But everyone knows I can only go down to Earth on Christmas Eve and not before. (**Santa to visiting children in his palace**)
- My dear Santa Claus, this year I behaved very well. I have been obedient and have studied very much. Please try to bring me.... a scooter, a cannon, a rocket, a bicycle, an atomic laboratory, a machine gun. Ohhhh! Golly! So be it! (**Santa, reading his mail aloud**)
- You hear those sirens? They're for you. The show is about to begin, and you will never get back before sunrise. Your reindeer will turn to powder. You will starve to death, and I will rule the Earth. (**Pitch to Santa after trapping him in a tree and summoning the fire department**)

Satan's School for Girls

1973   Rating: **   Roy Thinnes as the Devil

Spelling Productions. Written by Arthur A. Ross; Photographed by Tim Southcott; Edited by Allan Jacobs and Brian Brunette; Special Effects by Logan Frazee; Music by Laurence Rosenthal; Produced by Aaron Spelling and Leonard Goldberg; Directed by David Lowell Rich. Color, 73 minutes.

Annotated Cast List

Terry Lumley (*Martha Sayres*, student who commits suicide); Pamela Franklin (*Elizabeth Sayres*, her sister who investigates her death); Jo Van Fleet (*Jessica Williams*, headmistress of Salem Academy); Roy Thinnes (*Dr. Clampett*, art instructor, actually the Devil); Lloyd Bochner (*Professor Delacroix*, science instructor); Kate Jackson (*Roberta Lockhart*, student); Cheryl Ladd (*Jody Keller*, student); Jaimie Smith-Jackson (*Debbie Jones*, troubled student); Ann Knowland (*Kris*, student); Frank Marth (detective); Bill Quinn (gardener); Bing Russell (sheriff); Gwynn Gilford (*Lucy Dembrow*, Martha's friend).

Appraisal and Synopsis

Satan's School for Girls is a run-of-the-mill telefilm, mildly interesting and decently made but rather shallow and empty. The action centers on Salem Academy, an exclusive preparatory school for girls in Massachusetts. There is an undercurrent of unease in the school, and several students commit suicide. One of them, Martha Sayres, flies home to

California where she hangs herself. Believing she was actually murdered, her sister, Elizabeth, asks the sheriff to investigate, but he refuses. Her suspicions are further aroused after questioning Lucy Dembrow, Martha's friend and graduate of the school, who seems terrified of the place. Elizabeth decides to investigate on her own, assuming the identity of a student. Using the name Elizabeth Morgan, she applies and is accepted at Salem Academy.

Three students, Roberta Lockhart, Debbie Jones, and Jody Keller, greet Elizabeth when she arrives at the school. At first, everything appears normal. Dr. Clampett, the art teacher, is popular with the students. In class, Elizabeth sees a painting of her sister drawn by Debbie, a haunting portrait in which Martha is trapped in a mysterious dark room. Cranky Professor Delacroix, the science teacher, seems preoccupied with a psychological experiment involving rats in a maze. After the professor picks on her, Debbie collapses and is put to bed in her room. The students are further upset when news arrives that Lucy Dembrow has killed herself.

Elizabeth searches through the cellar of the school, an area which reportedly dates back to the time of the Salem witch trials. In legend, eight witches were concealed here to avoid capture. She locates the room depicted in Debbie's painting but is frightened away when Professor Delacroix mysteriously appears. The next day in class, the science teacher seems erratic and overwrought. That evening, Debbie commits suicide in the enigmatic room in the cellar. Roberta and Elizabeth find her and notify the headmistress, who only pretends to call the police. Delacroix goes wild after finding his lab animals were killed, and he jumps out of the window, hobbling away after landing on the lawn. Roberta and Elizabeth wake Dr. Clampett, who instructs the two students to go to his classroom and wait for him. Delacroix tries to cross the lake just outside the school grounds and drowns when several students in rowboats, including Jody, strike him with oars and poles.

Back at the school, Roberta speaks glowingly of Clampett. Elizabeth reveals her actual identity. The headmistress confronts Clampett, but he forces her to obey him, ordering that the school be evacuated. Seeing the school buses leave, Elizabeth alerts Roberta, but she seems unconcerned. She leads Elizabeth to the basement, where Clampett is gathered with seven students. He reveals that he is actually the Devil, seeking to gather eight replacements for the witches abandoned during the witch trials. That very evening they will travel with him to hell. He invites Elizabeth to become the eighth member and join them, revealing that he killed Martha, Lucy, and Debbie when they refused his invitation. She screams a refusal, tossing a lantern which bursts into flames. The students make no effort to escape, allowing the flames to consume them. Fleeing, Elizabeth encounters the headmistress, whose mind is in a fog as she goes about watering flowers. She drags the woman out of the burning building, and the fire department arrives too late to save the old building. In the cellar, the Devil is unharmed as he wanders about in the flames. Moments later, he appears outside the building, watching as it is totally consumed. He smokes a cigarette before fading into thin air, and the camera pans down to the singed ground where he once stood.

Satan's School for Girls basically leaves the viewer unsatisfied, since the Devil's purpose is never adequately explained or developed. Why did he wait almost 200 years to set his plan in motion? How does it relate to the original eight witches? Their actual fate is not revealed in the film. The Devil does not seem particularly concerned that he only recruited seven students instead of eight. At the conclusion, the only response possible by the viewer is a shrug of indifference. Oddly, this film was remade as another telefilm in 2000. Kate Jackson, who played Roberta in the original, then assumed the role of the headmistress.

Performances

Roy Thinnes is best remembered as the star of "The Invaders," a television series about a secret alien infiltration of Earth. As David Vincent, Thinnes played the sole human aware of the aliens' existence, since they were indistinguishable from men except for the fact that they couldn't bend their pinky fingers. In addition, Thinnes played Roger Collins in the short-lived evening version of "Dark Shadows" in 1991. Thinnes is adequate as the Devil, and it is interesting to see Satan enjoying posing as an art teacher. Thinnes is bland, self-assured, and low-key. The only indication that he is the Devil is his resistance to fire and his donning of a black robe in the final scene in the basement. In the final shot, watching the fire from the school grounds, he is again dressed as a professor with casual suit jacket. Except for the last scene, Thinnes is only mildly sinister, and he makes little impact overall. The other performers also make little impression, except for Lloyd Bochner and Kate Jackson, who got her start in the original "Dark Shadows." The telefilm provided an early role for Cheryl Ladd, who is billed as Cheryl Jean Stopplemoor in the credits.

Notable Quotes

- What the Devil is going on? (**Clampett to Roberta and Elizabeth**)
- I welcome what man rejects. I beckon what man despises. I forgive what man will not. (**the Devil to Elizabeth**)

Satan's Touch

1977   Rating: ***   Paul Davies as the Devil

Goodell Productions. Written by John Goodell; Photographed by John DeWitt; Special Effects by Optical Services; Edited by Peggy Keane and Ken Smith; Music by Steve Barnett and Bernie Wayne; Produced by Maury Grossman; Directed by John Goodell. Color, 87 minutes.

Annotated Cast List

James Lawless (*Jim Parish*, owner of Crocus Hill Food Market); Mikel Clifford (*Carol*, his wife); Adrienne and Kate Diercks (their daughters); Warren Frost (*Joe Donovan*, casino owner); Paul Davies (the Devil); Shirley Venard (*Sylvia Steele*, private detective hired by the casino); Michael Laskin (*Bill Gaggle*, gambler and systems expert); Lou Bellamy (*Fred Finch*, casino security); Bernard Erhard (*Tony*, casino manager who rigs the computer); Don Amendolia (*Angie*, government agent working at the casino); David Chase (drunken slots player); Patricia Mathews (*Sherri*, ex–chorus girl who tries to seduce Jim); Peter Goetz (*Charles Kotter*, gambler with computer wired into his suit); Nancy Nelson (*Debbie*, blackjack dealer); Jane

McDonough (*Mrs. Murphy*, elderly food market customer); Robert Shurson (poker game dealer); Carmine Pellosi (*Carmine*, lie detector expert); Richard Rundquist (roulette table operator); Earl Buys (pianist in Atlantic City); Reese Palley (Atlantic City china shop merchant); Candy Anderson (discotheque singer).

Appraisal and Synopsis

This low-budget comedy about gambling and the Las Vegas casino industry is clever and works on all counts. The only problem is that it runs out of gas about two-thirds of the way through the story and then tags on an extraneous episode in Atlantic City. At this point, it fumbles around a bit until it latches onto a fairly routine conclusion. On the whole, it manages to be far more successful than many more expensive films, and it is fairly entertaining and amusing without resorting to vulgarity or slapstick. Narrated by the Devil, the story begins as the Prince of Darkness contrasts two cities, Las Vegas and Crocus Hill, Iowa. In a mischievous experiment, Satan plans to bring elements of these two different worlds together. He selects Jim Parish, a humble grocer who always sticks up for the Devil when he is blamed for people's misdeeds, and endows him with a special power to win every gambling bet he makes. Then he arranges for Jim and his wife to win an all-expenses-paid vacation in Las Vegas.

Angie, a federal agent, is doing a gambling study for the government (a great example of our tax dollars at work). He approaches the Golden Nugget Casino to arrange to rig one slot machine so that it never pays off. A camera is then positioned to study how much time and money each gambler spends on this one-armed bandit. After one week, casino owner Joe Donovan is startled to learn that even though the rigged machine didn't pay out, his computer record reports a $3 shortage in the machine's income. Suspecting someone is tampering with the computer, he sends for Sylvia Steele, a private detective and mathematician, to investigate the matter.

Arriving at the Golden Nugget, Jim begins an incredible winning streak that comes to the attention of Tony, the casino manager, and Fred Finch, the security expert in charge of investigating patron cheating. Finch cannot explain how Parish always wins. Donovan asks Sylvia to keep her eye on Parish as well. Sitting next to him, she detects no system to his gambling. In fact, he seems quite an amateur, but he never loses, no matter which game he plays. The Devil blends in with the casino crowd to observe. Jim decides to remain in Vegas to gamble while his wife returns home to Iowa to care for their grocery store. Sylvia reports to Donovan, clearing Jim of any cheating, but the casino owner becomes obsessed with Parish's winning streak. He thinks he has either invented a foolproof system to win at gambling or, worse yet, he truly is a man so lucky he can never lose. Donovan hires Sherri, a former chorus girl, to seduce Jim, but nothing happens. Jim is merely friendly toward her. Donovan calls Parish to his office and questions him about his winning streak. A lie detector expert hired by the casino mogul concludes that Parish is entirely honest in his replies. When he learns that Sherri was hired by Donovan, Jim is deeply offended and decides to leave Vegas and head to Atlantic City.

Sylvia suspects that an insider, someone such as Tony, is skimming money from the casino winnings with a computer subprogram, which is why the rigged slot machine reported a shortage. Donovan, however, sends Sylvia to Atlantic City to keep her eye on Jim with whom she has struck up a friendship. Later the casino boss uncovers evidence that Tony has been banking large sums of money stolen from the casino, but the culprit has fled to Atlantic City, presumably to kill Sylvia. Donovan warns her by phone and promises to send help. When Tony arrives, he chases Sylvia and Jim along the boardwalk and through various hotels. They enter a discotheque where the Devil is acting as DJ. Tony is knocked out by Angie, who injects him with an anesthetic. Donovan arrives in Atlantic City and challenges Jim to a poker game. Sylvia advises Jim to lose on purpose. When the Devil observes Jim folding his winning hand containing four aces, he removes the spell from him. Jim now legitimately loses to Donovan at poker, and the casino owner realizes that Jim is a harmless man who simply had a remarkable winning streak. He allows him to retain some of his winnings, and a relieved Jim returns home.

Satan's Touch is unpretentious, except for some snazzy photographic effects in the first third of the film which are a little too flashy. The writing is interesting, and the plot moves quickly except for a dull patch in the last third. Perhaps the picture would have benefited by trimming an additional ten miniutes, because at 87 minutes, it is a bit overlong and padded toward the end.

Performances

Paul Davies plays a mellow, laid-back Satan who enjoys watching the results of his handiwork. Davies was a young man, in his early to midthirties when he made this picture. He has curly blond hair and a darker, neatly trimmed beard, and he wears no makeup as the Devil. He has a pleasant, mellifluous voice, which makes him an excellent narrator. Davies is at his best while making insightful observations as events unfold. For example, when Joe Donovan is discussing lie detectors, the Devil comments to the audience that thumb screws make good lie detectors. On the other hand, the role could have been improved if he had given it a more sinister air. He is a trifle too bland and smooth to be an effective Devil. Davies appeared in only a half dozen films, and he is not memorable. Most of his costars, with the exception of Warren Frost, are similarly inexperienced. Frost is best remembered as Dr. Hayward on "Twin Peaks." Most of the actors do a good job, particularly James Lawless as the good-natured grocer.

Notable Quotes

• Sunrise, generally a slow time for my business. Most places it's really too early or too late for truly inspired sinning. But here in Las Vegas it is still prime time. (**the Devil's opening narration**)

• I don't think we should blame the Devil. After all, he's just doing his job, isn't he? Tempting people, sending them to hell, is not a very pleasant job, and isn't it up to us to resist temptation? (**Jim Parish to his customer Mrs. Murphy upon catching her shoplifting**)

• Earthquakes? Of course we do earthquakes. No, no, acts of God is just an expression. (**Devil on the phone**)

Satan's Triangle

1975   Rating: *
Alejandro Rey, Kim Novak and Doug McClure as the Devil

Danny Thomas Productions. Written by William Read Woodfield; Photo-graphed by Leonard J. South; Edited by Bud Molin and Denis Verkler; Special Effects by Gene Grigg and Howard Anderson; Music by Johnny Pate; Produced by James Rokas; Directed by Sutton Roley. Color, 74 minutes.

Annotated Cast List

Kim Novak (*Eva*, lone survivor aboard the *Requite*, actually the Devil in disguise); Alejandro Rey (*Fr. Peter Martin*, priest found adrift on a raft, also the Devil in disguise); Doug McClure (*Jim Haig*, Coast Guard lieutenant); Michael Conrad (*Pagnolini*, Coast Guard commander and helicopter pilot); Jim Davis (*Hal Bancroft*, wealthy tourist who charters the *Requite*); Ed Lauter (*Jack Strickland*, captain of the *Requite*); Tito Vandis (*Salao*, crewman); Zitto Kazan (*Juano*, crewman); Peter Bourne (Swedish captain); Hank Stohl (*Dunnock*, Coast Guard captain); Tom Dever (Miami Rescue radio operator); Trent Dolan (Miami Rescue lieutenant).

Appraisal and Synopsis

This telefilm employs the Bermuda Triangle as the setting for a diabolical morality play, in which various people are tested in an unequal contest with the Devil. Unfortunately, there doesn't appear to be much rhyme or reason in the script penned by William Read Woodfield, one of the feature writers of the "Mission: Impossible" series. The Devil merely seems to be toying with people who can neither combat him nor find salvation. The modest effort is partially successful due to the creepy, foreboding atmosphere and the first-rate performances by the cast.

An emergency call to the Miami Rescue unit of the Coast Guard sets the story in motion. Two helicopters respond to the mayday. The first vehicle inexplicably suffers engine icing despite the warm temperatures and is forced to turn back. The second ship, piloted by Commander Pagnolini, continues on. When his partner, Jim Haig, informs him that the coordinates of their target are in the precise center of the Devil's Triangle, Pagnolini voices his opinion that supernatural forces are behind the trouble in that area.

They locate the *Requite*, the vessel that broadcast the SOS, which is an eighty-five-foot yacht apparently abandoned. Haig spots two dead bodies on the ship, one on deck and another hanging from the mast. Haig is lowered by cable to the *Requite* where he makes a detailed search. In the rear compartment of the vessel, the Coast Guardsman is shocked to find a body seemingly suspended in midair. He also finds a beautiful woman slumped in a corner in a state of shock. He tries to bring her back to the rescue copter, but the cable snaps as it attempts to lift them, dumping them into the ocean. They swim back to the *Requite*, and when Haig radios Pagnolini, the pilot informs him he is running low on fuel and will return in the morning.

The woman, Eva, feels the situation is hopeless. She recounts to Haig how their cruise began, when her wealthy friend Hal Bancroft chartered the boat so he could land a striped marlin that would outweigh the one recently caught by his stepbrother. It was a matter of honor and sibling rivalry for Hal. Strickland, captain of the yacht, would earn a $5,000 bonus if this feat were accomplished. When Hal hooks a huge marlin, one of the crew spots a man adrift in a lifeboat. The millionaire is peeved when he has to abandon his catch so the man can be picked up. Strange lightning plays around the ship as soon as the man is brought on board. He gives his name as Peter Martin, a priest who claims he was in a plane crash while accompanying a sick boy to a Miami hospital. The *Requite*'s crew abandons ship shortly afterward in a panic, proclaiming the vessel is doomed. After speaking to the priest, Hal resumes his quest for the marlin, finally succeeding. He and Strickland bring the huge fish aboard and store it in a refrigerated compartment next to the rear cabin. A violent squall suddenly erupts, the ship begins to flounder, and an automated SOS signal is activated as Strickland and Hal are mysteriously killed while trying to combat the storm. Eva becomes unconscious. When she awakens, the sea is calm, and Fr. Martin tries to comfort her, saying the Coast Guard should arrive soon. She is still despairing, admitting to the priest that she is a kept woman who stayed with Hal for money. When he hears the sound of the helicopter, he climbs the mast and fires a flare. He then falls, snapping his neck as he is tangled in the ropes. Eva sinks into shock.

Haig tries to find logical reasons for the strange deaths, even explaining that Hal's body is not really suspended in midair but impaled on the marlin's spear, since the fish had broken loose from its storage compartment. Eva is finally convinced by the Coast Guardsman's reasoning.

The next morning, a Coast Guard vessel arrives and rescues Haig and Eva. Pagnolini's rescue copter arrives and lands on deck. He then lifts off with his partner and Eva to fly them back to Miami. Meanwhile, the Coast Guard removes the bodies from the *Requite*. Lowering the body from the mast, they discover it is not a priest but a blonde woman. Captain Dunnock calls the helicopter at once to inform Haig of this development. As he hears this report, Eva transforms into Fr. Martin and pushes Haig out of the open hatch. Pagnolini tries to send a distress call, but the Devil tells him his radio will no longer work and that he is here to bargain for his soul. The Devil offers to save the pilot's life if Pagnolini will plead for it. Instead, Pagnolini deliberately crashes his helicopter into the sea. The Devil floats to the surface moments later and chuckles as he watches the dead body of Pagnolini. A Swedish ship arrives on the horizon, and the Devil transforms himself into the figure of Haig. He starts to wave as the captain spots him through his binoculars.

There seems to be no substance whatsoever behind the plot of this film. The Devil appears to act haphazardly, and instead of testing people as Fr. Martin suggests, he really does nothing to tempt them. There seems to be little consistency for his actions. Hal is selfish, Strickland is greedy, Eva is a prostitute, and Haig is a womanizer, but these traits seem unconnected to their fate. Pagnolini is an upstanding, virtuous man, and he is the only one who the Devil actually tries to pervert, but in vain. Pagnolini's sacrifice brings no redemption. Throughout this story, neither Eva nor Fr. Martin provide the slightest indication that the Devil has taken them over. Fr. Martin acts consistently in a priestly manner with Eva, reminding her, for example, that Mary Magdalene was also a prostitute. Likewise, when the Devil transforms himself into Eva to interact with Haig, he remains consistently in character throughout. Because of this, the film comes across as shallow, inconsistent, and insincere. The potential was certainly there for a far better film, but instead the filmmakers decided to use the Devil as only a gimmick, a surprise with which to end the story, but it is a hollow gesture.

Performances

It is difficult to assess the performances of Alejandro Rey and Kim Novak as the Devil, since they remain in character throughout. At the end of the film, Novak provides an elated smile as Haig is given the news that she is actually dead. Alejandro Rey is given a few brief moments as the Devil as he tries to entice Pagnolini, but he quickly becomes incomprehensible as he shouts and screams. Earlier in the picture, Rey is good, casting a somber mood on the ship, but his warnings about the Devil make little sense since he is the Devil all along. Kim Novak is the finest ingredient in this film, giving a warm, sensual, and heartfelt performance. But there is little difference between her rendition of the real Eva opposite Jim Davis and Alejandro Rey, and her satanic Eva opposite Doug McClure. Incidentally, McClure also plays the Devil, in the final shot of the picture as he is about to be rescued. His evil smirk in this brief scene is effective.

Notable Quotes

- I believe in God, Santa Claus, the Easter Bunny. But the Devil? That I can't quite swallow. (**Haig to Pagnolini**)
- Some people believe the triangle is the Devil's place, and when it is time for one to die, he tests us here, as he did the Lord in the wilderness. That's why the crew abandoned us. (**Fr. Martin to the others**)
- No, no, I reject you in God's name! (**Pagnolini to the Devil as he deliberately crashes his helicopter**)

The Sentinel

1977   Rating: **   Burgess Meredith as the Devil

Universal. Written by Michael Winner and Jeffrey Konvitz, based on the novel by Jeffrey Konvitz; Photographed by Richard C. Kratina; Edited by Bernard Gribble and Terry Rawlings; Special Effects by Albert Whitlock; Music by Gil Melle; Produced by Michael Winner and Jeffrey Konvitz ; Directed by Michael Winner. Color, 92 minutes.

Annotated Cast List

Christina Rains (*Allison Parker*, fashion model); Christopher Sarandon (*Michael Lerman*, her boyfriend, a lawyer); Burgess Meredith (*Charles Chazen,* the Devil); Ava Gardner (*Logan*, realtor); John Carradine (*Fr. Matthew Halliran,* blind priest and fifth floor tenant); Jose Ferrer (cardinal, sentinel project administrator); Arthur Kennedy (*Mgr. Franchino*, Brotherhood representative); Martin Balsam (*Gregor Ruzinsky*, language scholar); Mady Heflin (*Marshak*, Ruzinsky's student); Sylvia Miles (*Gerde Engstrom*, tenant); Beverly D'Angelo (*Sandra*, Gerde's roommate); Deborah Raffin (*Jennifer*, Allison's friend); Eli Wallach (*Gatz*, police lieutenant); Christopher Walken (*Rizzo*, police detective); Jerry Orbach (commercial director);

Jeff Goldblum (*Jack*, photographer); Hank Garrett (*James Brenner*, private eye); Diane Stillwell (his secretary); William Hickey (*Perry*, safecracker); Kate Harrington (*Anna Clarke*, cat party guest); Jane Hoffman (*Lillian Clotkin*, cat party guest); Robert Gerringer (*Hart*); Gary Allen (*Michael Stinnett*); Nana Tucker (apartment hunter); Tom Berringer (apartment hunter); Sam Gray (*Aureton*, doctor who attends Allison); Reid Shelton (pastor); Fred Stuthman (Allison's father); Lucie Lancaster (Allison's mother); Zane Lasky (*Raymond*); Ron McLarty (Michael's realtor).

Appraisal and Synopsis

The Sentinel is a major Devil movie that wound up a total debacle despite a sizable budget, a remarkable cast, and an intriguing premise. The principal culprit is director, producer, and coauthor Michael Winner. Author Jeffrey Konvitz also deserves much of the blame since he coproduced and co-wrote the screenplay. Konvitz's original novel had great potential, but as a screenplay the piece disintegrates into chaos. A last-minute recutting of the film only made matters worse.

Some culpability is due as well to the concept of the film (and the novel) which was never adequately thought out by the author. The central premise is that the entrance to hell exists underneath a brownstone in Brooklyn Heights overlooking the harbor of New York. In the novel, the location was West 89th Street. The denizens of the infernal regions are prevented from escaping to the world above by a sentinel, a guardian who monitors the entrance from the top floor of the building. Exactly how the sentinel is able to prevent any escapees is never explained. According to the novel, the first sentinel was Archangel Gabriel, who failed in his mission when Satan eluded his guard and slipped into the Garden of Eden. Since then God decided that human beings rather than angels would serve as sentinels. Of course, if the Devil were able to outwit an archangel, it would seem an ordinary mortal would be far easier to defeat. The Catholic church oversees the sentinel program, selecting its candidates from decent individuals who became victims of despair and attempted suicide. As the sentinels, these individuals become priests, nuns, or brothers, and they also lose their sight, gaining a special inner vision that enables them to identify the inhabitants of hell. The full dossier of each sentinel is maintained in church records dating back to the eighth century. It is not explained how the church managed this site centuries before the colonization of America. Who oversaw the sentinels before the church existed? One could assume the ancient legends of Roman or Phoenician visitors to the New World as an explanation, but how was the entrance guarded before then? Konvitz has no suggestions to plug up these loopholes. He could have done so, for for example, by envisioning a shift of locales for the entrance every millennium. Still, the concept of the entrance to hell being in the heart of Manhattan is clever, surreal, and wickedly humorous. It is a shame that Konvitz did not work the kinks out of his hypothesis beforehand, and similar flaws plague the main action of the film as well.

Critics of the picture concentrated their ire not on the illogic of the plot, but because Michael Winner employed people with actual physical deformities in the film as representing the legions of hell. The director was condemned for the exploitation of these people with hollow, righteous indignation. Not since Tod Browning's *Freaks* (1932) was such a commotion raised. These individuals, largely recruited from circuses, were not forced to do anything demeaning or degrading in the picture, but the critics ranted and raved merely because they appeared, and something in this

Burgess Meredith as the Devil summons up the hordes of hell in the controversial climax of The Sentinel.

critical reaction seems contrived and phony. The second issue concerned the role of the Catholic church in the sentinel project, and additional scenes were added to the television print with Jose Ferrer, which altered the group in charge to a renegade sect that was excommunicated by the church proper. But this rendered the story an even greater mess, and these inserts and scenes were later dropped when *The Sentinel* was released on video.

The original plot portrays Allison Parker, a New York fashion model, who is troubled after the death of her father. She rents an apartment in the mysterious brownstone. She makes friends with Charles Chazen, the charming and eccentric old man who is the colorful center of attention in the building. Later, Allison believes she is going mad when she explores the apartment directly over her own and finds her father there, alive and demented. She tells the story to her boyfriend, Michael, a lawyer, and the police investigate as well. Allison learns that she is actually alone in the building, except for the reclusive Fr. Halliran on the top floor. When she identifies the people who attended Charles Chazen's party for his cat, she learns they are all murderers who were executed for their crimes. Again, she believes she is going mad. Michael researches the building and finds it is owned by the Catholic church. He burglarizes the church's files and learns the secret of the sentinel project. He also discovers that Allison has been chosen to become the next sentinel. Michael questions Halliran but becomes infuriated when the priest fails to answer his questions. He attacks the priest, and Michael is himself killed by Monsignor Franchino, a church official who attends to Halliran.

Now dead and reanimated, Michael learns that Chazen is the Devil, who is plotting to have Allison kill herself before she can assume the role of sentinel. After Michael explains these revelations to Allison, the Devil calls up the legions of hell to persuade her to join Michael and the other damned in his kingdom. Allison resists, and as Fr. Halliran holds up his crucifix, the Devil and his cohorts descend back into hell. Halliran hands his crucifix over to Allison.

Months later, the brownstone is refurbished, and new tenants are renting an apartment in the building. They are told that a blind nun, Sister Therese, resides on the top floor. In fact, Therese is Allison, who has assumed the role of sentinel, and the film ends as the nun quietly sits in a chair by the window and maintains her vigil.

Performances

A major drawback to this film is that all of the main characters are either unlikable or actually repellent. We learn that Michael, played by Christopher Sarandon, murdered his first wife so that he could marry Allison, his mistress. Allison herself, played by Christina Rains, is cold, neurotic, and selfish. Perhaps a different actress could have made her more sympathetic. Jose Ferrer, Arthur Kennedy, Eli Wallach, Christopher Walken, Deborah Raffin, and the others also come across as heartless and unfeeling. This leaves Burgess Meredith as the most charming and sympathetic member of the cast, but since he is the Devil this could hardly be what the director intended. Meredith plays the role with an aura of sly enchantment, and his natural charisma makes him the most memorable character in the story. Meredith uses no makeup, and throughout the film he seems like a gracious, fun-loving, and appealing older gentleman. At the end of the film, when everyone realizes that he is the Devil, he still has the same charm, and one half expects Allison to join him as he requests. Single-handedly, Meredith salvages a good deal of the picture, making it seem tolerable and even interesting when he is onscreen. This performance is another feather in Meredith's cap, placing him among the most outstanding actors who have portrayed Satan.

Notable Quotes

• To thee thy course by lot is given charge and strict watch that to this happy place no evil thing approach or enter in. (**Gregor Ruzinsky, translating a text in Latin which only Allison is able to see in a blank book**)

What does it mean? (**Michael**)

You will have to check the book.... by Milton, the English religious writer, from his great work *Paradise Lost*. (**Ruzinsky**)

• Through me you go into the city of grief. Through me you go into the pain that is eternal. Through me you go among people lost. (**Michael, reading the message engraved in stone that was concealed behind a wooden panel in the vestibule**)

The entrance to hell! (**Halliran**)

• You are the chosen of the Lord God, the tyrant and our enemy. You are she who is to guard and protect the entrance to this earth. Now you must destroy yourself, kill yourself, be one with us. Be queen in our kingdom. Here, take it, take it my love, and remember, friendships can blossom into bliss. (**the Devil to Allison, handing her a knife**)

The Soldier's Tale

1964   Rating: ****   Robert Helpmann as the Devil

BHE Programmes. Written by Charles Ferdinand Ramuz as adapted by Michael Birkett, Kitty Black, and Michael Flanders; Photographed by Ken Nicholson; Edited by Richard Marden; Music by Igor Stravinsky; Produced by Leonard Cassini and Dennis Miller; Directed by Michael Birkett. Color, 61 minutes.

Annotated Cast List

Robert Helpmann (the Devil and narrator); Brian Phelan (*Joseph*, soldier); Svetlana Beriosova (princess); Melos Ensemble (band of traveling musicians).

Appraisal and Synopsis

While in Switzerland during the First World War, composer Igor Stravinsky came up with the idea of creating a theater piece for seven musicians and a small company of actors. He approached the writer Charles Ferdinand Ramuz with the idea of basing a scenario on Russian folklore about a soldier who deserts and his entanglement with the Devil. The resulting work was called *L'Histoire du Soldat*, and the music represented a dramatic change from his prewar style. Michael Birkett adapted it to the screen in 1964, expanding the property with exceptional flair and intelligence, including remarkable location footage. He brings *L'Histoire du Soldat* brilliantly to life.

The picture begins as Joseph, a soldier on leave, follows a band of musicians on a dusty road. Narration in rhyme provides a continual commentary. The soldier pauses to rest, taking out his violin from his knapsack. As he plays, he attracts the attention of an elderly butterfly collector. The old man approaches the soldier, offering a trade, Joseph's violin in exchange for a magic book that produces money. The soldier also must stay in the old man's home for three days to teach him how to play. The soldier complains that he only has a two-week leave but finally agrees. Of course, he doesn't realize it, but he has just made a deal with the Devil.

Joseph is wined and dined by the Devil for three days while the soldier teaches him the secrets of the instrument. On the third day, Joseph is driven in a coach by the Devil to the outskirts of his home village. Everyone reacts in horror when they see him. His mother shrieks, and his girlfriend has a husband and two children. Joseph discovers that he has been missing not for three days but for ten years. Only then does he realize the identity of his host. A black dog passes by and is transformed into a younger Devil as a hunter wearing a checkered deerstalker hat. When Joseph denounces him as a cheat, the Devil reminds him that he still has the book and should start using it.

After reading the book, the soldier begins to make a fortune. He starts as a peddler and quickly rises to become a wealthy financier. Joseph finds, however, that he is unable to achieve any happiness. The Devil visits him, this time in the guise of an old gypsy woman. She offers to sell him the contents of his original knapsack. He seizes the violin and, after playing a single note, finds himself back on the original dusty road. He keeps marching down it until he crosses the frontier into the next country. Joseph stops at a village inn, where he learns from another soldier that the king's daughter has sunk into a stupor from which she cannot be roused. He urges Joseph to see if he can help her. As Joseph heads off, the second soldier vanishes into thin air, yet another manifestation of the Devil. When Joseph arrives at the royal palace, he discovers that an elegantly dressed doctor is attending the princess. The doctor reveals himself as the Devil when he shows Joseph the violin. Joseph challenges Satan to a game of cards. He knows the Devil will cheat to win, but Joseph plans to lose the few coins he has. Once he loses all of the tainted money, the Devil will no longer have any power over him. The Devil passes out after his victory, and Joseph takes back his violin. He then goes to play for the princess. Enchanted by his playing, the beautiful woman rises from her slumber and dance. She then falls into Joseph's arms. The Devil awakens and, decked out with horns, a tail, and black tights, executes a furious dance to try to lure the princess away from Joseph, but she is repelled by him. The Devil finally collapses. The princess dances around the Devil's body which vanishes, but his voice rings out a curse, saying that if Joseph ever leaves this land, he will claim him forever.

Time passes, and Joseph's new bride has become bored. She wants to travel with her husband to see his home town and visit his mother. He rejects the idea, fearing Satan's curse, but she pleads and begs until he can no longer refuse. They head off, and as soon as they cross the frontier, the Devil reappears. He performs a spectacular dance of triumph. The princess looks on helplessly as the Devil takes off with Joseph to hell. She cries out his name as the story ends.

Performances

Robert Helpmann delivers the most incredible screen portrayal of the Devil in this little film, a unique and unparalleled *tour de force*. Helpmann appears in countless guises, from the butterfly collector and the gypsy woman to the disheveled soldier at the inn. He is magnificent and completely convincing in each variation, and then he tops it off with his dancing pyrotechnics. Of course, he was uniquely qualified to carry off the part, having been the lead dancer of the Sadlers Wells Ballet for over fifteen years. Helpmann also had extraordinary film experience, appearing and dancing in such memorable films as *The Red Shoes* (1948), *Tales of Hoffmann* (1951), and *Don Quixote* (1973), the unique ballet film directed by Rudolf Nureyev. Helpmann is also a riveting screen presence when he doesn't dance, such as his roles as Prince Tuan in *55 Days in Peking* (1963) and the Mad Hatter in *Alice's Adventures in Wonderland* (1972). Helpmann played the Devil again in an obscure comedy made in New Zealand called *Second Time Lucky* (1984). In this critically panned effort, Helpmann's Devil bets God (Robert Morley) that if Adam and Eve could start over again, they would again fall into sin. Adam and Eve are eventually placed in occupied France during World War II where they demonstrate the power of their love. Helpmann was knighted in 1968. Four years after his death, he was the subject of a documentary and tribute entitled *The Tales of Helpmann* (1990).

Notable Quotes

- Joseph finds the old man is as good as his word at the very least. In fact, it's a feast. He's quite at home in the Devil's dining hall, and after all, he's got his promise to keep as well, violin lessons in hell. (**narration**)
- We've got the world split down the middle. You've got the book, and I've got the fiddle. (**the Devil to Joseph**)
- He can't bear losing. He always cheats and wins. That's where your life begins. (**Joseph's thoughts**)
- Wisdom is knowing how to choose. Too much to possess is too much to lose. One blessing is happiness, just the same. Double the stake, and you've lost the game. (**closing narration**)

The Sorrows of Satan

1926   Rating: **   Adolphe Menjou as the Devil

Paramount. Written by Forrest Halsey, based on the novel by Marie Corelli as adapted by John Russell and George Hull; Photographed by Harry Fischbeck; Edited by Julian Johnson; Produced and Directed by D. W. Griffith. B&W, silent, 110 minutes.

Annotated Cast List

Adolphe Menjou (*Prince Lucio Riminez*, the Devil); Ricardo Cortez (*Geoffrey Tempest*, struggling writer and critic); Carol Dempster (*Mavis Clare*, writer in love with Geoffrey); Lya De Putti (*Princess Olga Godovsky*, exiled noblewoman who marries Geoffrey to be near Lucio); Ivan Lebedeff (*Amiel*, Lucio's servant); Lawrence D'Orsay (*Earl of Elton*, uncle of Princess Olga); Marcia Harris (Mavis' landlady); Dorothy Hughes (friend of Mavis); Nellie Savage (dancer); Eddie Dunn (marriage license clerk); Wildred Lucas (minister); Josephine Dunn, Claude Brooke, Jean Murga, Owen Nares.

Appraisal and Synopsis

Marie Corelli was the pen name of Mary Mackay (1863–1924), a popular novelist who was a favorite of Queen Victoria. Her novels were noted for their florid style and eccentric plots, and she was described as a female H. Rider Haggard. Her 1895 novel, *The Sorrows of Satan; or, The Strange Experiences of Geoffrey Tempest, Millionaire*, was filmed twice, in England in 1916 directed by Alexander Butler and in America ten years later by D.W. Griffith. The same novel inspired *Leaves from Satan's Book*, although little of that film was actually based on Corelli's story. The British version, which featured Cecil Humphries as the Devil, has not been seen in many years and is considered possibly lost. The 1926 adaptation of *The Sorrows of Satan* was initially prepared by Cecil B. DeMille, but the project fell to Griffith after DeMille left Paramount to form his own production company. Griffith reportedly disliked Corelli's novel but eventually warmed to the project after casting Adolphe Menjou as Prince Lucio Riminez (changed from Rimânez in the novel), the dapper Devil in a tuxedo, Ricardo Cortez as Geoffrey Tempest, and Carol Dempster as his mistress, who he had recently starred in *Sally of the Sawdust* (1925) with W. C. Fields. The character of Lady Sibyl, Lord Eaton's daughter, played in the 1916 British version by Gladys Cooper, was eliminated and replaced by a Russian niece, played by the exotic Lya De Putti, Hungarian actress and ballet dancer. Her character, Princess Olga, is a Russian emigré, which helps to make the film seem more topical. Griffith's lack of total commitment no doubt hurt the project, and as a whole the picture is old-fashioned, slow moving, and stodgy.

The picture opens with an impressive prologue, which was later removed from many prints, in which Lucifer is defeated in his celestial revolt and transformed from a pure white magisterial archangel into the dark, grotesque image of Satan. The visuals appear to be inspired by several prints by Gustave Doré. This action takes place on the massive steps outside the gates of heaven from which Lucifer and his companions have just been driven. The head

Geoffrey Tempest (Ricardo Cortez) is overwhelmed at his change of fortune after meeting Prince Lucio (Adolphe Menjou) in The Sorrows of Satan.

of the band of God's faithful, presumably Archangel Michael, informs Lucifer of his banishment. He is then charged with the task of tempting mankind throughout eternity. For every soul that resists him, however, he will be permitted one hour at the gates of heaven. Only at the end of time, when all men have turned from him, will he be forgiven and again resume his place at the right hand of God. Just as in *Leaves from Satan's Book*, this decree by God leaves the Devil with scant motivation to succeed in his task of corrupting humanity, yet he does succeed extraordinarily well, and rare are the occasions when he gets to spend an hour at the pearly gates due to failure. It seems as if Satan is honor-bound to do his best, but isn't he himself tempted to do a half-hearted job and earn more heavenly time?

The scene switches to modern times and introduces the audience to two poor, struggling writers, Geoffrey Tempest and Mavis Clare, who both live in the same rundown boardinghouse where they are perpetually struggling to pay their rent. So far, Mavis has only received rejection slips with her writing, and Geoffrey ekes out a living largely as a book critic. Their paths become entwined, the writers fall in love, and they spend the night together. Geoffrey pawns his watch to buy Mavis a bone china cup and saucer as a betrothal gift. The rest of the money he uses to obtain their wedding license. But when he goes to collect his check for his book reviews, he is told that his critiques are no longer wanted because he is out of sync with the public taste. Angry and depressed, Geoffrey proclaims he would sell his soul for money, if there were a Devil who would buy it. At that moment, a violent thunderstorm strikes. As Geoffrey struggles to plug the draft in his broken window, his door flies open and a dark figure enters his room. Turning, the writer is stunned to see an elegantly dressed man in a top hat and tuxedo. The man, Prince Lucio Riminez, hands Geoffrey a letter which explains that he is heir to a vast fortune left to him by a hitherto unknown uncle. As his late uncle's friend, Prince Lucio plans to take Geoffrey under his wing and introduce him to a new lifestyle. Geoffrey wants to tell the news at once to Mavis, but the prince advises him to wait until he learns all of the details. Displaying one of the weaknesses of silent film, this exchange between Geoffrey and the prince takes place right outside Mavis' room. She is waiting immediately behind the door for Geoffrey and should easily overhear this entire conversation but somehow does not. Lucio sweeps Geoffrey off to an ostentatious hotel dining room, where he is introduced to Princess Olga Godovsky, an emigré from Russia who is the niece of the Earl of Elton. While Geoffrey becomes overwhelmed by his sudden change in status, Mavis is puzzled and desperate over her fiancé's whereabouts. By the time Geoffrey and Prince Lucio return to his flat to transfer his belongings, Lucio has convinced Geoffrey to break off with Mavis and even dictates Geoffrey's farewell note to her, which his servant, Amiel, delivers. Mavis desperately tries to get Geoffrey's attention as he leaves the building, but the sound of Lucio's car drowns out her voice, and by the time she heads downstairs, the car has driven off. In vain, she runs after it.

Time passes, and Lucio maneuvers Geoffrey into a loveless marriage with Olga, who in reality is attached to Lucio and would do anything he asks. Meanwhile, Mavis, heartbroken over Geoffrey, starts to gain a modest success as a writer. Prince Lucio meets Mavis and offers to pave the way for her big literary breakthrough if she would be willing to become a friend and close companion to an elderly publisher. Mavis declines, clearly understanding the implications of the prince's proposal. Lucio shakes her hand sincerely, saying, "Though I can't help you, you have helped me," since her refusal has earned him an hour in paradise.

Olga finally throws herself at Lucio, who rejects her advances. Geoffrey overhears them and orders Olga to go to her room, where she kills herself with poison. Later, Geoffrey vents his anger and frustration over his unhappiness to the prince, who calls him a fool and reveals himself fully as the Devil with wings and horns. Geoffrey runs off in utter fear and panic. He returns to his old boardinghouse and seeks out Mavis. He pours out his heart to her, relating how he became the unwitting pawn of the Devil. She prays with him, and the shadowy image of the Devil which had followed him dissipates and leaves them in peace.

Most of *The Sorrows of Satan* is slow paced, ponderous, and heavy-handed. Much of it seems hollow and empty, reflecting images from Griffith's earlier work. For example, the bacchanal that Lucio prepares for Geoffrey is reminiscent of the bacchanal in *Orphans of the Storm* (1922). The rooming house also recalls Robespierre's boardinghouse in the same film. The scene where Mavis tries to get Geoffrey's attention, calling out and using fluttery gestures, resembles another scene in *Orphans of the Storm* where Lillian Gish calls down to her blind sister in the street below. At least in Gish's hands, the episode was heartrending. The matching sequence with Carol Dempster, however, is foolish and preposterous. The only first-rate moment of the picture, besides the introduction, is the scene when Lucio metamorphoses into the Devil. Done entirely in shadows, this effect is both creepy and sensational. It also serves to illustrate how dull and mishandled the rest of the film is in comparison. *The Sorrows of Satan* was also a financial failure, and it led to the termination of D. W. Griffith's contract with Paramount. Several later attempts at a comeback proved futile, and his last film was completed in 1931.

Performances

Adolphe Menjou, active in motion pictures from 1914, became a star after appearing in *A Woman of Paris* (1923), Charlie Chaplin's sophisticated social comedy intended to showcase Edna Purviance, his leading lady in countless comedies. Most of the acting plaudits went to Menjou, whose talent rose to the top under Chaplin's direction. Charlie himself only appeared in a bit part in this film. Unfortunately, most of Menjou's immense charm is not on display in *The Sorrows of Satan*, as he appears poker-faced and stoic throughout most of his scenes. He uses no special makeup as the Devil, since a stuntman acts in costume during the prologue and his transformation is accomplished entirely through the use of shadows. Menjou never really displays the "sorrows" of Satan onscreen, and the stodgy melodrama creaks along until Olga Tempest throws herself at Lucio. The expression of distaste on Menjou's face is magnificent, one of the highlights of the picture, as the Devil grows weary of earthly pawns, particularly after having been granted an hour in paradise when Mavis refused his temptation. The film misses an excellent opportunity by not staging the Devil's brief stopover in heaven and by not showing his personal reaction to it. The most disappointing aspect is that the potential is there for Lucio/Lucifer to have been outstanding, filled with mystery, wonder, and mixed emotions. Instead, the role is underplayed, and Menjou is reduced to a boring bystander and second fiddle in a hackneyed melodrama.

Notable Quotes

• Only when all men turn from thee canst thou resume thy glorious place at God's right hand, yet for every soul that resists thee, thou shalt have one hour at the gates of paradise. (**Archangel Michael to Lucifer**)

• Remember, I never stay in any man's company when he expresses a wish to be rid of me. (**the Devil, as Lucio, to Geoffrey during supper**)

• I am always meeting people who do not recall meeting me. (**Lucio to Mavis**)

• What sort of friend are you anyway? (**Geoffrey to Lucio**)

I never said I was your friend. Perhaps it is time to show you who I really am! (**Lucio's reply, as he transforms himself into the Devil**)

Sous le Soleil de Satan
AKA Under the Sun of Satan

1987   Rating: **   Jean-Christophe Bouvet as the Devil

Erato Films. Written by Sylvie Danton and Maurice Pialat, based on a novel by Georges Bernanos; Photographed by Willy Kurant; Edited by Yann Dedet; Music by Henri Dutilleux; Produced by Claude Abeille; Directed by Maurice Pialat. Color, 98 minutes.

Annotated Cast List

Gerard Depardieu (*Fr. Donissan*, devout French priest); Sandrine Bonnaire (*Mouchette Malorthy*, teenage girl who kills her lover); Alain Artur (*Marquis de Cadignan*, killed by Mouchette); Maurice Pialat (*Dean Menou-Segrais*, Donissan's spiritual advisor); Yann Dedet (*Dr. Gallet*, deputy who seduces Mouchette); Brigitte Legendre (Mouchette's mother); Jean-Claude Bourlat (Mouchette's father); Jean-Christophe Bouvet (the Devil, disguised as a traveler and horse dealer); Philippe Pallut (quarryman who helps Donissan); Marcel Ancelin (*Bishop Gerber*); Yvette Lavogez (*Marthe*, housekeeper): Pierre D'Hoffelize (*Pierre Havret*, father of dying boy); Corinne Bourdon (*Mrs. Havret*); Thierry Der'Ven (*Sabroux*, priest consoling Havret family); Vincent Peignaux (boy momentarily restored to life).

Appraisal and Synopsis

Sous le Soleil de Satan, written in 1926, was the first novel of Georges Bernanos (1888–1948), a mystical and poetic book about sin, redemption, and the presence of the Devil in the modern world. Bernanos became a prolific writer, who is best remembered for *Diary of a Country Priest* and *Dialogues of the Carmelites*. This film adaptation by Maurice Pialat is extraordinarily difficult to approach, particularly for casual viewers, since the picture is weighty and requires intense concentration. The presentation is static, and many long scenes occur in almost total darkness. The script is wordy, containing long philosophical and theological discourses that are hard to follow, particularly in translation. The intent of the story is often deliberately vague. Yet despite these significant obstacles, the film creates a powerful impression and sustains an intangible, ethereal mood that is unique. *Sous le Soleil de Satan* was the winner of the Golden Palm at the Cannes Film Festival in 1987. Less metaphysically inclined critics, however, have blasted the film as deadening and painful to watch.

The story is set in rural France in the 1920s Fr. Donissan is a sensitive and pious priest who is having difficulty determining how he can best serve God. His spiritual advisor, Dean Menou-Segrais, tries to help him channel his thoughts and energies. The scene shifts to Germaine Malorthy, known as Mouchette, who is a pregnant teenager carrying on affairs with two married men, the impoverished Marquis de Cadignan and Dr. Gallet, the local deputy to the national assembly. Mouchette visits the marquis in the middle of the night. They have a long discussion about their relationship which upsets Mouchette, who takes a shotgun and murders her lover.

When she visits Gallet, she confesses her crime to the unscrupulous politician, who begins to wonder about Mouchette's sanity.

The dean asks Fr. Donissan to help the elderly priest hear confessions in the nearby town of Etrapes. As he walks the eight miles to the neighboring village, Donissan becomes confused in the darkness accompanying a heavy rainstorm. He encounters a mysterious stranger, who suggests they rest in a stable. As the man talks, he reveals himself to be the Devil, and he offers the priest an opportunity for a vision in which he could see his own future and have his spiritual status revealed. Donissan refuses, and the Devil curses him, promising to test his mettle until his last breath. Donissan faints and is revived by a quarryman who helps guide the priest back to his own village. He then encounters Mouchette and is miraculously able to see into her soul. He speaks to her about her sins, particularly the murder of her lover. He attempts to help her seek redemption. Mouchette is first mocking and then frightened by the accuracy of the priest's revelations.

When Donissan reports to the dean, he tells him about his strange confrontation. The dean is puzzled by his diabolical encounter and is disturbed by his conversation with Mouchette. At her home, the girl thinks deeply about her situation and stabs herself in the neck with a knife. Donissan appears at this precise moment and carries her to the church, placing Mouchette before the altar where she dies.

Bishop Gerber instructs Menou-Segrais to transfer Donissan to a Trappist monastery, from which he will be assigned to a poor parish. Donissan leaves, and time passes in a dreamlike fashion. The priest meditates in a small chamber, and he is visited by the spirit of Mouchette who seems to be at peace. Later, Donissan is approached by a family whose son is dying of meningitis. By the time he arrives, the boy is dead. He has an involved philosophical discussion with Fr. Sabroux, and he tries to explain his dark vision in which he sees sin and the Devil triumphant everywhere. Donissan goes to see the corpse of the young boy, picks him up, and begs God to show him that He is more powerful than Satan. The boy revives momentarily and smiles at the priest. The boy's mother, witnessing this scene, proclaims Donissan to be a living saint. Dean Menou-Segrais seeks him out in the impoverished parish to which he was assigned. The dean is impressed that all of the peasants regard him as a holy man. Donissan is hearing confessions in his small church. The dean approaches the confessional and opens the door to find that Donissan has died, his face raised hopefully toward heaven.

Interpretations can vary widely as to the intent and meaning of almost every scene. The film can be regarded as allegorical, as surreal, or as a Kafkaesque black comedy. The protagonist, Donissan, appears at times to be hopelessly lost, a figure of despair, but at other moments, he seems filled with renewal and regeneration. Undoubtedly, viewers who evaluate and analyze this picture may easily come away with entirely different perceptions and conclusions. Perhaps the degree of success of this picture cannot be measured in usual terms but by the amount of thought that the picture inspires in its audience.

Performances

Jean-Christophe Bouvet is a shadowy Devil, thoroughly unpleasant and unlikable. The entire time he is on the screen, the film is extraordinarily dark and his countenance can barely be seen, except for his scruffy beard and piercing eyes. He reveals himself to be the Devil in a most unusual fashion, by kissing Donissan full on the lips without any warning of his action.

Depardieu barely moves a muscle during the entire scene, and the audience is unaware if he is conscious until he speaks toward the end of the encounter, rejecting the Devil and all of his works. Bouvet's Devil is totally lacking in charm. He is arrogant, self-assured, and repellent. Gerard Depardieu, the most illustrious French actor of the past thirty years, delivers a cerebral, dreamlike performance. His every movement is ponderous, and he stumbles, staggers, and faints throughout the film. His reading at times resembles his performance in *Danton* (1982) after his character has been condemned to the guillotine, and he sleepwalks through the final scenes of the picture. Sandrine Bonnaire, who became a major star in French cinema, was merely twenty when she tackled the complex role of Mouchette, and although she is extremely captivating, her performance is elusive and enigmatic, and the audience is uncertain about her motivation and choices. She goes through many different phases, yet none is truly convincing. Finally, director Maurice Pialat himself plays the key role of the dean, who is both devoted to and confused by his deeply troubled apprentice. He effectively conveys the dean's mixed feelings and deep concern about Donissan. His viewpoint is the prism through which the story of Donissan is relayed. It should be noted that Bernanos reportedly based his figure of Donissan on an actual French cleric who was worshiped by his parishioners.

Notable Quotes

- I sought you, hunted you ardently. [kisses Donissan] Ha, a friendly kiss, a trifle! I've kissed others, lots of others. Want to know something? I kiss you all! You know me in your flesh. None of you escape me! (**Satan to Donissan**)
- Man never fully knows what's going on in himself. You see yourself in enigmas, not clearly. (**Satan's philosophical observation**)
- Your prayers don't scare me. You were graced tonight. You'll pay heavily for it, my dear exorcist.... You will often fondle me thinking you are fondling the *other*. You are marked now with the sign of my hatred. (**Satan upon leaving Donissan, trying to confuse him in his love of God**)
- To God, you are not guilty of that murder. You are Satan's toy. (**Donissan to Mouchette**)

Speak of the Devil

1990   Rating: *   David Miller and Randal Leigh as the Devil

Delta Unique Media. Written by Raphael Nussbaum and Bob Craft; Photographed by Chuck Colwell; Edited by John Santos and Stephen Adrianson; Special Effects by Damon Allison and Richard M. Lca; Music by Gil Botcher; Produced and Directed by Raphael Nussbaum. Color, 99 minutes.

Annotated Cast List

Robert Elarton (*Jonah Johnson*, corrupt televangelist); Jean Miller (*Isabel Johnson*, his wife); Bernice Tamara Goor (*Eve*, Jonah's niece); Walter Kay (*Mort*, Jonah's cousin); Louise Sherill (*Mrs. Wigglesworth*, realtor); Shawn Patrick Greenfield (*Bobby Wigglesworth*, Her idiot son); Richard Rifkin (*Ben Tor*, rabbi); Mark Connor (IRS agent); David Campbell (*Gittens*, southern sheriff); Beverly Polcyn (*Ettie Gittens*, his mother); Denis de Boisblanc (*Steve Seligman*, L.A. cop); Dominick Daniels (the Hound of Hell); David Miller (the Devil); Randal Leigh (the Devil's voice); Sanford Hamton (*Skeeter Hipkins*, hillbilly father); Hilary Scott (*Lady Caligari*, Satanist); Miyako Kirksey (*Iris*, Caligari's assistant); Jay Schombing (*Juan*, handyman); Brandon Scott (*Carlos*, handyman); Dan Patrick Brandy (*Frank*); Tyler V. Bowe, Max Chain, Suzan Ellen, Troy Fromin (punk squatters); Doug Traer, Richard Tafilaw, Clark McLendon, Kenny Ellis (plumbers).

Appraisal and Synopsis

Watching *Speak of the Devil* could well serve as a punishment for denizens of the first circle of hell. It is one of the most abysmal Devil films ever made, with no redeeming features except for some decent makeup and costumes for Satan and his demonic Hound of Hell. Other than that, everything else in the production from the tinny electronic music score to the sophomoric script merits permanent consignment to the dustbin.

Rev. Jonah Johnson is a southern preacher whose phony healing television show is broken up simultaneously by the state police for fraud and by a hillbilly father seeking revenge for his daughter's pregnancy. Jonah and his wife, Isabel, flee, relocating in Los Angeles where they plan to open up another ministry. They purchase a rundown mansion at 666 13th Street, not knowing the building once served as headquarters for a cult of Satanists. They are pursued by debtors and the IRS when Lady Caligari, a wealthy eccentric, gives them a suitcase filled with money to start a new church devoted to the black arts. She also provides them with a Satanic manual, but first they have to clear out a gang of punk rockers, clean up the building, and deal with the haunted toilet on the second floor. The local rabbi warns them to leave, claiming their home is a hotbed of evil.

Johnson feels uneasy playing the role of Satanist, but Isabel goes at it with enthusiasm. They are joined by their niece Eve and cousin Mort, a former carnival showman, and they prepare for their opening service. They wind up conjuring a real demon, the Hound of Hell. Isabel makes a deal with the Devil and starts to grow younger. The punk rockers also return and become new recruits for Satan. Eve, an innocent, is unaware that her aunt and uncle have become Satanists, even though their new front is called the Church of Latter Day Sins. She befriends the local cop, Steve. At first, Jonah sacrifices chickens and goats at their services, but the Devil demands that Isabel arrange a human sacrifice, and she selects her niece Eve as the victim. Rabbi Ben Tor sneaks into their sanctuary and tries to exorcise it but is killed by the Hound of Hell. At the service, Jonah is reluctant to proceed, and the Devil himself materializes to insist. Jonah takes the ceremonial spear and plunges it through his chest, as well as that of the Devil standing behind him. The mansion erupts in flames and burns down, with only Eve and her policeman friend surviving. The mansion is completely destroyed except for the second-floor toilet. Unexpectedly, Jonah also emerges from the ashes. He later tries to atone and starts to hold services as a legitimate preacher, telling of his battle with Satan. The film concludes with a revival hymn.

The attempts at humor in this picture are clumsy and forced. When an IRS officer interrupts a service, the Hound of Hell urinates on his badge. There is also little wit, except maybe the name of the realtor, Wigglesworth, which refers to one of the Puritans from the era of the Salem witch trials, and Caligari, a tribute to the 1919 masterpiece of German expressionism. The special effects are dreadful, particularly the house fire at the end of the picture, as phony an effort as ever seen onscreen. But it is a welcome sight nevertheless, because it signals the end of this miserable picture.

Performances

David Miller's performance consists largely of being a talking head who tempts and controls Isabel. His appearance at the climax is not bad but far too short to bring any merit to the production. The voice of the Devil is provided by another actor entirely, and since even the lip sync is off, the effect is preposterous. The rest of the cast is equally inept, except for Jean Miller, who at least brings vitality and enthusiasm to her performance as Isabel. It is undetermined if Jean and David Miller are related.

Notable Quotes

• You all know it is hard to break Satan's evil spell upon this world, so won't you help us? (**Isabel at the revival meeting**)

• On your knees, mortals. Behold, I am Satan, your lord. Worship me and you shall profit. Fail me and you shall die! (**the Devil, speaking at one of Johnson's services**)

Spiritism
AKA Espiritismo

1961   Rating: ***   Guillermo Zetina as the Devil

Churubusco-Azteca. Written by Raphael Garcia Travesi and William Calderon Stell, inspired by the short story "The Monkey's Paw" by W. W. Jacobs; Photographed by Henry Wallace; Edited by Jorge Bustos; Music by Gustav C. Carrion; Produced by William Calderon Stell and K. Gordon Murray (English-language version); Directed by Benito Alazraki. B&W, 87 minutes.

Annotated Cast List

Jose Luis Jiminez (*Luis Howard*, businessman); Nora Vervan (*Mary*, his wife who becomes interested in spiritualism); Guillermo Zetina (the Devil); Rene Cardona, Jr. (*Rudolf*, their son); Mary Eugenia Saint Martin (*Aurora*, engaged to Rudolf); Jorge Mondragon (*Harry*, friend of Luis); Alicia Caro (*Amy*, his wife); Diana Ochoa (*Elvira*, psychic); Antonio Bravo (*Charles Pierpont*, head of occult society); Julissa Macedo (*Rosalee Pierpont*, his daughter); Beatriz Aguirre (*Stella Jean*, medium); Carmelita Gonzales (*Alice*, woman attending seance); Jorge Russek (*Larry Gray*, pilot employed by Rudolf).

Appraisal and Synopsis

K. Gordon Murray dubbed a large number of Mexican films for English-speaking audiences, beginning with *El Vampiro*

(1957), the film which sparked a fresh cycle of horror films in Mexico. Murray centered his operations at a sound lab in Coral Gables, Florida, where he also adapted Mexican serials, recutting them into feature films, as well as Westerns, fairy tales, and wrestling films featuring such popular figures as Santo, the masked hero of the ring, and *Las Luchadoras*, beautiful lady wrestlers. Murray remained active until the late 1960s. His productions featured nearly perfect lip sync but rather stilted dialogue, with "sir" used in practically every fifth sentence. "Excuse me, sir, but do you know the way to the haunted *hacienda*?" Murray's versions often anglicize or change the names of the characters, so in *Spiritism*, Amy was Carmen in the original, Stella Jean was Estercita, Charles Pierpont was Carlos Paz y Fuentes, and Larry Gray was Eduard Aguirre. The female name most commonly used by Murray is Martha, which seems to appear almost constantly, even when the name doesn't appear in the original production. These films became quite popular with numerous fans drawn by their wacky charm and brooding sense of atmosphere. *Espiritismo* is from the heyday of Murray's operations, and the picture was widely shown under the title *Spiritism*.

The opening scene shows Luis Howard ambling slowly into a church at night as his voice-over narrates the story of the cataclysm which has ruined his life. His tale begins at a psychic reading held by an acquaintance, Elvira, who goes into a trance and makes a series of tragic predictions about Luis and his wife, Mary. She warns that their lives will be upset by a crisis that will begin in a few weeks on their twenty-fourth wedding anniversary. Their son, Rudolf, will never wed Aurora, his fiancée, and Mary will have an encounter with the Prince of Darkness. If she resists him, all will be well, but if she falls for his temptations, then nothing can save her. Nonbelievers in the occult, Luis and Mary take these prophecies lightly, as do their friends, Harry and Amy, also at the seance.

On their wedding anniversary, Luis celebrates by handing his wife the paid-up deed on their home. After their party, Rudolf approaches them for a large loan, wanting to start his own crop-dusting business. Luis feels his scheme is too risky, but Rudolf badgers his mother into consenting to the idea. To finance their son, they again mortgage their home. In a short time, Rudolf's venture is on the ropes, and Mary has become fanatical about avoiding the loss of her home. While at church, she encounters Amy, who appears quite strange and unnatural. When Mary returns home, Luis tells her that Amy died the previous day. This loss unhinges Mary, changing her into a full-fledged spiritualist. She becomes a devoted follower of spiritualism and drags her reluctant husband to seances. During one elaborate seance, the spirit of Amy appears, convincing Luis that the medium is genuine. Mary decides to summon Satan to rescue her son's failing crop-dusting business. Mary is banned by the occult society after she invokes the Devil, who actually materializes and terrifies the group. They apparently drive him off, but a mysterious key appears in Mary's hand. Back at home, Luis falls into a trance, and the Devil comes to their door, bringing Mary a chest which he claims can solve her problems if she dares to use it. He explains that at one time he used the same box to test the disciples of Christ, implying that it corrupted Judas. The Devil leaves with a peal of thunder, reminding Mary that she received the key to it during the seance. When Luis awakens, he takes the chest and locks it away, saying, "There are some things man shouldn't touch."

The Devil then produces an overnight freeze that ruins the harvests of Rudolf's clients, who are unable to pay him. Financially ruined, he abandons his plans to marry Aurora. Desperate, Mary opens the box that evening and discovers a withered hand. Holding the hand, she wishes to receive a large sum of money. The fingers of the hand start to move as Luis enters the room. Astounded, he picks up the hand with tongs and places it in the fireplace. It crawls out of the flames and returns to the chest.

The next day, Luis and Mary learn that their son died in a plane crash while trying to fly home. A representative from the insurance company hands Mary a large check, payment in full from their son's insurance policy. Bereaved, Mary again turns to the withered hand to make another wish, that her son would return to her alive. He appears at their door moments later, disfigured, horribly mutilated, and in agony. Luis, shocked, grabs the hand and wishes his son back to the grave. Mary falls to the floor, and the chest and hand vanish as she dies of shock. Luis, his hair turned white, sobs in despair. The voice of a new narrator is introduced, warning of the dangers of spiritualism and other occult pursuits.

This picture, like most of K. Gordon Murray's films, is silly and absurd, yet enormously entertaining. The quality of the original Mexican production is rich in atmosphere and mood, and most of the performers play their roles with genuine relish. Other attempts to produce English-language versions of Mexican genre films, such as those by Jerry Warren, result in pictures that are literally unwatchable. Murray's versions, however, are fun and amusing in almost all cases, a tribute both to him and to the original filmmakers. Even purists who prefer the originals with or without subtitles respect Murray's products, which at the very least make these pictures available to a fresh audience, which probably never would have encountered them otherwise. In fact, the later Mexican genre films after 1970 remain virtually unknown north of the border, while the Murray versions have a cadre of fans. *Spiritism*, *Curse of the Doll People* (1960), *The Man and the Monster* (1958), and *The Witches' Mirror* (1960) are among the most colorful and diverting examples.

Performances

Guillermo Zetina was active in the Mexican film industry from 1943 through 1970, usually as a supporting cast member and character actor. His scene as the Devil is done without makeup, his diabolical countenance suggested purely by spotlighting from underneath, much the same effect that children use with a flashlight shining under the chin. Nevertheless, the minimal effect works. His dress is an ordinary, dark raincoat. Although he arrives in a downpour, his clothes are completely dry. The Devil speaks obliquely to Mary, promising nothing while giving her his poisoned gift, which he knows will only bring destruction. He doesn't even attempt to convince her to use it, merely comments that the decision is up to her. Although he arrives conventionally, ringing the doorbell, he leaves mysteriously, vanishing when Mary glances away. His scene lasts a mere two minutes, but it is the key moment of the film, the central event hinted at by Elvira in the opening scene. The irony is that the entire story hinges on crop dusting, which makes it all seem somewhat tongue-in-cheek. A number of Zetina's comments are odd as well and could be regarded as either straight drama or satire.

Notable Quotes

• If I thought it would help, I'd sell my soul to Satan.... After all, there is no such thing as the Devil in my opinion. (**Rudolf to his parents, speaking of raising money for a business scheme**)

• May all the benevolent spirits hear us. Turn back this sinister demon ... Form a wall around us to keep out the forces of evil. (**Charles Pierpont's response after Mary summons Satan**)

• This box you see here, it is Pandora's box. In its interior it contains all the virtue and all the wickedness in the world. (**the Devil, presenting his gift to Mary**)

• There are many who are helplessly driven by a desire to explore forbidden phenomenon. If with this picture, we are able to quench that unhealthy curiosity in some, we will consider our job well done. (**closing narration**)

Stay Tuned

1992   Rating: ***   Jeffrey Jones as the Devil

Morgan Creek. Written by Jim Jennewein, Tom S. Parker and Richard Siegal; Photographed by Peter Hyams; Edited by Peter E. Berger; Special Effects by John Nelson (supervisor); Music by Bruce Broughton; Produced by James G. Robinson; Directed by Peter Hyams. Color, 86 minutes.

Annotated Cast List

John Ritter (*Roy Knable*, TV addict); Pam Dawber (*Helen*, his wife); David Tom (*Darryl*, their son); Heather McComb (*Diane*, their daughter); Jeffrey Jones (*Spike*, the Devil); Bob Dishy (*Murray Seidenbaum*, neighbor trapped in Hell TV); Eugene Levy (*Crowley*, demoted demon); Erik King (*Pierce*, trainee); Don Calfa (*Wetzel*); John Blakewell Destry (*Sackler*, demonic assistant); Susan Blommaert (*Ducker*, demonic assistant); Gerry Nairn (TV announcer); Dale Wilson (*Guy Squirly*, game show host); Don Pardo (game show announcer); Lou Albano (wrestling ring announcer); Alan C. Peterson (referee); Ken Kramer (innkeeper); Gordon Maston (executioner); Janet Craig (*Miss Daisy*); Jimi DeFilippis (*Garf*); Colleen Winton (anchorwoman); Allen Schneider (android).

Appraisal and Synopsis

The plot of an earlier Devil movie, *Meet Mr. Lucifer* (1953), was conceived as a satire about television. Nearly forty years later, *Stay Tuned* tackled the issue far more successfully, adding a heaping dose of black humor. The approach of this film is reminiscent of "SCTV" which had several uproarious skits that were quite similar. One of their parodies was a game show called "Dante's Inferno" where contestants had to honestly admit their sins or they would be tossed into a fiery pit by demons. Another was a take-off on *The Exorcist* (1973) in which a possessed Linda Blair, played by Catherine O'Hara, hosted a fitness program where she rotates her head and tosses priests about for exercise. These same concepts are extended here to a feature-length story which is quite hilarious, if you enjoy black humor. The basic premise is that Mephistopheles, now known as Spike, has organized a multichannel television station to recruit fresh souls for Lucifer in hell. His main target is TV junkies, who he ensnares into signing a contract to test a new entertainment system. Of course, they fail to read the small print, and soon they are transported directly into their televisions where they face eternal damnation unless they are able to survive for twenty-four hours.

John Ritter plays Roy Knable, the ultimate couch potato, whose wife, Helen, feels completely neglected by him. She plans for them to spend a weekend away from their two kids, hoping to restore some romance to their marriage. Spike approaches Roy with his offer of a free trial of a home entertainment satellite system. Helen is outraged when she comes home to see the huge reception dish in the backyard, and while threatening to leave, both she and Roy are zapped into the dish, reappearing on a game show called "You Can't Win!" Helen's quick thinking enables them to win, and they advance to another program. At the control center, Spike is breaking in a new staff member, Pierce, explaining the intricacies of his grand design. When Crowley, another lackey, makes a comment about a soul who managed to survive, Spike becomes angry and demotes him to doing field work. He is exiled to the show, "Northern Overexposure," where he faces bitter cold and ravenous wolves. The Knables, surviving a match on a tag team wrestling show, also wind up on "Northern Overexposure," and Crowley teaches them a survival technique and instructs them on how to find and use conduits, passageways to another channel. Whenever things become too dangerous on one channel, they can escape to another. As the wolves attack, they plunge through a conduit.

At the Knable home, the children believe their parents have left on a weekend trip. Daughter Diane invites her friends over for a party, while son Darryl watches the new television. He is startled when he tunes in a Chuck Jones cartoon about two mice who look and sound like his parents. He quickly learns that they are trapped in the system, but his sister doesn't believe him when he tries to tell her.

The Knables become separated while escaping a cartoon cat. They eventually meet up in a *noir* detective film, and Diane finally spots her mother on the television. Darryl, a wiz at electronics, tries to construct a device that could recall them to the real world. Roy encounters Murray Seidenbaum, his neighbor who also became trapped in Hell TV. Murray gives Roy his remote control device after he is shot by a gangster with a tommy gun. Helen and Roy escape to a miniseries about the French Revolution called "Off with His Head," a parody of *The Scarlet Pimpernel*. They again bump into Crowley who tells them they only have to hide out for two more hours in order to survive. Roy is captured, however, and sentenced to the guillotine. Darryl manages to broadcast his voice onto the channel, and he imitates the voice of God, demanding that Roy be set free. The twenty-four hours expire, but Spike finds a loophole. He only signed a contract with Roy, who must be returned to the real world. But Helen was brought in by accident, so Spike figures that she has to find her own way out.

Back in the real world, Roy and his children plot to release Helen from Hell TV. She is transported to a Western by Spike, who ties her to a wagon filled with dynamite on the railroad tracks. Roy jumps back into the system to rescue her but gets diverted to a "Star Trek" episode, where he becomes Jean-Luc Picard, then shifts to a hockey game and a sitcom. Using his remote control to track down Helen, he finally has an epic sword fight with Spike, first on the set of an old swashbuckler and then in a music video. Roy finally transfers Spike to a channel controlled by Crowley. Roy saves Helen, and they return to reality by simply hitting the off button on the remote. Pierce, meanwhile, steps into Spike's shoes at Hell TV.

The best moments of *Stay Tuned* are the wild, crazy vignettes sprinkled throughout the film. The parody commercials are witty, and the Hell TV shows include "I Love Lucifer," "Meet the Mansons," "Three

Men and Rosemary's Baby," and "Driving Over Miss Daisy." Perhaps the grossest bit is a promo in which two elderly men fall victim to seizures with contrasting symptoms. As they collapse, the name of the show they are on is revealed as "Different Strokes." As the picture ends, upcoming shows for the next season of Hell TV are previewed.

Performances

Born in 1947, Jeffrey Jones is a versatile character actor who has played a wide variety of roles from Emperor Joseph II in *Amadeus* (1984) to the scene-stealing scientist possessed by an alien in *Howard the Duck* (1986) and Criswell the TV psychic in *Ed Wood* (1994). He plays an updated Mephistopheles who prefers his new moniker, Spike, as a ruthless, cutthroat executive desperate to please his boss, Lucifer. Jones' Devil is a nervous, insecure technocrat, always fearful that a single slip-up will cost him his position as the number one henchman in hell. His interplay with his control room lackeys can become a little tiring and one-note. Fortunately, he is drawn into the action confronting Roy in the last quarter of the picture, which is lively and clever, unlike the stagnant control room scenes. He also works well with "SCTV" alumnus Eugene Levy, who provides hilarious commentary throughout as Crowley. His name, no doubt, refers to Aleister Crowley, the self-proclaimed Satanist and black magician. John Ritter is somewhat inconsistent as Roy, but he does an adequate job overall. His most interesting moment is when he finds himself as Jack Tripper on "Three's Company," the role that made him famous. Ritter stares directly into the camera and screams, a priceless moment. He is also excellent in the French Revolution sequence, the longest segment in the film.

Notable Quotes

• Six hundred and sixty-six channels of heart-pounding, skull-blasting entertainment! Comedy! Drama! Hot oil aerobics! It's like nothing you have ever seen, brother.... Some people would give their souls for a system like this, figuratively speaking. (**Spike, making his pitch to Roy**)

• Of course, win or lose, every contestant takes home a set of *Encyclopedia Satanica*. (**game show announcer Don Pardo to the audience**)

The Story of Mankind

1957   Rating: *   Vincent Price as the Devil

Warner Brothers. Written by Irwin Allen and Charles Bennett, based on the novel by Hendrik Willem Van Loon; Photographed by Nick Musuraca; Edited by Gene Palmer and Roland Gross; Special Effects by Ruth K. Greenfield; Music by Paul Sawtell; Produced and Directed by Irwin Allen. Color, 100 minutes.

Annotated Cast List

Ronald Colman (the Spirit of Mankind); Vincent Price (*Mr. Scratch*, the Devil); Nick Cravat (his apprentice); Cedric Hardwicke (judge of the Heavenly Court); Don Megowan (primitive man); Burt Nelson (2nd primitive man); Nancy

Miller (primitive woman); John Carradine (*Khufu*, Egyptian pharaoh); Marvin Miller (*Armana*, Khufu's advisor); Francis X. Bushman (*Moses*); Dani Crayne (*Helen of Troy*); Charles Coburn (*Hippocrates*, father of medicine); Virginia Mayo (*Cleopatra*); Bart Mattson (Cleopatra's brother); Reginald Sheffield (*Julius Caesar*); Helmut Dantine (*Mark Antony*); Peter Lorre (*Nero*); Ziva Rodann (concubine); Cathy O'Donnell (Christian martyr); Melinda Marx (her child); David Bond (her male companion); Hedy Lamarr (*Joan of Arc*); Henry Daniell (*Bishop of Beauvais*); Leonard Mudie (inquisitor); William Schallert (*Earl of Warwick*); Tudor Owen (*Leonardo da Vinci*); Anthony Dexter (*Christopher Columbus*); Chico Marx (monk who advises Columbus); Agnes Morehead (*Queen Elizabeth I*); Cesar Romero (Spanish ambassador); Sam Harris (English nobleman); Reginald Gardiner (*William Shakespeare*); Edward Everett Horton (*Sir Walter Raleigh*); Groucho Marx (*Peter Minuit*); Harry Ruby (indian); Abraham Sofaer (chief); Eden Hartford (*Laughing Water*, chief's daughter); Harpo Marx (*Sir Isaac Newton*); Marie Wilson (*Marie Antoinette*); Franklin Pangborn (*Marquis de Varennes*); Dennis Hopper (*Napoleon Bonaparte*); Marie Windsor (*Josephine de Beauharnais*); Austin Green (*Abraham Lincoln*); Jim Ameche (*Alexander Graham Bell*); Bobby Watson (*Adolf Hitler*); George E. Stone, Alexander Lockwood, Richard Cutting, Toni Gerry, Angelo Rossitto.

Appraisal and Synopsis

It is fairly obvious that *The Story of Mankind* is a turkey, the only question is whether it is an entertaining one or not. For lovers of history, the picture can be aggravating with its blatant distortions and

The Devil (Vincent Price) points out one of his favorite individuals, Emperor Nero (Peter Lorre), as the Spirit of Mankind (Ronald Colman) seems more interested in his meal.

sweeping generalizations. Of course, Van Loon's books, such as *The Story of Mankind* and *Van Loon's Lives* offer a similarly distorted and often inaccurate portrait of events, which is why they are classified as fiction. If you regard the picture as an exercise in high camp, it is far easier to swallow, and on those terms it is a hoot, with Peter Lorre's cameo as Nero a hilarious high point of parody. Irwin Allen probably would have done better if he had done the whole film tongue-in-cheek as with the Marx Brothers' vignettes. Instead, when it attempts to be serious, it goes from being merely bad to being truly awful, with the Cleopatra, Joan of Arc, and Marie Antoinette segments being the poorest. On the other hand, Agnes Morehead and Cesar Romero bring the right semi-mocking tone to their portrayals of Queen Elizabeth and the Spanish ambassador. Bobby Watson's Hitler rendition is the only one that has a genuine ring.

The entire film is largely constructed around outtakes from many other pictures, such as *The Land of the Pharaohs* (1955), *Serpent of the Nile* (1953), and *Sign of the Pagan* (1954), with clips of the film's cast clumsily spliced in. Irwin Allen was so taken with the technique that years later he built a television series, "Time Tunnel," around the same concept. Some of Allen's cameos are clever, with Jim Ameche, Don Ameche's sound-alike brother who had a distinguished career as a radio personality, playing Alexander Graham Bell. The tone of the film-flip flops from being preachy to being silly to being just plain stupid. At times, the tenor seems anti-American, with most of the nation's history reduced to massacring Indians and promoting slavery. France is similarly maligned, with Napoleon, for example, depicted exclusively as a conquering madman instead of as a codifier of laws and champion of the rights of man. England, however, is given a pass for its national flaws, and one would never guess that the same England portrayed as "heroically" resisting Napoleon simultaneously was making war on America, attempting to stifle liberty while burning down the White House.

In a nutshell, this pseudosaga has a framing story with heaven deciding to hold a tribunal to judge whether mankind is worth saving and if Earth should be permitted to explode the super–H bomb, a new weapon promulgated by the Devil, which would destroy the planet. As spokesman for the human race, one person combining the essence of all mankind is selected to present the case for celestial intervention. Arguing against interference is Satan himself. The celestial high judge, played by Sir Cedric Hardwicke, who often sports Harry Potter-type glasses, permits the litigants to visit any period in history to make their case. Despite having total mastery over time, the court continues to rush the arguments, saying there is a deadline by which a decision must be made. Similar inconsistencies plague the entire plot. The Spirit of Mankind and the Devil skip and jump through human history, spending time with Khufu, Cleopatra, Joan of Arc, Leonardo da Vinci, Columbus, Sir Walter Raleigh, and Adolf Hitler. Each time the Spirit of Mankind discusses the progress of humans, the Devil counters with an equally powerful argument highlighting the evil of man. As a summary, the human advocate presents an infant, the man of tomorrow. The Devil notes that this last witness plays with a toy gun and toy sword, but the Spirit of Mankind notes the sword is merely a pencil case (although he doesn't explain what use are pencils to a baby). In the end, the court cops out and reneges on rendering a decision. This, of course, makes no sense because "at eleven o'clock" mankind was going to detonate the bomb and destroy itself. So it seems there had to be a reprieve after all, to allow the court more time to decide if man is more inclined toward evil or good. At this point, the film abruptly ends, leaving everything unresolved, making the whole purpose of the picture meaningless.

Performances

Vincent Price delivers the only completely successful performance in the entire film. It is his reading alone that retains the interest of the audience. Price's charming, sly, and unctuous Devil is nothing short of magnificent, and it is a shame his performance is wasted on such a third-rate production. He delivers all of his lines with zest and panache. Many of his comments have double and even triple meanings. For instance, while in the studio of Leonardo da Vinci, Price comments, "I never pretended to be an art expert." In real life, of course, Price's passion was fine art, and he was considered one of the nation's experts. Price is subtly made up as the Devil, with carefully manicured beard and a widow's peak, but no horns, tail, or other outward signs of his identity except for a pitchfork, which he ditches after his initial appearance. Price wears an elegantly tailored Edwardian suit with a cravat instead of a tie. Perhaps it is another inside joke since his apprentice is played by screen veteran Nick Cravat. A number of other oddities stand out in his part. Early in the film, he makes use of a phone without wires, seemingly the precursor of cell phones. He uses the name Mr. Scratch, just like Walter Huston in *The Devil and Daniel Webster*, and if the setting of this courtroom is heaven, then the Devil is certainly pleading his case in hostile territory. In the film's narration, the setting of the trial is described as being in outer space, which again lacks logic. The courtroom scenes are filmed among billowing clouds, but the judge has a substantial desk, and there is a mammoth clock floating in midair. About twenty spectators watch the trial, seated in a semicircle. These persons seem drawn from various periods of history. Perhaps they won some celestial lottery to view the proceedings. Neither Price, Colman, nor Hardwicke takes any notice of these spectators. A few years later, Price appeared as a guest star on Irwin Allen's TV series "Voyage to the Bottom of the Sea." Ronald Colman makes a sincere effort in this, his last film, but he is no match for Price in the proceedings. Colman seems tired and uninvolved for much of the picture. It is also interesting to note that this picture is the last one in which the Marx Brothers appear, although they have no scenes together. In addition, Groucho's young daughter Melinda and wife, Eden Hartford, appear in the film. Perhaps Groucho insisted on a package deal. Most of the cast seem stilted and artificial in their roles, and one can surmise that their performances were all done in one take, accomplished with the minimum of time and effort.

Notable Quotes

- As for me, I am quite a busy fellow. I have spent quite enough time getting man to see and do things my way.... Time is money, and man does not have a patent on evil. (**the Devil in his opening remarks**)

- This is the court of Nero, evil and depraved, whose debauchery and perversion surpassed even the wildest and wicked dreams of the most deluded. And this is Nero, nursed on a witch's venom, twisted by endless orgies, this madman knew no end to violence, no limit to lunacy. (**the Devil, introducing one of his favorites**)

- We therefore reserve judgment in order to allow mankind more time to set his house in order at the earliest possible date. (**the judge, postponing his verdict**)

The Student of Prague
AKA Der Student von Prag

1913   Rating: *****

John Cottowt as the Devil

Bioscop Films. Written by Hanns Heinz Ewers and Robert Lee (English titles); Photographed by Guido Seeber; Produced by Paul Davidsohn; Directed by Stellan Rye and Paul Wegener. B&W, silent, 60 minutes.

Annotated Cast List

Paul Wegener (*Balduin*, poor student of Prague and his mirror image); John Cottowt (*Scapinelli*, the Devil); Lothar Korner (*Count Schwarzenberg*, wealthy nobleman); Grete Berger (*Margit*, his daughter); Fritz Weidemann (*Baron Waldis Schwarzenberg*, Margit's cousin and fiancé); Lyda Salmanova (*Lyduschka*, gypsy dancer in love with Balduin).

Appraisal and Synopsis

This original version of *The Student of Prague* is one of the landmarks of world cinema. It has been cited by various film historians as the feature-length masterpiece that served as the springboard for the German school of film. Viewers expecting a stagy, studio-bound, primitive effort will be stunned by the sophistication, restrained and unexaggerated acting, and breathtaking location footage. The film is Gothic in flavor, a natural extension of nineteenth-century German Romanticism. It also prefigures the expressionistic style that became the trademark of the German silent film. Many diverse elements combined to create this milestone. Paul Wegener, a stage veteran who had worked since 1906 with the extraordinary director Max Reinhardt, had a natural instinct for the new medium of film. Wegener claimed he was convinced to launch his film career when he became intrigued with the onscreen concept of being able to play cards with his *Doppelgänger* (literally, "double walker" in German, referring to his twin self). With the use of a split screen, this effect could easily be achieved. Although the Danish filmmaker Stellan Rye was credited as sole director, most sources credit Wegener equally for the final film, which bore all the trademarks of pictures Wegener later directed, starting with *Die Augen des Ole Brandis* and *Der Golem*, both 1914. The scenario was written by Hanns Heinz Ewers, who years later became a devoted Nazi and helped to create the image of Horst Wessel as a symbolic martyr for the party. Ewers based his concept for *The Student of Prague* on various sources, including *Peter Schlemiel* by Adalbert von Chamisso, Edgar Allan Poe's "William Wilson" and various tales of E. T. A. Hoffmann, such as "The Doubles." The cinematography of Guido Seeber is breathtaking and features excellent use of location footage in Prague, as well as sophisticated techniques including the use of deep focus. The picture seems years ahead of its time in almost every regard, and it can be fully enjoyed today not as an example of antique filmmaking but as a fully developed *chef d'oeuvre*. The synopsis for the original is very similar to the 1926 remake with Conrad Veidt.

The story is set in Prague in 1820. Balduin (sometimes called Baldwin in English-language prints) is a popular and colorful student, the life of every party, and the best fencer in Prague. He is a spendthrift, however, and always broke. His predicament has caught the attention of Scapinelli, a notorious money lender who is actually the Devil. At a cafe, Balduin comments to Scapinelli that he needs to meet a rich heiress. Balduin is pursued by Lyduschka, a beautiful gypsy dancer who is infatuated with him.

Prague's most influential family is headed by Count Schwarzenberg. He has arranged for his daughter, Margit, to marry Baron Waldis Schwarzenberg, her cousin, in a loveless match. While participating in a fox hunt, Margit's horse runs wild, and she is thrown into a lake. Balduin, walking nearby with Scapinelli, plunges in and rescues her, and the grateful Margit gives him a medallion with her likeness as a keepsake. Balduin inquires after her the following day, but the impoverished student is given a cool reception by Count Schwarzenberg. Scapinelli visits Balduin in his room with an amazing proposal. He will give the student a small fortune in gold in exchange for the right to take anything he wants from his room. Looking around his shabby surroundings, Balduin comments that he has nothing of value and signs a contract with his visitor. Scapinelli selects Balduin's reflection in the mirror as his prize, and the reflection steps out of the mirror and walks off with his new master. Only at this moment does the astounded Balduin realize he has made a deal with the Devil.

Balduin uses his new wealth to secretly court Margit. He declares his amorous intentions to her, and she seems hesitant yet responsive to his advances. He slips her a note concealed in a handkerchief that suggests a secret rendezvous in the isolated old Jewish cemetery. Margit agrees to come. Lyduschka, spying on them, manages to obtain the incriminating note, which she brings to Baron Waldis. Balduin and Margit pledge their mutual love. Their tryst is interrupted by the appearance of Balduin's *Doppelgänger*. Baron Waldis confronts Balduin in his room, challenging him to a duel with sabers. When Count Schwarzenberg learns of this development, he visits the student and begs him not to kill Baron Waldis, his nephew and his only remaining relative bearing the name Schwarzenberg. Balduin gives his solemn promise to spare him.

At the appointed hour for the duel, Balduin encounters his double, carrying a bloodied saber. He is stunned to learn that his *Doppelgänger* replaced him in the dispute and killed the baron. As word of his betrayal of the count spreads, Balduin becomes an outcast. His regular card-playing companions walk away from their game. His double shows up, challenging him to gamble for his identity. Balduin goes to an inn where Lyduschka throws herself at him, but he spurns her.

The student sneaks into Margit's room at the Schwarzenberg estate, and they have a brief reconciliation. When she notices that her lover casts no reflection in the mirror, the young woman recoils in fear. The *Doppelgänger* appears, and Balduin rants at him while Margit faints. The student flees in terror as his reflection continues to stalk him. Returning to his room, Balduin loads his gun. When his reflection appears, he fires at him, and the image of his double vanishes. At first, the student is elated and shouts, "Redeemed." Then Balduin looks in the mirror to confirm that his reflection has returned to normal. He suddenly feels weak and realizes that he has been shot. In killing his *Doppelgänger*, he has only killed himself. Scapinelli enters the room in triumph. He tips his hat to Balduin's corpse and flamboyantly tears up his contract with the student. The final shot of the picture shows Balduin's ghostly figure fading into darkness as he sits astride his own grave.

The Student of Prague electrified the audiences of its day. The depiction of the *Doppelgänger* was flawless, and it took hold of the public's imagination. Writers of psychology even based treatises on it. In many ways, this motion picture paved the way for the richness and magic of numerous films to come. A portion of the critical accolades awarded by film historians to *The Cabinet of Dr. Caligari* (1919) are equally deserved by *The Student of Prague*.

Performances

John Cottowt made a mere handful of films, but they included some of the most memorable classics of the silent cinema. He was the exhibitor in the *Waxworks* (1924), Paul Leni's masterpiece of expressionism. He was Dr. Van Helsing in *Nosferatu* (1922), the prototype of all vampire films, as well as Scapinelli, the first Devil to appear in a feature film. His concept became the model for Werner Krauss as both Dr. Caligari and Scapinelli in the 1926 remake of *The Student of Prague*. The period from 1820 through 1850 is sometimes referred to as the Biedermeier period in terms of costume and style, named after the fictional Gottlieb Biedermeier, a satirical figure who later appeared in German magazines. Early German films enjoyed setting their action in this period, and Scapinelli typifies the dress of the Biedermeier-era villain, including dark frock coat, black top hat, and umbrella. Cottowt plays Scapinelli as a lively and clever Devil who delighted in laying the most extravagant traps, for his own enjoyment as much as to secure his goals. A number of sources referring to *The Student of Prague* mistakenly report that Balduin sold his soul to the Devil, which is untrue. Scapinelli is far more devious, creating a new wrinkle on an old ploy. The concept of selecting an item from a room is an old one, used in fairy tales, and the item selected is usually one completely unsuspected. John Cottowt's Devil is far craftier than anyone could anticipate. John Cottowt retired from films shortly after the appearance of sound, but he lived until 1949. Paul Wegener is both the strong and weak point of the film. His acting is restrained and excellent, but his bulky physique gives him the appearance of a middle-aged butcher, and it is simply too much to accept him as a young student. Lyda Salmanova was extraordinary as Lyduschka, and her acrobatics are impressive as she climbs inaccessible walls with ease. Her performance no doubt inspired Musidora in the role of Irma Vep for the French serial *Les Vampires* (1915). Salmanova became one of Wegener's five wives.

Notable Quotes

- I am no god nor can I a demon be,
  Yet scornfully I speak your very own name!
  For wherever you are shall I always be until the hour decreed,
  By your headstone and sit over your grave.

  (poem by Alfred de Musset that opens and closes the film)

- What an odd little fellow you are. Something from my poor little room? Take what you wish. (**Balduin to Scapinelli, before realizing he is the Devil**)

- Say what you will, who gives you the right to persecute me? (**Balduin to his *Doppelgänger***)

The Student of Prague
AKA The Man Who Cheated Life *and* Der Student von Prag

1926   Rating: ****   Werner Krauss as the Devil

Sokal Films. Written by Hanns Heinz Ewers and Henrik Galeen; Photographed by Gunther Krampf and Erich Nitzschmann; Produced by H. R. Sokal; Directed by Henrik Galeen. B&W, silent, 87 minutes.

Annotated Cast List

Conrad Veidt (*Balduin*, poor student of Prague, and his mirror image); Werner Krauss (*Scapinelli*, the Devil); Fritz Alberti (*Count Schwarzenberg*, wealthy nobleman); Agnes Esterhazy (*Margit*, his daughter); Ferdinand von Alten (*Baron Waldis Schwarzenberg*, Margit's cousin and fiancé); Elizza La Porte (*Lyduschka*, flower girl in love with Balduin); Erich Kober, Sylvia Tort, Max Maximilian, Marian Alma.

Appraisal and Synopsis

Although a masterpiece in its own right, the 1926 remake directed by Henrik Galeen is a less significant film than the earleir version overall. The 1913 *Student of Prague* was years ahead of its time, trailblazing new directions in cinema, but the 1926 version seems old-fashioned in concept and presentation. Its major strengths include a magnificent portrayal by Conrad Veidt as Balduin, and a more brooding, intense climax in the second half of the film. Conversely, the first half is less interesting than the original and gets bogged down somewhat with lengthy scenes of the students' partying and the Schwarzenbergs' hunting party, which delay the development of the main story. The plot is virtually identical, although Ewers fleshes out some of the scenes with greater detail. Balduin's disgrace after his double kills the baron is more pronounced. In fact, he is expelled from the university and totally ostracized. Another wonderful scene involves Balduin's appearance at a party, where he has to avoid the mirrored wall lest his missing reflection is noticed. There is also a beautifully filmed windstorm in which Scapinelli appears particularly diabolical. There are also a handful of minor changes. Margit doesn't fall into the lake, but Balduin stops her runaway horse and catches her when she is thrown. Scapinelli uses his supernatural powers more frequently, and he uses magic to maneuver Balduin's incriminating note to the ground in front of Lyduschka, who simply stole it in the first version. Lyduschka is presented more as a flower girl than as a gypsy, although her function in the plot is basically the same. Balduin's lateness to his duel with Baron Waldis is explained by the breakdown of his carriage, and Balduin races madly through the woods, while the editing intercuts to his double replacing him in the duel. This greatly improves the sequence from the original version in which Balduin just happens to be late. The most important differences involve the stalking by the *Doppelgänger* during the climax, which is far more deliberate, effective, and menacing in the remake. These scenes represent German expressionism in full bloom, with exceptional use of night photography. Incidentally, a third remake was filmed in 1935 by Arthur Robison in a version which downplayed the role of Scapinelli. This sound version was largely panned and quickly forgotten.

Performances

As Scapinelli, Werner Krauss makes an excellent Devil, but his performance is largely patterned after John Cottowt's 1913 reading, but his makeup makes Krauss' Scapinelli appear somewhat younger. He brings his own zest to the role which makes his performance more integral to the film, although in the second half, he disappears completely from the picture, leaving the *Doppelgänger* to do his dirty work. Scapinelli does not even reappear in Balduin's room after the student's demise, a serious shortcoming in the remake, since Scapinelli's moment of triumph was the highlight of the original film. Krauss is more diabolical than Cottowt on the whole, and he has to work harder to realize his aims. acting at moments like an orchestra conductor controlling events. His Devil doesn't seem to be able to relish events as much as Cottowt's Scapinelli, who has more fun with the part. Krauss was one of the major stars of the German silent screen, frequently appearing opposite Emil Jannings, one of the top actors of the era. Krauss played Maximilien Robespierre to Jannings' Danton in *Danton* (1921), Iago to Jannings' Othello in *Othello* (1922), and Orgon to Jannings' Tartuffe in *Tartuffe* (1925). Still, Krauss' most memorable role was as the sinister Caligari in *The Cabinet of Dr. Caligari* (1919). His bit as Jack the Ripper in *Waxworks* (1924) was also unforgettable. In his later years, Krauss worked in the Nazi-controlled German cinema, appearing in such productions as *Jud Süss* (1940) and *Paracelsus* (1943). Werner Krauss appeared in additional films through the mid-1950s, and he died in 1959. The exceptional Conrad Veidt is sensational as Balduin, bringing greater credibility, pathos, and genuine melancholy to the part than did Paul Wegener. He is also more ominous as the *Doppelgänger*. Fritz Alberti is somewhat more sympathetic as Count Schwarzenberg in this version, and Agnes Esterhazy makes a far more appealing Margit. Elizza La Porte, however, is rather insipid compared to Lyda Salmanova's smoldering Lyduschka.

Notable Quotes

• Here lies Balduin. He fought with the Devil and lost. (**epitaph on Balduin's tombstone, which opens and closes the film**)

• The Devil has his fingers in this game. (**friend's comment to Balduin as he abandons his card game**)

• The student Balduin is hereby dismissed. His motives for the duel with Baron Waldis were questionable, and his actions were unpardonable. (**notice by the dean of student affairs**)

Switch

1991   Rating: ***   Bruce Martyn Payne as the Devil

Warner Brothers. Written by Blake Edwards; Photographed by Dick Bush; Edited by Robert Pergament; Special Effects by Industrial Light and Magic; Music by Henry Mancini; Produced by Tony Adams; Directed by Blake Edwards. Color, 103 minutes.

Annotated Cast List

Perry King (*Steve Brooks*, Murdered ad executive); Ellen Barkin (*Amanda Brooks*, his female alter ego); Jimmy Smits (*Walter Stone*, Steve's best friend); JoBeth Williams (*Margo Brofman*, Steve's murderer); Lorraine Bracco (*Sheila Faxton*, owner of cosmetic company); Tony Roberts (*Arnold Friedkin*, Steve's boss); Bruce Martyn Payne (the Devil); Richard Provost (male voice of God); Linda Gary (female voice of God); Lysette Anthony (*Liz*, Margo's friend); Victoria Mahoney (*Felicia*, Margo's second friend); Basil Hoffman (*Higgins*, apartment house manager); Catherine Keener (Steve's secretary); Kevin Kilner (*Dan Jones*, new ad executive); J. M. J. Bullock (Margo's psychic); Diana Chisney (*Mrs. Witherspoon*, Steve's neighbor); David Loohl (*Caldwell*, defense attorney); Virginia Morris (assistant DA); Savant Tanney (*Harcrow*, trial judge); James Harper (*Laster*, police lieutenant); John Lafayette (police sergeant); Robert Clotworthy (bailiff); Ben Hartigan (minister); F. William Parker (barber); David Gale (doctor); Faith Minton (*Nancy*, bouncer in lesbian bar).

Appraisal and Synopsis

Switch is an amusing role-reversal comedy about the battle of the sexes by the talented veteran Blake Edwards. The entire success of the film rests on the performance of Ellen Barkin as an obnoxious male who finds his persona transformed into the body of a beautiful woman. Almost all of the humor is based on Barkin's unique, extravagant, and over-the-top reading. If you buy it, the picture is a total laugh riot. If you don't, it is repetitious and tedious. Barkin, by the way, was married at one time to Gabriel Byrne, the Devil from *End of Days* (1999).

The song "Both Sides Now" plays during the opening credits which appear over clouds in the sky. Womanizer Steve Brooks is invited to a surprise party by three of his former girlfriends, Margo, Liz, and Felicia. After luring him into a hot tub, they tell him the surprise is that they intend to kill him. They attempt to drown him and fail, so Margo shoots him in the chest as he lumbers after them. Steve suddenly finds himself in a black vacuum, and the voice of God, which has both a male and female half, explains that he deserves heaven except for the fact that he has treated women poorly his entire life. In fact, every woman he has ever known has disliked him. So God decides to return him to Earth in order to find one female with positive feelings for him. If he succeeds, he can proceed to heaven, otherwise he will be sent to hell. Steve awakens back in his apartment, where the Devil is waiting. He protests that God's test is unfair, because Steve will merely pour on his charm to win over a new conquest. Instead, the Devil suggests that Steve should be transformed into a woman while conducting his search. God agrees to Satan's proposal, and Steve is immediately changed into a beautiful blonde woman. Stunned by this development, Steve screams and passes out. The neighbors in his New York townhouse call the manager to investigate. Improvising, Steve says his name is Amanda, Steve's half sister, who is minding his apartment.

Amanda heads to Margo's house and demands her help. Since Margo killed Steve, Amanda now demands that Margo help him adjust to being a woman. At first doubtful, Margo is eventually convinced and helps find a wardrobe for Amanda. Next, Amanda cooks up an explanation for Steve's disappearance by claiming that he went to Tahiti like Gauguin to start a new life. Amanda manages to take over Steve's job as an ad executive, since she knows all about the misdeeds of the agency boss, Arnold Friedkin. Amanda reveals his true identity to Walter Stone, Steve's best friend, who also works at the agency.

Amanda's behavior is a comedy of errors, as all of her mannerisms remain masculine while her body is curvaceous and feminine. Amanda finds herself barely able to walk in high heels and still finds herself staring at every beautiful woman who passes by. Amanda undertakes a search to find a girl who liked him as Steve, but everyone from his secretary to his old high school dates report that Steve was a total creep. Amanda/Steve becomes confused as to his/her sexual identity when the job brings him into contact with Sheila Faxton, the owner of a cosmetic firm whose account is needed by the ad agency. Sheila is a lesbian who is attracted to Amanda, who finds the situation frightening and confusing. One night, the Devil shows up with a proposition that Amanda abandon her search since it is hopeless. He offers Amanda a job as one of his recruiters. When she refuses, the Devil proposes that she could bear his child in exchange for special treatment. Stunned, Amanda again refuses, and the Devil delivers a warning that time is running out.

At a local bar, Amanda and Walter get involved in a brawl, and Amanda brings her drunken friend home to spend the night. The next morning, Amanda learns that they had sex during the night and is outraged over the loss of her virginity. Steve's bullet-ridden body is found in the East River, where Margo, Liz, and Felicia dumped it after the murder. Margo plants the murder weapon at Amanda's apartment, and the police arrest Amanda as Steve's murderer. At the trial, Amanda reveals that she is really Steve, and she is committed to an asylum. Amanda learns she is pregnant but refuses an abortion. She reluctantly agrees to marry Walter for the sake of the child. When the baby is born, it is a girl who naturally responds to her mother. At this point, Amanda dies, and the love of the baby earns for Steve his place in heaven. As the film ends, Steve is uncertain whether to be a male or a female angel, and God grants him additional time to make a final decision.

The conclusion of the story is basically a cop-out, since the baby never knew Steve as Steve. She only responded to Amanda as her mother. The Devil would certainly have grounds for another complaint, but he seems to have given up this round with God as a lost cause. Edwards' screenplay, however, could provide no other possible resolution, and by the fade-out it appears that Amanda/Steve will spend eternity in sexual limbo. On the whole, Edwards manages his material fairly well, sometimes a bit obvious but nevertheless amusing as he explores the issue of sexual identity. The only other major flaw in his story was the overly brief screen time provided to Perry King as Steve. If the audience had been given more time to get to know Steve and understand his character, then the transformation would have been far more effective. As written, the switch is too abrupt to be fully successful.

Performances

Ellen Barkin totally dominates the film in a bravura reading that is unique. Jimmy Smits, as Walter, is exceptional in complementing her performance and helping to make it more believable. As the Devil, Bruce Martyn Payne appears too briefly to make a major impact on the story. There is nothing diabolical about his demeanor or dress, a casual dark suit. In his first scene, Payne merely looks up at the ceiling as he converses with God, who remains unseen. At one point, his expression suggests that he has taken this route before with God over Job. In his second appearance, his approach is more subtle. After Amanda fails to respond to his job offer to be one of his agents, he subtly endeavors to provoke Amanda/Steve's sexual confusion. Unfortunately, the script doesn't offer the Devil any additional opportunity to undermine his prey, and his last appearance is a brief glimpse of him on television in the guise of the newscaster who breaks the story of the discovery of Steve's body. Payne does well in the part, leaving the audience wishing for more. Payne appeared in many films, as well as on television in his native Great Britain. Among his credits with a supernatural theme are *The Keep* (1983), *The Howling VI* (1991), and *Necronomicon* (1994).

Notable Quotes

- I wish to lodge a complaint.... I have as much right to Steve Brooks' soul as you do. (**the Devil to God**)
- I'm going to get you anyway. Come along now, and I'll guarantee you a helluva time. (**the Devil to Amanda**)
- Do you want to hedge your bet with me? Make eternity a little less hellish? (**the Devil**)
  What did you have in mind? (**Amanda**)
  Did you see *Rosemary's Baby*? (**the Devil**)

Tales from the Crypt

1972   Rating: ***   Ralph Richardson as the Devil

Amicus. Written by Milton Subotsky; Photographed by Norman Warwick and John Harris; Edited by Teddy Darvas; Music by Douglas Gamley and Johann Sebastian Bach; Produced by Max J. Rosenberg and Milton Subotsky; Directed by Freddie Francis. Color, 92 minutes.

Annotated Cast List

Ralph Richardson (the Cryptkeeper, actually the Devil); Geoffrey Baldon (tour guide); Joan Collins (*Joanne Clayton*, woman lost in crypt); Ian Hendry (*Carl Maitland*, businessman lost in crypt); Robin Phillips (*James Elliot*, young man lost in crypt); Richard Greene (*Ralph Jason*, bankrupt collector lost in crypt); Nigel Patrick (*William Rogers*, retired major lost in crypt). **First story:** Marty Goddey (*Richard Clayton*, Joanne's murdered husband); Chloe Franks (*Carol Clayton*, Joanne's young daughter); Oliver MacGreevy (maniac dressed as Santa

Claus). **Second story:** Susan Denny (Carl Maitland's wife); Sharon Clere (Carl's daughter); Paul Clere (Carl's son); Angie Grant (*Susan Blake*, Carl's mistress). **Third story:** Peter Cushing (*Arthur Grimsdyke*, rubbish collector); David Markham (*Edward Elliot*, stuffy realtor); Edward Evans (*Ramsay*, town councilor); Dan Caulfield (postman); Ann Sears, Irene Gawne, Kay Adrian (neighbors). **Fourth story:** Barbara Murray (*Enid Jason*, Ralph's wife); Roy Dotrice (*Charles Gregory*, Ralph's solicitor). **Fifth story:** Patrick Magee (*George Carter*, group leader in Elmridge Home for the Blind); Tony Wall (attendant); Harry Locke (cook); Carl Bernard, John Barrard, Chris Cannon, Hugo de Vernier, Ernest C. Jennings, Louis Mansi (blind men).

Appraisal and Synopsis

This film was inspired by the comic book series created by Al Feldstein, Johnny Craig, and Bill Gaines. Screenwriter and producer Milton Subotsky takes a darker, more somber view of the Cryptkeeper, who in this version turns out to be the Devil. As originally conceived, the Cryptkeeper wasn't the Devil, but a campy, wise-cracking animated corpse who served as host and storyteller for a series of scary stories. This is how he was presented in the television series "Tales from the Crypt" and several later movies, such as *Demon Night* (1995). In the Amicus film, the Cryptkeeper does not engage the audience but painstakingly confronts his five "guests," explaining to them why they are there and preparing them for an eternity in hell.

The film begins with a montage of moody scenes of Highgate Cemetery in London, while Bach's *Toccata and Fugue in D Minor* thunders on the organ. A large group of people gather underground to take a tour of the catacombs to which the persecuted had fled during the bloody reign of terror of Henry VIII. The guide warns the crowd that the catacombs are dangerous labyrinths and to stick close to him. Five tourists get lost after one of them, Joanne Clayton, loses her brooch and goes back to retrieve it. They wander aimlessly for some time before descending into a cryptlike vault illuminated by flaming torches. The wall closes behind them, and they become trapped in the dark enclosure, which contains five stone blocks positioned in a semicircle before a larger object resembling a throne. A cowled man dressed all in black greets them mysteriously, explaining that all their questions will be answered in good time. He instructs them to sit and then addresses them one at a time, projecting images to them of their immediate plans.

These five visions are shared by the audience. The first story involves Joanne Clayton, wealthy socialite and mother. She is planning to murder her spouse on Christmas Eve. She sends her daughter to bed and then smashes her husband on the head with a poker. She throws his body into the cellar and tries to arrange the scene as if it were an accident. During her grisly task, she turns up the volume on the radio as it plays Christmas carols, so her daughter will not hear her. A radio bulletin broadcasts that a violent mental patient has escaped from the nearby asylum. He is believed to be wearing a Santa Claus outfit. Joanne locks all of the windows and doors and is alarmed when an intruder attempts to enter. Moments later, her daughter appears shouting, "He's here, Mommy. I let him in! It's Santa." The madman bursts in and overpowers Joanne, strangling her. A major clue in this story is that Joanne's Christmas gift from her husband is the same brooch that caused her to become lost. This would indicate to sharp-eyed viewers that the events of the story are set in the past, not the future.

The Cryptkeeper then turns to Carl Maitland, who claims he is on his way home to see his wife and children. His vision reveals that Carl is actually planning to run away with his mistress, Susan. As they head off, Susan takes the wheel, and Carl has a terrible dream that the car is in a crack-up. Stunned, Carl wanders home on foot, but his wife flees in horror from him. He goes to Susan's apartment and finds her blind and mourning for her lover who died in a car wreck. He awakens screaming in the car, and moments later Susan has the accident about which he dreamed.

The next story centers on the third guest, James Elliot, the stuck-up son of a wealthy realtor, who hates his neighbor Arthur Grimsdyke, the town rubbish collector. He undertakes a campaign to force the poor man to move, persuading the town council to fire him and turning the entire community against him. On Valentine's Day, he sends Grimsdyke a batch of hate mail disguised as Valentines. The poor man eventually commits suicide, but one year later his body rises from the grave and stalks James. The next morning, his father finds him dead with a Valentine poem and his torn-out heart on an adjacent table.

The fourth detainee, Ralph Jason, is a ruthless antiques collector facing bankruptcy. The image the Cryptkeeper shows him is a variant of W. W. Jacobs' "The Monkey's Paw." Jason discovers that the ancient Chinese figurine he owns has magic properties and can grant three wishes. His wife, Enid, wishes for a large sum of money. Shortly thereafter, Death, riding a motorcycle, claims Ralph while he is driving to visit his solicitor. His death in a car accident provides a large double-indemnity insurance settlement for her. She wishes for her husband to be returned to her, exactly as he was before his accident. His unblemished corpse in a casket is brought to her house. Since Ralph was actually claimed by Death before his accident, this wish is wasted. Enid wishes that Ralph would be recalled to life at once and never die. Ralph revives screaming, in total agony, since his veins are filled with embalming fluid instead of blood. He is doomed to face eternity in torment.

The fifth story concerns Major William Rogers, a cold-hearted retired officer who is appointed superintendent of the Elmridge Home for the Blind. He treats the men cruelly, cutting their rations and shutting off the heat at night. He uses the maintenance funds to decorate his office and to buy lavish meals for himself and his dog, a vicious German Shepherd named Shane. After he refuses to summon help for an ill resident who later dies, the blind men, led by George Carter, take revenge by imprisoning Rogers in the basement and setting up an elaborate trap in which Rogers must either run through a narrow passageway lined with exposed razor blades or be attacked by his own dog, who has been starved.

After this grisly tale, the Cryptkeeper opens up a passageway to a flaming pit, and the five unfortunate souls are informed they are in hell, for they all died unrepentant. The Cryptkeeper, revealed as the Devil, explains that the stories were true representations of how they died, and now they all understand why they are here. Bach's organ music swells as the Devil addresses the audience for the first time, waiting for his next victim.

The concept that the trauma of death causes souls to blot out the experience is a good one. A recent French film, *A Pure Formality* (1994) with Roman Polanski and Gerard Depardieu, effectively deals with a similar theme. Naturally, having the Devil perform the function of revealing why each one is damned also works well. Unfortunately, while most of the tales fit well into this scenario, the fourth story with the Chinese figurine does not, and it sticks out like a sore thumb. Milton Subotsky outwitted himself, because his trick ending of that tale disqualifies it from fitting in with the premise of the film. If each of these stories related by the Devil is accurate, then Ralph Jason is still alive and is incapable of dying. Therefore, it would not be possible for him to be there. Except for this glaring error, the rest of the film is fairly good, with the third story with Peter Cushing being the strongest and most entertaining.

Performances

Ralph Richardson is no stranger to horror films, since the distinguished actor made his screen debut in *The Ghoul* (1933) with Boris Karloff and Ernest Thesiger. His conception of the Devil is enigmatic, deliberate, and stately. Using detailed pronunciation, he manages to endow a simple word like "plans" with sinister connotations. At other points, he repeats an ordinary phrase, "And then?" and makes it sound like poetry. Few actors would be able to enrich a bare bones part with such a powerful aura of mystery. The other great performance in the film belongs to Peter Cushing, whose colorful junkman is filled with humor, compassion, and pathos. His scene after he rises from the dead rates with Boris Karloff's great revival scene in *The Mummy* (1932) as one of the most effective portrayals onscreen, of the revived dead. Other cast members also turn in fine performances, including Joan Collins, Richard Greene and the splendid Patrick Magee, who is best remembered on stage and screen as the sinister Marquis de Sade in *The Persecution and Assassination of Jean Paul Marat as Performed by the Inmates of the Asylum at Charenton under the Direction of the Marquis de Sade* (1967).

Notable Quotes

• I assure you I have a purpose. (**the Devil to his five guests**)
• You were mean and cruel right from the start. Now you really have no.... (**Grimsdyke's poem found next to Elliot's heart**)
• And now, who's next? Perhaps you? (**the Devil to the audience**)

Time Bandits

1981   Rating: ***   David Warner as the Devil

Avco. Written by Terry Gilliam and Michael Palin; Photographed by Peter Biziou; Edited by Julian Doyle; Special Effects by John Bunker (senior technician); Music by Mike Moran and George Harrison (songs); Produced by Terry Gilliam, George Harrison, and Denis O'Brien (executive); Directed by Terry Gilliam. Color, 116 minutes.

Annotated Cast List

David Rappaport (*Randall*, head time bandit); Kenny Baker (*Fidgit*, smallest time bandit); Malcolm Dixon (*Strutter*, studious time bandit); Jack Purvis (*Wally*, aggressive bearded time bandit); Tiny Ross (*Vermin*, time bandit); Mike Edmonds (*Og*, time bandit turned into a pig); Craig

Warrock (*Kevin*, youngster who joins the time bandits); David Daker (Kevin's father); Sheila Fearn (Kevin's mother); David Warner (*Evil Genius*, the Devil); Ian Holm (*Napoleon Bonaparte*); Sean Connery (*Agamemnon*, Mycenaean king); Juliette James (*Clytemnestra*, his queen); Ralph Richardson (the Supreme Being); Edwin Finn (the Supreme Being's image in cloud); Tony Jay (the Supreme Being's voice in cloud); John Cleese (*Robin Hood*); Peter Vaughan (*Winston*, ogre); Katharine Helmond (Winston's wife); Ian Muir (giant); Shelly Duval (*Pansy*, medieval lady, and girl on the *Titanic*); Michael Palin (*Vincent*, her inept beau, and boy on the *Titanic*); Jerold Wells (*Benson*, the Devil's first henchman); Derek Deadman (*Robert*, the Devil's second henchman); Roger Frost (*Cartwright*); Jim Broadhurst (*Compere*); John Young (*Reginald*); Terence Bayler (*Lucien*); Preston Lockwood (*Negley*); John Hughman (*The Great Rumbozo*); Myrtle Devengh (*Beryl*).

Appraisal and Synopsis

Many people assume that Terry Gilliam is British, but he was born in Minneapolis and didn't move to England until his late twenties, when he became involved with the zany BBC series "Monty Python's Flying Circus." *Time Bandits* was his first non-Python project, although other Python alumni such as John Cleese and Michael Palin were also closely involved. The film is stylish, unconventional, and offbeat with a handsome budget, but it is also uneven and choppy. Four years later, Gilliam would direct his phenomenal masterpiece, *Brazil* (1985), which owes a good deal of its brilliance to his work on *Time Bandits*.

The film opens with a map of the universe, and the camera pans forward to the planet Earth and to the British middle-class neighborhood of a bright youngster named Kevin. His parents are TV addicts, who pay scant attention to their intelligent son. Sent to his room, Kevin finds it invaded by a gang of six dwarves dressed in outlandishly colorful costumes who claim the youngster's room is the site of a time portal. Kevin learns that these diminutive adventurers, employees of the Supreme Being, decided to swipe the map that details the location of all the time portals that riddle all of creation. Suddenly the image of the Supreme Being in a cloud appears in the distance, and Kevin joins the group as they flee through another secret passageway.

Kevin's escapades with the time bandits lead him through various periods in history, encountering Napoleon as a young general who captures an Italian city, King Agamemnon in ancient Mycenae, and Robin Hood in medieval England. They even wind up on the ill-fated *Titanic*. Kevin takes photos with his instant camera, the only object he brought with him. The dwarves attempt to plunder wherever they go, but their plans always backfire. When they finally garner a decent haul, Robin Hood intervenes and distributes their booty to the poor. Meanwhile, the activities of the little vandals have come to the attention of the Devil, confined by the Supreme Being to the Fortress of Ultimate Darkness. He monitors their activities though a magic cauldron, and he instills in their minds the idea that the greatest fortune of all is concealed in the Fortress of Ultimate Darkness. Evil, as he prefers to be known, figures that if he can obtain the map, he can escape his prison and remake all creation as he chooses.

The gang eventually winds up in the time of legends on a boat piloted by an ogre and his wife. He captures the lot and plans to eat them. They manage to trick the pair into jumping overboard, and they set sail toward the Fortress of Ultimate Darkness. A giant lifts the boat out of the water, wearing it as a hat. When he falls asleep, Kevin and the gang get out and make their way to the nearby Devil's lair. As they breach the labyrinthian complex, the Devil poses as a game show host, similar to the favorite program of Kevin's parents. The dwarves enthusiastically rush to play the game and naively hand over their map. The Devil promptly imprisons them in a cage suspended over a bottomless cavern and heads off to examine the map. Kevin, however, has a photograph he had taken of the map and tells the others about the nearest time portal. They escape by catapulting from one cage to the next until they reach safety. Then they scheme to retrieve the map.

While the Devil conceives his grandiose plan to alter the world, the band steals back the map. In a fury, the Devil pursues them, turning one of them into a pig and killing Fidgit, the tiniest member of the group. He corners Kevin with the map, and the other dwarves use the time portal to bring reinforcements from every period in history. The Fortress of Ultimate Darkness is invaded by cowboys, medieval knights, ancient Greek archers, a World War II tank, and a jet. They each take turns attacking the Devil, but he defeats them all with his powerful magic. Finally, the Supreme Being himself arrives, turning the Devil into a stone, which explodes and scatters all over the large chamber.

The Supreme Being announces that he deliberately let the map be stolen by the dwarves so that he could test the power of evil. He revives Fidgit and rehires the dwarves with a cut in pay retroactive to the beginning of time. He then sets them to work cleaning up the stone fragments of Evil. Kevin questions the Supreme Being, who provides him with evasive answers. The Supreme Being then departs with the dwarves, leaving Kevin, who wakes up back at home in his bedroom as it fills with smoke. The house is on fire, and Kevin is rescued by a fireman who resembles King Agamemnon. The youngster wonders if his adventure was just a dream until he discovers his pocket filled with the photographs he took with his instant camera. As the firemen leave, Kevin's parents discover a stone fragment, and as they touch it they explode and vanish. Kevin watches dumbfounded as the camera pulls back until the Earth is a mere spot on the universal map. God's hands roll up the map and the picture ends.

On the whole, *Time Bandits* is an unsettling fantasy with the ambiguous message, that all creation is a mere diversion in the hands of a capricious God. Certainly the end is unique, as young Kevin is left abandoned on the street with no home, no family, and no resources. The various episodes of the film fail to hang together, and this inconsistency is the picture's principal flaw. The opening sequence with Napoleon, for example, is overlong, pointless, and rather flat. On the other hand, the Agamemnon sequence is excellent, and the historical detail is good as well. The difference is that Agamemnon is treated as a real human being, whereas Napoleon is nothing but a goofy caricature. The Robin Hood episode is a mixed bag, but the *Titanic* and ogre adventures are marvelous. The longest section, of course, is the encounter with the Devil, and the battle between the forces of good and evil at the climax is a clever reworking of the battle of the sorcerers with Boris Karloff and Vincent Price in *The Raven* (1962). As a wacky experiment in filmmaking, *Time Bandits* is fresh and entertaining, and even half-baked it is indeed far better than most of the rival comedies and adventure films made at the same time. The production values are good throughout. Former Beatle George Harrison served as executive producer and contributed some songs to the soundtrack. Mike Moran's score relies heavily on Mahler's *Sixth Symphony*, an unusual choice but it works very well. The cinematography is strong, particularly in the scenes set in ancient Greece. At times, the color relies heavily on red hues, which give the picture a distinct visual flair.

Performances

David Warner's character is billed in the credits as "Evil Genius" even though he is unmistakably the Devil in the course of the story, unlike Tim Curry, whose character in Ridley Scott's *Legend* (1985) is merely that of a demon. Warner is masterful in the role, fully the equal of Sean Connery for the best performance in the film. Warner uses his voice in an exceptional way, shading each comment with charm, eloquence, and diabolic intent. Dressed in an elaborate costume with headdress, Warner tosses off the best lines in the film as he complains about the doddering nature of the Supreme Being. Unfortunately, the film does not include a face-to-face confrontation between the two of them, as God disposes of the Devil before He Himself appears, another shortcoming of the scenario. The character of the Supreme Being is of a cold, supercilious corporate type, making the Devil more sympathetic by comparison even if he is concentrated evil. When challenged by Kevin, the Supreme Being hems and haws about the suffering he causes while engaging in His little experiments. One wonders if God rendered Kevin a destitute orphan at the end of the film because he dared to question Him.

Notable Quotes

- I am Evil. Evil existed long before good. I made myself. I cannot be unmade. I am all powerful. (**the Devil to his lackeys when one of them mentions that he was created by the Supreme Being**)
- God isn't interested in technology. He knows nothing of the potential of the microchip or the silicon revolution. Look how He spends His time.... forty-three species of parrots, nipples for men, slugs! (**the Devil**)
- I think it turned out rather well, don't you? (**the Supreme Being to Randall, referring to Evil**)

Torture Garden

1967   Rating: ***   Burgess Meredith as the Devil

Amicus. Written by Robert Bloch, based on four of his short stories; Photographed by Norman Warwick; Edited by Peter Elliott; Music by Don Banks and James Bernard; Produced by Max J. Rosenberg and Milton Subotsky; Directed by Freddie Francis. Color, 93 minutes.

Annotated Cast List

Burgess Meredith (*Dr. Diablo*, carnival showman, actually the Devil); Jack Palance (*Ronald Wyatt*, rare book collector); Michael Bryant (*Colin Williams*, playboy); Beverly Adams (*Carla Hayes*, Hollywood actress); Barbara Ewing (*Dorothy*

Endicott, Carla's cousin, a journalist); Michael Ripper (*Gordon Roberts*, Diablo's shill); Timothy Bateson (fairgrounds barker); Clytie Jessop (*Atropos*, waxen figure). **First story:** Maurice Denholm (*Roger Williams*, Colin's uncle); Catherine Finn (*Parker*, Roger's nurse); Niall MacGinnis (*Silversmith*, Roger's doctor); Michael Hawkins (constable). **Second story:** Nicole Shelby (*Millie*, Carla's roommate); David Bauer (*Mike Charles*, Carla's date); Robert Hutton (*Bruce Benton*, film star); John Phillips (*Eddie Storm*, film producer); Bernard Kay (*Dr. Heim*, brilliant scientist) **Third story:** John Standing (*Leo Winston*, concert pianist); Ursula Howells (*Maxine Chambers*, Leo's manager). **Fourth story:** Peter Cushing (*Lancelot Canning*, world's foremost Poe collector); Norman Claridge (book show exhibitor); Geoffrey Wallace (*Edgar Allan Poe*).

Appraisal and Synopsis

This anthology film of horror stories by Robert Bloch has a more interesting framework than usual. Dr. Diablo's Torture Garden is one of the top attractions of a British carnival. Dressed in an elaborate black costume with cape, Diablo performs a gruesome shock show, including the simulated execution of a felon in an electric chair. At the conclusion of the performance, the showman announces a private showing available for the select few, at a cost of five pounds. Five individuals, Gordon Roberts, Colin Williams, Carla Hayes, Dorothy Endicott, and Ronald Wyatt accept the invitation and proceed behind a curtain to Diablo's inner sanctum. Unseen by the others, Diablo burns the money he collected. Seconds later he enters and unveils the waxen image of Atropos, the Greek goddess of destiny, who carries the shears of fate. Diablo challenges each of them to step up to the image and stare at the shears, and Atropos will reveal the horror hidden inside them. The vision they see is a forewarning so they may possibly escape the consequences of their future misdeeds.

Colin Williams takes the challenge, and the first tale begins. Spendthrift Colin visits his elderly uncle Roger seeking money to settle his debts. Colin withholds medicine from his uncle when he suffers an attack, and the old man dies. He tears apart the house, searching for his uncle's hidden gold. Digging in the cellar, he exhumes a live cat encased in a buried coffin. The cat, named Balthazar, communicates with Colin by mental projection. Having demonic powers, Balthazar previously possessed Roger until he trapped and buried it. Now Balthazar controls Colin, forcing him to commit a series of murders, and Balthazar feeds off the flesh of the bodies. The cat also reveals the location of a chest of gold coins worth a fortune. Colin is caught by the police when the constable catches him moving a trunk leaking blood. Balthazar finally kills Colin as he sleeps in his jail cell. The vision ends, and Colin, shaken, refuses to share his revelation with the others in the Torture Garden.

Carla Hayes steps up before Atropos next, and the second tale shows how she deliberately burned her roommate's dress in order to replace her on a date with a Hollywood director, Mike Charles. Through him, Carla meets Bruce Benton, one of the film industry's longest reigning stars, and they form a bond. When Benton is kidnapped by gangsters, she discovers his body shot in the head. Producer Eddie Storm takes his corpse to Dr. Heim, a mysterious wonder-worker, and the following week Benton appears at the studio to complete his film. Carla investigates and learns his secret, discovering that Benton is actually a robot with a human brain, which had been removed from his aging body years earlier. To ensure her silence, Carla's brain is also placed in an artificial body, and in exchange, Power promotes her as the next superstar of the screen.

Subdued, Carla yields her place to her cousin, Dorothy Endicott. In her vision, the third tale, Dorothy seeks out an interview with Leo Winston, a famous but reclusive concert pianist. They fall in love, but Leo seems strangely attached to his piano, a final gift from his late mother. In fact, the piano is possessed by her spirit. When Dorothy is alone in the music room, the piano begins to stalk her. The instrument plays Chopin's Funeral March and rolls after Dorothy until she is forced out the window and killed as she crashes to the pavement below. Carla soothes Dorothy as she awakens from her trance with a cry of fear. Diablo is amused by her description of her revelation as a mere illusion. No one seems to notice, but Diablo's wardrobe has completely changed. Previously, he was dressed all in black, except for a white tie and a white flower in his lapel. Now he is dressed all in white, with a black tie and flower. With enthusiasm, Ronald Wyatt approaches the shears held by the figure of Atropos.

In the fourth prophetic tale, Wyatt attends a rare book exhibit where he meets Lancelot Canning, the world's foremost collector of Poe memorabilia. He wins Canning's confidence and is invited to his home. After inducing Canning to drink too much, Wyatt persuades him to show him his basement, where the most priceless treasures of his collection are stored. Wyatt is amazed to find unpublished stories written in Poe's own handwriting, but he questions Canning when he detects that these stories are written on modern paper. Canning reveals that his grandfather had unearthed Poe's body, and through black magic, brought the author back to life. Wyatt demands proof, and when Canning refuses, Wyatt kills the collector, striking him on the head with a heavy candlestick. He then opens an inner door in the basement where he discovers Edgar Allan Poe sitting in a chair. Poe claims he was revived because he had made a deal with the Devil, but he now wants to be released from the pact. He asks for Wyatt's help. After declaring he can be released by fire, Wyatt drops his candle and a conflagration begins. Wyatt, however, seems untroubled and even starts to smile as his surroundings go up in flames.

Wyatt is still smiling as his vision ceases. The last individual, Gordon Roberts, refuses to stand before the shears. Instead he grabs them and stabs Diablo in the chest. After the screaming customers flee the premises, Diablo gets up, assisted by Roberts, who is actually a shill, a carnival employee who is part of the show. The stabbing is only a gimmick to bring the private exhibition to an end. Roberts heads off to prepare for the next performance. Wyatt, however, has hidden behind a curtain and now approaches Diablo, saying he knows who he really is. Diablo asks if he is interested in making a deal. His features transform, becoming even more diabolical, and the Devil talks directly to the viewing audience, explaining that he operates this way for sport, and he wonders if we would be able to escape from his realm.

As with most anthology movies, the stories are inconsistent, varying in quality and interest. The story with the piano doesn't seem to fit, because, unlike the others, Dorothy commits no crime to merit her fate. Carla's misdeed is also a minor one, burning her roommate's dress to steal her date. The last story is also different because Wyatt seems to be aware that the events are not real and only a reverie, which is why he shows no fear of the fire. In fact, as the film ends, Wyatt is quite eager to ink his pact with the Devil. The concept of the Devil slumming at a side-show is not a stretch. The carnival setting has been utilized in films of terror including major efforts such as *The Cabinet of Dr. Caligari* (1919) and *Something Wicked This Way Comes* (1983). Most of the same people who created *Torture Garden* were later involved in *Tales from the Crypt* (1972).

Performances

Having played the Devil a number of times in his career, Burgess Meredith always manages to imbue the part with commanding style, wit, and sizzle. Meredith was an actor who always seemed to enjoy his work, he is having a ball with the role in this film, and he shares his glee with the audience at every opportunity. His Devil goes through an interesting set of changes as the film progresses. First we see him as a dapper showman, somewhat resembling his characterization as the Penguin from the "Batman" television series, with top hat and long-stemmed cigarette holder. After his performance, his wax moustache and Van Dyke beard are removed with a flourish as he slips into the persona of a slick hustler, treating the customers of his private viewing to a different performance than his theatrical presentation. None of the customers seems to notice the color change of his clothes, with the complete reversal of the black and white components of his attire. After he recovers from the phony stabbing routine, we see yet another guise, that of the backstage artist, reveling in his acting prowess and complimenting the work of his shill and accomplice. Finally, alone with Wyatt and then with the audience, the genuine Devil emerges, complete with narrow horns emerging from underneath the brim of his hat, raised eyebrows, and facial hair duplicating in a more elaborate fashion the stage moustache and beard that Diablo wore at the start of the picture. The differences in these variations are subtle but distinct, and Meredith appears to relish each gesture in his performance. The other supporting players are quite good, particularly Jack Palance and Michael Ripper. Peter Cushing plays his role more quietly than usual, but he is excellent nevertheless.

Notable Quotes

- What you have seen are imaginary horrors, but now I can let you experience real ones. Yes, ladies and gentlemen, I do have a private exhibit. It is for the true connoisseur.... Behind that curtain there you will find the real Torture Garden. It is not for the faint of heart. (**Diablo, hawking his special exhibit**)

- She is able to reveal to each and every one of you.... the secret, in fact, of your own evil. A very old-fashioned word nowadays, evil. You prefer, I see, the primordial monstrosities that lurk beneath the surface of the mind, but I prefer evil. (**Diablo, discussing the power of the image of Atropos**)

- If you liberate one who has made a pact with the Devil, you yourself become the Devil's slave. (**Poe's warning to Wyatt**)

- Of course I lose one or two along the line this way, but it's great for the sport. It's only fair, you know, to give them a chance to escape my domain. But will you? (**the Devil, addressing the camera**)

The Undead

1957   Rating: ***   Richard Devon as the Devil

American International. Written by Charles Griffith and Mark Hanna; Photographed by William Sickner; Edited by Frank Sullivan; Music by Ronald Stein; Produced and Directed by Roger Corman. B&W, 72 minutes.

Annotated Cast List

Pamela Duncan (*Diana Love*, modern-day prostitute, and *Helene*, medieval aristocrat); Richard Garland (*Pendragon*, knight in love with Helene); Allison Hayes (*Livia*, medieval witch); Billy Barty (Livia's imp); Val Dufour (*Quintis Ratcliff*, hypnotist who regresses Diana); Maurice Manson (*Ulbrecht Olinger*, psychic researcher and Ratcliff's teacher); Dorothy Neuman (*Meg Maude*, hag who helps Helene); Mel Welles (*Smolkin*, bewitched gravedigger); Bruno Ve Sota (*Scroop*, sly innkeeper); Richard Devon (the Devil); Aaron Saxon (*Gobbo*, jailer); Don Garret (knight who tries to capture Helene); Dick Miller (leper).

Appraisal and Synopsis

The Undead was originally titled *The Trance of Diana Love*. It is a hilarious Roger Corman concoction inspired by *The Search for Bridey Murphy* (1956) which was based on a true-life case of a woman who told about her experiences of an earlier life while under hypnosis. Of course, Corman's version includes actual regression to the past, witchcraft, magic, and the involvement of the Devil himself. The medieval setting is a total mish-mash, mixing clothes from various eras as well as the use of a Victorian hearse with plate glass windows. The time frame is only identified as the second year in the reign of the nonexistent French King Mark. The language is the most absurd element, a ludicrous parody of Shakespearean verse, including such contorted phrases as "Rest thy corpulence" and "Disturb me not, lummox." The makeup is ridiculously exaggerated, particularly for the character Meg Maude, whose putty nose and chin stick out absurdly. Livia and her imp companion transform themselves at every turn into phony-looking bats or spiders. All these madcap antics will either drive the audience crazy or into fits of uncontrollable laughter. If the success of a film is measured by its entertainment value instead of its quality, then *The Undead* is unquestionably a success.

The picture begins with the Devil appearing out of the flames and addressing the audience directly, a similar device to the opening of *Bait* (1954). The Devil intends the film to serve as an example of his working method. The scene dissolves to a foggy street, where psychic researcher Quintis Ratcliff approaches a streetwalker and brings her to the office of his old teacher, Professor Olinger. After seven years of study in Tibet, Quintis wants to demonstrate his ability to regress individuals to their previous lives. He proposes using the prostitute, Diana Love, as his guinea pig, considering her so weak-minded that she can easily be placed in a deep trance. Olinger reluctantly agrees. Diana finds herself back in the Dark Ages in the persona of Helene, an imprisoned French aristocrat condemned to die that very night for practicing witchcraft. Legally, witches can only be executed one night during the year. If Helene can escape and elude capture for only one night, she will have an entire year to prove her innocence. Diana is able to speak with her earlier self, and she advises her how to escape from Gobbo, her jailer. This escape, however, has unforeseen consequences since it alters history.

A number of people are affected by the change in events. Livia, the beautiful witch who framed Helene, schemes to ensure she is recaptured and executed. Meg Maude, an old hag who everyone assumes is a witch, hides Helene and tries to protect her. Even more colorful is Smolkin, the addle-brained gravedigger. His dementia was caused by Livia but blamed on Helene. Smolkin spends most of his time singing gruesome variations of popular nursery rhymes. Actually, Smolkin enjoys his bewitchment for it allows him to talk back to everyone, even the Devil himself. Livia tries to seduce Pendragon, Helene's noble sweetheart, but he resists her advances. Pendragon's friend Scroop, the innkeeper, is beheaded by Livia who plans to use his head as an offering to Satan.

Questioning Diana in her trance, Quintis becomes alarmed that if Helene escapes her appointed execution, all of her subsequent lives will be erased. He urges Professor Olinger to put him in a trance and uses a machine so he can match the brain wave frequency of Diana. By this method, Quintis returns to the past where he overpowers the knight who is tracking Helene and dresses in his suit of armor.

The Devil attends the meeting of the witches' sabbath, and he is pleased with the gift of Scroop's head. Many individuals sign his book, pledging their souls for his various diabolic favors. Satan conjures up three graveyard dancers in a scene that no doubt inspired Ed Wood's stripper film *Orgy of the Dead* (1965). A leper sells his soul to be cured. Livia brings Pendragon to Satan so he can make a deal to save Helene. Quintis arrives and persuades Pendragon not to sign the book. The hypnotist is startled when the Devil recognizes him and congratulates him for slipping the bonds of time. Quintis brings Pendragon to Helene's hiding place, and soon she is confronted with a deadly choice. If she submits to execution now, she will have many future lifetimes. If she chooses to avoid the execution, all future lives will be forfeit. The Devil urges her to live her full lifetime now and ignore any future ramifications. "Let the dawn slip by and live," he cajoles her slyly. Instead, Helene resists his temptation, and she voluntarily goes to the place of execution. Pendragon chases after her, and when Livia tries to stop him, he stabs her to death. The nobleman rushes to the block, but the axman's blade falls on Helene the moment he appears.

In modern time, Diana awakes, and she is now a reformed woman, brought to new awareness by her visit to the past. The body of Quintis has vanished, and only his empty suit remains. In the past, the Devil mockingly tells Quintis that he cannot return to his own time because his mental link to the future disappeared with the execution of Helene. He mocks Quintis and lets him know that he will collect his soul when his time is done, and the picture ends with the Devil's howls of laughter.

Performances

Richard Devon was a native Californian who broke into acting as a jack-of-all-trades in early television. He became a member of Roger Corman's informal troupe, later appearing as Stark the barbarian in *Saga of the Viking Women and their Voyage to the Waters of the Great Sea Serpent* (1957) and as Dr. Van Ponder and his alien duplicate in *War of the Satellites* (1958). His last appearance was as a

The Devil (Richard Devon) watches from the upper right as Pamela Duncan, Richard Garland, Dorothy Neuman, Allison Hayes, Val Dufour, and Mel Welles strike a publicity post for The Undead. *This scene does not occur in the film.*

cardinal in the apocalyptic thriller *The Seventh Sign* (1988). Devon plays the Devil as a hammy vaudevillian, with trimmed beard and Spock-like pointed ears. He wears a Tyrolean hat and carries a primitive three-pronged pitchfork. Devon seems to relish his meaty role, performing with great enthusiasm. Only Devon, Mel Welles, and Bruno Ve Sota deliver topnotch performances in the film. Welles' comic gravedigger is even cited with enthusiasm by critics who despise this film. Allison Hayes looks great, but her acting is clumsy and inconsistent. The three leads, Pamela Duncan, Richard Garland, and Val Dufour, are awkward throughout and were either too rushed or too unprepared to render anything but stilted readings. Dorothy Neuman and Billy Barty bring some sparkle to their roles, but they are such caricatures that one grows tired of them quickly. One of the film's finest moments, a superb vignette, is provided by Dick Miller as the leper who signs Satan's book. At first he is overjoyed to be cured of his disease, but a cloud passes over his face when he notices the Devil's mark permanently etched on his hand, and he warily glances at his new master as he backs away.

Notable Quotes

- Here is a story of my eternal work. It is a story of all ages, those dark and forgotten and those still to come. Behold the subtle working of my talents, and pray that I may never turn my interests upon you. (**the Devil's opening narration**)

• Quintis and I do bid thee stay. We will observe the future bend and split, then change with gay confusion. (**the Devil to Helene as she considers her choice**)

• I fear the joke's on thee, my brilliant friend. Here you are fixed, so make a local life with what comfort, joy, and sport thou may, and when thy present years are done, I'll come a-calling on thee. (**the Devil to Quintis**)

Up in Smoke

1957   Rating: *   Byron Foulger as the Devil

Allied Artists. Written by Jack Townley, based on a story by Elwood Ullman and Bert Lawrence; Photographed by Harry Neumann; Edited by William Austin; Music by Marlin Skiles; Produced by Richard Heermance; Directed by William Beaudine. B&W, 61 minutes.

Annotated Cast List

Huntz Hall (*Horace Debussy James*, Bowery Boy called Sach); Stanley Clements (*Duke Coveleske*, leader of the Bowery Boys); David Gorcey (*Chuck Anderson*, one of the Bowery Boys); Eddie Leroy (*Blinky*, Bowery Boy who wears glasses); Byron Foulger (the Devil); Dick Elliott (*Mike Clancy*, cafe proprietor); Judy Bamber (*Mabel*, cafe waitress in league with bookies); Ric Roman (*Tony*, top bookie); Ralph Sanford (*Sam*, hood who brings Sach to the bookie joint); Joe Devlin (*Al*, hood who poses as a race track broadcaster); James Flavin (cop who buys the jalopy); Earle Hodgkins (*Friendly Frank*, ued-car dealer); John Mitchum (desk sergeant); Jack Mulhall (police clerk); Fritz Feld (*Dr. Bluzak*, Sach's psychiatrist); Wilber Mack (*Drake*, druggist and gambler); Benny Rubin (*Bernie*, gambler who bets on Heel Plate).

Appraisal and Synopsis

Up in Smoke is the penultimate Bowery Boys film, when the series was in its dying stages. Leo Gorcey had already left the series the previous year, and the series producer, Ben Schwalb, had also just quit. The series went back a total of twenty years, with various name changes, to the film *Dead End* (1937) with Humphrey Bogart. Huntz Hall was the only member of the original troupe left, and reportedly the only reason the last two films were made was to play out Hall's contract. At this point, the Bowery Boys could no longer be considered a gang, only four middle-aged men who liked to hang out at Mike Clancy's cafe. It was thought that adding the Devil might make a worthwhile entry, but the series was so moribund at this point that nothing could enliven it. This is a tired film merely going through the motions of a successful formula that had completely dried up. It is appropriate, perhaps, that William Beaudine directed this effort, since he was noted for filming any project in a rapid manner, getting his scenes almost always recorded in one take.

The picture opens with the group reduced to four Bowery Boys, Duke, Sach, Blinky, and Chuck, raising money for a neighborhood youngster, Little Ozzie, who has polio. Sach is assigned to bring the money, $90, to the bank. A man gives him a ride to the bank, but his car breaks down in front of a bookie joint, and they swindle Sach out of the money. After telling the others, the depressed Sach plans to leave his friends and join the Foreign Legion. After Blinky brings him a hamburger, Sach vows to get even with the crooks and offers to sell his soul to do it. Satan immediately appears in his room and offers him a deal. He will give Sach the name of a long-shot winner at the races each day for an entire week in exchange for his soul. Sach hesitates, but the Devil easily talks him into the bargain. After getting his finger pricked for blood, Sach signs the contract. Satan gives him the name of Lazy Luke as the winner of the sixth race at Jamaica. Sach heads back to the bookies, but he is broke and they won't extend him credit. He plans to sell the jalopy jointly owned by the gang, and he takes it to Friendly Frank's used-car dealership. Unknown to Sach, the other boys had already sold the jalopy to a local cop to replace the lost funds intended for Little Ozzie. Sach is arrested and thrown in jail, and he misses the chance to gain any winnings from his tip.

Each day the Devil returns and gives Sach the name of a winning horse. Sometimes Lucifer appears to him in a disguise, such as an organ grinder's monkey. Sach now refers to him as Mr. Bub, short for Beelzebub. Sach never manages to make any money from the tips, either because events keep him from betting or because in one case, another gambler talks him into switching his wager.

Duke thinks his buddy has gone crazy and takes him to a psychiatrist, Dr. Bluzak. Sach's double talk totally confuses the doctor. When Sach summons the Devil, who takes over the form of the skeleton hanging in Bluzak's office, they hear him announce the name of another winning horse. They are convinced that Sach has indeed made a deal with Satan. The bookies also figure out that Sach is somehow getting surefire tips, and they try various schemes to learn about them, first by kidnapping Sach and Duke, but the Devil helps them escape, and later by installing a confederate, Mabel, to work as a waitress in Mike's cafe. The boys are smitten with the beautiful Mabel, and they invite her to come to the race track with them. The Devil turns up disguised as a soda vendor and informs Sach that the winning horse in the next race is called Rubber Check. Mabel sneaks off to tell the name to the bookies, who are also in the stands.

After learning that the polio fund will pick up all the medical expenses for Little Ozzie, Sach tells the Devil that he no longer needs the money. Satan replies that it makes no difference and that he will claim his soul after the next race. His only escape will be if Rubber Check loses the race. Sach goes to the jockey's locker room and substitutes as the rider for the horse. He does his best to lose the race, but the Devil ensures that he wins. When the Devil appears to escort Sach to hell, he is startled to hear the announcement that Rubber Check has been disqualified from the race due to an unauthorized rider. Sach is no longer bound by the contract, and the Devil is flabbergasted by the turn of events.

In an epilogue, the Devil winds up demoted and forced to work as a dishwasher at Mike's cafe. He complains to Sach, "After thousands of years of faithful service, they made me turn in my horns." The three bedraggled bookies come into the cafe and ask Mike for a free cup of coffee. Sach suggests that Satan redeem himself by signing on some new clients, pointing out the three crooks. The Devil is delighted as one of his two horns grows back. He tells Sach that he has actually grown fond of him and sets off to make a deal with the bookies.

This closing sequence is rather baffling because it is not revealed who demoted the Devil. The character in the film is presented as Satan himself, not one of his minions, so the infernal hierarchy is perplexing. It seems as if some higher power (surely not God!) has stepped in to punish the Devil for failing to ensnare Sach. Of course, the writers were merely trying to come up with a cute closer by reducing the Devil to a dishwasher, but the ramifications undermine the whole concept of the picture. It is simply a weak ending to a feeble comedy.

Performances

Byron Foulger was somewhat unusual casting for the Devil. Foulger was a veteran of over a hundred films in which he generally specialized in the role of an indecisive milquetoast. Nevertheless, Foulger tackled the role with relish. Note his glee when he describes himself as "a stinker!" There is also a gleam in his eye when the depressed Sach mumbles that for two cents he'd jump in the river, and Foulger places two pennies on the counter before him. Foulger's performance is the only worthwhile element in the film. His Devil is distinguished by his elegant dress and two small, protruding horns, which he keeps hidden under his hat. He simply pops into any place he visits out of thin air, but some of his appearances are never explained. There is no explanation why he shows up as an organ grinder's monkey, for instance. And who demotes him at the end of the picture? His performance is undermined by other inconsistencies. He refuses earlier to help Sach obtain money, but later he conjures a $100 bill out of thin air for Sach to find. The Devil also declines to aid Sach in getting out of jail, but then he rescues Sach and Duke when they are locked up in the back room of the bookies. It also doesn't make sense that the bookies set up Mabel to work at the cafe when they already are holding Sach prisoner.

Huntz Hall was a masterful comedian who was never given his rightful due, but in this film he has little good material to work with, and there seems to be little fire left in his portrayal of Sach. His best scene is not with the Devil, but with the psychiatrist, played with madcap enthusiasm by Fritz Feld, who usually specialized in playing loony French waiters. Stanley Clements is totally unsympathetic as Duke, lacking the timing, charm, and genius for spouting malapropisms of Leo Gorcey, who he replaced. David Gorcey, Leo's younger brother, makes no impression at all in the film. Of the other characters, only the sensational Judy Bamber adds some interest, and it is a shame she appears too late in the story to provide it with any real lift.

Notable Quotes

- Oh, I have so many names, Lucifer, Beelzebub, Diabolis, Satanis. It is really quite confusing at times, but I am generally known as the Devil. (**the Devil, introducing himself to Sach**)
- It won't be so bad. You'll meet a lot of new friends down there that you will absolutely hate. (**the Devil to Sach**)
- In more than twelve thousand years, nothing like this has ever happened to me. (**the Devil, in shock, when he learns that Sach is not bound by the contract**)
- And I want some of my blood back. You owe it to me. (**Sach as he walks off**)

Les Visiteurs du Soir
AKA The Devil's Envoys

1942   Rating: ****   Jules Berry as the Devil

Discina Paris. Written by Jacques Prevert and Pierre Laroche; Photographed by Roger Hubert; Edited by Henri Rust; Music by Maurice Thiriet; Produced by Andre Paulve; Directed by Marcel Carne. B&W, 116 minutes.

Annotated Cast List

Alain Cuny (*Gilles*, the Devil's envoy); Arletty (*Dominic/Dominique*, his companion, another envoy); Jules Berry (the Devil); Fernand Ledoux (*Baron Hugues*, feudal lord); Marie Dea (*Anne*, his daughter); Marcel Herrand (*Renaud*, Anne's fiancé); Gabriel Gabrio (executioner); Pierre Labry, Jean D'Yd, Roger Blin.

Appraisal and Synopsis

During the Nazi occupation of France (1940–1944), the French film industry operated under strict control and supervision. Director Marcel Carne was turned down when he submitted scripts set in the contemporary era, but he was given the go-ahead to proceed with this fifteenth-century fantasy with a basic theme of love and loss. Yet discerning viewers can detect clear observations about the contemporary scene. It certainly is not accidental that the year chosen, 1485, was a troubled era when the usurper, Henry Tudor, invaded England to overthrow Richard III, also considered a usurper by many. At the same time, the two young princes in the Tower disappeared, presumably slain by the duke of Buckingham, Henry Tudor, or possibly Richard himself. This was an era of international turmoil and the spilling of innocent blood, yet on the surface none of this appears to trouble the court of Baron Hugues. Their blissful repose will be upset soon enough.

The opening title card explains that in May 1485, the Devil sent two of his agents, Gilles and Dominique, to promote desperation in the hearts of men. Dominique, dressed as a man, pretends to be the brother of Gilles. They present themselves as troubadours at the court of Baron Hugues and entertain his daughter, Anne, and her fiancé, the blunt and boorish Baron Renaud. Gilles is assigned to seduce Anne and Dominique to arouse both Renaud and Hugues. Both Gilles and Dominique are actually lost souls who have signed contracts with the Devil, who has endowed them with special powers. The Devil is able to claim those who fall in love with them. Gilles occasionally uses his powers to do good. When he encounters an entertainer whose performing bear had been killed, he restores the animal to life. When Dominique asks why he bothers, Gilles replies that it amuses him.

At the dinner feast, three deformed dwarfs are also presented to the baron's guests. They are really imps, who can penetrate the disguises of Gilles and Dominique, and they serve as a Greek chorus during the first half of the film, commenting on the action as they dance and spin around. Early in the story, Gilles and Dominique stop time and bring Anne and Renaud into a dream world where they work their charms upon them. They then return them to the real world, and although Anne and Renaud have lost their memory of this encounter, they feel deeply drawn to the mysterious pair. They are invited to remain at the castle as guests, and Dominique reveals that she is a woman to both Hugues and Renaud, who become bewitched by her. Something goes wrong with the Devil's plans, however, when Gilles actually falls in love with Anne, and she with him. When Gilles reveals his mission to her, a violent thunderstorm breaks out, and the Devil himself appears at Hugues' castle in the guise of an elegant Renaissance prince. Vivacious and witty, the Devil soon manages to control Hugues and Renaud like puppets. He tricks them into intruding into Anne's chamber, where they catch her and Gilles in an embrace. Gilles is locked in the dungeon, and later the Devil goes to mock him for his efforts at defiance. Gilles insists that his love for Anne is pure.

The Devil sets out to seduce Anne, but she sees through him during their first meeting, when he appears in her room in the form of Gilles. She is aware at once that he is the Devil. Nevertheless, he uses every conceivable ploy to win her over. In a sense, Anne has now bewitched him. She also renounces Renaud and declares her love for the imprisoned Gilles. Meanwhile, inflamed by Dominique and provoked by the Devil, Hugues and Renaud fight a duel, and Renaud is slain. After this combat, Dominique explains to Hugues that she is no longer able to stay, and she rides off. The lovesick Hugues rides after her, abandoning his castle and his responsibilities.

Anne finally promises to become the Devil's consort if he will free Gilles from his contract and erase from his mind all memories of his dealings with the Devil, as well as herself. Satan does this, and Gilles, free from sin, delights in the fact that he is alive. He sees Anne and, failing to recognize her, still considers her the most beautiful woman in the world. He speaks with the Devil and finds he does not trust his smile. After Gilles sets off on his own, Anne tells the Devil that she intends to break her word, because everything is permitted for lovers. The Devil is stunned, but since Anne did not sign a contract, he is powerless to force her. He again tries to win her over. She requests to be allowed to meet Gilles one last time. He transports her to a fountain in the forest (one of their favorite meeting spots earlier in the picture), and when Gilles arrives moments later, they again fall deeply in love. After a few minutes, the Devil reappears and orders Anne away from Gilles. When she refuses, he turns them both into stone. Gazing at each other and smiling, they will remain statues for eternity. The Devil strikes at their figures with a whip when he hears their hearts still continue to beat, and he finally disappears into thin air.

Les Visiteurs du Soir is almost two different films. The first half has dreamlike photography, and each scene resembles a medieval book of hours brought to life. The costumes are lavish and the settings grand with seemingly no expense spared to make this a top-quality production. The stately storyline starts to drag, however, until the Devil arrives. Then everything changes like quicksilver. The dialogue is sharper and more clever, and the plot becomes more focused. As for the allegorical edge of the tale, if one envisions Anne as symbolic of the French nation, which is fervently courted by Satan, representing Hitler, then the meaning of the last scene has a poignant message. The Nazi overlords may harden France into stone, but they cannot still the French heart, which continues to beat for liberty and freedom. *Les Visiteurs du Soir* proved to be popular in its day, and the hidden message undoubtedly reached the French audience, as it eluded their German conquerors, who merely regarded it as escapist fantasy such as their own *Baron Münchhausen* (1943).

Performances

Jules Berry, born Jules Paufichet, was one of the French screen's leading performers. He actually made his film debut in 1908, but it wasn't until the sound era that his dazzling array of character roles brought him considerable popularity. He appeared in almost a hundred films, including Renoir's *Le Crime de Monsieur Lange* (1936) and the starring role in *Arsene Lupin, Detective* (1937). He continued to be in great demand up until his death in 1951. In no role did his presence so enliven the plot as it does in *Les Visiteurs du Soir*, and he completely dominates the film from his appearance halfway through. He is clothed in the garments of an elegant Italian Renaissance prince, a black costume with elaborate gold brocade on his chest, a ruffled fringe, and ribbons flapping from his sleeves. He also wears a fanciful cap which is tilted at a rakish angle. His manner is sly, and he seems an absolute master of human psychology. He observes Hugues' court seated at three elongated tables, and he lets out an infectious laugh. Soon, the entire court is in stitches, and then he stops, stares at them, and demands to know why they are laughing. It is a dextrous stroke that demonstrates his ability to manipulate each individual he encounters, until he confronts Anne, who parries and bests him easily in their scintillating conversations. Their give-and-take rates among the wittiest and most entertaining verbal duels in all of the Devil movies. When Berry is offscreen, however, the picture seems to deflate and sag. It is thrilling to watch Berry muster all the charm he can in these battles, yet he always falls short. His encounters with Alain Cuny and Arletty lack the edge of his scenes with Marie Dea, but they still are magnificent. Gabriel Gabrio is also quite good as the hangman. He is thrilled that Gilles refers to him as "my good man" in their initial encounter, as if no one before ever had a kind word to say to him. When Gilles is his prisoner, the executioner's hard facade melts again when Gilles sings a melancholy song, but he explodes in irritated anger when Gilles refuses to repeat the number for him. These vibrant touches also add to the richness and pageantry of this dark fantasy.

Notable Quotes

- I love fire, and it likes me too. See how friendly are the flames. They lick my hands as a dog would. How sweet. (**the Devil's chatter as he thrusts his hands into the fireplace in the baron's great hall**)
- I can hold the world in my two hands. Storms, snow, winds, shipwrecks, it's me! Wars, with their fine pleasures, plagues, hunger, crimes, jealousy, hatred, it's me, always me! (**the Devil to Anne, when she belittles his powers**)
- Even if you turned me into a dead snake, my love still would remain alive. (**Anne to the Devil**)
- Should you love me, I assure you that I'd change. Life would become easy and good. (**the Devil to Anne**)

Wholly Moses

1980   Rating: **   John Ritter as the Devil

Columbia. Written by Guy Thomas; Photographed by Frank Stanley; Edited by Sidney Levin; Special Effects by Chuck Caspar; Music by Patrick Williams; Produced by Freddie Fields; Directed by Gary Weis. Color, 101 minutes.

Annotated Cast List

Dudley Moore (*Harvey Orchid*, modern-day tourist in Israel, and *Herschel*, brother-in-law of Moses); Laraine Newman (*Zoey*, modern-day tourist, and *Zerelda*, Herschel's wife); James Coco (*Hyssop*, Herschel's father); John Ritter (the Devil); Paul Sand (angel); John Houseman (archangel); Madeline Kahn (merchant with cart in New Sodom); Dom DeLuise (*Shadrach*, wanderer in desert); Richard Pryor (pharaoh); Jack Gilford (tailor); David L. Lander (phony cripple cured by Herschel); Andrea Martin (*Ziparah*, Zerelda's sister); Richard B. Shull (*Jethro*, patriarch and shepherd); Jeffrey Jacquet (young pharaoh); Howard Mann (high priest); Sandy Ward (taskmaster); William Watson (bandit); Tanya Boyd (princess); Charles Thomas Murphy (bus tour guide); Stan Ross (*Mohammed*, bus driver); Walker Edmiston (voice of God).

Appraisal and Synopsis

Wholly Moses is a mildly amusing send-up of religious epics such as *The Ten Commandments* (1956), *David and Goliath* (1960), and *Sodom and Gomorrah* (1963). Not as irreverent as the Monty Python satire *Life of Brian* (1979), *Wholly Moses* is gentler yet more on target. It produces many smiles but few belly laughs.

The story begins with a bus load of tourists on a no-frills tour of Israel. Harvey Orchid is a language professor at City College in New York who goes on vacation whenever he is jilted in his love life. He makes the acquaintance of Zoey, another tourist. Her hat is carried off by a gust of wind when the bus stops for lunch at the site of Christ's forty-day fast. Harvey and Zoey track it down to the entrance of a small cave in the side of a mountain where they find an ancient clay vase containing an old scroll written in Aramaic. Harvey translates the text, which discloses the life of Herschel, the bumbling brother-in-law of Moses.

Herschel's life parallels Moses' in many ways. Both were simultaneously set adrift in baskets on the Nile as infants. Moses was rescued by the pharaoh's daughter, and Herschel was rescued by members of the Senmet family, artisans who carve and sell stone idols of pagan deities. Herschel's father, Hyssop, who set him adrift, apprentices himself as a slave to the house of Senmet and oversees the growth of Herschel, who is trained in the family business. When he is grown, Herschel becomes the young pharaoh's stargazer, and he is forced to cross the desert on foot when he displeases the pharaoh. He eventually is given refuge by the family of Jethro the shepherd, exactly as Moses was. Herschel marries Zerelda, one of Jethro's daughters, and he is assigned to hunt down the stragglers from the flock tended by his brother-in-law, Moses. While hunting for a lost lamb on Mount Sinai, Herschel hears the voice of God and believes Yahweh is addressing him. Actually, He is talking to Moses, hidden from Herschel's sight by a boulder. Herschel presumes that he has been chosen by God to set free the Hebrew slaves held by the pharaoh.

Zerelda and Herschel head off to Egypt, but get sidetracked by many misadventures. When they get separated, Herschel searches for his wife in New Sodom, the rebuilt city of wickedness. Here he encounters a group of angels planning to destroy the city again, since it has fallen back into its sinful ways. They permit Herschel and his wife to escape. Zerelda looks back at New Sodom as fire and brimstone descend on it, and she turns into a pillar of salt. The Devil arrives, waiting to collect the damned souls from New Sodom and escort them to hell. He casually chats with Herschel, complaining about God's temper. The Devil tells Herschel that he was behind the best ideas during Creation, such as trees and three of the four seasons.

When Herschel finally reaches Egypt, he goes to see the pharaoh and finds out that the slaves were already freed by Moses. Devastated to learn that Moses was the genuine chosen one, not himself, Herschel returns to Sinai. While Moses is meditating, Herschel carves the Ten Commandments on two tablets in an attempt to help. He then plans to contact God, sculpting an enormous stone idol as bait. When God arrives, Herschel demands to know why he allowed him to think he was chosen. God replies that he was chosen as God's instrument to carve the Ten Commandments. He also promises Herschel that his contribution will be made known to some people in the future.

Back in modern times, Harvey finishes reading the scroll to Zoey. When they attempt to bring their discovery down from the mountain, it disintegrates into dust. Harvey and Zoey resume their tour, wondering why they alone were chosen to learn the story of Herschel.

Performances

John Ritter appears as the Devil wearing a sterotypical red silken outfit with cape and hood. He has two black horns and carries a pitchfork. He acts nonchalant with Herschel, speaking with him simply to pass the time while waiting for the damned souls to gather from the newly redestroyed Sodom. He speaks disappointedly about God and reflects that he is actually puzzled why he was selected to serve as the Devil, a function he does not particularly enjoy. Ritter's appearance is brief. His last words to Herschel, commenting on his current occupation, are forlorn and wistful: "Sometimes it just tears you up." Ritter's easygoing manner provides one of the most interesting vignettes in the film, although his episode does nothing at all to advance the plot. Dudley Moore underplays Herschel and is good in the give-and-take scenes with Ritter, Laraine Newman, Dom DeLuise, James Coco, Richard Pryor, and particularly Paul Sand. At times, the comic material is thin, but Moore manages to be wry and engaging throughout.

Notable Quotes

- You've come to tempt me, Devil. (**Herschel**)

Man gives in to temptation freely enough without any help from me. (**the Devil's reply**)

- I've known Him longer than anyone. We started out together. We were partners. (**the Devil**)

How did you become the Devil? (**Herschel**)

It's very simple. God comes over to me and says, "Here, try this on." (**the Devil, indicating his clothes**)

Witch Academy
AKA Little Devils

1992   Rating: *   Robert Vaughan as the Devil

American Independent. Written by Mark Thomas McGee; Photographed by Gary Graver; Edited by Steven Nielson; Music by Chuck Cirino; Produced and Directed by Fred Olen Ray. Color, 78 minutes.

Annotated Cast List

Veronica Carothers (*Leslie Perkins*, plain-looking sorority applicant); Suzanne Ager (*Wanda Warden*, head sorority sister); Priscilla Barnes (*Edith Ott*, sorority den mother); Michelle Bauer (*Tara*, brunette sorority sister); Ruth Collins (*Darla*, blonde sorority sister); Robert Vaughan (the Devil); Don Dowe (*Neal*, Wanda's boyfriend); Jay Richardson (*Professor Lamar*, college professor).

Appraisal and Synopsis

Witch Academy is a sophomoric jiggle comedy about a college sorority of beautiful girls with no brains and sadistic streaks. Exploitation director Fred Olen Ray has been quoted as saying that a quick flash of female nudity is the best special effect. Every few minutes in this film, therefore, one of the starlets changes, her clothes permitting a glimpse of Ray's favorite special effect. Other than these assets, *Witch Academy* has little going for it, except for the charm of Robert Vaughan, who probably spent one day on the set during a five-day shoot. Almost everything about this film is a misfire. The story is sexist and puerile and the humor so forced and artificial that the effort is a total embarrassment. The characters are empty-headed caricatures who aren't funny. The real oddity of this quickie is that its story of the Devil exactly foreshadows the plot device used in the hugely budgeted *End of Days* (1999). In *Witch Academy*, the Devil becomes involved because he has an opportunity once every hundred years to regain his full powers by marrying a kind and gentle woman. In *End of Days*, Satan gets the same opportunity every thousand years. Could Andrew W. Marlowe, screenwriter of *End of Days*, have actually been influenced by this minor comedy? More likely it is the long arm of coincidence at work, since *Witch Academy* is almost unwatchable, except perhaps for diehard fans of scream queen Michelle Bauer.

The opening minutes of the film introduce the audience to Wanda, Tara, and Darla, three bubble-headed bimbos who comprise Sigma Gamma. Their sole activities consist of strutting around half dressed while trying to hurt each other with cruel practical jokes. When their costume party is canceled at the last minute, they decide to invite Leslie Perkins, a Sigma Gamma wannabe, over for some degradation games. Leslie is actually a goody two-shoes, totally unsuitable for this bad-girl sorority. They chain Leslie up in the basement for an hour as their opening prank. Their den mother, the sadistic Edith Ott, shows up and punishes the girls for allowing Leslie to park her car in front of their sorority house.

Leslie, meanwhile, is set free by the Devil who offers to transform her into a hot chick more desirable than any of the sorority sisters. She hesitates dealing with the Devil, put off by his bad reputation, but he offers her a deal that doesn't put her soul at risk. He gives her a free sample of the benefits of his deal by changing her into Becky, a steamy seductress. Becky, pretending to be Leslie's sister, introduces herself to the Sigma Gamma girls, and easily bests them in the art of one-upmanship. The story then fizzles as Becky occasionally becomes a demonic monster, who winds up killing Edith and two visitors to the sorority house: Neal, Wanda's boyfriend, and Professor Lamar, a regular visitor. Leslie is upset by her blackouts when she changes into a monster and begins to suspect that the Devil is using her in some larger scheme.

Satan finally admits that he is trying to win Leslie's consent to wed him so that his powers will reach their zenith, but Leslie refuses. Wanda, overhearing the Devil's plea, offers to replace Leslie and serve as the bride of Satan. Because Wanda is a rotten individual, a lightning bolt strikes when he weds Wanda. She is turned into a hag, and the Devil is transformed into a grotesque demon. Wanda and the Devil are cast into hell, with Wanda threatening to make the Devil suffer a hundred years of torment when they get home. Meanwhile, God restores the three dead victims back to life, and Leslie retains the beauty of Becky full time.

Performances

Robert Vaughan plays the Devil on his best behavior, on the surface as helpful as possible toward Leslie. This is revealed as a sham, as Satan is merely bidding for greater power. Except for his demonic appearance after the lightning bolt, Vaughan plays the Devil without makeup, merely sporting a dark suit with a red muffler draped around his neck. His performance is deft, light, and tongue-in-cheek. His dialogue is rather trite and empty, and Vaughan carries his role simply by his own natural charisma. His scenes are mildly amusing and provide the only entertainment in this threadbare and forgettable endeavor. No doubt Vaughan would have been smashing in the role if it had been more substantial. The demonic mask used at the end of the picture is fairly gruesome and effective, but by this point little can be done to salvage this film.

Notable Quotes

• Oh, my God! (**Leslie, after the Devil materializes before her eyes**)

Not quite. (**the Devil**)

• If you are the Devil, where are your horns? (**Leslie**)

Gone! The wonders of modern cosmetic surgery. (**the Devil's reply**)

• Hardly anyone believes in me anymore. Did you? (**the Devil to Leslie**)

Witchcraft through the Ages
AKA Häxan

1922   Rating: ***   Benjamin Christensen as the Devil

Svensk. Written by Benjamin Christensen; Photographed by Johan Ankerstjerne; Music by Daniel Humair (sound version); Produced by Ernest Mattison; Sound version produced by Anthony Balch, Directed by Benjamin Christensen. B&W, 126 minutes (silent version); 76 minutes (sound version).

Annotated Cast List

William S. Burroughs (narrator, sound version); Benjamin Christensen (the Devil); Maria Pedersen (*Marie*, seamstress accused of witchcraft); Clara Pontoppidan (*Sister Cecile*, nun clubbed by Satan); Elith Pio (young monk); Oscar Stribolt (fat monk); Johs Anderson (chief inquisitor); Tora Teje (mentally ill woman in 1920 sequence); Poul Reumert, Karen Winther, Kate Fabian, Astrid Holm, Gerda Madsen, Aage Hertel, Ib Schonberg, Emmy Schonfeld, Frederick Christensen, Ella La Cour, Elizabeth Christensen, Alice O'Fredericks.

Appraisal and Synopsis

In many ways, the Swedish film *Witchcraft through the Ages* is the granddaddy of all exploitation films. Controversial upon its initial release in 1922, the picture contained nudity, torture, cruelty, and violence, as well as surreal scenes where witches line up to kiss the Devil on his naked posterior just under his curled-up tail. It was considered unsuitable by many critics, which no doubt increased business in areas where the film was shown. *Witchcraft through the Ages* was banned, hacked, and re-edited in many countries so that many different versions exist, with the most complete one running slightly over two hours. The picture was frequently rereleased and set the standard for later exploitation campaigns. A major restoration was released in 1969 with narration by the controversial literary critic and novelist William S. Burroughs. The quality of the restoration is excellent, and the picture moves at a much brisker pace with most of the title cards eliminated. Unfortunately, a largely inappropriate jazz score was added which ruins many of the impressive visual images. Burrough's narration is somewhat stilted and ineffective as well. Nevertheless, this edition preserves most of the film in pristine condition and provides modern viewers with an opportunity to experience this bizarre effort.

The picture starts off as a straightforward documentary about the practices of witchcraft in medieval times using old engravings, woodcuts, and artwork by Pieter Breughel and Hieronymus Bosch as well as clever mechanical models to illustrate the presentation. A pointer is occasionally used to highlight details as they are discussed. The picture then switches to quick dramatized skits with actors, seeming like a diabolical version of "Laugh In." The first one is a rather tongue-in-cheek episode illustrating the usefulness of love potions by a homely woman to seduce an even more homely fat monk. The preparation of the potion by a witch is shown in detail, including the obtaining of a hanged robber's withered hand. The Devil makes his first appearance popping up in front of a monk sitting at a reading carrel. The startled cleric stumbles backward in utter panic. Next Satan is seen in a quick shot throttling a victim from behind, with flames roaring behind him. A few moments later he arrives in the bedroom of a sleeping couple. He gently knocks against the open door, awakening the woman and luring her, and she slips into his warm embrace. He escorts another woman in her sleep to his dream castle in hell called Apollyon, which is the Greek name of the Angel of Death quoted in Revelation 9:11.

The picture then settles down to its main story illustrating the persecution of witches by the church. A wealthy man, Jesper Le Reliem, falls ill, and his family believes it is due to a witch's curse. A poor elderly woman, Marie the seamstress, comes to the kitchen begging for a meal. Anna, Jesper's young wife, goes to the tribunal of the Inquisition to denounce her. Marie is seized and brought before the judges, and the seamstress is broken under torture. Desperate, the old woman denounces anyone and everyone she knows as being involved in witchcraft. She describes a diabolical feast of toads and unbaptized children cooked up by the Devil. In particular, Marie denounces the women and servants of Jesper's household as being passionately devoted to Satan. They are all arrested by the Inquisition, leaving the sick man alone with his son and a single servant. The young monk who Anna had first approached at the tribunal now confesses that he is troubled by impure thoughts, and he is ordered to endure flagellation as atonement. The monk then denounces Anna, who is tricked into confessing by an elaborate ruse, and she is condemned to burn at the stake. The message of this tale, clearly, is "what goes around, comes around." The story ends as the witch-hunting tribunal, having purged the town, moves on to the next city to set up shop.

Another sequence shows convents gripped in panic over the Devil. Satan appears before a nun, Sister Cecile, and beats her with a club when she resists him. She yields and helps Satan breach the sanctity of the convent until all of the nuns are infected with madness, and they dance in hysterical frenzy.

Finally, the film leaps forward to 1920 and describes how mental illness was mistaken for witchcraft in earlier eras. A succession of mentally ill women is depicted, and it is shown how each would have been mistaken for a witche. The picture ends as modern psychiatrists are seen as the remedy for the phenomenon of witchcraft.

Performances

The director and writer of this film, Benjamin Christensen, himself appears as the Devil in numerous episodes. He is bald with pointed ears and horns. Always naked, the color of his body is darkened by greasepaint. The Devil is hairless above the waist but hairy below, and he has a small, curly tail which rises above his buttocks. The other distinguishing feature is his tongue, which flutters and darts in and out of his mouth. Christensen received a modicum of fame for this film and was imported to Hollywood, where he had a modest career directing such films as *Mockery* (1927) with Lon Chaney. Another of his notable American efforts was *Seven Footprints to Satan* (1929), a film long considered lost until a complete print surfaced in Italy in the early 1990s. This film was based on a novel by Abraham Merritt of a diabolical supervillain in the Fu Manchu mode. In the film version, however, the characters of Satan and his entire entourage are revealed at the conclusion as hired players for an elaborate practical joke. Merritt was outraged and upset by this denouement, and he disowned the picture. Christensen returned to Europe with the dawn of sound films and later directed additional films in Denmark.

Notable Quotes

- Satan assumes many forms. He has been seen as a prince, a peasant, a friar, a dog, a pebble, a pitchfork, but as legend has it, never as a font of holy water. (**narration**)
- High in the celestial hell is the castle of Apollyon, and there Satan gratifies his unspeakable secret desires. (**narration**)
- The enigma of the Devil remains and will no doubt remain unsolved until the death of the last man or woman. (**closing narration**)

The Witches of Eastwick

1987   Rating: ***   Jack Nicholson as the Devil

Warner Brothers. Written by Michael Christofer, based on the novel by John Updike; Photographed by Vilmos Zsigmond; Special Effects by Michael Lanteri (supervisor); Edited by Richard Francis-Bruce and Herbert C. de la Bouillerie; Music by John Williams, Antonin Dvorak, Giacomo Puccini, and Wolfgang Amadeus Mozart; Produced by Don Devlin; Directed by George Miller. Color, 121 minutes.

Annotated Cast List

Jack Nicholson (*Daryl Van Horne*, the Devil); Cher (*Alexandra Medford*, sculptor); Susan Sarandon (*Jane Spofford*, teacher and cellist); Michelle Pfeiffer (*Sukie Ridgemont*, journalist and mother of six); Veronica Cartwright (*Felicia Alden*, Eastwick selectman); Richard Jenkins (*Clyde Alden*, her husband, editor of the town paper); Keith Jochim (*Walter Neff*, school principal); Becca Lish (Neff's wife); Carel Struycken (*Fidel*, Van Horne's servant); Helen Lloyd Breed (*Mrs. Biddle*, gift store owner); Ruth Maynard (her friend); Eugene Boyles (minister); Carol White (cashier); John Blood (deli clerk); Ron Campbell (ice cream vendor); Margot Dionne (nurse); Lansdale Chatfield, James Boyle (doctors); Babbie Green, Jane Johnson, Merrily Horowicz, Harriet Medin (townspeople).

Appraisal and Synopsis

A thoroughly delightful if somewhat uneven comic fantasy, this film owes most of its vitality to its four terrific leads. It is also boosted by top production values, including magnificent cinematography and a witty musical score by John Williams. The sets and location footage, such as at the Vanderbilt mansion "The Breakers" in Newport, Rhode Island, are superb. The prime weakness of *The Witches of Eastwick* is the screenplay, which has great difficulty at times blending together the film's diverse and sometimes contrary elements. The overuse of foul language makes the film less appropriate for younger audiences, which would have been drawn to the storyline. There are awkward shifts from slapstick to parody and from social commentary to horror. An absurd, overlong tennis game with juvenile sight gags completely stalls the plot at one point, breaking the rhythm of the story. Character development is weak, particularly with the three witches, who are given no opportunity in the script to react to the uncanny aspects of their relationship with their paramour. Only after the death of Felicia do they even mention an awareness of their supernatural powers. Time and again the film is forced to rely on the dynamic personalities of the main players to compensate for the script's awkwardness. Fortunately, they are able to do this rather well, and director George Miller keeps the action brisk enough for the most part. The satirical core of the picture never seems to gel. Miller is unable to provide a clear focus in what should have been a battle of the sexes with diabolical overtones.

The story is set in Eastwick, a small, upper-crust New England town dating back to 1640. Three women, unknown to themselves, are endowed with supernatural powers of witchcraft. All three, Alexandra, Jane, and Sukie, are sexually repressed, divorced, or widowed, and they are frustrated by the lack of suitable male companionship in Eastwick. One rainy night, the three friends conjure up the image of a desirable man, a tall, dark prince under a curse. Their powers are amplified by wishing together, and as a result the Devil, in the guise of millionaire playboy Daryl Van Horne, buys the Lennox mansion, the largest and most exclusive estate in town, and settles in the community. Eastwick's leading citizen, Felicia Alden, takes an immediate dislike to the flamboyant and cocky Van Horne. At a reception following a chamber music recital, the entire gathering is abuzz over Van Horne, who fell asleep and snored loudly during the concert. The annoyed Felicia trips and falls downstairs, breaking her leg.

Daryl sets out to seduce the three women one by one. He encounters Alexandra while birdwatching. He invites her to lunch. Vulgar, crude, but quite charming, Daryl is irresistible to Alexandra. Daryl visits Jane as she practices her cello. He rhapsodizes about her fingering but criticizes her bowing. He coaches her from the piano as they play Dvorak's *Cello Concerto*. Her cello actually starts to smoke in passion, and Jane falls into Daryl's arms the moment they finish playing. Finally, Daryl invites all three women to his mansion for a game of tennis. To the surprise of Alexandra and Jane, Daryl gives most of his attention to Sukie. Their tennis game gets out of control when the ball starts to behave contrary to the rules of nature. Later, when Sukie and Daryl go for a swim in his indoor pool, they wind up embracing each other passionately.

The three women become frequent guests at the mansion. Daryl fills the ballroom with balloons, and his guests and their children romp around while he plays the aria "Nessun Dorma" from Puccini's *Turandot*. A montage showing them all at play follows. Meanwhile, resentment starts to build in town against Van Horne and his three companions, largely fanned by a ranting Felicia. She forces her husband to fire Sukie from the newspaper.

Alexandra, Jane, and Sukie confront Daryl about how everyone in town is turning against them. He persuades them to eat cherries while concentrating on their resentment of Felicia. As they eat more and more cherries, the scene switches to Felicia's home where she predicts that the Devil is planning to have three sons to do his evil bidding on Earth. She inexplicably starts to spit up cherry pits. She goes into convulsions and dies. When the three girlfriends hear of her death, they panic and decide to avoid Daryl in the future.

Daryl is perplexed and annoyed when his three lovers give him the cold shoulder

Jack Nicholson shows his diabolic demeanor in The Witches of Eastwick.

and refuse to see him. The three women discover that each of them is pregnant. Daryl uses his supernatural powers to intimidate them. Alexandra gets a vision of snakes, Jane sees herself growing older, and Sukie gets attacks of sudden pain. They pretend to seek a reconciliation with Daryl, but after sending him off on an errand to fetch bagels and ice cream, they create a waxen image of him using hairs from his comb and other personal objects. They stick pins in this voodoo doll while concentrating their powers on sending Daryl back to hell. Daryl experiences wild and painful side effects as they launch their attack. He returns home and transforms into a raging demon before finally vanishing.

Eighteen months later, Alexandra, Jane, and Sukie find themselves missing Daryl, but they warn each other not to think of him when they are together lest they accidentally summon him. In the next room, their three infant sons are watching television when Daryl appears on the screen. Beaming, he calls to his children and talks to them. They gurgle with delight, but their mothers enter the room, shutting off the set by remote control as Daryl sighs, "Ah, ladies, come on."

Performances

Jack Nicholson's broad and exuberant frolic as the Devil is compelling, but his performance is similar to his interpretation of the Joker in *Batman* (1989). He is witty, charming, coarse, intelligent, uncouth, and inspiring all at the same time. For most of the film, Nicholson relies on no makeup, and the only unusual thing about his appearance is the unfashionable little pony tail he sports, no doubt a substitute for his demonic tail. When angered by his three acolytes, Nicholson's reading shifts more toward *The Shining* (1980) when Jack Torrance has his breakdown. At the climax, special effects take center stage as the enraged Devil reverts to his demonic form in a spellbinding sequence. The three leading actresses match Nicholson scene for scene, and their interplay with him is exceptional. Unfortunately, the script's stodgy development undercuts their performances somewhat. Veronica Cartwright is spectacular as the only one who seems aware from the start that Nicholson is the Devil and that he has a master plan to lead mankind astray with the three sons that he plans to sire with the witches. Carel Struycken, Lurch from *The Addams Family* (1991), is outstanding as the Devil's man Friday. The name of Keith Jochim's character, Walter Neff, is based on *Double Indemnity* (1944), in which Fred MacMurray played a murderous insurance salesman with the same moniker.

Notable Quotes

• Who are you? (**Alexandra to Daryl**)

Just your average, horny little Devil. (**his reply**)

• I know music. It is the one thing that makes me humble. (**Daryl to Jane**)

• Do you think God knew what He was doing when He created woman.... or do you think it was another of His minor mistakes like tidal waves, earthquakes, and floods? [gags] You don't think God makes mistakes? Of course He does. We all make mistakes. Of course when we make mistakes, they call it evil. When God makes mistakes, they call it nature. (**Daryl to the church congregation**)

Appendix One: Lost, Obscure, and Arcane Devil Films

This list contains additional Devil films not covered in the main section, mostly due to their relative obscurity. Since these films are lost, foreign, or generally unavailable at the current time, it is difficult to determine if they meet the criteria for inclusion in the book. All pre-1915 films are undoubtedly too short in length, but are listed in an attempt to be as comprehensive as possible. The names of the director and performer playing the Devil are included whenever possible, as well as the country of origin. This list is in chronological order.

The Devil's Manor (1896) Fr. Dir. by Georges Méliès; Georges Méliès as the Devil.
Faust et Marguerite (1897) Fr. Dir. by Georges Méliès.
Le Cabinet de Mephistopheles (1897) Fr. Dir. by Georges Méliès.
La Damnation de Faust (1898) Fr. Dir. by Georges Méliès.
Faust and Mephistopheles (1898) Brit. Dir. by George Albert Smith.
Le Grotte du Diable (1898) Fr. Dir. by Georges Méliès.
Le Diable au Convent (1899) Fr. Dir. by Georges Méliès; Georges Méliès as the Devil.
Faust and Marguerite (1900) US Dir. by Edwin S. Porter.
Guguste et Belzebuth (1901) aka *Clown vs. Devil*. Fr. Dir. by Georges Méliès.
Faust aux Enfers (1903) Fr. Dir. by Georges Méliès.
Faust et Mephistopheles (1903) Fr. Dir. by Alice Guy.
Les Filles du Diable (1903) Fr. Dir. by Georges Méliès.
The Merry Frolics of Satan (1906) Fr. Dir. by Georges Méliès.
Satan en Prison (1907) Fr. Dir. by Georges Méliès.
The Devil (1908) US Based on the play *Az Ördög* by Ferenc Molnár; Dir. by D.W. Griffith.
Faust (1909) US Dir. by Edwin S. Porter; William Sorrell as the Devil.
The Devil, the Servant and the Man (1910) US Dir. by Frank Beal.
Faust (1910) Fr. Dir. by Henri Andreani.
Bill Bumper's Bargain (1911) US Dir. by Francis X. Bushman; Francis X. Bushman as the Devil.
Dante's Inferno (1911) It. Dir. by Giuseppe de Liguoro.
Satan (1912) It. Based on *Paradise Lost* by John Milton; Dir. by Luigi Maggi.
Noch perd Rozhdestuom (1913) aka *The Night before Christmas*. Rus. Based on the short

story "Christmas Eve" by Nikolai Gogol; Dir. by Wladyslaw Starewicz; Ivan Mozzhukhin as the Devil.

Strashnaya Mest (1913) aka *A Terrible Revenge*. Rus. Based on a short story by Nikolai Gogol; Dir. by Wladyslaw Starewicz; Ivan Mozzhukhin as the Devil.

The Temptations of Satan (1914) US Dir. by Herbert Blanché; James O'Neill as the Devil.

The Devil (1915) aka *Satan's Pawn*. US Based on the play *Az Ördög* by Ferenc Molnár; Dir. by Thomas H. Ince and Reginald Barker; Edward Connelly as the Devil.

Rapsodia Satanica (1915) It. Dir. by Nino Oxilia; Giulio Bazzini as the Devil.

The Devil, the Servant and the Man (1916) US Remake of 1910 version; Dir. by Frank Beal.

The Devil's Toy (1916) US Dir. by Harley Knoles; Edwin Stevens as the Devil.

The Sorrows of Satan (1916) Brit. Dir. by Alexander Butler; Cecil Humphries as the Devil.

Faust des Riesen (1917) Ger. Dir. by Rudolph Bierbrach.

El Protegido de Satan (1917) Sp. Dir. by Jose Maria Codina.

The Warfare of the Flesh (1917) US Dir. by Edward Warren.

Restitution (1918) US Dir. by Howard Gaye; Al Ernest Garcia as the Devil.

To Hell with the Kaiser (1918) US Dir. by George Irving; Walter P. Lewis as the Devil.

Satanas (1919) Ger. Dir. by F. W. Murnau; Conrad Veidt as the Devil.

Unheimliche Geschichten (1919) aka *Weird Tales*. Ger. Dir. by Richard Oswald; Reinhold Schünzel as the Devil.

Kurfürstendamn (1920) Ger. Dir. by Richard Oswald; Conrad Veidt as the Devil.

The Devil* (1921) US Based on the play *Az Ördög* by Ferenc Molnár; Dir. by James Young; George Arliss as Dr. Muller, the Devil.

Don Juan et Faust (1922) Fr. Dir. by Marcel Herbier.

The Girl from Rocky Point (1922) US Dir. by Fred Becker; Walt Whitman (not the poet) as the Devil.

Faust (1923) Brit. Dir. by Bertram Phillips.

Puritan Passions (1923) US Based on the short story "Feathertop" by Nathaniel Hawthorne; Dir. by Frank Tuttle; Dwight Wiman as the Devil.

La Damnation de Faust (1925) Fr. Dir. by Victor Charpentier and Stephan Passet; Marcel LaPorte as the Devil.

The Soul Eater† (1925) Ger. Conrad Veidt as the Devil.

Liebe, Tod und Teufel (1934) aka *The Devil in the Bottle*. Ger. Based on the story "The Bottle Imp" by Robert Louis Stevenson; Dir. by Heinz Hilpert and Reinhardt Steinbicker.

Der Student von Prag (1935) Ger. Dir. by Arthur Robison; Theodore Loos as the Devil.

Pan Twardowski (1936) Pol. Dir. by Henryk Szaro: Kazimierz Junosza-Stepowski as the Devil.

Las Cinco Advertencias de Satanas (1938) aka *Five Warnings from Satan*. Sp. Based on the novel and play by Enrique Poncela; Dir. by Isidro Socias.

The Blood of Jesus (1941) US Dir. by Spencer Williams; James B. Jones as the Devil.

Himlaspelet (1942) aka *The Road to Heaven*. Swe. Dir. by Alf Sjöberg; Emil Fjellström as the Devil.

Big Showoff (1945) US Dir. by Howard Bretherton; Paul Hurst as the Devil.

Las Cinco Advertencias de Satanas (1945) aka *Five Warnings from Satan*. Mex. Based on the novel and play by Enrique Poncela; Dir. by Julian Soler; Alejandro Ciangberotti as the Devil.

---

*This lost film was recently discovered and is being restored.
†Different sources question if this film was ever completed.

Going to Glory, Come to Jesus (1946) aka *Fight with the Devil.* US Dir. by T. Meyer; John Watts as the Devil.

Der Apfel ist Ab (1948) aka *The Apple Fell.* Ger. Dir. by Helmut Käutner; Arno Assmann as the Devil.

Leggenda di Faust (1948) It. Dir. by Carmine Gallone; Italo Tajo as the Devil.

El Diablo No Es Tan Diablo (1949) aka *The Devil Is Not Such a Devil.* Mex. Dir by Julian Soler; Jose Antonio Vera as the Devil.

Der Fallende Stern (1950) aka *The Fallen Star.* Ger. Dir. by Harald Braun.

Gott, Mensch und Teufel (1950) aka *God, Man and the Devil.* Yiddish Dir. by Josef Zeiden; Gustav Berger as the Devil.

Ella, Lucifer y Yo (1952) Mex. Dir. by Miguel Morayta; Carlos Lopez Moctezuna as the Devil.

Glen or Glenda (1953) US Dir. by Edward D. Wood, Jr.; Captain DeZita as the Devil.

Retorno a la Juventud (1953) Mex. Dir. by Juan Bustillo Oro.

Que Lindo Cha Cha Cha (1954) Mex. Dir. by Gilberto Martinez Solares.

Toto all'Inferno (1955) It. Dir. by Camillo Mastrocinque; Nerio Bernardi as the Devil.

Misterios de la Magia Negra (1957) Mex. Dir. by Miguel M. Delgado; Reynaldo Rivera as the Devil.

El Fistol del Diablo (1958) Mex. 12-chapter serial recut as four feature films: *Duela a Muerte, Juego Diabolico, Trampa Fatal,* and *El Ataud Infernal;* Dir. by Fernando Fernandez; Roberto Canedo as the Devil.

Faust (1960) Ger. Dir. by Peter Gorski; Gustav Gründgens as the Devil.

Macario (1960) Mex. Dir. by Roberto Gavaldon; Jose Galvez as the Devil.

Jedermann (1961) Ger. Based on the play *Everyman* by Hugo Von Hofmannsthal; Dir. by Gottfried Reinhardt; Heinrich Schweiger as the Devil.

The Night before Christmas (1961) Rus. Based on the story "Christmas Eve" by Nikolai Gogol; Dir. by Aleksandr Rou; Georgi Millyar as the Devil.

Fan ger ett Anbud (1963) Swe. Dir. by Jan Molander; Heinz Hopf as the Devil.

Faust (1963) US Dir. by Michael Suman; Roban Cody as the Devil.

Mate Doma Iva? (1964) Czech. Dir. by Pavel Hobl; Raoul Schranil as the Devil.

Faustus XX (1966) Romania Dir. by Ion Popescu-Gopo; Jorj Voicu as the Devil.

Gregorio y Su Angel (1966) Mex. Dir. by Gilberto Martinez Solares; Tin Tan as the Devil.

Hissen som gick ner i Helvetet (1969) Swe. Dir. by Bengt Lagerkvist; Ake Fridell as the Devil.

Las Cinco Avisos de Satanas (1970) aka *Five Warnings from Satan.* Sp. Remake of 1938 film; based on the novel and play by Enrique Poncela; Dir. by Jose Luis Merino.

I Love My Wife (1970) US Dir. by Mel Stuart; Robert Kaufman as the Devil.

The Joys of Jezebel (1970) US Dir. by Peter Perry; Christopher Stone as the Devil.

Asylum of Satan (1972) US Dir. by William Girdler; the Devil played by unknown actor wearing rubber mask.

The Master and Margherite (1972) Yug. Dir. by Aleksander Petrovic; Alain Cuny as the Devil.

Birnbaum und Hollerstauden (1973) Ger. Dir. by Theodor Grädler; Alexander Golling as the Devil.

Poor Devil (1973) US NBC telefilm; Dir. by Robert Scheerer; Christopher Lee as the Devil.

Chi Sei? (1975) aka *The Devil within Her.* It. Dir. by Ovidio Assonitis; Richard Johnson performs a lengthy pre-credit narration as the Devil but plays an emissary of the Devil in the film proper.

Inquisition (1976) Sp. Dir. by Paul Naschy (directorial debut); Paul Naschy as the Devil.

Les Turlupins (1980) Fr. Dir. by Bernard Revan; Pierre Vial as the Devil.

Mo Deng Tian Shi (1981) HK Dir. by John Woo; Fat Chung as the Devil.
Dolina Issy (1983) Pol. Dir. by Tadeusz Konwicki; Jerzy Kryszak as the Devil.
Second Time Lucky (1984) N.Z. Dir. by Michael Anderson; Robert Helpmann as the Devil.
Andramelech (1985) Can. Dir. by Pierre Gregoire; Jean Petitclerc (Lucifer) and Bernard Meney (Mephistopheles) as the Devil.
Angela (1985) US Dir. by Rebecca Miller; Peter Facinelli as the Devil.
Parking (1985) Fr. Dir. by Jacques Demy; Jean Marais as the Devil.
Zorro vs. Satan (1985) Sp. Dir. by Felix M. Ruiz; ? as the Devil.
Mr. Boogedy (1986) US Dir. by Oz Scott; Kedric Wolfe as the Devil.
Australian Dream (1987) Aus. Dir. by Jackie McKimmie; Marlon Holden as the Devil.
Malefiche Presenze (1988) aka *Witchery*. It. Dir. by Fabrizio Laurenti and Rob Spera; Ely Coughlin as the Devil.
Narcosatanicos Asesinos (1989) Mex. Dir. by Jose J. Munguia; Roberto Ballesteros as the Devil.
Toxic Avenger III: The Last Temptation of Toxie (1989) US Dir. by Michael Herz and Lloyd Kaufman; Rich Collins as the Devil.
Eine Frau Namens Harry (1990) Ger. Dir. by Cyril Frankel; Charles Gray as the Devil.
Mi Nismo Andjeli (1992) aka *We Aren't Angels*. Serb. Dir. by Srdjan Dragojevic; Srdjan Todorovic as the Devil.
Back from Hell (1993) US Dir. by Matt Jaissie; Don Ruem as the Devil.
Young Goodman Brown (1993) US Based on a short story by Nathaniel Hawthorne; Dir. by Peter George; John P. Ryan as the Devil.
Come Again? (1994) US Dir. by Christopher Pappas and Matthew Silverstein; Paul F. Doering as the Devil.
Faust (1996) Swe. Dir. by Eva Bergman; Puck Ahlsen as the Devil.
Le Bassin de J.W. (1997) Port./Fr. Dir. by Joao César Monteiro; Hugues Quester as the Devil.
The Devil's Child (1997) US ABC telefilm; Dir. by Robby Roth; Thomas Gibson as the Devil.
The Good Book (1997) US Dir. by Matthew Giaquinto; Barry Gerdsen as the Devil.
Faust (1997) Ger. Dir. by Cordula Tranter; Norbert Mahler as the Devil.
The Book of Life (1998) Can. Dir. by Hal Hartley; Thomas J. Ryan as the Devil.
Dirty Work (1998) Can. Dir. by Bob Saget; Adam Sandler as the Devil.
Mensch Jesus (1999) Ger. Dir. by Cornelius Meckseper; Gustav-Peter Wöhler as the Devil.
Ricky 6 (1999) Can. Dir. by Peter Filardi; Gerald Wong as the Devil.
G-Men from Hell (2000) US Dir. by Christopher Coppola; Robert Goulet as the Devil.

Appendix Two: Television Devils

The Devil has made numerous appearances in television productions, mostly anthology shows such as "The Twilight Zone" (1959–1964), and it is certainly germane to consider a number of these depictions in this study of Satanic portrayals. Unless noted otherwise, each episode is a half hour in length.

Florenz Ames Ames plays a crafty Devil in an episode of "Four Star Theater" (1951–1954) called "Devil to Pay," in which he hires cantankerous efficiency expert Charles Boyer to straighten out the office backlog in hell. Boyer brings modern business practices to the inferno and winds up discovering his own lost file, announcing his own death as imminent. For his punishment, the Devil assigns him an office in hell where he will spend eternity making big deals which all fall through. This clever episode was directed by Robert Florey.

Fred Astaire Portraying a humorous Devil for "Alcoa Premiere" (1961–1963), a program he normally hosted, in a segment called "Meet Mr. Lucifer," Astaire undertakes seven transformations as Satan attempts to bring hell more up-to-date for the modern world. This hour-long episode is unrelated to the film with the same title.

Jack Benny Comedian Benny made three appearances as himself on Danny Thomas' sitcom "Make Room for Daddy" (1953–1965). In one episode, "That Old Devil Jack Benny," he also plays the Devil during an extended dream sequence, offering a contract to Thomas that would guarantee him comedic success: the use of the word "gee" as a surefire laugh, just as Jack Benny has the rights to the word "well."

Sebastian Cabot In "The Twilight Zone" episode "A Nice Place to Visit," slain gambler Larry Blyden assumes he is in heaven when he encounters Cabot as the jovial Mr. Pip, who endeavors to grant his every wish. He soon becomes bored and questions Pip if he should be sent to "the other place" instead. Pip finally responds, "This is the other place!"

Gary Cole "American Gothic" (1995–1996) is set in a mysterious southern town dominated by its sheriff, Lucas Black (Cole), who is the Devil in disguise. This offbeat drama only lasted one season.

John Emery One of the finest episodes of Boris Karloff's "Thriller" (1960–1962), "The Devil's Ticket" concerns failed artist MacDonald Carey, who pawns his soul to the Devil (Emery) for ninety days in exchange for artistic success. To redeem his soul, he must paint a portrait of such quality that it captures the subject's soul. Carey tricks Satan by using him as his subject, but he is consigned to hell when his wife burns his overcoat, which contained the Devil's pawn ticket. This episode was written by Robert Bloch.

Theodore J. Flicker The noted director/author of *The President's Analyst* (1967) and countless television shows played the Devil in "Hell's Bells," an episode he made for the Rod Serling–hosted series "Night Gallery" (1970–1973). John Astin plays a hippie who dies in an auto crash and winds up in the netherworld which consists of sedate, wallpapered rooms filled with Lawrence Welk fans. When Astin confronts the Devil, wanting to encounter fire and brimstone, he is told that this section is meant to be hell for him, but for others the identical room is paradise.

Robert Foulk "The Hunt" is a backwoods folktale from "The Twilight Zone." Hunter Arthur Hunnicutt and his hound dog drown while on a raccoon hunt. They arrive at the pearly gates, and the gatekeeper (Foulk) welcomes the hunter, but refuses to allow his dog to enter. Hunnicutt stomps off and later meets an angel, who tells him that he actually bypassed the entrance to hell. The angel explains, "Even the Devil can't fool a dog!"

John Glover Glover was a regular as Satan in the series "Brimstone" (1998–1999), in which the Devil dispatches a recently deceased cop, Ezekiel Stone, back to Earth to track down and retrieve the 113 souls who escaped from hell. The unusual hour-long show lasted only a single season.

Thomas Gomez In "Escape Clause," an early "Twilight Zone" entry, hypochondriac David Wayne is offered a deal by the Devil, who uses the name Cadwallader. Wayne wishes to be made immortal and indestructible. He is later arrested for the death of his wife, and after being sentenced to life imprisonment without parole, Wayne implores the Devil to activate the escape clause and take his soul at once. Gomez is best remembered as a *film noir* villain.

Robin Hughes "The Howling Man" is perhaps the best single television episode featuring the Devil. In this "Twilight Zone" classic, Hughes plays a mysterious prisoner at a remote monastery in Europe after World War One. Hiker H. M. Wynant, seeking refuge at the monastery during a storm, winds up freeing the meek-looking man who instantly transforms into a caped, horned Devil. John Carradine costars as the monk who captured the Devil. Hughes also played the beheaded sorcerer in "The Thing that Couldn't Die" (1958).

Burgess Meredith In "Printer's Devil," an hour-long episode of "The Twilight Zone," Burgess Meredith gives one of his most memorable performances, comparable to Walter Huston in *The Devil and Daniel Webster*. A small-town newspaper on the verge of bankruptcy is saved when a crafty new employee named Smith joins the staff. He alters the linotype machine so that anything typed on it comes true, and he creates a series of made-to-order disasters. Smith then tells the editor, Robert Sterling, that he is the Devil and induces him to sign his contract. Sterling eventually tricks the Devil by typing out a linotype story that Smith's contract is null and void.

Duane Morris The Gothic soap opera "Dark Shadows" (1966–1971) featured one episode in which Satan himself appears, using the name Diabolos. The witch Angelique (Lara Parker), cursed with vampirism by her mentor, the warlock Nicholas Blair (Humbert Allen Astredo), goes to hell to appeal to Satan to free her from his spell. She claims he has fallen in love with a mortal woman. Blair himself is summoned, and the Devil gives him forty-eight hours to sacrifice his beloved at a black mass. Several episodes later, Blair fails and is consumed by the flames of hell under the watchful eyes of his adversary, Barnabas Collins (Jonathan Frid). As the Devil, Morris wears a monk's cowl, which hides his features, and speaks in a melodramatic voice with frequent laughter.

Julie Newmar   Perhaps the most beautiful of all Devil portrayals, Newmar is stunning in "Of Late I Think of Cliffordsville," another one-hour episode of "The Twilight Zone." Ruthless business tycoon Albert Salmi wants to relive his youth and his career of business triumph. He signs a deal with Miss Devlin to return to Cliffordsville in 1910, but the lovely Devil tricks him by restoring only his appearance of youth, while his stamina and health remain that of a seventy-five-year old. When Salmi renegotiates to return to 1963, he winds up as a poor janitor instead of a wealthy corporate leader.

Mickey Rooney   Rooney appears in a one-man episode of "The Twilight Zone" called "The Last Night of a Jockey." He plays Grady, an embittered jockey who was recently suspended for throwing a race. The Devil appears to him in the form of his own reflection in the mirror. He offers to grant his greatest wish, to become big. At first, Rooney is delighted to be transformed into a giant, but when he learns that he is cleared by the racing commission, he falls into despair because giants cannot be jockeys.

George C. Scott   A 1960 episode of "Play of the Week," a two-hour show produced by David Susskind, featured a modern-dress dramatization of the third act of George Bernard Shaw's *Man and Superman*, which is entitled "Don Juan in Hell." This role was originally intended to be played by Vincent Price, who toured in the play, but a scheduling conflict prevented his appearance, and he was replaced by Scott.

Jean Shepherd   Author, humorist, and radio personality Jean Shepherd had a long-running PBS series called "Jean Shepherd's America." In a 1985 episode, Shepherd assumes the role of the Devil in a fantasy travelogue of the city of New Orleans. Decked out in an elaborate cape, Shepherd provides a surreal tour of the city interspersed with monologues about the seven deadly sins and the fine art of temptation.

David Wayne   *The Devil and Daniel Webster* was dramatized several times on television and radio, with one of the best versions being an hour-long 1955 presentation on "Breck Showcase Theater" with Wayne as Mr. Scratch and Edward G. Robinson as Daniel Webster.

Index

Note: Performers with asterisks have played the Devil.
*Numbers in **boldface** refer to pages with photographs.*

Aaron, Caroline 60
Abbott, George 54
Abbott, John 132
Abeille, Claude 255
Abraham, Marc 108
The Absent-Minded Professor (1961 film) 28
Ackerman, Forrest J 112, 114
Acts of the Apostles (Bible N.T.) 133
Adagio for Strings (orchestra composition) 133
Adam 226–229, 250
Adams, Beverly 281
Adams, Tony 273
Adan y Eva (1956 film) 228
The Addams Family (1991 film) 303
Adelsten, Paul 39
Adler, Gordon 95
Adler, Richard 54
Adolphson, Kristina 89
Adrian, Kay 276
Adrianson, Stephen 257
Agamemnon (king of Mycenae) 279, 280
Agar, John 28
Ager, Suzanne 296
Aguilar, Rosa Maria 235
Aguirre, Beatriz 259
Aguirre, Jose Luis *see* Trotsky
Ahlsen, Puck* 308
Airplane (1980 film) 233
Alazraki, Benito 259
Alba 36
Albano, Lou 262
Albert, Eddie 101, 104
Alberti, Fritz 271, 272
Albigenses 195
Albright, Hardie 21
Alcoha Premier (TV series) 309
Alcoha Presents *see* *One Step Beyond*

Alda, Robert 180
Alexander, Richard 165
Alexander, Stone (Devil pseudonym) 217–220
Alexander, Van 226
Alexander the Great 105, 107
Alfred Hitchcock Presents (TV series) 95
Alhazred, Abdul (character) 113
Ali, Muhammad 221
Alias Nick Beal (1949 film) 4, 9–17
Alice in Wonderland (1988 film) 124
Alice's Adventures in Wonderland (1972 film) 250
Alien (1979) 77
Aligheri, Dante *see* Dante Aligheri
All in the Family (TV series) 57
All My Children (TV series) 155
All That Money Can Buy *see* *The Devil and Daniel Webster*
Allegret, Catherine 197
Allen, David 112
Allen, Gary 246
Allen, Irwin 264, 266, 267
Allen, Mel 204, 206
Allen, Rae 54
Allen, Woody 60–62
Allesandroni, Allesandro 98
Alley, Kirstie 60
Allison, Damon 257
Allred, Gloria 201
Alm, Gita 95
Alma, Marian 271
Alma Tedema, Lawrence (artist) 133
Alper, Murray 22
Alpert, Trevor 39
"The Alphabet Song" (song) 130
Alten, Ferdinand von 271
Alvarez, Jacinto Molina *see* Naschy, Paul

Amadeus (1984 film) 264
Ameche, Don 142, **143**, 145, 266
Ameche, Jim 265, 266
Amendola, Claudio 157
Amendolia, Don 240
American Gothic (TV series) 309
Ames, Florenz* 309
Ames, Leon 135
Ames, Michael 142, 145
The Amityville Horror (1979 film) 116
Amoni, Tony 208
Ancelin, Marcel 255
The Ancient Mariner (1925 film) 60
And Then There Were None (1945) 33
Anderson, Candy 241
Anderson, Eddie "Rochester" 44
Anderson, Howard 243
Anderson, Johs 298
Anderson, Michael 308
Anderson, Michael, Jr. 132
Anderssen, Bibi 89
Andrada, Jenny 160
Andramelech (1985 film) 308
Andreani, Henri 305
Andrew, Kory L.* 78, 79
Andrews, Julie 36
Andrews, Tod *see* Ames, Michael
Angel Heart (1987 film) 17–21
Angel on My Shoulder (1946 film) 21–24, 91
Angela (1985 film) 308
Angels and the Devil (theme) 121–122, 127–129, 169–170, 185, 231–233
Animal House (1978 film) 202
Anka, Paul 226, 229
Ankers, Evelyn 114
Ankerstjerne, Johan 298
Ansara, Michael 132
Anspach, Susan 69

313

314 • Index

Anthology films 78, 95, 171, 201, 275, 281, 298
Anthony, Lysette 273
Antichrist 4, 127, 188, 218, 220
Antony, Mark 265
"Any Fool Can See" (song) 72
Anzel, Hy 61
Der Apfel ist Ab (1948 film) 307
Apollyon (Devil's dream castle) 299, 300
The Apple Fell see *Der Apfel ist Ab*
Applegate (Devil pseudonym) 54–57
Aquilon, Raymond 197
Aragorn (character) 232
Arana, Tomas 168
Arata, Ubaldo 189
Arbus, Allan 51
The Archdevil see *The Devil in Love*
Archerd, Army 69, 233
Archibald, Dawn 49
L'Arcidiavolo see *The Devil in Love*
Argo, Victor 168
Aristocracy and the Devil (theme) 34–35, 100–101, 173–175, 250, 251–254, 269, 271, 291, 292
Arlen, Harold 43
Arletty 291, 293
Arliss, George* 306
Armstrong, Louis 44, 45, 46
Armstrong, R. G. 176
Arngrim, Stefan* 126, 129
Arno, Sig 80
Arnold, Benedict 63, 65. 66, 68
Arnold, Edward* 62, 66, 68
Arnova, Alba 118
Arquette, Lewis 183
Arquette, Patricia 183
Arrighi, Niké 75, 77
Arriola, Armando 235
Arsene Lupin, Detective (1937 film) 293
Art and the Devil (theme) 14, 86, 93–94, 96, 180, 183, 209–212, 238, 239, 267, 309–310
Arthur, Johnny 80, 81
Artuffo, Riccardo 189
Artur, Alain 255
Arvedson, Ragnar 89
As Good As It Gets (1997 film) 43
Asa the Black Monk 65
Ashley, John 30, 31
Ashton, James 101
Askin, Leon 135
Asmodeus (Devil pseudonym) 113–115
Asner, Ed 139, 141, 142
Assmann, Arno* 307
Assonitis, Ovidio 307
Astaire, Fred* 309
Astin, John 310
Astredo, Humbert Allen 310
Asylum of Satan (1972 film) 3, 307
El Ataud Infernal (1958 film) 307

Athletes and the Devil (theme) 40, 54–57, 93, 118–120, 185
Atropos (mythological figure) 282–284
Attila the Hun 146, 147, 152
Auer, Mischa 118, 120
Die Augen des Ole Brandis (1914 film) 268
Auger, Claudine 73, 74
August, Joseph 58, 62
El Aulloido del Diablo see *Howl of the Devil*
Austin, Frank 63
Austin, William 288
Australian Dream (1985 film) 308
Australian films 308
Autopsia de un Fantasma (1967 film) 4, 25–27
Autopsy of a Ghost see *Autopsia de un Fantasma*
Avellana, Joe Mar 160, 163
Avery, Val 176
Axton, Hoyt 176, 177
Az Ördög (play) 305, 306

Babylon Five (TV series) 203
Bach, Johann Sebastian 53, 66, 124, 275, 276, 277
Back from Hell (1993 film) 308
Back to the Future (1985 film) 148
Bacon, Toni 226
Bacque, Andre 91
The Bad Seed (1956 film) 156
Badaraco, Jacob A. 165
Baggot, King 214
Bahl, Ellen 194
Bailey, G. W. 157, 159
Bailey, John 51
Bailey, William 44
Bait (1954 film) 28–30, 285
Bakalyan, Richard 132, 135
Baker, Buddy 69
Baker, Caroll 132, 135
Baker, Kathy* 197, 200, 201
Baker, Kenny 278
Baker, Rick 83
Bakey, Ed 115
Bakker, Jim 234
Bakker, Tammy Faye 234
Balaban, Bob 60
Balch, Anthony 298
Baldon, Geoffrey 275
Baldwin, Walter 63
Balin, Ina 132
Ballad of Hillbilly John see *Legend of Hillbilly John*
Ballesteros, Robert* 308
Ballhaus, Michael 167
Balpetre, Antoine 91
Balsam, Martin 245
Baltzell, Deborah 69
Bamber, Judy 288, 290
Banks, Don 281
Baphomet (form of the Devil) 76, 77, 104

Barbareschi, Luca 157
Barbariccia (king of hell) 189–191
Barber, Gillian 204
Barber, Samuel 132, 133
Barboni, Leonida 118
Barcelon, Ben 30
Barclay, Eric 121
Barker, Reginald 306
Barkin, Ellen 273, 275
Barnes, Jonvon 78
Barnes, Priscilla 296
Barnes, Susan 201
Barnett, Steve 240
Baron, J. B. 221
Baron, Robert 69
Baron Münchhausen (1943 film) 293
Barr, Sharon 87
Barrard, John 276
Barrel (character) 237
Barrett, James Lee 132
Barrie, Michael 201
Barsaraba, Gary 168
Bartkowiak, Andrzej 83
Barton, Hollis 217
Barty, Billy 285, 287
Barwise, Patrick 105
Baskin, Sonny 230
Le Bassin de J.W. (1997 film) 308
Bassoff, Lawrence 151
Bates, Alan 197, 201
Bates, Florence 142, 143
Bates, Michael 36
Bateson, Timothy 282
Batman (1989 film) 131, 220, 303
Batman (TV series) 284
Battistrada, Lucio 25
Bauchens, Anne 165
Bauer, Christopher 84
Bauer, David 282
Bauer, Michelle 296
Bava, Mario 179, 180, 182, 183
Baxter, Anne 21, 23, 24
Bayler, Terence 279
Baywatch (TV series) 153
Bazzini, Giulio* 306
Beal, Frank 305, 306
Beal, Nick (Devil pseudonym) 9–17
Beasley, John 186
The Beast see *Equinox*
Beast of Hollow Mountain (1956 film) 25
Beast of the Apocalypse 211, 220
Beast of the Yellow Night (1971 film) 30–32
Beat the Devil (1954 film) 120
Beatty, Ned 233, 234
Beatty, Warren 144
Beaudine, William 288
La Beauté du Diable (1950 film) 32–35
Beauty and the Devil see *La Beauté du Diable*
Beck, Billy 154

Becker, Fred 306
Beckett, Scotty 142
Bedazzled (1967 film) 35–39
Bedazzled (2000 film) 39–43
Bedelia, Bonnie 204
Bedoya, Ingrid 95
Beelzebub 4, 11, 38, 105–108, 129, 148, 179, 289, 290, 305
Been, Michael 168
Beezle (Devil pseudonym) 146–148
Beggar My Neighbor (play) 191
Belcher, Charles 165
Belfagor:The Devil Who Took a Wife (novel) 73
Belgian films 98
Bell, Alexander Graham 265, 266
Bell, Karina 171
Bellamy, Diana 51
Bellamy, Lou 240
Belle du Jour (1967 film) 196
Belmore, Lionel 165
Benét, Stephen Vincent 62, 63
Benguigui, Catherine 208
Benjamin, Adrian 105
Benjamin, Richard 61
Bennett, Charles 264
Bennett, Joan 22
Benny, Jack* 44, 309
Berger, Grete 268
Berger, Gustav* 307
Berger, Howard 183
Berger, Mel 135
Berger, Peter E. 262
Bergerac, Cyrano de (character) 26
Bergese, Micha 49
Bergin, Patrick* 146, 148
Bergman, Andrew 214
Bergman, Boris 197
Bergman, Eva 308
Bergman, Ingmar 89, 90, 134
Bergosa, Jose 194
Beriosova, Svetlana 249
Berlin Film Festival 138
Berlioz, Hector 2
Bernanos, Georges 255
Bernard, Carl 276
Bernard, James 75, 281
Bernardi, Nerio* 307
Bernstein, Herman 130, 131
Berraoui, Ichrak 157
Berringer, Tom 246
Berry, Jules* 291, 293
Berryman, Michael 154
Bertheau, Julien 194
Best, Willie 44
Between Two Worlds (1944 film) 141
Bey, Said 157
The Bible 1, 16, 87, 132–135, 157, 166, 216, 218, 227, 229, 230
Biedermeier, Gottlieb (character) 270
Bierbrach, Rudolph 306

Big Showoff (1945 film) 306
Bill, Tony 139
Bill and Ted's Bogus Journey (1991 film) 162
Bill Bumper's Bargain (1911 film) 305
Billy Budd (1961 film) 50
Biondi, Lee 201
Birkett, Michael 249
Birnbaum und Hollerstauden (1973 film) 307
Birney, Frank 126
The Birth of a Nation (1915 film) 60
Birthday (play) 142
Bismarck, Prince Otto von 152
Bisset, Jacqueline 157
Biziou, Peter 278
Björnstand, Gunnar 89
Black, Kitty 249
Black, Lucas (Devil pseudonym) 309
The Black Cat (1934 film) 89, 158
Black Fist (1976 film) 221
The Black Hole (1979 film) 2, 69
Blackenstein (1973 film) 221
Blacula (1972 film) 221
Blade af Satans Bog see *Leaves from Satan's Book*
Blair, Janet 114
Blair, Joan 21
Blair, Linda* 225, 233, 234, 262
Blair, Nicholas (character) 310, 311
Blair Witch Project (1999 film) 78, 113
Blake, Robert 132
Blake, William 230
Blanchard, Rene 91
Blanchard, Susan* 223, 225
Blanché, Herbert 306
Blandick, Clara 142
Blank, Erika 99, 101
Blankfield, Mark 201
Blewitt, David E. 135
Blin, Roger 291
Blinn, Stephen 217
Bliss, Thomas 108
Bloch, Robert 281, 282, 310
Blocker, Dirk 223
Blofeld, Ernst Stavro (character) 134
Blomberg, Jan 95
Blommaert, Susan 262
Blood, John 300
The Blood of Jesus (1941 film) 306
Bloodbath at the House of Death (1983 film) 116
Bloody Chamber and Other Stories (fiction collection) 49
Bloom, Verna 167
Blossom, Roberts 168
Blount, Lisa 204
The Blue Angel (1930 film) 123
Blyden, Larry 309
Bochner, Lloyd 238, 240

Böcklin, Arnold (artist) 127
Boers, Frank, Jr. see Bonner, Frank
Bogart, Humphrey 24, 120, 288
Bogart, Paul 214
Bogosian, Eric 61
Bogris, Yannis 108
Boguski, Thomas "Doc" 230
Bohem, Endre 9
Boisblanc, Denis de 258
Boito, Arrigo 2, 54, 118, 119
Bolin, Nick 87
Bolin, Shannon 54
Bonaparte, Napoleon see Napoleon I
Bond, David 265
Bond, James (character) 26, 43, 134
Bone, George Harvey (character) 145
Bonet, Lisa 17
Bonnaire, Sandrine 255, 257
Bonner, Frank 112
Bonny, Steve 65
Book collectors and the Devil (theme) 208–213, 281, 283
The Book of Life (1998 film) 308
Boone, Pat 132, 135
Boorman, Charley 197
Booth, John Wilkes 39, 42
Booz, Emmanuel 208
Border, W. K. 230
Borgnine, Ernest* 101, **103**, 104
Bosch, Hieronymus (artist) 102, 141, 162, 298
Botcher, Gil 257
Botorf, Inga 95
The Bottle Imp (short story) 92, 306
Bouillere, Herbert C. de la 300
Bourdon, Corinne 255
Bourlat, Jean-Claude 255
Bourne, Peter 243
Bouvet, Jean-Christophe* 255–257
Bowe, Tyler 258
Bowery Boys 288–290
Bowie, David 167, 170
Boyd, Tanya 294
Boyd, William 165
Boyer, Charles 309
Boyle, James 300
Boyles, Eugene 300
Boyne, Hazel 63
Boys Town (1938 film) 83
Bracco, Lorraine 273
Bracht, Frank 54
Bradbury, Ray 204
Bradley, Helen 146
Brahms, Johannes 36
Bram Stoker's Dracula (1992 film) 212
Brandy, Dan Patrick 258
Braun, Harald 307
Bravo, Antonio 259

316 · Index

Bray, Thom 223
Brazil (1985 film) 279
Breck Showcase Theater (TV series) 311
Breed, Helen Lloyd 300
Bregnone, Guido 189, 191
Brenguier, Dominique 197
Bresnard, Nicole 32
Breterton, Howard 306
Brett, Alan 124
Breughel, Pieter (artist) 133, 298
Breye, Brian 221
Briant, Shane 48
The Bride of Frankenstein (1935 film) 193
Bridges, Beau 135, **137**, 138
Bridges, Kenneth 146
Bridges, Lloyd 139, **141**, 142
Briggs, Harlan (character) 207
Bright, Matthew 129, 130
Brill, Stephen 183
Brimstone (TV series) 310
Brinckerhoff, Burt 132
Brismee, Jean 98
Brissen, Frederick 54
Bristol, Robert* 46, 48
British films 39, 49, 75, 105, 191, 197, 249 251, 252, 275, 278, 281, 305, 306,
Brittany, Morgan 201
Broadhurst, Jim 279
Brokhim, Albert 130
Bromfield, Valri 204
Bron, Eleanor 35, 38, 43
Bronson, Lillian 87
Brook, Claudio 101, 194
Brook, Jesus 235
Brook, Stanley 69
Brooke, Claude 251
Brooks, Alan* 165–167
Brooks, Norville 112
Broström, Gunnel 95
Brotherhood, J.C. 17
Broughton, Bruce 262
Broussard, Eddie 226
Brown, Chris 49
Brown, Jimmy 49
Brown, Ralph 95
Brown, Russ 54
Brown, T. K. 139
Brown, W. Earl 186
Browning, Tod 246
Brownjohn, John 208
Brunette, Brian 238
Bruun, Hugo 171
Bryant, Leonora 226
Bryant, Michael 281
Bub, Mr. (Devil pseudonym) 289
Buchanan. Ruby 49
Buck, George 18
Buckingham, Duke of 291
Buckles, Jeffrey Scott 78
Budd, Julie 69
Buferd, Marilyn 118, 120
Bulik, Richard 46

Bulloch, J. M. J. 273
Bumpus, Joyce 126
Bunker, John 278
Buñuel, Luis 194–196
Buono, Victor* 115–117, 132, 135
Bupp. Sonny 63, 68
Burgos, Julio 149
Burke, Joseph 69
Burke, Patrick 112
Burmeister, Leo 168
Burn Witch Burn (1962 film) 114
Burns, George* 38, 45, 214, **215**, 216, 217
Burroughs, William S. 298
Burt, Dick 126
Burton, Clarence 165
Burton, Richard* 105, 106, **107**, 108, 135, **137**, 138, 199, 200, 225
Burton, Tim 237
Bus-Fekete, Laszlo 142
Bush, Dick 273
Bush, Rebeccah 151
Bushman, Francis X.* 265, 305
Busoni, Ferruccio 2, 54
Bustos, Jorge 235, 259
Butler, Alexander 251, 306
Butler, Captain Walter 65, 68
Butt, Lawson 58
Buys, Earl 241
Bwana, Ugh-Fudge 130
"By the Light of the Silvery Moon" (song) 143
Byers, John 146
Byington, Spring 142
Byrne, Gabriel* 108, 109, 111, 273
Byron, George Gordon, Lord 111

Cabaret (1972 film) 220
Cabin in the Sky (1943 film) 43–46
Le Cabinet de Mephistopheles (1897 film) 305
The Cabinet of Dr. Caligari (1919 film) 130, 259, 270, 272, 284
Cabiria (1914 film) 189
Cable, Debbie 78
Cabot, Sebastian* 34, 309
Cabrera, Susana 25
Cadell, Jean 192
Cadiente, Jeff 230
Cadwallader (Devil pseudonym) 310
Caesar, Julius 265
Calfa, Don 262
Calhern, Louis 142, 145
Caligari, Dr. (character) 130, 259, 270, 272
Calloway, Cab 131
Calvo, Manolo 235
Camacho, Ahui 25
Campani, Carlo 118
Campbell, David 258
Campbell, Ron 300
Can Do (song) 214, 216
Canadian films 203, 308
Canedo, Roberto* 307

Cannes Film Festival 180, 255
Cannon, Chris 276
Caper, John 112
Capers, Hedges 176
Capri, Agnes 194
The Car (1977 film) 3
Caras, Paul 1
Carbajal, Carlos 25
Cardona, Rene 235
Cardona, Rene, Jr. 259
Cardwardine, Richard 105
The Caretaker (1964 film) 134
Carey, Harry, Jr. 51
Carey, Leonard 142
Carey, MacDonald 309
Carlin, John 115
Carliner, Mark 51
Carlson, Erika 101
Carmichael, Ian 192
Carminati, Tullio 32
Carne, Marcel 92, 291
Carney, Art 192
Carnival (opera) 3
Carnival of Sinners see *The Devil's Hand*
Caro, Alicia 259
Carothers, Veronica 296
Carpenter, John 223, 225
Carpenter, Thelma 87
Carradine, John* 25, 26, **27**, 245, 265, 310
Carrie (1976 film) 129
Carriere, Augusta 194
Carriere, Jean-Claude 194
Carrion, Gustav C. 259
Carroll, Christopher 184
Carroll, Janet 217
Carter, Angela 49, 50
Cartwright, Hoss (character) 177
Cartwright, Veronica 300, 303
Carvey, Dana 183
Casablanca (1942 film) 24, 44
Casanova (1976 film) 101
Caspar, Chuck 294
Cassel, Seymour 23
Cassell, Jean-Pierre 197, 201
Casseus, Gabriel 39
Cassidy, Joanna 153, 156
Cassini, Leonard 249
Cassini, Tatiana 73
Castellucci, Teddy 183
Castillo, Cecile 163
Castle of Death see *The Devil's Nightmare*
Castro, Arturo 25
The Cat People (1942 film) 94
Cataclysm (1980 film) 46–48
Caton, Juliette* 167, 170
Caulfield, Dan 276
Cavaliere, Salvatore 183
Cavanaugh, Lawrence J. 51
Cavell, Marc 132
Cazotte, Jacques 208, 212
Cecil B. DeMille's The King of Kings see *The King of Kings*

Centenera, Andres 30
Cepek, Petr* 124, 125
Cerberus (mythological creature) 148
Cerdan, Marcel 118, 120
Cerval, Claude 194
Chabot, Amadee 25
Chae, Sunny 61
Chain, Max 258
Chambliss, Woody 101
Chamisso, Adalbert von 2, 268
Chan, Charlie (character) 3, 45, 83
Chan, Kim 84
Chanel, Helene 73
Chaney, Lon* 95, 96, **97**, 98, 114, 149
Chaney, Lon, Sr. 299
Chao, Stephanie 184
Chaos theory 200
Chaplin, Ben* 186, 188
Chaplin, Charlie 81, 94, 130, 254
Charles V (Holy Roman Emperor) 105, 106
Charlie Chan at the Opera (1936 film) 3
Charlie Chan in London (1934 film) 83
Charmarat, George 91
Charon (mythological character) 146, 147, 190
Charpentier, Victor 306
Chase, David 240
Chatfield, Lansdale 300
Chazen, Charles (Devil pseudonym) 245–248
Cher 300
Chi Sei? (1975 film) 307
La Chienne (1931 film) 34
Children of the Devil (theme) see Offspring of the Devil
Chinese films 308
Chisney, Diana 273
Chitty, Erik 36
Chopin, Frederic 283
Chopra, Ram 105
Christ see Jesus Christ
Christensen, Benjamin* 298–300
Christensen, Elizabeth 298
Christensen, Frederick 298
Christie, Agatha 33
Christmas and the Devil (theme) 233, 235–238, 276, 305, 306
A Christmas Carol (short story) 58
Christmas Eve (short story) 306, 307
Christmas Vacation (1989 film) 202
Christofer, Michael 300
Christopher (saint) 196
Christopher, Robin 112
The Chronicle of St. Albin (illustrated manuscript) 95
C.H.U.D. II: Bud the Chud (1989 film) 203
Chung, Fat* 308
Ciangberotti, Alejandro* 306
Las Cinco Advertencias de Satanas (1938 film) 306

Las Cinco Advertencias de Satanas (1945 film) 306
Cinco Avisos de Satanas (1970 film) 307
Cinesite Hollywood 186
Cirino, Chuck 296
Citizen Kane (1941 film) 68, 127
City of Lost Children (1995 film) 101
Civilization (1916 film) 159
Clabaugh, Richard 230
Clair, René 32, 33
Clampett, Dr. (Devil pseudonym) 238–240
Claridge, Norman 282
Clarieux, Jean 194
Clark, Asa 21
Clark, Blake 183
Clark, Fred 9
Claus, Santa 235–238, 245, 275–276
Clay, Andrew Dice 201, 202
Cleese, John 279
Clementi, Pierre* 194, 196
Clements, Stanley 288, 290
Clemmons, Ted 221
Cleopatra (queen of Egypt) 59, 146, 147, 265, 266
Cleopatra (1963 film) 136
Clere, Paul 276
Clere, Sharon 276
Clergy and the Devil (theme) 11–16, 26, 51, 90, 93–94, 139–141, 161–163, 172–173, 187–188, 195–196, 205, 230, 233–234, 244, 247–248, 255–256, 257–259, 299
Cleveland, George 21, 62
Clifford, Mikel 240
Clift, Faith 46, 48
Clotworthy, Robert 273
Clown vs. Devil see *Guguste et Belzebuth*
El Club Dumas (novel) 208, 209
Clueless (1995 film) 159
Clute, Chester 22
Clute, Sidney 176
Clytemnestra (queen of Mycenae) 279
Coburn, Charles 142, 265
Coco, James* 151, 153, 294, 295
Cocteau, Jean 196
Codina, Jose Maria 306
Cody, Roban* 307
Coe, George 217
Coghill, Ambrose 105
Coghill, Neville 105, 106
Cohen, Herman 118
Cole, Gary* 309
Coleman, Majel 165
Collard, Jacques 208
The Collector (1965 film) 50
College (1927 film) 74
Collins, Angelique du Pres (character) 310
Collins, Barnabus (character) 89, 311

Collins, Joan 275, 278
Collins, Monte 165
Collins, Rich* 308
Collins, Roger (character) 240
Collins, Ruth 296
Colman, Ben 139
Colman, Ronald 264, **265**, 267
Columbus, Christopher 265, 266
Colwell, Chuck 257
Come Again? (1994 film) 308
The Company of Wolves (1984 film) 49–50
Concierto de Aranguez (guitar concerto) 182
Conde, Antonio Diaz 235, 237
Conde, Antonio Diaz, Jr. 235
Conforto, Emily 230
Conjure Wife (novel) 114
Conlan, Frank 63
Connell, Edward 112
Connelly, Edward* 306
Connery, Sean 279, 281
Connor, Mark 258
Conrad, Michael 243
Considine, John 132
Contact Man see *Alias Nick Beal*
Conte, Richard 132
Contla, Nacho 25
Contracts with the Devil (theme) 14–16, 19–20, 32–35, 36–38, 51–53, 54–57, 64–68, 102–104, 106–108, 122, 125, 136, 151–153, 161–163, 204–207, 214–217, 222, 268–270, 271–272, 283, 285–287, 310, 311
Cooder, Ry 51, 53
Cook, Peter* 35, 36, 38, 39, 43
Cook, Randall William 146
Coolidge, Philip 132
Cooper, Alice 223, 225
Cooper, Barry 126, 129
Cooper, Betty 36
Cooper, Gladys 251
Cooper, Len 95
Coppola, Christopher 308
Coquelin, Jean 91
Cordy, Raymond 32
Corelli, Marie 171, 172, 251
Corey, Jeff 63
Corman, Roger 32, 285, 286
Cornthwaite, Robert 87
Corrigan, Shirley 99
Cortese, Leonardo 118, 120
Cortex, Tony 102
Cortez, Ricardo 251, **252**
Cosby, Bill* 69, 72
Costello, William 165
Cotten, Joseph* 87, 88
Cottowt, John* 268, 270, 272
Coughlin, Ely* 308
Courage Mountain (1992 film) 170
Courtland, Jerome 69
Couture, Suzette 157
Covert, Allan 183
Covington, Toni 226

Craft, Bob 257
Craig, Alec 63
Craig, James 62, 68
Craig, Janet 262
Craig, Johnny 276
Cravat, Nick 264, 367
Craven, Wes 153, 154
Crawford, John 95, 132
Crayne, Dani 265
Cregar, Laird* 24, 91, 117, 142, 143, 145
Crenna, Richard 115, 117
Cribbs, Squire (character) 83
Le Crime de Monsieur Lange (1936 film) 293
Criminals and the Devil (theme) 12, 21–24, 222, 289, 290
Crispino, Amando 25
Criswell (TV psychic) 264
Croft, Bill 204
Cromwell, James 214
Cronjager, Edward 142
Crossroads (1986 film) 4, 51–53
Crossroads (TV show) 51
"Crossroads Blues" (song) 52
Crosswhite, Jerry 78
Crothers, Scatman 53
Crouch, Matthew 217
Crowden, Graham 49
Crowley, Aleister (satanist) 264
Crumb, Misty 78
Crystal, Billy* 60, 62
Cthulhu Mythos 113
Cuenco, Ernani 163
Cuenet, James 32
Cullen, James V. 101
Culp, Robert 201
Cumming, Dorothy 165
Cummings, Robert 22
Cummins, Jack 203
Cummins, Peggy 191
Cundy, Dean 153
Cuny, Alain* 194, 195, 291, 293, 307
Curiel, Juan Luis 46
Curry, Tim 162, 281
Curse of the Demon (1957 film) 92
Curse of the Doll People (1960 film) 261
Cushing, Peter 276, 278, 282, 284
Cutting, Richard 265
Cyler, Catherine 197
Cyphre, Louis (Devil pseudonym) 17–21
Czech films 124, 307

Dacomine, Jacques 208
Dafoe, Willem 167, 170
Daindridge, Ruby 44
Daker, David 279
D'Albrook, Sidney 165
Dale, Governor Thomas 65
Dali, Salvador (artist) 196
Dallas (TV series) 153

D'Amato, Senator Alphonse 84, 86
Damn Yankees (1958 film) 54–57
La Damnation de Faust (1898 film) 305
La Damnation de Faust (1925 film) 306
La Damnation de Faust (oratorio) 2
Dandelion Wine (novel) 204
Danforth, Jim 112
D'Angelo, Beverly 245
D'Angelo, Salvo 32
Dangerfield, Rodney* 54, 183, 185
Daniel (Bible O.T.) 170
Daniel, David, Sr. 78
Daniell, Henry 265
Daniels, Dominick 258
Daniels, Leroy 221
Danischewsky, Monja 191
Danish films 171
Dano, Royal 166
Danson, Randy 168
Dante, Peter 183
Dante Alighieri 1, 58, 59, 148, 190, 191
Dante Symphony (symphony) 2
Dante's Inferno (1911 film) 58, 305
Dante's Inferno (1924 film) 58–60
Dante's Inferno (1935 film) 58
Dante's Inferno (1987 film) 58
Dante's Inferno (TV skit) 43, 262
Dante's Peak (1997 film) 129
Dantine, Helmut 265
Danton (1921 film) 272
Danton (1982 film) 257
Danton, Georges 123, 272
Danton, Sylvie 255
Danza del Infierno (orchestral composition) 237
Daquin, Michel 194
Darden, Severn* 176, 178
Dark, Johnny 233
Dark Circle see Alias Nick Beal
Dark Shadows (TV series) 89, 240, 310–311
Darvas, Teddy 275
Darwell, Jane 62, 68
Davao, Charlie* 163, 164
David and Goliath (1960 film) 294
Davidsohn, Paul 268
Davies, Freeman A. 51
Davies, Paul* 240, 242
da Vinci, Leonardo see Leonardo da Vinci
Davis, Bette 24
Davis, Don S. 204, 207
Davis, Jim 243
Davis, Judy 60
Davis, Sammy, Jr. 77
Davis, Ted 201
Dawber, Pam 262
Dax, Danielle 49
Dea, Marie 291, 293
Dead End (1937 film) 288

Deadman, Derek 279
Debney, James 108
Deception (1946 film) 24
Decillis, Patricia 126
Deckard, Be 146
Deconstructing Harry (1997 film) 60–62
Dedet, Yann 255
DeFilippis, Jimi 262
De Fina, Barbara 167
Defru, Paul 98
De Grasse, Sam 165
DeGroot, Maurice 99
Dejjiti, El Housseine 157
Delavanti, Cyril 132
Delgado, Miguel M. 307
Dellafemina, Michael 146
Dellas, Dave 233
The Delomelanicon (text written by Satan) 209
Delong, Jorge 25
DeLory, Al 101
De Luca, Michael 183
DeLuise, Dom 294, 295
DeMauro, Gino 153
Demetrau, Georges 197
DeMille, Cecil, B. 165–167, 226, 251
Demon Night (1995 film) 276
Dempster, Carol 251, 254
Dempter, Austin 35
Demy, Jacques 308
Denholm, Maurice 282
De Niro, Robert* 17, **18**, 20, 21
Denker, Jenry 132
Denman, Trevor 204
Denny, Susan 276
Depardieu, Gerard 255, 257, 277
Depp, Johnny 208, 212, 213
De Putti, Lya 251
Derleth, August 176
Derr, Richard 30
Der'Ven, Thierry 255
Desiderio, Robert 214
Des Jardin, John 108
Despeauz, Jean 91
Destry, John Blakewell 262
Detective (1985 film) 213
Detectives and the Devil (theme) 17, 46
Deuteronomy (Bible O.T.) 187
Devengh, Myrtle 279
Dever, Tom 243
The Devil (1908 film) 305
The Devil (1915 film) 306
The Devil (1921 film) 306
The Devil and Daniel Webster (1941 film) 62–69, 123, 310
The Devil and Daniel Webster (TV adaptation) 267, 311
The Devil and Max Devlin (1981 film) 69–72
The Devil and the Dead see *Lisa and the Devil*
"Devil Defying" (song) 177, 179

Devil Dog, Hound of Hell (1978 film) 3
"Devil in a Blue Dress" (song) 234
Devil in female form (theme) 39–43, 50, 105–108, 153–156, 157–160, 167–170, 196, 199–200, 208–213, 223–225, 233–234, 243–245, 311
The Devil in Love (1966 film) 73–34
The Devil in the Bottle see *Liebe, Tod und Teufel*
The Devil Is Not Such a Devil see *El Diablo No Es Tan Diablo*
The Devil Rides Out (1968 film) 75–77
Devil Souls (1997 film) 78–80
The Devil, the Servant and the Man (1910 film) 305
The Devil, the Servant and the Man (1916 film) 306
Devil to Pay (TV episode) 309
The Devil Walks at Midnight see *The Devil's Nightmare*
The Devil with Hitler (1942/43 film) 80–83
The Devil Within Her see *Chi Sei?*
The Devil's Advocate (1997 film) 83–87
The Devil's Bride see *The Devil Rides Out*
Devil's Cabaret (1931 short subject) 4
The Devil's Child (1997 film) 308
The Devil's Daughter (1987 telefilm) 87–89
The Devil's Envoys see *Les Visiteurs du Soir*
The Devil's Hand (1942 film) 4, 91–94
The Devil's Longest Night see *The Devil's Nightmare*
The Devil's Manor (1896 film) 305
The Devil's Messenger (1960/62 film) 95–98
The Devil's Nightmare (1971 film) 98–101
The Devil's Partner (1957 film) 3
The Devil's Rain (1975 film) 101–105
The Devil's Son in Law see *Petey Wheatstraw*
The Devil's Ticket (TV episode) 309
The Devil's Toy (1916 film) 306
The Devil's Wanton (1949 film) 89
Devincentis, Chris 126
Devlin (Devil pseudonym) 310
Devlin, Don 300
Devlin, Joe 80, 83, 288
Devon, Richard* 286, **287**
Dew, Eddie 63
DeWitt, John 240
Dexter, Anthony 265
DeZita, Captain* 307
D'Hoffelize, Pierre 255

Le Diable Amoureau 208, 209, 212
Diable au Convent (1899 film) 305
Diablo, Dr. (Devil pseudonym) 281–284
El Diablo No Es Tan Diablo (1949 film) 307
Diabolis 290, 31
Dialogues of the Carmelites (novel) 255
Diamon, Hyman 130
Diary of a Country Priest (novel) 255
Al Diavolo la Celebrita see *Fame and the Devil*
Diaz, Joko 160
Diaz, Paquito 163
Diaz, Vic* 30, 31
Dickens, Charles 58
Dickinson, Desmond 191
Dickson, Malcolm 278
Di Credico, Paolo 73
Diehl, John 186
Diercks, Adrienne 240
Diercks, Kate 240
Dieterle, William 62, 66, 121, 123
Dietrich, Marlene 123
Different Strokes (TV show parody) 264
Di Leo, Mario 115
Dionne, Margot 300
DiPalma, Carlo 60
Dirty Work (1998 film) 184, 308
The Discrete Charm of the Bourgeosie (1972 film) 196
Dishy, Bob 262
Disney, Walt 69
DiStefani, Angel 235
Divina, Vaclav 28
The Divine Comedy (poem) 1, 58, 59
Djävulens Öga see *The Devil's Eye*
Dr. Black and Mr. Hyde (1975 film) 221
Dr. Crippen (1962 film) 134
Dr. D (Devil pseudonym) 151
Doctor Faustus (play) 2, 35, 105, 121, 124, 125
Doctor Faustus (1967 film) 105–108
Dr. Jekyll Jr. (1979 film) 120
Doering, Paul F.* 308
Doff, Red 226
Doktor Faust (opera) 2
Dolan, Trent 243
Dolina Issy (1983 film) 308
Dolores Claiborne (1995 film) 131
Don Juan (character) 74, 89–91
Don Juan et Faust (1922 film) 306
Don Juan in Hell (play) 90, 311
Don Juan und Faust (play) 124
Don Quixote (1973 film) 250
Donahue, Tim 214
Donaldson, Tex 51
Donen, Stanley 35, 54
Donovan, King 9
Donovan's Brain (1953 film) 95

Doolittle, Alfred (character) 193
Doolittle, John 214
Doppelgänger (theme) 268–270, 271–272
Doré, Gustave (artist) 59, 115, 190, 251
D'Orsay, Lawrence 251
Dotrice, Roy 276
Double Indemnity (1944 film) 303
The Doubles (short story) 268
Doucette, Jeff 39
Dougherty, Charles 151
Douglas, Buddy 146
Douglas, Gordon 80
Douking, Georges 91, 194
Doukkali, Karim 157
Doumanian, Jean 60
Dowe, Don 296
Down, Carl 135
Doyle, Brian 39
Doyle, Julian 278
Doyle, Patrick 203, 206
Doyle, Patsy 63
Dracula (1974 telefilm) 77
Dracula, Count (character) 75, 77, 212
Dracula: Prince of Darkness (1966) 77
Dragojevic, Srdjan 308
Dragstrip Girl (1957 film) 30
Drake, Judith 18
Dreyer, Carl Theodor 171, 172
Driving Over Miss Daisy (TV show parody) 264
Düberg, Axel 89
Duboi Digital Effects 208
DuBrey, Claire 142
Ducceshi, Maria 208
Dudley, Robert 63
Duela a Muetre (1958 film) 307
Dufour, Val 285, **287**
Duke, Vernon 43
Dulo, Jane 214
Dumas, Alexandre 212
Dumas, Roger 91
Dun, Dennis 223, 225
Dunaway, Stephen 214
Duncan, Ian 157
Duncan, Pamela 285, **287**
Dundee, Jimmie 22
Dune (1984 film) 213
Dunham, Joanna 132
Dunlop, Vic 69
Dunn, Eddie 251
Dunn, Josephine 251
Duplay, Eleonore 182
Duran, Jim 112
Durden-Smith, Richard 105
Durond, Erneste (Devil pseudonym) 173–175
Durst, Eric 108
Dutilleux, Henri 255
Duval, Shelly 279
Dvorak, Antonin 300, 301
D'Yd, Jean 291

Easton, Robert 204
Eastwood, Clint 77
Eaton, Marjoire 135, 138
Eccles, Jeremy 105
Eckhard, Lt. William (character) 220
Eclair Numerique 208
Ed and His Dead Mother (1992 film) 111
Ed Wood (1994 film) 264
Eddington, Paul 75
Eden, Daniel 126
Edesen, Robert 165
Edlund, Richard 39
Edmiston, Walker 294
Edmonds, Mike 278
Edwall, Allan 89
Edward Scissorhands (1990 film) 131
Edwards, Blake 273
Edwards, Darren Mark 146
Edwards, Lou 46
Edwards, Sarah 62
Efroni, Yehuda 217
Eisen, Robert S. 28
Eklund, Allan 89
Ekman, Gösta 121, 123
Elarton, Robert 257
Elfman, Danny* 129–131, 212, 237
Elfman, Marie-Pasquale 130, 131
Elfman, Richard 129, 130
Elizabeth I (queen of England) 265, 266
Ella, Lucifer y Yo (1952 film) 307
Ellen, Suzan 258
Ellington, Duke 43, 44, 45
Elliott, Dick 288
Elliott, Peter 281
Ellis, Christopher 201
Ellis, Kenny 258
Ellis, Ron 78
Ellsworth, Robert 165
Emery, John* 309
Emilfork, Daniel* 98–101
Emmanuelle, Colette 99
Emmett, Fern 63
The Empire Strikes Back (1980 film) 170
Encyclopedia Satanica (parody reference set) 264
End of Days (1999 film) 48, 108–112, 186, 188, 273, 296
English, Elaine 157
Englund, Bryan 151
Englund, Jan 28
Equinox (1967/71 film) 112–115
Eraser (1996) 109
Erhard, Bernard 240
Erhmann, Jean-David 194
Erwin, Bill 153, 156
"Escape Clause" (TV episode) 310
Espinoza, Joe 135
Espiritismo see *Spiritism*
Essoe, Gabe 101
Esterhazy, Agnes 271, 272

Estgregan, George 163
Etcheverry, Michel 194
Evans, Charles 9
Evans, Edward 276
Evans, Rex 80
Evans, Roy 49
Eve 226–229, 250
Everett, Lee 201
Everyman (play) 307
The Evil Dead (1982 film) 47
The Evil (1978 film) 115–117
Ewers, Hanns Heinz 268, 271
Ewing, Barbara 281
Exodus (Bible O.T.) 170
Exorcist (1971 film) 4, 187, 188, 233, 234, 262
Exorcist II: The Heretic (1977 film) 225, 234

Fabian, Kate 298
Facinelli, Peter* 308
Fajardo, Eduardo 179, 183
Falla, Manuel de 172
The Fallen Star see *Der Fallende Stern*
Falling Angel (novel) 17, 18
Fallon, Phillipa 226
Fame and the Devil (1949 film) 118–121
Famous Monsters of Filmland (magazine) 114
Fan ger ett Anbud (1963 film) 307
Fann, Al 51
Fantasy Island (TV series) 72, 139
Farfan, Frederico 101
Farley, Dot 165
Farley, Jim 63
Farnsworth, Richard 146
Farr, Jamie 132, 133
Farrow, John 9, 16
Farrow, Mia 16
Faust (1909 film) 305
Faust (1910 film) 305
Faust (1923 film) 306
Faust (1926 film) 115, 121–124
Faust (1960 film) 307
Faust (1963 film) 307
Faust (1994 film) 124–126
Faust (1996 film) 308
Faust (1997 film) 308
Faust (legend) 2, 32, 51, 54, 63, 121, 138
Faust (opera) 2, 3, 26, 54, 123, 125
Faust (oratorio) 2
Faust (play) 2, 9, 121, 124, 136
Faust and Marguerite (1900 film) 305
Faust and Mephistopheles (1898 film) 305
Faust aux Enfers (1903 film) 305
Faust des Riesen (1917 film) 306
Faust et Marguerite (1897 film) 305
Faust et Mephistopheles (1903 film) 305

Faust Overture (orchestral composition) 2
Faust Symphony (symphony) 2
Faustus XX (1966 film) 307
Favorite Deadly Sins see *National Lampoon's Favorite Deadly Sins*
Faye, Julia 165
Faylen, Frank 80
Fear No Evil (1981 film) 126–129
Fearn, Sheila 279
Feathertop (short story) 306
Fein, Irving 214
Feld, Fritz 288, 290
Feldstein, Al 276
Der Fellende Stern (1950 film) 307
Fellini, Federico 50, 101
Fenton, George 49
Ferguson, Cason 165
Ferguson, Jessie 223, 225
Ferguson, Jessie Lawrence 223, 225
Fernandez, Fernando 307
Ferrer, Jose 132, 135, 245, 247, 248
Ferzetti, Gabriele 73
Ffrangcon-Davies, Gwen 75
Fields, Freddie 294
Fields, W. C. 83, 179, 251
55 Days in Peking (1963 film) 250
Fight with the Devil see *Going to Glory, Come to Jesus*
Filardi, Peter 308
Filipino films 30, 160, 163
Les Filles du Diable (1903 film) 305
A Fine Madness (1966 film) 170
Finn, Catherine 282
Finn, Edwin 279
Fiore, Mauro 186
Fiorentini, Inginio 167
The Firm (1993 film) 84, 154
Firth, Julian 39
Fischbeck, Harry 251
Fischer, Gunnar 89
Fischer, Thomas L. 101
El Fistol del Diablo (1958 serial) 307
Fitzgerald, Edward F. 28
Fitzsimmons, Art 46
Fitzsimmons, Courtland 80
Five Warnings from Satan see *Las Cinco Advertencias de Satanas*
Fjellström, Emil* 306
Flaherty, Joe 126
Flanders, Michael 249
Flash Gordon (1936 serial) 60
Flavin, James 21, 142, 288
Fleisher, Max 130
Flicker, Theodore J.* 310
Florek, Dann 18
Floyd, Count (character) 126
Fontelieu, Stocker 17
For Heaven's Sake (1950 film) 22
Foraker, Lois 201
Forbidden Zone (1980 film) 129–131

Ford, Harrison 159
Ford, Lita 146
Forke, Farrah 201
Fors, Len 95
Fosse, Bob 54, 57
Foster, Susan 139
Foulger, Bryan* 288, 290
Foulk, Robert* 310
Fouquier-Tinville, Quentin 171, 174
Four Horsemen of the Apocalypse (1921 film) 45
Four Star Playhouse (TV series) 309
Fowley, Douglas 80
Fox, Charles 233
Fox, William 58
Foxworth, Robert 87
Franci, Carlo 118
Francis, Anne 139, 142
Francis, Freddie 275, 281
Francis, John 157
Francis-Bruce, Richard 300
Franco, David 109
Franco, Larry J. 223
Frankel, Cyril 308
Franken, Steve 217
Frankenheimer, John 230
Frankenstein and the Monster from Hell (1974 film) 48
Frankenstein Meets the Wolfman (1943 film) 95, 96
Frankenstein Monster (character) 96, 150, 191
Frankenstein's Daughter (1959 film) 30
Frankeur, Paul 194
Franklin, Pamela 238
Franks, Chloe 275
Frantic (1988 film) 213
Fraser, Bill 192
Fraser, Brendan 38, 39, 42, 43
Fraser, Duncan 204
Eine Frau Namens Harry (1990 film) 308
Frazee, Logan 238
Frazee, Terry D. 183
Freaks (1932 film) 246
Freed, Arthur 43, 44
Freeman, Jeff 233
Der Freischütz (opera) 2, 124
French films 32, 91, 194, 197, 208, 255, 270, 291, 305, 306, 307, 308
Fresco, John 115
Fresney, Pierre 91
Frey, Nathaniel 54
Frid, Jonathan 87, 89
Friday (character) 192
Fridell, Ake* 307
Fridh, Gertrud 89
Fromin, Troy 258
Frontiere, Dominic 135, 139
Frost (Devil pseudonym) 197–201
Frost, Roger 279
Frost, Warren 240, 242

Frye, Soleil Moon 153, 156
Fu Manchu (character) 21, 75, 150, 299
Fuest, Robert 101
The Fugitive (1993 film) 159
Fuller, Robert 233
Fundquist, Georg 89
Fusco, John 51
Fütterer, Werner 121

G-Men from Hell (2000 film) 308
Gable, Clark 2
Gabriel (archangel) 126–128, 230–232, 246
Gabriel, Peter 167
Gabriello, Andre 91
Gabrio, Gabriel 291, 293
Gadler, Steve 197
Gael, Josseline 91
Gaerlan, Edmundo 160
Gagano, Ambassador Charles 84
Gaines, Bill 276
Gale, David 273
Galeen, Henrik 271
Galliano, Dino 167
Gallini, Matt 109
Gallion, David 230
Gallo, Lillian 139
Gallone, Carmine 307
Galvadon, Gilberto 307
Galvez, Jose* 307
Gamblers and the Devil (theme) 43–45, 216, 231–242, 268–269, 271–272, 309
Gamley, Douglas 275
Garcia, Al Ernest* 306
Garcia, Eddie 30
Garcia, Stella 226
Garden, Yvonne 99
Garden of Delights (painting) 102
Gardiner, Reginald 265
Gardner, Ava 245
Gardner, Jimmy 49
Gardner, Pierce 186
Garfield, Allen 208
Garland, Richard 285, **287**
Garner, Martin 214
Garret, Don 285
Garrett, Hank 246
Garroway, Lloyd 108
Garson, Willie 233
Gary, Linda 273
Garzoni 91
Gassman, Vittorio* 73, 74
Gates, Madelyn 69
Gates, Maxine 9
Gaudin, Christian 91
Gaunt, Leland (Devil pseudonym) 203–207
Gawne, Irene 276
Gaye, Howard 58, 60, 306
Gayle, Rozelle 87
Geerling, Georgia 46
Gehenna 216
Geier, Camille 60

Gelbert, Larry 39
Gelin, Daniel 197
Gelin, Xavier 197
Genesis (Bible OT) 226, 228, 229
George, Peter 308
George, Wally 233
George Washington (TV miniseries) 232
Gerdsen, Barry* 308
German films 121, 268, 271, 306, 307, 308
Gerringer, Robert 246
Gerry, Toni 265
Gertz, Jami 51
Gesatin (Devil pseudonym) 81, 83
Gevisser, Peter 157
Ghostbusters (1984 film) 39
The Ghoul (1933 film) 278
Giaquinto, Metthew 308
Giarraputo, Jack 183
Giatti, Ian 214
Gibson, Thomas* 308
Gidley, Pamela 146
Gielgud, John 58
Gilchrist, Gilly 157
Gilford, Gwynn 238
Gilford, Jack 294
Gill, Beverly 139
Gillespie, A. Arnold 132
Gilliam, Terry 278, 279
Gilroy, Tony 83
Giotto di Bondonne (artist) 133
Girdler, William 307
Girl from Rocky Point (1922 film) 306
Girney, "Renegade" Simon 65, 68
Giroud, Roland 197, **199**
Gish, Lillian 123, 254
G'Kar (character) 203
Glaser, Bedrich 124
Gleason, Jackie 34, 192
Glen or Glenda (1953 film) 307
Glick, Michael S. 101
Glover, Brian 49
Glover, John* 310
Goat of Mendes *see* Baphomet
Gobbi, Tito 120
God and the Devil (theme) 23, 34, 37–38, 44–45, 78, 80, 172, 175, 196, 214–217, 250, 251–252, 273–275, 280, 281
God, Man and the Devil see *Gott, Mensch und Teufel*
Godard, Jean-Luc 212
Goddey, Marty 275
Godfather (film trilogy) 86, 109
God's Army see *The Prophecy*
Goebbels, Joseph 80
Goethe, Johann Wolfgang 2, 9, 121, 124, 125, 204
Goetz, Peter 240
Gogol, Nikolai 306, 307
Going to Glory, Come to Jesus (1946 film) 307
Gold, Brandy 214

Gold, Toby 126
Goldberg, Adam 230, 232
Goldberg, Iddo 157
Goldberg, Leonard 238
Goldblum, Jeff* 197, **199**, 200, 246
The Golden Age (1930 film) 196
Goldway, Elliot 109
Der Golem (1914 film) 268
Golling, Alexander* 307
Gomez, Chema 149
Gomez, Nicholas 230
Gomez, Thomas* 310
Gonzales, Carmelita 259
The Good Book (1997 film) 308
Goodell, John 240
Goodich, Fred 126
Goodin, Chalmers 95
Gooding, Cuba, Jr. 2, 105
Goodman, Hazelle 60
Goor, Bernice Tamara 257
Gorcey, David 288, 290
Gorcey, Leo 288, 290
Gorchow, Michelle 201
Gordon, Phil 130
Gordone, Charles 17
Gori, Mario Cecchi 73
Göring, Hermann 80
Gormley, Peggy 168
Gorski, Peter 307
Gorss, Saul 22
Gothic (1986) 111
Gott, Mensch und Teufel (1950 film) 307
Gottfried, Gilbert 146, 148
Gould, Elliott 69, 72
Goulding, Edmund 58
Goulet, Robert* 308
Gounod, Charles 2, 3, 26, 54, 123, 124, 125
Gourney, Howard 36
Goursaud, Anne 186
Gourson, Jeff 183
Gout, Alberto 228
Grabbe, Christian Dietrich 2, 124, 125
Grädler, Theodor 307
Graff, Alan 51
Graham, C. J. 146
Graham, Gerrit* 201, 203
Grand Canyon Suite (orchestral suite) 162
Grandmaison, Maurice 46
Grant, Angie 276
Grant, Arthur 75
Grasmere, Robert 223
Graver, Gary 296
Gray, Bruce 154
Gray, Charles* 75, 77, 308
Gray, Gloria 58
Gray, Pamela 84
Gray, Sam 246
Graytak, Eugene 233
The Great Dictator (1940 film) 81, 83
The Great Escape (1963 film) 134

The Great White Hope (1970 film) 141
The Greatest Story Ever Told (1965 film) 132–135, 207
El Greco (artist) 133
Greco, Paul 168
Green, Austin 265
Green, Babbie 300
Green Eyes (Devil pseudonym) 208–213
Green Mansions (1937 film) 45
Greenberg, Richard 83
Greene, Leon 75, 77
Greene, Richard 275, 278
Greenfield, Ruth K. 264
Greenfield, Shawn Patrick 257–358
Greenquist, Brad 186
Gregoire, Pierre 308
Gregorio y Su Angel (1966 film) 307
Gregory, Andre 167
Gremlins (1984 film) 109
Greys, Tamara 149
Gribble, Bernard 191, 245
Grieg, Edvard 206
Grier, Pam 30
Griffith, Charles 285
Griffith, D. W. 172, 251, 254, 305
Griffiths, Fred 192
Grigg, Gene 243
Griggs, Loyal 132, 133
Grofé, Ferde, Jr. 160, 162
Gross, Denise 78
Gross, Roland 264
Grossman, Maury 240
Le Grotte du Diable (1898 film) 305
Groundhog Day (1993 film) 39
Grubman, Alan 84
Gründgens, Gustav* 307
Grunseld, Ernie 84
Guardino, Harry 166
Guarracino, Umberto* 189, 191
Guerra, Saverio 202
Gugino, Roslyn 126
Guguste et Belzebuth (1901 film) 305
Guidry, Deborah 221
Guilbert, Yvette 121, 123
Guild, Leo 95
Guilomar, Julien 194
Guinness Book of World Records (reference book) 70
Guiterrez, Conchita 221
Gullo, Jeff 108
Gunn, Moses* 139, 141
Guy, Alice 305
Guyer, Murphy 84
Guys and Dolls (musical) 214
Gwenn, Edmund 22
Gwynn, Alfred 95
Gwynne, Anne 114
Gwynne, Olga 192

Haas, Hugo 28, 29
Haber, Paul 126
Hackford, Taylor 84
Haggard, H. Rider 251
Hagney, Frank 22
Haig, Sid 30
Hale, Jonathan 21
Hall, Alfred 142
Hall, Cecelia 221
Hall, Huntz 288, 290
Hall, Kevin Peter 146
Hall, Philip Baker 186
Hallelujah Chorus 133
Halloween (1978 film) 225
Halloween 3 (1983 film) 154
Halsey, Forrest 251
Hambling, Gerry 17
Hamilton, Lois 153
Hamlet (1948 film) 193
Hamlet (play) 1, 26, 106
Hamley-Clifford, Molly 192
Hamlisch, Marvin 69
Hammersmith (Devil pseudonym) 135–138
Hammersmith Is Out (1972 film) 135–138, 199
Hammond, Roger 157
Hampton, Grayce 142
Hamton, Sanford 258
Hancock, John 51
Handel, George Frederick 132, 133
Handl, Irene 192
Hangover Square (1945 film) 145
Hanna, Mark 285
Hannibal 189
Hanson, Erling 171
"Happiness Is a Thing Called Joe" (song) 44
Harapos, Mario Garcia 25
Harben, Philip 192
Harding, Gilbert 192
Hardwicke, Cedric* 28, 29, 264, 266, 267
Harlem Globetrotters 184, 185
Harman, Peter 105
Harpe, Micajah 65
Harpe, Wiley 65
Harper, James 273
Harriman, Doug 146
Harrington, Kate 246
Harrington, Laura 84
Harris, David 201
Harris, Ed 204, 207
Harris, Jack H. 112, 113
Harris, John 275
Harris, Johnny 115
Harris, Marcia 251
Harris, Sam 265
Harris, Sean 157
Harris, Violas 61
Harrison, George 278, 280
Harrison, Rex 194
Harrison, Richard 105
Harrison, William Henry 68
Harryhausen, Ray 176

Hart, Frederick 86
Hart, Roxanne 214
Hart, William "Buck" 230
Hartford, Eden 265, 267
Hartigan, Ben 273
Hartley, Hal 308
Harts, Sara 95
Hassner, Eva 95
Hasso, Signe 142
Hathorne, John 62, 64, 65, 66, 68
The Haunting (1963 film) 116
Haunts of the Very Rich (1972 film) 139–142
Hautecoeur, Louisette 194
Hawdon, Robin 36
Hawkins, Michael 282
Hawthorne, Nathaniel 64, 306, 308
Häxn see *Witchcraft through the Ages*
Hayes, Allison 285, **287**
Hayes, Barton 176
Hayes, Bobby Lee 230
Hayes, Gloria 160
Hayward, William Dr. (character) 242
Heartbreak Ridge (1986 film) 141
Heaven Can Wait (1943 film) 24, 91, 142–145
Heaven Can Wait (1978 film) 144
Hedison, David 132, 133
Heermance, Richard 288
Heflin, Mady 245
Heflin, Van 132, 133
Hegge, Malcolm 126
Heidi (character) 170
Heifetz, Jascha 66
Heine, Heinrich 2
Helen of Troy 105–108, 265
Helgeland, Brian 146
Helleman, Hallander 171
Heller, Mary Cristina 157
Hell's Bells (TV episode) 310
Hellzapoppin' (1941 film) 4, 190
Helmond, Katharine 279
Helpmann, Robert* 237, 249–250, 308
Helsengreen, Emil 171
Helton, Percy 9
Hemingway, Mariel 61
Hender, Frederique 99
Hendry, Ian 275
Henesy, Sharon 176
Henreid, Paul 24
Henry VII (king of England) see Tudor, Henry
Henry VIII (king of England) 123, 276
Hensen, Gladys 192
Herbier, Marcel 306
Hercules (mythological character) 189
Here Comes Mr. Jordan (1941 film) 22, 118, 141
Herlihy, Tim 183

Herlth, Robert 121
Herman, Paul 168
Herrand, Marcel 291
Herrera, Ricardo 163
Herring, Craig 39
Herrmann, Bernard 62, 66, 72, 131
Hershey, Barbara 23, 167
Hertel, Aage 298
Herts, Kenneth 95, 96
Herz, Michael 308
Herzinger, Charles 63
Heston, Charlton 132, 207
Heston, Fraser C. 203, 207
Hewitt, Barbara 112
Hickey, William 246
Hickman, Darryl 9
Hidden Faces (musical group) 146
Higgins, Colin 87
Higgins, Michael 17
Highway, Tom (Devil pseudonym) 78
Highway to Heaven (TV series) 230
Highway to Hell (1990 film) 146–148
Hilario, Teofilo 30
Hilbeck, Fernando 149
Hill, Phyllis 139
Hill, Robert 226
Hillebrandt, Carl 171
Hilpert, Heinz
Himlaspelet (1942 film) 306
Himmler, Heinrich 80
Hinn, Michael 95
Hippocrates 265
Hissen som gick ner i Helvetet (1969 film) 307
L'Histoire du Soldat (musical theater piece) 249
Histoires Extraordinaires see *Spirits of the Dead*
The History of the Devil and the Idea of Evil (book) 1
Hitchcock, Alfred 72, 95
The Hitchhiker (TV series) 156
Hitler, Adolf 14, 16, 80–83, 92, 94, 146, 147, 148, 152, 184, 185, 200, 220, 265, 266, 292
The Hitler Gang (1944 film) 83
Hjortsberg, William 17, 18
Hoag, Robert 132
Hobl, Pavel 307
Hobley, MacDonald 192
Hobson, Miles C. 157
Hodge, Jim 214
Hodgkins, Earle 288
Hodson, Donald 168
Hoff, Halvard 171
Hoffa, Jimmy 146
Hoffman, Basil 273
Hoffman, Elizabeth 126, 129
Hoffman, Jane 61, 246
Hoffmann, Carl 121
Hoffmann, E. T. A. 268
Hofmannsthal, Hugo von 307

Hogge, Nigel 160
Holden, Marlon* 308
Holden, Nolle 171
Holland, Anthony 135, 138
Holland, Jack 126
Holland, Rodney 49
Holloway, Stanley* 191, 193
Holm, Astrid 298
Holm, Ian 279
Holmes, Christina 230
Holmes, Leon 165
Holocaust 2000 (1978 film) 4, 218
Holst, Gustav 47, 48, 172
Holt, Willy 208
Holy Ghost 225
The Honeymooners (TV series) 192
Hong Kong films 308
Hood, Harry 63
Hootkins, William 217, 220
Hoover, Mike 112
Hopf, Heinz* 307
Hopman, Gerald 101
Hopper, Dennis 265
Horn, Camilla 121, 123
Horne, Lena 44, 45
Horowicz, Merrily 300
Horton, Edward Everett 265
The Hot Rock (1971 film) 141
Hot Shots (1990 film) 233
Houdini, Harry 224
House of Evil see *The Evil*
House of Exorcism see *Lisa and the Devil*
House of Rothschild (1934 film) 82
The House of the Seven Gables (novel) 64
The House on Haunted Hill (1958 film) 116
Houseman, John 294
Howard, Anne Marie 223
Howard, Clifford 165
Howard, Clint 183
Howard, James Newton 83
Howard, Sandy 101
Howard the Duck (1986 film) 264
Howarth, Alan 223
Howell, Elizabeth 54
Howells, Ursula 282
Howl of the Devil (1988 film) 149–151
"The Howling Man" (TV episode) 310
Howling VI (1991 film) 275
Hoyer, Edgar 171
Hubert, Roger 291
Huene, Walter von 109
Huerta, Chris 149
Hughes, Dorothy 251
Hughes, Robin* 310
Hughes, Roddy 192
Hughman, John 279
Hull, George 251
Humair, Daniel 298
Humbard, Brenda 221
Humphrey, Harry 63

Humphries, Barry 36
Humphries, Cecil* 306
The Hunchback of Notre Dame (1959 film) 101
Hunk (1987 film) 151–153
Hunnicutt, Arthur 310
"The Hunt" (TV episode) 310
Hunter, Jeffrey 166
Hunter, Tab 54, **56**, 57
Huntley, Raymond 192
Hurley, Elizabeth* 38, 39, 40, **41**, 42, 43
Hurst, Paul* 306
Hurt, John 186,188
Huskins, Curtis 78
Huss, Toby 39
Huston, Walter* 62, **67**, 68, 267, 310
Hutton, Robert 282
Hyams, Peter 108, 262
Hyde, Edward (character) 149, 150
Hyman, Greg 60
Hytner, Steve 230

"I Am the Antichrist" (song) 127
I Love Lucifer (TV show parody) 263
I Love My Wife (1970 film) 307
I Married a Witch (1942 film) 32
I Wake Up Screaming (1941 film) 145
Iago (character) 272
Ifans, Rhys 183, 185
Iglesias, Pompin 25
I'll Never Heil Again (1941 short subject) 80
Imboden, David 165
In Harm's Way (1965 film) 193
In Service to the Devil see *The Devil's Nightmare*
In the Hall of the Mountain King (orchestral composition) 206
Ince, Thomas H. 159, 306
Incontrera, Annabella 73
The Incredible Shrinking Man (1958 film) 226
Incubus (1965 film) 3
Industrial Light and Magic 273
Inferno (Divine Comedy, Part One) 1, 58, 59
Inferno (novel) 38
Inflation (1942 short subject) 68
Ingle, John H. 233
Ingram, Rex* 43, 44, 45
"Inner Light" (TV episode) 169
Innocent VIII (pope) 73
Inquisition (1976 film) 307
Intellectuals and the Devil (theme) 33–35, 36, 47, 61–62, 105–108, 116–117. 118–120, 121–125, 218–220, 294, 296
Intolerance (1916 film) 172
The Invaders (TV series) 240
Invitation to Hell (1984 film) 153–156

Invocation of Darkness see *The Delomelanicon*
Ironside, Michael 217, 220
Irving, Amy 60
Irving, George 306
Iscariot, Judas see Judas
The Island of the Dead (1945 film) 127
The Island of the Dead (painting) 127
Issyanov, Ravil 217
It Happened Tomorrow (1944 film) 32
Italian films 73, 98, 118, 179,189, 305, 306, 307, 308
The Italian Straw Hat (1927 film) 32
Ito, Robert 217
Ivan (Devil pseudonym) 174, 175
Iverson, Floyd 65
Ivey, Judith 84

Jablin, David 201
The Jack Benny Program (radio show) 44
Jack the Ripper 55, 144, 272
Jackson, Dee Jay 204
Jackson, Gordon 192
Jackson, Kate 238, 240
Jacobs, Allan 238
Jacobs, W. W. 259, 277
Jacobson, Peter 61
Jacquet, Jeffrey 294
Jaissie, Matt 308
Jak, Lisa 135
James, Juliette 279
James, Mark 129
James, Nicholas 130
Jamison, Bud 58, 60
Janelli, Tommy 201
Jannings, Emil* 121, 123, 272
Jansenism 195, 196
Järrel, Stih* 89–91
Jason, Peter 223, 225
Jaws of Satan (1978 film) 3
Jaws II (1978 film) 87
Jay, Tony 279
Jean Shepherd's America (TV series) 79, 311
Jedermann (1961 film) 307
Jefford, Barbara 208, 213
Jenkins, Arlene 9
Jenkins, Richard 300
Jennewein, Jim 262
Jennings, Ernest C. 276
Jeopardy (TV series) 186
Jeremiah (Bible O.T.) 216
Jessop, Clytie 282
Jessup, Sioux-z 230
Jesus (2000 film) 157–160
Jesus Christ 47, 50, 95, 106, 108, 126, 128, 132–135, 157–160, 165, 166, 167–171, 172, 174, 194, 195–196, 207, 294
Jesus of Nazareth (1977 film) 220

Jetter, Claude 194
Jiminez, Jose Luis 259
Jingle Bells (song) 237
Joan of Arc (saint) 265, 266
Job (Bible O.T.) 1, 122
Jochim, Keith 300, 303
John (Bible N.T.) 134, 220
John (saint) 132, 157, 165, 168, 171
John the Baptist 132, 157, 166, 167–169, 216, 220
Johnson, Arnold 214
Johnson, Bruce Douglas 230
Johnson, Carolyn Key 201
Johnson, Chic 190
Johnson, Douglas 230
Johnson, J. Macmillan 132
Johnson, Jane 300
Johnson, Julian 251
Johnson, Lorimer 58
Johnson, Michael see Michael York
Johnson, Noble 21, 165
Johnson, Richard* 307
Johnson, Robert 51, 52, 53
Johnson, Russell 132
Johnson, Steve 146
Johnstone, Shane 49
Joker (character) 303
Jolson, Al 57
Jones, Chester 176
Jones, Chuck 263
Jones, Daniele 186
Jones, Dicky 142
Jones, J.J. 87
Jones, James B.* 306
Jones, James Earl 141
Jones, Jeffrey* 84, 86, 262, 264
Jones, Jessica (Devil pseudonym) 153–156
Jones, Marvin 221
Jones, Neal 84
Jones, Orlando 39
Jones, Spike 130
Jones, Trevor 17
Jong, Ate de 146
Jordan, Bert 80
Jordan, Neil 49
Joseph II (emperor of Austria) 264
Joseph, Paul A. 115
Josephine (empress of France) 265
Joslyn, Allyn 142
"Journey to Babel" (TV episode) 72
Joyce, John 112
The Joys of Jezebel (1970 film) 307
Jud Süss (1940 film) 272
Judas 132–134, 157, 165, 166, 167–170, 171, 172, 191, 220, 260
Judd, Rainer 108
Judd, Robert* 51, 53
Judgment Day (1988 film) 160–163
Juego Diabolico (1958 film) 307
Junosza-Stepowski, Kazimierz* 306
Jurassic Park (1993 film) 200
Just the Ten of Us (TV series) 115

Kaczmarek, Jan A.P. 186
Kadler, Karen 95, 96
Kahn, Madeline 294
Kahn, Michael 101
Kallista, Jaromir 124
Kaminski, Janusz 186, 187
Kane, Erica (character) 155, 156
Karate Kid (film series) 53
Karloff, Boris 3, 89, 158, 278, 280, 309
Kartaphilos (character) 95
Kastner, Elliott 17
Katch, Kurt 21
Kato, Seiko 226
Kaufman, Famie 25
Kaufman, Lloyd 308
Kaufman, Robert* 307
Käutner, Helmut 307
Kavner, Julie 61
Kay, Bernard 282
Kay, Walter 257
Kazan, Zito 243
Kazantzakis, Nikos 167, 168
Keane, Edward 22
Keane, Peggy 240
Keane, Robert Emmett 63
Keaton, Buster 74, 205, 207, 237
Keen, Geoffrey* 191, 193
Keener, Catherine 274
Keener, Eliott 17
The Keep (1983 film) 275
Keitel, Harvey* 167, 170, 183, 185
Keith, Brian 201, 202
Keith, Ian 80
Kelber, Michel 32
Kell, Ayla 217
Kellaway, Cecil 94, 226, 229
Kellaway, Roger 176
Kelly, Gene 83
Kelsey, Tamsin 204
Kemper, Steven 108
Kendall, Elaine Corall 109
Kendall, Kay 192, 193, 194
Keni, Deranne 221
Kennedy, Arthur 245, 248
Kennedy, John F. 177
Kennedy, Ted 233
Kennett, George 226
Kenobi, Obi-Wan (character) 234
Kershner, Irvin 168, 170
Keyes, Anthony Nelson 75
Keymas, George 28
Kharis (character) 77
Khondji, Darius 208, 212
Khufu (pharaoh) 265, 266
Kibbe, Gary B. 223
Kibbee, Roland 21
Kidd, Captain William 65
Kier, David 94
Kier, Udo 108
Kilar, Wojciech 208, 212
Kiley, Richard* 23
The Killing of Satan (1983 film) 163–165
Killum, Guy 51

Kilner, Kevin 273
King, Don 84, 86
King, Erik 262
King, Perry 273, 274
King, Stephen 72, 203, 204, 206
The King of Kings (1926 film) 165–167
King of Kings (1961 film) 166, 213
Kipper Kids 130
Kirgo, George 23
Kirksey, Miyako 258
Kirschner, Jack 115
Klein, Robert 58, 60
Kline, Richard H. 135
Klinger, Friedrich 2
Knapp, Sebastian 157
Knell, David 69
Knoles, Harley 306
Knowland, Ann 238
Kober, Erich 271
Kobota, Tak 69
Kobrin, Rob 203
Kohlund, Christian 157
Kojack (TV series) 182
Komack, James 54
Konvitz, Jeffrey 245, 246
Konwicki, Tadeusz 308
Kopelson, Anne 84
Kopelson, Arnold 83
Korner, Lothar 268
Koscina, Sylvia 179, 182, 183
Kosloff, Theodore 165
Koteas, Elias 186, 230
Koufax, Sandy 206
Kovacs, Ernie 130
Krabbé, Jeroen* 157–159
Kraft, Tenna 171
Kramer, Ken 262
Kramer, Steve 109
Krampf, Gunther 271
Kratana, Richard C. 245
Kraus, Jan 124
Krauss, Werner* 270, 271, 272
Kress, Harold F. 43, 132
Kronen, Ben 233
Kryszak, Jerzy* 308
Kudla, Vladimir 124
Kuecher, Robert Watson *see* Watson, Bobby
Kuhn, Robert 126
Kuhn, Roberta 149
Kulle, Jarl 89
Kuran, Peter 126
Kurant, Willy 255
Kurfürstendam (1920 film) 306
Kurtz, David 151
Kurtzman, Robert 183
Kusatsu, Clyde 201
Kyser, Hans 121

Labry, Pierre 291
La Cour, Ella 298
Ladd, Cheryl 238, 240
Ladd, Diane 87
Lafayette, John 273

Lafferty, Sandra 230
Lagerkvist, Bengt 307
Lagerwall, Sture 89
Lahlou, Omar 157
Lake, Veronica 32
LaLanne, Jack 233
Lally, Mike 22
LaLoggia, Charles M. 126
LaLoggia, Frank 126, 127
LaLoggia, Joe 126
Lamarr, Hedy 265
Lancaster, Burt 35
Lancaster, James 186
Lancaster, Lucie 246
Land of the Giants (TV series) 129
Land of the Pharaohs (1955 film) 266
Landau, Martin 132, 135
Lander, David L. 294
Landis, Winifred 58
Landor, Rosalyn 75
Lane, Campbell 204
Lang, Fritz 206
Langella, Frank 208, 213
Langlouis, Hervé 197
Lansbury, Angela 49, 132
Lanteri, Michael 300
La Porte, Elizza 271, 272
LaPorte, Marcel* 306
Lara, Graciela 235
Laroche, Pierre 291
Larquey, Pierre 91
Lary, Pierre 194
LaSardo, Robert 201
Laskin, Michael 240
Lasky, Zane 246
Lassie (film series) 153
The Last Laugh (1924 film) 121, 123
"Last Night of a Jockey" (TV episode) 311
The Last Temptation of Christ (1988 film) 167–171
Lathrop, Philip 226
Latimer, Jonathan 9
Latouche, John 43
Laugh In (TV series) 298
Laughton, Charles 34
Laurenti, Fabrizio 308
Laurentiis, Dino de 106
Laurey, Maurius 194
Lauter, Ed 243
Lavat, Queta 235
Lavdiere, Hervé 197
LaVey, Anton Sandor 102
LaVey, Diane 102
Lavista, Raul 25
Lavogez, Yvette 255
Lawless, James 240, 242
Lawrence, Bert 288
Lawrence, Keith 160
Lawrence, Marc 46, 48, 109
Lawson, Sarah 75
Lawyers and the Devil (theme) 9–16, 63–68, 84–87, 247–248

Lea, Richard M. 257
Leachman. Cloris 139, 142
Leary, Denis 201, 202
Leaves from Satan's Book (1918/21 film) 171–175, 251, 252
Lebedeff, Ivan 251
Le Chanois, Jean-Paul 91
Lecocq, Charles 98
Lecter, Hannibal (character) 200
Lederer, Francis 30
Lederer, Otto 165
Ledoux, Fernand 291
Lee, Christopher* 75, 77, 307
Lee, Pio C. 163
Lee, Robert 268
Lee, Robert E. 60
Leffert, Joel 61
Legend (1985 film) 163, 281
Legend of Hell House (1973 film) 116
Legend of Hillbilly John (1973 film) 176–179
Legendre, Brigitte 255
Leggenda di Faust (1948 film) 307
Legiardi, Edmund 118
Lehar, Franz 182
Leiber, Fritz 22, 112, 114, 115
Leigh, Randel* 257, 258
Lembeck, Ann 201
Lembeck, Michael 139
Lemkin, Jonathan 83
Lenard, Mark 132
Lenau, Nicolas 2
Leni, Paul 270
Lennon, Jarrett 146
Leonard, Jack E. 203
Leonardo da Vinci (artist) 74, 133, 265, 267
Leone, Kathy 179
Leone, Sergio 179, 180
Lerer, Shifra 61
Leroux, Maxime 197
Leroy, Eddie 288
Lesser, Robert 109
Lestocq, Humphrey 192
Leuw, Raymond A. de 69
Levant, Oscar 3
Levay, Sylvester 153
Leviathan 129
Levin, Sidney 294
Levine, Steve 197
Levinthal, Malcolm 115
Levitt, Steve 151
Levy, Elliott 157
Levy, Eugene 262, 264
Levy, Melvin P. 176
Lewis, Denise D. 109
Lewis, Jerry* 54
Lewis, Ralph 58, 60
Lewis, Ted 57
Lewis, Walter P.* 306
Lewton, Val 92, 127
Liebe, Tod und Teufel (1934 film) 306
Life of Brian (1979 film) 294

"Life's Full O'Consequences" (song) 44
Lifestyles of the Rich and Famous (TV series) 152
Liguoro, Giuseppe de 58, 305
Lilith 226, 228, 229
Lincoln, Abraham 39, 42, 265
Lindley, Giselle 130
Lindo, Delroy 84
Lindon, Lionel 9
Lindsey, Hal 218
Lindsey, Jason 95
Lindstrom, Viggo 171
Linville, Albert 54
Lion, Mickey *see* Bava, Mario
Lipscomb, Dennis 51
Lipstein, Harold 54
Lisa and the Devil (1979 film) 179–183
Lish, Becca 300
Lister, Tom "Tiny," Jr. 183, 186
Liszt, Franz 2, 51
Litchenstein, Irving L. 112
Little Devils see Witch Academy
Little Engine That Could (children's story) 186
Little Nicky (2000 film) 183–186
Little Red Riding Hood (fairy tale) 50
Little Shop of Horrors (1986 film) 2
Livus, Titus 189
Lloyd, Charles 36
Lloyd, Eric 60
Lloyd, Julie 214
Loaded Weapon (1993 film) 202
Lock (character) 237
Locke, Harry 276
Lockhart, Gene 62
Lockwood, Alexander 265
Lockwood, Preston 279
Lockyear, Tom 157
The Lodger (1944 film) 145
Loftus, Bryan 49
Logan, Bob 233
Logan, Jacqueline 165
Logan, Kristopher 201
Loggia, Robert 132
London, Tom 165
Loohl, David 273
Looking for Richard (1996 film) 86
Loos, Theodore* 306
Lopez, Fernando 149
Lopez, Javiern 25
Lopez, Sylvia 184
Lord, Mindret 9
Lord of the Rings (2001 film) 232
Lord's Prayer 128
Lorimer, Alan E. 39
Lorre, Peter 135, 265, 266
The Lost Continent (1968 film) 77
Lost Souls (2000 film) 186–189
Loughran, Jonathan 183
Louie, Viola 165
Louis XV (king of France) 123
Louis XVI (king of France) 173

Louis-Dreyfus, Julia 61
Lovecraft, H. P. 113, 176
The Loved One (1964 film) 86
Lovejoy, Ray 197
Lovitz, John 183
Lovsky, Celia 132, 135
Lowe, Chad 146, 148
Lubitsch, Ernst 142, 143, 144
Lucas, Alex 135
Lucas, Wilfred 251
Lucci, Susan* 153, 155, 156
Las Luchadoras (lady wrestlers) 260
Lucidi, Renzo 118
Lucifer 4, 16, 20, 29, 33, 121, 123, 126–129, 145, 170, 175, 183, 185, 190, 191, 193, 203, 209–212, 219, 222, 223, 230, 232, 233, 235, 237, 238, 251–254, 262, 264, 287, 290 307, 308, 309
Lugosi, Bela 89, 126
Luke (Bible N.T.) 47, 134, 159, 167, 220
Lulli, Folco 118
Lumley, Terry 238
Lupino, Ida 101, 104
Lurch (character) 303
Lurie, John 168
Lustig, Aaron 39
Luze, Herve de 208
Lycanthropus: The Moonlight Murders (1996 film) 149
Lynch, Brad 197
Lynch, Conrad Jimmy 221
Lynn, Emmett 28
Lynne, Donna 226

M (1931 film) 206
Mabitol, Alberto 160
Mabitol, Romeo 160
Macari, Ruggero 73
Macario (1960 film) 307
MacDonald, Jeannette 2, 3
MacDonald, Peter 49
Macedo, Julissa 259
MacGinnis, Niall 282
MacGreevy, Oliver 275
Machiavelli, Niccolo 73, 74
Machio, Ralph 51, 53
Maciste (1915 film) 189
Maciste all'Inferno see Maciste in Hell
Maciste e il Nipote d'America (1924 film) 191
Maciste in Hell (1926 film) 189–191
Maciste in Hell (1962 film) 190
Maciste's American Relative see Maciste e il Nipote d'America
Mack, Wilbur 288
Mackay, Mary *see* Corelli, Marie
MacKey, Paul 146
MacMurray, Fred 303
MacNeil, Regan (character) 233, 234
MacPherson, Jeannie 165

Macready, George 9, 16
Mad Hatter (character) 250
Mad Max (1979 film) 148
Madsen, Gerda 298
Madsen, Virginia 230
Magana, Delia 35
Magee, Patrick 276, 278
Maggi, Luigi 305
The Magician (1926) 45
Maguelon, Pierre 194
Maguire, Tobey 61
Mahler, Gustav 2, 281
Mahler, Norbert* 308
Mahoney, Victoria 273
Maillet, Christian 99
La Main du Diable see *The Devil's Hand*
Maines, Marlene 142
Maistre, François 194
Make Room for Daddy (TV series) 309
Makeham, Eliot 192
Malefiche Presenze (1988 film) 308
Malenotti, Maleno 118
Malet, Arthur 214
Malone, A. Jay 221
Maly, Svatopluk 124
Man and Superman (play) 90, 311
The Man and the Monster (1958 film) 261
Man of La Mancha (1972 film) 153
The Man Who Cheated Life see *The Student of Prague*
The Man Who Knew Too Much (1956 film) 72
Manchu, Fu see Fu Manchu
Mancini, Henry 273
Manfredini, Harry 217
Mann, Howard 294
Mann, Peter 132
Manni, Ettore 73
Manning, Ruth 69
Mansi, Louis 276
Manson, Maurice, 285
Mantegna, Joe 201, 202
Mantle, Mickey 55, 204, 206
Manuel, Denis 194
Marais, Jean* 196, 308
Marat, Jean Paul 278
La Marca del Hombre Lobo (1967 film) 149
Marcarelli, Robert 217
March, Frederic 32
Marchal, Georges 194
Marden, Richard 35, 249
Marduke (Devil pseudonym) 176–179
Margolen, Janet 132
Margolis, Mark 108
Margoyles, Miriam 108, 111
Margulles, Michael D. 233
Marie Antoinette (queen of France) 171, 173, 174, 265, 266
Marinaro, Ed 201
Marino, Dan 184

Mark (Bible N.T.) 167, 120
Markham, David 276
Markham, Monte 160
Markoe, Bruce 46
Marks, Leo* 168, 170
Marley, Jacob (character) 58
Marley, Peverel 165
Marlowe, Andrew W. 108, 109, 296
Marlowe, Christopher 2, 35, 105, 109, 121, 124
Marr, Sally 69
Marsen, Edward 49
Marshak, Daryl A. 46
Marshak, Philip 46
Marshall, Alan 17
Marshall, Mike 197
Marshall, Trudy 142
Marter, Ian 105
Marth, Frank 238
Martin, Al 80
Martin, Andrea 294
Martin, Edie 192
Martin, Elizabeth 46
Martin, Gregory Mars 146
Martin, Julie 221
Martin, Marion 21
Martin, Rudolf 39
Martin, Todd 139
Martinez, Fernando 25
Martinson, Mark L. 129
Marty (1955 film) 104
Marvella, Un Gapo 163
Marx, Chico 265
Marx, Groucho 234, 265, 267
Marx, Harpo 265
Marx, Melinda 265, 267
Marzi, Franca 118
Mascara, Melissa 109
Masche, Jacquelyn 233
*M*A*S*H* (TV series) 133
The Masked Marvel (1941 serial) 81
Mason, James 165
The Master and Margherite (1972 film) 307
Mastrocinque, Camillo 307
Matarazzo, Heather 84
Mate Doma Iva? (1964 film) 307
Mather, Aubrey 142
Matheson, Richard 75
Mathews, Patricia 240
Matras, Christian 194
Matthew (Bible N.T.) 167, 196
Matthew (saint) 132, 157, 165
Mattison, Ernest 298
Mattson, Bart 265
Max Headroom (TV series) 125
Maximilian, Max 271
Maxwell, Edwin 142
Mayhand, Ernest 221
Maynard, Ruth 300
Mayo, Archie 21, 24
Mayo, Virginia 265

Maze, Edward 95
McAllen, Kathleen Rowe 126
McCalla, Irish 25
McCallum, David 132, 133
McCarthy, Kevin 153, 156
McClaren, Vincent 49
McClure, Doug* 243, 245
McComb, Heather 262
McCormack, Muriel 165, 167
McCormack, Patty 153, 156
McCracken, Charlie 78
McDonough, Jane 241
McDowall, Roddy 132, 133
McEvoy, Anne Marie 153
McGarry, Parnell 36
McGee, Mark Thomas 112, 296
McGhee, Brownie 17, 21
McGowan, Tom 46
McGuire, Dorothy 132, 135
McGuire, Josh 157
McGuire, Zach 157
McHale's Navy (TV series) 104
McIntosh, Angus 105
McIntosh, David 105
McKay, Michael Reid 146
McKean, Michael 183
McKee, Robert 165
McKerras, Ross 217
McKimmie, Jackie 308
McKinnon, Ray 204
McLarty, Ron 246
McLean, Michael 142
McLendon, Clark 258
McLeod, Kenneth 160
McLernon, Harold 165
McQueen, Butterfly 44
McWhorter, Richard 105
Meara, Ann 146, 148
Meckseper, Cornelius* 308
Medici, Lorenzo de 73, 74
Medin, Harriet 300
The Medusa Touch (1978 film) 200
Meeker, George 21
"Meet Mr. Lucifer" (TV episode) 309, 262
Meet Mr. Lucifer (1953 film) 191–194
Meet the Mansons (TV show parody) 263
Mefistofele (opera) 2, 119
Megowan, Don 264
Mei, Wei 84
Meier, Shane 204
Melennec, Patrice 197
Méliès, Georges* 1, 121, 305
Melin, Lee 95
Melle, Gil 245
Mellor, William C. 132, 133
Melos Ensemble 249
Menaugh, Michael 105
Mendez, Jose Carlos 235
Meney, Bernard* 308
Menjou, Adolphe* 251, **252**, 254
Mensch Jesus (1999 film) 308
Mephisto Waltz (1971 film) 3, 154

Mephisto Waltz (tone poem) 3
Mephistopheles 3, 4, 21, 23, 32, 33, 34, 35, 38, 105–108, 121–123, 124–126, 262, 264, 305, 308
The Merchant of Venice (1952 film) 34
Meredith, Burgess* 245, **247**, 248, 281, 284, 310
Merino, Jose Luis 307
Merlin, Joanna 223
Merlin the Magician 235, 236
Merrick, Doris 142
Merritt, Abraham 299, 300
The Merry Frolics of Satan (1906 film) 305
"The Merry Widow Waltz" (orchestral composition) 143
Mertes, Raffaele 157
Mesa, William 214
The Messiah (oratorio) 133
Messing, Debra 157
Metcalfe, Ken 30, 32
Metternich, Prince Clemons 82
Mexican films 25, 228, 235, 259, 307, 308
Meyer, Johnnes 171, **173**
Meyer, T. 307
Mi Nismo Andjeli (1992 film) 308
Michael (archangel) 121–124, 126–128, 230, 232, 252, 254
Michaels, Beverly 28
Miele, Luciano 108
"A Mighty Fortress Is Our God" (hymn) 11, 16
Mikros Images 208
Milchan, Aaron 84
Miles, Sylvia 245
Milkis, Edward K. 87
The Milky Way (1969 film) 194–196
Milland, Ray* 9, **10**, **12**, 16
Miller, Barry 168
Miller, David* 192, 257, 259
Miller, Dennis 249
Miller, Dick 285, 287
Miller, George 300
Miller, Jean 257, 259
Miller, Marvin 265
Miller, Nancy 264–265
Miller, Rebecca 308
Miller, Thomas L. 87
Le Million (1931 film) 32
Mills, Ann 153
Mills, Donna 139
Millyar, Georgi* 307
Milner, Martin 226, 229
Milton, John 2, 61, 86, 175, 190, 212, 248, 305
Milton, John (Devil pseudoym) 84–87
Mineo, Sal 132, 133
Minnelli, Vincent 43, 44
"Minnie the Moocher" (song) 131
Minos (mythological character) 190

Minton, Faith 273
Minuit, Peter 265
Mireless, George 221
Mirkovitch, Steve 223
Mission: Impossible (TV series) 243
Mr. Boogedy (1986 film) 308
Mr. Frost (1990 film) 197–201
Misterios de la Magia Negra (1957 film) 307
Mitchell, Cameron 25, 26, 46, 48
Mitchell, Thomas 4, 9, 16, 66, 68
Mitchum, John 288
Mo Deng Tian Shi (1981 film) 306
Moanoogian, Peter 201
Mockery (1927 film) 299
Moctezuna, Carlos Lopez 307
Modern Times (1936 film) 130
Modot, Gaston 32
Molander, Jan 307
Molin, Bud 243
Molina, Jacinto *see* Naschy, Paul
Molina, Sergio 149, 150
Moll, Charles *see* Moll, Richard
Moll, Giorgia 73
Moll, Richard 46, 48
Molnár, Ferenc 305, 306
Moloch 216
Monahan, Greg 154
Mondale, Eleanor 201
Mondragon, Jorge 259
Monk, Debra 84
The Monkey's Paw (short story) 259, 277
Monroe, Marilyn 228
Monseu, Jacques 99
Monsieur Verdoux (1947 film) 114
Monteiro, Joao César 308
Montesanto, Frank 126
Montgomery, Belinda J. 87
Montgomery, Robert 22, 141
Monticelli, Mario 118
Monty Python's Flying Circus (TV series) 279, 294
Moody, Lynne 115
Moore, Cleo 28, 29
Moore, Demi 61
Moore, Dicky 142
Moore, Dudley 35, 36, 38, 39, 42, 43, 294, 295
Moore, Evelyn 36
Moore, Rudy Ray 221
Mora, Danny 214
Morales, Manuel Trejo 25
Moran, David* 60
Moran, Mike 278, 280
Morayta, Miguel 307
Morehead, Agnes 265, 266
Moreland, Mantan 44, 45
Moreno, Belita 214
Moreno, Jose Elias 235, **236**
Morgan, Sherill 73
Morley, Robert 250
Morris, Duane* 310
Morris, Kirk 190

Morris, Pam 126
Morris, Virginia 273
Morse, Robert 151
Morse, Susan E. 60
Mortensen, Viggo* 230, 232
Morton, Joe 51
Morton, Thomas 65
Mortorff, Lawrence 217
Moses 207, 265, 294–295
Il Mostro di Frankenstein (1920 film) 191
Motorcycle Gang (1957 film) 30
Mowbray, Alan* 80, 81, **82**, 83
Mower, Patrick 75, 77
Mozart, Wolfgang Amadeus 300
Mozzhukhin, Ivan* 306
Mudie, Leonard 265
Muerin, Dennis 112
Muir, Ian 279
Mulhall, Jack 288
Mulholland, Jim 201
Muller, Dr. (Devil pseudonym) 306
Muller, Lilian 69
Müller-Stahl, Armin 157
The Mummy (1932 film) 278
The Mummy (1959 film) 77
Munguia, Jose J. 308
Muni 194
Muni, Paul 21, 24
Munoz, Tito 160
Munro, Caroline 149
Munro, Lochlyn 204
A Murder of Crows (1998 film) 2, 105
Murga, Jean 251
Murnau, F. W. 121, 123, 306
Murphy, Charles Thomas 294
Murray, Barbara 192, 276
Murray, K. Gordon 235, 259, 261
Muse, Clarence 142
Musicals 54, 129, 176
Musicians and the Devil (theme) 19–21, 44–45, 51–53, 118–120, 131, 177–179, 214–217, 249–250, 283, 301
Musidora 270
Musset, Alfred de 270
Mussolini, Benito 16, 38, 80, 81, 83
Musson, Bernard 194
Musuraca, Nick 264
Muthel, Lothar 121
My Fair Lady (1964 film) 193
My Favorite Martian (TV series) 57
My Tail Is Hot (1964 film) 4
Mystic Knights of the Oingo Boingo (theater ensemble) 130

Nader, George 30
Nairn, Gerry 262
Naked Gun (film series) 234
Nalder, Reggie* 69, **71**, 72

Napoleon I (emperor of France) 265, 266, 279, 280
Narcisse, Jarret 18
Narcosatanicos Asesinos (1988 film) 308
Nares, Owen 251
Naschy, Paul* 149, 150, 307
Nascimbene, Mario 105, 106
National Lampoon (magazine) 202
National Lampoon's Favorite Deadly Sins (1995 film) 201–203
Nealon, Kevin 183
Neanderthal man 191
"Nebuchadnezzar" (song) 177
Necromancy (1972 film) 154
Necronomicon (1994 film) 275
Necronomicon (Cthulhu Mythos book) 113, 114, 115
Needful Things (1993 film) 134, 203–207
Needful Things (novel) 203, 204
Neff, Walter (character) 303
Negret, François 197
Neiderman, Andrew 83
Neill, James 165
Nelson, Albert 230
Nelson, Argyle, Jr. 132
Nelson, Burt 264
Nelson, Craig T. 84
Nelson, John 129, 262
Nelson, John Allen 151, 153
Nelson, Nancy 240
Nelson, Shawn 230
Nero (emperor of Rome) 55, 228, 265, 266, 267
Nero's Mistress (1956 film) 120
Nerval, Gerard de 91
Nessun Dorma (opera aria) 301
Neumann, Harry 288
Never Bet the Devil Your Head (short story) 50
The Neverending Story (1984 film) 156
New Zealand films 250, 308
Newland, John 176
Newman, Alfred 132, 133
Newman, David 39
Newman, Dorothy 285, **287**
Newman, Laraine 294, 295
Newmar, Julie* 311
Newmara, Tammy 95
Newsweek (magazine) 152
Newton, Isaac 265
"A Nice Place to Visit" (TV episode) 309
Nichols, Dandy 192
Nicholson, Jack* 300, **302**, 303
Nicholson, Ken 249
Nicholson, Martin 129
Nicodemus 44
Nielsen, Christian 171
Nielsen, Connie 84, **85**
Nielsen, Leslie 233, 234
Nielson, John C. 109
Nielson, Steven 296

The Night Before Christmas (1913 film) see *Noch perd Rozhdestuom*
The Night Before Christmas (1961 film) 307
Night Court (TV show) 48
Night Gallery (TV series) 139, 310
Night Has a Thousand Eyes (1948 film) 9
Night Train to Terror (1985 film) 46
Nightbreed (1990 film) 131
The Nightmare Before Christmas (1993 film) 131, 237
The Nightmare Never Ends see *Cataclysm*
Nightmare of Terror see *The Devil's Nightmare*
Nightmare on Elm Street (1984) 154
Ninchi, Carlo 32
The Nine Gates of the Kingdom of Shadows (Satanic guidebook) 209, 210, 212, 213
The Ninth Gate (1999 film) 208–213
Nissen, Helge 171, **173**, 175
Nitzschmann, Erich 271
Niven, Larry 38
Noah's Ark (1929 film) 226
Noch perd Rozdestrom (1913 film) 305
Nocturnal Procession (tone poem) 2
Norman, Josephine 165
Norris, Peter 165
Northern Overexposure (TV show parody) 263
Nosferatu (1922 film) 121, 270
A Nous la Liberté (1931 film) 32
Novack, Ivana 99
Novadine, Abedelouhahad 157
Novak, Kim* 243, 245
Nowell, Wedgwood 80
Nureyev, Rudolf 250
Nussbaum, Raphael 257

O Ugly Bird (short story) 176
Oakie, Jack 83
Obi-Wan Kenobi see Kenobi, Obi-Wan
O'Brien, Denis 278
O'Bryne, Bryan 233
Ochoa, Diana 259
O'Connor, Derrick 108
O'Connor, Donald 83
O'Connor, Frances 39, 43
O'Donnell, Cathy 265
O'Donovan, Elizabeth 105
Oedipus Rex (play) 21
Of Late I Think of Cliffordville (TV episode) 311
Off with His Head (TV miniseries parody) 263

Offspring of the Devil (theme) 44–45, 83–86, 87–89, 109–111, 137, 183–186, 221–223, 303
O'Fredericks, Alice 298
Oh, God! (1977 film) 214
Oh God! You Devil (1984 film) 38, 214–217
O'Hagan, Michael 108
O'Hanlon, George 115
O'Hara, Catherine 237, 262
O'Hara, David 157
Oingo Boingo (musical group) 130, 131
Okerlund, "Mean" Gene 233, 234
The Old-Fashioned Way (1934 film) 83
Old Ones (ancient gods) 113, 114
Oldman, Gary 157–159
Olin, Lena 208
Oliver, Barret 153, 156
Olivier (Devil pseudonym) 46–48
Olivier, Dennis 130
Olivier, Lawrence 193
Olsen, Flemming 176
Olsen, Ole 190
Olstead, Rebecca Renee 109
Los Olvidados (1950 film) 196
The Omega Code (1999 film) 4, 188, 217–220
Omen (1976 film) 4, 77, 220
One Step Beyond (TV series) 95, 176
O'Neil, Don 126
O'Neill, Frank 132
O'Neill, Henry 9
O'Neill, James* 306
Oogie Boogie (character) 131, 237
Optical Services 240
Orange, Gerald 18, 21
Orano, Alesso 179, 182
Orbach, Jerry 245
Order of the Silver Serpent (satanist group) 210, **211**, 212, 213
O'Reilly, Robert 217
Orestes, Daniel 84
Orfei, Liani 73
Orgon (character) 272
Orgy of the Dead (1965 film) 286
Ornitz, Kim 186
Oro, Juan Bustillo 307
Oropesa, Elizabeth 163
Orphans of the Storm (1922 film) 253, 254
Orpheus (1949 film) 196
Orpheus in the Underworld (Greek myth) 146, 148
Ortin, Polo 235
Osborne, Ozzy 184, 185
Ostrand, Tracey 184
O'Sullivan, Maureen 16
Osunn, Norman 165
Oswald, Richard 306
Othello (1922 film) 272
Othello (character) 123
Ottensen, John 60

Otto, Henry 58
Oursler, Fulton 132
Out of the Past (1947 film) 92
The Outer Limits (TV series) 130
Outward Bound (1930 film) 141
Overbeck, Kevin 78
Oxenberg, Catherine 217, 220
Oxford University Drama Society 105, 106
Oxilia, Nino 306

Pacino, Al* 83, 84, **85**, 86, 111
Packard, Clayton 165
Padden, Sarah 21
Paganini (operetta) 182
Paganini, Nicolo 51
Pagano, Bartolomeo 189, 191
Page, Mary Anne 146
Paiva, Nestor 9
Palacios, Manuel 25
Palance, Jack 77, 281, 284
Palau, Pierre* 91, 94
Palette, Eugene 142
Palin, Michael 278, 279
Paller, Gary 203, 204
Palley, Reese 241
Pallut, Philippe 255
Palmer, Gene 264
Palmer, Maria 146
Pals in Paradise (1926 film) 166
Pan Twardowski (1936 film) 306
Pangborn, Franklin 265
Paniagua, Cecilio 179
Panza, Sancho (character) 153
Pappas, Christopher 308
Paracelsus (1943 film) 272
Paradise Lost (poem) 2, 84, 175, 212, 248, 305
Pardo, Don 262, 264
Parker, Alan 17, 19
Parker, F. William 273
Parker, Gretchen 51
Parker, Jameson 223
Parker, Lara 310
Parker, Tom S. 262
Parking (1985 film) 308
Parnell, Emory 80
Parrish, Julie 69
Passet, Stephan 306
The Passion of Joan of Arc (1928 film) 172
Pate, Johnny 243
Patrick, Nigel 275
Patterson, Sarah 49
Paufichet, Jules *see* Berry, Jules
Paul (saint) 167, 169
Paul, Edna Ruth 126
Pauley, Rebecca 208
Paulino, Justo 30
Paulve, Andre 291
Payne, Bruce Martyn* 273, 275
Pazuzu (demon) 4, 233
Peale, Norman Vincent 98
Pearl, Natasha 51
Pearson, Sydney 191

Peck, Bob 58
Peck, Gregory 77
Pedersen, Maria 298
Pegg, Ann Warn 204
Peignaux, Vincent 255
Pelissier, Anthony 191
Pellosi, Carmine 241
Pendelton, Steve 9
Penguin (character) 284
Peres, Marcel 194
Peretz, Susan 214
Perez, Jennifer 160
Perez, Pepito 9
Perez-Reverte, Arturo 208, 209
Pergament, Robert 273
Perkins, Gil 22
Perry, Joe 132
Perry, Peter 307
The Persecution and Assassination of Jean Paul Marat as Performed by the Inmates of the Asylum at Charenton under the Direction of the Marquis de Sade (1967 film) 278
Persephone (mythological character) 189, 190
Persoff, Nehemiah 132, 168
Pession, Gabriella 157
Pete the Cutthroat 65
Peter (Saint) 36, 37, 132, 134, 157, 165, 168, 194, 201, 202
Peter I (Bible N.T.) 80
Peter Schlemiel (novella) 268
Peter the Great (tsar of Russia) 123
Petersen, Robert C. 87
Petersen, Vilhelm 171
Peterson, Alan C. 262
Petey Wheatstraw (1977 film) 221-223
Petitclerc, Jean* 308
The Petrified Forest (1936 film) 24
Petrovic, Aleksander 307
Pettet, Joanna 115, 117
Pettingell, Frank 192
Pfeiffer, Michelle 300
Phantasm (1979 film) 47
Phantom of the Opera (1925 film) 2
Phantom of the Opera (1943 film) 114
Phantom of the Opera (character) 150
Phelan, Brian 249
Philbin, Regis 184
Philibosian, Robert 201
Philipe, Gérard* 32, 33, 35, 203
Philipps, Robin 275
Phillips, Alex, Jr. 101
Phillips, Bertram 306
Phillips, Don 230
Phillips, James 112
Phillips, John 282
Pialat, Maurice 255, 257
Piat, Jean 194

Picard, Jean-Luc (character) 169, 263
Picardo, Robert 214, 217
Piccoli, Michel 194
Picker, Si 61
Pickup (1950 film) 28
Pilate, Pontius 95, 132, 157–159, 165, 167, 170
A Pilgrim's Progress (prose allegory) 195
Pilkington, Steve 78
Pilon, Daniel 194
Pinal, Silvia* 196
Pinar, Carlos 25
Pine, Linda 108
Pinney, Clay 186
Pinon, Efren C. 163
Pio, Elith 171. 298
Pip (Devil pseudonym) 309
Pipitine, Nino, Jr. 142
Piria, Paolo 157
Pitch (Devil) 235–238
Pittack, Robert 80
Pittard, Robert 63
Pizzie, Carl 157
The Planets (orchestral suite) 47
Play of the Week (TV series) 311
Playtime (1967 film) 195
Pleasence, Donald* 132, 134, 223, 225
Plummer, Amanda 204, 207, 230, 232
Plus Longues Nuit du Diable see The Devil's Nightmare
Pluto (mythological character) 189, 190, 191
Poe, Edgar Allan 50, 268, 282, 283
Poff, Lon 58, 60
Pogany, Gabor 105
Pogson, Katharyn 49
Pohlkotte, Tanya 202
Poinson, Danny 221
Poitier, Sidney 132
Polacco, Caesare 118
Polaire, Pauline 189, 191
Polanski, Roman 208, 212, 213, 277
Polcyn, Beverly 258
Polet, Philippe 197
Polish films 306, 308
Politicians and the Devil (theme) 9–16, 22–24, 63–68, 118–120
Polk, Oscar 44
Pollak, Kevin 108
Pommer, Erich 121
Ponce, Luis Daniel 214
Poncela, Enrique 306, 307
Pontoppidan, Clara 298
Poor Devil (telefilm) 77, 307
"Pop Goes the Weasel" (song) 65, 66
Pope, Bill 39
Pope, Robert 60
Popescu-Gopo, Ion 307
Poppe, Nils 89
Porkins (character) 220

Porrett, Susan 49
Porter, Edwin S. 305
Porter, Jean 80
Porter, Steven M. 201
Portillo, Adolfo Torres 235
Portugese films 308
The Postman Always Rings Twice (1946 film) 302
Potter, Harry (character) 266
Pounder, C.C.H. 108, 112
Pournelle, Jerry 38
Powell, Buddy 214
Powell, Dick 33
Powell, Eddie* 75, **76**, 77
Powell, Stephanie 83
Pozzetto, Dominique 208
Prange, Gregory 153
Prather, Joan 101
Predator 2 (1990 film) 109
Preminger, Otto 193
The President (1919 film) 171
The President's Analyst (1967 film) 310
Presson, Jason 154
Pretorius, Dr. (character) 193
Prevert, Jacques 291
Price, Vincent* 264, **265**, 267, 280, 311
The Prince (book) 73
Prince, John T. 165
Prince of Darkness (1987 film) 223–225
Prine, Andrew 115
Printer's Devil (TV episode) 310
Prinz, Isabella 149
Prison (1988 film) 232
The Private Lives of Adam and Eve (1959 film) 226–229
Prophecy (1979 film) 230
The Prophecy (1995 film) 230–233
Prophecy II (1999 film) 232
Prophecy III (2000 film) 232
Protegido de Satan (1917 film) 306
Provost, Richard 273
Pryor, Richard 294, 295
Psychiatrists and the Devil (theme) 116–117, 135–138, 197–202, 285–287, 289
Psycho (1998 film) 232
Das Psycho Rangers (motorcycle club) 146
Puccini, Giacomo 300, 301
Pulley, B. S. 203
Punky Brewster (TV series) 156
A Pure Formality (1994 film) 277
Puritan Passions (1923 film) 306
Purviance, Edna 254
Purvis, Jack 278
Pyle, Denver 176

Qualen, John 62
Qualtro, Van 109
Quartorze Juillet (1934 film) 32
Quasimodo (character) 149, 150, 186

Quatermass, Martin *see* John Carpenter
Que Lindo Cha Cha Cha (1954 film) 307
Quester, Hugues* 308
Quezadas, Cesareo 235
Quezadas, Lupita 235
Quibell, Kevin 223
Quinn, Anthony 101
Quinn, Bill 238
Quinn, J. C. 230
Quixote, Don (character) 177

Rae, Cassidy 201
Raffin, Deborah 245, 248
Raft, George 135
Ragan, Russell 157
Ragsdale, William 201
Ragtime (1981 film) 141
Raimbourg, Lucien 99
Rains, Christina 245, 248
Rains, Claude* 21, 22, 23, 24, 91, 118, 132, 135, 141
Rais, Asil 208
Raleigh, Sir Walter 265, 266
Ralph, Hanna 121
Rambo, John (character) 234
Rameau, Hans 121
Ramey, Betty 223
Ramirez, Ruben 235
Ramis, Harold 38, 39, 42, 43
Rampling, Charlotte 17, 21
Ramsay, Todd 146
Ramuz, Charles Ferdinand 249
Rand, Sally 165
Randale, Kenneth 202
Raoul, Dale 201
Raphael (archangel) 126–129
Raphaelson, Samson 142
Rappaport, David 278
Rapsodia Satanica (1915 film) 306
Rash, Dennis 78
Rasputin, Grigori 149, 150, 175
Rathbone, Basil 25, 26, 27
The Raven (1962 film) 280
Rawlings, Terry 245
Ray, Frankie 109
Ray, Fred Olen 296
Ray, Joey 9
Ray, Nicholas 166
Raymond, Gary 132, 135
Rea, Stephen 49
Red Dust (1926 film) 166
The Red Shoes (1948 film) 250
Reddy, Brian 186
Redmond, Harry, Jr. 21
Reed, Oliver 58
Reed, Robert 139, 142
Reedy, Mike 69
Reel EFX 233
Reese, Tom 132
Reeve, Spencer 75
Reeves, Keanu 84, 86
Regalbuto, Joe 153
Reiner, Carl 214

Reinhardt, Gottfried 307
Reinhardt, Max 268
Reisenfeld, Hugo 165
Rembrandt Van Rijn (artist) 14
Remick, Lee 200
Renoir, Jean 293
Repossessed (1990 film) 233–235
Requa, Charles 165
Restitution (1918 film) 306
Retorno a la Juventud (1953 film) 307
Reumert, Poul 298
Revan, Bernard 307
Revelation (Bible N.T.) 1, 109, 117, 188, 220, 230, 231, 299
Rexiane 91
Rey, Alejandro* 243, 246
Reynolds, Helene 142
Rhomm, Patrice 98
Ricci, Elena Sofia 157
Rich, Adam 69
Rich, Allan 201
Rich, David Lowell 238
Richard III (king of England) 86, 186, 291
Richard, Frieda 121
Richards, Addison 21
Richards, Dick 165
Richards, Stewart 63
Richardson, Jay 296
Richardson, Ralph* 275, 278, 279,
Richardson, Sy 221
Richman, Lucas 160
Richman, Mark Peter* 160–162
Richter, Bernard 208
Richter, Jeff 126
Richter, Marrinette 208
Richter, W. D. 203, 206
Rickles, Don 203
Ricky 6 (2000 film) 308
Riddle, Jay 186
Riddle, Tod Curtis 78
The Riddle of the Sands (1979 film) 220
Ridley, Arnold 191
Rifkin, Richard 258
Rigoletto (1954 film) 120
Riminez, Prince Lucio (Devil pseudonym) 251–254
Ripper, Michael 282, 284
Ritter, John* 262, 263, 264, 294–295
Rivera, Reynaldo 307
Rivers, Fletcher 44
Rivilla, Ramon 163
Rizzio, Gianni 118
Roach, Hal 80
Road to Heaven see *Himlaspelet*
Roberts, Randy 214
Roberts, Tanya 201
Roberts, Tony 273
Robespierre, Maximilien 182, 253, 272
Robin Hood (character) 279, 280
Robinson, Edward G. 311

Robinson, James G. 262
Robinson Crusoe (play) 192
Robison, Arthur 272, 308
Robles, Nestor 30
Rocca, Stefania 157
Rocha, Fr. Michael 109
Roche, Eugene 214, 217
Rodann, Ziva 226, 265
Rodero, Jose Lopez 208, 213
Rodgers, Eric 191
Rodis-Ryan, Maureen 142
Rodrigo, Joaquin 179, 182
Rodriguez, Ismael 25
Rodriguez, Percy 176
Rogers, Charles 21, 80
Rogers, Mary 69
Rogers, Sheila 69
Röhreig, Walter 121
Rojo, Jose Antonio 149
Rokas, James 243
Roland, Rita 87
Roley, Sutton 243
Roman, Ric 288
Romanian films 307
Romero, Cesar 160, 163, 265, 266
Romero, Eddie 30
Rooney, Mickey* 73, 74, 226, **227**, 229, 311
Root, Nancy 226
Root, Lynn 43
Roper, Jack 22
Roquemore, Bryan L 221
Roquemore, Cliff 221
Roquemore, Clifford II 221
Roquevert, Noel 91
Rosander, Oscar 89
Rose, Colin 124
Rose, Joshua 201
Rose, Virginia 130
Rosemary's Baby (1968 film) 3, 84, 220, 275
Rosenberg, Alan 168
Rosenberg, Brandon 183
Rosenberg, Max J. 275, 281
Rosenthal, Lawrence 87, 238
Rosenzweig, Barney 176
Ross, Arthur A. 238
Ross, Jerry 54
Ross, Stan 294
Ross, Tiny 278
Rosseter, Thomas 60
Rossetti, Dante Gabriel (artist) 58
Rossitto, Angelo 265
Rosza, Miklos 131
Roth, Adam 201
Roth, Philip 61
Roth, Robby 308
Roth, Stephanie 61
Rothstein, Richard 153, 156
Rou, Aleksandr 307
Roublcek, George 124
Rouillard, Jacqueline 194
Rourke, Mickey 17, 21
Roxanne (paramour of Alexander the Great) 105, 107

Roy, Philip E. 126
Royalty and the Devil (theme) *see* Aristocracy and the Devil
Royce, Coaster 151
Rubens, Paul 237
Rubin, Benny 288
Ruby, Harry 265
Rudin, Lou 84
Ruem, Don* 308
Ruggeri, Manuela* 157–159
Ruginis, Vyto 84
Rundquist, Richard 241
Rusia, Akosoa 51
Russ, Tim 51, 53
Russek, Jorge 259
Russel, Del 168
Russell, Bing 238
Russell, John 251
Russell, Ken 58, 111
Russell, Robert 36
Russell, Robyn 46
Russian films, 305, 306, 307
Russo, James 208
Rust, Henri 291
Ryan, John P.* 308
Ryan, Meg 186,188
Ryan, Robert 115, 166
Ryan, Thomas J,* 308
Ryder, Alfred 176
Ryder, Winona 186, 188
Rye, Stellan 268

Sachs, Alice 126
Sachs, Andrew 124–126
Sade, Marquis Donatien de 194, 195, 196, 278
Sadlers Wells Ballet 250
Sadowsky, Nina R. 186
Saga of the Viking Women and Their Voyage to the Waters of the Great Sea Serpent (1957 film) 286
Sager, Lynn Marie 108
Saget, Bob 308
Saint Martin, Mary Eugenia 259
Saito, James 84
Saks, Gus 60
Sala, Franz 189
Salacron, Armand 32
Salcedo, Leopoldo 30
Salem's Lot (1979 film) 72
Sally of the Sawdust (1925 film) 251
Salmanova, Lyda 268, 270, 272
Salmi, Albert 311
Salo, Mario 189
Sammeth, Barbara 87
San Francisco (1936 film) 2
San Jose, Francisco Garcia 149
Sand, Paul 294, 295
Sandberg, Carl 132
Sanders, Sherman 63
Sandkovich, John 230
Sandler, Adam* 183, 184, 186, 308
Sandler, Jana 184

Sandor, Gregory 129
Sanford, Erskin 21
Sanford, Ralph 288
Sangra, Elena 189
Sangster, Jimmy 69
Santa Claus (1959 film) 235–238
Santa Claus Conquers the Martians (1964 film) 235
Santiago-Hudson, Ruben 84
Santo (wrestler) 260
Santoni, Espartaco 179
Santos, John 257
Sarandon, Christopher 245, 248
Sarandon, Susan 300
Sartor, Fabio 157
Satan (1912 film) 305
Satan en Prison (1907 film) 305
Satanas (1919 film) 306
Satanico Pandemonium (1978 film) 4
Satanis 290
Satanism (theme) 47, 75–77, 87–88, 102–105, 110, 158, 187–188, 208–211, 258, 260, 261, 264
Satan's Pawn see *The Devil* (1915)
Satan's School for Girls (1973 film) 238–240
Satan's School for Girls (2000 film) 240
Satan's Touch (1977 film) 240–242
Satan's Triangle (1975 film) 243–245
Satin, Barney (Devil pseudonym) 69–72
Saturday Night Live (TV series) 184
Saunders, J. Jay 151
Savage, Nelly 251
Savage, T. J. 46
Savalas, Telly* 132, 179, 182
Savina, Carlo 179
Sawaya, George 102
Sawtell, Paul 264
Sax, Guillaume de 91
Saxon, Aaron 285
Scapinelli (Devil pseudonym) 268–270, 271–272
Scarlatti, Domenico 89
The Scarlet Pimpernel (novel) 263
Scarpia, Baron (character) 34
Schallert, William 265
Scheerer, Robert 307
Schell, Ronnie 69
Schiavelli, Vincent 197, 200, 201
Schildkraut, Joseph 132, 135, 165, 167
Schildkraut, Rudolf 165, 167
Schilinsky, Estanislao 25
Schleuter, William 160
Schnéevoigt, George 171
Schneider, Allen 262
Schneider, Eric 204
Schoengarth, Russell 176
Scholander, Sven 171

Scholars and the Devil (theme) *see* Intellectuals and the Devil (theme)
Schombing, Jay 258
Schonberg, Ib 298
Schonfeld, Emmy 298
Schoonmaker, Thelma 167
Schrader, Paul 167
Schranil, Raoul 307
Schrank, Joseph 43
Schreiber, Avery 151
Schroyer, Sonny 69
Schubert, Franz 206
Schuck, John 135
Schumann, Robert 2
Schwab, Lana 233
Schwab, Martin 28
Schwalb, Ben 288
Schwartz, Jan Stuart 130
Schwartz, Thomas Wayne 151
Schwarz, Howard 69
Schwarzenegger, Arnold* 108, 109, 111
Schweiger, Heinrich 307
Sciorra, Annabella 202
Scob, Edith 194
Scola, Ettore 73, 74
La Sconfitta di Satana see *Alias Nick Beal*
Scorsese, Martin 167, 168, 170
Scott, Brandon 258
Scott, Frederick Daniel 233
Scott, George C.* 90, 311
Scott, Hilary 258
Scott, Linda Gaye 135, 138
Scott, Martha 87
Scott, Oz 308
Scott, Ridley 281
Scott, William 58
Scratch (Devil pseudonym) 51–53, 62–68, 264–267, 311
Scrooge, Ebenezer (character) 58, 59
SCTV (TV show) 38, 39, 126, 262, 264
Seacrist (Devil pseudonym) 139–142
The Search for Bridey Murphy (1956 film) 285
Sears, Ann 276
Seawright, Roy 80
Seay, John 126
Sebastian (saint) 105, 106
Second City Television (TV show) *see SCTV*
Second Time Lucky (1984 film) 250, 308
Seeber, Guido 268
Segall, Harry 21, 22
Seigner, Emmanuelle 208, 212, 213
Seizure (1974 film) 89
Seldes, Marian 132
Sellers, Peter 184
Selzer, Milton 115
Seneca, Joe 51, 53

The Sentinel (1977 film) 154, 245–248
Seraphim see *The Prophecy*
Serbian films 308
Sergeant, Brett 160
Serling, Rod 310
Serpent of the Nile (1953 film) 266
Serra, Domenicco 189
Serre, Henri 197
Sersen, Fred 142
Sertner, Robert M. 153
Servais, Jean 99
Setbon, Philip 197
Seven, Johnny 132
The Seven Deadly Sins (1952 film) 203
Seven Footprints to Satan (1929 film) 4, 299
The Seventh Sign (1988 film) 217, 287
Severe, Peggy 18
Seversin, Michael 17
Seyrig, Delphine 194
Shafer, Robert 54
Shaft (1971 film) 221
Shakespeare, William 105, 106, 265, 5
Shamada, Chuck 69
Shanklin, Doug 151
Sharp-Bolster, Anita 142
Sharpe, Thom J 233
Shatner, William 101, 104
Shaw, G. Tito* 212, 213
Shaw, George Bernard 90, 311
Shaw, Peter* 193
Shearer, Jack 109
Sheba and the Gladiators (1958 film) 191
Sheena, Queen of the Jungle (TV show) 25
Sheffield, Reginald 265
Sheiner, David 132
Shelby, Nicole 282
Shelton, Deborah 151, 153
Shelton, Reid 246
Shenah, Emma 230
Shepard, Hilary 151
Shepherd, Jean* 79, 311
Sheppard, William Morgan 204
Sheridan, Joe 208
Sherill, Louise 257
Sherman, Robert M. 214
Sherriden, Jo 197
The Shining (1980 film) 303
Shire, David 214
Shirley, Anne 62, 68
Shirley, John 105
Shock (character) 237
Shue, Elizabeth 60
Shull, Richard B. 294
Shumway, Lee 22
Shur, Miriam 39
Shurson, Robert 241
Shylock (character) 34
Sidi, Nicholas 157

Siegal, David R. 21
Siegal, Richard 262
Siegel, Eve 108
Siegmann, George 165
Sign of the Pagan (1954 film) 266
Silberg, Tussie 49
Silberman, Serge 194
The Silence of the Lambs (1991 film) 200
Silent films 58, 121, 165, 171, 189, 251, 268, 271, 298, 305, 306
"Silent Night" (carol) 237
Silvani, Aldo* 118, 120
Silver, Ron 214, 217
Silver John the Balladeer (book) 176
Silvera, Frank 132
Silverstein, Matthew 308
Silverthorn, Richard J.* 126, 129
Simon, Christine 194
Simon, Michel* 32, 33, 34, 35
Simon, Simone 62, 68
Simon of the Desert (1965 short subject) 4, 196
Simons, Robert 183
Simpson, Mari Anne 126
Sims, Joan 192
Sinatra, Frank 86
Singin' in the Rain (1952 film) 83
Sinthia the Devil Doll (1968 film) 4
Siodmak, Curt 95
Sirola, Joseph 132
Sisto, Jeremy 157, 159
Sjöberg, Alf 306
Sjöberg, Gunnar 89
Skeppsteadt, Carl-Olaf 95
Skerrit, Tom 101, 104
Skiles. Marlin 288
Skywalker, Luke (character) 234
Sleeping with the Enemy (1991 film) 148
Slezak, Victor 186
Slifer, Clarence 132
Sloane, Olive 192
Slowe, Georgia 49
Smigel, Robert 184
Smith, Andrea 226
Smith, Bee-Be 201
Smith, David Anthony 160
Smith, George Albert 305
Smith, Gerald Oliver 142
Smith, Ken 235, 240
Smith-Jackson, Jaimie 238
Smithee, Alan (pseudonym for disgruntled directors) 180
Smithson, Clark 230
Smits, Jimmy 273, 275
Snyder, Moriah Shining Dove 230
Socias, Isidro 306
Socrates 25
Sodeke. Soji 160
Sodom and Gomorrah (1963 film) 294
Sofaer, Abraham 132, 135, 265
Soijin 165
Sokal, H. R. 271

Solares, Gilberto Martinez 307
Solares, Raul Martinez 235
The Soldier's Tale (1964 film) 237, 249–250
Sole, Francisco 212
Soler, Julian 306, 307
"Some of These Days" (song) 130
Something Wicked This Way Comes (1983 film) 284
Something Wicked This Way Comes (novel) 204
Somewhere in Time (1980 film) 87
Sommer, Elke 179, 180, 182, 183
The Song and Dance Man (1926 film) 83
Sony Pictures Imageworks 208
Sophocles 21
Sorrell, William* 305
The Sorrows of Satan (1916 film) 306
The Sorrows of Satan (1926 film) 172, 251–254
The Sorrows of Satan; or, The Strange Experiences of Geoffrey Tempest, Millionaire (novel) 251
Sosa, Guillermo Bravo 235, 238
The Soul Eater (1925 film) 306
Soul selling (theme) *see* Contracts with the Devil
Sous le Soleil de Satan (1987 film) 255–257
Sousa, Lino Ribeiro de 208
South, Leonard J. 243
Southcott, Tim 238
Souza, Emory 116
The Space Between Us (1999 film) 159
Spaceballs (1987 film) 233
Spafford, Robert 168
Spain, Fay 226, 229
Spanish films 149, 196, 306, 307, 308
Spartacus (1960 film) 213
Speak of the Devil (1990 film) 257–259
Spear, Bernard 36
Special Effects Unlimited 233
Speed (1994) 109
Spelling, Aaron 238
Spence, Gerry 202
Spencer, Dorothy 142
Spencer, Douglas 9
Spencer, Kenneth 44, 45
Spera, Rob 308
Spiegel, Howard 61
Spigott, George (Devil pseudonym) 35–39
Spinell, Joe 130
Spiritism (1961 film) 259–262
Spirits of the Dead (1968 film) 50
Spock (character) 237, 287
Sprunck, Paul 165
Spy Hard (1996 film) 234
Stahl, Betsy 186
Staiver-Hutchins, Michael 75

Stamp, Terence* 49, 50
Standing, John 282
Stanley, Frank 294
Stanton, Harry Dean 167, 170
Stapleton, Jean 54, 57
Star Trek (TV series) 72
Star Trek: The Next Generation (TV series) 169, 263
Star Trek: Voyager (TV series) 53, 217
Star Wars (1977 film) 164, 220, 236
Starewicz, Wladyslaw 306
Starke, Anthony 233
Starke, Pauline 58
Stay Tuned (1992 film) 262–264
Steen, Tor 95
Steiger, Rod 108, 109, 112
Stein, Ronald 285
Steinbricker, Reinhardt 306
Steiner, Max 131
Steinfeld, Jake 233
Steinkampf, Frederic
Stell, William Calderon 235, 259
Steno 118, 120
The Stepford Wives (1974 film) 154
Stern, Stephen Hilliard 69
Sternberg, Nicholas Joseph von 221
Stevens, Edwin* 306
Stevens, George 132, 133
Stevens, Onslow 21
Stevenson, Klint 46
Stevenson, Robert Louis 92
Stewart, Jimmy 207
Stewart, Paul 132
Stewart-Conner, Kalie 184
Stigmata (1999) 109, 188
Stiller, Amy 146
Stiller, Ben 146
Stiller, Jerry 146, 148
Stockdale, Carl 63
Stohl, Hank 243
Stoltz, Eric 230
Stone, Christopher* 307
Stone, George E. 80, 81, 265
Stone, Harold J. 132
Stone, Oliver 89
Stoppa, Paolo 32
Stopplemoor, Cheryl Jean *see* Ladd, Cheryl
The Story of Mankind (1957 film) 264–267
La Strada (1954 film) 120
Straight on 'Til Morning (1972 film) 48
Strandin, Ebon 171
Strange, Robert 63
Strange Fascination (1952 film) 28
Strangelove, Dr. (character) 184
The Strangler (1964 film) 117
Strasberg, Susan 176
Strashnaya Mest (1913 film) 306
Strauss, Johann 206
Strauss, Peter 23

Stravinsky, Igor 249
Streisand, Barbra 33
Stribolt, Oscar 298
Striker, Joseph 165
Strock, Herbert L. 95, 96
Stroke, Adam 146
Struycken, Carel 300, 303
Stuart, Mel 307
The Student of Prague (1913 film) 268–270
The Student of Prague (1926 film) 271–272
Der Student von Prag (1935 film) 306
Stuthman, Fred 246
Sublett, John William 44
Subotsky, Milton 275, 276, 278, 281
Succubus *see* *The Devil's Nightmare*
Suchy, Jiri 124
Suicide Kings (1998 film) 159
Sullivan, Frank 285
Suman, Michael 307
Summoning the Devil (theme) 33, 75–77, 103, 106, 108, 122, 125, 210–211, 213, 260, 301
Sunrise (1927 film) 123
Superman (1978 film) 185
Superman II (1980 film) 50
Susskind, David 311
Svankmajer, Jan 124, 125
Svengali (1931 film) 24
Swanson, Kristy 146, 148
Swedish films 89, 95, 298, 306, 307
Swickert, Josef 58
Switch (1991 film) 273–275
Sydow, Max von* 45, 132–134, 203, 204, **205**, 207
Syncopation (1930 film) 83
Szaro, Henryk 306
Szgetti, Cynthia 151
Szwarc, Jeannot 87

Tafilaw, Richard 258
Tagliavini, Ferrucio 118, 120
Tajo, Italo* 307
"Takin' a Chance on Love" (song) 44, 45
Talbot, Larry (character) 96, 151
A Tale of Two Cities (1935 film) 114
Taleb, Mohammed 157
Tales from the Crypt (1972 film) 97, 275–278, 284
Tales from the Crypt (TV series) 276
The Tales of Helpmann (1990 film) 250
Tales of Hoffmann (1951 film) 250
Tales of the Unexpected (TV series) 139
Tallas, Greg 46
Tamburro, Charles A. 109

Taming of the Shrew (1967 film) 220
Tanney, Savant 273
Tarantino, Quentin 183
Tarr, Cynthia 214
Tartuffe (1925 film) 272
Tati, Jacques 195
Taylor, Duke 22
Taylor, Elizabeth* 105, 107, 108, 135, **137**, 138
Taylor, Ferris 63
Taylor, Frank 95
Taylor, Jack 208
Taylor, Samuel W. 28
Taylor, Wally 51
Tchaikovsky, Peter Illyich 172
Tejada, Hermanes 25
Teje, Tora 298
Television and the Devil (theme) 190, 192–193, 262–264, 279, 303
Tempest, Troy 146
The Temptations of Satan (1914 film) 306
The Ten Commandments (1923 film) 166, 226
The Ten Commandments (1954 film) 207, 294
Ten Little Indians (play) 33
Tenser, Marilyn Jacobs 151
Teomi, Oded 217
Teresa (saint) 195
Terminator II: Judgment Day (1991 film) 53
A Terrible Revenge see *Strashnaya Mest*
Terror Is a Man (1959) 30
Terzano, Massimo 189
Terzieff, Laurent 194
Terzon, Lorenzo 99
Teuber, Andreas* 105, **107**
Texiere, Jacob 171
Thalberg, Irving 166
Thall, Benj 233
That Nazty Nuisance (1943 short subject) 80, 81
"That Old Devil Jack Benny" (TV episode) 309
Theron, Charlize 84
Thesiger, Ernest 192, 193, 278
The Thief of Baghdad (1940 film) 45
The Thing That Couldn't Die (1958 film) 310
Thinnes, Roy* 238, 240
Thirard, Armand 91
Thiriet, Maurice 291
13 Demon Street (TV series) 95
Thomas, Danny 243, 309
Thomas, Guy 294
Thomas, Mark 87
Thomas Aquinas (saint) 111
Thompson, Galen 115, 116
Thompson, Jamie 201
Thomson, Kenneth 165
Thornton, Randy 146

"Those Were the Good Old Days" (Devil's song) 55, 57
Three Men and Rosemary's Baby (TV show parody) 263–264
The Three Musketeers (1973 film) 220
The Three Musketeers (novel) 212
Three Stooges 80
Three's Company (TV series) 264
Thriller (TV series) 72, 309
Thunderball (1965 film) 74
Tierney, Gene 142, 145
Tilton, Charlene 201
Time (magazine) 152
Time Bandits (1981 film) 4, 278–281
Time Tunnel (TV series) 266
Tin Tan* 307
Tinti, Gabriel 179, 183
Tiomkin, Dimitri 21, 22
To Die For (1995 film) 131
To Hell with the Kaisar (1918 film) 306
Toby Dammit see *Spirits of the Dead*
Toccata and Fugue in D Minor (organ piece) 276
Tocci, Franco 179
Todd, Lisa 102
Todorovic, Srdjan* 308
Tojo, Hideki 81
Tolan, Michael 132
Tolan, Peter 39
Tolsky, Susan 69
Tom, David 262
Tomelty, Joseph 191, 193
Toney, Theodore 221
Tonti, Aldo 73
Tophet, Harry O. (Devil pseudonym) 214–217
Torah (sacred Jewish texts) 218
Torchia, Aristede (character) 209
Tormé, Mel 226, 229
Torn, Rip 166
Torney, Jim 63
Torrance, Jack (character) 303
Torrence, Ernest 165
Tort, Sylvia 271
Torture Garden (1967 film) 281–284
La Tosca (1940 film) 34
Totheroh, Dan 62
Toto all'Inferno (1955 film) 307
Totter, Audrey 9, **12**, 16, 17
Touch of Evil (1958 film) 226
Touched by an Angel (TV series) 77, 230
Tourneau, Jacques, 92, 94
Tourneau, Maurice 91, 92, 94
Townley, Jack 288
Townley, Toke 192
Toxic Avenger III: The Last Temptation of Toxie (1989 film) 308
Tracy, Spencer 2, 58
Traer, Doug 258

Traffic (1972 film) 195
Tragical History of the Life and Death of Doctor Faustus see *Doctor Faustus* (play)
The Train (1964 film) 35
Tramcourt, Jeanne 171
Trampa Fatal (1958 film) 307
The Trance of Diana Love see *The Undead*
Tranter, Cordula 308
Travesi, Raphael Garcia 259
Travolta, John 101, 102, 104
Traylor, William 176
Treasure Island (novel) 205, 206
The Treasure of Sierra Madre (1947 film) 68
Tremors (1990 film) 225
Trent, William 17
Treuberg, Franz von 179, 163
Trikonis, Gus 115
Trioano, William G. 95
Tripper, Jack (character) 264
Triska, Jan 217
Troobnick, Eugene 61
Trost, Ron 217
Trotsky* 235, **236**, 237
Trovaioli, Armondo 73
Trubshawe, Michael 36
Tryon, Glenn 80
Tubbs, William 118
Tucci, Stanley 61
Tucker, Jack 221
Tucker, Nana 246
Tudor, Henry 291
Tudor, Owen 265
Tunie, Tamara 84
Tunney, Robin 108, 111, 112
Turandot (opera) 301
Les Turlupins (1980 film) 307
Turner, Anna 36
Turner, Frank C. 204, 207
Tuttle, Frank 306
TV Dante (1989 telefilm) 58
Twilight Zone (TV series) 95, 182, 195, 309, 310, 311
Twin Peaks (TV series) 207, 242
Twitchell, Archie 21
Two Episodes from Lenau's Faust (tone poems) 2
"Two Lost Souls" (song) 55
The Two of Us (1967 film) 35
Tyler, John 68
Tyng, Christopher 201
Tyrrell, Susan 130

Ufland, Harry 167
Ullman, Elwood 288
Umall, Erlyn 163
The Undead (1957 film) 285–288
Under the Sun of Satan see *Sous le Soleil de Satan*
Unger, Bertil 69
Unger, Gustav 69, 95

Unheimliche Geschichten (1919 film) 306
Unholy Trinity 129
Up in Smoke (1957 film) 288–290
Updike, John 300
Urbiz, Enrique 208
Urich, Robert 153, 156
Ustinov, Peter 135, 136, 138
Uziel (angel) 230, 231

Vai, Steve 51
Valére, Simone 32
Valli, Alida 179, 182
Valvestito, Carcello 73
Vampire Playgirls see *The Devil's Nightmare*
Les Vampires (1915 serial) 270
El Vampiro (1957 film) 259–260
Vampyr (1932 film) 172
Van Cau, Christian 194
Vanderbilt, Cornelius 300
Van De Sande, Theodore 183
Van Dine, Casper 217, 220
Vandis, Tito 243
Van Doren, Mamie 226, 229
Van Fleet, Jo 238
Van Helsing, Abraham (character) 270
Van Horne, Daryl (Devil pseudonym) 300–303
Van Kline, Joe 230
Van Loon, Hendrik Willem 264, 266
Van Loon's Lives (book) 266
Vannucchi, Luigi 73
Van Trees, James 21
Vanzina, Carlo 120
Vanzina, Stefano *see* Steno
Varconi, Victor 165
Varennes, Andre 91
Varnardo, Victor 108
Vattier, Robert 91
Vaughan, Peter 279
Vaughan, Robert* 296–297
Veidt, Conrad* 268, 271–272, 306
Velez, Kimberly 184
Venard, Shirley 240
Ventura, Jesse "The Body" 233, 234, 235
Vep, Irma (character) 270
Vera, Jose Antonio* 307
Verdi, Giuseppe 132
Verdon, Gwen 54, **56**, 57
Verebes, Erno 9
Verkler, Denis 243
Verley, Bernard 194
Vernier, Hugo de 276
Vernon, Howard 149
Vervan, Nora 259
Ve Sota, Bruno 28, 285, 287
Vial, Pierre* 307
Vichy France 92, 249, 291
Victor, Charles 192
Victor, Henry 80
Victoria (queen of England) 251

Vidgeon, Robin 146
Vigota, Abe, 87, 89
Viharo, George 115
The Villain Still Pursued Her (1940 film) 83
Villechaize, Hervé 130
Vinaro, Boy 163
Vince, Pruitt Taylor 17
Vincent, David (character) 240
Vincent, Louise 197
Vincent, Virginia 153, 156
Vincz, Melanie 151
Virgil 58, 60
Vision Art 217
Les Visiteurs du Soir (1942 film) 92, 195, 291–293
Viva 130
Vlad, Roman 32
Voedemann, Stella 217
Vogel, Tony 157
Voicu, Jorj* 307
La Voie Lactée see *The Milky Way*
Voyage to the Bottom of the Sea (TV series) 133, 267

Wade, Lindy 62
Wagers with the Devil (theme) 50, 52, 65–66, 122, 147, 216, 250
Wagner, Christie 46
Wagner, Richard 2
Wagner, Sidney 43
Wagrowski, Gregory 217
Wakeham, Debra 204
Walden, Barbara 226
Walken, Christopher 230, 232, 245, 248
Walker, Vernon L. 62
Wall, Aina 197
Wall, Geraldine 9, 16
Wall, Tony 276
Wall Street (1987 film) 50
Wallace, Geoffrey 282
Wallace, George 183
Wallace, Henry 259
Wallace, Robert 102
Wallach, Eli 245, 248
Wallen, Lennart 95
Wallop, Douglass 54
Walls, Audubon 221
Walsh, Edward 51
Walsh, J. T. 204
Walston, Ray* 54, **56**, 57
Walther, Hertha von 121
Walton, Bill 184
Walton, Herbert C. 192
Wandering Jew (legend) 95
War of the Satellites (1958 film) 286
Ward, Edward 80
Ward, Sandy 294
Warden, Rick 157
The Warfare of the Flesh (1917 film) 306
Warner, David* 4, 49, 278, 279, 281

Warner, H. B. 62, 68, 165, 167
Warner, Mark 83
Warren, Eda 9
Warren, Edward 306
Warren, Gene 176
Warren, Jerry 261
Warrilow, Peter 160
Warrock, Craig 278, 279
Warwick, Norman 275, 281
Washburn, Bryant 165
Washington, George 82
Wass, Ted 214, 217
The Waterboy (1998 film) 184
Waters, Ethel 44
Waters, Russell 75
Watling, Jack 191
Watson, Bobby 80, 81, **82**, 83, 265, 266
Watson, Bobs 83
Watson, William 294
Watts, John* 307
Waxman, Franz 9, 11
Waxman, Michael 146
Waxworks (1924 film) 270, 272
Wayne, Bernie 240
Wayne, David* 310, 311
Wayne, John 132, 135
We Aren't Angels see *Mi Nismo Andjeli*
Weathers, Carl 184
Webb, Clifton 22
Webb, David 78
Weber, Carl Maria von 2, 124
Webster, Daniel 62–68, 223, 310, 311
Webster, Nicholas 235
Weddle, Vernon 69
Wegener, Paul 268, 270
Weidemann, Fritz 268
Weird Science (TV series) 203
Weird Tales see *Unheimliche Geschichten*
Weird Woman (1944 film) 114
Weis, Gary 294
Weisenberg, David
Weissman, Benjamin 157
Welch, Raquel 35, 38
Weld, Tuesday 226, 229
Weldon, Ben 22
Welk, Lawrence 310
Weller, Mary Louise 115
Welles, Mel 285, **287**
Welles, Orson 166
Wellman, Maly Wade 176, 177
Wells, Jerold 279
Wendkos, Paul 139
Wenger, Carol 101
Wessel, Horst 268
West, Chrissy 78
West, Lockwood 36
Westerberg, Fred 165
Westman, Tony 203
Westover, Richard E. 151
"What Is There About Me?" (song) 45

Whatever Happened to Baby Jane? (1962 film) 117
"Whatever Lola Wants" (song) 54, 55, 56
Wheatley, Dennis 75
Wheel of Fortune (TV series) 235
Where Eagles Dare (1968 film) 77
Whilhoite, Kathleen 18
Whitcraft, Elizabeth 17
White, Carol 300
White, Ebony 221
White, Roman 78
Whiteman, Russ 22
Whitlock, Albert 245
Whitman, Ernest 44
Whitman, Walt* 306
Whitmore, Stanford 135
Who Fears the Devil? see *Legend of Hillbilly John*
Wholly Moses (1980 film) 294–295
Widen, Gregory 230
Widlund, Ann Catherin 95
Wiehe, Emma 171
Wiehe, Viggo 171
Wieth, Carlo 171
Wieth, Clara 171
Wilcox, Mary 30, 32
Wild Man Steve 221
The Wild Wild West (TV series) 72, 138
Wilen, Max 95
Wiley, Sharon 226
Wilkinson, June 226, **227**
William Wilson (short story) 268
Williams, Andrew (Devil pseudonym) 126–129
Williams, Billy Dee 164
Williams, Brook 135
Williams, David C. 230
Williams, Gary Anthony 108
Williams, JoBeth 273
Williams, Joe 221
Williams, John 300
Williams, Patrick 157, 294
Williams, Randy 221
Williams, Robin 61
Williams, Rose Jewel 221
Williams, Spencer 306
Williams, Tudor **3**
Williams-Hurner, Jeremy 230
Williamson, Walter 217
Wilson, Dale 262
Wilson, Dooley 44
Wilson, Jeannie 69
Wilson, Marie 265
Wiman, Dwight* 306

Windsor, Marie 265
Winge, Torsen 89
Wingreen, Jason 214
Winkler, Henry 184, 185
Winner, Michael 245, 246
Winston, Helene 69
Winters, Shelley 74, 87–89, 132
Winther, Karen 298
Winton, Colleen 262
Wise, Robert 62, 66
Witch Academy (1992 film) 296–297
Witchcraft Through the Ages (1922 film) 298–300
Witchery see *Malefiche Presenze*
The Witches' Mirror (1960 film) 261
The Witches of Eastwick (1987 film) 300–303
The Witch's Curse (1962 film) 190
Witherspoon, John 183
Witherspoon, Reece 183
Witten, Brian 183
Wizan, Steve 233
WKRP in Cincinnati (TV series) 115
Wöhler, Gustav-Peter* 308
Wolfe, Ian 87, 89
Wolfe, Kedric* 130, 308
Womack, Gail 221
A Woman of Paris (1923 film) 254
Women Devils see Devil in female form
Wong, Gerald* 308
Wong, Victor 223, 225
Woo, John 308
Wood, Cyrus 58
Wood, Edward D. Jr. 264, 286, 307
Wood, William 139
Woodard, Alfre 186
Woodfield, William Read 243
Woods, Jack* 112–115
Woodworth, Marjorie 80
Wooley, Stephen 49
Worth, Nicholas 154
Wright, Charles Julian 146
Wright, Ken 223
Wyda, Emmy 121
Wyngarde, Peter 114
Wynn, Ed 132, 133
Wynn, Keenan 101
Wynter, George 84
Wynter, Sarah 186

Xena the Warrior Princess (TV series) 157

Yaru, Marina* 50
Yates, Cassie 115
Yates, Peter 203
Yeaman, Steven Arthur 46
The Year the Yankees Lost the Pennant (novel) 54
Yen, Ann 223
Yiddish films 307
Yordan, Phil, Jr. 46
Yordan, Philip 46
York, Michael* 217, 220
You Can't Win! (TV show parody) 263
"You Got to Have Heart" (song) 54, 55
You Nazty Spy (1939 short subject) 80
You Only Live Twice (1967 film) 134
Young, Casey 46
Young, James 306
Young, John 279
Young, Roger 157
Young Americans (1993 film) 232
Young Goodman Brown (1993 film) 308
Young Goodman Brown (short story) 64
Yugoslavian films 307
Yulin, Harris 176

Zacpal, Antonin 124
Zadora, Pia 201
Zall, Andy 214
Zane, Bartine 69
Zanuck, Darryl F. 226
Zanussi, Lucia 189
Der Zarewitsch (operetta) 182
Zavitz, Lee 28
Zeffirelli, Franco 220
Zeiden, Josef 307
Zemanova, Marle 124
Zenda, John 154
Zerneck, Frank von 153
Zerneck, Frank von, Jr. 154
Zetina, Guillermo* 259, 261
Ziegler, Ted 69
Zimmerman, Jerry 157
Zingaretti, Luca 157
Zinnemann, Tim 51
Zinner, Peter 217
Zorro vs. Satan (1987 film) 308
Zsigmond, Vilmos 300
Zucchero, Joe 160
Zugsmith, Albert 226

www.ingramcontent.com/pod-product-compliance
Lightning Source LLC
Chambersburg PA
CBHW081537300426
44116CB00015B/2668